Albert Edward P.

Colonel Xth Royal Hussars

THE

TENTH ROYAL HUSSARS

Printed and bound by Antony Rowe Ltd, Eastbourne

THE MEMOIRS

OF THE

TENTH ROYAL HUSSARS

(PRINCE OF WALES' OWN)

HISTORICAL AND SOCIAL

COLLECTED AND ARRANGED

BY

COLONEL R. S. LIDDELL

LATE COMMANDING TENTH ROYAL HUSSARS

WITH ILLUSTRATIONS BY OSCAR NORIE

LONDON

LONGMANS, GREEN, AND CO.

AND NEW YORK: 15 EAST 16th STREET

1891

DEDICATED

BY SPECIAL PERMISSION

TO

FIELD-MARSHAL H.R.H. ALBERT EDWARD

PRINCE OF WALES, K.G.

COLONEL TENTH ROYAL HUSSARS

PREFACE

THE compiler of these memoirs is aware that his work
is to some extent an experiment in regimental history.   In addition to the official record of the services
and movements of the 10th Hussars which will be
found contained in its pages, an endeavour has been
made to give the volume an interest by the introduction of episodes and anecdotes illustrative of the daily
life of the regiment.   Much of the history of the Tenth
is bound up with the history of the country.   Much
of its social life is connected with names well known
to the public.   Its campaigns, and the changes which
have taken place from time to time in its organisation,
dress, and accoutrements, are identical with those of
many other regiments.   On these grounds it seems
not unreasonable to hope that the book may become
acceptable beyond the immediate connection of the
regiment.

   To the numerous officers, non-commissioned officers,
and privates of the Tenth, past and present, who have
rendered him valuable aid, as well as to the relatives
of many who have served in the regiment, the compiler desires to express his obligations for the assistance
they have given him and for the unbounded confidence
they have reposed in him.   To name them all would be
impossible, but it will hardly be invidious to express his
special acknowledgments to a few.

Without the help and encouragement he received from H.R.H. the Prince of Wales he could not have persevered in his difficult undertaking. From first to last His Royal Highness has manifested his sympathy in the most practical way, and assisted him with his invaluable counsel.

The earlier portion of the memoirs owe not a little to Mr. William Douglas, formerly a private in the regiment, who was himself engaged upon a history of the Tenth, but who agreed to surrender his enterprise and offered the writer every assistance. Extracts have also been made from a work published by him, entitled " Soldiering in Sunshine and Storm."

The Diary of the late Dr. Jenks, surgeon of the regiment in the Peninsula and at Waterloo, has been laid under large contribution for the incidents of a period in regard to which much difficulty was experienced in obtaining information.

The Diary of General Sir John Slade, written during the Corunna campaign in 1808–9, has also been placed at the disposal of the compiler, through the kindness of his son, Mr. Wyndham Slade.

Special thanks are due to Dr. Thomas Fraser, whose service of twenty-seven years in the Tenth constituted him an invaluable authority for its history, and to whose labour in supervising the work it owes whatever of literary merit it may be found to possess.

Acknowledgment must also be made of the kind assistance rendered in its revision by Major Arthur Griffiths, author of " The English Army," &c., who was at one time attached to the Tenth from the Staff College.

CONTENTS

---⋆✶⋆---

CHAPTER I

PAGE

RAISING OF THE REGIMENT—TITLES BORNE—CAUSES OF EMBODI-
MENT—POLITICAL SITUATION—WARRANT FOR RAISING THE REGI-
MENT 1

CHAPTER II

ORIGIN OF THE BRITISH CAVALRY—LIST OF OFFICERS—PRICES OF
COMMISSIONS—PAY OF NON-COMMISSIONED OFFICERS AND MEN—
DRESS 7

CHAPTER III

MOVEMENTS OF THE REGIMENT—REVIEW BY GEORGE I.—BRIGADIER-
GENERAL GORE—AUGMENTATION—REVIEW BY GEORGE II.—LORD
SEMPHILL'S HIGHLANDERS—LORD COBHAM APPOINTED COLONEL—
GENERAL CHURCHILL 13

CHAPTER IV

THE REBELLION OF 1745—BATTLE OF FALKIRK—DUKE OF CUMBER-
LAND SENT TO COMMAND—BATTLE OF CULLODEN—MEDAL STRUCK
—REGIMENT REDUCED 21

CHAPTER V

SIZE OF DRAGOON HORSES—ESTABLISHMENT DECREASED—DEATH OF
LORD COBHAM — FIRST CLOTHING WARRANT — THE LIGHT OR
HUSSAR TROOP FORMED—WARS IN INDIA AND AMERICA . . 29

CHAPTER VI

WAR WITH FRANCE—AUGMENTATION OF THE ARMY—EXPEDITIONS ON
THE FRENCH SEA-COAST—HUSSAR TROOPS SENT ON SERVICE—
REGIMENT EMBARKS FOR GERMANY—THE SEVEN YEARS' WAR—
BATTLE OF MINDEN 36

CHAPTER VII

PAGE

BATTLE OF WARBURG—CHARGE OF MAJOR DAVENPORT—PURSUIT OF
THE FRENCH—THE REGIMENT CROSSES THE RHINE—BATTLE OF
CAMPEN — KIRCH-DENKERN — MARCH TO HANOVER — SURPRISE
OF THE FRENCH CAMP AT GREBENSTEIN—CONCLUSION OF THE
SEVEN YEARS' WAR 46

CHAPTER VIII

THE REGIMENT REDUCED—REVIEW BY GEORGE III.—DEATH OF SIR
JOHN MORDAUNT—THE TENTH MADE "THE PRINCE OF WALES'S
OWN "—ROYAL ESCORTS—MOVEMENTS OF THE REGIMENT—WAR
DECLARED BY FRANCE—AUGMENTATION OF THE REGIMENT . . 56

CHAPTER IX

INTEREST OF THE ROYAL FAMILY IN THE REGIMENT—HIS ROYAL
HIGHNESS THE PRINCE OF WALES APPOINTED COMMANDANT—IN-
CREASE IN THE CAVALRY—BEAU BRUMMELL—THE PRINCE OF
WALES APPOINTED COLONEL—GENERAL SIR AUGUSTUS PITT . . 63

CHAPTER X

NAPOLEON BUONAPARTE — THE ESTABLISHMENT RAISED — REGIMENT
MADE HUSSARS—TROOPS DESPATCHED TO PORTUGAL . . . 71

CHAPTER XI

THE REGIMENT PROCEEDS ON ACTIVE SERVICE—EMBARKATION—
SAHAGUN—ADVANCE OF NAPOLEON—RETROGRADE MOVEMENTS—
MAYORGA—BENEVENTE—CAPTURE OF A FRENCH GENERAL BY A
PRIVATE HUSSAR—ASSISTANT-SURGEON DENNY—RETREAT ON AND
BATTLE OF CORUNNA 81

CHAPTER XII

RETURN OF THE ARMY TO ENGLAND—THE REGIMENT AT BRIGHTON—
THE HEALTH OF GEORGE III.—THE PRINCE OF WALES APPOINTED
REGENT—THE REGIMENT STYLED "ROYAL"—PREPARATIONS FOR
ACTIVE SERVICE—ARRIVAL AT LISBON—CAMPAIGNS OF 1810-11-12—
LORD WORCESTER 95

CHAPTER XIII

THE HUSSAR BRIGADE — CAMPAIGN OF 1813—MORALES DEL TORO — FALL OF BURGOS—BATTLE OF VITTORIA 103

CHAPTER XIV

MARSHAL SOULT APPOINTED TO COMMAND THE FRENCH—POSITION OF THE ARMIES AFTER VITTORIA—BATTLES OF THE PYRENEES—FALL OF ST. SEBASTIAN—THE ENGLISH ENTER FRANCE . . . 114

CHAPTER XV

BATTLE OF ORTHEZ—PURSUIT OF THE ENEMY—COMBAT OF TARBES — ARRIVAL OF A SQUADRON FROM THE DEPÔT—THE BATTLE OF TOULOUSE—PEACE—THE TENTH MARCH THROUGH FRANCE . . 121

CHAPTER XVI

NAPOLEON'S ESCAPE FROM ELBA—THE REGIMENT ORDERED ON ACTIVE SERVICE—POSITION OF THE ENGLISH ARMY BEFORE WATERLOO— THE CAVALRY FORCE—NAPOLEON TAKES THE FIELD—THE BATTLES OF LIGNY AND QUATRE BRAS 133

CHAPTER XVII

THE PRUSSIANS RETREAT—THE ENGLISH FALL BACK UPON WATERLOO —AFFAIR AT GENAPPE—THE NIGHT BEFORE WATERLOO . . 142

CHAPTER XVIII

THE FIELD OF WATERLOO—POSITIONS OF THE CAVALRY BRIGADES— COMMENCEMENT OF THE BATTLE—CHARGES OF SOMERSET'S AND PONSONBY'S BRIGADES—VANDELEUR'S AND VIVIAN'S BRIGADES TAKE GROUND TO THE RIGHT 147

CHAPTER XIX

THE PRUSSIANS UNDER BLÜCHER ARRIVE—VIVIAN'S BRIGADE ORDERED TO ADVANCE—THE TENTH CHARGE THE IMPERIAL GUARD—DEATH OF MAJOR HOWARD—LINES BY AN OFFICER OF THE TENTH— BYRON'S "CHILDE HAROLD"—LIST OF OFFICERS PRESENT—LIST OF KILLED AND WOUNDED 154

CHAPTER XX

PAGE

PURSUIT OF THE FRENCH—LOSSES—REWARDS—SILVER TRUMPET—
LIEUTENANT SLAYTER SMITH ORDERED TO RECONNOITRE—THE
OCCUPATION OF PARIS—MARCH TO BOULOGNE—EMBARKATION AT
CALAIS 168

CHAPTER XXI

BIOGRAPHIES OF OFFICERS WHO SERVED IN THE REGIMENT DURING
THE PENINSULAR AND WATERLOO CAMPAIGNS   177

CHAPTER XXII

THE TENTH AT BRIGHTON—REVIEW BY THE PRINCE REGENT—REGI-
MENT REDUCED—GOLD LACE INTRODUCED—DEATH OF GEORGE III.
—THE PRINCE REGENT—LORD STEWART APPOINTED COLONEL—
LIEUTENANT HODGSON EMPLOYED IN AID OF THE CIVIL POWER IN
SCOTLAND—REVIEW BY KING GEORGE IV.   194

CHAPTER XXIII

CENTRE-PIECE PRESENTED BY KING GEORGE IV.—SILVER GILT SOUP
TUREENS—DRESS REGULATIONS—REGIMENT ORDERED TO IRELAND
FOR THE FIRST TIME—SIR GEORGE QUENTIN RETIRES—LORD
LONDONDERRY'S INSPECTION—DUEL   208

CHAPTER XXIV

EXPEDITION TO PORTUGAL—BRIGHTON—REVIEW IN HYDE PARK—
DEATH OF GEORGE IV.—CHANGE OF DRESS 210

CHAPTER XXV

REDUCTION OF THE REGIMENT — IN IRELAND — DEATH OF KING
WILLIAM IV.—ESTABLISHMENT INCREASED—LORD THOMAS CECIL—
CORONATION OF HER MAJESTY QUEEN VICTORIA—REVIEW BEFORE
THE QUEEN — THE FIRST GRAND MILITARY STEEPLECHASES —
THE MARQUIS OF LONDONDERRY — MAJOR-GENERAL THE HON. H.
BEAUCHAMP LYGON APPOINTED COLONEL   215

CHAPTER XXVI

ORDERS RECEIVED FOR SERVICE IN INDIA—REGIMENT AUGMENTED—
EMBARKATION—ARRIVAL IN BOMBAY—MARCH TO KIRKEE   .   . 228

CHAPTER XXVII

PAGE

THE CANTONMENT OF KIRKEE—DRESS REGULATIONS—ARRIVAL OF
TROOP HORSES—FIRST MOUNTED INSPECTION 236

CHAPTER XXVIII

SPORTS AND AMUSEMENTS — A DRAFT ARRIVES FROM ENGLAND —
RACQUET COURT BUILT—ATTACK OF CHOLERA—REVIEW BY THE
COMMANDER-IN-CHIEF 244

CHAPTER XXIX

COLONEL BONHAM RETIRES—DEATH OF THE DUKE OF WELLINGTON
—A CAMP OF EXERCISE—COLONEL TRITTON'S CAREER—RUMOURS
OF WAR IN EUROPE—WAR DECLARED BY ENGLAND AND FRANCE
AGAINST RUSSIA 252

CHAPTER XXX

THE LANDING OF THE ALLIED ARMY IN THE CRIMEA—ORDERS FOR
THE REGIMENT TO LEAVE INDIA FOR THE SEAT OF WAR—LAST
CHRISTMAS AT KIRKEE—DEPARTURE FROM BOMBAY . . . 260

CHAPTER XXXI

MARCH FROM SUEZ—ARRIVAL AT CAIRO—THE VICEROY ENTERTAINS
THE REGIMENT—VISIT TO HAMIL PASHA—REVIEW OF THE 10TH
HUSSARS BEFORE THE VICEROY 269

CHAPTER XXXII

DEPARTURE FROM CAIRO—MARCH TO ALEXANDRIA—A CHALLENGE
FROM AN ARAB SHEIK—REGIMENT EMBARKS—ARRIVAL AT BALAC-
LAVA—FIRST ENCAMPMENT—REDUCED CONDITION OF THE BRITISH
CAVALRY DIVISION 276

CHAPTER XXXIII

A RECONNAISSANCE—DAILY DUTIES OF THE CAVALRY—ARRIVAL OF
THE SARDINIAN ARMY—THE QUEEN'S BIRTHDAY—THE LINE OF
THE TCHERNAYA OCCUPIED—THE SECOND BOMBARDMENT OF
SEBASTOPOL—AN ADVANCE UNDER GENERAL DE LA MARMORA . 285

CHAPTER XXXIV

PAGE

THE REGIMENT JOINS OMAR PASHA—STORM AT BALACLAVA—OUT-
BREAK OF CHOLERA—RETURN TO KARANI—DEATH OF LORD
RAGLAN—BATTLE OF THE TCHERNAYA—SIEGE OF SEBASTOPOL . 296

CHAPTER XXXV

EXPEDITION TO KERTCH — CAPTAIN PERCY SMITH — THE CAVALRY
DIVISION LEAVES THE CRIMEA—THE TENTH AT ISMID—PROPO-
SALS FOR PEACE—OCCUPATIONS AT ISMID—DEPARTURE FOR
ENGLAND 304

CHAPTER XXXVI

THE REGIMENT REDUCED—IN THE MIDLAND COUNTIES—CHANGE IN
THE DRESS OF HUSSARS—COLONEL PARLBY—REDUCTION OF THE
REGIMENT—THE INDIAN MUTINY AND CONSEQUENT INCREASE—
ALDERSHOT — COLONEL WILKIE — FIRST REGIMENTAL STEEPLE-
CHASES—COUNTRY QUARTERS 317

CHAPTER XXXVII

YORK—DEATH OF THE PRINCE CONSORT—A SECOND WINTER AT
YORK—THE EARL BEAUCHAMP TRANSFERRED TO THE 2ND LIFE
GUARDS—H.R.H. ALBERT EDWARD PRINCE OF WALES APPOINTED
COLONEL—THE REGIMENT MOVES TO IRELAND—DUBLIN—THE
CURRAGH — NON-PIVOT DRILL INTRODUCED — CAHIR — GENERAL
ELECTION 330

CHAPTER XXXVIII

THE PRINCE OF WALES VISITS IRELAND—ESCORTS OF THE TENTH—
IN AID OF THE CIVIL POWER—THE FENIAN MOVEMENT—FLYING
COLUMNS—SECOND VISIT OF THE PRINCE OF WALES . . . 340

CHAPTER XXXIX

THE TENTH RETURNS TO ENGLAND — MARCH TO ALDERSHOT —
VOLUNTEER REVIEW—THE CROWN PRINCE OF PRUSSIA INSPECTS
THE TENTH—SQUADRON ORGANISATION—REGIMENT PROCEEDS TO
SHORNCLIFFE — REGIMENTAL RACES — AUTUMN MANŒUVRES —
PRINCE OF WALES TAKES COMMAND OF A CAVALRY BRIGADE—
ILLNESS OF THE PRINCE OF WALES 349

CHAPTER XL

PAGE

SALISBURY MANŒUVRES—ORDERS TO PREPARE FOR INDIA—FAREWELL
DINNER GIVEN BY THE PRINCE OF WALES—THE 7TH HUSSARS'
DINNER—COLONEL VALENTINE BAKER 360

CHAPTER XLI

THE REGIMENT EMBARKS FOR INDIA—FROM BOMBAY TO MUTTRA—
DURBAR AT AGRA—LIFE AT MUTTRA—THE PRINCE OF WALES'S
VISIT TO INDIA — THE CAMP AT DELHI — AGRA — LIEUTENANT-
COLONEL THE HON. C. C. MOLYNEUX 371

CHAPTER XLII

THE IMPERIAL ASSEMBLAGE—PROCLAMATION OF HER MAJESTY EM-
PRESS OF INDIA—MARCH TO RAWUL PINDI—DIFFICULTIES IN
AFGHANISTAN—THE TENTH ORDERED ON SERVICE—HOSTILITIES
COMMENCE—SQUADRON IN THE KURRAM VALLEY—PEIWAR KOTAL
—KHOST VALLEY—THE SQUADRON MARCHES TO JOIN HEAD-
QUARTERS AT JELLALABAD—MOVEMENTS OF THE HEAD-QUARTERS
—ALI MUSJID—JELLALABAD 386

CHAPTER XLIII

AN EXPEDITION ORDERED AGAINST THE KHUGIANIS—DISASTER IN
THE CABUL RIVER—LIST OF THOSE DROWNED—ACTION OF FUT-
TEHABAD—TELEGRAMS FROM THE QUEEN AND PRINCE OF WALES—
DEATH OF SHERE ALI—TREATY OF GUNDAMUCK—WITHDRAWAL
OF TROOPS TO INDIA—CHOLERA—HONOURS GRANTED FOR THE
CAMPAIGN 400

CHAPTER XLIV

THE TREATY OF GUNDAMUCK—OUTBREAK OF SECOND CAMPAIGN—
OFFICERS AND NON-COMMISSIONED OFFICERS OF THE TENTH EM-
PLOYED—THE REGIMENT MARCHES TO MIAN MIR—BRIGADED WITH
THE 15TH HUSSARS—LUCKNOW—LORD RALPH KERR—VISIT OF THE
DUKE AND DUCHESS OF CONNAUGHT — ORDERS FOR ENGLAND
RECEIVED 418

CHAPTER XLV

THE NATIVE CAVALRY REGIMENTS PRESENT THE TENTH WITH A
CUP—EMBARKATION AT BOMBAY—STOPPED AT ADEN—ORDERED
TO THE EASTERN SOUDAN—PREPARATIONS FOR A CAMPAIGN—

a

PAGE

ARRIVAL AT SUAKIM—GENERAL VALENTINE BAKER—THE REGI-
MENT MOUNTED—PROCEEDS TO TRINKITAT—CAUSES OF THE EX-
PEDITION—EL TEB 428

CHAPTER XLVI

AFTER THE ACTION—THE TENTH HORSES—TROOPER HAYES—" A TALE
OF THE 10TH HUSSARS "—MARCH TO TOKAR—THE REGIMENT DE-
STROYS THE ARMS AND AMMUNITION OF THE ENEMY—RETURN TO
TRINKITAT AND SUAKIM—TAMAII 441

CHAPTER XLVII

CONVOY DUTIES—AN ADVANCE INLAND—THE CAMPAIGN BROUGHT
TO A CLOSE—HONOURS AWARDED—ARRIVAL AT PORTSMOUTH—
SHORNCLIFFE—THE DUKE OF CAMBRIDGE INSPECTS THE TENTH
—THE PRINCESS OF WALES PRESENTS THE MEDALS TO THE
REGIMENT—OFFICERS ORDERED ON THE NILE EXPEDITION . . 451

CHAPTER XLVIII

PRINCE ALBERT VICTOR APPOINTED TO THE REGIMENT—RETURN OF
THE OFFICERS AND MEN FROM THE NILE EXPEDITION — THE
REGIMENT INSPECTED BY THE PRINCE OF WALES—COLONEL E. A.
WOOD 460

CHAPTER XLIX

THE JUBILEE OF HER MAJESTY QUEEN VICTORIA—CELEBRATION OF
THE FIFTIETH ANNIVERSARY OF HER ACCESSION—PRINCE ALBERT
VICTOR PROMOTED TO BE CAPTAIN—HIS IMPERIAL HIGHNESS
PRINCE WILLIAM OF PRUSSIA VISITS THE REGIMENT—JUBILEE
REVIEW AT ALDERSHOT—COLONEL R. S. LIDDELL . . . 470

CHAPTER L

VISCOUNT DOWNE APPOINTED TO COMMAND—INSPECTION BY H.R.H.
THE DUKE OF CAMBRIDGE—THE REGIMENT MARCHES TO YORK—
VISIT OF H.R.H. THE PRINCE OF WALES 476

APPENDIX I 485

APPENDIX II 545

LIST OF ILLUSTRATIONS

———•>◦<—————

FIELD-MARSHAL H.R.H. ALBERT EDWARD PRINCE OF WALES,
K.G., COLONEL 10TH ROYAL HUSSARS FROM 1863. (FROM A
PHOTOGRAPH BY MESSRS. DOWNEY, LONDON) . . . *Frontispiece*

10TH DRAGOONS FROM 1715 TO 1783 . . . . *To face page* 16

THE LIGHT TROOP—FROM 1756 TO 1763 . . . ,, 34

10TH LIGHT DRAGOONS FROM 1783 TO 1803 . . . ,, 60

10TH LIGHT DRAGOONS (ROYAL HUSSARS) 1811 TO 1819 . ,, 76

H.R.H. THE PRINCE REGENT, K.G., COLONEL 10TH LIGHT
DRAGOONS (HUSSARS) FROM 1793 TO 1820 . . ,, 130

10TH ROYAL HUSSARS FROM 1819 TO 1831 . . . ,, 196

10TH ROYAL HUSSARS FROM 1831 TO 1840 . . . ,, 216

10TH ROYAL HUSSARS FROM 1846 TO 1855 (INDIA) . . ,, 240

10TH ROYAL HUSSARS, 1855–56 (CRIMEA) . . . ,, 306

10TH ROYAL HUSSARS FROM 1856 TO 1873 . . . ,, 332

10TH ROYAL HUSSARS FROM 1873 TO 1884 (INDIA) . . ,, 408

H.R.H. PRINCE ALBERT VICTOR OF WALES, K.G., CAPTAIN
10TH ROYAL HUSSARS. (FROM A PHOTOGRAPH BY
MESSRS. LAFAYETTE, DUBLIN). . . . . ,, 460

10TH ROYAL HUSSARS FROM 1884 . . . . . ,, 470

10TH ROYAL HUSSARS FROM 1886 . . . . . ,, 482

R. Norie.

1715 - 83.

1756 – 63.

The Light Troop.

Litho W Greve, Berlin.

O.Norie

Litho W Greve Berlin.

1783 – 1803.

C. Norré.

Litho W. Greve, Berlin.

1811–19.

O.Noue

Litho. W. Greve, Berlin.

1819 - 31

O. Norie

Litho. W. Greve, Berlin

1831–40.

1846 – 55.

(India.)

Lith. W Greve Berlin

O. Norie

1855-56.

(Crimea.)

Litho W Greve, Berlin.

1856 - 73

O. Norie

Litho. W. Greve, Berlin

O.Nolte

1873–84.

Litho. W. Greve. Berlin.

1884 - 91.

(Jubilee - day.)

O. Nouve

Litho. W. Greve. Berlin.

O. Norie

Litho. W. Greve, Berlin.

1886-91.

MEMOIRS

OF

THE TENTH ROYAL HUSSARS

CHAPTER I

RAISING OF THE REGIMENT —TITLES BORNE—CAUSES OF EMBODI-
MENT — POLITICAL SITUATION — WARRANT FOR RAISING THE
REGIMENT

THE 10th Regiment of Dragoons, now bearing the
distinguished title of "The Prince of Wales's Own
Royal Hussars," is one of the regiments of cavalry
which were raised at the close of the first year of the
reign of King George I.

Since that period it has seen much and varied service; and although it has inscribed on its insignia
only the historical names of "Peninsula," "Waterloo,"
"Sebastopol," "Ali Musjid," "Afghanistan 1878–79,"
and "Egypt 1884," other famous victories and military
operations in which it took part might justly be added
to the list of those the regiment thus officially bears,
as will appear in the course of the following memoirs.
At Culloden and Minden, at Warbourg, Campen,
Kirch-Denkern, during the retreat on Corunna, at
Sahagun, Mayorga, and Benevente, at Morales and

*B

Vittoria, in the Pyrenees at Orthez and Toulouse, the Tenth was afforded the opportunity of upholding its reputation, took an active share, and not unfrequently bore a distinguished part in the various operations which rendered these names famous in military history. The causes which led to the first embodiment of the regiment will be best understood by a brief reference to the history of the time.

Though the political aspirations of the Jacobite party in England had received a check in the death of James II. at St. Germain's in 1701, the hope of eventually restoring the Stuart dynasty to the throne was by no means extinguished. The late King's son—James Francis Edward—was looked upon by the adherents of the dethroned family as the future monarch, and at his residence at Bar-le-Duc, on the borders of Lorraine, where he held his Court, he received kingly honours, having his royal palace and Guards. In 1716 he married the Princess Maria Clementina Sobieska, granddaughter of the famous John Sobieski, King of Poland, and her dowry, which amounted to over one million sterling, placed him amongst the wealthiest persons of the time in Europe. Ample means were, therefore, not wanting to enable him to prosecute an attempt to recover the English throne, and in England itself the large number of dissatisfied Roman Catholics, who were naturally disposed to the cause of the Stuarts and ready to afford it material aid, gave additional encouragement to his hopes of restoring the dynasty of his family. Many of the reigning families of Europe, moreover, recognised his claim to the throne and warmly espoused his cause. Louis XIV., who had always maintained close relations with the exiled Stuarts, was prepared to give tangible proofs of his goodwill by sending troops to assist the partisans of the family in their attempt to

place the Pretender—as the son of James II. was designated by the Protestants—on the throne, to the exclu-
sion of the House of Hanover.

These plans, which were possibly matured even
before the death of Queen Anne in 1714, were not
brought prominently forward until George I. had
ascended the throne. But shortly after that event riots
and disturbances took place in various parts of the
country. Hardly had George I. been formally proclaimed King before the Jacobite party was ready to
dispute by an appeal to arms his title to the throne.

In July 1715 matters came to a crisis. The King,
when in the act of giving his assent to several bills in
the House of Lords, was informed that already a rebellion threatened his kingdom, and that an invasion from
abroad menaced the safety of his throne. But the
death of Louis XIV. at this juncture, and the doubt as
to the light in which the Jacobite cause might be regarded by his successor, produced a certain amount of
delay. It was not until September in that year that
the standard of the " Pretender " was raised in Scotland
by the Earl of Mar. The defeat of the Earl, however,
at Sheriffmuir, and the surrender of Preston a few
weeks afterwards, put an end to this first attempt to
restore the Stuart family. At this critical period prompt
measures were needed and were taken to meet the
danger which threatened both Protestantism and the
Hanoverian dynasty. The standing army was augmented by several regiments of horse and foot; and
Brigadier-General Humphrey Gore, an officer of repute
and a staunch Protestant, who commanded a regiment
of foot during the reign of Queen Anne, was among those
ordered to raise, organise, and equip one of the proposed
new regiments of cavalry.

On the 23rd July, 1715, the following Warrant

B 2

under the sign-manual was issued to this officer, authorising him " to raise, form, and discipline a regiment of dragoons of six troops."

GEORGE R.

Whereas we have thought fit that a Regiment of Dragoons [1] be forthwith Raised under your command for Our Service, which is to consist of six troops of one Sergeant, two Corporals, one Drummer, one Hautbois [2] and Thirty private Dragoons, including the Widdowsmen [3] in each troop. These are to authorize you by beat of Drumm or otherwise to raise so many Voluntiers as ſhall be wanting to compleat the said Regiment to the above numbers. And when you ſhall have Listed fifteen men fitt for service in any of the said Troops, You are to give notice to Two of Our Justices of the Peace of the town or Country wherein the same are, who are hereby Authorized and Required to view the said Men and Certify the Day of their so doing, from which Day the said fifteen Men and the Commission and Non-Commission

---

[1] Dragoons appear to have been of French origin. The name then given to them, according to one authority, was " Dragon," taken from the arm they carried of that name, a short piece with a barrel of sixteen inches. Lord Orrery says they were so called, as they fought in the air or on the ground, mounted or on foot. One man held ten horses, while his comrades (the riders) fought on foot. Their long carbines were called " dragons " from the cock being made in that shape.

[2] "The 'hautbois' (oboe, Italian and Spanish) seems to have been a French invention, and was introduced into the English army after the Restoration. It was used in the infantry and dragoons. It appears to have been a large flageolet or clarionet and gave a sound louder than all other instruments, except the trumpet, and apparently was well adapted as an accompaniment to the drum. In 1759 they were again exchanged for trumpets."—*The British Army*, by Sir Sibbald Scott, Bart.

[3] The following extract from a Warrant of George I., dated 26th April, 1717, explains the object of the " Widdowsmen," showing that the widows of officers who were killed or died in the service received a pension from a fund accumulated for them by means of the pay drawn for these " Widdowsmen," who existed only on paper :—

" Our Commissary-General of the Musters to pass and allow upon the Muster, one man out of each respective Troop or Company of Our forces, both at home and abroad, to be and to remain as a fund for the payment thereof, of which Royal Bounty we do hereby Establish, Direct, and Appoint you to be the receiver and paymaster."—*Military Miscellany Books*.

Officers of Such Troops are to enter into our pay, and you are to cause the said Voluntiers to be Raised and Levy'd as aforesaid to march under the Command of such Commission Officers as you ſhall direct to Hertford, appointed for the Rendezvous of the Said Regiment, and all Magistrates, Justices of the Peace, Constables and other Our Officers who it may concern are Hereby required to be Assisting unto You in providing Quarters, Impressing Carriages and otherwise, as there ſhall be Occasion.

Given at Our Court at St. James' this 23rd day of July, 1715. In the first Year of Our Reign.

By His Majesty's Command,

(Sd.) Wm. Pulteney.[1]

To our Trusty and well beloved Brigadier Gore and Colonel of one of our Regiments of Dragoons.[2]

The instructions in the above Warrant were speedily acted upon, and the regiment raised in Hertfordshire and the adjoining counties. So successfully were its ranks recruited to the authorised strength, that in a very short time Brigadier-General Gore was enabled to report his corps complete and fit for service, whereupon its numbers were augmented from thirty to forty men per troop (" Widdowsmen" included).

As the several troops were embodied they were assembled at Hertford, and the head-quarters established there for the first time, but on the 30th September they were moved to Marlborough. The corps thus raised has been continued in the service to the present day, and is that now known as " The 10th, or Prince of Wales's Own Royal Hussars."

---

[1] *War Office Military Miscellany Books*, Record Office.

[2] At the same date the following dragoon regiments were also raised :—

Bowles' Dragoons.	Rich's Dragoons.
Pepper's ,,	Dormer's ,,
W. Stanhope's ,,	Churchill's ,,
Munden's ,,	Newton's ,,
Tyrrell's ,,	Honywood's ,,

1715

Lieutenant-Colonel Peter Hawker was appointed on the 22nd July as lieutenant-colonel commanding, but at that time the full colonel of the regiment took a very active part in its affairs, and often accompanied it on service in the field.

CHAPTER II

ORIGIN OF THE BRITISH CAVALRY—LIST OF OFFICERS—PRICES OF
COMMISSIONS—PAY OF NON-COMMISSIONED OFFICERS AND MEN
—DRESS

BEFORE proceeding further with the regimental history, 1715
it may be well to examine the origin and progress of
the mounted branch of our army, its composition, arms,
dress, pay, &c.

The formation of the present army commenced
after the Restoration in 1660, with the establishment of
regular corps of horse and foot. The horsemen were
cuirassiers, but only wore armour on the head and
body. The arms which they carried are described in
the Regulations of Charles II., 5th May, 1663 :

> Each Horseman to have for his defensive armes, back, breast
> and pot, and for his offensive armes, a sword and a case of
> pistolls, the barrels whereof are not to be under fourteen inches
> in length ; and each Trooper of Our Guards to have a carbine,
> besides the aforesaid armes.

In the first year of the reign of King James II.
several regiments of horse and dragoons were raised,
and the former were armed with a short carbine in
addition to the sword and pair of pistols. The
dragoons had "Snaphause musquets, strapt, with
bright barrels of three foote eight inches long,
bayonetts, &c." After several years' experience little
advantage was found to accrue from having cavalry

formed almost exclusively for engaging the enemy on foot, and, the horse having laid aside their armour, the arms and equipment of horse and dragoons were so nearly assimilated that there remained little distinction besides the name and rate of pay.[1]

In 1715 the cavalry consisted of four troops of Horse Guards, each troop commanded by a colonel; two troops of Horse Grenadier Guards; the Royal Horse Guards Blue; the King's, Queen's, and 4th Regiments of Horse, which became in 1746 the 1st, 2nd, and 3rd Dragoon Guards; three other regiments of horse, and the King's Carabiniers, which became in 1788 the 4th, 5th, 6th, and 7th Dragoon Guards, and fourteen regiments of dragoons.

At this time (1715), and for many years afterwards, all regiments bore the name of the Colonel-in-Chief. It was, however, then, as now, the custom to select a particular corps to bear the designation of "The Prince of Wales's Own." A cavalry regiment raised in the same year by Colonel Charles Churchill, but dis-

[1] Cannon's *Records of the 2nd Dragoon Guards.*

1715

banded in 1718, was so styled, as is shown by a Royal Warrant issued on the 8th March, 1716, authorising the sum of 600*l.* to be paid " to Colonel Charles Churchill, as Colonel of Our most dear son, George Augustus, Prince of Wales's Own Regiment of Dragoons, in consideration of their losses by horses killed and disabled, and other extraordinary expenses in their long and continued marches in a very rigorous season, in pursuit of the rebels who were taken prisoners at Preston." We shall, by-and-by, see how and when the 10th Dragoons succeeded to this greatly prized distinction.

The following are the names of the officers first appointed to the regiment :

Colonel and Captain Humphrey Gore.

Lieutenant - Colonel and Captain Peter Hawker.
Major and Captain Paston Knyvet.
Captain Balthazar Guidet.
  „ George Treby.
  „ John Wittewrong.
Captain and Lieutenant Israel Presley.
Lieutenant Henry Gore.
  „ John Jordain.

Lieutenant Robert Blount.
  „ Andrew Purcell.
  „ Henry Courtney.
Cornet Francis Boucher.
  „ William Prosser.
  „ William Stannus.
  „ Peter Chaban.
  „ Thomas Hincks.
  „ Thomas Crawley.[1]

It will be noticed that the three field officers commanded troops. They also received pay for them. The senior lieutenant held the rank of captain, and evidently commanded the colonel's troop.

The system of promotion of the officers by purchase was at this time fully sanctioned, and the prices paid for commissions in Gore's Dragoons were laid down in

[1] List of officers taken from records in the Military Secretary's Office, Horse Guards.

a Regulation dated "Whitehall, 27th February, 1719–20, by His Majesty's command.

(Sd.) GEORGE TREBY."

The prices were as follows :

Colonel and captain, 6,000*l.* ; lieutenant-colonel and captain, 2,700*l.* ; major and captain, 2,200*l.* ; captain, 1,500*l.* ; captain-lieutenant, 850*l.* ; lieutenant, 680*l.* ; cornet, 520*l.* ; adjutant, 172*l.*

As a provision for officers the sale of commissions on retirement[1] had been recognised as early as the reign of Charles II.[2]

In the Estimates for His Majesty's land forces in 1716, Brigadier Gore's regiment is shown as consisting of six troops of forty-nine men each, officers included, and the grant to the regiment for 366 days is given as 12,849*l.* 13*s.* This sum maintained the regiment in pay, arms, clothing, accoutrements, forage, &c.[3] The whole of this money was disbursed by the colonel, who was held responsible for its covering all the expenses of his regiment. As regards the pay of the non-com-

---

[1] In March 1755 a Warrant signed " H. Fox " throws some light on the manner of promotion and retirement then existing :—" The sum of 5*s.* a day is granted to Major Chaban for the term of his natural life, on his being replaced in the 10th Dragoons by the promotion of Captain William Augustus Pitt of the same regiment, to be allowed out of the pay of the said Major Pitt, or the major of our said regiment for the time being, and that upon his death the major for the time being shall receive pay conformable to the establishment."—*War Office Miscellany Books*, Record Office.

[2] " The Duke of Buckingham, in a speech in the House of Commons during that reign, says: ' I had a regiment, which was Sir G. Scott's, and, not knowing the law of England, I gave him 1,500*l.* for it.' The Warrant of Charles II. (7th March, 1683–4) deals with the system as one established, and the assent of the Crown gave it legality."—Clode, *Military Forces of the Crown.*

[3] War Office Library.

missioned officers and men, a Warrant was issued in 1717 1715
regulating the pay and stoppages of the cavalry :—

				s.	d.		s.	d.
	Sergeant's full pay per week	.					14	0
				s.	d.			
	Deductions { To his Landlord	.	5	3				
	For Corn .	.	.	1	5½			
	To the Farrier .	.	0	3½				
				7	0——7	0		
In winter quarters or in the House .							7	0
	Corporals and Drums, each .	.	10	6				
	Deductions, as above .	.	7	0				
				3	6——3	6		
	Dragoons . . .	.	8	2				
	Deductions, as above .	.	7	0				
				1	2——1	2		

While the horses were at grass, which period varied from sixteen to twenty weeks, the pay for man and horse was subject to further stoppages for " medicine money," &c.[1]

As regards the dress of regiments at this time, very great latitude was given to the colonel, but from pictures of the period the uniform of the 10th Dragoons resembled in nearly every particular what is described later on in the Warrant of 1751, except that instead of the royal arms the accoutrements bore the crest of the colonel.

The chivalric costumes of the Stuarts' reigns had gradually disappeared in the time of William and Mary and Queen Anne. The effect of the Marlborough wars was to introduce the Ramilies cocked hats and large boots. The hair, which had hitherto been worn in long perukes, in Queen Anne's time was formed into a tail, with a bow at the top called a Ramilies tie, which

---

[1] *War Office Miscellany Books*, Record Office.

is said to have been first introduced by the famous Lord Bolingbroke.

No great changes took place in dress during the reign of George I., but it is difficult to follow the various fashions in wearing the hair. Luard, in his "History of the Dress of the British Soldier," says: "To the catalogue of wigs we find added the tie-wig and the bob-wig, the latter sometimes worn without powder. The Ramilies tail was followed by the pig-tail, which was adopted about the year 1745. The military wore powder, with the head well larded; at one time long tails, at another a thick tail clubbed, as it was called, which was turning it up, leaving a great knob below and securing it with a leather strap." The dressing of the hair and the cock of the hat were very much thought of during the reign of George II. and the early part of George III. "The military and the mercantile cock of the hat were very different."

The French Revolution in 1789 had its influence on these fashions, and " the three-cornered hat was laughed out of fashion by the nicknames of ' Egham, Staines, and Windsor,' being compared to the triangular direction-post which pointed to those places." The Chelsea pensioners are now the sole supporters of this head-dress. "Wigs also diminished in size at the same period, and the practice of frizzing, plastering, and powdering the hair came into fashion. The poor soldiers, who had always been compelled to follow fashion, however ugly and unfit for military purposes, were not yet released from the tortures of hair-dressing. Stiff curls were worn on each side, and a long tail behind, the whole plastered and powdered. In 1804 an order was issued to reduce the tails to seven inches, and in 1808 they were abolished."[1]

[1] The above extracts are taken from Luard's *History of the Dress of the British Army.*

CHAPTER III

MOVEMENTS OF THE REGIMENT—REVIEW BY GEORGE I.—BRIGADIER-
GENERAL GORE—AUGMENTATION—REVIEW BY GEORGE II.—LORD
SEMPHILL'S HIGHLANDERS—LORD COBHAM APPOINTED COLONEL
—GENERAL CHURCHILL

ALTHOUGH the regiment was not employed in Scotland during the rebellion headed by the Earl of Mar, it rendered good service in England by suppressing tumults and maintaining order. The performance of these disagreeable and arduous duties was highly commended by the authorities at that time. In October 1716 the head-quarters of the regiment moved from Marlborough to Exeter. When tranquillity had been restored to the country during the following year, a reduction in the strength of the army was made. In 1718 several of the regiments raised in 1715 were disbanded, but Gore's regiment of dragoons was not one of them. For some years it was quartered in turn in every part of England, having, in 1717, been stationed in Yorkshire; in 1719, in Gloucestershire and Worcestershire; and in 1720 it occupied extensive cantonments in Devonshire and Shropshire; while in 1721 its troops were again distributed through the counties of Worcestershire and Gloucestershire.

On the 8th March, 1720, Major Charles Powlett was appointed lieutenant-colonel commanding the regiment, *vice* Lieutenant-Colonel Hawker, who resigned. Major

1716–
1721

Powlett had up to this time served in Lord Mark Kerr's
regiment of foot.

In 1722 some uneasiness began to be felt throughout the kingdom in consequence of the Jacobites
renewing their plots and intrigues for the restoration
of the Stuarts to the English throne; but the measures
taken by the Government in keeping the army in readiness for any emergency proved sufficient to prevent an
outbreak.   In May of that year the 10th Dragoons
was encamped near Marlborough, whence it marched
to Salisbury Plain.   Here, with a number of other
regiments, it was reviewed by George I. on the 30th of
August, and after the review a detachment of the regiment had the honour of escorting His Majesty on the
first stage of the road to Portsmouth.   From Salisbury
Plain the regiment marched into camp near Chippenham, remaining there until the 1st October, when it
moved into cantonments at Cirencester, &c.

On the 12th January, 1723, Brigadier-General Gore
was removed to the Royal Dragoons, and the colonelcy
of the Tenth was bestowed upon Colonel Charles
Churchill, who had raised the regiment of dragoons
already referred to, known as the " Prince of Wales's
Own," in 1715.   The colonelcy of that corps he sold to
Sir Charles Hotham in 1717 ; but twelve months afterwards it was disbanded.

Lieutenant-General Humphrey Gore obtained his
first commission as ensign in a regiment of foot about
the year 1689, and served with distinction in the wars
of King William III., until the treaty of Ryswick in
1697.   He also did good service during the reign of
Queen Anne, having by that time obtained the rank
of lieutenant-colonel.   Appointed colonel of a newly
raised regiment of foot on the 1st February, 1707, he
proceeded with it in 1709 to Spain, where, on the

1st January following he received the command of a brigade.

Brigadier Gore next took part in the battles of Almanara and Saragossa in 1710, besides being engaged in the advance upon Madrid and the subsequent retreat towards Valencia. Being in the unfortunate affair of Brihuega, where General Stanhope's force, after standing one of the severest sieges on record, was obliged to surrender, Brigadier Gore was made prisoner by the French. He was subsequently released, but, his regiment being disbanded at the peace of Utrecht, he was not again employed until 1715, when, as we have seen, he was elected by King George I. " to raise a regiment of dragoons." Removed to the Royal Dragoons in 1723, he was appointed major-general on the 6th March, 1727, and lieutenant-general on the 29th October, 1735. He died on the 18th August, 1739.

In the summer of 1723 the 10th Dragoons was removed into quarters in Leicestershire, where the regiment remained until the spring of 1724, when it was sent again into Yorkshire. In the following year it was quartered in the counties of Gloucester and Hertford, finding detachments for duty on the Hampshire coast in aid of the Excise. After these detachments had been called in, the regiment marched into quarters near Hounslow in April 1726. In May, George I. reviewed the Tenth on Hounslow Heath, the regiment marching immediately afterwards into Gloucestershire. During the winter it was employed in suppressing riots in Somersetshire and Wiltshire. In this year a Warrant, dated 16th February, was issued, making the following provisions :—

That Dragoon Regiments should have the same exercise on horseback and on foot.

That every troop should consist of one Quartermaster, two

1723–
1727

Sergeants, three Corporals, two Drummers, one Hautbois, and forty-seven effective private dragoons.

That as the Colonels have represented that there are no sword blades to be had in England, His Majesty has been pleased to send orders to the Lord Commissioner of the Treasury to permit sword blades to be imported from Germany.[1]

(Signed)   H. PELHAM.[2]

1727–
1728

In 1727, in anticipation of hostilities breaking out between this country and Germany, the Tenth was augmented[3] by three troops and directed to be held in readiness to embark for Holland; but in consequence of the death of George I., combined with a more favourable turn of affairs between this country and Germany, the embarkation did not take place.

On the 4th May, 1728, the regiment, having returned to Hounslow, was reviewed on the Heath by George II. in brigade with the 4th Dragoons, when the two corps, as we are informed by the "London Gazette," "made a very fine appearance." After the review the Tenth marched to Scotland, where it was stationed nearly two years. During this time its establishment was reduced to its former complement of six troops. Returning to England in March 1730, the regiment remained in Yorkshire until April 1732, when it moved into Lancashire.

1733

On the 21st May, 1733, Major Philip Gery succeeded to the lieutenant-colonelcy and command of the regiment, *vice* Powlett, promoted into the 1st troop of Horse Guards. Major Gery had been in the 10th Dragoons since 1717.

In this year (1733) the regiment was quartered in Leicestershire, and whilst there an order was received, dated 18th February, 1733–34, " to cause six corporals

---

[1] *War Office Miscellany Books*, Record Office.   [2] Secretary for War.
[3] Cannon's *Records*.

and fifty-four effective men to be added to the 10th Dragoons—viz. one corporal and nine privates to each troop, with horses.—(Signed) WM. STRICKLAND." [1]

From Leicestershire, in the spring of 1734, the regiment marched into Cheshire, going back to Yorkshire in 1735, where it was stationed until 1738.

A Clothing Warrant was issued on the 20th May, 1736, by which it would appear that Government was by degrees taking the management of the clothing of the army more into its own hands, instead of its being left to the entire control of the colonels of regiments. This order lays down specified times for issue and the articles to be supplied, viz.:—

New Boots to be supplied every third Cloathing to the whole Regiment.

New Headstalls, Reins, Breastplates, &c., &c., every third Cloathing, new Housings and Caps every fifth Cloathing.

New Accoutrements of the best Buff that can be had in England, a Shoulder Belt with a Pouch and Waste Belt sufficient to carry the Sword, with place to receive the Bayonet and Sling for the Arms, such as the General Officers appointed to inspect the Cloathing shall approve of, every Tenth Cloathing.

The Second Mounting to consist of new laid Hats, Gloves and Collars.—By His Majesty's command.

(Sd). WILL YONGE. [2]

On the 9th July, 1737, Major Anthony Lamelonière was appointed from the second troop of the Horse Grenadier Guards as lieutenant-colonel commanding the 10th Dragoons in the place of Lieutenant-Colonel Gery, deceased.

On the 5th September, 1739, a Warrant was issued to increase " each troop of the eight regiments of dragoons by one sergeant and ten private men, so as

[1] *War Office Miscellany Books.* [2] *Ibid.*, Record Office.

to make their strength three sergeants, three corporals, two drummers, and fifty-nine effective private men," and authorising the colonels, in order to defray the expense of clothing, an assignment of the arrears of the pay from the June previous until June 1741.[1]

In the summer of 1740 the Tenth formed part of a force assembled under Lieutenant-General Wade, near Newbury, and was encamped there for some weeks. In 1741 hostilities broke out on the Continent, and the next year a British army proceeded to Flanders. The Tenth, however, was retained in Great Britain.

On the 4th February, 1741, Major John Jordain was promoted lieutenant-colonel commanding the regiment, *vice* Lieutenant-Colonel Lamelonière, who was transferred to the third troop of Horse Guards.

It was in 1739 that Lord Semphill raised his regiment of Highlanders, formed of what was termed " independent companies," in which, among other inducements held out to recruits, was a promise that the corps should never be required to go on foreign service. However, the army at this time being much reduced, this regiment was sent in May 1743 to Gravesend, for the purpose of being despatched to Flanders. On being ordered to embark a report was circulated amongst them that their destination was the West Indies. They at once burst out into open mutiny. One hundred and fifty of them, fully armed and accoutred, deserted, and marched off in a body towards Scotland. A squadron of Wade's 3rd Dragoon Guards and Churchill's 10th Dragoons were ordered in pursuit of the Highlanders, whom they overtook in Ladywood, near Oundle, and after much persuasion they were prevailed upon to surrender. Three ringleaders were tried by court-martial and shot, while the remainder of the mutineers

[1] *War Office Miscellany Books*, Record Office.

were drafted into different colonies abroad. When the Highlanders knew their destination was Flanders instead of the West Indies, no objection was made by any of the remainder to embark. It is almost needless to add that in the Netherlands, and subsequently in Germany, Lord Semphill's Highlanders, now the 42nd Highlanders, laid the foundation of a fame the brilliancy of which has never been lessened, but ever since steadily increased.[1]

During 1744 the Tenth gave a number of volunteers, also horses, to the dragoon regiments on foreign service. On the 14th May, 1745, Lieutenant-General Churchill died, and was succeeded in the colonelcy of the Tenth by Field-Marshal Viscount Cobham, from the 6th Horse, now the 5th Dragoon Guards.

Lieutenant-General Charles Churchill was a son of an elder brother of the great Duke of Marlborough. Entering the army in 1693, he saw much service in the Low Countries under his relative during the wars of King William III. and Queen Anne. Appointed captain and lieutenant-colonel in 1704 in the 2nd Foot Guards, he proceeded to Portugal to serve under the Earl of Galway, then in command of a body of troops in that country. Finding, however, that he was missing great opportunities through being absent from the Netherlands, he soon applied for and obtained permission to join the British forces there. In March 1706 he was appointed regimental major of the 3rd Foot (the Buffs), of which his father, General Charles Churchill, was colonel. At the battle of Ramilies, fought on the 23rd May, 1706, he especially distinguished himself by driving with his battalion three French regiments into a morass, where most of them either perished or were taken prisoners. Promoted for his gallantry on this occasion

---

[1] See Cannon's *Historical Records of the 42nd*, p. 32.

c 2

to the rank of colonel, he in 1709 succeeded Colonel Johnson in the command of a regiment of foot, which was, however, disbanded at the peace of Utrecht in 1713. Two years afterwards he raised a regiment of horse, which was styled "The Prince of Wales's Own Regiment of Dragoons." This being disbanded in 1718, His Majesty in 1723 appointed him colonel of the Tenth. In 1727 Colonel Churchill was appointed brigadier-general, major-general in 1735, and lieutenant-general in 1739. He was likewise Governor of Plymouth, one of the Grooms of the Bedchamber to King George II., Deputy Ranger of St. James's Park, and represented Castle-Rising in Parliament. He died, as already stated, on the 14th May, 1745.

CHAPTER IV

THE REBELLION OF 1745—BATTLE OF FALKIRK—DUKE OF CUM-
BERLAND SENT TO COMMAND—BATTLE OF CULLODEN—MEDAL
STRUCK—REGIMENT REDUCED

ALTHOUGH the rebellion of 1715 had been easily put   1745
down, the supporters of the Stuarts had not lost heart.
The battle of Fontenoy and the reverses that England
had experienced in Flanders excited fresh hopes in
the mind of Charles Edward, the son of the Chevalier St. George and grandson of James II.[1]   Known
in England as " the Young Pretender," in Scotland
almost idolised under the name of " Bonnie Prince
Charlie," it scarcely needed his mother's immense
fortune, besides numerous adherents, to make him
formidable to the House of Hanover.   Imagining that
the British army was so weakened by its losses that it
could not oppose him in any formidable numbers, this
prince resolved to seek the coast of Scotland alone, and
throw himself upon his friends.   The Court of France,
without openly approving this attempt, secretly favoured
it.   Landing in Scotland on the 25th July, Charles reached
Perth at the head of 2,000 men, and on the 4th September proclaimed his father, James III., King of Great
Britain.[2]   On the 17th September he took possession of
Edinburgh, and on the 21st defeated the royal army
under Sir John Cope at the battle of Preston Pans.

In consequence of the growing insurrection, Mar-

[1] Cust, *Annals of the Wars.*   [2] Russell's *Memoirs of Europe.*

shal Wade was despatched to Newcastle to collect as many troops as possible, several regiments were re-called from Flanders, and the Duke of Cumberland, who had been summoned from Germany in great haste, at once undertook the formation of another army, which was assembled on Finchley Common.[1] The 10th (or Cobham's) Dragoons formed part of this force.

On the last day of October the young prince, now master of the whole kingdom of Scotland, with the exception of the castles of Edinburgh and Stirling, commenced his march into England, which was carried out with considerable skill.[2] After possessing himself of Carlisle, he advanced on Preston and Manchester, and finally reached Derby on the 4th December, thus interposing himself between the Duke of Cumberland's army and London. The royal army, on which the defence of England principally rested, lay at Lichfield, Coventry, Stafford, and Newcastle-under-Lyne. The rebels now found themselves in a critical position, as the Duke of Cumberland, with a large disciplined force, was in their rear and Marshal Wade on their flank. The Highland chiefs therefore urged the necessity of instantly returning to Scotland, and, the young prince at last acceding, the insurgent army began its retreat on the 6th December, pursued by the English cavalry. The 10th Dragoons, taking part in the general advance, made several long marches, and finally arrived in the middle of January 1746 at Edinburgh.

1746   The Duke of Cumberland had been recalled from Carlisle to guard the southern coast against an apprehended invasion from France, and Marshal Wade, who had succeeded him as commander-in-chief of the royal forces, was now replaced by General Hawley. Under

[1] Cust's *Annals of the Wars.*   [2] Russell's *Memoirs of Europe.*

his orders were Major-General Huske, Brigadiers Cholmondeley and Mordaunt, three regiments of dragoons,
a small force of artillery, and twelve regiments of
infantry, most of which had served on the Continent.
Thinking this force sufficient to destroy the rebels,
who were now occupied in the siege of Stirling Castle,
General Hawley set out from Edinburgh, and on the
16th January encamped in a field on the west of the
town of Falkirk.   Charles, hearing of his approach, left
a few hundred men to continue the siege, and advanced
to meet the royal troops, but the English remained in-
active.   On the morning of the 17th the royal troops
were joined by Cobham's regiment of dragoons (the
Tenth) and a thousand Argylshire Highlanders.   About
eleven o'clock the same day a body of the rebels was
observed advancing on the Stirling and Falkirk road.
Hawley being away from the camp, General Huske was
left in command, and evidently had his attention attracted in this direction,[1] while Charles himself crossed
the Carron, and marched in the direction of some high
ground called Falkirk Muir.   General Hawley, now
arriving, ordered three regiments of dragoons to endeavour to anticipate the rebel Highlanders, and for some
time it appeared a race between the two who should
get soonest to the top of the hill.   At this moment the
day became overcast, and before the cavalry could
advance a storm of great violence beat in their faces,
which so much impeded them that the Macdonald
Highlanders were the first to reach the ground, and
were soon followed by the rest of the insurgent forces,
who now formed in order of battle in two lines.

The royal army likewise formed in two lines, the
dragoons in front, facing the right and centre of the
Highlanders.   There was a ravine or gully which

---

[1] Cust's *Annals of the Wars* and Russell's *Memoirs of Europe.*

separated the right of the King's army from the left of the rebels. No artillery was employed on either side, as the insurgents had left theirs to take part in the siege of Stirling, while that of the English[1] had stuck in a bog while crossing the moor and could not be extricated in time.

The battle commenced with an attack on the rebels by the three regiments of dragoons under Ligonier. The Keppoch Highlanders let the cavalry come within ten paces, when they opened fire, and a desperate struggle ensued, the Highlanders throwing themselves on the ground and stabbing the horses. The infantry on both sides then approached one another, and the rebels, after exchanging fire with their opponents, threw down their muskets and attacked the English troops sword in hand. Nearly blinded by the wind and rain, the royal troops did not stand firm. The left gave way, the centre followed the example, and the second line as well as the first was thrown into confusion. Hawley himself was swept down the hillside, not knowing whether any regiments remained firm or not.[2] On the extreme right of the royal army the result was different. The 4th Regiment, the 14th and 48th, afterwards joined by the 3rd Buffs, stood like rocks. Cobham's dragoons, too, had rallied and advanced to the support of these gallant regiments. General Huske, who was in command of this portion of the royal force, took advantage of the ground he held, and poured a destructive fire on the Highlanders, who retired rapidly, spreading the most disastrous tidings. Charles himself, who, from his commanding position, observed this movement, placed himself at the head of the Athol brigade, and forced Huske to withdraw from the field. This he was enabled to do in good order, as he was

---

[1] Cust's *Annals of the Wars.*   [2] Russell's *Memoirs of Europe.*

protected by two squadrons of the 10th Dragoons.[1]
Hawley, leaving behind him twenty officers and 400
men killed, and some 400 prisoners, retired through
Falkirk towards Linlithgow. The battle, as already
stated, was fought without artillery, and the seven
pieces belonging to the English, which had stuck fast in
the bog, were abandoned. The storm continued to rage
during the whole of the next day, while the English
retired to Edinburgh and the rebels recommenced the
siege of Stirling.

When the news of the battle of Falkirk reached
St. James's (it was on the day of a Drawing Room) great
consternation prevailed. The Duke of Cumberland was
sent to the North, and assumed command of the royal
forces in Edinburgh on the 30th January. His presence
gave great encouragement to the troops, with whom His
Royal Highness was very popular, and within thirty
hours of his arrival he set out to give battle to the
insurgents. His army, consisting of fourteen battalions,
the Argyleshire men, and Cobham's and Lord Mark
Kerr's Dragoons, advanced in two columns. The two
dragoon regiments formed the advanced guard. On
the 31st the Duke arrived at Linlithgow, and on approaching Falkirk he learnt that the rebels had raised
the siege of Stirling Castle and retreated northwards.

In February Charles Edward took possession of
Inverness, and made it his head-quarters, and about the
same time the Duke of Cumberland arrived at Aberdeen.
Early in March the English army drew more closely
round the Highlanders, and, amongst other engagements,
the 10th Dragoons were employed in a surprise on
the rebels in the neighbourhood of Strathbogie. The

---

[1] " The enemy did not pursue, which was owing to the gallant behaviour of two squadrons of Cobham's (10th) Dragoons."—*London
Gazette.*

regiment remained at this place for some weeks. In April the English again advanced, crossing the Spey. As they approached Speymouth the Tenth engaged a party of hussars[1] of the insurgents' force, who retired before them. Charles was lodged on the 14th April at Culloden House, and, hearing that the royal troops would not advance that day, and were celebrating the birthday of the Duke of Cumberland, he determined to attack them at Nairn. Under cover of night he advanced, but his Highlanders, half-starved and exhausted, were unable to reach the striking point before daylight. It was then decided to retire to their original position on Culloden Moor and await the attack.

At eight o'clock on the morning of the 16th April information reached Charles that the Duke's army was in full march towards him. He immediately formed up his army in two lines on Drummossie Muir. The King's army was also drawn up in two lines, with a reserve— the Duke of Kingston's Light Horse and one squadron of Cobham's Dragoons (the Tenth) on the right of the first line, a regiment of dragoons and two squadrons of Cobham's on the left. "Two field-pieces were placed in the intervals between the battalions, and did great execution. About two o'clock the Highlanders, impatient of the fire of the artillery, commenced the attack,"[2] descending from the strong position they held, traversing the marshy land below, and charging their opponents sword in hand. They succeeded in breaking through two regiments of English in the first line, but on reaching the second were received with so terrible a fire from Semphill's regiment "that great numbers fell, and nearly all the rest turned back." While this was going on

---

[1] This is the first mention of hussars in Great Britain. Evidently a portion of the foreign levies employed by the Pretender.

[2] Russell's *Memoirs of Europe.*

General Bland, who commanded the cavalry, having broken down a wall on the right of the rebel army, entered with the 10th Dragoons and other cavalry, and, driving back the Highlanders posted behind it, got on their flank and rear. The flight of the latter now became general, and they were followed in pursuit by the English cavalry, who completed the victory. Prince Charles, after leaving the field, crossed the river Nairn, where he dismissed two troops of horse which had accompanied him, and proceeded himself to Gorthlech, to take counsel with Lord Lovat.

The number of English troops in the action of Culloden was about 8,000, the Highlanders not exceeding 5,000. The loss of the royal army amounted to about 310 killed and wounded ; that of the insurgents to about 1,000.

Although the chiefs of the clans were prepared to make a further resistance, the Prince declined their offers. For some months Charles wandered among the Western Isles, and, despite the 30,000*l.* offered for his capture and the privations he underwent, he was enabled at length to escape in safety to France.

To commemorate the victory of Culloden the King caused medals to be struck. They were oval in shape, in gold, silver, and in bronze, with garnished edge, and pierced loop for suspension. On the obverse side is the head of the Duke of Cumberland, " Cumberland " above. On the reverse " Apollo " standing ; at his feet a dragon pierced with an arrow : " Actum est ilicet periit." Exergue : " Præl. Colod. Ap. XVI. MDCCXLVI." There also appears to have been another medal struck in bronze—circular, with pierced ornamental loop— supposed to have been worn by those who fought at Culloden. On the obverse, the Duke of Cumberland on horseback, a battle in the distance. Above : " Gul.

1746   Aug. Cum. Terror Reb." Exergue : " 1746."[1] Reverse
plain.   It would seem that, although the oval medal
had a ring, as if intended for suspension, there is no
account of its having been conferred as an honorary
distinction to be worn.[2]

After the battle of Culloden the 10th Dragoons
were employed on the coasts of Scotland for some
months, preventing the escape of the rebels, and after
remaining in quarters for a short time in that country
returned to England in 1747.

[1] Gibson's *British Military and Naval Medals.* The above medals
can be seen in the British Museum.

[2] " Although the custom of striking medals to commemorate victories
may be traced to the ancients, and the Moguls are believed to have granted
them in the twelfth century, it is only in modern times that they have
been issued in order to be worn as personal decorations. There is no proof
of medals being conferred in England for services in the field earlier than
the time of Charles I., who in May 1643 authorised a badge for such
soldiers as might distinguish themselves in " forlorn hopes." For the
battle of Edgehill a medal was also issued. The example set by the
King was followed by his enemies, and Cromwell issued a medal for
Naseby and Dunbar. This medal is the first ever given to both officers
and men, as is the present practice, until that for Waterloo was authorised.
With the restoration of the Monarchy, the practice of awarding medals
for military and naval services appears to have fallen into abeyance, and
was not resumed until the reign of William and Mary, when a gold
medal was given to each of the officers engaged in the defeat of the French
fleet at the battle of La Hague on the 24th May, 1692. The medals of
succeeding reigns appear to have been confined to naval services.
Although medals were struck in commemoration of the victories of the
great Duke of Marlborough, it is certain that they were not worn by
either officers or soldiers. It was not so, however, with the naval service."
—Carter's *Medals of the British Army.*

CHAPTER V

SIZE OF DRAGOON HORSES—ESTABLISHMENT DECREASED—DEATH
OF LORD COBHAM—FIRST CLOTHING WARRANT—THE LIGHT OR
HUSSAR TROOP FORMED—WARS IN INDIA AND AMERICA

AT the end of the campaign in Scotland a Warrant 1746-
appeared in 1746–47, issuing an order relating to the 1747
size of dragoon horses.

It is H.R.H. the Duke's Orders that for the future no Horse
shall be bought to mount the Dragoons above the Size of Fifteen
hands, at most, and that the Officer or Officers, who are appointed
to Buy, choose, or receive such Horses have very strong Instructions given them to buy or take very Nimble kind of Horses that
can Gallop, with short backs, broad Fillets for carrying of Forage,
Small clean Legs, and as clear of Hair as possible. And to prevent the Excuse of Horses growing after they are Bought, it is
His positive orders that no Horse be bought for any Regiment
that is not rising five years old at least ye next Grass, and as
they are for immediate Duty, if they were rising Six Years old, it
would be better for the Service, and His Royal Highness gives
this further notice that if notwithstanding these orders, any
Horses are bought above the size or under the age here directed
and found so, when Received, by whom His Highness shall
appoint, it shall be to the Loss of the Buyer, receiver or chooser.
It is H.R.H.'s opinion that the Sergeants of Dragoons should
be mounted upon a much Lighter Nimbler kind of horse than
the Dragoon.

During 1747 war was continued on the Continent,
but the 10th Dragoons were not called upon to take

part in it. The year 1748 opened with vigorous preparations for war in every quarter; but the preliminaries of a general pacification at Aix-la-Chapelle were commenced in April, and on the 18th October the peace was signed. A disarmament throughout Europe then took place, and amongst the reductions in England, amounting to 1,900 men, the establishment of the Tenth was lowered to 285 men. A few years of peace followed the treaty of Aix-la-Chapelle, and public business in England continued to flow in a calm and unbroken current. On the 15th March, 1748, Lieutenant-Colonel Henry Whitley succeeded to the command of the regiment, *vice* Jordain, who was appointed to the colonelcy of a regiment of Marines.[1]

1749
On the death of Field-Marshal Viscount Cobham in 1749, the colonelcy of the Tenth was given to Major-General Mordaunt, his commission being dated the 1st November of the same year. Sir Richard Temple, afterwards Viscount Cobham, served under King William III. in the Netherlands, and subsequently under the great Duke of Marlborough during the wars of Queen Anne. At the sieges of Venloo and Ruremonde, at the battle of Oudenarde, and at the siege of the important fortress of Lisle, he equally distinguished himself, and in January 1709 he was promoted to the rank of major-general. His conduct at the sieges of Tournay and Mons, as well as at Marlborough's crowning victory, Malplaquet, was rewarded in the following year by the rank of lieutenant-general and the colonelcy of the 4th Dragoons. Continuing to serve under Marlborough, in 1711 he took part in forcing the French lines at Arleux and the capture of the fortress of Bouchain. On the accession of King George I. he was

---

[1] Several instances occur at this period of cavalry officers being transferred to the Marines.

created Baron Cobham, and after having been sent
with General Stanhope in 1714 as joint ambassador to
Vienna, was appointed in 1715 colonel of the Royal
Dragoons. Two years later he was made Governor of
Windsor Castle, and in 1718 advanced to the dignity
of Viscount Cobham. Removed to the King's Horse
(now 1st Dragoon Guards) in 1718, he was made about
the same time a Privy Councillor and Governor of the
island of Jersey, but resigned his appointments in 1733.
In 1742 he was promoted to the rank of field-marshal,
and in December of the same year King George II. conferred upon him the colonelcy of the first troop of
Horse Grenadier Guards. In 1744 he was transferred
to the 6th Horse (now 5th Dragoon Guards), and in
1745 to the 10th Dragoons, the colonelcy of which he
retained until his death in 1749.

Previous to 1751 great latitude had been given to
colonels in the clothing of their regiments, and there
is no doubt that in details each was permitted to con-
sult his individual taste, although a board of general
officers was appointed periodically to supervise the
matter. Up to this date it is extremely difficult to
give authority for the dress of the army; but as very
few changes took place during the reigns of George I.
and II., it is almost certain that the dress now autho-
ritatively laid down by Warrant was in all essentials
identical with the dress worn by the regiment when
first raised in 1715, unless that at that time the appointments, &c., bore the crest of the colonel, instead of, as
now ordered, the royal arms.

On the 1st July, 1751, a Royal Warrant was issued
as follows :—

No Colonel to put his Arms, Crest, Device or Livery on any
part of the Appointments of the Regiment under his Command.

No part of the Cloathing or Ornaments of the Regiment to

be altered after the following Regulations are put in Execution, but by Us, or Our Captain General's Permission.

By this Warrant the Tenth was ordered to be equipped and accoutred as follows :—

Coats—scarlet, double breasted, without lappels, lined with deep yellow; slit sleeves, turned up with deep yellow; the button holes worked up with white lace; the buttons of white metal, set on three, four and five together; a slash pocket in each skirt; and a white worsted aiguillette on the right shoulder.

Waistcoats and Breeches—deep yellow.

Hats—bound with silver lace, and ornamented with a black cockade and a white metal loop.

Boots—of jacked leather.

Cloaks—of scarlet cloth, with a deep yellow collar, and lined with deep yellow shalloon; the buttons set on white frogs or loops, with a green stripe down the centre.

Horse Furniture—of deep yellow cloth: the holster-caps and housing having a border of white lace, with a green stripe down the centre; X.D. embroidered on each corner of the housing, on a red ground, within a wreath of roses and thistle; the King's cypher, with the crown over it, and X.D. underneath, embroidered on the holster caps.

Officers—to be distinguished by silver lace, their coats and waistcoats bound with silver embroidery; the button-holes worked with silver and a crimson silk sash worn across the left shoulder.

Quarter Master—to wear a crimson sash round the Waist.

Drummers and Hautboys—Clothed in deep yellow coats, lined with red, and ornamented with white lace, having a green stripe down the centre, their waistcoats and breeches of red cloth.

Sergeants—to have narrow silver lace on the cuffs, pockets, and shoulder straps; silver aiguillettes, and deep yellow and green worsted sashes tied round the waist.

Guidons—the first, or King's Guidon, to be of crimson silk, embroidered with silver and green; in the centre the rose and thistle conjoined; and crown over them, with the motto " Dieu et mon Droit" underneath; the white horse, the emblem of the house of Hanover, in a compartment in the first and fourth corners, and X.D. in silver characters on a deep yellow ground in the second and third corners. The second and third guidons to be of deep yellow silk, with silver and green fringe; in the centre X.D. in silver characters on a red ground, within a wreath of roses and thistles on the same stalk; the White horse on a red ground in the first and fourth corners, and the rose and thistles conjoined upon a red ground in the second and third corners.

The banners of the kettledrums and trumpets to be the colour of the Faceing of the Regiment, with the Badge of the Regiment in the Centre of the Banner on the Kettledrums, as in the second guidon.

The Drums of Dragoons to be of brass, the Front to be painted with the Colour of the Faceing of the Regiment, &c.

The Bells of Arms to be painted in the same manner as the Drums.

Given at our Court of Kensington this 1st day of July, 1751, in the 21st year of Our Reign. By His Majesty's Command.

H. Fox.[1]

In the spring of 1753 the 10th Dragoons was stationed in Scotland. On the 21st of April it was reviewed near Edinburgh by Lieutenant-General Churchill, "and went through the exercise with great applause."[2] The regiment returned to England in the following year, and occupied quarters in 1755 at Romford and other towns in Essex.

Although in Europe peace existed in 1750 between France and England, the interests of the two countries in the East Indies clashed to such a degree that hostilities may be said to have been carried on without interruption. In 1751 Clive attacked and captured Arcot, and from that time until war was declared in 1755 fighting continued. In North America, the limits

[1] *War Office Miscellany Books*, Record Office.
[2] Cannon's *Records*.

1754–
1755

of our colony in Nova Scotia had been a cause of angry discussion in France. In like manner, the line of demarcation between the French provinces of Canada and the British territory of New England was by no means free from cavil. Collisions followed, neither slight nor few. These, culminating in a skirmish in which Major George Washington[1] was worsted by the French, combined with the hostilities between the English and French in the East Indies, led to war again breaking out between the two countries.[2] An augmentation immediately took place in the English army, and the House of Commons granted a million of money as a vote of credit.

1756

On the 29th January, 1756, a Warrant was issued by His Majesty's commands, signed " Barrington," ordering one troop of light dragoons[3] to be added to all the following regiments :—

1st, 2nd, and 3rd Regiments of Dragoon Guards.

1st Royal Regiment of Dragoons, Colonel Hawley.

2nd Royal Regiment of North British Dragoons, Lieutenant-General Campbell.

3rd King's Own Regiment of Dragoons, Lord Albemarle.

4th Regiment of Dragoons, Sir Robert Rich.

6th Inniskilling Regiment of Dragoons, Lord George Cholmondeley.

7th Queen's Regiment of Dragoons, Lieutenant-General Cope.

10th Regiment of Dragoons, Lieutenant-General Sir John Mordaunt.

11th Regiment of Dragoons, the Earl of Ancram.

Another Warrant was issued on the 14th April, fixing the establishment of these light troops at—

One Captain, one lieutenant, one cornet, one quartermaster, two sergeants, three corporals, two drummers, 60 private light

---

[1] Afterwards General George Washington.

[2] Lord Mahon's *History of England.*

[3] These troops are sometimes spoken of as " hussar " troops.

dragoons, including a farrier. The Corporals and private men to be from 5 ft. 6½ in. to 5 ft. 8 high and light active men. The size of the horses 14.3, and not under, well turned, nimble Road horses as nigh the colour of the Regiment as can be got. The arms of the men to be a Carbine with Ring and Bar, 4 ft. 3 inch long, with a bayonet of 17 inches in length. One pistol of 10 inches in the barrell, and of Carbine bore. A strait cutting Sword, 34 inches long in the Blade.

For accoutrements they are to have tanned leather Shoulder-belts and belt for Sword bayonet, and tanned leather Cartouche Box with a double row of holes to contain 24 Cartridges. The saddle to be with small Cantles behind, as the Jockey saddles are, and to be 22 inches long in the Seat. On the right side the Holster for the Pistol; on the left a Churn, in which a Spade and felling Axe, or a spade and woodman's Bill is to be carried.

The Cloathing and Cloaks of the Light Dragoons to be the same as the rest of the regiment; only instead of Hats, the men are to have Jacked leather caps. The men to wear light Jockey boots with small Stiff tops.

We are pleased to allow £5. 16. 9. for the accoutrements, horse furniture and other appointments for each N.C.O. and Private, and three pounds Levy money. Likewise £12 for each horse.

By His Majesty's Command, this 14th day of April, 1756.

(Signed)   BARRINGTON.[1]

In pursuance of the above order a seventh troop was added to the 10th Dragoons, of which Lieutenant Robert Atkinson was appointed captain, Lord Wallingford lieutenant, and Frederick Caldwell cornet, their appointments bearing date 25th December, 1755, and this troop was designated the " Light Troop."

[1] *War Office Military Miscellany Books*, Record Office.

CHAPTER VI

WAR WITH FRANCE—AUGMENTATION OF THE ARMY—EXPEDITIONS
ON THE FRENCH SEA-COAST—HUSSAR TROOPS SENT ON SERVICE
—REGIMENT EMBARKS FOR GERMANY—THE SEVEN YEARS' WAR
—BATTLE OF MINDEN

1756–
1757

IN May 1756 the 10th Dragoons marched from Essex to Dorchester, and on passing through London had the honour of being reviewed by King George II. in Hyde Park. Subsequently it formed part of the force which had assembled at Blandford for training under Lieutenant-General Sir Charles Howard. Returning thence to Dorchester, the camp broke up in October. The Tenth remained at Dorchester until April 1757, when it proceeded to Canterbury. While stationed here the regiment furnished seventeen detachments to aid the revenue service on the coasts of Kent and Sussex.

1758

With the following year, 1758, came vigorous preparations for carrying on a harassing warfare with France by means of flying squadrons of ships with troops on board. These vessels, sailing from point to point, were intended either to attack by sea the towns on the coast, or, disembarking the land forces, to assail them from the shore. These descents were planned by Mr. Pitt, the Prime Minister, in the belief that they would be the most effectual means of serving our German allies, by drawing the attention of the enemy to their own internal defences.[1] No efforts were spared to make them thoroughly successful. Lord Anson was

----

[1] Russell's *Modern Europe.*

even called away from his post at the Admiralty to take the command, with Hawke and Howe as his subordinates. The force of cavalry, artillery, and infantry ordered to accompany the expedition was certainly composed of the *élite* of their respective services. A battalion from each regiment of the Guards, and the grenade companies of all other regiments in England, making in all sixteen battalions, together with six thousand picked Marines, gave a force of foot second to none of any country; the artillery, with sixty pieces of cannon and fifty mortars of various kinds, was equally well represented; while the horse, which was commanded by Eliott (afterwards Lord Heathfield, the hero of Gibraltar), consisted of nine of the light troops recently added to cavalry regiments, these having been specially selected for this service.[1] The whole force was under the command of Charles, second Duke of Marlborough, with Lord George Sackville as second in command. In May of this year the light troop of the Tenth marched to Portsmouth, where it was formed into a brigade with the light troops of other regiments, ready for embarkation. So great was the enthusiasm of the nation that many noblemen and gentlemen, who had been unable to obtain commissions, voluntarily accompanied the expedition as private soldiers. "Lord Downe, Sir James Lowther, Sir John Armitage, the Hon. W. Berkeley and others, volunteered their services with the Tenth."[2]

The squadron under Commodore Howe sailed from Spithead, and on the 5th June anchored in the Bay of Cancale. Lord Anson also embarked with the expedition, but Hawke proceeded with the larger ships in order to spread more widely the alarm and watch the French squadron in Brest Harbour.

[1] *Life of Lord Howe.*　　　　[2] *Ibid.*

The fortifications at St. Malo proving too strong for a *coup de main*, the Duke of Marlborough landed his force in the bay, and the next morning the whole army marched in two columns towards St. Malo, and encamped a little more than a mile from the town. The light horse advanced to the walls, and were saluted by the guns from the ramparts, which killed a few horses, without any other loss. At night the same party, with the piquet of foot, made their way close under the walls to the harbour, where they found a 50-gun ship, two 36-gun frigates, upwards of twenty privateers, and seventy to eighty merchant ships. To these the troops set fire with combustibles provided for that purpose. The naval stores suffered the same fate.[1] On the completion of these operations the troops were re-embarked, and after appearing before Granville and Cherbourg, which they were unable to attack owing to the weather, the fleet returned to St. Helens, and anchored there on the 1st July.

The success of this expedition by no means answered the ardour of public expectation, and, although contrary to the opinion of King George II., the Prime Minister was not deterred from making another attempt. The King remarked of this expedition: "I never had any opinion of it; we shall brag of having burnt their ships, and they of driving us away." Next month, however, the new expedition sailed under the command of General Bligh, the Duke of Marlborough and Lord George Sackville volunteering to serve in Germany in preference to "buccaneering." Prince Edward Augustus Duke of York, next brother to the Prince of Wales, accompanied this second expedition to the coast of France.

The troops having landed near Cherbourg, and the town being forsaken on their approach, they proceeded

[1] Barrow's *Life of Lord Howe*.

to destroy the forts and the basin. Over 100 pieces of cannon were destroyed, twenty-two brass ordnance were brought away, and afterwards carried with great pomp and procession through the city of London to the Tower. While these operations had been going on in Cherbourg several skirmishes took place at a short distance inland, where the French troops had formed, and in one of these Captain Lindsey, a most active, brave, and intelligent officer, in command of the light troop of the Greys, was killed by a musket shot.[1]

The troops having re-embarked, the fleet sailed to the westward of St. Malo, where a second landing was made. The troops then marched from the Bay of St. Cas to the village of Matignin, where they encountered the French troops. At length, news having arrived of the approach of the Duke d'Aiguillon at the head of about 10,000 men, it was considered necessary to fall back on the ships. The re-embarkation was covered by the Grenadier regiment and the 1st Regiment of Foot Guards. This gallant body formed and faced the greatly superior enemy. About 600 were killed, amongst them General Drury, and 400 were taken prisoners. The expedition then returned to England.

While the light or hussar troop of the 10th Dragoons was thus engaged on the enemy's shore, the six heavy troops had moved to Hounslow, where they were encamped on the Heath, and on the 10th July, in brigade with the Royal Horse Guards (Blue) and the 1st Dragoon Guards, were reviewed by King George II. in Hyde Park, when His Majesty was graciously pleased to express his approbation of the fine appearance and discipline of the troops. Shortly afterwards the Tenth embarked for Germany and joined

---

[1] Barrow's *Life of Lord Howe*; Lord Mahon's *History of England*; Russell's *Modern Europe.*

the force under Charles, Duke of Marlborough, which had been sent to defend the Electorate of Hanover from the inroads of the French. To avert this threatened invasion of the French in 1756, King George II. had entered into subsidising treaties with Hesse-Cassel, who bound herself to supply 8,000 men. Russia at the same time engaged herself to bring 55,000 men into Livonia. The King of Prussia also gave up his French alliance.

The attack on the 17th May by the French on Minorca, then in possession of Great Britain, brought about a declaration of the war known afterwards as the Seven Years' War.

The campaign in Germany was opened on the part of the Allies by Frederick, King of Prussia, entering Saxony and taking possession of Dresden. At the same time Marshal Schwerin and Marshal Keith appeared in Bohemia to overawe the Austrians. In 1757 Frederick entered Bohemia, and the battle of Prague was fought. The French in April crossed the Rhine and the Weser, and the Duke of Cumberland, in command of about 40,000 Hessians and Hanoverians and 6,000 Prussians, retired before them and waited to receive the French at Hastenbech, where a battle of an undecided character took place. The Allies, however, afterwards retired, and the Duke of Cumberland signed the Convention of Closter-seven, which was most unfavourable to him in its terms. The kingdom of Prussia being now a prey to the barbarities of Russia, who had turned against her, and an Austrian army having presented itself before Berlin, Frederick found his difficulties still further increased by the defeat of the Allies in Hanover. At the same time England was in the greatest depths of despondency. Not only on account of losing Minorca to the French, and having to give up the Electorate of Hanover to be pillaged by the French Marshal de Richelieu, but her undertakings in other parts of the world, especially in North America, were meeting with anything but success.

Affairs, having reached this pass, now suddenly changed. Frederick the Great repulsed his enemies on all sides. In England, a new Ministry having been formed, the Government became more energetic, and people entered into the enthusiasm. A new agreement was signed in 1758 in London between the King of Prussia and His Britannic Majesty. Amongst other arrangements, it was resolved to send a body of British troops to join the army under Prince Ferdinand of Brunswick.

The 10th Dragoons, amongst others, embarked for Germany in the middle of July of this year, and, having arrived off Embden on the 1st August, it landed on the 3rd, and encamped till the 5th on some waste ground a few miles above the town. Having shortly afterwards joined the Hanoverian, Hessian, and Brunswick troops under Prince Ferdinand, the regiment was reviewed by His Serene Highness on the 20th at Coesveldt. The season being now far advanced, Prince Ferdinand decided to go into winter quarters, while the French army, under Contades, deemed it more prudent not to follow him across the Rhine, as the heavy rains had rendered its passage difficult.[1] The 10th Dragoons passed the winter in the Bishopric of Paderborn.

It was at this time that Lieutenant-Colonel Henry Whitley, who had commanded the regiment for eleven years with honour to himself and advantage to the service, was rewarded with the colonelcy of the 9th Dragoons, by commission dated 6th April, 1759. He was succeeded by Lieutenant-Colonel William Augustus Pitt,

---

[1] Russell's *Modern Europe*; Cust's *Annals of the Wars*; Mahon's *History of England*.

an officer who had been in the regiment more than fifteen years.[1]

The campaign in Germany opened for the Allies in 1759 with brighter promise. The British arms in every part of the world had proved victorious—in the conquest of Canada, in the naval victories of Boscawen and Hawke, and in the successful prosecution of the war in the East Indies. Frederick the Great at the close of the last campaign had obliged the Austrians to evacuate Saxony, while his generals compelled the Russians and Swedes to retire towards their own frontier. He now commenced the present campaign with vigour, in concert with Prince Ferdinand of Brunswick. Besides the Hanoverians and Hessians in British pay, the latter had under his orders from 10,000 to 12,000 British soldiers commanded by Lord George Sackville, the cavalry of which was composed of the Royal Horse Guards, 1st Dragoon Guards, 3rd Dragoon Guards, the Scots Greys, the Inniskillings, and the 10th Dragoons.

The French for their part sent large reinforcements into Germany, and early in the year surprised Frankfort-on-Maine, a neutral city, and made it the place of arms for their Southern army. This gave them the great advantage of securing the course of the river Maine and the Upper Rhine. From this position it was of the greatest moment for Prince Ferdinand to dislodge them. Leaving behind him his British and Hanoverians, to the number of 25,000, to observe Marshal Contades, he marched with 30,000 men towards Frankfort and met the French army, under the Duke de Broglie, encamped at Bergen. Here a battle took place, in which Prince Ferdinand was worsted and fell back. De Broglie and Contades, now joining hands, reduced the towns of Cassel, Munster, and Minden, and again

---

[1] Cannon's *Records*.

it appeared as if the whole of the Electorate of Han- 1759
over was to fall to the French.

As Prince Ferdinand fell back from Minden, and
united to his army the British and Hanoverians, he
decided to pursue a bold line of conduct, and bring the
matter to an issue by giving battle to the enemy. The
main body of the French had encamped near Minden,
to which town its right extended. On its left was a
steep hill, and in its front was a morass. From this
strong position Prince Ferdinand desired to entice
his opponent, and for this purpose he left a body of
troops, consisting of about 5,000 men, under General
Wangenheim, entrenched on the banks of the Weser,
in hopes of drawing the French out. At the same
time he marched with his main body to Hille. Contades, thinking that he now saw the Allies divided,
and that the opportunity presented itself of placing his
army between Prince Ferdinand and the river Weser,
broke up his camp and directed the Duke de Broglie to
march forward and profit by the seeming blunder.
Accordingly, on the 1st August De Broglie advanced
until he reached a neighbouring height, whence he
beheld, not entrenchments defended by a small body,
but the whole army of the Allies, which had marched
in the night and was now formed up in excellent order.
He at once called Contades to his aid, who was forced
to accept battle in a disadvantageous position between
a river and a morass. The French army was, however,
without loss of time formed up, the two wings consisting of infantry, the cavalry in the centre. At five in
the morning the allied army advanced to the attack.
The left of the French position was first assailed by the
Germans, while the British troops threatened the centre.
The French cavalry were then ordered to advance and
throw themselves upon the English and Hanoverian

infantry. These, however, successfully met this, the principal shock of the battle, repulsing each attack of horse and foot that came against them; while the Hessian cavalry, with some regiments of Prussian and Hanoverian dragoons, completed the enemy's discomfiture, and forced them to flight. "At that instant Prince Ferdinand sent orders to Lord George Sackville for the British and Hanoverian horse, which was on the right, to advance to the charge."[1] "Had these orders been duly fulfilled, it is acknowledged by French writers that their army must have been utterly destroyed;"[2] but whatever was the cause, through misinterpretation of orders or being imperfectly understood, the pursuit did not take place, and the French were permitted to retire.[3] Meanwhile Prince Ferdinand sent orders to the Marquis of Granby, who commanded the second line, to advance at once, but much of the opportunity was lost. The French, however, retired the same night behind the Weser, and the next day the garrison of Minden surrendered. Their losses in the battle were computed at 8,000 men killed, wounded, or taken prisoners, with thirty pieces of artillery and seventeen standards. The military chest and the carriages of the marshals were also captured in the flight across the Weser. Further serious losses were sustained by the breaking down of the pontoon bridges. The loss of the Allies was estimated at 2,000.

Great rejoicings took place in England on the victory of Minden. Prince Ferdinand received the Order

---

[1] Russell's *Modern Europe*.   [2] Lord Mahon's *History of England*.

[3] "Lord George Sackville on his return to England was at once dismissed from all employment—the command of a regiment, a post in the Ordnance, and the rank of general. A year later a court-martial took place and found him guilty of disobeying Prince Ferdinand's orders, and that he was unfit to serve His Majesty in any military capacity whatever."—Lord Mahon's *History of England*.

of the Garter, a gift of 20,000*l*., and a pension of 2,000*l*. a year. The success of this action was much enhanced by the brilliant generalship of Ferdinand, who had detached a force of 10,000 men on the 28th July, under his nephew, to act in rear of the French. This Prince attacked a force under the Duke of Brissac, utterly routed it, and thus became master of the passes, so that the French under Contades were compelled to continue their retreat in disorder, and were rapidly driven from their recent conquests of Cassel, Munster, and Marburg, and forced to take up their winter quarters in the city of Frankfort. It is said that on the day Prince Ferdinand was invested by the King of England with the Order of the Garter in recognition of his services, Marshal Contades, hearing of it, drew up the French army, and paid his opponent the compliment of ordering a general salute on the occasion.

Nothing further of great importance took place during the campaign of this year, Ferdinand's army being considerably reduced by his sending his nephew with some 12,000 men to the assistance of Frederick the Great, who was very much pressed by the Russians, Austrians, and Swedes, and in January 1760 both armies went into winter quarters, the French between the Maine and the Lahn, and the Allies near Marburg.

CHAPTER VII

BATTLE OF WARBURG—CHARGE OF MAJOR DAVENPORT—PURSUIT
OF THE FRENCH—THE REGIMENT CROSSES THE RHINE—BATTLE
OF CAMPEN—KIRCH-DENKERN—MARCH TO HANOVER—SURPRISE
OF THE FRENCH CAMP AT GREBENSTEIN—CONCLUSION OF THE
SEVEN YEARS' WAR

1760   GREAT preparations were made on all sides for the
coming campaign.   One large Austrian army entered
Silesia, assisted by the Russians, while another entered
Saxony.   The French, on their part, augmented their
forces in Westphalia to nearly 100,000 men under the
Duke de Broglie, while a smaller force under the Count
de St. Germain was collected upon the Rhine.   England at the same time determined to prosecute the war
with energy, and, owing to the British victories in
North America and in the East and West Indies, the
nation entered with enthusiasm into the ensuing campaign.   In addition to giving the aid of 25,000 British
troops, two millions sterling was voted by Parliament
in subsidies to Germany.

The allied army being less in number than that of
the Duke de Broglie, Prince Ferdinand was compelled
at first to act on the defensive.   He fell back before
the French advance, as De Broglie entered Hesse with
his grand army, and retreated towards the river
Diemel.   St. Germain at the same time invaded the
Duchy of Westphalia and made a junction near Corbach with De Broglie.   Unaware of this concentration
on the part of the French, Prince Ferdinand had sent

1760

his nephew, the Hereditary Prince, with a strong force consisting of his own corps and some English battalions and squadrons in the direction of Corbach. The young Prince, thinking that he had St. Germain alone in front of him, took the offensive, and was repulsed with some loss. A few days later, however, on the 16th July, hearing that a French detachment was advancing, he attacked it at Emsdorff in front and rear with six battalions and some cavalry, to which was added a British cavalry regiment lately arrived from England, Eliott's Light Horse [1] (now the 15th Hussars). The French were taken by surprise and were speedily driven back, on which the Prince, placing himself at the head of Eliott's Light Horse, charged them, and broke them up completely. Besides the great losses the French suffered in this action, the general commanding, Glaubitz, 177 officers and 2,282 soldiers laid down their arms, and the whole of the artillery and baggage was captured. [2]

While these transactions were taking place, the Duke de Broglie remained at Corbach. The Chevalier de Muy, now his second in command in the place of St. Germain, received orders to cross the Diemel with 35,000 men and threaten the communications of the Allies. To meet this movement Prince Ferdinand also passed this river on the 30th July. De Broglie encamped that day at Zieremberg, and De Muy near Warburg. Seeing that these two forces were too far apart to support one another, the Prince determined to attack that of the Chevalier de Muy. He accordingly sent the Hereditary Prince to turn the left wing, while he himself advanced against the centre. Meeting with

---

[1] In 1759 the first two regiments of light dragoons were raised in England—viz. the 15th and 16th Light Dragoons.

[2] The 15th Hussars now include "Emsdorff" amongst their honours.

great resistance, and finding that he was making but slow progress with the infantry, partly owing to the intense heat, the Prince sent orders to Lord Granby to bring up the British cavalry.

The Tenth was now in brigade with the 6th Dragoons, under command of Brigadier-General the Earl of Pembroke, the whole of the cavalry being under the immediate orders of Lord Mostyn. The cavalry and artillery were at this time posted some distance in rear under cover of a wood. On receipt of the orders to advance, they were brought rapidly forward, and found the French cavalry pressing hard upon Prince Ferdinand's columns. The British cavalry immediately charged and entirely routed the French, and, continuing to advance, drove everything before them and scattered the enemy in all directions.

In the rapidity of this operation many squadrons became detached from their regiments. One of these, the left squadron of the Tenth, commanded by Major Davenport, fell in with a German [1] grenadier regiment of the enemy. At first mistaking it for our allies, the Hessians, Major Davenport halted his squadron within seventy yards of the enemy, who, taking advantage of this error, poured in upon it not only a volley of musketry but the fire of two pieces of brass ordnance. From this unexpected fire its commander fell dead, pierced by four bullets. Another officer, Cornet Ratcliffe, was shot through the body, two more had their horses killed under them, leaving Captain Mordaunt the only effective officer with the squadron. Without a moment's hesitation this gallant officer called upon his squadron to advance, and charging home, in spite of a second volley and the firmness with which the

---

[1] In these operations the French had several regiments of Saxons fighting for the liberation of their country.

Grenadiers held the ground, overcame them, capturing 300 prisoners, two mules with ammunition, three waggons with military stores, and two brass guns which are now in the Tower of London. The officer commanding the Grenadiers surrendered to Captain Mordaunt.

Prince Ferdinand of Brunswick, who witnessed the gallantry of our dragoons, expressed himself much pleased with the conduct of the regiment, and he published in his orders of the day that " the British cavalry performed prodigies of valour." The enemy was now driven from the field, with the loss of 1,500 killed and wounded, 1,500 taken prisoners, ten pieces of artillery, and ten stands of colours, " the day being decided against them mainly by a charge of Lord Granby and the British horse." [1] In his despatch after the battle this officer says : " I should do injustice to the general officers and to every officer and private man of the cavalry if I did not beg His Lordship would assure His Majesty that nothing could exceed their gallant behaviour." The loss of the Allies was about 1,200 killed and wounded. The 10th Dragoons had two officers and one private killed, ten wounded, four horses killed and twelve wounded. By this victory Prince Ferdinand, being ensured the command of the Weser and the Diemel, was enabled to maintain his communications with Westphalia, and prevent the enemy from entirely overrunning the Electorate of Hanover.[2]

After joining in the pursuit of the French for several miles beyond the Diemel, the 10th Dragoons was encamped with the other cavalry corps and twelve battalions of British infantry, under the Marquis of

[1] Lord Mahon's *History of England.*
[2] Russell's *Modern Europe.*

E

Granby, upon the heights of Wilda, four miles in front of Warburg.

Prince Ferdinand continued to occupy this place for a month, and the French did not attempt to attack him in so formidable a position, but remained at Cassel and Göttingen. With the exception of some raids into the enemy's country under the Hereditary Prince, in which the Greys and Inniskillings took part,[1] nothing occurred of importance until the end of September, when Prince Ferdinand detached a force under his nephew, consisting of twenty battalions and ten squadrons, about 15,000 men, to the Lower Rhine, on the borders of the United Provinces, to undertake the siege of Wesel. On the other hand, the Marquis de Castries was sent with 25,000 men to oppose him, and took up his post near the Convent of Campen.

On the 15th October the young Prince attempted a surprise in the night. For this purpose he marched at ten P.M., and endeavoured at first to obtain possession of the Convent. This led to firing, which brought up the French army, and an obstinate fight ensued, the enemy successfully holding their ground from five in the morning till nine at night. "The Hereditary Prince seeing no prospect of success withdrew his troops and left the field of battle to the enemy." His loss is variously estimated between twelve and sixteen hundred men, and he was compelled to raise the siege of Wesel.

The 10th Dragoons was employed during this action with the force under the personal command of the Hereditary Prince, which was led to attack the main body of the French in their camp at Rhinberg, while the detached force was attacking the Convent. The fight was of a most determined nature, and was carried

[1] Cust's *Annals of the Wars.*

on with varied success. The Tenth was engaged through-out the day, and in the final charge the commanding officer, Colonel William Augustus Pitt, was wounded and taken prisoner. Lieutenant Richard Briscoe and four private troopers were killed, Lieutenant Peter Renouard and three rank and file wounded. Lieutenant Charles Erskine, Quartermaster Dobson, three sergeants, and twenty-seven rank and file fell into the hands of the enemy. The loss in troop horses was thirty-three killed, seven wounded, and eleven missing.[1] On the other hand, the French General de Ségur, many other French officers and soldiers, a standard, and several guns were captured. The principal loss on the side of the Allies occurred amongst the British troops. Lord Downe, who had served with the Tenth light troop during the raids on the French coasts in 1758, was wounded and taken prisoner in this action. He after-wards died of his wounds.

On withdrawing from the field the Prince retired towards the Rhine, and finding that the bridge of boats which spanned the river, and by which he had intended to cross, was much damaged by floods, he caused it to be removed lower down. While this was being done, the 10th Dragoons, in skirmishing order, so successfully kept the enemy in check that no attempt was made to prevent the retreating force from crossing the bridge when completed. On the 18th October the regiment followed the army across the Rhine, and afterwards encamped at Brunnen, from whence it moved to Klein Reckum, and subsequently into cantonments. This was the last remarkable incident in the campaign. Both armies now went into winter quarters. The French were left in possession of Hesse and the whole country east of the Weser. The British troops were cantoned

---

[1] Cannon's *Historical Records.*

in the Bishopric of Paderborn, where they suffered great hardships from scarcity of forage and provisions. On the 25th October, two days after the news of the surrender of Berlin to the Russians, King George II. died.

The King of Prussia, who had commenced his campaign in 1760 by acting on the defensive, soon afterwards was compelled to take more active measures, and in August defeated the Austrians at Lignitz. In October he advanced to the relief of Berlin, and, having effected this, he again turned his attention to the Austrians. On the 4th November, after a bloody battle, he defeated them at Torgau, and this victory gave him once more command of the provinces of Saxony. The severity of the season now rendered campaigning impossible, and all the armies went into winter quarters.

During February of the opening year, the 10th Dragoons, with other troops, in spite of the hard winter, was employed on an incursion into the French cantonments, when several towns and villages were occupied and extensive magazines seized. These enterprising measures prevented any renewal of hostilities on the part of the French until the end of June, when one division, under the Prince de Soubise, from the Rhine, and another, under the Duke de Broglie, from Cassel, marched to form a junction, and attacked the Allies near the village of Kirch-Denkern. At this time the 10th Dragoons was formed in brigade with the 1st and 6th Dragoons, under Major-General Eliott, and employed on reconnoitring duties in front of the river Asse, but on the approach of the French armies this brigade was advanced beyond Kirch-Denkern and took up its post in the centre of the allied position.

On the 16th July the French troops, on advancing to the attack, found the Allies strongly posted, the left

wing commanded by the Marquis of Granby and the
centre by General Conway. " On the previous evening
De Broglie had assailed Granby, but was driven back."
The next morning before daybreak the attack was resumed by Soubise, "who was also defeated, and the
whole French army fell back with a loss of 4,000 men,
and did not halt until the division under Broglie arrived
at Cassel and that of Soubise had crossed the river
Rohr."[1] Notwithstanding this check, the French were
enabled almost immediately to resume the offensive,
and met with some successes, so that this campaign
closed leaving the opposing armies much in the
same positions as at the commencement.[2] The 10th
Dragoons was employed subsequently in operations on
the Diemel and other parts of the Bishopric of Paderborn, and in November in the Electorate of Hanover,
where several skirmishes occurred. The cavalry then
went into winter quarters in East Friesland.

Early in this year war was declared between England
and Spain, but in spite of this renewed preparations
were made for vigorous measures in Westphalia. In
other parts of the world England had been victorious,
more especially in naval engagements, and the country
was more determined than ever to bring this war to a
satisfactory conclusion. The alliance between Russia
and Austria being ended, Frederick the Great found
his task in Saxony and Silesia much lessened, and during this year met with successes that tended towards
producing peace.

In Westphalia the French had determined to make
the most powerful efforts. The Duke de Broglie had
been disgraced, and the Prince de Soubise now commanded their army assembled on the Weser, in con-

---

[1] Russell's *Modern Europe* ; Mahon's *History of England.*
[2] Cust's *Annals of the Wars.*

junction with Marshal d'Estrées ; that on the Lower Rhine being under the Prince de Condé. On the side of the Allies the Hereditary Prince was posted in the Bishopric of Munster to observe the movements of Condé, while Prince Ferdinand lay behind the Diemel with the main body in order to oppose the Grand Army. During this campaign the 10th Dragoons was brigaded with the Scots Greys, under the command of Colonel William Augustus Pitt, the lieutenant-colonel of the Tenth. Having taken the field about the middle of May, the brigade was encamped in the first instance at Brackel, and subsequently on the heights of Tissel.[1]

In June the Prince de Soubise was strongly posted near Grebenstein, on the frontier of Hesse, and on the 24th of this month Prince Ferdinand took him by surprise and drove him from his position. The attack was commenced by the corps under General de Spörcken, under whose orders the British troops were placed, and after a sharp engagement the enemy retreated, and was pursued into the woods of Wilhelmstal, where between two and three thousand prisoners were made. Several other advantages were gained by the Allies, and the French retired before them to Cassel. This place also was reduced, and while following the enemy the 10th Dragoons was constantly employed in harassing their retreat, until the 3rd November, when intelligence was received of the signature of the preliminaries of peace. A few days later the principal conditions of peace were agreed to. These were that in Spain and Portugal each country should preserve the same limits as before the war ; in Germany the French troops were to restore whatever territories they held in Hesse and Hanover ; Minorca was to be exchanged for Belleisle ; and in

---

[1] Cannon's *Historical Records.*

America France was to cede to England the provinces of Canada, Nova Scotia, and Cape Breton.

After the military operations were thus arrested, the 10th Dragoons remained for several weeks in the Bishopric of Munster. It was during its stay there that the thanks of Parliament were received by the army for its conduct in the war. The regiment commenced its march through Holland to Williamstadt in February 1763, and embarked for England. It landed at Harwich about the middle of the month, and marched into quarters at Dorchester and Blandford.

Thus terminated the Seven Years' War, in which the Tenth had had the good fortune to take so prominent a part. The regiment passed nearly five years in Germany, was present at all the principal actions that took place during the four summer campaigns, and suffered considerable hardships during the severe winters spent in that country; but up to the present time (1890) no record appears amongst the honours permitted to be worn by the regiment to show that the 10th Dragoons participated in any way in these hard-fought campaigns.[1]

---

[1] The English cavalry regiments employed in the Seven Years' War were the Royal Horse Guards (Blue); the 3rd and 4th Regiments of Horse; the 1st, 2nd, and 3rd Dragoon Guards; the 2nd, 6th, 10th, 11th, and 15th Dragoons.

CHAPTER VIII

THE REGIMENT REDUCED—REVIEW BY GEORGE III.—DEATH OF SIR
JOHN MORDAUNT—THE TENTH MADE "THE PRINCE OF WALES'S
OWN"—ROYAL ESCORTS—MOVEMENTS OF THE REGIMENT—WAR
DECLARED BY FRANCE—AUGMENTATION OF THE REGIMENT

1763–
1766

ON the conclusion of the treaty of peace, which took place at Fontainebleau, considerable reductions were made in the army, and amongst others the light troops of dragoon regiments were disbanded and the establishment of the six heavy troops was lowered. To supply the place of the disbanded troops eight men per troop were subsequently equipped as light dragoons. On the 25th March a Royal Warrant was issued, signed " W. Ellis," ordering that all the privates of the disbanded light troops were to be treated with great liberality. Each man who had served one year was to receive " the Horse which we have paid for by the Levy Money, we being pleased to grant Our whole Right in such Horse to the Dragoon." They were also to receive six days' pay, and to take away with them their cloaks and clothing.[1]

On the 30th April, 1764, the regiment was reviewed by King George III. in brigade with the 7th Dragoons, and His Majesty's approbation was afterwards expressed in orders.

At this time some slight alterations were made in the appointments of the army. The aiguillettes of

---

[1] *War Office Miscellany Books*, Record Office.

dragoons were discontinued, and epaulettes introduced, 1764–1766
and the large cumbersome jack-boots were replaced by
a lighter kind. At the same time a Warrant was issued
prohibiting the docking of the horses' tails :—

His Majesty having been pleased to order that all His Regiments of Horse and Dragoons, except the Light Dragoons, shall
be mounted on such horses as shall have their full Tails, without
the least part taken from them, all Breeders and Dealers in horses
for the Service of the Army are desired to take notice that for the
future no Horses, but such as shall have their full Tails, without
the least part taken from them, will be bought for any of the
Regts. of Horse or Dragoons except the Light Dragoons.

During the three succeeding years the Tenth was
stationed in different parts of England.

A Warrant was issued in 1767, increasing the amount 1767–1774
to be paid for remount horses to twenty-two guineas.[1]
This year the Tenth marched to Scotland, returning to
England in 1768. On the 5th October, 1770, Lieutenant-
Colonel T. Osbert Mordaunt succeeded to the command
of the regiment ; but beyond occasional reviews there
is no record during this period of any regimental interest. The Tenth was quartered in various parts of
England until 1773, when it again went to Scotland for
one year, coming back to England in 1774.

Differences had for a long time existed between 1775–1781
Great Britain and her North American colonies, and at
length, in 1775, war broke out. At first this seems to
have caused no change in the establishment of the army ;
but when, in 1778, the revolted provinces were joined
by France, the strength of the army was raised, and
thereupon the 10th Dragoons received orders to recruit,
eight men being added to each troop.[2] During the summer of this year the regiment was encamped near Bury

---

[1] In 1801 this was raised to 25*l*.

[2] *War Office Military Miscellanies*, Record Office.

St. Edmunds with the 3rd, 4th, and 7th Dragoons, and two battalions of Militia, under Major-General Warde.

In 1779 a Warrant appeared by which orders were given for the light dragoons of all the regiments to be formed into separate corps, which were severally named the 19th, 20th, and 21st Light Dragoons.[1] In the same year the Tenth marched to Scotland, where it remained until 1781.

On the 23rd October of the previous year (1780) General Sir John Mordaunt, who had commanded the 10th Dragoons for thirty-one years, died at his country seat, Bevis Mount, near Southampton. Entering the army in August 1721, he was appointed, after several years' service, a captain and lieutenant-colonel in the 3rd Foot Guards. He commanded a brigade of infantry at Falkirk, served in the Netherlands under the Duke of Cumberland, and, distinguishing himself at the battle of Val, he was rewarded with the rank of major-general and by appointment to the colonelcy of the 12th Dragoons. He was transferred in July 1749 to the 4th Irish Horse (now 7th Dragoon Guards), and in November following to the 10th Dragoons. He was promoted lieutenant-general in 1754, and commanded the land forces of the expedition to Rochefort in 1757. He was promoted to the rank of general in 1770, and also rewarded with the K.C.B., and made Governor of Berwick. He was many years a member of Parliament, and died at the age of eighty-three. Sir John Mordaunt was succeeded in the colonelcy of the Tenth by Lieutenant-General Sir William Augustus Pitt, an officer who had served in the regiment from the day he first joined the army in 1744 until his appointment as colonel of the 12th Dragoons in 1775.

[1] Warrant signed " C. Jenkinson," *Record Office.* These regiments were disbanded in 1783.

At the end of 1782 negotiations were commenced for the acknowledgment of the independence of the North American Colonies, and in the following year the Peace of Versailles was signed.

The army again underwent a reduction, and the troops of dragoon regiments had their establishments fixed by a Warrant at one captain, one lieutenant, one cornet, one quartermaster, two corporals, one hautbois, one trumpeter, and twenty-eight privates. At the same time the 19th, 20th, 21st, and 22nd Light Dragoons were disbanded.

From further experience gained through the American war the value of light dragoons was fully confirmed, and an order was issued in 1783 for the 7th, 9th, 10th, 11th,[1] 13th, and 14th to be formed into light dragoons, and the light troops attached to the heavy regiments were transferred to and incorporated with the newly-raised corps. At the same time at change of clothing and equipment took place more appropriate to the designation of light dragoons. I was then that the 10th Dragoons was honoured with the distinction of receiving the title of the " 10th or Prince of Wales's Own Regiment of Light Dragoons."[2] In consequence of this change of equipment and designation, the dress was altered the following year from scarlet to blue, and the Prince of Wales's plume with the Rising Sun and the Red Dragon became the badges of the regiment, with " Ich Dien " as the motto.[3]

[1] The 12th had been formed into light dragoons in 1768.

[2] *Orders.*   "Adjutant-General's Office, 27 September, 1783.

" It is His Majesty's pleasure that the Tenth Regiment of Light Dragoons shall in future be called the Tenth or Prince of Wales's Own Regiment of Light Dragoons.   " WILLIAM FAWCETT, Adj.-General."

[3] The three ostrich feathers of the Prince of Wales's plume are supposed to have been derived from the badge of Queen Philippa (the

1784–
1786

At this time apparently the first mention of rations of any kind being issued to the soldier appears, as seen in the following extract from a Royal Warrant in 1784 : " Non-commissioned officers and every Private man shall be allowed Bread at the Public charge, to the amount of Tenpence halfpenny per week." [1]

In 1785 the Tenth was stationed at Hounslow and out quarters, and performed the escort duties to the royal family.[2] A detachment employed at Portsmouth at this time received the thanks of the Secretary at War for good conduct.

On the 10th May, 1786, Lieutenant-Colonel William Newton succeeded to the command of the regiment.

1787–
1790

For the next few years the Tenth remained in the south of England, during which time there is no record of any special interest. On the 21st May, 1788, it was reviewed by King George III. on Blackheath, and after the review it proceeded to Norwich, and later in the year to Leicester and Nottingham. On the 25th May, 1790, His Majesty reviewed the 10th Dragoons on Hounslow

mother of Edward the Black Prince, the first Prince of Wales), being the appanage of the eldest son of the House of Hainault. The Rising Sun and the Red Dragon are ancient badges of Wales.

[1] *War Office Miscellany Books*, Record Office.

[2] At the commencement of the reign of George III. the household troops were relieved from carrying out travelling escorts, which duty was ordered in future to be performed by light dragoons. The following orders show how the escorts were employed at this period :—" His Majesty will leave Kew on Monday morning at 6 o'clock precisely, and will travel at the rate of 10 miles an hour. This information will enable you to calculate the exact time of the King's arrival at the several posts of the Detachments under your command, so you will accordingly have the escorts in perfect readiness to fall in, and proceed to their respective points of relief."—H. C., A.-G. A similar order appears on His Majesty proceeding from Windsor to Weymouth, the escorts to be found by the 10th Light Dragoons, relieved at Basingstoke by the 15th Light Dragoons, and at Andover by the 16th Light Dragoons.

Heath, and subsequently it was stationed at Windsor. On its removal the King graciously expressed his approval of its conduct and bearing. Of the movements or proceedings of the regiment during the years 1790 or 1791 there is no record, beyond the change of quarters from Windsor to Richmond, and again to Lewes. On the 21st May, 1792, their Royal Highnesses the Prince of Wales and the Duke of York reviewed the regiment, and later in the summer it marched to Wickham Bushes, afterwards to Elvesham, and in August to Brighton Downs, at all of which places it was under canvas.

It was natural that so disturbing an event as the French Revolution should arouse the hostility of all monarchical countries, and during 1792 Louis XVI. was forced into war with Austria, and later on with Sardinia. At the end of that year France declared herself against all established Governments. The French armies in the North advanced as far as Antwerp, and invaded the Dutch territory in pursuit of the beaten Austrians, this aggression causing the greatest alarm throughout Great Britain.[1]

Until the end of this year England had been at peace, with the exception of the continued hostilities in India; but the course of the French Revolution, followed by the execution of Louis XVI., determined her to declare war and join the confederacy against the Government of France. An augmentation of the army in England in consequence took place, and a Warrant dated 12th December, 1792, signed "George Yonge," increased the troops of the 10th Light Dragoons by ten men each; and in 1793 it was ordered that " the esta-

---

[1] Alison's *History of Europe.*

blishment of three troops, consisting each of three sergeants, three corporals, and a trumpeter, forty-seven private men and horses with the usual number of Commissioned officers be added to the Tenth " and other cavalry regiments.[1]

[1] *War Office Miscellany Books*, Record Office.

CHAPTER IX

INTEREST OF THE ROYAL FAMILY IN THE REGIMENT—HIS ROYAL
HIGHNESS THE PRINCE OF WALES APPOINTED COMMANDANT—
INCREASE IN THE CAVALRY—BEAU BRUMMELL—THE PRINCE
OF WALES APPOINTED COLONEL—GENERAL SIR AUGUSTUS PITT

THE long period during which the Tenth had remained   1793
in the southern counties of England had given King
George III. repeated opportunities of becoming personally acquainted with the regiment and its conduct,
both in quarters and in the field. At the several
reviews in which it took part, Her Majesty the Queen,
the Princes and Princesses, were frequently present, and
graciously expressed their interest in the regiment,
besides taking notice of the parties employed on escort
duty. Owing to this, no doubt, and to the title of the
Tenth, His Royal Highness the Prince of Wales was
pleased to express a wish to be at the head of the
regiment which bore his name, and in 1793 he was
appointed Colonel Commandant.[1]

---

[1] Cannon's *Records.*

In this year (1793) the following regiments of light dragoons were
raised :—

21st Light Dragoons. Disbanded, 1820.				24th Light Dragoons. Disbanded, 1802.			
22nd ,,	,,	,,	1802.	25th ,,	,,	,,	1820.
23rd ,,	,,	,,	1802.				

In 1795 eight more regiments of light dragoons were formed, viz. :—

26th Light Dragoons. Disbanded, 1817.				30th Light Dragoons. Disbanded, 1796.			
27th ,,	,,	,,	1819.	31st ,,	,,	,,	1796.
28th ,,	,,	,,	1802.	32nd ,,	,,	,,	1796.
29th ,,	,,	,,	1819.	33rd ,,	,,	,,	1796.

In 1794 the Tenth was again stationed at Hounslow, and during that and the following year performed the duties of the royal escort. In this year Lieutenant-Colonel William Cartwright succeeded to the command, *vice* Newton.

During 1795 an officer was appointed to the regiment who, although it cannot be said that he earned a military reputation, yet he achieved such remarkable notoriety by his peculiarities, follies, and eccentricities, that a memoir of the Tenth might perhaps be considered by some incomplete unless his name found a place in it. Captain Gronow, in his " Reminiscences and Recollections," mentions Beau Brummell as follows :—

"Amongst the curious freaks of fortune there is none more remarkable in my memory than the sudden appearance in the highest and best society in London of a young man whose antecedents warranted a much less conspicuous career. I refer to the famous Beau Brummell. He was endowed with a handsome person, and distinguished himself at Eton as the best scholar, the best boatman, and the best cricketer, and, more than all, he was supposed to possess the comprehensive excellences that are represented by the familiar name of good fellow. . . . He made many friends amongst the scions of good families . . . and his reputation reached a circle over which reigned the celebrated Duchess of Devonshire. . . . At last the Prince of Wales sent for Brummell, and was so much pleased with his manner and appearance that he gave him a commission in his own regiment, the 10th Hussars. Unluckily, Brummell, soon after joining his regiment, was thrown from his horse at a grand review at Brighton, when he broke his classical Roman nose. This misfortune, however, did not affect the fame of the Beau, and, although his nasal organ had undergone a slight transformation, it was forgiven by his admirers, since the rest of his person remained intact.

"In the zenith of his popularity he might be seen at the bay window of White's Club, surrounded by the lions of the day, laying down the law, and occasionally indulging in those witty remarks for which he was famous.

"His house in Chapel Street corresponded with his personal 'get-up.' The furniture was in excellent taste, and the library contained the best works of the best authors of every period and of every country. His canes, his snuff-boxes, his Sèvres china were exquisite ; his horses and carriage were conspicuous for their excellence ; and, in fact, the superior taste of a Brummell was discoverable in everything that belonged to him."

Another account of him mentions that "George Bryan Brummell, when at Eton, was known as ' Buck Brummell,' and there he devoted himself more to the study of dress than of the classics. The wearing of a gold buckle in the white stock was a fashion he introduced amongst his schoolfellows, and no doubt was much admired at the time. From Eton he went to

F

Oriel College, Oxford, for a few terms, but, failing as a competitor for a prize poem, he left the University, after which he received his commission in the Tenth.

" By his good nature and agreeable manners, his witty conversation, his taste in dress, and his perfect assurance, he gained the favour of the Prince Regent, who was then in command of the Tenth. He soon became the leader of the fashionable world. In fact, at that time no party in London was considered complete without him." Many of his sayings have been preserved in " The Wits and Beaux of Society " and other books.

" All the world watched Beau Brummell to imitate him and order their clothes of the tradesman who dressed that sublime dandy. One day a youthful beau approached Brummell and said : ' Permit me to ask you where you get your blacking ? ' ' Ah,' replied Brummell, gazing complacently at his boots, ' my black- ing positively ruins me. I will tell you in confidence, it is made with the finest champagne.' [1]

" His gloves were made by two different artists, one being appointed to provide ' thumbs,' the other the fingers and hands." His valet carrying down the load of crushed handkerchiefs which the Beau had not suc- ceeded in squeezing with his chin down into the proper folds, and carelessly describing them as " our failures," is an old, well-worn legend. " He believed, with strict economy, dressing might be done on eight hundred a year." [2]

Colonel Kelly, of the 1st Foot Guards, also one of the greatest dandies of the day, met his death at a fire at the Custom House, where he lived with his sister. On the news of his death becoming known all the dandies were anxious to secure the services of his valet, who possessed the mystery of inimitable blacking.

---

[1] Captain Gronow.   [2] *Post and Paddock.*

Brummell lost no time in discovering his place of residence, and asked what wages he required. The servant answered, his late master gave him 150*l.* a year, but it was not enough for his talents, and he should require 200*l.*; upon which Brummell said, " Well, if you will make it guineas, *I* shall be happy to attend upon *you.*" [1]

Brummell often used to be a guest of the Duke of Rutland at Cheveley Park at the same time as the Duke of York, during the race meetings, and had a bedroom sacred to him both there and at Belvoir. He generally dressed for the course in a tight green shooting-coat, leathers, and top-boots, and was rather a carriage man than one of the regular Newmarket cavalry. His pleasantries were the salt of the Cheveley *battues*, but he was not known as a good shot.[2] Once, being reproached by the father of a young man who had lost money at cards while in his company, he merely replied, " Why, sir, I did all I could for your son; I once gave him my arm all the way from White's to Brookes's!" Being asked why he had not entered the lists of matrimony, he explained how one attempt had been frustrated: " What could I do, my dear fellow, when I actually saw Lady Mary eat cabbage?" It is said that he never could master the names of the men of his troop; indeed, he could only recognise his own troop by one old soldier, who had a bottle nose, and was always placed in the front rank. Unfortunately for Mr. Brummell, one day his troop, being the junior, was broken up and mixed with the others. Coming on parade late, after the colonel, and when the regiment was formed up, he rode rapidly to where he expected to find his troop, but, being thoroughly puzzled, he galloped up and down, until he came opposite his blue

[1] Captain Gronow.   [2] *Post and Paddock.*

1795   nose, when he placed himself in front of it.   " How
now, Mr. Brummell?" vociferated the colonel, "You
are with the wrong troop!"   " No, no," said Brummell, turning round in his saddle, " I know better than
that; a pretty thing, indeed, if I did not know my
own men."

After serving little more than three years he left the
regiment.   It is said his retirement took place on the
Tenth being ordered to Manchester.   His excuse was
that he could not possibly go on foreign service, and be
so far removed from London.   " Established in London,
he surrounded himself with all the elegancies of life.
Yielding to every whim of his eccentric mind, he
aspired to lead the fashionable world, and soon became
its despotic ruler."   His days, however, were ended in
misery.   Having run through all his fortune, he was
compelled to leave his own country, and retired to
France, where he was appointed Consul at Caen, in
Normandy.   For many years he lived in poverty at
Calais, and died at Caen at the age of sixty, his body
having survived his mind.[1]

1796   On the 18th July, 1796, General Sir William Augustus
Pitt, K.C.B., was promoted to the colonelcy of the 1st
or King's Dragoon Guards, and H.R.H. the Prince of
Wales, to the gratification of all serving in the regiment,
was appointed colonel of the 10th Light Dragoons.
General Pitt had been connected with the Tenth from
the 1st February, 1744, when he joined as cornet, and
he may be said to have gained all his reputation while
in the regiment.   Proceeding with the Tenth to Germany
in the summer of 1758, he took a distinguished part in
almost every general engagement and skirmish during
the Seven Years' War until the battle of Campen, where,
as already narrated, he was severely wounded and taken

[1] *Wits and Beaux of Society.*

prisoner. Promoted to the rank of colonel in 1762, and
to major-general in August 1770, he obtained in the
October following the colonelcy of the 12th Light
Dragoons, from which he was transferred to the 3rd
Irish Horse (now the Carabiniers). In 1777 he became
lieutenant-general, and on the death of Sir John Mordaunt in 1780 was given the colonelcy of his old
regiment, the 10th Light Dragoons. Created a K.C.B.
in 1792, he was promoted general in 1793, and appointed Governor of Portsmouth in the year following.
He died in 1810.

In this year (1796) veterinary surgeons for the first
time were appointed to cavalry regiments as commissioned officers. In 1797 the pay of the private soldier
was fixed at one shilling per diem, with a daily stoppage
of $6\frac{1}{2}d.$ on home service.[1]

From 1796 to 1799 the Tenth was stationed in
various parts of Surrey, Dorsetshire, and Kent, but
nothing of interest concerning the regiment at that time
remains on record. In 1798 a carbine and bayonet
was issued in place of the musket. In August 1799
H.R.H. the Prince of Wales reviewed the regiment on
Hounslow Heath in presence of King George III.[2]
In the autumn of 1799 eight troops of the regiment
went to Ramsgate to embark for foreign service, but
the order was countermanded. In May 1801 H.R.H.
the Duke of Cumberland inspected the regiment, and
in June it moved to Windsor, Hounslow, and Hampton Court to perform the usual escort duty. In April
1803 the Tenth marched to Brighton, where it again

---

[1] "A Warrant was issued on the 13th March, 1800, ordering that the
issue of small beer to troops when stationed in barracks or when billeted
in settled quarters should cease, and in lieu a pecuniary compensation of
1d. a day in addition to the pay should be made."—Record Office.

[2] A picture of this review was painted and is now to be seen in
Hampton Court Palace.

1803   carried out the duties of the Court, which at that time occupied the Pavilion, the marine residence of the Prince of Wales. While stationed here His Royal Highness often took command of the regiment in the field.

In this year field officers ceased to hold troops, and additional captains were appointed to command them, as the following order shows :—

In future each Troop throughout the army shall have an effective Captain, and consequently the Field Officers of the several regiments shall no longer have troops.

(Sd.)   H. CALVERT, A.-G.

Although rifles had been issued as early as 1680 to the Household Cavalry, it was not until 1803 that rifled carbines were heard of, and the 10th Light Dragoons was the first regiment to receive these, as the Rifle Corps, or present Rifle Brigade, was the first infantry regiment to receive rifles in 1800.[1]

The Hon. Frederick Ponsonby entered the 10th Light Dragoons in 1800, and had a most distinguished military career. In 1806 he was promoted captain in the regiment. In 1807 he became major in the 23rd Light Dragoons, and was present in its famous charge at Talavera. He commanded the 12th Lancers at Salamanca and throughout the Peninsular War. In the charge of the 12th Lancers at the battle of Waterloo, Colonel Ponsonby was severely wounded, and, lying on the ground, received a lance thrust as a French lancer regiment passed over him. He was appointed Aide-de-Camp to the King in 1814, a major-general in 1825, and Colonel of the Royal Dragoons in 1836.

[1] " In the year 1803 a target was fired at 200 yards distance by command of his present Majesty, then Prince of Wales, with a rifle barrel 22 inches in length; and from its accuracy was adopted for the use of the 10th Light Dragoons."—*Twenty-two Years' Practice and Observations with Rifle-barrelled Guns* (p. 85), Ezekiel Baker, gunmaker (London, 1803).

CHAPTER X

NAPOLEON BUONAPARTE—THE ESTABLISHMENT RAISED—REGIMENT
MADE HUSSARS—TROOPS DESPATCHED TO PORTUGAL

NAPOLEON BUONAPARTE, who from a general of division 1803
had in 1799 become First Consul, in other words, Dicta-
tor of France, inaugurated his rule by making proposals
of peace to the various powers, and while the negotiations were proceeding made enormous preparations
for war. England and the other belligerents declined
the terms offered, war was continued, and early in 1800
Napoleon invaded Italy, and won the hard-fought
battle of Marengo. In the same year the English took
Malta from the French, and in November an expedition, under Sir Ralph Abercrombie, was despatched to
Egypt to expel the troops of France from that country. In March 1801 he defeated them at the battle
of Alexandria, but was himself mortally wounded. By
this time Russia had been won over from the confederacy by the policy of Napoleon, and the menac-
ing attitude towards England of the other Northern
powers (Sweden and Denmark) resulted in a British
fleet under Sir Hyde Parker, with Lord Nelson as
second in command, being sent to act against this
coalition.

In the following year (1802), after much negotiation, a treaty of peace was signed at Amiens, but, as
might have been expected with so restless a ruler in
France, this truce was of no long duration, and in 1803

Buonaparte found a pretext for a quarrel with England in her refusal to evacuate Malta. War was declared in March.

In 1804 Napoleon proclaimed himself Emperor, and was crowned by the Pope. At this period he contemplated carrying out his scheme for the invasion of England, and assembled an army of 160,000 men on the shores of the Channel, in the neighbourhood of Boulogne. To meet this, great preparations were made in England, and the strength of the army was largely increased. Fortunately, at this time, there was a considerable force of cavalry and infantry in Great Britain, and they were held in readiness to assemble at any threatened point. On the 28th June the House of Commons voted 50,000 additional men to the army, and the King was empowered to call out a *levée en masse* if the invader should land.[1] The 10th Light Dragoons, whose establishment was raised to ten troops, was stationed at Blatchington, Rye, Eastbourne, and Bexhill. In December an augmentation of one lieutenant, one sergeant, one corporal, and nineteen privates was made to each troop.

Lieutenant-Colonel George Leigh succeeded to the command of the regiment on the retirement of Colonel William Cartwright, promoted a major-general in 1804. General Cartwright entered the service at the early age of fifteen as an ensign in the 61st Foot. He was present at most of the memorable actions of 1813 and 1814 in the Peninsula and South of France. The first standing orders known to exist and handed down in the regiment were compiled by this officer. A copy in manuscript, presented by H.R.H. Albert Edward Prince of Wales, is now in the possession of the regiment. General Cartwright was appointed Colonel of the 23rd

[1] Cust's *Wars of the Nineteenth Century.*

Light Dragoons in 1804, to the 3rd Dragoons in 1807, and the 1st Dragoon Guards in 1821. He died in 1827.

As might be expected when so much ardour was manifested by all classes, the Heir-Apparent would not be behindhand in volunteering his services, and the Prince of Wales made most strenuous efforts to obtain an important command beyond that of his regiment.[1] After repeated applications on the part of His Royal Highness, it was finally decided not to permit the heir to the throne to proceed on active service.

In September 1805 the French Emperor suddenly gave up his design of invading England, and transferred his army to the seat of war in Germany. In consequence of this the measures for defence in England were relaxed, and the troops returned to their various quarters. The Tenth was removed to Essex, where the regiment remained during this year, the head-quarters in Romford Barracks.

In 1805 the pay of regimental officers and non-commissioned officers was increased. Privates also received additional pay of 1*d.* per diem after ten years' service, and 2*d.* after seventeen years'.

In 1806 the Tenth marched to Richmond and the neighbourhood, but remained there only one week, returning again to Essex—head-quarters to barracks at Romford, with the detachments in quarters or permanent billets in the surrounding villages.[2]

---

[1] *Vide* Royal Correspondence with the Right Hon. H. Addington, Secretary of State.

[2] "The quartering of troops was one of the main difficulties which Ministers of the Crown had to contend with at this time. It was the most obvious course that a soldier should have his residence provided for him by the Crown, but when a regular army was first formed in England Parliament would not consent to have the men drawn away from the affairs of civil life. In many instances they were permitted to work in trade, and the horses of the cavalry were turned out to grass, therefore the opponents of a standing army would not sanction the erection of

1806   At this time a bill was introduced into Parliament
by Mr. Wyndham abolishing unlimited service in the
ranks; but two years later a clause was introduced
permitting men to enlist for life, and such inducements
were held out to men doing this, that practically unlimited service remained the rule, although the two
systems went on side by side.[1]

His Royal Highness the Prince of Wales, who at all
times had taken great interest in the regiment of which
he was head, in this year obtained official sanction from
His Majesty that it should be clothed and equipped as
hussars. This was shortly afterwards followed by the
7th and 15th Light Dragoons being also converted in
the same manner, and thus was formed the Hussar
Brigade which afterwards did such excellent service in
the Peninsula.[2] The 18th Dragoons became hussars
in the same year. The men of these new hussar regi-

sufficient barracks. In 1718 there was an increase made in the barrack
accommodation, the rooms being calculated for five beds for ten men. In
1792 the barracks of Great Britain held about 20,000 men of artillery
and infantry. Whenever the army was augmented the troops were put
under canvas, however inclement the weather. In Ireland barracks were
proceeded with more rapidly. The billeting of a large standing army was
a great hardship on the people, and when William III. arrived in England, by his order, only those persons holding victualling houses, &c., were
liable to find billets. The gradual erection of barracks removed the
greatest impediment that had existed to a standing army, as the people
would not endure the quartering of troops in permanent billets."—Clode.

[1] In 1829 the option of limited service was entirely removed, but a
Warrant introducing pensions was issued. Unlimited service then continued until 1847, when an Act was passed dividing the service into a first
and second period. Infantry—First period, 10 years; second period, 11
years; total, 21 years. Cavalry and Artillery—First period, 12 years;
second period, 12 years; total, 24 years. In 1867 an Act made all
branches of the army—First period, 12 years; second period, 9 years;
total, 21 years; and in 1870 long service of 12 years, and short service of 6 years with colours and 6 reserve was brought in.

[2] Although 1806 has hitherto been fixed as the year in which the Tenth
became hussars, there can be no doubt that as early as 1803 the regiment
was clothed in this manner, as the Clothing Regulations at the Record

ments were furnished with pelisses, sashes, fur caps, 1806
leather pantaloons, and Hessian boots. Carbines of a
lighter description than formerly used were issued, and
the officers and soldiers were directed to wear mustachios on the upper lip.[1]

Hussars, for some years, had been formed in nearly
every European state, in emulation of those renowned
troops raised in Hungary and Poland, known in the
former country as hussars and in the latter as Uhlans.
The word " hussar " was derived from two Hungarian
words, " husz," signifying twenty, and " ar," pay. When

Office for that year show the issue of the hussar dress to the Tenth, but
to no other regiment :—

" *Clothing Regulations, 22nd April,* 1803. *For* 10*th Light Dragoons.*

" Once every four years—1 pelisse, 1 dress-jacket, 1 hussar cap. Once
every 8 years—1 sash.

" (Sd.)   JAS. PULTENEY."

As has already been stated, great latitude was given to the colonels in
the dress of their regiments, and the Prince Regent in the first instance
clothed his own regiment as hussars, the 7th, 15th, and 18th Light
Dragoons following his example in 1805. *Vide* Cannon's *Records* of
these regiments. It was not until the 18th April, 1811, that the Warrant
was published giving official sanction for all four regiments to be clothed
and equipped as hussars, dating from the 25th December, 1807. This
order was signed, " In the name and on behalf of His Majesty. Approved.
(Sd.) GEORGE P. R." The Tenth, therefore, was the first regiment of English
hussars formed in this country. But in 1803 a regiment of the German
Legion (the 1st Light Dragoons) was already equipped as hussars. The
8th Light Dragoons, at this time serving in India, was not converted into
hussars until its return to England in 1824. The 11th Light Dragoons
became hussars in 1840 ; the 3rd, 4th, 13th, and 14th Light Dragoons
twenty years later. At the inspection, 20th October, 1820, the general
reports that "the standards were deposited in the Pavilion at Brighton
when the regiment became hussars."

[1] Other cavalry regiments by degrees adopted the wearing of a moustache, until a general order, issued on the 2nd August, 1830, forbade
them in all regiments except the Life Guards, Horse Guards, and Hussars.
All cavalry appear to have worn them after 1841, and by a Horse Guards
Circular, dated the 21st July, 1854, " the wearing of a moustache, which
privilege has been until this time confined to the cavalry, is sanctioned
also for the infantry."

1806   Matthias Corvinus succeeded to the throne of Hungary
he decreed that one man out of every twenty should
be enrolled as a cavalry soldier, and that the families
which supplied him should also provide for him.
These men thus enrolled were the first hussars.
Uhlans, who had much in common with hussars, took
their name from one of their first leaders, Huland, a
Lithuanian nobleman. In the wool mantle worn by
these Uhlans[1] we have the pelisse, and the whips carried
by them were also to be found attached to the bit reins
of the Tenth and some other of our light cavalry regiments until a recent date, and at present are still
retained by the 11th Hussars.

1807   The 10th Hussars was inspected in its new equipment by the Duke of York on the 3rd July, 1807, on
Hounslow Heath, and in the September following, while
stationed at Ipswich, by the Duke of Cumberland. The
Tenth, in brigade with the 7th and 15th Hussars, with
two troops of Horse Artillery, was at this time placed
under the command of Major-General Lord Paget.
This brigade of fifteen squadrons formed the first hussar brigade ever brought together in England, and
movements newly introduced were carried out by them
with greater rapidity than formerly. On the 5th October H.R.H. the Duke of York inspected this brigade on
Rushmore Heath.

The Tenth remained until the following spring in
Essex. On the 16th June it marched to Richmond,
and occupied quarters at that place and in the surrounding villages, and after being inspected by the
Commander-in-Chief marched on the 30th of the same
month to Brighton. On the 12th August a review of
all the troops in Sussex took place in presence of the

---

[1] Hungarian shepherds also have from time immemorial worn a sheep-
skin over their shoulders.

Prince of Wales on Newmarket Hill. The Tenth formed
part of the Cavalry Brigade.

Up to this time the army of England had taken
but little share in the struggle that was going on in
Europe ; but the English navy, under Nelson, held command of the seas, and the victory of Trafalgar compen-
sated for the defeats sustained by the Allies on land
in 1805. Still, the battle of Austerlitz may be said to
have restored the balance of power back to France,
and when, in October of the next year, Napoleon
entered Berlin, defeating the Prussians at Jena and
Auerstadt, and following up his success by the invasion
of Russia, he found the whole of Europe at his feet,
with England alone left to resist his further progress.
He now turned his attention to this country, and determined to destroy its maritime power by uniting the
fleet of France with those of other countries. To
counteract this the British Government sent a fleet of
seventeen ships, accompanied by transports conveying
20,000 troops under Sir Arthur Wellesley, to Denmark,
and on the 15th August, 1807, Copenhagen was taken
and the Danish fleet seized, to prevent its being used
against us by the French. Napoleon now returned to
Paris, and having secured, by the treaty of Tilsit, all
he desired in Northern Europe, he occupied himself
with the completion of his system in the South. To
carry this out he embroiled the royal family of Spain
in such a manner as to give an excuse for sending
troops into that country under pretence of preserving
the peace of a neighbouring state. A treaty was soon
afterwards concluded between France and Spain for
the conquest of Portugal, and a French army under
Junot marched by Valladolid and Salamanca upon
Lisbon, which place he occupied in November 1807.
Buonaparte's scheme of taking possession of the Por-

tuguese fleet was, however, frustrated by the presence of the British ships under Sir Sidney Smith, which enabled the two admirals to effect a junction, and the English and Portuguese fleets combined left the Tagus.

The Spaniards now found their country occupied in all directions by French troops, and this was soon followed by the dethronement of the Spanish monarch and the entry of Murat into Madrid to take military possession of it. The occupation of the Peninsula was soon completed by Napoleon in placing his brother Joseph on the throne of Spain and appointing Junot as Governor of Portugal. "Not a shot was fired, not a sword drawn to effect this vast transfer."[1] The English Government upon this determined to despatch troops to the aid of the Spanish and Portuguese, and a force consisting of about 9,000 men was collected at Cork, and sailed from that port on the 12th July, Sir Arthur Wellesley being appointed to command them. Thus "commenced that long and bloody contest in the Peninsula which was destined to terminate in such a glorious manner."

Finding that the enemy's position at Lisbon was too strong to permit his landing in that neighbourhood, the English commander resolved to disembark his force at Mondego Bay, between Oporto and Lisbon. This was carried out on the 1st August, and another British division under General Spencer, arriving two days later from Cadiz, raised the effective strength of Wellesley's army to 12,300 men.[2] With this force he advanced against the French, who were worsted at the combat of Rorica and retired before him. Junot himself now arrived with reinforcements and attacked the English in their position at Vimiera, and was defeated. The

---

[1] Alison.   [2] Cust's *Annals of the Wars*.

French then proposed a conference, which resulted in the Convention of Cintra.

Although the Tenth took no part in this short campaign, it was represented by a young officer whose military career as well as his character as a sportsman made him a prominent figure at that time. This was Colonel Henry Francis Mellish, of Blythe Hall, then a captain in the regiment and aide-de-camp to Sir Ronald Ferguson. He was at a later period assistant-adjutant-general to Sir Arthur Wellesley, and was present at the battles of Talavera, Busaco, Badajos, Fuentes d'Onore, and Salamanca. His excellent talents stood him in good stead during these campaigns, and he was so much appreciated by his chief that he was often entrusted with the drawing up of despatches. During the war it was reported one day to Sir Arthur that Mellish was taken prisoner. He replied, "They'll not keep him long," and the next day he was seen riding into camp on a donkey. On one occasion his brother-officers began laughing at him, it is said, for bestriding so sorry an animal as a charger, declaring it was not worth 5*l.* " I'll make it worth 35*l.* before long," was his answer, and he forthwith rode straight towards the enemy's lines. Fire was opened on him, and his horse shot, when he returned on foot and claimed the Government compensation. While serving in the Peninsula he was appointed (27th April, 1812) Equerry to the Prince of Wales. On his return to England after the battle of Salamanca he took up his residence at Hodsock Manor, where he was known not only as the best judge of a race-horse, but also as the best gentleman rider and whip of the day. Lord William Lennox, in his "Reminiscences," mentions that once at Newmarket, "when a rider was thrown during a race, Colonel Mellish caught the horse, jumped on his back, and brought him in second at the finish." " Few people in England," says a writer in " Sporting Anecdotes," " have filled a larger space in the public notice of the time than Colonel Mellish, and it was not confined to one class of men, but every part of society had seen, known, or heard of him." He was the possessor of many famous race-horses—Sir Lancelot, Luck's All, Stockton, &c. Two years running he won the St. Leger with Sancho and Staveley. In 1806 he entertained the Prince of Wales and the Duke of Clarence for a fortnight at Blythe Hall, and kept open house for the Doncaster meeting. In 1807 he fought a duel with Martin Hawke, in a field by the roadside, as they were returning in their respective drags from the Yorkshire election. On this occasion he was wounded near the elbow-joint, and on perceiving it he immediately ran up to his opponent and said, " Hang it, Hawke, you've winged me, but give me your hand." They were rival whips, and some ill blood on the point as well as election matters brought about this extempore determination to fight.[1] He was always well known as a successful cattle-breeder, carrying off all the chief prizes at the shows. Possessed of abilities as a painter and a musician, and happily married to an accomplished woman, his future seemed full of promise, but he died at the early age of thirty-five.

[1] *Post and Paddock.*

CHAPTER XI

THE REGIMENT PROCEEDS ON ACTIVE SERVICE—EMBARKATION—
SAHAGUN—ADVANCE OF NAPOLEON—RETROGRADE MOVEMENTS—
MAYORGA—BENEVENTE—CAPTURE OF A FRENCH GENERAL BY A
PRIVATE HUSSAR—ASSISTANT-SURGEON DENNY—RETREAT ON AND
BATTLE OF CORUNNA

FOR some months previous to the campaign of 1808 great preparations had been made in England to put the army on a war footing, and a considerable increase had been made in its numbers. In May 1807 the 10th Hussars received orders to be in readiness for foreign service, and its eight troops were each raised to a strength of eighty rank and file. But it was not until September of the following year that a notification came, ordering the regiment to be in immediate readiness for embarkation. In October the Tenth, under command of Lieutenant-Colonel George Leigh, marched in four divisions from Brighton and Lewes, and on the 17th and 18th embarked at Portsmouth on board the transports in presence of H.R.H. the Prince of Wales. It was on this occasion that His Royal Highness took off his sabre, and gave it to Brigadier-General Slade, with his hussar jacket and pelisse. General Slade, who had served in the Tenth until he attained the rank of second lieutenant-colonel, now proceeded to Spain in command of the Hussar Brigade, consisting of the 7th, 10th, and 15th Hussars. The ships were detained in Stokes Bay until the 31st, when they set sail and

1808

G

arrived off Corunna on the 10th November. On that and the two following days the regiment disembarked, swimming the horses to the shore. When all had landed they marched to the barracks of St. Lucia, where they remained until the rest of the division arrived, ten days later.

Cornet George FitzClarence, 10th Hussars, eldest son of the Duke of Clarence, was appointed Extra Aide-de-Camp to General Slade.

The command of the British army in Portugal, vacated by the return of Sir Arthur Wellesley to England after the Convention of Cintra, had been placed in the hands of Sir John Moore. This general, by bringing up Sir David Baird's division from Corunna and Hope's from the Escurial, found himself at the head of nearly 25,000 men, with sixty guns, of which force 2,000 were cavalry. With these he determined to advance into Spain, as he was aware of the immi nent danger that threatened Madrid, and he trusted to create a favourable diversion for the defenders of the Spanish capital by throwing himself on the enemy's communications. " The forward march of the English forces, however, was continued with preparations for a retreat,[1] " as Moore knew that Napoleon's forces amounted to no less than 200,000 men. After reaching Salamanca on the 13th November, his march was directed on Valladolid, but, hearing of the fall of Madrid on the 14th December, the columns were moved on Toro and Benevente.

The Tenth, with the remainder of the Hussar Brigade, left Corunna on the 22nd November, with orders to join the army under Sir John Moore as soon as possible, and, proceeding in three divisions by way of Betanzos, Astorga, and Benevente, arrived at Zamora

[1] Alison's *History of Europe.*

on the 8th December.[1] On arriving at Zamora the inhabitants met the troops with great joy, shouting "Long live the English!" The following morning the brigade marched to Toro, which was reached after dark. The women came to their balconies with flambeaux to light the soldiers through the town, the church bells ringing.

On the 14th the Hussars moved to Tordesillas, a town, like Zamora and Toro, standing on an eminence above the river Douro. The country around was perfectly open, not a tree or a bush or hedge of any kind to be seen. This was the most distant point reached in Spain. On the 15th the brigade moved to La Motta, on the 17th to Villa Braxima, and on the 18th to Villa Pando, where Sir John Moore, Sir David Baird, and the other generals were holding a council of war as to the line of conduct to be adopted.

On the 14th the main body, under Sir John Moore, arrived at Mayorga, where the junction with Sir David Baird was fully effected on the 20th. Learning that Soult, with only two divisions of infantry and two cavalry brigades, in all about 18,000 men, was lying in unsuspecting security in the valley of the Carrion, Moore made preparations to attack him, fairly cal-

---

[1] General Slade, writing in his diary of this march, states that the Hussar Brigade halted at Betanzos on the 20th, at Guitirz on the 21st, and came to Lugo on the 22nd. At this place an order reached him from Lord Paget to reduce the baggage, as the enemy had advanced to Astorga. The marches were made at night, and the cold was very great. On the 24th the brigade proceeded to Negales, and, in consequence of the baggage mules not arriving, bivouacked in the open. The march from Travedelos to Rogalos passed through the mountains, the road being only a mountain path, with a precipice on one side. One horse of the brigade fell down, and was found dead at the bottom of the valley. Villa Franca, Membibre, and Astorga were the next halting-places, and on the 6th December Benevente was reached. The palace at this town appears to have been very beautiful, built by the Moors, and contained a good armoury.

culating that he could overcome Soult before rein-forcements could reach him. The cavalry of the two armies now came into contact. The Hussar Brigade left Mayorga at twelve midnight of the 20th December. The weather was extremely cold; snow lay on the ground, the roads were covered with ice, and many men had to dismount and lead their horses. Between five and six on the morning of the 21st the advance parties of the 15th Hussars fell in with a French patrol and took five prisoners. The remainder escaped, and, galloping off, gave the alarm, so that the surprise of the enemy was prevented. The 15th Hussars, ac-companied by Captain Thornhill and twelve men of the 7th Hussars, were then directed to move along the left bank of the Cea, with a view of intercepting the French dragoons, some seven or eight hundred strong, under Brigadier-General Debelle, and of occupying Sahagun. The Tenth, with four guns, under General Slade, were at the same time to advance direct upon the village, as ordered in the following memorandum from Lord Paget to General Slade : —

The 10th Hussars with 4 guns will march from the Monas-teries so as to arrive at the Bridge of Sahagun at half-past six in the morning. . . . The object of this movement is to surprise Sahagun. The picquet at the Bridge will be driven in briskly. If serious resistance is shewn, a squadron or more may be dis-mounted, who, followed by a mounted squadron, will enter the town, make for the General's and principal officers' quarters to make them prisoners. The grand object is to drive the enemy through the town, on the other side of which Lt.-General Lord Paget will be posted with the 15th Hussars. The moment this object is in way of being accomplished two squadrons of the Tenth must be detached to the left, where the enemy has a piquet of from 60 to 100 men. These must be briskly attacked and made prisoners. This done they will return to Sahagun. (Sd.) Paget.

Morgel de Alaxo : 20th Dec., 1808, ½ 9 p.m.

General Slade writes in his Diary:

" A more dreadful night troops could not be exposed to, as it was particularly dark, a severe frost, with sleet falling, and the snow drifted in many places to the depth of four feet. Many horses fell, and one man had his leg broken. We arrived at the bridge at the hour fixed, but the French were gone. We followed through the town and found that the 15th had not ten minutes charged and put them to the rout. We joined in the pursuit, when 140 prisoners were made. One of the lieutenant-colonels taken is said to be a relation of the Empress Josephine. The French were prepared for the attack, and were drawn up ready to receive the 15th. I must here observe that the French load their baggage every night, and keep their horses bridled and saddled, the men sleeping in the stables. Had we surprised them, the regiment under my command would in all probability have had hot work, as they were all in a convent, where they could very easily have defended themselves. This convent the Hussar Brigade occupied on the night of the 21st."

The 15th Hussars, under the personal command of Lord Paget, on reaching the rear of the position and finding the French dragoons in line ready to receive them, charged at once, broke them up, and pursued them for some distance.[1] "Twenty killed, two lieutenant-colonels, eleven other officers, and 154 men prisoners, was the result of this victorious action. Debelle retired, the English infantry occupied Sahagun, and head-quarters were established there."[2] This was known as the action of Sahagun.[3]

---

[1] "On the 21st, Lord Paget, at the head of the 10th and 15th Hussars, fell in with, and after a short and brilliant action totally defeated, a body of 700 French cavalry, &c."—Alison.

[2] Napier.

[3] For this action Lord Paget received a medal, and the 15th Hussars

Soult, now seriously alarmed, hastily called in his detachment, while Napoleon, immediately suspending the expeditions into the other provinces of Spain, promptly marched at the head of 50,000 men, including the Imperial Guard, to oppose himself to Moore.[1] In the evening of the 21st December the Hussar Brigade marched to Cal, and on the 23rd two squadrons of the Tenth under Major Quentin, moving forward, reconnoitred the position of Marshal Soult at Saldanha, and drove in the French piquets. The remaining two squadrons proceeded the same day to St. Nicholas. As soon

as Napoleon heard of the forward movement of Sir John Moore, he ordered Soult to fall back before him, and endeavour to draw the English general on, while he himself marching from Madrid cut off the retreat of the English army on Portugal. Moore, however, at once awoke to his danger, and gave orders for an immediate retreat. On the 24th the English retired as far as Sahagun. "On the 25th, at three in the morning, we marched back to Sahagun, but how different the treat-

was permitted to inscribe "Sahagun" amongst its honours. The Tenth, however, has no record of this brilliant affair.

[1] Alison, *History of Europe*.

ment to that we received on advancing ! No more ringing of bells, no longer did the air resound with 'Long
live the English !' All the shops were shut, and not
anything to be got. I may truly say it was the most
unpleasant Christmas Day that could be spent." [1]

On the 26th December Buonaparte, advancing from
the Escurial, reached Tordesillas with the advance of
his cavalry, sending strong detachments to Mayorga.
At this place our troops were enabled to measure
strength with their opponents.[2] Seeing the enemy
drawn up on the brow of the rising ground, threatening
the line of retreat, apparently waiting to cut off any
stragglers, Lord Paget, who was at Mayorga, instantly
directed Colonel Leigh, at the head of two squadrons of
the Tenth, to dislodge them. " Colonel Leigh, forming
his small force into two lines, rode briskly forward, one
squadron leading and the other supporting, till he
gained the top of the hill. Here the men were commanded to rein up for the purpose of refreshing the
horses after the ascent, and they did so under a smart
fire from the French. But the horses had no sooner
recovered their wind than the word to 'charge' was
given, and in a few minutes the French were overthrown. Many were killed, many more wounded, and
upwards of ninety prisoners taken. This was known as
the action of Mayorga." [3]

From Sahagun the Hussar Brigade proceeded to

[1] General Slade's *Diary*.

[2] " On the 26th, Baird's troops crossed the Esla, while Moore with the
rear guard was protecting the passage of the stores and baggage. . . . He
was at this time threatened by a large body of Ney's horsemen, when
Lord Paget, with two squadrons of the Tenth, charged and overthrew
them. . . . Indeed, the superiority of the English horse had become so
apparent, that they set all odds at defiance, never hesitated to attack the
enemy's cavalry, though threefold in number, and had already made 500
prisoners, during the few days they had been engaged in active operations."
—Alison.   [3] Lord Londonderry's *Narrative of the Peninsular War*.

Valderas, where the captured French horses were destroyed, as well as several of the horses of the brigade
that were unable to travel, and thus commenced the
famous retreat on Corunna.[1] Napoleon was now rapidly
advancing, although the passes of the Guadarama
Range were choked with snow. On the 26th he had
reached Tordesillas, whence he wrote to Soult : " Our
cavalry scouts are already at Benevente. If the
English pass to-day in their position they are lost; if
they attack you with all their force, retire one day's
march ; the farther they proceed the better for us. If
they retreat, pursue them closely." When this was
written Moore had already given his orders to fall back,
and on Napoleon's arrival at Valderas, to his mortifica-
tion, he found he was twelve hours too late. Continuing
the retreat, the cavalry arrived at Benevente on the
27th December, after crossing the Esla and destroying
the bridge at Castro Gonzalo. Cavalry piquets were
left to watch the ford of the Esla, and the army was
given two days' rest at Benevente.[2] Early in the morning of the 29th a French officer was observed reconnoitring the fords near the destroyed bridge, and presently between five and six hundred cavalry of the
Imperial Guard crossed the river. The piquets,
under Lieutenant-Colonel Loftus Otway,[3] of the 18th
Hussars, retired before them, fighting until joined by
the supports, composed of the 3rd German Hussars,

[1] " On the 26th we marched to Valderas—we were thirteen hours on
horseback—and a most severe day it was. I should conceive that not less
than forty horses sunk from fatigue and were obliged to be shot."—General
Slade's *Diary*.

[2] " *27th December*.—Marched to Benevente. It rained the whole of
this day, which after the frost made the roads almost impassable. No
ploughed field, after the breaking up of a frost, could be in a worse state.
The exertions of the artillery and the difficulties they encountered exceed
everything I could have conceived."—Extract from General Slade's *Diary*.

[3] Afterwards Lieutenant-General Sir Loftus William Otway.

when the whole charged the leading French squadrons with some effect.   Brigadier-General the Hon.
C. Stewart then took the command, but though the
ground was obstinately disputed the enemy still advanced.   "At this moment the plain was covered
with stragglers, baggage, mules, and followers, the
town was filled with tumult, the distant piquet and
vedettes were seen galloping in from the right and left,
the French were pressing forward boldly, and every
appearance indicated that the enemy's whole army had
come up and was passing the river." [1]

At length the enemy's cavalry, under General Lefèvre-Desnouettes, a dashing officer who had already
distinguished himself in previous campaigns, had been
drawn sufficiently far into the plain, when the 10th
Hussars, who were formed up out of sight, concealed by
some houses, suddenly appeared, and, receiving orders
from Lord Paget to charge, bore down upon the enemy
at full speed.   The piquets, seeing the Tenth coming forward to support them, gave a loud cheer, joined in the
attack, and overturned the enemy in a headlong rush.
The French fled fast towards the river, followed so
closely by the Tenth, covered by the 7th Hussars, that
the French squadron plunged into the stream and
crossed to the other side.   Their loss was fifty-five
killed, seventy wounded, besides their general, many
officers, and seventy men taken prisoners, making a
total loss of two hundred excellent soldiers.   It is said
that Napoleon himself was an eye-witness of this *ren-
contre* from the opposite heights, on which he stood.[2]
" During the pursuit in the plain an officer was observed

---

[1] Napier.

[2] A medal was struck for Sahagun and Benevente, but the honour of
bearing the names of these actions amongst its records has not been
granted to the Tenth.

to separate from the main body and make towards another part of the river. He was followed by two men of the Tenth, and refusing to stop was wounded and brought in a prisoner."[1] This was the French General Lefèvre-Desnouettes, and the man by whom he was captured was Private Levi Grisdall, of the 10th Hussars.[2] This gallant affair was known as the action of Benevente.[3] The British loss was also severe, being about fifty killed and wounded.[4] Sir John Moore, in detailing the operations of the army, spoke in terms of commendation of the conduct of the hussars, adding: "Our cavalry are very superior to any the French have, and the right spirit has been infused into them by the example and instruction of their two leaders, Lord Paget and Brigadier-General Stewart.[5] The Hussar Brigade maintained their posts on the Esla under an occasional cannonade until the evening, and then withdrew to La Baneza.[6] After our cavalry, acting as the rear guard of the army, had evacuated

---

[1] Alison, Cust, Napier, Cannon's *Regimental Records.*

[2] This man, by order of the Prince Regent, was promoted to the rank of sergeant. General Desnouettes was sent as a prisoner to England, and was treated with great consideration, and received many privileges. He lived at Cheltenham and Malvern on parole, but in May 1812 he escaped to France.

[3] Lord Londonderry in his *Narrative of the War in Spain and Portugal*, speaking of the action of Benevente, says: "This was the most serious affair in which we had yet been engaged. The cavalry opposed to us formed part of the Imperial Guard. They were all tried soldiers, and they fought in a manner not unworthy of the reputation which they had earned in the North of Europe."

[4] "It was a most spirited conflict, most creditable to the English cavalry. . . . This was the most serious affair in which the British cavalry had yet been engaged."—Cust.

[5] Afterwards the Marquis of Anglesey and the Marquis of Londonderry.

[6] "Previous to evacuating Benevente, the Commissary stove three puncheons of rum and set fire to all the stores, such as tents, blankets, &c."—General Slade's *Diary.*

Benevente, Mr. Denny, the assistant-surgeon of the Tenth, re-entered that town with a guard of twenty men lent to him by Brigadier-General Slade, and selecting our wounded from those of the enemy in the convent, brought them safely away. On the 30th the British General reached Astorga, and continued his retreat. Napoleon joined the head-quarters of Soult at that place on the 1st January, 1809, but hearing there that the Austrians were preparing to take the field he gave up the pursuit of the British to his Marshal and returned to Paris.

Soult, with an army consisting of 70,000 strong, including 10,000 cavalry, now vigorously pressed the pursuit. The weather was dreadful. Rain and snow rendered the roads almost impassable, but, in spite of all, every position was disputed, every opportunity taken to stand and fight. General Slade states in his Diary : " On the 31st, at Astorga, it was reported the French were advancing upon us. The Hussar Brigade assembled at our alarm posts at eight P.M., where we remained till midnight. We then marched to Membibre, arriving at two P.M. the following afternoon. The many delays were owing in the first instance to the depth of the snow, and also from the frequent interruptions we met with from carriages being overturned, artillery waggons burning, &c." In the Tenth alone, Captain Darby and seventeen private soldiers died of fatigue, while sixty horses were destroyed to prevent their falling into the hands of the enemy. " On the 2nd January the French came in upon us in such force at Villa Franca that Sir John Moore ordered the whole army to retreat to Lugo, a distance of sixteen leagues (sixty-six miles). The cavalry marched from Villa Franca at four P.M., halted for a couple of hours at Hewerias, and reached Lugo between ten and eleven the following night. On the

4th we remained quiet, but at three P.M. on the 5th the whole army was under arms and marched about a league on the Villa Franca road, conceiving that the French meditated an attack, but nothing passed beyond a little skirmishing, and the cavalry returned to Lugo at eight P.M.[1]" On the 6th January Moore halted at Lugo, and, strongly posted, was prepared to give the enemy battle, but, Soult declining it, the English again retired. "The Tenth, under General Slade, was ordered to occupy the bridge of Robardo, on the road to Corunna, over which the whole of the army passed by seven A.M. the next morning, when it was blown up, but not so effectually but that the advanced guard of the French contrived to harass our rear most exceedingly. On the 7th we marched to Constantine and remained in bivouac till seven in the evening, when we again resumed our march, and arrived at Betanzos about four in the afternoon of the 8th. This was a most fatiguing march, as we did not go above two miles an hour, being obliged to regulate our pace by the infantry, and it rained incessantly full thirty-six hours."[2] On the 10th, the rear guard halted at Betanzos, where there was a slight affair of outposts, and on the 11th the army reached Corunna, without a gun or a colour having fallen into the hands of the enemy. As the transports were not yet in sight, Moore took up a strong position to offer battle; but on the evening of the 14th the ships arrived, the dismounted cavalry, the sick, the best horses and fifty pieces of artillery were embarked, and preparations were made for evacuating Corunna and placing the whole army on board on the 16th. "On the 16th we went on with embarking the cavalry, but, from the time being so limited, Sir John Moore directed me not to allow more than thirty horses per regiment to embark, the remainder

[1] General Slade's *Diary*.   [2] *Ibid*.

to be destroyed."[1] "All the encumbrances were shifted in the morning, when about two o'clock a general movement of the French line gave notice of an approaching battle, and the British infantry, 14,500 strong, occupied their positions."[2] The battle of Corunna lasted until dark, and resulted in the French being driven back from their most advanced ground, and being unable to molest the embarkation of the troops. This was completed on the 18th, under the orders of General Hope, who had assumed command of the army on the death of Sir John Moore.

General Slade, writing in his diary of this day, says: "About one P.M. this day, as I was superintending the embarkation of the 18th Hussars, I heard a firing from our lines that indicated a general action, and though I had no cavalry remaining I went to the army to offer my services to Sir John Moore, but almost at the moment of my arrival I found he had received a wound from a cannon ball which he only survived about three hours. Almost at the same instant the second in command, Sir David Baird, received a musket shot through the upper part of his left arm, and was obliged to leave the field. The command of the army devolved upon Lieutenant-General Hope. The action lasted about four hours. The object of the French in the action appears to have been to get possession of a hill which entirely commanded the harbour, from which they could have done our shipping a great deal of mischief, as here were nearly 300 sail of transports. The wind fortunately favoured our getting away, or there is no saying what might have been the consequences.

"It is not in the power of language to do justice to the exertions of the navy in getting us off. It is evident

[1] General Slade's *Diary*.   [2] Napier.

to me that without their aid we should have been obliged to have left many thousands behind." [1]

Previous to the battle it had been found necessary, as already mentioned, to destroy the greater portion of the horses of the British cavalry. The ground around Corunna was rocky and unsuited to the movements of horses that had already become tender in the feet from their long march through Portugal, without the possibility of bestowing proper care on their shoeing, so that they could not be employed in the action. This painful measure was therefore adopted in order to prevent the horses falling into the hands of the French, and some thousands were shot on the seashore. The Tenth, which had left England with over six hundred horses, returned with only thirty.

[1] General Slade's Diary has been most kindly given to be used in these memoirs by his son, Mr. Wyndham Slade.

CHAPTER XII

RETURN OF THE ARMY TO ENGLAND—THE REGIMENT AT BRIGHTON
—THE HEALTH OF GEORGE III.—THE PRINCE OF WALES AP-
POINTED REGENT—THE REGIMENT STYLED "ROYAL"—PREPARA-
TIONS FOR ACTIVE SERVICE—ARRIVAL AT LISBON—CAMPAIGNS
OF 1810–11–12—LORD WORCESTER

THE fleet sailed from Corunna Bay on the 18th January,   1809
and the troops were disembarked at various ports in
England during the first week in February. The depôt
of the Tenth had been stationed at Brighton during the
campaign, and as the various detachments of the head-
quarters arrived they proceeded to that place. On the
26th March, the whole being assembled, the regiment was
inspected by Lieutenant-General Lord Charles Somerset.
The officers and men of the 10th Hussars at this time received the thanks of H.R.H. the Prince of Wales for
their conduct on active service, which was again
repeated when His Royal Highness reviewed the regiment with the other troops in the district on the 12th
August. A magnificent piece of gold plate was presented by the officers of the Hussar Brigade to their
distinguished commander, Lord Paget, to commemorate
his skilful leadership in the brilliant operations of the
cavalry in Portugal during the campaign of 1808–9.

" Corunna" was inscribed on the colours of the in-   1809–
fantry regiments that took part in this campaign, but   1810
no cavalry regiment was allowed this distinction. Some
officers of the Tenth received the gold medal. At this

time medals for all ranks were not granted, and decorations were limited to generals, staff officers, and officers
commanding regiments, who were selected by the Commander-in-Chief himself as particularly deserving, but
no special mark was bestowed to show the part taken
by cavalry regiments in this campaign.

In 1810 Lieutenant-Colonel George Quentin succeeded to the command of the regiment in succession
to Lieutenant-Colonel Leigh.

Colonel George Leigh joined the 10th Light Dragoons in 1790, and received such rapid promotion that
he commanded the regiment in nine years. When the
Tenth proceeded to Spain in 1808 to take part in the
campaign under Sir John Moore, Lieutenant-Colonel
Leigh was in command. He had many opportunities of
distinguishing himself. He was awarded the gold medal
for Sahagun and Benevente, and was promoted to a
brevet colonelcy. He retired from the army in 1810.

The losses on foreign service were speedily replaced,
and after passing the summer at Brighton the regiment
marched to Essex, having head-quarters at Romford.
Remaining in this county during the winter months, it
moved again on the 10th April, 1810, and went into
billets in the eastern suburbs of London, with head-
quarters at Islington. This last change was in consequence of the riots which had taken place between the
6th and 9th April owing to the committal of Sir
Francis Burdett to the Tower by the order of the House
of Commons. While in London the regiment was
reviewed on the 16th April by H.R.H. the Duke of
York. On the 2nd May it returned to Romford, and
on the 16th marched to Brighton, with out-quarters
at Lewes.

A change in the position of non-commissioned officers was at this time made by troop quartermasters

being abolished and troop sergeant-majors appointed.
One regimental quartermaster, promoted from the
ranks, whose commission was not to be purchased, had
already been given to each regiment.[1] From the 25th
September a trumpet-major was borne on the strength
of a cavalry regiment, in accordance with a general
order dated 20th October.

Towards the close of the year the health of King
George III. became seriously affected, and the death of
his favourite daughter, Princess Amelia, greatly aggra-
vating his disease, it became necessary to form a
Regency. Accordingly, in February 1811, the Prince
of Wales was appointed Regent of the United Kingdom.
Upon this His Royal Highness on the 6th March was
pleased to confer, in the name and on behalf of His
Majesty, the designation " Royal " upon his regiment,
directing that in future it should be called " The 10th,
the Prince of Wales's Own Royal Regiment of Hussars."
At the same time the facings of the uniform were
changed from yellow to red.[2]

The regiment remained stationed at Brighton at
this time for two years—namely, from the 16th May,
1810, until 16th May, 1812. As His Royal Highness
took up his residence during the summer months at the
Pavilion, he saw a great deal of the Tenth, often taking
command of the regiment in person in the field. He
also honoured the officers by constantly inviting them

---

[1] " All troop quartermasters with forty years' service or over to be
retired on full pay, the remainder gradually to be paid off. Troop sergeant-
majors to be distinguished from the other sergeants by an additional
chevron. The regimental sergeant-major to be distinguished by a crown.
By the Commander-in-Chief's command, HARRY CALVERT, Adj.-Gen."

[2] The Tenth after this was often called the " Prince Regent's Regiment
of Hussars," but no official sanction ever appears to have been given for
this title. In a picture of the Prince Regent in the uniform of the regiment, now in the Pavilion at Br'ghton, the shabracque is shown with
" G.P." on one place and " P.R." on another.

1811   to participate in the hospitalities of the Pavilion, and to join in the sports and amusements in which he engaged. On one of these occasions, when His Royal Highness, accompanied by the officers of his regiment, had taken out his pack of beagles, and all efforts to find a hare having proved a failure, he proposed extempore races to be ridden over the hurdles used for night folding the sheep, which are to be found in considerable numbers on the Downs. These races proved a great success, and are said to have been the first introduction of hurdle-racing in this country.[1]

" Brighton will never see such picturesque Watteau-like groups again as those which were then presented by the Prince's Court as it sallied forth from the Pavilion for the evening promenade on the Steyne, the ladies with their high head-dresses and spreading ' peacock tails,' and the two ' Manners,' Sir Bellingham Graham, Colonels Mellish and Leigh, all of the Tenth, as their esquires. In those days the Prince made Brighton and Lewes Races the gayest scene of the year in England. The Pavilion was full of guests, and the Steyne was crowded with all the rank and fashion from London. Lord Foley and Colonel Mellish, two of the great supporters of the turf, were looked to for all the best racing information of the day. The Prince himself would make his appearance in the crowd later, dressed in a green jacket, a white hat, and light nankeen pantaloons and shoes, distinguished by his high-bred manner and handsome person ; he was generally accompanied by the Duke of Bedford, Lord Jersey, Charles Wyndham, Shelley, Brummell, Mr. Day, and Churchill." [2]

1812   Several changes of quarters took place in 1812.

---

[1] Blaine's *Encyclopædia of Rural Sports.*
[2] *Post and Paddock.*

The right wing (four troops) of the regiment marched from Brighton to Guildford on the 16th May, and on the 24th July the head-quarters moved to Hounslow and were stationed there, with detachments at Hampton Court and Windsor.

The Prince Regent reviewed the 10th, 15th, and 18th Hussars, in brigade, on Hounslow Heath on the 17th August, 1812, on which occasion Her Majesty Queen Charlotte and H.R.H. the Commander-in-Chief were present.

On the 21st October, four troops—viz. B, D, E, and G—marched to Knightsbridge Barracks, and took over the guards and escorts connected with the Court and the metropolis from the Life Guards on the embarkation of the latter for foreign service to reinforce the army in the Peninsula. The Tenth, however, had only performed these duties for a few weeks when six troops of the regiment were ordered to hold themselves in readiness to proceed to the seat of war. The order of preparation for these troops was received on the 29th November, and in the following month the troops that had been at Knightsbridge marched to Guildford, where the whole regiment was now assembled. The strength detailed for foreign service was 2 field officers, 6 captains, 12 subalterns, 1 acting adjutant, 4 staff officers, 1 regimental sergeant major, 2 troop quartermasters, 4 troop sergeant-majors, 29 sergeants, 24 corporals, 6 trumpeters, 513 privates, and 523 troop horses.

When these head-quarter troops had been thus completed, the four remaining troops, under the command of Major the Hon. Frederick Howard, marched on the 11th December to York, and formed the depôt of the regiment. While stationed there, during the early part of 1813, they were engaged in recruiting and purchasing horses. They also were employed in sup-

1813   pressing the Luddite riots,[1] and kept the peace at the public execution which afterwards took place, when fourteen of the ringleaders were hanged. But in the course of the summer the depôt was moved to Brighton, where it joined the depôt of the 15th Hussars.

On the 24th January, 1813, orders were received for the six service troops to proceed to Portsmouth. Arriving there in three detachments on the 26th, 27th, and 29th, they at once embarked, and by two P.M. on the 29th the transports had set sail for Lisbon. Lieutenant-Colonel Palmer was in command of the regiment, with Major Robarts as second. Colonel Quentin did not sail with the Tenth, but joined it some months afterwards in Spain. On the 13th February the ships anchored in the Tagus, and by the 16th all had disembarked. On landing, the regiment marched to Belem Barracks, and remained there until the 6th April, occupying itself with preparations for the coming campaign in the spring, and for the march to join the army under Lord Wellington. On the 18th February 550 pistols, just arrived from England, were issued.

On the 6th and 7th April the troops marched from Belem to Villa Franca. Continuing their route on the 21st, they entered the valley of the Mondego, and, advancing towards the frontier of Spain, joined the army of Wellington, now lying on the banks of the Coa and Agueda.

1809–   Between the departure of the 10th Hussars in 1809,
1810   after Corunna, and their return in 1813, many important events had taken place in the Peninsula. The British Government, having determined to hold Portugal, had in March 1809 made arrangements with the Government of that country for placing the whole

---

[1] These riots commenced in 1811, and were an expression of the people's feelings in York against the introduction of machinery.

of their army under the orders of an English officer, and for its thorough reorganisation. General Beresford, who was selected for this post, was, on his arrival in Lisbon, appointed a field-marshal, and placed in command of the Portuguese army. At the same time troops were again despatched from England, and in April Sir Arthur Wellesley, who had been chosen as the most fitting person to fill the post of commander of the forces, arrived in Lisbon, where he was nominated by the Regency Marshal-General of the Armies of the Kingdom of Portugal.

After the battle of Corunna, Marshal Soult had advanced through Galicia into Portugal and occupied Oporto. Sir Arthur Wellesley now commenced his operations against that place, while Beresford marched towards the Upper Douro. Having gained possession of Oporto, Sir Arthur moved next into Spain, and, after effecting a junction with the Spanish forces under Cuesta, encountered the French troops under Joseph Buonaparte (King of Spain) at Talavera, a battle which he won on the 29th July, and with it the title of Lord Wellington. After this victory, finding that he met with no support from the Spaniards, the English commander fell back upon Portugal, and in August took up a defensive position on the frontiers of that kingdom.

In 1810 the campaign re-opened with increased vigour. At this moment enthusiasm ran high in England. Volunteers of all ranks joined the army, anxious to take part in the coming struggle, and amongst these was the Marquis of Worcester, who then held a commission in the Monmouth and Brecon Militia. His father having refused to put him into the regular army, Lord Worcester shipped himself and three horses on board a merchant ship proceeding to Lisbon. On arrival in the Tagus he at once joined

Lord Wellington, who placed him on his staff, and in this position he was present at the battle of Busaco. In August 1811 he received a commission in the 10th Hussars, but, the regiment being still at home, he remained on the staff of Lord Wellington. When, however the Tenth landed in Lisbon in 1813, Lord Worcester joined them and took part as a regimental officer in all the operations of that and the following year.

The defence of Portugal occupied Lord Wellington during 1810. In September of that year the French commenced their third invasion of that country, and the English army withdrew to Busaco, a position which Massena, now in command of the French troops, attacked in force. The Allies eventually retired, Wellington falling back upon the lines of Torres Vedras, which he occupied during the winter. The principal events of the campaign of 1811 were the retreat of Massena from Portugal, the battles of Fuentes d'Onore and Albuera.

The year 1812 opened with the capture of Ciudad Rodrigo and Badajoz. On the 13th June, Wellington advancing passed the Agueda and marched towards the Tormes. On the 22nd July the battle of Salamanca was fought, resulting in the defeat of Marmont, who had superseded Massena, a victory which gained for Wellington the title of Marquis. At Valladolid the English army turned to meet Joseph, who was driven before them, and Wellington entered Madrid in triumph.

In September the English forces again marched to Valladolid, and forced the French back to Burgos. Here Wellington's successes for this campaign ended. Finding himself greatly overmatched in numbers by the French, he determined to fall back again on the Portuguese frontier, and place his army in cantonments in the neighbourhood of Ciudad Rodrigo.

CHAPTER XIII

THE HUSSAR BRIGADE—CAMPAIGN OF 1813—MORALES DEL TORO—
FALL OF BURGOS—BATTLE OF VITTORIA

THE feeling had become general in England that the moment had at length arrived for the total expulsion of the French from the Peninsula, and preparations were now made on a large scale to compass it. The French were losing heart. Napoleon had withdrawn large contingents from the South to cover the disasters in Russia, and his brother Joseph, who commanded the armies in Spain, had failed to inspire confidence there. Wellington, on the other hand, animated the Spaniards as well as his own troops with the greatest enthusiasm. Before spring arrived, the allied army, thoroughly recruited in health and vigour after the many hardships of the last campaign, and largely reinforced from England, especially in cavalry, was prepared to take the field in greater strength than it had done since the commencement of the Peninsular war.[1]

Early in 1813 the "campaign of Vittoria" was undertaken, a campaign in which the Tenth played a conspicuous part. On the 18th May the Hussar Brigade, consisting of the 10th, 15th, and 18th, was reviewed by the Marquis of Wellington at Trexada. On the 22nd the march began; head-quarters were estab-

1813

---

[1] " Nearly 200,000 allied troops were in readiness in the whole Peninsula, of whom 44,000 were British, with 90 guns, and 6,000 horse."—Alison.

lished at Ciudad Rodrigo on the 23rd, from which date
the army continued its advance on the Douro in three
columns. The left column, 40,000 strong, under Sir
Thomas Graham, had orders to turn the right of the
French line on that river, a difficult operation, which
obliged it to cross the mountainous country of the
Tras-os-Montes, and to encounter and overcome many
obstacles.[1] The Hussar Brigade, which formed part of
this force, acted as its advanced guard. In passing the
Douro, a feat accomplished by Graham's force in six
hours, three horses of the Tenth fell out of the boats,
but were brought safely to the shore by Troop Sergeant-
Major Kirkee, who jumped into the water after them.
Graham continued his advance in the direction of Bra-
ganza, so as to open communication with Galicia, and
wheeling to his right prepared to cross the Esla. On
the 27th and 28th the centre and right of the army
crossed the Douro at Zamora and Toro. Wellington
himself passed this river in a basket slung on a rope
from rock to rock in the neighbourhood of Miranda,
and joined Graham's force on the Esla.

On the 31st May the Hussar Brigade crossed this
last-named river, using the Almendra ford. They entered the river with infantry hanging on to their stirrups, but the water was so deep and the current so strong
that several men, being unable to hold on, were drowned.
The cavalry, however, pushed on, surprised a French
piquet, and captured an officer and thirty men at Per-
drices. Sir Thomas Graham, having now effected a
junction with the rest of the army, and the French
position being thus turned, the enemy began to retreat,

---

[1] "Graham had overcome many difficulties . . . . but by his vigour
and perseverance 40,000 men had been transported in ten days through
200 miles of the most broken, rugged country in the Peninsula, and on
the 3rd June the whole army was in communication on the northern
bank of the Douro, between Toro and the river Esla."—Alison.

followed closely by the Allies. On the 1st June the head of the allied army entered Zamora, and the enemy retired through Toro, after destroying the bridge.

At this time the Marquis of Wellington noticed that Sir Colquhoun Grant, who was in command of the Hussar Brigade, marched every day left in front, which placed the junior regiment, the 18th, always in advance. He called the attention of the brigadier to this, who immediately ordered that each regiment in its turn should lead; and as the brigade pursued the French through Toro the Tenth had the satisfaction of being in front. At the village of Morales the rear guard of the French was overtaken on the 2nd June by the Hussar Brigade. The French horsemen immediately passed a bridge and a swamp under fire, and then, facing about in two lines, gave battle. Major Robarts, with the Tenth, followed them, and, forming up with a squadron of the 18th echeloned on his flank, and the remainder of that regiment in support, charged the French dragoons with such effect that their first line was at once overthrown, and, becoming a confused mass, galloped back on to their supports. Following up their success, the Tenth, with the 18th still in support, the 15th in reserve, attacked the second line; this soon broke and fled, the pursuit being carried on for two miles. In addition to their loss in killed and wounded, two officers, 202 non-commissioned officers and men of the enemy, and an equal proportion of horses, were captured. Their shattered squadrons finally took refuge behind a large body of cavalry, infantry, and guns posted on the heights in front of Morales del Toro. The loss of the Tenth on this occasion was Lieutenant Cotton, Private Rogers, and four horses killed, nine rank and file and five horses wounded, Captain Lloyd, Quartermaster Cowley, Sergeant Roper, and Private Shackleford taken prisoners, and ten horses missing. Captain Lloyd, being severely wounded, was left at Pedrosa del Rey on parole, and, on an exchange having been arranged for him, resumed his duty there. Quartermaster Cowley was left at Burgos on the retreat of the French from that place. He was found in the gaol, released, and thereupon rejoined his regiment.

In a letter from the Marquis of Wellington, dated Toro, 2nd June, 1813, addressed to Lieutenant-General Sir Thomas Graham, K.B., His Lordship says : " The Tenth had a very handsome affair this morning with the enemy's cavalry between this and Morales. Their loss is small, but they must have destroyed the enemy's 16th Dragoons, of whom they took about 200 prisoners. The enemy showed in great strength in cavalry about Pedrosa del Rey." In His Lordship's despatch to Earl Bathurst, dated Amperdin, 6th June, 1813, he reports : " The troops have continued to advance since the 31st of last month, and were on the 1st at Zamora, and on the 2nd they arrived at Toro. The English hussars, being in the advanced guard, fell in between Toro and Morales with a considerable body of the enemy's cavalry, which were immediately attacked by the Tenth, supported by the 18th and 15th. The enemy were overthrown and pursued for many miles, and 210 prisoners, with many horses and two officers, fell into our hands. I enclose Colonel Grant's report of this gallant affair, which reflects great credit upon Major Robarts and the 10th Hussars and upon Colonel Grant, under whose directions they acted."

The following brigade order was issued on this occasion, dated Morales del Toro, 2nd June, 1813 :—

It is with the utmost satisfaction that Colonel Grant returns his best thanks to Major Robarts for the gallant manner in which he led the 10th Royal Hussars in the affair with the enemy this day. He requests Major Robarts will explain to the officers and men of that corps his entire approbation of the discipline and bravery they evinced, and he feels extreme pleasure in paying this tribute to their steady and excellent conduct, as well as to the decided and irresistible impetuosity with which they overthrew the enemy's ranks. 1813

The young Marquis of Worcester, who was an officer of the leading squadron, has left on record how they came across a French piquet near Morales del Toro, which they drove in on its supports, and how, as soon as the whole of the Tenth came up, it charged the French dragoons so fiercely that they were completely routed : " It then became a chase across country over the prickly-pear hedges, the pace being so good that the rest of the Hussar Brigade in support could not get up; and nearly the whole of the enemy's dragoons were destroyed or taken prisoners." Captain Surman, who later on was ridingmaster and adjutant of the Tenth, and was afterwards the Prince Regent's ridingmaster, has stated that at Sahagun, in 1809, when the 15th Hussars, supported by the Tenth, as previously described, met and destroyed nearly the whole of a French cavalry regiment of the Guard, Napoleon, who was present, became so indignant that he removed them from the Guard, and they became the 16th Dragoons of the line. This regiment the Tenth now met at Morales, and it again sustained a similar defeat.[1] Following up the pursuit of the retiring enemy, the Hussar Brigade left Morales on the morning of the 3rd June, and, a junction with the rest of the army having been made, the whole moved forward on the 4th, the right wing, under Sir Rowland Hill, being directed along the main road to Burgos.

[1] Letter from the Duke of Beaufort, dated the 17th September, 1877.

Arriving at Hormillas on the 12th June, the Hussar
Brigade, in advance, continued to march to Burgos,
and was engaged with the rest of the troops in the capture of that town. The enemy had taken up a position
behind the Hormaza, and offered battle, but the Hussar
Brigade and Major-General Ponsonby's brigade, with
artillery, followed by the Light Division, turned the
right of their line, while the other divisions advanced
against their front, and forced them to fall back into
the town of Burgos. This, however, they abandoned
during the night, and blew up the Castle. " Scarcely
had the echoes of the explosion at Burgos ceased when
the army was again in motion towards the sources of
the Ebro." [1] Graham in one march passed the Ebro,
the centre of the army followed, and the right wing,
under Hill, crossed the river at the Puente Arenas. By
this movement the French were cut off from the sea-
coast, and English vessels entered the port of Santander.
A depôt and hospital station were established at this
place, and a new base of operations opened.

From the 15th to the 21st the march continued
through a rocky and mountainous country. " The whole
crest of the mountains between the Ebro and the sea
was soon in their possession; hill and valley, every difficulty of an Alpine region was met and surmounted,
when at length joyfully the men descended the sunny
vales and the scarlet uniforms were to be seen in every
valley. No words can do justice to the exquisite
beauty of the scenery through which the British troops
passed during this memorable march, and often the
men rested on their muskets, gazing on the lovely
scenes spread far beneath their feet." [2]

On the 19th the Tenth, with the rest of the Hussar
Brigade, arrived at Savagetta, within a day's march of

[1] Napier.   [2] Alison.

Vittoria, and, the whole army following under Wellington, the French were forced to retreat behind Salinas de
Anara. Joseph, seeing that the English were concen-
trating on his right and rear, lost no time in uniting his
divisions, and marched up the left bank of the Zadora
in order to gain the basin of Vittoria. The French
General Reille was left at Subijana de Morillas to protect the retreat, but, his position being turned by two
English divisions, he too was compelled to cross the
Zadora and also fall back, with some loss. This crisis,
in which the Allies nearly prevented the French from
entering the passes, being over, the combat ceased, and
the Allies pitched their tents on the Bayas.[1]

The Marquis of Wellington had now under his command 60,000 English and Portuguese and above 20,000
Spanish auxiliaries, his whole army numbering more
than 80,000 combatants. The French army, under
Joseph Buonaparte, formed up in the valley of Vittoria,
numbered less than 70,000.

The moment had at length arrived when the enemy,
whose whole movements since the commencement of
the campaign had been those of retreat, was compelled
to make a final stand on Spanish territory, if only to
allow time for the immense baggage trains of King
Joseph to retire into France. The ground on which
the decisive battle of Vittoria was fought lies in a basin
about eight miles in length by six in breadth, the town
of that name being at the northern end. The river
Zadora, running southward, after passing Vittoria, with
many turns and rugged banks, divides this basin un-
equally. The position taken by the French was a
strong one, its right resting on the Zadora, its left on
the Puebla Mountains. Fifty pieces of artillery were
massed in front, pointing to the bridges of Mendoza,

[1] Napier's *History of the Peninsular War*.

Tres Puentes, Villoda, and Nanclares, which the Allies must cross, and which formed the great strength of the French position. Wellington divided his army into three distinct parts. Graham with the left wing advanced by the Bilbao road to turn the French right; Hill was to attack the left; while Wellington, in the centre, with 30,000 men, forced his way in front.

On the morning of the 21st June, the weather being rainy, the allied troops had moved from their camps on the Bayas. About one o'clock Hill's attack was developed, while at the same time " a curling smoke faintly seen far up the Zadora on the enemy's extreme right showed that Graham was at work." [1] Upon this the retreat of the French commenced, and the Hussar Brigade was ordered to the centre of the line to assist in forcing the enemy back, then retiring towards the town of Vittoria. As soon as Lord Wellington saw the hill in front of Arinez denuded of French troops, he advanced the cavalry to that post, the Tenth being in support. Up to this time the regiment had not been much employed owing to the unfavourable nature of the ground, but now the Hussar Brigade was ordered to advance towards the left of the town, on which the enemy was falling back in great confusion. Continuing the pursuit, the brigade entered Vittoria at full gallop, and turning to the right passed through the eastern gate along the road leading to Pampeluna. There it fell in with the great body of the enemy's baggage, the guard of which was charged and dispersed by a squadron of the Tenth, led by Captain Henry Wyndham and the Marquis of Worcester. [2] While engaged in securing prisoners, &c., some of the enemy's cavalry came out of the town and formed in its rear with the

---

[1] Napier.   [2] *Regimental Digest of Services.*

intention of attacking. The men of the Tenth, however, were soon rallied, and, being formed into two squadrons, kept their ground, although a column of French infantry was advancing. The latter, after firing a volley into our squadrons, which killed and wounded a few men and horses, retired, but, the ground being much intersected with ditches and ravines, the regiment was prevented from charging, although it frustrated every attempt of the enemy to carry off the baggage which had been captured.[1] While the other squadrons were assisting in securing the fruits of the battle, Captain Wyndham continued the pursuit, and, coming up with the carriage of Joseph Buonaparte, is said to have fired into it as the occupants were making their escape.[2] The whole regiment, which throughout the battle had been under the command of Major Robarts, now followed the flying enemy with the rest of the British cavalry until after sunset, and bivouacked on the Pampeluna road for the night.

Writing of this great battle Napier says : " Never was a victory more complete. The French carried off but two pieces of artillery. Jourdan's marshal's bâton, Joseph's private carriage[3] and sword of state, one hundred and forty-three pieces of cannon, ammunition, treasure, everything fell into the hands of the victors. The loss of the French was about 6,000 killed and wounded, that of the Allies 5,176."

The Tenth suffered but slightly—four rank and file, eight horses killed ; one sergeant, one trumpeter, two

[1] Diary of Dr. Jenks, late 10th Hussars.

[2] " Joseph himself narrowly escaped being made a prisoner : a squadron of dragoons pursued the carriage and fired into it, and he had barely time to throw himself out and escape on horseback under shelter of a troop of horse."—Alison.

[3] " In this carriage were found a number of most valuable pictures, among which was the beautiful Correggio of ' Christ in the Garden,' which now adorns Apsley House."—Alison.

corporals, six privates and seven horses wounded, five horses missing—Privates Bryant, Pinder, Inglefield, and Crawton killed ; Sergeant Wilson, Corporals Smith and Whalebone, Trumpeter Dickinson, Privates W. Miles, Fartlin, Farlen, Exall, and Skinner wounded.[1] This victory gained for the British commander the bâton of a field-marshal, which was notified to him in a most flattering letter from the Prince Regent. " You have sent me among the trophies of your unrivalled fame the staff of a French marshal, and I send you in return that of England." [2]

While Graham was despatched with his division to invest St. Sebastian, Wellington followed the French army into the Pyrenees and blockaded Pampeluna. " In this campaign of six weeks Wellington marched with 100,000 men six hundred miles, passed six great rivers, gained one decisive battle, invested two fortresses, and drove 120,000 veteran troops from Spain." [3]

On the 22nd June the Tenth, with the rest of the Hussar Brigade, left its bivouac and continued the pursuit of the enemy, halting at night a league from Salvatierra. On the succeeding day it continued its march in the direction of Pampeluna, and after several movements went into cantonments at Olite, in Navarre, about twenty miles south of Pampeluna, as part of a

[1] Attention may here be drawn to the fact that, while some regiments have the privilege of numbering " Vittoria " amongst their honours, the Tenth and others do not do so. The same has already been said of the cavalry action of " Benevente " in 1809, while " Sahagun," an action of an exactly similar nature, and at which the Tenth were also present, is only borne by one regiment." The gallant action of Morales del Toro, in which the Tenth took the prominent part, has also remained unacknowledged.

[2] " It is a remarkable fact that 500 years before a battle was fought by the Black Prince on the same ground near Vittoria in the cause of the rightful monarch of Spain, and a hill on the field is still called the 'English Hill.' "—Alison.

[3] Napier.

corps of observation during the investment of that place. After the arduous marches both before and after the battle of Vittoria, a rest was absolutely necessary both for man and horse, and it was with great satisfaction that the cavalry was permitted to remain at Olite until the 27th July. On the 25th of that month Colonel Quentin joined from England and took command of the regiment.

I

CHAPTER XIV

MARSHAL SOULT APPOINTED TO COMMAND THE FRENCH—POSITION
OF THE ARMIES AFTER VITTORIA—BATTLES OF THE PYRENEES
—FALL OF ST. SEBASTIAN—THE ENGLISH ENTER FRANCE

1813   MARSHAL SOULT, sent by Napoleon from Germany, now
took command of the French army, which again acted
on the offensive.   The English troops were of necessity
much scattered throughout the Pyrenees, owing to the
sieges of St. Sebastian on the left and Pampeluna on
the right, these two places being fifty miles apart.   In
consequence of this, the cavalry duties in maintaining
the communications were very considerable.   " The
theatre of Wellington's operations at this time was a
trapezoid, having Bayonne, St. Jean Pied-de-Port, St.
Sebastian, and Pampeluna, all fortresses in possession
of the French, at the angles.   The interior, broken by
savage mountains, narrow craggy passes, deep water-
courses, precipices and forests, appeared a wilderness
which no military combinations could embrace. . . .
The allied forces were formed, as it were, into three
distinct armies, one occupied in besieging St. Sebastian,
another blockading Pampeluna, while the third remained
in a central position ready to support either.   The
French general was thus given an opportunity of con-
centrating against any part of the English line in
stronger numbers.   Soult determined to operate on
Wellington's right." [1]   For this purpose he assembled

[1] Napier.

at St. Jean Pied-de-Port on 24th July 60,000 troops to force the passes of Roncesvalles and Maya. To guard these passes from the impending attack, Wellington placed 20,000 men under Generals Byng and Morillo; while other divisions were placed in support and to watch the lateral passes, the cavalry division remaining on the Ebro. On the 25th Soult placed himself at the head of his troops and led them against Byng's division posted on the rocks of Altobiscar, and thus commenced with the combat of Maya what have since been termed the battles of the Pyrenees.

The English divisions having been successfully concentrated in time, the advance of the French was checked both at Maya and at Roncesvalles. On the 27th the Hussar Brigade moved from Olite to Haarte, and took part in the operations in support of the right of the British line. Captain Harding's troop of the 10th Hussars was sent forward and skirmished with the enemy, who showed an intention of turning the right flank. Captain Harding received a wound from a musket-shot in the groin. Private Altride was taken prisoner, his horse having fallen with him. Lieutenant Seymour's charger was wounded, as also were two troop-horses. The regiment threw out strong piquets and went to the village of Ardanez for the night.

The first battle of Sauroren took place on the 28th July, when after a most severe engagement the British infantry were victorious. "While this action was being fought on the mountain, the French cavalry beyond the river Guy passed a rivulet, and with a fire of carbines forced the 10th Hussars to yield some rocky ground on Picton's right; yet the 18th Hussars, having better firearms than the Tenth, renewed the combat, killed two officers, and drove the French over the rivulet

I 2

again."[1] The French acknowledged to a loss in this battle of two generals and 1,800 men killed and wounded, while that of the Allies amounted to 2,600. On the 29th both armies rested in position without firing a shot, but the cavalry was still employed on outpost and reconnoitring duties. " On Wellington's side the crisis was now over. He had held his position and concentrated his divisions. Soult's position was proportionately difficult ; he had sent his artillery and part of his cavalry and his wounded back to France."[2] On the 30th July the combat of Buenza took place, in which General Hill was compelled to fall back from his position. On this day the right and centre squadrons of the Tenth, under Colonel Quentin, were ordered to cross the mountain ridge into the next valley and join the Third Division under Picton, which after many difficulties they effected. The left squadron, under Captain Wyndham, remained at Illurdos. The two squadrons under Colonel Quentin were advanced along the Val de Zubiri and attacked the left flank of the French under General Foy, this movement being the opening of the second battle of Sauroren. In this action and the combat of Buenza the Allies lost 1,900 killed and wounded. On the French side the loss was enormous ; two of their divisions were completely disorganised, and Foy was entirely separated from the main body ; more than 2,000 were killed and wounded, and 3,000 prisoners taken. The French now fell back, followed by the Allies, Picton's division being ordered to occupy the Pass of Roncesvalles. The two squadrons of the Tenth advanced on the 31st to the village of that name at the head of the pass, and piquets were at once sent forward. On the 1st August they were employed in reconnoitring and patrolling in the moun-

[1] Napier. [2] *Ibid.*

tains, and in the evening, after posting piquets among the lofty heights, returned to Roncesvalles and unsaddled, having been in marching order since the morning of the 27th. The operations termed " the battles of the Pyrenees," which took place between the 25th July and 1st August, were now brought to a conclusion—a short but brilliant campaign, with hard work, exposure, and severe fighting, in which the Tenth had the honour to take an active part. Lord Welling-

ton's despatches after these actions were sent home by the Marquis of Worcester, lieutenant of the 10th Hussars.

After this the regiment continued to furnish patrols in the mountains, and on the 7th August a sergeant's party, proceeding in the direction of St. Jean Pied-de-Port, where the French had a strong garrison, was intercepted by a detachment of the enemy's infantry, which had got in its rear. The Hussars dashed upon this body, and forced their passage through, with the exception of one man, Private Frame, whose horse was shot and himself made prisoner. Another private, Springhall, was wounded by a musket-shot in the knee. Sergeant Gander, who commanded the patrol, particularly distinguished himself. On the 10th August the 14th Light Dragoons relieved the Tenth from patrol duty, the latter withdrawing to Zubiri and Tafalla. On the 31st August a successful assault was made on the fortress of St. Sebastian, and on the 8th September the citadel surrendered.

At this time information was received from England that the establishment of the Tenth had been increased to twelve troops, the additional troops being designated L and M.

The regiment suffered a serious loss owing to the transport " Margarita," carrying stores and new clothing for the men, entering by mistake the harbour of Santona, which was still occupied by the French. The ship and everything it contained was captured by the enemy. The loss to the regiment was thirty cases, containing forage-caps, overalls, 300 pistols, &c.

Throughout September both armies rested, Wellington being occupied in reorganising the allied army before carrying the war into France. After the battle of Vittoria and the taking of St. Sebastian some relaxation had been given to the army, and both officers and men took advantage of it to participate in field sports, both shooting and hunting. Two packs of hounds were kept at St. Jean de Luz—one by Lord Wellington, the other by an officer of the Commissariat, Marsden by name. No less than 200 officers assembled at the meets, some well mounted, but mostly on ponies, or even mules. One day, in the midst of a run, the fox crossed the Bidassoa, the hounds following, and entered the enemy's position; the field remained on the English side. The French, not understanding what was taking place, turned out under arms; but on Marsden, the master, advancing with his white handkerchief as a flag of truce, and explaining, he was permitted to cross and bring back the hounds. On the 18th October three troops of the Tenth marched from their cantonments in Navarre to the vicinity of Pampeluna, to assist in the blockade of that place, which surrendered shortly afterwards.[1] The remaining three troops arrived, and the whole regiment proceeded to Lizasso. At this time a draft of twenty-eight men and fifty horses, under Lieutenant Powell, arrived from England. On the 12th November, in consequence of a forward movement of the army, the Tenth re entered the mountains and was stationed at Doña Maria and its vicinity, but, being unable to procure forage, it again returned to Lizasso.

During the operations in the Pyrenees Marshal Soult was observed on one occasion to make a movement in front of our right centre, which the general took for a reconnaissance. As the French general perceived we had ordered preparations to receive him, he sent a flag of truce to demand a cessation of hostilities, saying that he wanted to shoot an officer and several men for acts of robbery committed by them, with every sort of atrocity, on the farmers and peasantry of the country. The execution took place in view of both armies, and a terrible lesson it was.

The army on the left of the allied line, released from the siege of St. Sebastian, had crossed the Bidassoa on the 7th October, and established itself on French territory.

---

[1] Regimental Sergeant-Major and Assistant-Adjutant Wells was sent into the Arsenal of Pampeluna to select seventy French carbines for the use of the regiment.

Being near the sea and in a good climate, it was in comparative comfort, but the troops still in the mountains suffered considerable hardships, with indifferent shelter and scant supplies on Alpine heights. On the 10th November, after weeks of heavy rain, Wellington, having now under his command 90,000 men, descended from the Pyrenees with this force and entered France, and the battles of the Nivelle then took place. The Tenth, however, remained in the neighbourhood of Pampeluna until December. On the 12th of that month the regiment received 500 carbines from England, and returned the old ones into the store of Pampeluna. On the 16th it marched to the front by the Tolosa Pass and crossed the Bidassoa by a pontoon bridge, and, entering France, crossed the Nive at Cambo, and arrived at Halcoy on the 22nd December. Here Major the Hon. F. Howard joined from England. On the 30th the Tenth took over the outpost duties from the 7th Hussars, with cantonments at Ocuraye, and remained on this duty until the 9th January, 1814, when, on being relieved by the 15th Hussars, it fell back on Cambo. On the 12th February the regiment again took up the advanced duties, and a few days later the whole army was put in motion, the Tenth covering the right division, which was employed in dislodging the French from Hellette. On the 18th the division arrived at Bidache, and occupied both banks of the Gave d'Oleron, which was the advanced post of the army. On the 24th the army again pushed forward, and on the 25th the regiment forded the Gave de Pau at Salvatierra.

CHAPTER XV

BATTLE OF ORTHEZ—PURSUIT OF THE ENEMY—COMBAT OF TARBES
—ARRIVAL OF A SQUADRON FROM THE DEPÔT—THE BATTLE OF
TOULOUSE—PEACE—THE TENTH MARCH THROUGH FRANCE

MARSHAL SOULT having collected his forces at Orthez,   1814
took up a strong defensive position, where he was
attacked by the Allies on the 27th February.   The
main body under Wellington crossed the Gave below
Orthez, and attacked the right and centre of the
French, and at the same time the division under Hill
forded the river above that town, with the object of
cutting off their retreat.   The cavalry, under Sir Stapleton Cotton and Lord Edward Somerset, closely followed
on their flank ; but the only opportunity that occurred
during the battle for the action of cavalry was taken by
Cotton, who charged with the 7th Hussars, supported
by Somerset's dragoons, and took 300 prisoners ; 2,000
more threw down their arms, but made good their escape.
The enemy lost 3,900 killed, wounded, and prisoners, and
six guns in this battle ; the Allies, 2,300.   The Tenth had
a few men slightly wounded, and one man and horse severely, by the bursting of a shell.   In the pursuit the regiment was employed with the advanced guard, and drove
before it the French rear guard.   On the 28th the right
squadron, composed of Captain Harding's and Captain
Lloyd's troops, A and F, under Lieutenant-Colonel Palmer,
being considerably advanced, came in contact with a
body of French cavalry formed on the road.   Captain

Harding's troop, supported by Captain Lloyd's, immediately charged, broke the enemy's ranks, killing several
men, and took thirty-four French dragoons prisoners,
at the same time capturing eight horses. The centre
and left squadrons, under Colonel Quentin, which were
in support, came up and drove the remainder of the
French rear guard across the Adour. Captain Harding
and five privates were severely wounded, four horses
killed, and eight wounded. The regiment bivouacked
that night on the banks of the river. In reference to
this affair the following order was published :—

Dane : 1st March, 1814.

Major-General Lord Edward Somerset will be pleased to convey his best thanks to Lieutenant-Colonel Quentin and the officers
and men of the 10th Royal Hussars for their gallant and steady
conduct yesterday.

(Signed)   STAPLETON COTTON.

About six A.M. on the 29th the advanced parties of
the Tenth, under Lieutenant Eversfield, felt the enemy in
the direction of St. Sever. This officer was called from
his piquet by Sir Stapleton Cotton and sent with three
or four men to follow the enemy, while the remainder
of his party fell in and awaited the supports. These
orders he carried out, until a squadron of the regiment,
under Lieutenant-Colonel Palmer, coming up with two
guns of Major Gardner's battery of horse artillery caused
the enemy to retire. The Tenth forded the Adour at
St. Sever on the 1st March, the bridge having been
burnt by the enemy during the previous night, and
after several marches arrived at St. Gaime on the 8th.
The main body of the Allies was now concentrated about
Aire and Barcelonne, with the cavalry advanced to La
Cassade.

At this point Marshal Soult, collecting his divisions,

advanced in force, pushing back the English cavalry posts. Amongst those driven in was a piquet of the Tenth, but Captain George FitzClarence (afterwards the Earl of Munster), who commanded the outlying piquets of the regiment, on the 13th March attacked the position thus taken possession of and regained the lost ground. The Tenth had one man (Private Maiden) and one officer's horse wounded. On the 14th Wellington concentrated his troops on his right, and the cavalry posts were drawn down the Adour, the Hussar Brigade falling back on Barcelonne. The enemy, however, did not attack, and Soult, hearing of the fall of Bordeaux, determined to retire. On the 16th the Tenth was advanced to Saint Germain, and on the 18th the left squadron crossed the Adour and pursued the rear guard of the French for some miles. On the 19th the whole regiment forded the Adour and proceeded to Hartez, where coming in contact with the enemy next day it forced them to retire. On the 21st the Hussar Brigade was employed in covering the Third Division, and took part in the combat of Tarbes.

On the 22nd March a squadron of the Tenth, under command of Captain Joseph Smyth (afterwards Smyth-Windham), which had left England in December 1813, joined the head-quarters with the following strength :—Captains Smyth and Turner, Lieutenants Richardson, Jackson, Meynell and Crawford, Assistant-Surgeon Jenks, Quartermaster Sired, 1 troop sergeant-major, 7 sergeants, 8 corporals, 2 trumpeters, 146 privates, and 162 horses. This detachment sailed with other troops in a fleet of twenty-six transports under convoy of Captain Palmer, R.N., commanding His Majesty's ship "Hebrus," brother of Lieutenant-Colonel Palmer, of the Tenth. Having landed at Passages, a small port near St. Sebastian, this reinforcement marched across the Pyrenees, descended into France by St. Jean de Luz, crossed the Gave de Pau and marched by Peyrehorade to Dax. As the army was moving daily in pursuit of the French, no certain information could be obtained of its exact position. Captain Smyth, with his squadron, proceeded from Dax to St. Sever, and, keeping the left bank of the Adour, reached Plaisance, and, to the great satisfaction of all, shortly afterwards joined the head-quarters of the regiment, which they found in brigade with the 7th and 18th Hussars at Devies, under command of Lord Edward Somerset.

Marshal Soult was retreating slowly and in good order upon Toulouse, and in following him up it was necessary that every inch of country should be carefully patrolled. There were skirmishes almost daily, and by constant practice both officers and men had acquired great proficiency in outpost duties. Lieutenant-Colonel Palmer, who was a most enterprising officer and an admirable horseman, gained much distinction in this campaign, and the gallant conduct and skilful leading under very arduous circumstances of the following officers was also brought to official notice: Captains Gordon, Harding, Lloyd, Simeon, Stuart, and George FitzClarence ; Lieutenants Horace Seymour, Fitzgerald, Eversfield, Henry FitzClarence, Charles Wyndham, Augustus Berkeley, and H. Somerset. The men also had become experts on outpost and advanced cavalry duties, many were first-rate shots, and one man in particular, named Farmer, greatly distinguished himself as a marksman.[1]

Continuing to follow the enemy, the 10th Hussars arrived at the banks of the Garonne on the 3rd April, after a fatiguing night march, with incessant rain. On

[1] Dr. Jenks's *Diary.*

the 4th April the regiment, with a considerable part of the army, crossed the river at Grenade, on a bridge of boats, and drove in the enemy's piquets. Two deserters with their horses surrendered to the Tenth patrols. On the following day it became necessary to remove the floating bridge owing to the floods and large masses of timber that were being washed down the stream, and for three days the army lay divided by an impassable river. The French, however, did not take advantage of this critical position of the Allies, and on the 8th, the river having subsided, the whole army was united, and advanced. The Hussar Brigade was employed in front, and the advanced parties of the Tenth were engaged with the enemy and drove their piquets back close to Toulouse. In this affair Lieutenant Charles Wyndham,[1] Private Workman, and two horses were wounded.

The battle of Toulouse was fought on the 10th April. During the forenoon the Hussar Brigade was drawn up on the right of the line, but in the early part of the afternoon it was suddenly called upon to move in front of the Third and Fourth Divisions, under Marshal Beresford, who was ordered to the left of the position. To effect this it was necessary to traverse a narrow swampy plain, within range of the artillery of the French redoubts, bounded on the other side by the river Ers, a small, impassable stream. This the hussars crossed by the only bridge left undestroyed and ran the gauntlet of the enemy's fire. Having

---

[1] A younger brother of Captain Henry Wyndham (afterwards Sir Henry Wyndham) already mentioned. He joined the Tenth when very young (between fifteen and sixteen). A story was told of him, that he was a very good-looking young boy, and in one of the cavalry engagements he was at the mercy of the colonel of a French cavalry regiment, who, instead of cutting him down, lowered his sword, saying, "Allez, petit diable d'Anglais."

reached the other bank, they drove Berton's cavalry before them, and in doing this the Tenth lost Captain Gordon, Privates Venn, Baker, Newell, and Deamer killed; Captain FitzClarence, Privates Schasby, Kay, Manley, Stone, Parrott, and Corporal Lucas wounded; fifteen horses killed, one missing, and six wounded. After a severe combat of many hours, the fortune of the day was in favour of the Allies, and the French withdrew within the suburbs. The loss on both sides was very severe—greater on that of the Allies, as might be expected from the strong position of the French behind their entrenchments. The loss of the allied army was 4,558 men killed and wounded; that of the French, 3,200.

Soult retreated from Toulouse on the 12th in the direction of Carcassonne. The same day Wellington entered the town and met with a most brilliant reception. "The Mayor of Toulouse had retired with the army, but the Bourbon party raised the white flag and the mass of citizens adopted the Bourbon colours. Wellington entered the city amidst the most joyous acclamations. When he dismounted from his horse in the courtyard of the Capitole, he was carried through the halls out to the balcony, and was hailed as the deliverer of France by the crowds below. In the evening the play of 'Richard Cœur de Lion' was presented at the theatre, and the audience rose to greet with the loudest applause the conqueror when he entered his box." [1] The news now arrived of the taking of Paris, the dethronement of Napoleon, and the proclamation of Louis XVIII. "The British soldiers were received by the inhabitants with great joy, and were decorated with the royalist colours. From the day the army entered France, it had been well received by the people, every-

[1] Clinton's *Peninsular War.*

thing being paid for and no violence permitted. During the hostilities the troops fared as to quarters sometimes well, sometimes ill—one day in a château, another in a hovel; at other times under worse shelter, or it might be none. Protection of some kind for the night, however, was desirable, for the season was exceptionally wet and few escaped a daily soaking. Rations were supplied as a rule regularly, but forage was often a serious difficulty." [1]

The Hussar Brigade had been sent on the 12th April to follow the French, and on the 18th, at Puylaurens, the Tenth vedettes received an officer with a flag of truce from Marshal Soult. This officer was conducted by Lieutenant Somerset to the head-quarters of Lord Wellington, and soon afterwards the news of peace became known. A convention having been entered into for a suspension of hostilities, the British cavalry was withdrawn to the neighbourhood of Toulouse and went into cantonments in the surrounding villages. " The British infantry embarked at Bordeaux—some for America, some for England—and the cavalry received orders to take shipping at Boulogne." [2] The Portuguese and Spaniards returned to the Peninsula from France across the Pyrenees. Wellington proceeded to Paris, where he was cordially received by the allied sovereigns, and after taking part in the definitive treaty of Paris returned to England. To the army which had carried out his plans, he issued an order of the day from Bordeaux expressing his thanks.

The head-quarters of the Hussar Brigade were at Villandrique, and they remained cantoned in this neighbourhood until the end of May, giving them an opportunity of getting the horses into condition for the long march through France now before them. Thirty-nine

---

[1] Dr. Jenks's *Diary*. [2] Napier.

troop horses of the Tenth were cast and sold at Toulouse on the 20th May, and the following week the dismounted men marched for Bordeaux, under the command of Lieutenant-Colonel Palmer and Lieutenant Berkeley, where they embarked for England. The head-quarters commenced the march from Villandrique to Boulogne on the 2nd June. The route taken was by Montauban to Cahors, where the river Dordogne was crossed in boats. From thence by Limoges, Orleans, Etampes, Neufchâtel, Abbeville, Montreuil, and Boulogne, which was reached on the 11th July. "Everything was well organised by the French authorities as to billets and rations, and the march was conducted throughout in perfect order, and without any collision with French troops." [1]

On arrival at Boulogne, and after delivering up to the French Government twenty-one horses, the 10th Hussars embarked for England on the 15th and 16th July, landed at Dover and marched to Brighton, where it arrived on the 24th.

At the close of the Peninsular campaign no medal was distributed generally to officers and men, but, on a medal being issued after Waterloo to all alike, officers and men, it was only natural that the hopes of those who had served in the several actions of the Peninsular war should be stimulated to obtain a similar recognition; but it was not till the 1st June, 1847, that this omission was repaired by Her Majesty Queen Victoria, who ordered a " medal to be struck to record the services of her fleets and armies during the wars commencing in 1793 and ending in 1814, and that one should be conferred upon every officer, non-commissioned officer, and soldier of the army who was present

[1] Dr. Jenks's *Diary*.

at any battle or siege." The war medal has on the obverse the head of the Queen, with the date 1848, and on the reverse Her Majesty crowning with a laurel wreath the Duke of Wellington. The ribbon is red with blue edges, and a bar was given for each battle or important action. The rank and name of the recipient was engraved round the edge of the medal.[1]

On the 3rd May, 1814, Wellington had been created Marquis of Douro and Duke of Wellington in the British peerage. A further grant of 400,000*l.* and for the twelfth time the thanks of Parliament were now voted to him; Generals Beresford, Graham, and Hill received peerages, and some minor honours were bestowed on the heroes of the Peninsula both in the higher and the lower ranks.[2] The honour of bearing "Peninsula" on its appointments was granted to the 10th Hussars in recognition of its services during the campaigns of 1809 and 1813–14, but no special engagement in which the regiment took a prominent part was recorded. Neither the retreat on Corunna in 1809, nor the actions of Sahagun, Mayorga, and Benevente, nor the gallant action of Morales del Toro in 1813, the battle of Vittoria, the battles of the Pyrenees, nor Orthez nor Toulouse, have as yet (1890) found any official recognition, but are still dearly prized services, and are handed down with pride in the regiment's history.

As a result of the war a formal treaty was concluded between Napoleon and the allied powers. By it Napoleon renounced the empire of France and the kingdom of Italy. The island of Elba was selected by him as his place of residence, and 100,000*l.* a year was provided for him as an income. On the 30th May a treaty was signed at Paris. between the Government of

---

[1] Carter's *Medals of the British Army.*
[2] Clinton's *Peninsular War.*

K

France and the Allies, which provided that France should be reduced to its original limits. Malta was ceded in perpetuity to Great Britain, and many countries in Europe were made independent.

The following are the names of the officers on the return of the regiment from the Peninsula:—

10th or the Prince of Wales's Own Royal Regiment of Light Dragoons (Hussars).

Colonel: H.R.H. the Prince Regent, K.G.; Lieutenant-Colonels: George Quentin, Charles Palmer; Majors: Hon. Frederick Howard, G. J. Robarts; Captains: A. De Grammont, J. R. Lewis-Lloyd, B. Harding, Simeon H. Stuart, George FitzClarence, Joseph Smyth, Ed. Page Turner, Robert Giveen, Charles Synge, Lord Arthur Hill, Samuel Bromley; Lieutenants: Edward Fox FitzGerald, Henry Marquis of Worcester, Charles Eversfield, Charles Holbern, George Wombwell, Charles Wyndham, Horace Seymour, Henry Somerset, F. Page Turner, Augustus Fitzhardinge Berkeley, Henry FitzClarence, John H. Powell, Josias Jackson, J. A. Richardson, F. E. Meynell; Cornet: J. Edward Moreton Douglas; Paymaster: John Byng Wilkinson; Quartermaster: James Rogers; Surgeon: Charles Morrison; Assistant-Surgeons: W. R. Rogers, George S. Jenks; Veterinary Surgeon: H. C. Sannerman.

The depôt of the regiment had remained at Brighton since May 1813, and during the visit of the allied sovereigns to England in June 1814 had furnished a guard of honour of 100 rank and file to the Emperor of Russia and the King of Prussia on their arrival at Portsmouth.

Soon after the return of the troops from active service the establishment of the regiment was reduced from twelve to eight troops, and on the 12th September it left Brighton and marched to Romford, Hornchurch,

and Ilford, where it passed the winter. On the 6th March, 1815, three squadrons marched to London to assist in preserving the peace during the riots caused by the passing of the Corn Bill, returning to Romford on the completion of this duty.

At this time an event of serious moment to the regiment occurred, which must be mentioned here, as it was followed by extensive changes in the *cadre* of the Tenth, and has become a matter of history. At the close of the campaign of 1814, many of the officers addressed a letter to the second in command containing animadversions on the conduct of Colonel Quentin during the war. This officer demanded a court-martial, which was granted, and the court assembled at Whitehall on the 17th October, 1814. After due investigation of the charges preferred against him, Colonel Quentin was acquitted. In consequence of this all the officers who had signed the letter were removed and appointed to other regiments. As a finale to this affair Colonel Quentin sent a cartel to Colonel Palmer, the second in command, who had forwarded the letter. The two colonels met in France. Colonel Palmer received his adversary's fire and discharged his pistol in the air. Both the officers who left and those who were appointed to the regiment in their place received the sobriquet of the "Elegant Extracts," but it is doubtful to whom this could be most properly applied, whether to those officers who left or those who were taken from other regiments and brought in. The rank and names of the officers composing the regiment after this occurrence were as follows :—

Colonel : H.R.H. the Prince Regent, K.G., &c.; Lieut.-Colonels : George Quentin, Lord Robert Manners ; Majors : The Hon. Frederick Howard, the Hon. H. Cecil Lowther ; Captains : Samuel Bromley, Thomas W.

1815 Taylor, H. C. Stapylton, John Grey, John Gurwood, Charles Wood, Valentine Jones, Henry Floyd, Arthur Shakespeare, Hon. John Jones; Lieutenants: Charles Holbern, Francis Edward Meynell, Robert Curtis, John Whitehill Parsons, William Slayter Smith, Henry John Burn, Robert Arnold, Christopher I. Allingham, William Cartwright, Samuel Hardman, George Orlando Gunning, J. C. Wallington, E. Hodgson, William C. Hamilton, Anthony Bacon; Cornets: W. Paxton Jervis, William Lindsay; Paymaster: James Tatton; Adjutant: Samuel Hardman; Quartermaster: James Rogers; Surgeons: Charles Morrison, W. R. Rogers; Assistant-Surgeon: George Samuel Jenks; Veterinary Surgeon: Henry C. Sannerman.

CHAPTER XVI

NAPOLEON'S ESCAPE FROM ELBA—THE REGIMENT ORDERED ON
ACTIVE SERVICE—POSITION OF THE ENGLISH ARMY BEFORE
WATERLOO—THE CAVALRY FORCE—NAPOLEON TAKES THE FIELD
—THE BATTLES OF LIGNY AND QUATRE BRAS

THE news of Napoleon's escape from the isle of Elba
and his progress towards Paris became known throughout Europe at the beginning of March 1815. " If a
thunderbolt had fallen amidst the Congress of Vienna
then sitting, greater consternation could not have
been excited than the announcement that Napoleon
had secretly left Elba. All minor differences that had
ensued throughout the nations of Europe owing to the
treaty of Paris the year previous were immediately
forgotten. . . . All lesser subjects of alarm were ab-
sorbed in the pressing danger arising from the return
of Napoleon to the throne of France." [1] A declaration
signed by all the powers was forthwith drawn up pro-
scribing Napoleon as a public enemy, and expressing
their determination to employ the whole forces at their
disposal to prevent Europe from being again plunged
into the abyss of revolution. The Russian troops in
Poland were ordered to prepare to march. Austria
put on a war footing her armies in Italy and Germany,
and Prussia called out the Landwehr. England being
now delivered from the pressure of the American war,
and thus in a position to employ her resources more

1815

---

[1] Alison.

freely, poured troops into Flanders, and provided at the same time for the equipment of the newly-raised forces of the Belgians. Levies were also raised in Hanover. These troops, brought together for the defence of the Belgian frontier, were placed under the command of the Duke of Wellington, and a Prussian army under Prince Blücher took the field to co-operate with him.

In April great additions were made to the English army. Amongst these, on the 6th of that month the 10th Hussars was augmented by two troops, and the regiment received an order for three squadrons to hold themselves in readiness for embarkation for active service. On the 9th they commenced their march, the depôt moving to Brighton, and on the 16th the first detachment embarked about two in the morning and landed at five the same evening at Ostend. The remainder of the six troops sailed on the following day, but did not complete their disembarkation until the 18th. On the 20th, the whole regiment marched to Bruges, and afterwards took the following route :—21st, Eccloo ; 22nd, Ostacher and other villages near Ghent ; 23rd, Oudenarde ; 24th, Berghem, where a halt of some days was made. Upon arrival at Aspelaer, near Ninove, on the 2nd May, after a long march in very hot weather, it was found that the orders for the regiment's cantonment had been changed, consequently the right squadron, with head-quarters, moved to Oultre and the remaining squadrons to Voorde. In these villages the regiment remained several weeks.[1]

The force under the Duke of Wellington at this time was scattered over a great extent of country in order to facilitate the subsistence of the troops. On the left the Allies were connected with the Prussians

---

[1] Dr. Jenks's *Diary.*

near Charleroi, while their centre and right were at Mons and Tournai.

The cavalry of the Anglo-Allied army, commanded by the Earl of Uxbridge, consisted of seven brigades. Of these, the British and King's German Legion cavalry, with the Hanoverian brigade, were stationed at Grammont and Ninove and the villages in the neighbourhood. The sixth or Hussar Brigade was commanded by Major-General Sir Hussey Vivian. It consisted of the 10th Hussars, 390 strong, under Colonel Quentin; the 18th Hussars (396), under Lieutenant-Colonel the Hon. H. Murray; and the 1st Hussars of the King's German Legion (493), under Lieutenant-Colonel von Wissell.[1]

" As there was little expectation of a change of quarters for some weeks, the officers had many opportunities of visiting Brussels, about eighteen miles from the cavalry head-quarters. The monotony of the regimental camp life also was enlivened by amusements arranged among officers of their own brigade and the Guards. Horse-racing was established, and many successful meetings held. Perhaps the most successful of these was one that took place on the 23rd May, during which the officers of the Tenth gave a grand *fête*. About 200 sat down at this entertainment, amongst the number Lord Hill and Lord Uxbridge. Again, on the 30th, another race meeting was held, when the regiment again entertained its friends at luncheon, when the Prince of Orange and also Sir Sidney Smith were present. These races were held near Grammont, the stewards being Major-General Sir Hussey Vivian, Lord Robert Manners, and Sir Noel Hill. The last of these meetings appears to have taken place on the 1st June, when Lord Uxbridge presented a cup to be run for. On this day the 10th and 18th Hussars gave a parting *fête* to the 7th Hussars,

[1] Siborne's *Waterloo Campaign*.

as the latter regiment was now told off to serve in a different brigade. At the same time drills were constantly held, and the brigades were exercised three times a week under their respective commanders." [1]

On the 6th May the Hussar Brigade was inspected by Lieutenant-General the Earl of Uxbridge. On the 29th the Duke of Wellington reviewed the whole of the British cavalry in the presence of Field-Marshal Prince Blücher, the Duc de Berri, and other distinguished officers. " The troops were drawn up with the 7th, 10th, 15th, and 18th Hussars, with Horse Artillery, in the first line, each half squadron taking a squadron interval (this line was commanded by Generals Grant and Vivian); the 1st Life Guards, the Blues, 2nd Life Guards, and 1st Dragoon Guards in second line, under Lord E. Somerset, and the 1st Royal Dragoons, Inniskillings, and Greys, under General Ponsonby; the 11th, 12th, 13th, 16th, and 23rd Dragoons, under Vandeleur, in the third line. On the arrival of the Duke of Wellington and Marshal Blücher a salute was fired." Captain Charles Wood in a letter says: " Old Blücher, upon passing my troop, recognised me immediately and gave me his hand," [2] &c. &c. " We brought into the field 5,600 swords besides the Horse Artillery, thirty-six guns, all looking in first-rate condition."

On the afternoon of the 1st March, Napoleon had reached the Gulf of St. Juan and landed on French territory with 400 of his Old Guard. He marched first on Grenoble, where on the 6th March he met troops detached from the garrison of that place sent to arrest his progress. Advancing to the front of his own men, he

---

[1] Extract from letter from Captain Charles Wood, 10th Hussars, to his brother, Colonel Wood, of Littleton.

[2] Captain (afterwards Colonel) Wood had served under Lord Stewart at the battle of Leipzig, and had been specially noticed by Marshal Blücher.

called upon the soldiers to join him. This the whole garrison did with the greatest enthusiasm, and Napoleon's force was brought up to 3,000 men. Daily adding to these numbers, he continued his march, and reached Lyons on the 12th. At this place he was joined by Marshal Ney, who had been sent by Louis XVIII. to oppose him, but who came over to his side with the whole army under his orders. This act virtually gave him back the government of the country. On the 20th Louis XVIII. abdicated, and at nine o'clock the same night Napoleon arrived at the Tuileries. "Nothing which vigour and activity could do was wanting on the part of the Emperor Napoleon to provide the means to oppose the phalanx of enemies ready to overwhelm him." [1] He restored to the old regiments their numbers, provided arms and ammunition, and by rousing the national spirit revived the worn-out finances of the country. All this he accomplished in three months, and, having collected an army with the greatest rapidity, early in June decided to take the field against the Allies in Belgium. He selected the direct route to Brussels by Charleroi for his main line of advance, the road on which Blücher's right and Wellington's left rested,[2] intending by striking between them to defeat the Prussians in the first instance and then fall upon the English.

"On the 12th June, Colonel von Wissell, whose regiment, the 1st Hussars of the German Legion, formed an extensive line of outposts in front of Tournai, supported by the remainder of the Hussar Brigade, reported to Sir Hussey Vivian that he had received information of the French army having assembled on the frontier." On the 14th, Napoleon himself arrived on the scene of operations and took command of his forces, now con-

[1] Alison. [2] Siborne.

centrated on the right bank of the Sambre. At sunrise on the 15th he moved forward in three columns, and by eleven o'clock was in full possession of Charleroi. The Prussians fell back fighting, and concentrated at Ligny by nightfall. About five o'clock the same afternoon the Duke of Wellington received information of the advance of the French, and orders were at once issued for the British army to march in the direction of Quatre Bras, while the Prussians concentrated on the left at Ligny.

"The intelligence of the arrival of Napoleon upon the scene of operations was known to few in Brussels beyond the Duke and his immediate staff, and on the evening of the 15th the famous ball, of which so much notice has been taken, and which has become historical, was given by the Duchess of Richmond in a house in the Rue de la Blanchisserie. The Duke of Wellington and all the officers in and near Brussels attended ; amongst them Lord Robert Manners and other officers of the 10th Hussars were present. It had been hinted to the generals of division and brigade that one by one, as the night drew on, they should take their leave. Orders likewise had been issued to the troops to hold themselves in readiness to march. . . . By-and-by general after general withdrew from the Duchess's party, some on the plea that their commands were far away, others because duty or private business called them. The Duke remained until a late hour, and returned thanks after supper for the health of the Prince Regent, which was proposed by the Prince of Orange. He soon afterwards retired, and the company broke up. A bugle call, heard first in the Place d'Armes, and taken up and echoed back through various quarters of the town, roused all classes of people in a moment. Regiments were seen to muster by the dim light of the stars in square, street, and alley, and as they were ready marched off in the direction of the Forest of Soignies."[1]

The Tenth received its orders at midnight, and the Hussar Brigade, breaking up its cantonments, moved towards Nivelles in the early morning of the 16th. On arriving at that place an express was received, ordering the brigade to proceed on the Namur road to Quatre Bras, which, after a long and harassing march, hampered with many obstructions, was reached the same evening.

Marshal Ney, having arrived at the French headquarters on the night of the 15th, was placed by Napoleon at the head of a force of about 17,000 men, and the next day advanced to attack the English at Quatre Bras, with a view to preventing their concentration. Napoleon himself, with the main portion of his army, attacked the Prussians at Ligny. About two o'clock on the 16th the two battles commenced. The Prussians were defeated, and fell back in the direction of Wavre. The English held their ground, and throughout the day continued to receive reinforcements as the troops came up from their various cantonments, so that Wellington, commencing with about the same numbers as Ney, had assembled an army of 30,000 men before the day was over. With this force he was able to drive the French back and remain in possession of the field. By nine P.M. the whole of the British cavalry, whose cantonments had been on the extreme right of the extended position of the allied army, arrived at Quatre Bras and bivouacked on the field.

To secure the position taken up by the Hussar Brigade Sir Hussey Vivian threw out two strong piquets —one, under Captain Croker, from the 18th Hussars, on the Namur road ; the other, under Major the Hon.

[1] Gleig's *Battle of Waterloo.*

Frederick Howard, from the 10th Hussars, in front; and also from the latter regiment a smaller piquet, under Lieutenant Arnold, on the right of the Namur road. But during the night (the 16th) the bivouac on the field of Quatre Bras remained undisturbed, save from some firing caused by outpost affairs brought on by a cavalry patrol passing between the adverse lines.[1]

Wellington, arriving early in the morning of the 17th, found this brigade posted as described; but Sir Hussey could give little information to the Duke beyond the fact of the firing above mentioned, for the French continued quiet, and as yet no forward movement was indicated. In the direction of Fleurus a French vedette was visible, probably thrown out after last night's battle from Marshal Ney's extreme right. But there was no intelligence of Blücher; so Captain Grey's troop from the 10th Hussars was sent along the Namur road, accompanied by Lieutenant Bacon and Lieutenant-Colonel the Hon. Sir Alexander Gordon, A.D.C. to the Duke, in order to gain information. Advancing cautiously, the patrol discovered a French vedette posted on rising ground about a mile and a half beyond Petit-Marbais. Captain Grey now detached Lieutenant Bacon with a few men to explore, while with the remainder of the troop, placed in concealment, he awaited the result. On perceiving Bacon's party the enemy's piquet mounted and galloped back to their supports. As the French showed no further disposition to advance, Captain Grey began to retire, and soon afterwards struck into a cross-road that led towards the Prussian line of retreat. Here he fell in with General Ziethen, commanding the rear guard of the Prussians, retiring on Wavre. Gordon obtained satisfactory information from the general, which he immediately reported to the Duke

[1] Siborne.

of Wellington. The patrol, however, did not return to Quatre Bras until half-past seven in the evening.

The left troop of Howard's squadron, under Captain Wood, was also sent to patrol in the direction of Wavre, and subsequently this officer laid claim to having been the first to convey to the Duke the intelligence of the Prussian retreat to Wavre. Hence arose a difference of opinion as to which troop was the first to give this important information, and after a patient and thorough investigation Captain Siborne has decided in favour of Captain Grey's troop, accompanied by Sir Alexander Gordon.[1]

[1] Siborne; Dr. Jenks's *Diary.*

CHAPTER XVII

THE PRUSSIANS RETREAT—THE ENGLISH FALL BACK UPON WATER-
LOO—AFFAIR AT GENAPPE—THE NIGHT BEFORE WATERLOO

1815   NAPOLEON's victory at Ligny having caused Marshal
Blücher to retire with his army, the Duke was obliged
to make a retrograde movement on Waterloo, in order
to keep touch with the Prussians.   Selecting a position
in which be could rely on Blücher's co-operation from
Wavre, Wellington issued his orders for the allied army to
be drawn up in front of Mont St. Jean, at the junction
of the Charleroi and Nivelles roads leading to Brussels.

Marshal Ney, perceiving the British in retreat, at
once pushed forward his cavalry.   Thereupon Vivian
moved the 10th Hussars across the slope above the
Namur road, and there posted them in echelon of
squadrons.   At that moment Wellington with his staff
rode up and halted in front of the regiment, and it
was from this point that the Duke soon afterwards saw
the advance of the enemy's cuirassiers, preceded by
lancers.   Scouting parties from the 10th and 18th
Hussars were sent out, but, being unable to check the
French advance, the piquets fell back, and the 10th
Hussars took up their proper position in the line.   Then
Vivian, forming in a new alignment, threw back his
left, so as to present a front to the enemy, and also to
protect the left of the whole line.   Vandeleur's brigade
was during this movement in the right rear of Vivian's
and close to Quatre Bras.

As soon as Wellington discerned Ney's intention to molest his retreat, it became a question of deep consideration whether it would be advisable to offer a serious resistance to the enemy's advance. When, however, Lord Uxbridge made the remark that the defiles in rear as well as the distance of the allied infantry would prevent their co-operation, the Duke without hesitation ordered the cavalry to continue its retreat. To carry this into effect the Earl of Uxbridge immediately formed his cavalry into three columns, and retired in the following order :—The right column, consisting of Grant's and Dörnberg's light cavalry brigades, by the ford a little above the town of Genappe ; the centre column, composed of all the heavy cavalry, along the Brussels high road ; and the left column, formed of Vandeleur's and Vivian's brigades, across the bridge over the river Genappe at Thuy.[1]

Scarcely had these dispositions been made than the piquet of the 18th Hussars was driven in by two or three squadrons of French cavalry. Vivian, however, opened fire with his battery of horse artillery, and checked their further advance. The French then hastily brought up their artillery and fired upon the Hussar Brigade. But Vivian, who had received instructions from Lord Uxbridge to retire, coupled with an intimation that he would be supported by Vandeleur, then in his rear, perceiving the enemy's cavalry pressing forward in great numbers, not only in his front, but on his left flank, put his brigade about and retired in line, covered by skirmishers. On nearing Vandeleur's brigade, Vivian was surprised to find the second line also in retreat ; for he had expected to retire through the intervals of that brigade, and was not aware of the instructions given to Vandeleur " to leave the road

[1] *See* Siborne, p. 163.

clear." He immediately occupied the ground thus vacated, and ordered the 18th to charge the French as soon as they came within reach. " It was now that a violent storm of thunder and rain broke over the field of battle. The 18th Hussars were just preparing to charge, and only waiting till the guns of the brigade had created disorder in the enemy's ranks. At the first discharge of artillery the heavens burst forth with peals of thunder, and poured down torrents of rain." [1] In a few minutes the ground became so saturated with water that rapid movements of cavalry were impracticable. In consequence of this state of the ground, Vivian determined to retire on the Brussels road. He despatched at once his battery of horse artillery towards the bridge over the Genappe at Thuy, and sent an aide-de-camp to request Vandeleur to move his brigade across with all rapidity, so as to leave the bridge clear for the passage of his guns and cavalry. The enemy still closely followed the left column, and, as there was some difficulty in passing the squadrons over the bridge, Vivian ordered a portion of the 10th Hussars to dismount as soon as they had reached the opposite bank of the river, and there to be prepared with their carbines to defend the passage of the remainder of the brigade, should their retreat be hardly pressed. So bold, however, was the enemy's attack that a squadron of the 1st German Hussars was cut off from the bridge and compelled to pass the Genappe at a point lower down the stream. Meanwhile, having ascertained that all was ready, Vivian galloped over the bridge with the remainder of the 1st German Hussars, followed by the French loudly cheering; but the fire from the dismounted men of the Tenth, together with the sight of the remainder of the regiment and the

[1] Siborne.

whole of the 18th Hussars formed up on the rising ground beyond, checked the pursuit. After remaining in this position for some little time, Vivian's brigade continued its retreat without further molestation along a narrow cross-road leading through the villages of Glabois, Frischermont, Smohain, and Verd-Cocou.[1]

While Vivian fell back with his brigade, the 7th Hussars were left in Genappe to check the pursuit, and were hotly engaged with the enemy in covering the retirement of the army. Wellington at the same time fell back with the whole of his troops towards the forest of Soignies, where he took up a position on either side of the high road from Charleroi to Brussels at Mont St. Jean, in front of the village of Waterloo. Napoleon followed with the great bulk of his forces, and formed them nearly opposite to the English on both sides of the same high road, with his head-quarters at La Belle Alliance. Thirty-two thousand French under Grouchy were detached to observe the Prussians retiring on Wavre, while the numbers remaining with Napoleon himself were about 72,000,[2] with 248 guns. Wellington's force numbered about 68,000[3] strong, with 156 pieces of artillery. Included in this total were nearly 16,000 cavalry on the French side, and between 12,000 and 13,000 on that of the Allies.[4]

"Never was a more melancholy night passed by soldiers than that which followed the halt of the two armies in their respective positions on the evening of the 17th. The whole day had been wet and cloudy, but towards evening the rain fell in torrents."[5] The two armies bivouacked in their respective positions, the space between them in some places not exceeding

---

[1] *See* Siborne, p. 168.   [2] *Ibid.*   [3] *Ibid.*
[4] Alison.   [5] *Ibid.*

L

1,500 yards. In the early morning the vedettes of the opposing sides might be seen withdrawing, while the drying and cleaning of firearms became general, and soon the troops on each side were moved to the several posts assigned to them.

CHAPTER XVIII

THE FIELD OF WATERLOO—POSITIONS OF THE CAVALRY BRIGADES—
COMMENCEMENT OF THE BATTLE—CHARGES OF SOMERSET'S AND
PONSONBY'S BRIGADES—VANDELEUR'S AND VIVIAN'S BRIGADES
TAKE GROUND TO THE RIGHT

THE selection of the ground on which battle was to be
given to such a formidable opponent was carefully made
by Wellington. Although the choice was in every respect limited, the Duke displayed the skill, judgment,
and forethought for which he was always so pre-emi-
nently distinguished in determining the British position
at Waterloo. Several conditions had to be taken into
consideration. Firstly, the Prussians posted at Wavre,
ten miles off, ought to have facility in affording timely
aid to the British; secondly, the ground ought not to
be too favourable to cavalry and artillery, in which
arms the enemy was greatly superior; and, lastly, the
position must afford shelter to the new and hastily combined elements of the allied army, so as not to expose
them unnecessarily at the commencement of an engagement. Yet all these conditions were fulfilled. Moreover, the right flank, resting on the village of Merbe-
Braine, was well secured by a ravine; while the left
flank was protected by the hamlets of La Haye and
Papelotte. In front of the right was the now historical
farmhouse of Hougoumont, and in advance of the
centre the scarcely less famous buildings of La Haye
Sainte.

1815

The incidents of this great and decisive battle, which replaced the legitimate sovereign on the throne of France and restored tranquillity to Europe, are generally so well known that it will be only necessary here to allude to the movements of other corps when they form a connecting link with the operations of the one regiment especially dealt with in these memoirs.

To render the cavalry actions intelligible, a brief account must here be given of the places occupied by the brigades in the line of battle. The allied cavalry, consisting of seven brigades of British and King's German Legion (8,373 men strong), and Hanoverian and Brunswick (2,604 strong), and Dutch-Belgian (3,505 strong), was under Lord Uxbridge. These brigades, formed by regiments mostly in close columns of squadrons at deploying intervals, were posted on the reverse slopes of the main ridge or in hollows screened from the enemy. On the extreme right, near to the Nivelles road, stood the Fifth Brigade, consisting of the 7th and 15th Hussars and 13th Light Dragoons, under Major-General Sir Colquhoun Grant. On his left was the Third Brigade, under Major-General Sir William Dörnberg, consisting of the 23rd Light Dragoons and of the 1st and 2nd Light Dragoons of the King's German Legion. In the rear of this brigade stood the Cumberland Hanoverian Hussars, under Lieutenant-Colonel Hake. In the right rear of Alten's division, further to the left, stood the 3rd Hussars of the King's German Legion, under Colonel Sir Frederick Arentschildt. On the right of the Charleroi road, and in rear of Alten's division, Major-General Lord Edward Somerset's 1st or Household Brigade was drawn up—the 1st and 2nd Life Guards, the Royal Horse Guards (Blue), and 1st King's Dragoon Guards. On the left of the Charleroi road, in rear of Picton's division, stood the Second or Union Brigade—1st Dragoons (Royals), 2nd Dragoons (Scots Greys), and 6th Dragoons (Inniskillings), under Major-General Sir William Ponsonby. Again to the left the Fourth Brigade was posted—the 11th, 12th, and 16th Light Dragoons, under Major-General Sir John Vandeleur; and upon the extreme left of the whole army the Sixth Brigade, consisting of the 10th and 18th Hussars and 1st Hussars of the German Legion, under Sir Hussey Vivian. The reserves consisted of the Dutch, Belgian, the Brunswick and Hanoverian cavalry, and were posted in rear of the centre within the roads from Charleroi and Nivelles.

On the morning of the 18th a reconnoitring party was sent out from the Sixth Cavalry Brigade, by order of Sir Hussey Vivian, to guard the left flank of the British army, which was much exposed, and also in hopes of gaining some intelligence of the near approach of the Prussians. This patrol was taken from the 10th Hussars, and was under the command of Major Taylor, who proceeded with it in the direction of Ohain, and placed his piquets at Ter la Haye and Frischermont. About ten in the morning a Prussian patrol was met with, when the officer in charge of it informed Major Taylor that General Bülow was at St. Lambert, advancing with his corps d'armée. Major Taylor immediately despatched this important intelligence by Lieutenant Lindsay to the Duke's head-quarters, besides reporting it to Sir Hussey Vivian.

About eleven o'clock the massive divisions of the enemy were seen advancing.[1] The infantry in two lines, covered by skirmishers and flanked by regiments of lancers, moved forward to the music of their regimental bands. Thus formed, it presented a magnificent

[1] Napoleon delayed his attack until so late, owing to the deep state of the ground after the rain, which was much against his strongest arm, the artillery.

and imposing sight. Cuirassiers followed in the rear of the centre of each infantry wing, lancers and chasseurs marched behind the cuirassiers on the right wing, and behind the left were the grenadiers and dragoons of the Imperial Guard, supported by the Sixth Corps of cavalry. No less than 246 pieces of ordnance were distributed along the front and on the flanks of the first line, and these were kept in readiness to open fire on the British position.

At 11.30 A.M. Prince Jerome's division attacked Hougoumont, on the English right. Attack quickly succeeded to attack, each made with the impetuosity characteristic of the onset of French troops, but all without avail, and their finest efforts proved ineffectual. The British left was next attacked by the French about 12.30 P.M. "Upon the extreme left of the first or main line," says Siborne, "was stationed Vivian's Light Cavalry Brigade, comprising the 10th and 18th Hussars and the 1st Hussars of the King's German Legion. The two former regiments were in line in rear of the Wavre road, and withdrawn a little from the crest of the ridge; the right of the Tenth resting upon a lane leading from Smohain in the direction of Verd-Cocou. The 1st Hussars, King's German Legion, were also in line and formed in reserve. The left of the brigade was completely *en l'air* upon high, open, and flat ground. . . . On the right of Vivian's brigade, and having its own right resting upon a narrow lane, forming a slight hollow way lined with hedges, stood Vandeleur's brigade of light cavalry, consisting of the 11th, 12th, and 16th British Light Dragoons, in columns of squadrons. The lane on which its right rested, descending the interior slope of the position, joined the other lane which led from Vivian's right to Verd-Cocou. This advance of the French troops was confronted by

Vandeleur's dragoons and the Tenth Hussars, whilst the remaining regiments formed the reserve." [1]

The Earl of Uxbridge, seeing that a favourable opportunity presented itself for the use of his cavalry, gave orders for a simultaneous charge of the two heavy cavalry brigades under Lord Edward Somerset and Sir William Ponsonby, the former against the enemy's cavalry, the latter against the masses of French infantry. Somerset charged the enemy's cuirassiers, who were suddenly thrown out of their speed by coming on to a hollow way. Being taken in flank as well as in front, they were broken up, driven back, and pursued by the 2nd Life Guards. No sooner did Ponsonby perceive the Household Brigade with the King's Dragoon Guards in motion, than he led on his own brigade, the Royals and Inniskillings in the first line, the Greys in support. With these he attacked the French infantry division advancing under General Allix. The Greys, coming up on the left of the front line, charged with it, and our dragoons, having the advantage of the descent of the hill, bore down the mass of men in front of them. The whole were in a moment jammed together, when gradually a scattering flight from the rear loosened the unmanageable mass, which now rolled back. The charge of the Union Brigade having thus succeeded, the three regiments then rallied and fell back before the large bodies of the French cavalry brought to bear upon them.

Vandeleur's brigade now moved up in support, as Ponsonby's brigade was suffering severely from the lancers and chasseurs under Jaquinot. It was just at the right moment that the 12th and 16th Light Dragoons, in columns of divisions, rapidly moved over the crest of the hill. When half way down, forming

[1] Siborne.

line to the right, they dashed through a column of
French infantry so as to reach the right flank of the
French lancers, whom they drove down the hill in
complete disorder and confusion.

Perceiving Ponsonby's brigade in disorder, Vivian
had ridden forward from the extreme left and descended some distance down the slope to gain a better
view for his own personal guidance. With practical
judgment he soon came to a conclusion what the result
of this affair might be, and immediately despatched
orders to the 10th and 18th Hussars to move up along
the hollow way to the right, leaving, however, the
1st Hussars, K.G.L., to protect the left flank. But as
the charge of Vandeleur's brigade had succeeded without the active aid of its own support, the 11th Light
Dragoons, the further advance of the 10th and 18th
Hussars was stayed. They continued, however, in
their new position on the right of the lane leading
to Verd-Cocou.

It was now about half-past three o'clock, and
Napoleon, finding that his infantry had been able to
make little or no impression upon the British position,
determined to try the effect of repeated charges by his
splendid cavalry under Marshal Ney upon the British
centre and left.

By this time Vivian's brigade had been drawn still
further from the left to strengthen the centre of the
line. It had scarcely taken up its new position when
Colonel Quentin, at the head of the Tenth, was wounded
in the ankle, and the command of the regiment devolved on Lieutenant-Colonel Lord Robert Manners. Immediately after this occurrence the enemy made another
desperate attack upon the British centre, which had so
far succeeded as to dislodge and drive back some
battalions of Brunswick infantry. Just then the Sixth

Brigade, with the 10th and 18th Hussars in front and 1st Hussars, K.G.L., in reserve, drew up in rear of these troops (the Brunswick infantry), relieving the exhausted remnant of the Scots Greys and 3rd Hussars, King's German Legion. The presence and appearance of this fresh cavalry tended very considerably to restore confidence to that part of the line. The allied infantry were, however, on the point of once more giving way. The Nassauers were falling back *en masse* right against the horses' heads of the 10th Hussars, but these, by keeping their files closed, prevented further retreat. Vivian, and Captain Shakespeare, of the Tenth (who was acting as his extra aide-de-camp), rendered themselves conspicuous at this moment by their endeavours to halt and encourage the Nassauers.[1]

The Hanoverians, with the German Legion on the left, led by Kielmansegge, now resolutely dashed forward at the double, their drums beating. The Brunswickers took up the movement, as did also the Nassauers; Vivian and his aide-de-camp cheering them on, whilst the 10th Hussars followed in close support. His brigade, by its proximity to these troops, against which so close and unremitting a fire of musketry was maintained, was placed in a very trying position for cavalry, and suffered much in consequence. It was here that Captains Grey, Gurwood, and Wood, of the Tenth, were wounded.

[1] Siborne.

CHAPTER XIX

THE PRUSSIANS UNDER BLÜCHER ARRIVE—VIVIAN'S BRIGADE ORDERED TO ADVANCE—THE TENTH CHARGE THE IMPERIAL GUARD—DEATH OF MAJOR HOWARD—LINES BY AN OFFICER OF THE TENTH—BYRON'S "CHILDE HAROLD"—LIST OF OFFICERS PRESENT—LIST OF KILLED AND WOUNDED

1815   DURING all this terrible conflict the Prussians from Wavre were struggling steadfastly on to Wellington's assistance. The muddy, bad roads all but stopped their progress, and had it not been for the determination of "Old Marshal Forward," as his soldiers named Blücher, their commander, he and his army would not have reached the field of Waterloo that night. When the Prussians were seen and their guns heard on the British left, Napoleon made a final effort to break Wellington's line by bringing up his Old Guard, which as yet had taken no part in the battle. This was certainly the most critical part of the action.

It is well known how Napoleon's last charge failed, and how with more and more fresh battalions he strove eagerly to incite the Imperial Guard to renewed efforts. Then it was that the Duke at last found himself enabled to become the assailant. Knowing that his left was now protected by the Prussians, and that he had the Hussar Brigade under Vivian fresh and ready at hand, he, without a moment's hesitation, launched them against the cavalry near La Belle Alliance. The charge was as successful as it was daring. The best description of the part taken by the Tenth in this memorable charge is found in the following passages from Siborne:—

"Vivian, the moment he received the order to advance, wheeled his brigade half squadrons to the right. Thus the 10th Hussars became the leading regiment, the 18th Hussars followed, the 1st Germans moving off in rear of all. As the column passed by the left front of Vandeleur's brigade it was saluted by the latter with cheers of encouragement, and in a similar manner by Maitland's brigade of Guards as it passed their flank. On arriving about midway, Vivian observed bodies of French troops on the left of La Belle Alliance, posted as if fully prepared to resist the threatened attack, and he at once decided upon attacking them. Continuing the advance in the same order, he, with the view of turning the left of the enemy's cavalry, ordered the 10th Hussars to incline to the right, a command which was followed by 'Line to the front on the leading troop in succession by regiments,' the two corps behind being ordered to follow in support of the Tenth. The rapid pace which had been maintained by the head of the column, combined with the incline to the right which had been made, rendered it difficult for the rear troops to get up into line, and as Vivian sounded the 'charge' as soon as the first squadron was formed, it was executed not in line but by echelon of squadrons, which, under the circumstances, was the preferable and most desirable formation, for before the left squadron of the Tenth had dashed in among the enemy's cavalry the latter were in full flight. Seeing the success of the charge, Vivian at once ordered the 'halt' and 'rally' for the Tenth, while he directed the 18th Hussars to attack the chasseurs and grenadiers à cheval. When the charge of the 18th began, some French artillery attempted to cross the front at a gallop, but the attempt failed, and after capturing the guns the 18th bore down upon the cavalry, who were soon driven from their position and flying along the high road. Just as the ' halt ' and ' rally ' had sounded for the Tenth, the right squadron, under Major the Hon. F. Howard, was attacked on the flank by a body of cuirassiers and forced about a hundred yards away to the left, while the other two squadrons, not being aware of Vivian's order to halt, continued the pursuit under Lieutenant-Colonel Lord Robert Manners.

" Sir H. Vivian having seen the 18th charge, and being satisfied with its success, was hurrying to bring up the remaining regiment of his brigade, the 1st German Hussars, when he met with Major Howard's squadron, close to a square of the French Grenadiers of the Guard. General Vivian doubted for a moment how far it might be advisable to attack the square, but seeing one of our infantry regiments advancing, and calculating on its immediately charging the face and angle of the square next to it, ordered Major Howard to charge the face and angle to which he was opposed. This was executed with the greatest gallantry and determination, Vivian himself joining in the charge on the right of the squadron. The hussars charged home to the French bayonets, when a fierce conflict ensued, Major Howard being killed at the head of his men. He was shot in the mouth, and fell senseless on the ground, when one of the Imperial Guard stepped out of the ranks and beat his head with the butt end of his musket. Two other officers—Lieutenants Arnold and Bacon—were wounded, and Cornet Hamilton, who rode as a serrefile, brought the squadron out of action. Lieutenant Gunning was killed immediately previous to the attack. In consequence of the infantry regiment not joining in the attack, the square, a very strong one, cannot be said to have been broken by the shock, for the veteran soldiers of whom it was composed knew too well their power of resistance against such a handful of horsemen; still the square fell slowly back until it reached the hollow way formed by the narrow road that led from the causeway in rear of La Belle Alliance towards the left of the French position, into which, descending in confusion, the Guards went to swell the hosts of fugitives, hurrying along the general line of retreat of the French army."

Meanwhile the remainder of the 10th Hussars, consisting of the left and centre squadrons, had, under Lord Robert Manners, continued its course down into the valley south-east of the Hougoumont enclosures, and drove back the French cuirassiers. They now came upon the retreating infantry, many of them wearing the large bearskin caps, showing them to be the Imperial Guard. They seemed seized with a panic as their routed cavalry dashed past them, and they commenced throwing down their arms, numbers of them loudly calling out " Pardon." [1] Then crossing the same narrow road before mentioned, the Tenth brought up their right shoulders and ascended the height in rear of the hollow way. Upon the slope of the hill about half a battalion of French Guards had rallied and formed, with some cavalry close behind them, and opened a sharp fire upon the Tenth. Lord Robert Manners halted for a minute when within about forty paces from them, to allow his men to form up. He then gave a cheer and charged, when the Imperial Guard and the cavalry instantly turned and fled. The very forward movement of Vivian's brigade, and the vigorous attack which it made against the centre of the French position, having

[1] Siborne.

1815 rendered an immediate support imperative, Vandeleur's brigade was despatched across the ridge in column of half squadrons, right in front, at the moment of the general advance in line. So, as Siborne goes on to tell us, "Vivian's brigade, which had not only broken but completely pierced the centre of the French position, had its right effectually protected by Vandeleur's advance, while its left was secured by the advance of Adam's brigade of infantry, which, operating along the left side of the Charleroi road, was pushing the enemy's routed forces further and further from the field of battle." [1]

The following extracts are taken from some lines written by an officer of the 10th Hussars who was present at the repulse of the last attack made by the French :—

'Tis Vivian, pride of old Coimbra's halls,
His veins th' untainted blood of Britons fills.
Him follows close a Manners, glorious name,
In him a Granby's soul aspires to fame,
Or such as erst, when Rodney gained the day,
Ebbed from his kinsman's wound with life away.

---

[1] Napoleon and his aide-de-camp, Gourgaud, both ascribe the loss of the battle to this happy charge of Vivian's brigade on the flank of the Old Guard. "Le soleil," says Gourgaud, "était couché; rien n'était désespéré, lorsque deux brigades de cavalerie ennemie, qui n'avaient pas encore donné, pénétrèrent entre La Haie Sainte et le corps du général Reille. Elles auraient pu être arrêtées par les huit carrés de la Garde, mais, voyant le grand désordre qui régnait à la droite, elles les tournèrent. Ces trois milles chevaux empêchèrent tout ralliement."—Alison. To the same purpose Napoleon says in his despatch : "Sur les huit heures et demie, les quatre bataillons qui avaient été envoyés pour soutenir les cuirassiers marchèrent à la baïonnette pour enlever les batteries. Le jour finissait, une charge faite sur leur flanc par plusieurs escadrons Anglais les mirent en désordre. . . ."—Napoleon, *Bulletin sur la Bataille de Mont Saint-Jean*, 21 Juin, 1815. Marshal Ney also states : "There still remained to us four squares of the Old Guard, advantageously placed to protect the retreat. These brave grenadiers, the choice of the army, forced successively to retire, only yielded ground foot by foot, till, finally overwhelmed by numbers, they were almost entirely annihilated."

Then pierced the fatal ball young Gunning's heart;
Headlong he fell, nor felt one instant's smart;
Calm, pale as marble form on tombs, he lay
As days had sped since passed his soul away.
His charger onward, on the squadron's flank
To battle rushed, keeping its master's rank.

Charge! Howard, charge! and sweep them from the field;
To British swords must their bayonets yield.
To high emprise, upon the battle's plain,
When was the name of Howard call'd in vain?
Worthy his great progenitors, he heard
Vivian's call exulting, then, with ready word,
"Tenth Hussars, charge!" he cried, and wav'd on high
His gleaming sword: forward at once they fly.

Thus rushed the gallant squadron on the foe,
Yet firm they stood, their arms in levell'd row,
Their volleying thunders poured our ranks among,
Where foremost blade on foremost musket rung.
Three gallant youths, the van, exulting led,
Three by the deadly volley instant bled.

Arnold and Bacon fall, again to rise,
From three fell wounds brave Howard's spirit flies.
Full many a warrior on that dreadful day,
Brave, generous, gentle, breathed his soul away,
But one more gentle, generous, or brave,
Never in battle found a soldier's grave.

As the moon rose and gradually shed its light over the field, the retreating line of the vanquished foe became by degrees perceptible. Wellington, who had led the advance of Adam's infantry, and had seen how complete and crushing was the defeat, returned to his main body. When he reached La Belle Alliance, he gave the command for the whole army to bivouac upon the field of battle. Adam's brigade passed the night on the spot it had reached; Vandeleur's on the right near the woods of Cellois; while Vivian, inclining somewhat to his right, led his hussars much further in advance of the army, establishing his bivouac close to the hamlet of Hilaincourt.

The following is a list of officers of the 10th Hussars who were present in the actions on the 16th, 17th, and 18th of June :—Lieutenant-Colonels: George Quentin (severely wounded), Lord Robert Manners (Brevet Colonel); Major: Hon. F. Howard (killed); Captains: T. W. Taylor (Brevet Major), H. C. Stapleton, J. Grey (wounded), J. Gurwood (wounded), C. Wood (severely wounded), H. Floyd, A. Shakespeare (acting A.D.C. to Sir Hussey Vivian); Lieutenants: J. W. Parsons, C. Gunning (killed), W. S. Smith, H. J. Burn, R. Arnold (wounded), W. Cartwright, J. C. Wallington, E. Hodgson, W. C. Hamilton, A. Bacon (severely wounded), W. H. B. Lindsay ; Paymaster : J. Fulton ; Lieutenant and Adjutant : J. Hardman ; Assistant-Surgeon : J. S. Jenks ; Veterinary Surgeon : H. C. Sannerman.

The casualties in the Tenth were : Killed, two officers and twenty-one rank and file, and fifty-one horses. List of killed : Major the Hon. F. Howard, Lieutenant C. Gunning, Privates John Falea, Richard Freemantle, Robert Kent, George Hemming, Evan Price, Edward Rosewell, Thomas Gadson, John Taylor, Charles Porter, John Taites, Joseph Wyatt, Samuel Deacon, John Dowling, James Ashwin, Robert Swingler, Henry Gander, Samuel Jenkins, William Wanstill, Samuel Lee, W. Green, Joseph Derry.

The wounded were six officers, one troop quartermaster, one trumpeter, thirty-eight rank and file, and thirty-five horses. Missing, one trumpeter, twenty-five rank and file, and forty-one horses.

On the morning after the battle a party under Lieutenant W. Slayter Smith, consisting of Sergeant Plowman and six men, were sent back to the field of action to bury the dead of the regiment and to bring away any 1815 who were wounded. In the execution of this duty the party found the body of Major Howard, which they interred beneath two trees near the spot where he fell.

Lord Byron, in a note to " Childe Harold," thus describes the place : " My guide, from Mount St. Jean, over the field seemed intelligent and accurate. Where Major Howard fell was not far from two tall and solitary trees (there was a third cut down or shivered in the battle), which stand a few yards from each other at a pathway's side. Beneath these he died and was buried. The body has since been removed to England. A small hollow for the present marks where it lay, but will probably now be effaced; the plough has been upon it, and the grain is now ripening. After pointing out the different spots where Picton and other gallant men had perished, the guide said: 'Here Major Howard lay; I was near him when he received his death wound.' I told him my relationship, and he seemed then still more anxious to point out the particular spot and circumstances. The place is one of the most marked in the field, from the peculiarity of the two trees above mentioned." Lord Byron has immortalised the death of his kinsman in the following lines :—

> Their praise is hymned by loftier harps than mine,
> Yet one I would select from that proud throng,
> Partly because they blend me with his line,
> And partly that I did his sire some wrong,
> And partly that bright names will hallow song ;
> And his was of the bravest, and when showered
> The death-bolts deadliest the thinn'd files along,
> Even where the thickest of war's tempest lowered,
> They reached no nobler breast than thine, young gallant
> Howard !

M

There have been tears and breaking hearts for thee,
And mine were nothing, had I such to give,
But when I stood beneath the fresh green tree
Which, living, waves where thou didst cease to live,
And saw around me the wild field revive
With fruits and fertile promise, and the spring
Come forth, her work of gladness to contrive
With all her reckless birds upon the wing,
I turned from all she brought to those she could not bring.[1]

APPENDIX

The following letters are appended, and, from having
been written on the spot, will prove of considerable
interest :—

A Short Account of the Battle of Waterloo.

*Letters from General William Cartwright, then a Lieutenant in
the 10th Royal Hussars, aged Eighteen.*

> Waterloo, near Brussels : 19th June
> (Monday after Waterloo).

MY DEAR FATHER, — Although I have seen many battles in
my life, I assure you they were a complete farce to one for this
last three days. Bony, against us, fought like a tiger; we fought
like *Englishmen*, and, thanks to God, repelled him with great
loss. Our cavalry behaved so finely that everyone when they saw
us were quite thunderstruck. Poor Gunning is killed, as also
Bouverie. I only wonder we were not all killed. I have lost
all my baggage, and therefore intend taking Gunning's, and you
will pay Mr. Gunning, I have no doubt. Thank God, I have

---

[1] *Childe Harold.* Major the Hon. F. Howard was the second son of
the Earl of Carlisle. His family were so anxious, if possible, to recover
the body of their relative, that the Duke of York wrote to the Duke of
Wellington that every effort should be made to do so. On inquiry it was
found that two sergeants of the 10th Hussars who had assisted in burying
him could undertake to find the spot. They were sent from Paris,
and were fortunate enough to find the remains, which were despatched
from Brussels to England.

been lucky enough to escape. I commanded a troop on this occasion. We charged four or five times our numbers—the men in armour—but we made a pretty hole in them; there are not above six officers left with the regiment. I command a squadron now. We have been fighting since the 16th. I will give you another account in a day or two, but in the meantime excuse this scrawl. We are within three leagues of Brussels.

In haste, &c., &c.,

Your most affectionate Son,

WM. CARTWRIGHT.

[SECOND LETTER.]

Three days after Waterloo—on the advance.

MY DEAR MOTHER,—Having at length a day's halt, I take the opportunity of writing to you, to give you some account of our proceedings, which commenced on the 16th, which day about 4 o'clock A.M. we were routed out and marched to Nivelle. It was just about 7 P.M. when we reached that place, but as the scene of action was two leagues on, we trotted in and got into the field of action just before dusk. We bivouacked there the whole night, and the next morning the skirmishing again commenced. This lasted till about 10 o'clock, from 4 in the morning, when the Duke, our noble commander, having heard that Blücher (who was on our left) had been repulsed, he determined to retreat in order to communicate with this old gentleman. Accordingly, the infantry all went to the rear, and the Hussars —for they are always more employed than any other cavalry— were to cover the *retreat*. The Hussars' General, Sir Hussey Vivian, appointed our regiment and the 7th to this unpleasant duty, for such it is. We showed front to the enemy for two or three hours after the army had retreated, till at last the enemy brought up a very large force of Cuirassiers, who are all in armour. We were then forced to retreat, and of course these fellows followed us up. We fought and retired, and so on, till at length we came up to our infantry, who were in position. We then took our post, and a great deal of cannonading, &c., ensued. We bivouacked on the top of the position this night (17th), and a pretty rainy one it was. I was never so wet and miserable in my life. The next morning of course we expected an attack, but 9 o'clock passed, and nothing new, so nothing till 11, when our piquet was driven in. Of course we all turned out immediately, and took our place in our position, which I assure you was rather formidable. The enemy then brought on very heavy columns, both of infantry and cavalry. All of ours awaited the attack, which was conducted by Napoleon himself and with great vigour; they made attacks every moment, bringing on fresh troops every time; but our fellows, fighting more like lions than men, managed to keep them down. He had about 130,000 in the field; we had not more than 70,000, including *everything*, Hanoverians, &c. Of course numbers will tell at last, and our right began to waver—this was on the main road. We then moved from the left, which was our former place in the position, to the right, and supported the infantry in some style. We were kept under the heaviest fire that ever was heard, both of musketry and cannon, for some time. (About 7 P.M.) However, the Prussians at length made their appearance on the left and began with the enemy. This gave us double spirit, and we went on like tigers—we actually went up to the mouth of the cannon. While we were thus engaged, the enemy heard the Prussians on the left; this they did not seem to like, and we of course pushed on the more. However, our commandant of the brigade, Sir Hussey Vivian, ordered us to form in column right in front; this brought me, as I was commanding the right troop, in front. We then went on, and the enemy formed squares—we did not mind this, but deployed as steady as if we were at a field day. It was just here that poor Gunning was killed. We then moved on and came to the charge. The squares of course made a desperate resistance, but our valour soon extinguished their squares. Their cavalry then came down with *Lancers*, *armour*, &c., enough to frighten us, but we charged them, though twice our number, and quite panic struck them; some ran off, others were tumbling off their horses, others attempted to defend themselves, and so on. We however gave a pretty fair account of them. After this they brought on more cavalry, but we played them the same trick. We took an immense number of prisoners, cannon, &c., &c., and flatter ourselves we were the means of saving the day. I will give you a copy of

the orders issued by our commander, as follows :—" Major-
General Sir Hussey Vivian begs to express in the strongest
possible terms to the brigade he has the honour and pleasure to
command, the infinite admiration with which he beheld the conduct of the regiments composing it in the memorable and glorious
battle of yesterday. The attacks of the 10th and 18th Hussars
were made with that spirit that ensured success, and the second
attack of the 10th Hussars, on a square of infantry, was a proof
of what discipline and valour can accomplish. The Major-
General desires that every individual officer, and those engaged
on the plains of Waterloo, will, together with the strongest
expressions of his approbation, accept his very best thanks for
their valour and steadiness. (Sd.) HUSSEY VIVIAN, Major-
General." What can be more satisfactory than the above
order ? Besides this there is a letter despatched to the Prince
about the regiment. We have just been giving them a taste
of the new Tenth. Having lost everything I had, horses included, I have just got poor Gunning's baggage up. I must
take it, and intend getting it valued by our adjutant, which is
the regular manner, and then send the account to my father.
We intend to be in Paris in a fortnight. Nobody knows where
Buony is. They say we are to have another battle at Laon,
where he is making a stand. The rascals killed all the prisoners
they took. We are not working on their principle. The Prussians are following them up on our left. You will see by the
" Gazette " that the cavalry had a very fair share in the battle. I
must now conclude, as I am going to put on a clean shirt for
the first time since we began.

Adieu, my dear mother. Pray excuse this scrawl, and for-
give all faults, and believe me, &c., &c.,

WM. CARTWRIGHT.

The following are extracts from letters of Captain
Charles Wood, 10th Hussars, after he was wounded in
the battle :—

I got hit just as the Duke moved to the attack and bled like
a pig. I took up my stirrups into the hunting seat and made
the best of my way back to Waterloo. With the assistance of

a dragoon I afterwards got into Brussels, and found a lodging in the Rue Royale. Arnold [1] will come home with me. He was shot through the lungs. They tell me he must not eat meat for six months. He says, "Wait till I get to Northampton with five hunters next November. . . ." Quentin is going to Paris to-morrow in a carriage . . . . Bob Manners was struck in the shoulder by a lance, and did not find it out till the next day. . . . . You should have seen us all the night before the fight. Every one wet through. We had a shower that came down like a wall. Our horses could not face it, and all went about. It made the ground up to the horses' fetlocks. We got into a small cottage close to our bivouac, about a mile in rear of the position, most of us naked, and getting our things dry at the fire. I managed to get "Paddy" [2] a shop for the night. Old Quentin burnt his boots, and could not get them on. . . . We had to feed on what we found in the hut, beginning with the old hens for supper and the young chickens for breakfast. I see the English papers say, "The Light Dragoons could make no impression on the French Cuirassiers." Now our regiment actually rode over them. Give me the boys that will go at a swinging gallop for the last seventy yards, applying both spurs when you come within six yards. Then if you don't go right over them I am much mistaken. . . . I have found the ball which went through my thigh into the pad of my saddle, very high up. I think it hit the bone, which drove it upwards.

Letter from Lieutenant Lindsay to his Mother, Lady G. Lindsay, written on the field of Waterloo; it was sealed with a wafer made of pinched bread.

Monday, 19th.

MY DEAREST MOTHER,—We have just had the happiness of giving the French the most complete drubbing they ever got, having beaten them on the heights of Waterloo, destroyed nearly their whole army, taking nearly an hundred pieces of cannon. They drove in a piquet of the Tenth on which I happened to be at ten o'clock, and a charge of the Tenth on the 18th decided the fate of the day. Nearly the whole of their

---

[1] Wounded in the charge on the French square.   [2] His charger.

officers have either been killed or wounded, and, thank God, I
escaped without the least accident. I write this in the most
shocking place you ever saw, but you must be satisfied with
it till I can write a fuller account. We are about to pursue
them immediately. The Prussians have saved us that trouble,
for they have followed them. Eight officers are the whole we
can muster. Most are killed or wounded. Adieu, my dearest
mother, with thousand loves to all.

W. F. B. LINDSAY.

CHAPTER XX

PURSUIT OF THE FRENCH—LOSSES—REWARDS—SILVER TRUMPET—
    LIEUTENANT SLAYTER SMITH ORDERED TO RECONNOITRE—THE
    OCCUPATION OF PARIS—MARCH TO BOULOGNE—EMBARKATION
    AT CALAIS

1815   THE pursuit of the French on the evening of Waterloo
was left to Blücher, whose troops had not suffered
much in the battle, and Ziethen with the Prussian
cavalry continued to follow them during the whole
night. Thus ended the battle of Waterloo. The loss
of the Allies was 22,378 killed, wounded, and missing.
Of the French army, scarcely 40,000 recrossed the
Sambre, carrying with them only twenty-seven guns.

In commemoration of the battle of Waterloo a silver
medal was struck and bestowed on all ranks. That
year of service was allowed to count as two in reckon-
ing the pensions of soldiers, and each corps present was
granted permission to add the word "Waterloo" to its
honours. Two hundred thousand pounds were voted
by the House of Commons and presented to the Duke
of Wellington,[1] and he was created Prince of Waterloo
by the King of the Netherlands.

A silver trumpet, now in the Officers' Mess of the

---

[1] "It is impossible to convey an idea of the universal interest and
transports of joy excited throughout the British Empire by the brief but
stirring campaign of Waterloo, and when Wellington's letter was read
aloud to crowds in every street by whoever was fortunate enough to have
obtained first a copy of the *London Gazette*."—Alison.

10th Hussars, is a valued record of the part taken by the regiment in the great battle, and bears the following inscription :

PURCHASED
BY DESIRE OF THE
SOLDIERS OF THE TENTH OR PRINCE REGENT'S OWN
ROYAL HUSSARS
WITH PART OF THE PRIZE MONEY
ARISING FROM THE ENEMY'S HORSES
CAPTURED BY THEIR BRIGADE
UNDER THE COMMAND OF
MAJOR-GENERAL SIR H. VIVIAN, K.C.B.
AT THE BATTLE OF
WATERLOO.
18 JUNE, 1815.

The wounded of the Tenth were all well cared for after the battle, and, with the exception of Colonel Quentin, all the officers were lodged together, owing to the exertions of Dr. Jenks of the regiment, in a large house in the Rue Royale, facing the Park, in Brussels.

The allied forces followed up the French without intermission, and on the 20th Vivian's brigade was cantoned at Merbe Ste. Marie. Two days later it moved forward to Le Cateau. On the 25th the advanced guard formed by the Hussar Brigade had reached Crésour, near St. Quentin, and the following day the Tenth advanced to Mattiquies, in the valley of the Somme, having its outlying piquets on that river. Vivian had on this day sent forward Lieutenant Slayter Smith, of the 10th Hussars, as far as Nesle, with directions to proceed if practicable to Roge, and gain information concerning the movements of the French army. Lieutenant Smith, having reached the latter place, ascertained that the French troops had left the town the night before, and that a body of gendarmerie had marched out at one end of the town whilst he and his party had entered by another. On returning from Nesle, he had proceeded but a short distance when he perceived a carriage moving rapidly and coming from a cross road. He ordered the driver to halt, and found in the carriage a military looking man, who, after some evasive answers to his questions, acknowledged himself to be General Lauriston, aide-de-camp to Napoleon, and stated that he was going in the first instance to his country seat at Vaux, near Le Cateau, and then to join the King, Louis XVIII. He added that he had gone to Paris to raise an army for His Majesty, that he had not only failed in the attempt but had narrowly escaped being arrested. Having given this explanation, he entreated Lieutenant Smith to allow him to continue his route, but the latter, considering it his duty to make him a prisoner, took him that night to Sir Hussey Vivian, who then desired Lieutenant Smith to proceed with the general to the Duke of Wellington. On reaching His Grace's quarters at one o'clock in the morning, and intimating his errand, a curious incident occurred. There was no guard at the house, not even a sentry, and Smith had some difficulty in rousing a sleepy servant from among his fellows to announce him. The Duke was engaged in conversation with a Frenchman. On a table in the room appeared the *débris* of a repast. Having explained to the Duke the name and rank of the individual he had brought with him, His Grace said " Bring him in." On hearing the name of Lauriston, the Frenchman before mentioned, who had been sent to the Duke by Fouché to treat for a cessation of hostilities, became greatly alarmed, and begged to know how he might escape without being recognised. His Grace remarked, " There is but one door and one window, take your choice." He preferred the door, and escaped by passing behind the Duke's back as Lauriston entered.

An animated conversation ensued between the two generals, and an hour had elapsed in this way, when the Duke gave his orders to Lieutenant Smith for the disposal of the general, whom he subsequently sent to the King, much to his annoyance, since he was thus obliged to appear before His Majesty as a prisoner instead of a volunteer. On the 28th June the advanced guard was at Auteuil, and on the 30th the Tenth reached Vanderlen. The Prussian army crossed the Seine, and established itself at Issy on the 2nd July, while the British were formed on the left bank of the river, and the capital thus became invested.[1]

Paris capitulated on the 4th July, and on the 7th the allied armies entered the city. Napoleon had fled to Rochefort, the wreck of his army had retired beyond the Loire ; no list of killed and wounded had appeared, and the official journal of Paris had made out that the great imperial army at Waterloo had gained a great victory. No one knew whether they had lost relations and friends in the battle.

During the occupation the 10th Hussars were quartered at Puteaux and Neuilly-sur-Seine. On the 16th a draft of the regiment joined from England, consisting of Captain V. Jones, Lieutenant Meynell, Cornet Gale, Assistant-Surgeon Rogers, Regimental Sergeant-Major Wells, two corporals, fifty-five privates, and seventy-nine horses, and two days later Major the Hon. H. C. Lowther, two privates, and two troop horses also joined. Every third day the regiment went on duty in Paris during their stay at Puteaux.

On the 24th the Tenth was present at a grand review held at St. Denis before the allied sovereigns

---

[1] " With such expedition was the pursuit conducted that ten days after the Allies fought at Waterloo they were grouped round the walls of Paris." —Alison.

and other distinguished foreigners assembled at Paris.[1] " At an early hour on a fine summer morning there were seen issuing from the various roads which centre on the plains of St. Denis numerous English, Russian, Prussian and Austrian regiments of horse and foot, in heavy marching order, with their bands playing, and finally a mass of men, numbering not less than 200,000, took up their positions. About twelve o'clock the Duke of Wellington, commander-in-chief of the allied army, approached. Immediately behind, the Emperors of Austria and Russia, the Kings of Prussia, Holland, Bavaria, and Wurtemberg, several German princes and general officers, forming one of the most illustrious, numerous staffs ever brought together. The review lasted two hours; then the men marched home to their quarters through a crowd of spectators which included the whole population of Paris. The most mournful silence was observed throughout on the part of the French." [2]

The Foot Guards were encamped in the Bois de Boulogne, the Highlanders in the Champs-Elysées. In those days the former place was a wild pathless wood, swampy, and entirely neglected; the latter contained only a few scattered houses, and the roads and pathways were ankle-deep in mud. The only attempt at lighting was the suspension of a few lamps on cords which crossed the roads. The Boulevards had handsome houses, isolated, with gardens interspersed, and the roads were bordered on both sides with stately spreading trees, some of them probably one hundred years old. There was but an imperfect pavement, and the road showed nothing but mother earth, in the middle

[1] " The British army before this had been greatly strengthened by the arrival of troops from Canada, mostly Peninsular veterans, and by the recovery of a large part of the wounded from Waterloo, and it now mustered 60,000."—Alison.

[2] Captain Gronow.

of which a dirty gutter served to carry the impurities of the city to the river. The people in the streets appeared sulky and stupefied. The theatres all this time, as may easily be imagined, were not well attended; in fact, all the best places in the house were empty.

Louis XVIII. arrived on the 26th July, and, as he was escorted by the Garde du Corps, was received with the wildest joy and cries of " Vive le Roi!" After the restoration of the Bourbons, thousands of English flocked to Paris, and our countrymen and countrywomen, having been so long excluded from French *modes*, had adopted fashions of their own, and were easily recognisable in the streets. The dress of the British military, in its stiff formal ugliness, was equally peculiar. An order had been given to the managers of all the theatres to admit a certain number of soldiers of the Army of Occupation free of expense. One play, entitled " Les Anglaises pour Rire," gave offence to the English soldiers, and on one occasion a sergeant and his men charged the stage, and on the gendarmes interfering were driven out of the theatre. The English soldiers walked about Paris in parties of a dozen, and were quiet and well-behaved. They usually gathered every day on the Boulevard du Temple. Stage coaches and four-in-hand teams were introduced into Paris in 1815 by Captain Bacon, of the 10th Hussars (afterwards a general in the Portuguese service), Sir Charles Smith, and Arnold of the Tenth. They used to meet opposite Demidoff's house, afterwards the Café de Paris, and drive to the Boulevard Beaumarchais, and then back again, proceeding to the then unfinished Arc de Triomphe. Races were also established in the neighbourhood of Vincennes. All the officers of our several cavalry and infantry regiments contributed their efforts to make these races a success.

At this time England was represented by Sir Charles

Stuart, one of the most popular ambassadors ever sent to Paris. The British Embassy was a centre where all English gentlemen collected, and dinners, balls, and receptions were given throughout the season. The presence of the Allies no doubt was irritating to the French soldiers, and many mutual insults took place, and duels were of daily occurrence, not only between the various nationalities but between the French officers themselves, those of Napoleon's army and the Bourbon officers of the Garde du Corps.

On the 30th the Hussar Brigade marched to Beauvais. At this place the officers appear to have obtained comfortable quarters, and they established an excellent mess, through the good management of Captain Valentine Jones, who made a requisition on the Préfet, and was abundantly supplied with plate, linen, &c.[1]

A curious duel took place at Beauvais between a Captain B——, of one of our cavalry regiments quartered in that town, and a French officer. The Frenchman would not fight with pistols, B—— would not fight with swords; so at last it was agreed that they should fight on horseback with lances. The duel took place in the neighbourhood of Beauvais. B—— received three wounds, but eventually killed his man.[2] After passing the whole of August and part of September at Beauvais, the regiment moved to Poix, and afterwards to Grandvilliers, Abbeville, Pont de Remys, and Boulogne, at each of which places it remained some time. On the 27th October the 10th Hussars, 16th Light Dragoons, and 23rd Light Dragoons received orders of readiness to march for embarkation for England. Before leaving Boulogne these regiments transferred horses to those remaining in France, so as to complete their establishments to 420 horses each.

---

[1] Dr. Jenks's *Diary*.　　　[2] Captain Gronow's *Reminiscences*.

A treaty of peace was concluded in November 1815 between France and the allied powers, by which the frontier of France was restored as it stood in 1790. 28,000,000*l*. was to be paid to the Allies for the expenses of the war, and it was stipulated that an army of 120,000 men, composed of 30,000 each from England, Russia, Austria, and Prussia, was to occupy for not less than three years the frontier fortresses, to be maintained by the French Government. Large indemnities were also paid to each power, that received by England being 5,000,000*l*., but this she surrendered to the King of the Netherlands.[1]

In January 1816 the regiment, with 448 rank and 1816 file, marched to Calais for embarkation. On the departure of the Tenth from Boulogne the civil authorities presented the commanding officer with an address, complimenting the regiment on the good conduct of the men during its stay there : [2]—

Boulogne : le 2 Janvier, 1816.

Le Sous-Préfet du 1er arrondissement du Dépt. du Pas-de-Calais certifie que pendant le séjour de plus de trois semaines que vient de faire à Boulogne le Dixième régiment de Hussards de l'armée de S.M. Britannique il n'a pas donné lieu à la plus légère plainte. L'exacte discipline que le corps a constamment observée est digne de tout éloge, et lui a attiré l'estime des habitans de cette ville.

Fait à Boulogne le jour, mois, et an que dessus.

Le Sous-Préfet,   ED. HERMAN.

The first transport, the " Resolution," sailed from Calais on the 4th January with the head-quarters of the regiment, and had not proceeded far when she encountered a severe storm. She was caught in such a furious gale that she took two days and two nights

---

[1] Alison.
[2] The original of this letter is in the Orderly Room of the regiment.

in crossing the Channel, and narrowly escaped being wrecked upon the Goodwin Sands. The whole of the horses she carried, thirty-seven in number, were washed overboard. The remainder of the regiment, following a few days later, made a good passage. The several detachments landed at Dover and Ramsgate, and marched from there to Brighton on the 11th.

Soon after its arrival a reduction of two troops of the regiment took place; the establishment of each troop being—one captain, two lieutenants, two cornets, four sergeants, four corporals, one trumpeter, one farrier, two boys, seventy-one privates, seventy-two horses.

CHAPTER XXI

BIOGRAPHIES OF OFFICERS WHO SERVED IN THE REGIMENT DURING
THE PENINSULAR AND WATERLOO CAMPAIGNS

As a sequel to the description of the campaigns in the Peninsula and Waterloo, a few sketches of the careers of the most prominent members of the 10th Hussars who took part in these wars are here introduced.

General Sir John Slade, Bart., G.C.H., entered the service on the 10th May, 1780, as a cornet in the 10th Dragoons, and became second lieutenant-colonel in that regiment on the 29th April, 1795. On the 18th October, 1798, he exchanged into the Royal Dragoons, obtained the command, and continued in it till May 1803, when he was placed upon the Staff as a brigadier. In the month of May 1806 he was removed from the Staff of England to that of Ireland, and was appointed to the command of the cavalry in Dublin. This he held till the 14th August, 1808, when he was appointed to a brigade of infantry ordered on foreign service, consisting of the 3rd battalion of the Royals, 2nd battalion of the 23rd, and the 2nd battalion of the 81st, and embarked at Cork in the following September, under the command of Lieutenant-General Sir David Baird. The transports put into Falmouth, when orders met the Brigadier-General to repair to Portsmouth, and to take the command of the 7th, 10th, and 15th regiments of Hussars. It was here that the Prince of Wales took the

1780-
1859

N

sabre which he wore from his side and gave it to the brigadier, with his hussar jacket and pelisse. On the 8th November he landed at Corunna. The Brigadier-General continued in command of the Hussar Brigade until the army re-embarked, when he acted as a volunteer at the short but sharp affair of Corunna, where he was in conversation with Sir David Baird at the time that officer received the wound which made it necessary to amputate his left arm. Sir John Hope, in his official letter giving an account of the action, dated H.M.S. "Audacious," off Corunna, 16th January, 1809, writes thus: "I was indebted to Brigadier-General Slade during the action for a zealous offer of his personal services, although the cavalry was embarked." On the 25th February the Brigadier-General was again placed on the Irish Staff, and remained in Ireland till the 17th August following, when he was placed once more upon the Staff in Spain. He was appointed to the command of a brigade of cavalry, consisting of the Royals and 14th regiment of Light Dragoons. During Massena's retreat from before the lines of Lisbon the Brigadier-General, in consequence of Sir Stapleton Cotton being in England, commanded the cavalry. At the affair of Fuentes d'Onore the Brigadier-General had his horse shot under him, and was obliged to ride a troop horse during the remainder of the day. At this time the French General Montbrun advanced from Ciudad Rodrigo with 4,000 men, and drove back the Light Division, under the command of General Crawford. Brigadier-General Slade had only from 300 to 400 men to oppose them, and for the gallant manner in which he performed this duty he was mentioned in the despatches of Sir Brent Spencer. In June 1813, in consequence of Major-General Clinton being given the local rank of lieutenant-general in Spain, and General Slade being

senior to that officer, he was ordered home. The Major-
General was again placed upon the Staff in Ireland,
where he remained till the 24th June, 1814, when he
was promoted to the rank of lieutenant-general. On the
20th July, 1831, Lieutenant-General Slade was appointed
to the colonelcy of the 5th Dragoon Guards, and in the
September following His Majesty King William was graciously pleased to create him a baronet in reward for
his services in the Peninsula, and shortly after made
him a Knight Grand Cross of the Royal Hanoverian
Guelphic Order. He was appointed Equerry to H.R.H.
the Duke of Cumberland in the year 1779 on the formation of His Royal Highness's household. He was
honoured three times with the thanks of Parliament.
He received the gold medal and clasp for Corunna and
Fuentes d'Onore, the silver medal and two clasps for
Sahagun and Busaco. Sir John Slade died at Monty's
Court on the 13th August, 1859, aged ninety-seven, and
was buried at Norton Fitzwarren, near Taunton.

1780-
1859

Lieutenant-General Sir George Quentin, K.C.B., received his first appointment in the 10th Light Dragoons
as cornet on 25th February, 1793. He was afterwards
appointed Ridingmaster, an office which he discharged
much to the satisfaction of H.R.H. the Prince Regent,
with whom he was a great favourite. He served as major of
the Tenth during the campaign in the Peninsula, 1808–9,
and was present at the action of Benevente, for which
he afterwards received the silver medal with one clasp.
He commanded the regiment in the Peninsular campaign
from 25th July, 1813, until the end of the war in 1814,
and was awarded the gold medal and clasp for the
battles of Orthez and Toulouse. He served also in the
campaign of 1815, and commanded the regiment at
Waterloo until severely wounded. He received the
Waterloo medal, the Companion of the Bath, and was

1793 -
1851

N 2

1793–
1851
afterwards made a K.C.B. He was appointed A.D.C. to the Prince Regent in 1811, promoted major-general in 1825, and lieutenant-general in 1838. He was well known as an admirable horseman, and for his remarkably upright figure. He died in 1851, upwards of eighty years of age.

1787–
1842
Colonel John Grey, who was born at Buckworth, in Northumberland, in December 1787, joined the 3rd Light Dragoons as cornet in 1805. After serving abroad for some years he was brought into the 10th Hussars as captain in November 1814. He proceeded with his regiment to Belgium in 1815, and after the battle of Quatre Bras was employed on outpost duty, and has received the credit of being the first to discover and report the retreat of the Prussians from Ligny. He was present at the battle of Waterloo, and there wounded, but rejoined the regiment and served during the occupation of France by the Allies. He received the Waterloo medal. In 1821 he was promoted to a majority in the Scots Greys, which regiment four years later he commanded. He sold out in 1839, and died 21st December, 1842.

1796–
1851
Major-General Charles Palmer joined the 10th Light Dragoons as cornet on the 17th May, 1796; was promoted, after three years' service as a subaltern, to the rank of captain, and became major in 1805. He served with the Tenth during the Peninsular war, and was promoted lieutenant-colonel in 1810. He was appointed A.D.C. to the Prince Regent in 1811. He proceeded to Spain in command of the regiment in 1813, and remained in that position until the return of Colonel Quentin. He took a most distinguished part during the advance of the army through the Pyrenees and in the battles in the South of France, and earned the name of a most forward cavalry officer. After the peace in

1814 he retired on half-pay, was promoted colonel, and on the 27th May, 1825, became a major-general. After this he sold his commission and retired from the army, and sat in Parliament for some years. He died on the 17th April, 1851. 1796--
1851

In 1798 Lord Robert Manners entered the army as cornet in the 10th Light Dragoons, at the age of seventeen. In 1808 he proceeded with his regiment to Portugal as a captain, and took part in the campaign under Sir John Moore, and was present with it in the affair at Benevente. He was employed on the Staff in the Walcheren expedition in 1809, and was present at the siege of Flushing. In this campaign he acted as A.D.C. to Lieutenant-General the Earl of Chatham, commanding the forces. He became major in 1810; the following year was promoted to a lieutenant-colonelcy in the 2nd Foot, and commanded that regiment at the battle of Fuentes d'Onore. On the 2nd July, 1812, he was placed in command of the 23rd Light Dragoons, but on that regiment being disbanded after the peace in 1814, he was brought back to his old regiment, the 10th Hussars, as lieutenant-colonel and second in command. He was present at the battle of Waterloo, and on the commanding officer, Colonel Quentin, being wounded early in the day, he took the command, and led the regiment in the decisive charge at the close of the battle. For this he received the Companion of the Bath and the Waterloo medal. Lord Robert himself received a slight bayonet wound on the day of Waterloo, but no official record was made of it, and he did not bring it to notice. In 1819 Lord Robert retired on half-pay, was promoted colonel in 1821, major-general in 1830, and this closed his military career. He sat in Parliament as member for Leicestershire from 1806 to 1835. He was a fine horseman and 1798--
1835

1798–
1835

an excellent sportsman. There is an admirable portrait of Lord Robert on horseback in hunting-dress, painted by Fernsley, at Belvoir Castle. An engraving of this picture is also in the possession of the officers of the 10th Hussars, and is hung in the ante-room of their mess. He is galloping with the heel well down, the stirrup touching the ball of the foot, the figure upright, the right hand holding the hunting-whip, in which is set an eyeglass, to his eye. An old brother officer describes him " as distinguished for his courtesy and geniality in the camp as for his gallantry in the field. He was regarded as an excellent specimen of a commanding officer. In private life he was a high-minded man, a faithful friend, an agreeable companion, and a thorough sportsman." He died on the 15th November, 1835.

1798–
1855

Lord Charles Manners joined the 10th Light Dragoons on the 7th February, 1798, and served with it until he became major in 1808. He was present with his regiment during the campaign under Sir John Moore, and received the silver medal with clasp for Benevente. He was employed in the Walcheren expedition in 1809. He was Aide-de-Camp to the Duke of Wellington from 1811 until the army entered Madrid in 1812. He was then placed in command of the 3rd Light Dragoons, and remained present with that regiment till the war closed in 1814. During this last campaign Lord Charles was nearly taken prisoner, having entered the French lines by error, and approached the enemy's piquets too closely. On being pursued he put his mare at a wide stream, and being mounted on a hunter he had received only a few days before from England, and knowing her jumping qualities, he knew he might safely trust her to carry him safely over. On landing on the other side he took off his cap and said, " Adieu, Messieurs," and rode to his

own lines. He heard the clicking of the French carbines, and the commanding officer's voice calling out,
" Non, ne tirez pas." He met with an accident in this
campaign, causing a wound which, perhaps, cannot be
better described than by giving a copy of a letter from
the Duke of Wellington to his mother the Duchess of
Rutland, now in the possession of the Duke of Rutland
at Belvoir Castle. This letter shows also the thoughtful
kindness of the great Duke :—

I don't know whether Lord Charles will be able to write
to you by this occasion, notwithstanding that he is quite well,
in consequence of a little accident he met with yesterday. We
were pursuing the enemy after the action of the 22nd, and,
having by accident lost his sword on the preceding night, he
was taking one from a Frenchman who was a prisoner ; while
in this act a dragoon of the 11th, believing that he was a
Frenchman, cut him over the shoulder and gave him a slight
wound. He is, however, quite well, and has been constantly
with me since that time, and, indeed, would not know that he
was wounded if it was not necessary to keep his arm in a sling.
I have the honour to be your Grace's
Most obedient and faithful humble servant,
(Sd.)   WELLINGTON.

He received the gold medal and three clasps for Salamanca, Vittoria, and Toulouse. He was not present at
Waterloo, but, in command of his regiment, joined the
army at Paris, and remained there during the occupation. He was appointed Aide-de-Camp to the Prince
Regent in 1817. He was promoted major-general in
1825, was created a K.C.B., became lieutenant-general
in 1838, and general in 1854. Lord Charles sat in
Parliament for some years as member for Cambridge-
shire, until the Reform Bill, when he was defeated. His
constituents presented him with a magnificent silver
gilt candelabrum, which is now an heirloom at Belvoir

1798–
1855

Castle. He succeeded his brother Robert in 1835 as member for Leicestershire, and held his seat till 1852. He died on the 25th May, 1855.

1803–
1829

Lieutenant-Colonel George James Robarts, C.B., was appointed cornet in the 23rd Light Dragoons on the 8th December, 1803. He joined Hompesch's Mounted Rifles on the 19th October, 1804, and the next month was transferred as a captain to the 10th Light Dragoons. He was employed as a Deputy-Assistant Adjutant-General with the army under Sir John Moore in 1808–9, and was present at all the actions of that campaign and at the battle of Corunna. In 1811 he was promoted major, and proceeded to Spain with the regiment in 1813, and was in command at the affair at Morales del Toro on the 2nd June. For this he was promoted lieutenant-colonel. He was present at Vittoria in command of the Tenth, for which he received the gold medal and became a Companion of the Bath. He was present at several actions in the Pyrenees. Lieutenant-Colonel Robarts retired on half-pay in 1814. He sat in Parliament for some years, and died in 1829.

1814–
1815

Major the Hon. Frederick Howard served in the campaign in the South of France in 1814, and was present with the 10th Hussars at the battles of Orthez and Toulouse. He accompanied his regiment to Belgium in 1815, and was killed at Waterloo at the head of his squadron when charging a square of the French Imperial Guard. He was buried at the time on the field, but afterwards his body was conveyed to England and finally laid at his own home, Castle Howard, in Yorkshire. His memory has been perpetuated in verse by his kinsman, Lord Byron.[1]

1815–
1839

Colonel Robert Arnold was brought into the Tenth as a lieutenant from the 16th Light Dragoons. He

[1] *Vide ante*, page 161.

had seen much active service in the Peninsula, was wounded at the storming of Badajos with the grenadiers of the 4th Regiment, and was afterwards at the battle of Vittoria with the 16th Dragoons. He accompanied the 10th Hussars to Belgium, and at Waterloo took part with Major Howard's squadron in the charge on the Imperial Guard. He received a musket ball through the lungs as well as a gun-shot wound in the fore-arm. He was promoted to be captain in 1818 and to the majority of the Tenth in 1825. He was appointed to the command of his original regiment, the 16th Lancers, in 1826, and proceeded to India. In 1838 he commanded a brigade of cavalry which formed part of the force that proceeded to Afghanistan under Sir John Keane, and was present at the capture of Ghuznee and the occupation of Cabul. He died on the 20th August, 1839, at Cabul, and was buried in the Armenian burial-ground at that place.

Major-General Taylor, C.B., entered the army in 1804, receiving a commission in the Carabiniers. In 1805 he went to the Mediterranean as D.A.A.G. under Sir James Craig. In 1807 he received the appointment of Military Secretary to the Governor-General of India (Lord Minto), and remained in that country for seven years. During this period—in 1812 —he took part in the expedition to Java as A.D.C. to General Gillespie. In 1814 he returned to England, and shortly afterwards was appointed to a troop in the 10th Hussars, went with them to Flanders, and took part in the Waterloo campaign. He was on piquet on the morning of the 18th June, 1815, with his squadron on the extreme left of the allied army, and it was to him that a Prussian staff officer, patrolling, brought the report of the advance of Blücher. This important intelligence Captain Taylor conveyed himself with the

1815– 1839

1804– 1854

1804–
1854

greatest despatch to the Duke of Wellington. At the close of the battle his squadron was engaged in the pursuit subsequent to the repulse of the French Guard. By the death of Major Howard in the action he obtained the majority of the regiment and a brevet lieutenant-colonelcy. He went on half-pay in 1825, but the following year was appointed Commandant of the Cavalry Riding Establishment at St. John's Wood, which appointment he held until 1831. In 1833 he became Groom of the Bedchamber to His Majesty King William IV., and in 1837 was appointed Lieutenant-Governor of the Royal Military College, Sandhurst; in 1853, Colonel of the 17th Lancers. He received the silver medal and clasp for Java, the Waterloo medal, and Companion of the Bath. He died on the 8th January, 1854.

1806–
1860

General Sir Henry Wyndham, K.C.B., joined the army in 1806 as ensign in the 31st Regiment, but was transferred the following month to the Foot Guards. In 1808 Lieutenant Wyndham proceeded to Portugal, and was A.D.C. to the Duke of Wellington at the battles of Vimiera and Rorica. He was A.D.C. to Sir John Moore during the campaign of 1808–9, and brought home despatches after the battle of Corunna. He also escorted as prisoner to England the French General Lefèvre. He was promoted a captain into the 71st Regiment in June 1809, and in July was transferred to a troop in the 10th Hussars. Captain Wyndham was employed in the Peninsula during the campaign of 1811 in the Portuguese cavalry, and was present at the battle of Albuera. In 1813 he served with his regiment, and was present at the brilliant affair of Morales del Toro. At the battle of Vittoria and in the subsequent pursuit he took a prominent part with his squadron, as has been already mentioned.[1] He was also present with the

---

[1] See *ante*, p. 110.

10th Hussars throughout the battles of the Pyrenees, until promoted a major in the 60th Regiment. He became a lieutenant-colonel in " Dillon's " regiment on the 20th January, 1814, a captain and lieutenant-colonel in the Coldstream Guards in July of the same year. At the battle of Waterloo he took part with his regiment in the defence of Hougoumont. When the gates of that farm-house were forced by the French, he assisted in expelling them, and with three other of the Coldstreams closed the gates upon the enemy. He was severely wounded in the battle, and afterwards, when lying at Brussels, there was some intention of amputating his arm, but he would not allow this to be done without first consulting the doctor of his old regiment. Dr. Jenks, of the 10th Hussars, was sent for, who gave it as his opinion that the operation was not necessary, so it was not carried out, and the arm was saved. Sir Henry Wyndham never ceased to remember his debt of gratitude, and Dr. Jenks mentions in his diary that many years afterwards, when he was a candidate for surgeon to the Brighton Hospital, General Wyndham came a long journey on the Derby Day to record his vote for him. On the 11th July, 1816, Lieutenant-Colonel Wyndham was appointed to the command of the 19th Lancers, and this he held until the regiment was disbanded, and in 1821 went on half-pay. On the retirement of Sir George Quentin in 1824 he was selected for the command of the 10th Hussars. On the 27th May, 1825, he became a brevet colonel and aide-de-camp to the King. He commanded the cavalry in Portugal in the expedition in 1827 under Sir William Clinton. In 1833 he retired from the Tenth, and was placed on half-pay. He became a major-general in 1837, commanded the Dublin District from 1843 to 1846, promoted a lieutenant-general in November 1846,

1806–
1860　　appointed Colonel of the 11th Hussars on the 19th November, 1847, and promoted to general in 1854. He was
created a K.C.B., received the war medal with four
clasps—Rorica, Vimiera, Albuera, and Vittoria—also
the Waterloo medal and the Spanish medal for Albuera.
He died on the 2nd August, 1860.

1812　　Dr. Jenks became assistant-surgeon of the Tenth
Hussars in 1812. He embarked in 1814 with a squadron proceeding from the depôt at Brighton to join the
head-quarters, serving with the army in the Peninsula.
He accompanied this squadron in its march through the
Pyrenees and the South of France until at length the
regiment was reached a few days after the battle of
Orthez. He was present during the remaining actions
of the campaign and at the battle of Toulouse. After
the declaration of peace he marched with the Tenth
through France and embarked with it for England at
Boulogne. He was present with the regiment at the
battle of Waterloo, and owing to his excellent arrangements the wounded officers and men of the Tenth were
well housed and cared for in Brussels. Dr. Jenks, after
retiring from the service, lived at Bath until a ripe old
age, and to the last took the greatest interest in his
old regiment, and contributed largely by his notes to
these memoirs.

1808–
1845　　Colonel John Gurwood, C.B., entered the army as
ensign in the 52nd Foot on the 30th March, 1808. He
served in the Peninsula from that year until 1812. At
the attack on Ciudad Rodrigo in 1811 he received a
wound in the skull from a musket ball, from the effects
of which he suffered for the rest of his life. Having
taken the Governor of that place, General Banier,
prisoner, he was presented by the Duke of Wellington
with his sword. In July 1812 he was transferred to
the 9th Lancers as a captain. He served during the

remainder of the war in Spain as brigade major to the Household Cavalry. He was present at the battles of Vittoria, Nivelle, Nive, Orthez, and Toulouse. He was transferred to the 10th Hussars in 1814, and served with that regiment throughout the campaign of 1815, and was again severely wounded at the battle of Waterloo. He was promoted to a majority in 1817, lieutenant-colonel in 1827, and colonel in 1841. He was private secretary to the Duke of Wellington, and will always be remembered in connection with his great chief as the compiler of the Wellington Despatches. He died in 1845.

Lieutenant-Colonel Charles Wood was gazetted to the 52nd Light Infantry as ensign on the 16th March, 1809. He proceeded at once to Portugal and joined his regiment at Truxillo, as the army was falling back after the battle of Talavera. He served throughout the following campaign with the Light Division, was present at the battle of the Coa, and was wounded when carrying the King's colour of the 52nd at Busaco. He was present at the battle of Fuentes d'Onore. In 1811 he was A.D.C. to General Robert Craufurd, and was with him at his death at the storming of Ciudad Rodrigo. He was appointed Deputy-Assistant Adjutant-General at the head-quarters of the Duke of Wellington, and was present at the capture of Badajos, the battle of Salamanca, and the siege of Burgos. On the 17th September, 1812, he was promoted a captain in the 68th Foot. In 1813 Captain Wood accompanied Lord Stewart to Germany as A.D.C., and afterwards took part with the Prussians in the campaign against the French. He was present at the battles of Gross-Beeren, Donnewitz, Wittemberg, and Leipsic, when the French under Napoleon were totally defeated by the Allies. On this occasion, for his report on the evening of the

18th October that the French were retiring, and for
saving a Prussian general and his staff from being captured, he was decorated by the King of Prussia with
the military order of merit. After this victory he was
present at all the subsequent engagements in France,
and finally entered Paris with the Allies in 1814. In
July 1813 he had been posted to the 18th Hussars, but
he did not join them, and was transferred to the 10th
Hussars in November 1814. He proceeded with his
regiment to Belgium in 1815, and took part in the
Waterloo campaign. When in command of a piquet
on the 17th June, he was one of the first to discover
the retreat of the Prussians from Ligny, and he immediately reported this circumstance to the Duke of Wellington. He was severely wounded at the head of his
troop on the 18th at Waterloo. The following letter
was written by Lord Stewart (afterwards Marquis of
Londonderry) to Colonel Wood on this occasion :—

Hamburg: July 3, 1815.

It was only this minute from a letter from young Paget at
Brussels that I hear of our young hussar's[1] wound. Thank
Heaven he is doing well. I must envy his being winged on
such a day. I am sure now the danger is over you will glory
at it, and that his majority will be easy now. I am quite
miserable to be out of this and not with my own old friends.
I am painfully anxious about Harris,[2] who, I hear, is in great
danger. Dashwood was also wounded. Every one of my old
staff.   (Sd.)   STEWART.

After the peace he was appointed Brigade Major on
the Staff of the Northern District at Pontefract. Colonel
Charles Wood to the end of his life displayed an un-
abated interest in his old regiment. He made several
presents to the officers' mess, which are still much
valued. Amongst them are pictures of old officers and

---

[1] Charles Wood.   [2] Lost an arm and died.

uniforms, the Wellington Despatches, the Life of Ziethen, and other interesting books.   He died on the 13th December, 1877, at the age of eighty-seven.

1809–
1877

Captain William Slayter Smith entered the army as ensign on the 25th December, 1806.   He exchanged to the 13th Light Dragoons on the 12th February, 1810, and was transferred to the 10th Hussars, 12th November, 1814.   He served in the Peninsula from February, 1810 ; was present on the left of the position at Busaco, and was with his regiment while it was covering the retreat of the army through the lines of Lisbon.   He received a sabre cut in the head and a pistol shot through the body in the celebrated charge made by the 13th Light Dragoons at Campo Mayor, when two squadrons overthrew 880 French cavalry.   Lieutenant Slayter Smith returned home on account of his wounds and went out again in 1812, and was engaged in a variety of minor affairs.   On one occasion, whilst on piquet, he was left without support for forty-eight hours, but succeeded in keeping his position in presence of D'Erlon's Corps ; during this time he received a carbine shot wound and had his horse shot under him.   He returned to England in consequence of ill health, and joined the senior department of the Royal Military Academy in October 1813, where he remained till the Tenth went to Belgium in 1815.   Lieutenant S. Smith was present at the cavalry actions that took place as the army fell back from Quatre Bras on the 17th June, during which he was taken prisoner, but soon made his escape.   After Waterloo he commanded a small party of observation, and whilst so engaged he took General Lauriston prisoner and conveyed him, by desire of Sir Hussey Vivian, to the Duke of Wellington (see *ante*).   Lieutenant Smith after this was sent to the head-quarters of Blücher, making constant reports to Sir H. Vivian on

1806–
1865

1806–
1865

the movements of the Prussian army. Captain Slayter
Smith died at Ripon, in 1865, aged seventy-two, after a
long service as Adjutant of the Yorkshire Hussars.

Captain Ellis Hodgson served for many years in the
10th Hussars, and took part with it in the Waterloo
campaign. In 1820, when the regiment was quartered
in Scotland, he was employed in command of a detachment of his own regiment as well as some Yeomanry
against a large body of rioters. On this occasion he
was wounded,[1] and in recognition of his conduct he was
appointed to a troop in the 3rd Dragoons. He was
living at York in 1861–2, when his old regiment was
stationed there, and a cordial reception was accorded
to him on his coming to the barracks.

1814

Lieutenant Anthony Bacon commenced his service
in the 16th Light Dragoons, and was transferred to the
Tenth in 1814. He proceeded to Belgium with his
regiment in 1815, and was severely wounded at the
battle of Waterloo. In after years he took service with
the Portuguese Government, and held the rank of
lieutenant-general.

In addition to the above slight sketches of the
careers of officers of the Tenth who took part in the
Peninsular and Waterloo campaigns, many names might
be added. Some have already been mentioned in the
pages of this book ; of the services of others it has been
found impossible to obtain details. Amongst them the
following may be alluded to as having earned distinction
either in their military career or in civil life as members
of Parliament, country gentlemen, sportsmen, magistrates, and so forth :—Captains Lloyd, Harding, and
Stuart (afterwards Sir Simeon Stuart, Bart.), George
FitzClarence (afterwards the Earl of Munster), G. Smyth-
Windham, Page Turner (afterwards Sir Edward Page

[1] See p. 200.

Turner, Bart.), Giveen, Synge, Lord Arthur Hill (after-   1815
wards Lord Sandys), Fitzgerald, the Marquis of Worcester (afterwards Duke of Beaufort), H. Somerset
(afterwards General Sir Henry Somerset, Governor of
the Cape, &c.); G. Wombwell (afterwards Sir George
Wombwell, Bart.), Charles Wyndham, Horace Seymour,
Augustus Berkeley, T..H. Powell, Jackson, Richardson,
Green, Cornet Palliser, Lieutenant and Adjutant Wells.

CHAPTER XXII

THE TENTH AT BRIGHTON—REVIEW BY THE PRINCE REGENT—
REGIMENT REDUCED—GOLD LACE INTRODUCED—DEATH OF
GEORGE III.—THE PRINCE REGENT—LORD STEWART APPOINTED
COLONEL—LIEUTENANT HODGSON EMPLOYED IN AID OF THE
CIVIL POWER IN SCOTLAND—REVIEW BY KING GEORGE IV.

1816-
1817
AT this time smuggling was carried on extensively on the coasts of England, and troops had to be made use of in order to suppress it. It fell to the lot of the Tenth immediately on its return home, on account of being stationed at Brighton, to be engaged on this duty at various points from Chichester to Winchelsea. At first only one squadron was employed, but on the 13th February two more squadrons were sent out and stationed at Worthing, Hastings, and other suitable localities to assist in the prevention of the contraband trade.

On the 17th January, 1817, being still at Brighton, the Tenth Hussars was there reviewed by H.R.H. the Duke of York, in presence of the Grand Duke Nicholas (afterwards Emperor of Russia), Prince Esterhazy, and other distinguished personages. A fortnight later a squadron marched to Croydon Barracks to be in readiness for some disturbances expected in London, but on the 22nd February it returned to Brighton. On the 26th June two squadrons marched from Brighton to Brentford, and from there were moved on the 19th July to King Street Barracks, London, and performed the duties in London while the Life Guards were being reviewed. On the completion of that service they moved to Hounslow Barracks, and the head-quarters and the remaining two squadrons joined them from Brighton and the out-stations where detachments had been employed on coast duty. Three troops were stationed at Hampton Court, and an escort party at Kensington Barracks under Lieutenant Hodgson. On the 19th November the regiment, in review order, took part in the funeral procession of H.R.H. the Princess Charlotte. In December new pelisses, lace jackets, and shakos were received.

Towards the end of the year 1817, on the disbanding of the 23rd Light Dragoons, thirty-five men of that corps volunteered to the Tenth. Twenty-four men were therefore allowed to claim their discharge from the service by paying the bounty of a similar number of men from the 23rd, so that no expense fell upon the Government.

On the 26th May, 1818, H.R.H. the Prince Regent, accompanied by the Prince of Hesse-Homburg and other personages of high rank and distinction, reviewed the 10th Hussars on Hounslow Heath, and on the following day the regiment commenced its march by separate squadrons to Canterbury. On its arrival, one squadron was detached on coast duty to Deal, Hythe, and the neighbouring villages. On the 14th June the whole of the regiment was moved to Ramsgate, Margate, and Broadstairs, to be out of the way during the election of a member of Parliament for the city of Canterbury, returning to their former quarters as soon as that was over. This was in obedience to a constitutional rule prohibiting the military from participating in or even being present during electioneering proceedings. On the 11th September two squadrons marched to Bristol and Radipole Barracks, Weymouth, and ten days later were followed by the remainder. From these stations numerous detachments were employed on revenue duty in Hampshire and Dorset, while two troops were stationed at Brecon and Abergavenny, in Wales.

On the return of the Tenth Hussars from active service in 1816 a reduction in the number of troops had been made ; but on the 28th October, 1818, an order was received making a further decrease in the numbers of men, and the following became the establishment :—One colonel, one lieutenant-colonel, two majors, eight captains, eight lieutenants, eight cornets, one quartermaster, one paymaster, one adjutant, one surgeon, one assistant-surgeon, one veterinary surgeon, one regimental sergeant-major ; and one troop sergeant-major, two sergeants, three corporals, one trumpeter, one farrier, forty-two privates, and thirty-four horses per troop.

Having passed the winter in the South of England, the Tenth received orders to proceed to Scotland in the spring, and on the 10th May commenced the march. During a halt at Gloucester six troops were inspected by Major-General Sir Robert Bolton on the 20th May. From the 14th to 17th June the regiment was in quarters at Dalkeith, and by the 21st the several squadrons completed their march and occupied Piershill Barracks, Edinburgh. On the 26th it was inspected on Portobello Sands by Major-General Hope, commanding the forces in North Britain. Three troops proceeded to Perth, Cupar-Angus, and Forfar on the 30th June, and on the 11th August three more troops were sent to Glasgow on account of serious disturbances amongst the weavers of that city. In October another detachment, under Lieutenant Ellis Hodgson, was despatched to Paisley in aid of the civil power, and received the thanks of the Provost of that town for the manner in which the duty was performed.[1] During the winter constant moves of portions of the regiment were made between head-quarters and Perth, Falkirk, Hamilton, Glasgow, &c. ; but beyond these and the inspection by Major-General Sir Thomas Bradford, there is nothing of importance to record.

1819

In the year 1819 the " Army List " shows gold lace on the uniforms for the first time, and the dress of the 10th Hussars was as follows :—" A shako, larger in circumference at the top than at the bottom, made of red cloth with an upright feather or plume and gold lace. Pelisse blue, with black fur. Jacket blue, and cross loops and olivets in gold ; blue facings. Girdle, crimson and gold. Trousers, blue with double gold stripe." In 1820 the shakos were changed to blue, and the chain belt [2] now worn by the officers appeared for the first time. Leopard skins were also carried on the saddles of officers, and shell ornaments were introduced on the bridles, breast-plates, and cruppers, and, although they were part of the kit of an officer of hussars in 1812, they do not appear to have been brought into universal use until this time, but only worn on special occasions.

1820

In consequence of the death of His Majesty King George III., which took place at Windsor on the 29th January, 1820, and the accession of the Prince Regent to the throne as George IV., a vacancy in the command of the 10th Hussars as a matter of course ensued. The colonelcy had been now held by His Royal Highness for nearly four and twenty years. He had been placed

---

[1] Regimental records in orderly room.

[2] From this belt is supposed to originate one of the many familiar nicknames given to the regiment, " The Chainy Tenth." This has sometimes been confused with another sobriquet soon afterwards applied, " The China Tenth."

at the head of the 10th Hussars as commandant in
1793. He was appointed Colonel in July 1796, and
he continued in command throughout his regency,
making in all twenty-seven years' service with the
regiment. Thus from his earliest years the Prince
Regent had been associated with the Tenth, and he
never ceased to evince the warmest interest in its
welfare. His Royal Highness was succeeded as Colonel
of the regiment by Lieutenant-General Charles Vane,
Lord Stewart, G.C.B., afterwards Marquis of Londonderry. In the order conferring the appointment, dated
the 3rd February, 1820, it was directed that the title
of the regiment should continue to be "The 10th, or the
Prince of Wales's Own Royal Regiment of Hussars."

Lord Stewart was at this time His Majesty's repre-
sentative at the Court of Vienna, and he addressed a
letter to the commanding officer, the original of which
is now kept in the orderly room :—

Vienna : 25th February, 1820.

SIR,—I cannot resist requesting of you to convey to the
regiment under your command the very high sense I entertain
of the distinguished honour conferred upon me by being placed
at its head.

So signal a mark of the King's personal favour, as well as
professional approbation, is more highly prized by me than the
richest gift the Crown has to bestow. To find myself the successor of your illustrious Prince, and now beloved sovereign, in
the command of a corps which has enjoyed his special parental
care, and which has ever been as conspicuous for its distinguished
conduct in the field as famed for the name it bore, overpowers
me with sensations I am inadequate to describe.

I know full well that the loss sustained by the 10th Hussars
can never be repaired ; let me, however, entertain the hope that
my best recommendation to them, after the royal nomination,
will be found in my unwillingness to yield to any of them in

duty, devotion, and affection to the illustrious personage whose   1820
loss they deplore, and in my deep anxiety to preserve that
excellent *esprit de corps* which has been infused into the regiment by its royal commander.

Inadequate as I am to stand in the place of that royal and
dearly beloved commander, I hope you will allow me to unite in
the prayer that it may still be the united effort of the regiment
to be emulous beyond all other corps of his royal approbation
and protection, while we remain, like all others of the British
army, steadfast in our loyalty and obedience to the service of the
best of kings and the happiest of countries.

I have, &c.,

(Signed) VANE STEWART, Lieutenant-General,

Colonel 10th Hussars.

To the Officer Commanding the 10th Hussars.

The head-quarters remained at Edinburgh during
the winter of 1819–20, but, owing to continued disturbances in the neighbourhood of Glasgow, were
ordered to that place in the spring of 1820. At the
same time the squadron from Perth marched to
Stirling in consequence of some armed bands having
collected between that place and Kilsyth, and having
intercepted orderlies employed between those towns.
On the arrival of the squadron at Kilsyth on the
morning of the 5th April, after a forced march, Lieutenant Ellis Hodgson and nine men were at once
mounted on horses belonging to the Kilsyth troop
of Yeomanry, and, accompanied by Lieutenant David-
son and nine of the Yeomanry Cavalry, they made a
rapid march of about ten miles, and, meeting the
offenders, received their fire and, charging upon them,
cut down and made prisoners the whole band. For
the performance of this duty they were thanked in
orders by Major-General Sir Thomas Bradford, who
added :—

The General cannot but notice, as a circumstance highly creditable to the zeal of the Kilsyth troop, that the hussars were mounted for the occasion on horses lent them by the Yeomanry, in consequence of their own having made a forced march ; and he will take care that the owner of the horse upon which Lieutenant Hodgson rode, and which was killed, shall be indemnified for his loss.

(Sd.)   JAMES DOUGLAS, D.Q.M.G.

Lieutenant Hodgson received a pike wound through the hand, and Sergeant Saxelby two pike-wounds in the side. Lieutenant-Colonel Taylor, at this time temporarily in command, and the troops of the 10th Hussars at Glasgow, were also thanked by the Lord Provost and magistrates of that city for their zeal and moderation during the disturbances in the manufacturing districts of Scotland.

After spending twelve months of considerable activity in the North, orders to return to England were received. Leaving Edinburgh on the 1st of May, the Tenth reached Carlisle on the 9th, and thence proceeded to Peterborough and Stamford. On the 26th it marched from these two towns—three troops and head-quarters to Romford, two troops to Norwich, two troops to Ipswich, and one troop to Lynn. After two months at these stations the regiment again moved, now to Richmond and Twickenham, head-quarters being at the former place.

On the 4th August the 10th Hussars had the honour of being reviewed by His Majesty King George IV. on Hounslow Heath, and afterwards marched into quarters at Hampton Court and Kingston. On the 7th, head-quarters and five troops moved into Hounslow Barracks, and took over the royal escort duties, leaving three troops at Hampton Court. From the 17th August to the 13th November, during the investigation of the conduct of Queen Caroline by the House of Lords, piquets were furnished by the Tenth at the Riding House, Pimlico.

On the 28th October the regiment was inspected by Major-General Lord Edward Somerset (the Inspector-General of Cavalry). On the 28th November four troops marched to Knightsbridge for the purpose of assisting the police during the procession of the Queen to St. Paul's, returning to Hounslow on the 30th.

On the 11th May, 1821, the regiment was inspected by Lord Edward Somerset.

On the 16th July it moved from Hounslow to Pimlico, Chelsea, and Knightsbridge, and on the 19th was on duty at the coronation of His Majesty King George IV., returning on the following day to its previous quarters.

On the 23rd it marched in five divisions from Hounslow and Hampton Court to Brighton, Arundel, Eastbourne, and Hastings ; head-quarters and five troops being at Brighton. In August seventeen detachments were sent out and distributed among the villages along the Sussex coast to assist the revenue officers in the prevention of smuggling.

On the 25th an order was received reducing the establishment by two troops. In consequence of this reduction the two junior captains would have had to retire on half-pay. These were Cartwright and Hodgson, but the former was permitted to remain on the active list as another officer—Captain Grey—was voluntarily retiring at the same time. Captain Cartwright went on half-pay in 1822, and the following year was appointed to the 8th Hussars. In this regiment he obtained the rank of lieutenant-colonel, was promoted a colonel in 1851, major-general in 1857, lieutenant-general in 1863, and general in 1871. He served in the campaigns of 1813 and 1814, including the battles of the Pyrenees, Orthez, and Toulouse, in the 3rd Hussars, and received the silver medal with five clasps. He served in the campaign of 1815 with the 10th Hussars, and was present at the battle of Waterloo. He died on the 5th June, 1873.

On the 26th September Lieutenant-General Lord Stewart made his first inspection of the Tenth since his appointment as its colonel-in-chief, and a month later Lord Edward Somerset made his half-yearly inspection.

CHAPTER XXIII

CENTRE-PIECE PRESENTED BY KING GEORGE IV.—SILVER GILT
SOUP TUREENS—DRESS REGULATIONS—REGIMENT ORDERED TO
IRELAND FOR THE FIRST TIME—SIR GEORGE QUENTIN RETIRES
— LORD LONDONDERRY'S INSPECTION—DUEL

THE 10th Hussars remained with head-quarters at   1822
Brighton throughout the winter, 1821–22, and on the
13th May, 1822, marched to Richmond, Twickenham,
and Isleworth. On the 1st June the Household Brigade,
10th Hussars, the 14th Light Dragoons, 15th Hussars,
and three batteries of Horse Artillery, under General the
Earl of Cathcart, were reviewed on Hounslow Heath by
H.R.H. the Duke of York, Commander-in-Chief of the
Army. On the same day His Majesty was very graciously
pleased to present to the regiment a magnificent centre-
piece of silver gilt, " as a memorial of his favourable
sentiments towards the corps he had commanded from
the year 1793 till his accession to the throne in 1820."
The centre-piece consists of a large pedestal surrounded
by candelabra, with the following memorial inscription
engraved on one of its panels :—

THE GIFT OF
HIS MAJESTY
KING GEORGE IV.
TO THE
10TH OR PRINCE OF WALES'S
OWN ROYAL REGIMENT
WHICH HE COMMANDED
FROM THE YEAR 1793
UNTIL HIS ACCESSION
TO THE THRONE.

On another panel the most important recent engagements in which the regiment had taken part are inscribed, viz. :—

BENEVENTE.

CORUNNA.

MORALES DEL TORO.

VITTORIA.

ORTHEZ.

TOULOUSE.

WATERLOO.

While on the third panel is the Prince of Wales's plume. Each corner is adorned with an allegorical figure, the whole supporting a statuette of George IV. dressed as a Roman emperor. In honour of this occasion the Marquis of Londonderry, Colonel of the Tenth, gave a grand banquet at his residence in St. James's Square, which was attended by H.R.H. the Commander-in-Chief and many distinguished officers. Having, in the name and on behalf of His Majesty, presented this splendid gift to the 10th Hussars, he took the opportunity in commemoration of the event to supplement the royal present by giving on his own part to the regiment two large richly embossed silver-gilt soup tureens, which, with other gifts received before and since, form the service of gold plate now used by the officers' mess.

The first "Dress Regulations" brought out in their present form were published in 1822. By these it appears that the dress of the 10th Hussars was as follows :—

Jacket.—Blue, Prussian collar, full three inches deep. Five rows of buttons, richly trimmed with dead gold gimp, chain loops.

Pelisse.—Blue cloth, white fur collar.[1]

---

[1] The 10th Hussars is allowed to continue white fur, and the 15th Hussars to continue black fur.

Pantaloons.—Fine scarlet web.[1]

Boots.—Hessian, gold lace binding and tassels.

Cap and Feather.—According to established regimental patterns.

Cravat.—Black silk.

Sabre.—Curved, with Mameluke hilt, gilt crop; scabbard, fish skin.

Sash.—With crimson and gold barrels.

Pouch-belt.—Half-inch gold lace, scarlet cloth edging.

Trousers (full dress).—Scarlet cloth Cossacks, with regimental lace up the seams.[2]

Undress Trousers.—Blue-grey Cossacks.

Undress Boots.—Ankle.

On the 5th June the Tenth marched in two wings from Richmond to Bristol, *en route* for Ireland, where for the first time it was to be stationed.[3] Reaching Bristol on the 13th, it embarked in ten hired vessels and sailed for Waterford. Arriving on the 17th, it marched to the following stations : Head-quarters and two troops to Cahir, one troop to New Ross, one to Fethard, one to Carrick-on-Suir, and one to Clogheen. On the 16th October General Sir John Elley made his half-yearly inspection. In these quarters the regiment remained until the following spring without any note-

[1] The 7th Hussars is allowed to continue to wear blue pantaloons and trousers.

[2] The 7th and 10th Hussars wear gold, the 8th and 15th wear silver lace.

[3] Previous to the union of Great Britain and Ireland in 1800, troops on the British establishment were distinct from those on the establishment of Ireland. The pay of the former was voted by the English Parliament ; that of the latter by the Irish. Appointments, promotions, &c., in the army in Ireland were dealt with by the Commander-in-Chief in that country and not by the Horse Guards. There was a difference also in the establishments and pay of the regiments. The " Army List " of 1764 contains the half-pay granted to officers in the British and Irish establishments. Before 1800 certain regiments were never stationed in Ireland. It is for this reason that the Tenth had not served in that country previous to 1822.

worthy occurrence taking place beyond the ordinary routine of regimental duties. On the 9th March, 1823, an inspection was made by His Excellency Lieutenant-General Lord Combermere.

During this year Captains Gurwood, Valentine Jones, and E. F. Meynell retired. They were succeeded by Lieutenants W. C. Drummond, R. Burdett, and W. C. Hamilton. At the same time Lord Muncaster, Lord James FitzRoy, and T. Surman (promoted from the ranks), were gazetted as cornets.

On 28th April the route was received for the Tenth to march to Dublin, and a detachment to be sent to Newbridge. On the 10th May it arrived at these stations, the head-quarters being at the Portobello Barracks, Dublin. This was the first occasion on which the Tenth had been quartered in the capital of Ireland. To judge from contemporary prints and caricatures, as well as from the squibs and anecdotes of the time, its first stay in that popular garrison evoked much humorous comment, and the many good-natured hits and the several sobriquets which have been handed down originated then. It was now, no doubt, that the well-known saying " The Tenth don't dance " was first heard of, and became a popular sarcasm. The regiment for some years, while on home service, had been so constantly stationed either at Brighton or in the neighbourhood of London, that it got the credit, though no doubt quite undeservedly, of not appreciating any provincial society. The story is told that at a ball given by the Lord Mayor of Dublin to the garrison, the Tenth officers who attended, in order to escape introductions, declared that " the Tenth don't dance." As might be expected, this anecdote, which most probably had some very slight foundation in itself, soon became improved upon, and various editions and additions have since appeared. The nickname also of the "China Tenth" was apparently introduced in Dublin, as it was supposed the regiment was thought so precious that it required to be taken care of, in the same manner as valuable china, in being moved from one station to another.

On the 14th May the 10th Hussars was inspected by Major-General Sir Colquhoun Grant, and on the 21st June it was reviewed, with the 4th and 6th Dragoon Guards, in the Phœnix Park by the Lieutenant-General (Lord Combermere) Commanding the Forces.

On the 1st August 335 pistols were issued from the Pigeon House Fort, Dublin, to replace the same number found unserviceable. The regiment paraded in review order on the 8th August, and proceeded to Sir John Rogerson's Quay to escort the body of Major-General Sir Denis Pack, K.C.B., which had been brought over from England for interment at Kilkenny. The winter of 1823–24 was passed in Dublin.

In March 1824 Colonel Sir George Quentin retired from the command, and was succeeded by Lieutenant-

1824   Colonel Henry Wyndham, who was brought in from half-pay.[1]

In May 1824 the Marquis of Londonderry came over from England in order to see his regiment, and reviewed it in the Phœnix Park. A picture of this review is now in the Officers' Mess, representing Lord and Lady Londonderry, both in the uniform of the Tenth, the latter wearing a busby on her head, although

1824–   the regiment appears with shakos.[2] During this visit a
1825   matter of discipline connected with a young officer of the name of Battier was brought before Lord Londonderry for his decision, and, as he gave it against him, this officer considered himself aggrieved and sent a challenge to His Lordship. Lord Londonderry could with all honour, even in the days of duelling, have declined the challenge, but, waiving his rank and other objections, he went out, and, having received his adversary's fire, fired his own pistol in the air. Sir Henry Hardinge was Lord Londonderry's second in this affair. Very serious notice was taken of this duel by the Commander-in-Chief, a severe reprimand being sent to Lord Londonderry, and Cornet Battier was gazetted out of the service.[3]

On the 17th of July the Tenth left Dublin, and head-quarters were stationed at Ballinrobe, the out-quarters being at Athlone, Gort, and Loughrea. After remaining nearly three years in Ireland, it returned to England in the spring of 1825. Marching by Clonmel to Waterford, it embarked there in twelve vessels on the 27th April for Bristol, but owing to contrary winds it

[1] For biographical sketch, see p. 186.

[2] This picture was taken at the time by an artist in Dublin, from whom it was purchased in 1863 by Lieutenant (afterwards Colonel) Liddell, 10th Hussars.

[3] "The matter is referred to in a letter written by the Duke of Wellington to Lord Londonderry, April 19th, 1824."—*Wellington's Despatches*, vol. xiv.

was the 11th of May before all the squadrons arrived, having lost thirteen horses during the passage. The regiment was detained at Bristol two months, a detachment being employed at Stroud in quelling disturbances amongst the weavers.

On the 12th July it was inspected by Major-General Sir Hussey Vivian in marching order on Durdham Downs, and afterwards the books were examined at the Bush Inn, Bristol.[1] On the conclusion of the inspection the regiment was ordered to Exeter, and on the 29th July commenced its march. Head-quarters remained at this place until March the following year, sending a squadron to Devonport and Truro in aid of the revenue officers on the coast.

In March 1826 the regiment left the Western District, with orders to march to Norwich and Ipswich, but on its arrival at Sherborne, in Dorsetshire, received a fresh route to proceed to Nottingham and Northampton. In April three troops were employed in aid of the civil power at Manchester, in consequence of great disturbances in many parts of Lancashire, and in May the head-quarters also were sent to Bury to assist in this duty, returning again to Nottingham.

[1] *Regimental Digest of Services* in the Orderly Room.

P

CHAPTER XXIV

EXPEDITION TO PORTUGAL—BRIGHTON—REVIEW IN HYDE PARK—
DEATH OF GEORGE IV.—CHANGE OF DRESS

1826-
1827

AT this time the attention of the country was seriously drawn to the position of Portugal, which appeared to be threatened by the neighbouring country of Spain, and the English Government, having failed in arranging matters by negotiation, was compelled at last to intervene. On the 11th December, 1826, a message was presented to the House of Commons, stating that "His Majesty had received an earnest application from the Princess Regent of Portugal, claiming, in virtue of the ancient obligations of alliance and amity subsisting between Great Britain and Portugal, His Majesty's aid against a hostile aggression from Spain."[1] In consequence of this Mr. Canning announced, in a celebrated speech to the House of Commons, that troops would be immediately despatched from England. Accordingly, a force of 5,000 men was brought together to form this expedition, and placed under the command of Lieutenant-General Sir William Clinton. The 10th Hussars and 12th Lancers composed the Cavalry Brigade, commanded by Colonel Wyndham, of the Tenth.

In November the 10th Hussars had marched from Nottingham *en route* to St. Albans, but on the road their destination was altered, and they were sent to Oxford.

[1] Knight's *History of England.*

At this place the orders were received to prepare two squadrons for active service, and the third to be formed into a depôt. On these arrangements being completed, the service squadrons marched on the 23rd December to Portsmouth, and the depôt to Hounslow Barracks. The former embarked at Portsmouth on the 3rd January, 1827, and disembarked at Lisbon between the 11th and 19th of the same month, and, not for the first time, occupied Belem Barracks.

On the 29th January the English troops were reviewed on the Campo de Freiras before Her Royal Highness the Infanta of Portugal, and three days later the Cavalry Brigade advanced inland, and after a ten days' march arrived at Coimbra. After being inspected by Major-General Sir Edward Blakeney, the regiment was cantoned along the east bank of the Mondego River, occupying a distance of about six miles. On the approach of the British regiments the Spaniards withdrew, and declared a friendly disposition towards the Portuguese Government. The British troops, however, were kept in Portugal until the spring of the following year, and the cavalry were employed principally on escort and convoy duty. In April three troops of the regiment marched to Leira, then the head-quarters of the army, leaving one troop, under command of Captain Wallington, at Coimbra. In August a troop, under command of Captain the Hon. R. Watson, was despatched to Cintra for the purpose of escorting Her Royal Highness the Infanta Regent from that place to Belem.

The Infante Dom Miguel came back from England to Portugal in February 1828 in an English frigate, and the troops of the expeditionary force were paraded in review order to receive him on his arrival. This appears to have closed the services required of the English force in Portugal, and on the 11th March the

1828   Tenth embarked on board five transports, and arrived at Portsmouth on the 22nd and 23rd, and thence proceeded to Brighton to join the depôt. The squadron forming the depôt in England, after remaining a short time at Hounslow, had marched to Ipswich in January 1828, and after several other changes of quarters moved to Brighton in March to await the arrival of the service troops from Portugal. The regiment, being now assembled at Brighton, was inspected on the 7th May by Major-General Sir Hussey Vivian, and on the 11th of the same month the Marquis of Londonderry, as Colonel of the Tenth, held a review and complimented the regiment on its appearance on its return from foreign service.

The changes in the commissioned ranks this year were as follows :—Major Arnold, Captains Burdett and Harvey, Lieutenant Knox and Paymaster Wardell, left ; Captain Drummond was promoted ; Lieutenant and Adjutant Wells was appointed Paymaster, and Cornet Preston became Adjutant.

During the time the Tenth was stationed at Brighton a guard, consisting of one subaltern, one sergeant, and twenty-two privates, was mounted at the Royal Pavilion, the residence of the King. In August H.R.H. the Duke of Cambridge inspected the Tenth in watering order. After passing another year at Brighton, with one squadron at Chichester, the regiment proceeded to Hampton Court Barracks in May 1829, leaving a detachment under an officer as a guard to the Pavilion at Brighton. The Tenth had during the past few years been quartered frequently at Brighton, but, on leaving at this time, it was not to return for more than forty years. A memento of its occupation of the Preston Barracks in 1828–29 still remains in the Fives Court, shown by an inscription on a slab at the summit stating that the

building was erected by the officers, under the direction
of "Sergeant Stone, of the 10th Hussars."

On the 27th May the regiment took part in a grand review in Hyde Park of all the troops in and near London in honour of the Duke of Orleans, afterwards Louis Philippe, King of France, at which the Duke of Wellington and many other illustrious persons were present. On this occasion the Marquis of Londonderry assumed command of the Tenth, and afterwards entertained the Duke of Orleans and the other distinguished personages who had been present at a grand banquet at Holdernesse House. In June the head-quarters and four troops were moved from Hampton Court to Hounslow Barracks, and were stationed there during the following winter. In April 1830 the regiment marched into Yorkshire and Lancashire, the head-quarters being at Leeds.

On the 26th June His Majesty King George IV. died at Windsor Castle after a short illness. Although his connection with the 10th Hussars had ceased on his ascending the throne in 1820, the unremitting interest he always took in everything that concerned the regiment, losing no opportunity of associating himself with it, had endeared him to all ranks, and the announcement of his death was received with deep regret. The 10th Hussars paraded in review order, and was in attendance at the Market Place, Leeds, on the 3rd July, when the authorities there proclaimed the accession of King William IV.

On the 18th May, 1831, a general order was issued,
ordering the colour of the hussar pelisses to be scarlet instead of blue, and the fur to be changed from white to black; and in August of the same year another general order appeared affecting the dress of the cavalry, and ordering " the mustachios of the cavalry to be

abolished, except in the Life Guards, Royal Horse
Guards, and Hussars," and " the hair of the non-commissioned officers and soldiers to be cut close to the sides,
and at the back of the head, instead of being worn in
that bushy and unbecoming fashion adopted by some
regiments. The four regiments of hussars to be dressed
perfectly alike. Their officers to have one dress only,
and that of a less costly pattern, which will forthwith
be prepared." The latter part of this order does not
appear to have been acted upon. In March 1831 the
overalls of light cavalry were ordered to be blue in
place of grey.

In June 1831 the Tenth embarked at Liverpool for
Ireland, and, after occupying quarters in Dublin for
eleven months, was removed to Longford in the summer
of 1832, to Newbridge in 1833, and Dundalk in 1834.

On the 25th March, 1832, the regiment suffered a
great loss in the death of Mr. Sannerman, the veterinary surgeon, an officer who had served in it many
years, and was present at the battle of Waterloo.

Some changes amongst the officers at this time
took place. Captain the Hon. R. Watson retired from
the service, and was succeeded by Lieutenant Osborne.
On the 22nd of March, 1833, Lieutenant-Colonel Wyndham [1] retired from the regiment, which he had commanded from March 1824, and was succeeded by
Lieutenant-Colonel Gore, half-pay, 9th Lancers. This
officer sold out in the following April, when Major Lord
Thomas Cecil was appointed to the command.

---

[1] For biographical sketch see p. 186.

CHAPTER XXV

REDUCTION OF THE REGIMENT—IN IRELAND—DEATH OF KING
WILLIAM IV. — ESTABLISHMENT INCREASED — LORD THOMAS
CECIL — CORONATION OF HER MAJESTY QUEEN VICTORIA—
REVIEW BEFORE THE QUEEN—THE FIRST GRAND MILITARY
STEEPLECHASES — THE MARQUIS OF LONDONDERRY — MAJOR-
GENERAL THE HON. H. BEAUCHAMP LYGON APPOINTED COLONEL

DURING the time the head-quarters remained at New- 1833
bridge, in 1833, several troops were employed at out-
stations in aid of the civil power in those districts
which were proclaimed under the first Coercion Act.

In July of this year black sheepskins were issued
for the first time to the Tenth to be worn on the troop
saddles.

On the 14th August the head-quarters and two
squadrons marched to Dublin, remaining there a month.
While stationed there they took part, in brigade with
the 5th Dragoon Guards and the 14th Light Dragoons, in a review before Lieutenant-General Sir Hussey
Vivian, commanding the Forces in Ireland.

In January 1834 instructions were received reducing 1834
the number of rank and file of the 10th Hussars to 274.
In this year new blue jackets and scarlet pelisses were
issued, also new black shakos.[1] The following Dress
Regulations were issued in 1834 for the hussars :—

Jacket.—Entirely of blue cloth, richly trimmed with dead
gold gimp chain loops, extending the full width of jacket across
breast, and about three inches wide at bottom.

[1] *Regimental Digest of Services Book.*

Pelisse.—Scarlet cloth, braided similarly to jacket.

Waistcoat.—Scarlet, with half-ball buttons, and ornamented with gold cord.

Cap.—Black beaver, bell-shaped; crown six inches deep; black sunk glazed top, eleven inches in diameter; gold lace of two inches wide round the top; an inch-wide black leather binding round the bottom; black patent leather peak, edged with gold embroidery.

Plume.—Black cocktail, drooping sixteen inches in front, eight inches at back.

Trousers.—Blue cloth, with a stripe of gold lace, one inch and a half wide down the outward seam.

Boots.—Ankle.

Sash.—Gold and crimson barrelled; large acorn at the end of the cord.

HORSE FURNITURE.

DRESS.

Shabracque.—Of scarlet cloth, of a diagonal shape in the fore part, twenty-five inches and a half deep, embroidered with double cypher " W. R." and imperial crown.

UNDRESS.

Shabracque.—Of the spotted tiger-skin, round in front, sixteen inches and a half deep; square behind, fifteen inches deep, one yard six inches long.[1]

In March head-quarters and three troops were stationed at Dundalk, Captain Wood's troop on detachment at Belturbet, Captain Lord Fincastle's at Ballyshannon, Captain Ward's at Monaghan; one subaltern and twenty men being sent to Belfast. During the twelve months passed by the Tenth in the North of Ireland constant moves were made to various towns to assist the civil power at elections and during other disturbances.

In March 1835 the regiment sustained another

---

[1] The 15th Hussars has special permission to wear a scarlet cap instead of black beavers; also a red forage cap instead of blue.

severe loss in the death of Captain William Wood, who died while on a visit to Lord Enniskillen. This officer was one of three brothers—Thomas, William, and Robert—who served in the Tenth. He also had an uncle in the regiment, Charles Wood, who has already been mentioned as commanding a troop at Waterloo. One nephew, Edward A. Wood, joined twenty-three years later and commanded it, and another is at the present time (1890) senior major and second in command. Captain William Wood was known as a very fine horseman and a good draughtsman. Lieutenant and Adjutant Preston, who had been promoted from the ranks, and had served in the Peninsular War and at Waterloo, succeeded to the troop. Lieutenant Sir James Gardiner Baird was appointed Adjutant.

Many regiments in the service had introduced a "non-commissioned officers' medal,"[1] apparently subscribed for and bestowed by themselves on their comrades who had won their universal esteem throughout their service. Although there was no official sanction given for this custom, it was known and recognised, but its distribution was left entirely in the hands of the sergeants. The silver non-commissioned officer's medal had in the Tenth on the obverse side a mounted hussar surrounded by roses, thistles, and shamrocks, with date beneath. Reverse, "The Prince of Wales's Own" in an oval garter, enclosing his crest and motto; below, on a scroll, "The Royal Hussars," within a wreath. This medal was first issued when the regiment was in Dublin, about 1835, and was continued until 1860, when Regimental Sergeant-Major Hickman was the last recipient.[2]

[1] Some of these regimental medals may be seen in the United Service Institution.

[2] Extract from Captain Tancred's work, *Decorations of the British Army and Navy.*

1836

Between the 7th and 13th April the 10th Hussars marched in small detachments from its different stations to Belfast and embarked for Scotland. By the 19th, head-quarters and five troops were assembled at Glasgow Barracks; the sixth troop, Captain the Hon. Percy Moreton's, being sent on detachment to Hamilton. In January 1836 this latter troop was relieved by Captain Houston's troop, and in addition the troops of Captains Lyster Kaye and Rowley were sent to Hamilton, so that it was equally divided between Glasgow and Hamilton until May, when the whole regiment moved to England, head-quarters and three troops being stationed at York and three troops at

1837

Newcastle. On leaving these stations in May 1837 the head-quarters proceeded to Nottingham, sending detachments to Sheffield and Derby under Captain Quentin[1] and Captain Lyster Kaye.

On the 9th June the Tenth was inspected by Major-General Sir R. D. Jackson, commanding the district.

On the death of His Majesty King William IV. the regiment paraded on the 21st June to hear Her Majesty Queen Victoria proclaimed Queen. On the 6th August authority was received for the cypher " V. R." to be used on the accoutrements in the place of " W. R."

1838

In January 1838 an order was received increasing the establishment to 335 rank and file, and in April three horses were added to each troop, bringing up the total to 271.

On the 15th June, 1838, Colonel Lord Thomas Cecil retired upon half-pay and was succeeded by Colonel John Vandeleur, who had been some years on half-pay from the 12th Lancers. Lord Thomas Cecil, son of the tenth Earl and first Marquis of Exeter, at an early age entered the Royal Navy and served in it for four years. He then

---

[1] Son of Sir George Quentin, late commanding 10th Hussars.

obtained a commission in the army, and on the 24th 1838 October, 1816, was appointed as cornet in the 10th Hussars. In 1820 he was promoted to a lieutenancy, and in the following year became a captain, in 1827 major, and in April 1833 succeeded Colonel Wyndham in command. He took part in the expedition to Portugal in 1827, but beyond that the rest of his service was passed in the United Kingdom. Besides his excellent qualities, a good drill and a strict disciplinarian, he was a fine horseman, and a most forward rider in the hunting-field. He rode in the first Grand Military Steeplechases in Ireland when major of the regiment, and won the race, carrying the well-known Exeter colours. After twenty-two years' service in the Tenth, he retired on half-pay in June 1838, and sold out of the army in 1846, when he was made a full colonel. In the year he left the regiment he married Lady Sophia G. Lennox, youngest daughter of the fourth Duke of Richmond and of Charlotte his duchess, who gave the historical ball at Brussels the night before the battle of Quatre Bras. Lord Thomas was in Parliament as member for Stamford from 1808 till 1832, and his attendance there took him away from his regiment to a certain degree. He was opposed by Mr. Tennyson, the Radical candidate, at the election of 1831, and one day, during the contest, being offended at some remarks made by his opponent, called him out. They fought a duel at Wormwood Scrubs at 6 P.M. the same evening, but without any serious consequences.

" He always took warm interest in his old regiment in after years, and in the society of his late brother-officers, especially the Marquis of Winchester, Sir John Trollope (afterwards Lord Kesteven), Sir Robert Burdett, Sir Bellingham Graham, Sir James Baird, the Hon. Archibald Macdonald, the Hon. Richard Watson, Dr.

Jenks, and all the family of the Woods. The last occasion on which he saw the Tenth was at Brighton Barracks in 1870, when it was under the command of Colonel Valentine Baker, and the appearance and perfection of drill it had been brought to by that officer gave him the greatest satisfaction." [1]   He died in London on the 29th November, 1873.

In June the 10th Hussars marched to Hounslow and took up the duties of the royal escort on the 23rd of that month.

On the 25th it moved into quarters at Putney, Fulham, &c., and had the honour of being on duty at the coronation of Her Majesty Queen Victoria. On this occasion the regiment lined the streets from Waterloo Place through Pall Mall East and Charing Cross to Northumberland House, the regimental band being placed north of the Duke of York's Column. After the ceremony was over it returned to Hounslow.

On the 4th July the Tenth marched to Woolwich for a review, returning to Hounslow on the 6th. On the following day it moved temporarily to its former quarters at Putney, Fulham, &c., for the purpose of being present at a grand review held before Her Majesty in Hyde Park. The troops present on this occasion were the three regiments of Household Cavalry, the 10th Hussars, 12th Lancers, three troops of Horse Artillery, three batteries of Field Artillery, four battalions of Foot Guards, and two battalions of the Rifle Brigade, the whole commanded by General the Marquis of Anglesey.

On the 2nd August the Tenth furnished the detachments which escorted Her Majesty from London to Windsor. On the 18th September the regiment marched to Windsor and was present at a review before the Queen, returning to Hounslow the same day. In No-

[1] Letter from Lady Sophia Cecil.

vember escorts were found from Staines to Hampton
Court on Her Majesty proceeding from Windsor to
Brighton.

On the 9th November the band and ninety-eight men
took part in the Lord Mayor's procession.

Lieutenant and Adjutant Sir James Baird was pro-
moted to a troop, on which Troop Sergeant-Major G.
Webb, from the 12th Lancers, was appointed Cornet and
Adjutant. Cornets H. E. Surtees, John Wilkie, and
Lord G. Beauclerck joined.

In March 1839 thirty horses were received from the
15th Hussars on that regiment being ordered to India.
In April the head-quarters of the Tenth marched
from Hounslow to Dorchester, and the detachments
were sent to Exeter and Bradford. Several changes of
quarters were made during the summer; troops were
despatched in aid of the civil power to Frome, Clifton,
and other places, and the troop of Captain Sir James
Baird was employed in escorting Chartist prisoners
from Trowbridge to Devizes Gaol. During the following
winter fresh disturbances took place at Chepstow, Newport, and Cardiff, where other troops of the regiment
were sent to assist in restoring order. The most serious
of these riots was at Newport, for their connection with
which the Chartist leaders, Frost, Williams, and Jones,
were tried and transported. The military came into
collision with the mob, and many of the people were
shot. D troop of the Tenth, under Captain Lyster Kaye
and Lieutenant W. Cavendish (afterwards Lord Chesham), was employed at this place.

On the 10th February, 1840, the 10th Hussars
paraded with the rest of the troops at Dorchester, and
a *feu de joie* was fired in honour of the marriage of Her
Majesty Queen Victoria with Prince Albert of Saxe-
Coburg Gotha.

On the 14th March an order was received changing the colour of the pelisses from scarlet to blue.

On the 24th March the whole of the men of the Tenth at Dorchester were employed in extinguishing a very destructive fire at Fordington, and rendered such good service that they afterwards received a vote of thanks from the inhabitants.

In May the Tenth changed its quarters. It moved to Birmingham on the 14th of that month, remaining there until relieved by the Scots Greys three weeks later. The head-quarters then marched to Coventry, sending detachments to Northampton and Weedon. While stationed at Coventry the regiment had the misfortune to lose an excellent officer, Captain Rowley, who died in barracks of small-pox after a short illness.

In this year (1840) the Grand Military Steeplechase meeting was held for the first time in England, and its locality was selected in Northamptonshire. The Tenth, being quartered in the county, naturally took great interest in its success, and took a prominent part in its inauguration. Captain Sir James Baird, whose troop was stationed at Northampton, had the satisfaction of winning the first gold cup, riding his brown horse Carlow. Twenty horses started. This, however, was not the first time that an officer of the Tenth had won a military race. In 1832 the Irish Grand Military Steeplechase was won near Dublin by Lieutenant the Hon. H. Saville's mare Modesty, ridden by Major (afterwards Colonel) Lord Thomas Cecil.

In May 1841 the 10th Hussars, from its several stations in Northamptonshire, marched to Liverpool, and there embarked for Ireland. On arrival at Dublin it was quartered in Portobello Barracks, and on the 7th June was inspected by Lieutenant-General Sir E. Blakeney, commanding the Forces.

At this time O'Connell was at the height of his influence and popularity in his efforts to effect the repeal of the Union. The country was in consequence in a very unsettled state, and the services of the military were everywhere required. The several troops of the Tenth were dispersed in aid of the civil power to Belfast, Dundalk, and Newry. The election at Carlow, however, gave the Government the greatest anxiety, as the defeat of O'Connell by Colonel O'Brien by a few votes had caused intense excitement amongst the people. A squadron of the Tenth had been sent there from Dublin on the 8th June, and on arrival found already assembled four troops of the Carabiniers, under Colonel Jackson, a squadron of the 12th Lancers, a troop of Horse Artillery, and the 98th Regiment, under Lieutenant-Colonel Colin Campbell (afterwards Lord Clyde). On the conclusion of these duties the regiment was again assembled at Portobello Barracks.

On the 11th November the 10th Hussars took part in a review of all the troops in the Dublin garrison, when a *feu de joie* was fired in honour of the birth of His Royal Highness Albert Edward Prince of Wales.

On the 8th February, 1842, Captain S. Wells, paymaster of the Tenth, died at the age of sixty-one. He entered the army in 1798, was promoted sergeant in the Tenth in 1800, regimental sergeant-major in 1808; was acting-adjutant during the campaign of 1813 in the Peninsula, adjutant in 1816, and paymaster 1826, making a total service of forty-three years.[1] Sir James Baird, when riding this year (1842) in the Grand Military Steeplechases near Dublin, had the misfortune to meet with a bad accident. He shortly afterwards retired from the service. Cornets R. G. Townley, Francis Leigh, and Thos. Carlyon joined.

---

[1] *Regimental Digest of Services.*

1842　　On the 19th March 335 busbies were served out in place of the shako, which in various shapes had been the headdress of the Tenth and other hussar regiments since 1822.[1]

On the 18th June the Tenth paraded in review order, and took part in a field day in the Phœnix Park in commemoration of the battle of Waterloo. In August it marched to the South of Ireland. Head-quarters

were established at Ballincollig, and two troops at Cork, until April 1843. The regiment was then re-moved to Cahir in Tipperary, and during its stay at

[1]　　　　　　　　　　　"Horse Guards: 6th August, 1841.

"Sir,—By desire of the General Commanding-in-Chief, I have the honour to acquaint your Lordship that Her Majesty has been graciously pleased to approve of the 10th, or the Prince of Wales's Own Royal Regi-ment of Dragoons (Hussars), resuming the fur hussar cap formerly worn by that regiment.—I have, &c.

"(Signed) John Macdonald, A.G.

"General the Marquess of Londonderry, G.C.B.,
　　Colonel of the 10th Hussars."

this place the various troops were kept constantly 1843 moving in aid of the civil power until September 1844, when it again changed its head-quarters, and was stationed at Newbridge.

During this year Captains Robert Blücher Wood and A. Wellesley Williams left the 10th Hussars. The former officer went on half-pay, and was soon after appointed military secretary to Lord Hardinge, Governor-General of India. He afterwards commanded the 80th Regiment at the battle of Ferozeshah, where he was badly wounded, and received the C.B. After holding staff appointments at the Horse Guards and in Ireland and the commandantship at Maidstone, as a major-general he commanded at Colchester, and afterwards at Malta. Captain Cathcart also left the Tenth, and exchanged with Captain Broadley Harrison into the 11th Hussars. Cornets C. F. Surtees, Lord Garvagh, and E. Shelley were gazetted to the regiment.

In June 1843 the Marquis of Londonderry was transferred from the colonelcy of the 10th Hussars, which he had commanded for twenty-three years, to that of the 2nd Life Guards.[1] His Lordship was born at

---

[1]
" 25th June, 1843.

"BROTHER HUSSARS,—There may be many among you to whom I am personally unknown, for Time who steals our years away steals our service also; still, none that I address can be ignorant of the eventful records of this distinguished corps. The connection of George Prince of Wales with the corps forms a bright page in its history, and if a Prince of Wales is again placed at your head, your glorious banner and plume of feathers and 'Ich Dien' will once more, under royal command, become the pride and glory of the Army; but for this object the *esprit de corps* which has ever animated you must never slumber—your deeds must be the same, your conduct as meritorious. Let the memory of the past lighten your hopes for the future, and let the actions on the plains of Castille and Estremadura, of the Esla, Benevente and Morales, and, above all, of glorious Waterloo, be ever before your eyes. It is now my painful duty to take leave of you. I cannot deny whatever distinction or honour awaits me. I leave you with sincere regret; for more than twenty years I have been at your head. Always a hussar since their first establishment in our

Q

Dublin in 1778, and at fourteen years of age entered the army as ensign in the 108th Foot, and in 1794 accompanied Lord Moira in his expedition to Holland. He served with the Austrian armies from 1795 to 1797, and was severely wounded at the battle of Donauwerk. After rising through the various grades of his profession, he joined Sir John Moore in the Peninsula in 1808 as brigadier-general, and took a distinguished part in covering the retreat of the British force on Corunna with the Hussar Brigade. He held the post of Adjutant-General of the army in Portugal, under Sir Arthur Wellesley, from 1809 to 1813. For his services in these campaigns he received the thanks of the House of Commons, and was created a Knight of the Bath and of various foreign orders. In 1813 he left the army in Spain and was sent as Ambassador to Berlin. During the summer of this year he acted as military commissioner to the armies of the allied sovereigns. In 1814 he was raised to the peerage with the title of Baron Stewart, was appointed Ambassador to Austria, and one of the plenipotentiaries at the Congress of Vienna in 1814–15. On the 3rd February, 1820, he was appointed Colonel of the 10th Hussars, on the accession of the Prince Regent to the throne as George IV. In 1822 he succeeded his brother in the Irish marquisate. In 1843 he

---

service, I have thought little of any other arm. A separation under such circumstances must be felt; but when I also recollect I was selected by the Prince Regent to succeed him in the command of the corps, I have ever thought it the prominent feature of my humble career. You will know before this reaches you that the Queen has been graciously pleased to confer upon me the high distinction of the Household Brigade by placing me in command of the 2nd Life Guards. Sensible of the high promotion, and grateful for this mark of favour, I now in dutiful obedience bid you farewell. My parting words have been dictated by that interest and affection I must ever feel for the 10th Royal Hussars, for whose military fame and welfare I shall ever offer up an earnest prayer.

"(Sd.) VANE LONDONDERRY."

was transferred to the colonelcy of the 2nd Life Guards. He died 1st March, 1854. Major-General the Hon. H. Beauchamp Lygon, afterwards Earl Beauchamp, was appointed Colonel of the 10th Hussars in succession to the Marquis of Londonderry.

After passing the winter at Newbridge, the head-quarters, with four troops and the troop that was detached at Athy, moved up to Dublin in the beginning of May 1845. The dismounted men, with one troop and the hospital, were left at Newbridge till the 29th May, when they too joined the Dublin garrison, and were divided between Island Bridge and the Portobello Barracks. After having been for about a month brigaded with the Royal Dragoons and the 8th Hussars at Dublin for the purpose of field manœuvres, the right wing of the regiment, with head-quarters, embarked at the North Wall on the 4th June to return to England, and landed at Liverpool at an early hour next morning. The steamer that conveyed this wing returned to Dublin for the remaining part of the regiment, and the whole corps had crossed over by the 8th. On arrival the Tenth was broken up into detachments, and these proceeded at once by route march to their respective destinations as follows :—Head-quarters, with C troop, commanded by Captain Bonham, and E troop, commanded by Captain Harrison, to York; B troop, under Captain Tolmin, and F troop, under Captain Lord George A. Beauclerck, to Newcastle; A troop, under Captain Quentin, to Leeds, and D troop, under Captain Wilkie, to Bradford.

Changes in officers' ranks in 1845 :—Left—Lieutenant Leigh, retired by sale of commission; Assistant-Surgeon Arthur Anderson, M.D., promoted in Rifle Brigade. Appointed—Lieutenant Charles Freville Surtees, by purchase; Assistant-Surgeon T. Fraser, M.D.

CHAPTER XXVI

1846   THE year now commenced may be said to have formed almost a new epoch in the annals of the regiment. Although it had enjoyed its full share of all the active service in which the English army had been engaged upon the continent of Europe from the time that it was raised, now for the first time it was to be called upon for a tour of service in a tropical climate. Early in the month of March 1846 it received orders, quite unexpectedly, to prepare for service in the East Indies. Up to this date no change had taken place in its distribution as it stood at the close of 1845, but now the squadron at Newcastle was brought in to head-quarters at York and the troop at Bradford was ordered to join that at Leeds, while further preparations for foreign service were at once commenced. All the troop horses were given over to other regiments or sold at York, with the exception of the number required to mount a depôt troop. The officers also parted with their chargers, and all was ready by the 2nd April. On that date the head-quarters and the four troops collected at York proceeded by rail to Canterbury, halting one night at Leeds *en route* to pick up the two troops stationed there, and the whole arrived together the next day. The depôt troop, with its horses, marched by road, under the command of Lieutenant Carlyon, and arrived at Canterbury about ten days later. According to the custom for regiments proceeding on service to India, a considerable increase in the numbers both of officers and men was now made. The Tenth was raised at Canterbury from six to nine troops—that is, eight service troops besides the depôt troop. This augmentation necessarily caused great and very important changes in its composition, to such an extent indeed as almost to constitute it a new corps. They were as follows :—

APPOINTED—Major J. Tritton, by transfer from 3rd Light Dragoons; Captains Dungan, by transfer from half-pay; Petrie-Waugh, by transfer from 16th Lancers; T. Lloyd, promoted from 4th Light Dragoons; Lieutenants E. Finch, transferred from half-pay, 13th Light Dragoons; R. Walsh, transferred from 74th Highlanders; M. L. Meason, transferred from 40th Regiment; R. S. Parker, transferred from 13th Foot; R. C. Holmes, transferred from 95th Foot; R. Playne Smith, transferred from 74th Highlanders; C. P. Rosser, promoted from 14th Light Dragoons; Theodore Wirgman, promoted from Royal Dragoons on augmentation. J. Wycliffe Thompson, appointed from 3rd Dragoon Guards by purchase; T. S. Little, transferred from 39th Foot; R. E. Blake, transferred from 22nd Foot by purchase; A. J. Loftus, transferred from 97th Foot by purchase; Lord J. de Burgh Browne, transferred from 9th Lancers by purchase; Cornets J. Walrond Clarke, by purchase; Charles McMahon, transferred from 71st Foot on augmentation; R. Clements, promoted from Regimental Sergeant-Major, 10th Hussars, on augmentation; Butler M. Giveen, B. A. Branfill, John D. Drummond, J. Stopford Blair, appointed on augmentation. Theodore Williams, by purchase; Edward Stacey, by purchase; Surgeon M. J. M. Ross, by exchange from 44th Foot; Assistant-Surgeon J. M. Stephens, M.D., from 16th Lancers on augmentation; Veterinary-Surgeon J. Robertson, by exchange from 11th Hussars; Quartermaster J. Fenn, promoted from Sergeant-Major 10th Hussars.

It was not in officers alone that the regiment was so largely transformed at this time. It had to be provided with additional non-commissioned officers and men to raise its ranks to the Indian establishment over and above what was required to fill up the blanks occasioned by the discharge of men considered unfit for service in a tropical climate on account of age, long service, or other disability. In those days cavalry soldiers were expected to serve twenty-five years before being entitled to claim discharge, and there were several old soldiers in the regiment fit for service at home whom it was not considered desirable to take to India. They were therefore discharged "invalided." In addition to these there was a certain number of men who were allowed to leave by the purchase of their discharge. The numerous vacancies thus caused could only be filled within the limited time available by volunteering from other corps. Accordingly, soon after the arrival of the Tenth at Canterbury, drafts to make up its ranks to the required strength began to arrive in small detachments and in varying numbers from the following regiments—the Royal Dragoons, the Scots Greys, the 4th Light Dragoons, the 6th Inniskilling Dragoons, the 7th, 8th, and 11th Hussars, the 13th Light Dragoons, and 17th Lancers. The Tenth was thus quickly raised to the required Indian strength. The newly appointed officers also joined, so that before the end of the month it was possible to report it complete at all points and ready for embarkation. The Adjutant-General (Sir George Brown) thereupon came down from the Horse Guards to Canterbury to inspect it. After doing so, and seeing it march past, he complimented it very highly, and remarked that the men of the 10th Hussars for height and size much more resembled Lifeguardsmen than Light dragoons. They were at that time to a large extent picked men and remarkably tall, the average height being 5 feet $9\frac{1}{2}$ inches; and the volunteers who had just joined well matched their new comrades in that respect, being also all of them tall fine men and excellent specimens of the English cavalry soldier of that period, so that the observation of the General on their appearance was not unwarranted.

The 10th Hussars being now pronounced fit to proceed on the service for which it was selected, and the transports for its conveyance to India being ready at Gravesend, the first detachment left the Cavalry Barracks on the 30th April. This consisted of C and D troops, under the command of Captain Wilkie. They marched dismounted to Herne Bay, a distance of eight miles, and from there were conveyed in small steamers to Gravesend, where they were embarked on board the " Brahmin." The head-quarters and four troops left Canterbury on the 5th May, and proceeded in the same manner as the previous detachment—first by road to Herne Bay and then by steamer to Gravesend. The head-quarters, with A and B troops, under the command of Colonel Vandeleur, embarked on board the " Larkins," and E and H troops, under command of Captain Broadley Harrison, on board the " Hindostan," both vessels sailing early next morning. F and G troops, under Captain R. Hugh Smith-Barry, followed on the 7th May, embarking on board the " Persia." No delay took place, each vessel sailing on the morning after the embarkation of the troops, and by the 8th of May the whole of the regiment was on its way to India, *vid* the Cape of Good Hope. The ship which was the last to leave England was the first to reach its destination, arriving in Bombay on the 21st August. All the ships, however, came in some days later at short intervals, and the whole regiment was disembarked and landed in Bombay by the 26th August. On landing, the troops were provided with temporary accommodation in the barracks at Colaba, and the officers were put up at the British Hotel in the Fort. After the disembarkation of the baggage, a large chest of the officers' mess plate, consisting principally of silver forks and spoons, was found to be missing, and although a careful search was made no trace of it was ever obtained.

At that season of the year it is very undesirable for troops newly arrived in the country to make a prolonged stay in Bombay. The monsoon being then little more than half over, the climate is very trying to Europeans, more especially the unacclimatised, on account of the excessive heat and the depressing effects of the moisture-laden atmosphere. The necessary arrangements for the move up country were therefore quickly made, and the Tenth left Bombay for its final destination at Kirkee on the 29th August, three days after the arrival of the last ship. Embarking at the pier in Bombay Harbour in large open boats, it was conveyed across the arm of the sea lying between the island of Bombay and the mainland and up the estuary of the Panwell River to Panwell. Here it was landed within no great distance of the site appointed for the first encampment. The passage took about six hours, and the departure had to be so timed that the arrival at Panwell should be when the tide was at its highest there, for only at full tide could boats of such size as those used in this service get up the river so far. Panwell and the surrounding country is flat, low-lying, and marshy at all times, and a favourite resort for snipe-shooting later in the season; but during the monsoon it is a complete swamp, and it was not an easy matter to find a dry spot on which to pitch the tents. Notwithstanding, however, the unsuitableness of the ground and the situation, it was found necessary to remain here the following day, as the required transport for regimental baggage, &c., was not fully forthcoming. The result was a good deal of sickness before the troops marched out at an early hour on the second night. Between sunset and reveillé, which sounded about two A.M., many cases of choleraic diarrhœa of rather a severe type appeared.

The first march from Panwell was to Chowk, and the next, on the 1st September, to Kolapoor, at the foot of the Khandalla Ghât. The sickness that had commenced at Panwell kept daily increasing. This was attributable to the malarious condition of the country at that period of the year all the way from Panwell to the foot of the Ghâts. Still, the novelty of the scene and all the circumstances, the excitement and good spirits of all from being once more on land after so many weary months on board ship, the feeling that every day brought them nearer to the destination which was to be for a time their home, caused a general cheeriness, and each day's march was accomplished merrily. The next day's stage was short, by a steep zigzag road cut in the precipitous face of the Bhore Ghât up to Khandalla, a station situated at its summit. Every one rejoiced on arrival at Khandalla on the morning of the 2nd September. The worst was considered to be over. The malaria-laden atmosphere of the Concan swamps was left behind, and men were breathing the purer, drier air of the elevated plain of the Deccan. Khandalla is about 2,500 feet above the level of the Concan, as the seaboard is called, and the rise is very abrupt, in most places precipitous. Here the aspect of the country becomes wholly changed. Partially or wholly submerged paddy fields and swamps were exchanged for lovely scenery, composed of tree-covered eminences and slopes intersected with dark precipitous rocky ravines, the hollows of which were thickly overgrown with a jungle of thorny and other shrubs of all sorts, in many places impenetrable and the known resort of tigers, bears, and other wild animals, all, now, in the rainy season, presenting an appearance of rich luxuriance of green foliage in varying shades. It was decided that the regiment should again halt for a day at this lovely spot before proceeding further. This, it was hoped, would tend to neutralise the effects of the recent exposure and improve the condition of the sick. Great was the disappointment on finding that this expectation was to be but partially realised. In the course of the forenoon, shortly after arrival at Khandalla, a case of genuine Asiatic cholera was reported in the person of a native follower, a Portuguese troop cook, the disease having been evidently contracted in the plain below on the march from Panwell. Very shortly afterwards this formidable malady broke out amongst the troops. From Khandalla the march was continued on the 4th September to Karlee, and at Wirgaum, the next encamping ground to Karlee, two men died of cholera and were buried there. This occurrence cast a serious gloom over the whole regiment. The disease was, in its rapidly fatal course, altogether new to officers and men, and its appearance amongst them so early after their arrival in the country was very discouraging. The march, however, was continued the next day (the 6th) from Wirgaum to Akourdie, and on the 7th September the regiment arrived at its destination at Kirkee, when another case of cholera proved fatal, but after that the disease spread no farther.

On the march from Khandalla to Kirkee there was no object of special interest to attract attention with the exception of the cave temples in the neighbour-

hood of Karlee. Being within easy reach of where
the regiment was encamped, these were duly visited
by a certain number both of officers and men. These
temples are similar to the more famous rock temples
of Elephanta near Bombay, but on a much smaller
scale.

1846

CHAPTER XXVII

1846   KIRKEE was at that time the cavalry station of the
Bombay Presidency, and there the whole of its first
tour of service in India was passed by the 10th Hussars,
and, as it was a period of perhaps a longer continued
peace than has existed in that country either before or
since, there will not be much to record in these pages
beyond the ordinary uneventful cantonment life of a
regiment in India. It was universally regarded as a
most pleasant and, for India, a remarkably healthy
station, and, next to Bangalore, one of the most coveted
in the country. It had now been occupied for many
years, first by the 4th and after them by the 14th
Light Dragoons. The latter had moved out of it on
being ordered for service in the Bengal Presidency
some months before the arrival of the Tenth. The
distance of Kirkee from Bombay was reckoned to be
about 120 miles, and from the neighbouring military
station of Poona about four miles.

The cantonment of Kirkee was laid out very much
after the same manner as would be an encampment
under canvas, but it naturally extended over a greater
area and was on a much larger scale. The lines in
which the horses were all picketed in the open without
any shelter were in front. Then came the troop lines,

with married soldiers' quarters on either flank. In rear of the troop lines, and between them and the first line of officers' bungalows, was the general foot parade-ground, which served also as a cricket ground. Then came the subalterns', the captains', and the field officers' lines in succession. The cantonment was intersected and traversed by excellent macadamised roads, along which were planted trees already grown to a considerable size. These, besides adding greatly to the beauty of the place, were valuable for their grateful shade. The mess-house, centrally situated in the field officers' lines, was a large separate building, provided with detached mess sergeants' quarters and other necessary outbuildings. The Tenth purchased the mess property from the 14th Light Dragoons just as it stood. The only change subsequently made in it was the addition to the mess-house of a large room for a second billiard table, which was also used as a library. The cantonment was thus found by the regiment on its arrival at Kirkee completely provided with all the requisite accommodation, mess-house and officers' quarters all ready for use and immediate occupation, and the lines beautifully laid out and ornamented.

In the annual reliefs of cavalry in India as now carried out it is the custom that the corps returning to England should leave its horses behind to be taken over by the one coming out, but on this occasion it was not so. The Tenth did not replace a regiment returning home, but was sent out to augment the force already in India. It was, therefore, necessary to provide it with fresh remounts. To meet this requirement a small detachment, consisting of the riding-master, the veterinary surgeon, and a party of rough-riders, with a captain in command, was sent out overland so as to arrive some months in advance, with the view of purchasing and preparing horses ready to mount the regiment immediately on arrival in the country. The officers selected for this service were Captain Lloyd, promoted into the Tenth on augmentation from lieutenant and adjutant 4th Light Dragoons, Lieutenant Wirgman, Ridingmaster and Veterinary Surgeon Robertson. Captain Lloyd, having had many years' experience in India whilst serving there with the 4th Light Dragoons, was considered especially well qualified to undertake this duty; but the result was not satisfactory. By the time the Tenth had arrived no horses had been procured, the reason being that at that season of the year there are none in the Bombay market of the description or class which supplies remounts. Arrivals from the Persian Gulf do not come in till the monsoon is quite over, and this is usually not before the end of October. Orders had preceded the regiment that remounts should be procured from the Cape also, but from neither source had any been obtained. It therefore remained dismounted for some months after its arrival; but there was plenty of occupation both for officers and men. The great number of volunteers brought in from so many different sources immediately before embarkation, the large number of officers of whom so considerable a proportion came from infantry regiments, and who were accordingly unpractised in cavalry drill, besides a number of young officers who had never undergone any drill at all, kept every one busy. At the same time, it is not to be supposed that sports and amusements were neglected. Cricket, of course, became early established, and every spare moment was devoted to it. Every troop had its cricket club, and played matches against each other, the officers taking part with their respective troops, and in course of time matches took place between the Tenth and the regiments in the neighbouring station of Poona, both 1846 at Kirkee and on their own grounds.

Colonel Vandeleur, after having brought the Tenth out to India, remained in the country only sufficiently long to see it comfortably settled in its new quarters. Having effected an exchange with Lieutenant-Colonel Parlby, of the 4th Light Dragoons, he returned to England and retired from the service before the end of the year. Colonel Vandeleur had served in the Peninsula as a subaltern in the 71st Foot, and was severely wounded in the battle of Fuentes d'Onore. He was then transferred to the 12th Light Dragoons, in which he attained the rank of major, and, after having been on half-pay for some time, was gazetted lieutenant-colonel in the 10th Hussars in 1838. He received the Peninsular medal, with clasps for Fuentes d'Onore, Vittoria, Pyrenees, Nivelle and Nive, and the medal for Waterloo.

In the Dress Regulations published in 1846 the dress of the 10th Hussars is given as follows :—

Busby.—Nine inches deep, and the same size at top and bottom. Scarlet fly and plaited top.[1]

Plume.—White egret with scarlet bottom.[2]

Trousers.—Blue cloth, with a stripe of gold lace one inch and a half wide down the outward seam.[3]

Pouch Belt.—The 10th Hussars are permitted to wear, both in dress and undress, a pouch and pouch belt of black patent leather, according to regimental pattern.

Undress Belts and Slings.—10th Hussars' Russian leather.

Although the above was the officially recognised

---

[1] The busbies of this period were taller than the modern ones, and worn "rakishly" on one side of the head, instead of straight up and down.

[2] The 10th Hussars while serving in India will wear a shako of regimental pattern.

[3] The 10th and 11th Hussars are permitted to wear two stripes of gold lace, each three quarters of an inch wide, with a light between.

1846   dress of the 10th Hussars while serving in Europe, it was not found suitable for the Indian climate. The busby was replaced by a shako, and with as little delay as possible after arrival at Kirkee the regiment was provided with white cotton clothing for ordinary wear. It consisted of a stable jacket and overalls made of cotton material called American drill, and a white cotton quilted cover worn on the shako, with a curtain hanging down, and sufficiently forward to protect the temples as well as the back of the head and neck. At balls and on dress occasions, the officers still appeared in the lace jacket with pelisse slung and scarlet overalls, and at mess the blue stable jacket was always worn.

Before the end of 1846 a draft was received from England, though the regiment had only been a few months in the country. It arrived on the 2nd of December, and consisted of two sergeants and thirteen rank and file. The following changes took place during this year :—

LEFT.—Lieutenant-Colonel Wallington ; Captains Dungan, McDonough, Tomline, Hyder, and Lieutenants Pate and Finch, retired by sale of commission ; Surgeon D. Murray, M.D., by exchange to 44th Foot ; Veterinary-Surgeon T. Gloag, by exchange to 11th Hussars ; Quartermaster McClellan, retired on half-pay.

1847   On the departure of Colonel Vandeleur for England, Lieutenant-Colonel A. F. Bonham succeeded to the command, and on the 16th January, 1847, the first inspection in India took place. It was made by Major-General McNeil, who was at that time in command of the Poona Division. The parade was on foot, for as yet there were no horses. The General expressed himself very much struck with the height of the men, just as General Sir George Brown had done on inspecting the regiment at Canterbury before embarkation.

In this year a change was made in the Enlistment
Act, by which the service of the soldier was divided into
a first and second period, the first to be for twelve
years in cavalry and ten years in infantry. On completion of the first period a soldier might retire, but
without any consideration for the service so far rendered,
or re-engage to serve for a further period to complete a
total of twenty-one years for infantry or twenty-four
for cavalry, with the prospect of a pension, the amount
of which was regulated by certain conditions.

For the first quarter of this year the drilling and
general instruction of the regiment had still to be
limited to what could be carried out on foot, and the
announcement that a considerable number of horses had
at length been procured was hailed with general satisfaction, as the further training proper to cavalry soldiers could now be commenced. But it was nearly the
middle of April before the first batch of remounts,
numbering about 200, was received—that is, more than
seven months after the Tenth landed in India. The
remounts included 150 more or less pure Arabs and
Persians, but only about fifty Cape horses. The failure
to get a larger proportion of the latter was at first much
regretted, as the Cape horse was a bigger and apparently a stronger animal than the Arab, and, so far as
appearance went, bore a better proportion to the height
of the men and did not look so puny under them as did
the Arab horses. But it was soon found what the Arab
horse lacked in size and robustness was made up for by
spirit and power of endurance. These horses were at
once taken in hand by the rough-riders and the old
soldiers of the regiment, and the work of breaking them
in, at least to a sufficient extent, did not take long.
The first mounted inspection took place on the 11th
June—that is, some six weeks after the first of the

R

remounts had arrived. The inspecting officer on this occasion was Brigadier-General Pennefather, who expressed himself highly satisfied with the progress that had been made, and especially commended the Riding-master, Lieutenant Wirgman, for the pains he must have taken to have developed such proficiency in riding among officers and men. At that time there was no covered riding school at Kirkee, but steps were taken to provide one in time to be available before the riding drill of many of the officers was considered quite finished. It was a large, airy, solidly built structure of handsome appearance, and proved not only a comfort to all concerned but also a great convenience, inasmuch as, being lofty, airy, and well roofed, riding drill could be carried on at all seasons well sheltered from sun and rain.

It may be mentioned here with regard to the Arab horses that, though they were found so amenable to breaking in as troopers, yet, being all entire, they gave a great deal of trouble by their indomitable spirits—biting, kicking, and occasionally fighting with one another, both in and out of the ranks. The men, however, became very fond of them, and as in India it is possible to keep the same man permanently in charge of the same animal, it became the rule that a man was never parted from his horse, unless it was absolutely necessary on some good ground, either for service purposes or on account of bad conduct and neglect of his horse on the part of the man. The consequence was that in course of time each man came to look upon his particular troop horse as his own property, and called him by a pet name in addition to the name given by the troop officer. Picketed in their lines, the horses stood at all seasons of the year unprotected from sun or rain save by their clothing, which consisted of a coarse

woollen material of native manufacture lined with a par- 1847
ticular kind of thick felt called a "numnah." During the
heavy rains in the monsoon these coverings kept their
backs perfectly dry, and the horses were maintained in
good condition throughout this trying season. Some,
however, did suffer severely from an almost incurable
kind of sore called "bursatti," and also from sore heels,
both of which affections were considered in large
measure attributable to exposure to wet.

On the occasion of the first mounted inspection by
Brigadier-General Pennefather the regiment was seen
by troops, in "riding-school" order, in the open
manèges, but very shortly afterwards the horses were
brought together in the field, and, after a few pre-
liminary drills by the adjutant, commanding officer's
field days followed, and before long the regiment took
part in divisional field days in Poona. Thus it now
commenced what was to be the regular routine of
work during its stay at Kirkee.

CHAPTER XXVIII

SPORTS AND AMUSEMENTS—A DRAFT ARRIVES FROM ENGLAND—
RACQUET COURT BUILT—ATTACK OF CHOLERA—REVIEW BY THE
COMMANDER-IN-CHIEF

1847   As the drill and equitation of the regiment were
now gradually perfected, more leisure was afforded
for other occupations than the regular routine of
regimental work.   In addition to cricket, pigeon shooting and boating were added, and formed the chief
resources in the way of outdoor amusements during the
monsoon—that is, from about the beginning of July
onwards, the most pleasant season of the year at Kirkee,
though perhaps not the most healthy.   At the latter
end of the monsoon and during the winter months pig-
sticking was much patronised; during the hot months
large-game shooting was to be had on the Western
Ghâts, forty miles from the cantonments, and antelope
were to be found in considerable numbers within quite
a short distance.   In addition to these amusements
the sport of horse-racing remained.   Preparations for
it were speedily undertaken.   A racecourse was found
already in existence; it could hardly be said to have required making; in fact, the flat level plain (" Maidan ")
of considerable extent just outside the cantonment
and adjoining the field drill-ground was naturally well
adapted and readily available for the purpose, needing
little more than the selecting and marking out of the
proposed course.

Amongst the junior officers who first came out with

the regiment to India was one who had been well
known in England both in the hunting field and as a
steeplechase and flat-race rider. This was Lieutenant
Wardrop. Both before and after joining he had ridden
in several important races, and was in great request as
a light-weight rider. His health unfortunately failed
in the climate of India, and he was sent home on sick
leave, but, not becoming sufficiently restored to return
to India, he after a time retired by the sale of his commission. Not many months afterwards, however, the
Tenth obtained a distinguished successor as a racing
celebrity in Lieutenant Thomas Townley. These two
are mentioned, as they were justly considered a good
deal above the average in their attainments as race
riders; but besides them there were many excellent
riders amongst the officers, who were often in the saddle
at the race meetings which continued to be held at
Kirkee annually with great success during the stay of
the Tenth in India.

Amongst the outbuildings in the troop lines, which
were all temporary structures at that time, one was
found that was considered adaptable for the purposes
of a theatre. It was accordingly appropriated to the
Dramatic Society, and was successfully converted so as
to form a sufficiently comfortable little house, if not
exactly all that could be desired. A latent fund of
dramatic talent was found to exist among the men, especially the bandsmen, and very soon an excellent company of actors was evolved. The performances were
most creditable, and drew crowds of patrons both from
the civil and military community of Poona and the station. The theatre of the Tenth proved a source of great
entertainment and amusement not only to the actors themselves and their comrades, but to the *élite* of the fashionable society which assembled from all parts at Poona

1847 and in its neighbourhood in the so-called rainy season. Amongst them were the Governor and the Commander-in Chief and their respective staffs and heads of departments, civil and military. During "the season" the station of Poona is very gay with the usual social entertainments, Government House, then at Dapoorie, setting the example with balls, dinners, public breakfasts, &c. In these festivities the Tenth was not behindhand, and, its mess-house being well adapted for the purpose, gave beside other entertainments a grand ball annually, which was not the least appreciated event of the season.

During this year the following changes took place amongst the officers:—Lieutenant Walsh died at Kirkee on the 1st February, a few months after his arrival in India; Lieutenant Lord James de Burgh Browne also died in February, at sea, without having joined; Captain Richard Townley exchanged into the 16th Lancers, but before he was able to leave the country he succumbed to disease of long standing affecting the spine, and died at Khandalla on the way down to Bombay to proceed to England; Lieutenant Shelley exchanged into the 16th Lancers; Captain Smith-Barry retired from the service by the sale of his commission; and Captain Carlyon was appointed to the 3rd Dragoon Guards. The fresh appointments in the course of the year were Captains Methuen Stedman and William Murray, Lieutenant J. Percy Smith, Cornets T. H. Dury, Henry Alexander, and J. R. Cuthbert. All these in due course joined head-quarters in India with the exception of Cornet Dury, who exchanged into the 3rd Light Dragoons.

1848 On the 31st January, 1848, a strong draft joined from England. It consisted of one captain, three subalterns, one sergeant, two corporals, and 107 privates, principally recruits, and was always spoken of as the " hundred and ten draft." The officers were Captain

Stedman, in command, Lieutenant Blake, and Cornets 1848 Clements and Stacey.

There are no occurrences of any importance to record for this year. The usual routine of duties went on with little or no variation from what has been already described. The sports and pastimes of the officers also continued much the same, with the exception that in the course of this year an addition was made to their resources in that way by the institution of a racquet club, and the erection by its members of a splendid court for the practice of the game. It was built in convenient proximity to the mess-house, but formed no part of the mess premises, being the exclusive property of the subscribers and members of the club.

On the 2nd June the regiment was inspected by Major-General Auchmuty, C.B., and in December by Major-General Manson, the generals commanding the Poona Division at these respective periods.

The following were the changes amongst the officers in 1848 :—Paymaster E. B. Frith exchanged into the 13th Light Dragoons; Cornet T. H. Dury exchanged into the 3rd Light Dragoons; Lieutenant Parker retired by the sale of his commission. And the new appointments were Paymaster R. T. Elrington, from the 13th Light Dragoons; Cornet H. Fraser Dimsdale, from the 3rd Light Dragoons; Cornet F. B. H. Carew.

On the 4th February, 1849, a draft arrived from 1849 England, consisting of two cornets, one sergeant, and twenty-nine privates.

Sir Willoughby Cotton, who was the Commander-in-Chief of Bombay at this time, took very great interest in everything that concerned the Tenth, not only in regard to its general efficiency, its mounting when that was in progress, and its preparation for the field, but also in furthering its sports and amusements. He was a

1849   regular attendant at the race meetings organised by the regiment, being usually about the first to arrive on the course, and he made himself very popular with both officers and men.   On his inspection in July of this year he expressed himself in very flattering terms, and called Lieutenant Wirgman to the front and highly complimented him on the equitation.   It may be mentioned here that Lieutenant Wirgman came into the English service from the Austrian army, in which he served for several years in a hussar regiment.   He was highly educated (a graduate of Trinity College, Cambridge) and a most accomplished officer, well read in military literature and an excellent linguist.

On the 28th November another draft, consisting of one sergeant, one corporal, and thirty-three privates, joined from England. In this year there were the following changes amongst the officers :—Lieutenant Wardrop retired from the service by the sale of his commission ; Lieutenant J. Stopford Blair exchanged into the 13th Light Dragoons ; Cornet Fraser Dimsdale was appointed to the 1st Dragoons ; and the new appointments to the regiment were :—Lieutenant R. W. Hatfield, from the 13th Light Dragoons ; Cornet Thomas Manners Townley ; Cornet Fred Marshall, afterwards Colonel of the 2nd Life Guards.

1850   On the 28th January, 1850, Captain Lloyd, an officer who had seen much service in India whilst in the 4th Light Dragoons, died at Bombay from dysentery. The death of this officer caused very deep and universal regret in the regiment.   He was a favourite with every one, and his long experience of Indian service was of great value to a corps new to the country, as was the case with the Tenth when he joined.   The senior lieutenant (George Webb), for many years the adjutant, was promoted without purchase to the vacant troop.

This officer had considerable seniority by this time, and very shortly after getting this step sold out and went home. He had served many years in the 12th Lancers, in which he had risen to be regimental sergeant-major, and from that position was promoted to a cornetcy in the Tenth in 1839. Lieutenant T. Percy Smith, formerly of the 16th Lancers, who had served many years and seen much active service in India, and was an officer of high reputation before coming into the Tenth, was appointed to the adjutancy.

It has been seen that the Tenth had a very early experience of cholera after arrival in the country on the march from Bombay, but fortunately on that occasion the disease prevailed to a very limited extent, and there were only three deaths, as, in fact, after arrival at Kirkee the cholera season was over, and the disease disappeared. It usually broke out about the commencement of the monsoon, and only two seasons passed without some cases occurring. In 1850 a serious visitation of the disease took place, the monsoon being late in its arrival, and the hot season consequently unusually protracted. A good deal of sickness prevailed, but not of a nature to give any forewarning of what was coming. All at the hospital appeared much as usual one evening, but before seven o'clock next morning several deaths had occurred of men admitted in the course of the night, and the number of cases increased so rapidly that the medical officers never left the hospital night or day. The exertions of Surgeons Ross and Fraser were unremitting, and it was mainly due to their never-failing kindness, sympathy, and devotion to their duty that a still further spread of this calamity was prevented. The troop officers were also constantly in the hospital, as well as the chaplain, the former encouraging, the latter comforting the sufferers.

1850   The total number of deaths was considerable, though the proportion of recoveries was regarded as being above the usual average. After the first heavy fall of rain the disease gradually disappeared. With the exception of these short outbreaks of cholera and a certain amount of fever prevalent at some seasons, and in some years more than others, the general health of the regiment during the period of more than eight years that it was stationed at Kirkee was good.

Amongst the events of this year may be mentioned a visit paid to Poona by the Gaekwar of Baroda on the 21st February. Two squadrons of the Tenth in review order were ordered out to meet and receive him, and to escort him to his camp. On the following day the Tenth was reviewed in his presence.

In the course of 1850 the following changes took place:—Brevet Major W. Petrie Waugh exchanged to half-pay; Captain T. Lloyd died; Captain George Webb retired from the service by the sale of his commission; Cornet F. B. H. Carew was transferred to the 16th Lancers; and the following cornets were appointed:— Hamilton Beckett, John Edmund Severne, Edward M. Roper Stapylton, Arthur Herbert Cass.

1851   On the 17th January, 1851, a draft arrived from England, consisting of Cornets Beckett and Severne, one sergeant, two corporals, and sixty-two privates; and on the 17th April Cornets E. M. Stapylton and A. H. Cass joined head-quarters from England " overland."

On the 23rd May of this year the Tenth lost a much valued and respected non-commissioned officer by the death of Regimental Sergeant-Major Peck after a few days' illness. He was brought up in the regiment, was well known to all, and universally regretted.

On the 16th September the Tenth was reviewed in

the presence of His Excellency the Commander-in-Chief, Lieutenant-General Sir John Gray, who succeeded Sir Willoughby Cotton in the command of the Bombay Army. On the 26th October Lieutenant R. Playne Smith rejoined the regiment after an absence of two years in England, passed in going through a course of studies at the Royal Military College, Senior Department, the equivalent in that day of the present Staff College. On the 15th November Captain Bowles joined head-quarters from England on exchange from the 7th Hussars. On the 18th November a draft arrived from England, consisting of Captain Lord George Beauclerk (in command), Cornet Webster, two sergeants, one corporal, and sixty-two privates.

The following changes took place amongst the officers in 1851:—Left by sale of commission—Captain Sir Thomas Munro, Bart., Lieutenant M. L. Meason, and Lieutenant MacMahon ; Captain Lord Garvagh exchanged into the 7th Hussars; Lieutenant Fred Marshall appointed to 2nd Life Guards. Resigned— Assistant-Surgeon Stephens, M.D. Joined—Captain Charles Bowles, Cornets W. G. Bridgeman, W. M. Hathway, Musgrave Bradley Dyne, and Guy Webster, Assistant-Surgeon J. Macbeth, M.D.

CHAPTER XXIX

COLONEL BONHAM RETIRES—DEATH OF THE DUKE OF WELLINGTON
—A CAMP OF EXERCISE—COLONEL TRITTON'S CAREER—RUMOURS
OF WAR IN EUROPE—WAR DECLARED BY ENGLAND AND FRANCE
AGAINST RUSSIA

1852   IN February 1852 Lieutenant-Colonel Bonham left the
regiment, retiring on half-pay. He was in England at
the time, having been sent home on sick certificate
some months previously, when the command devolved
temporarily on Lieutenant-Colonel Parlby, the second
lieutenant-colonel.   Now, however, on the retirement of
Colonel Bonham, Colonel Parlby succeeded to the command permanently.   Two years later Colonel Bonham
was made a brevet colonel and appointed to the command of the Cavalry Depôts at Canterbury and Brighton.
He entered the army as a cornet in the 10th Hussars
in 1829.   He succeeded to the command in 1846 shortly
after the arrival of the Tenth in India, on the departure of Colonel Vandeleur to England, and continued
to command it until his health failed and he was obliged
to leave the country, as already stated, some time in
1851.   He died in 1856 at Brighton.

On the 17th March, 1852, the regiment was inspected
by Major-General Staveley, C.B.

On the 16th September the death of the Duke of
Wellington took place, and he was succeeded in the
chief command of the army by Lord Hardinge.   On
this occasion the Tenth, in common with the remainder

of the army, went into mourning in accordance with the general order of 23rd September.

Cornets Hathway and Dyne joined head-quarters, the former on the 19th January and the latter on the 16th March, 1852, and Cornet Benson, with a draft of two sergeants, four corporals, and seventy-two privates, arrived from England on the 9th December, 1852.

In the course of this year Lieutenant-General Lord Frederick FitzClarence was appointed to the chief command in the Bombay Presidency, and assumed office on the 24th November. On the 14th December he made an inspection of the Tenth in marching order. Lord Frederick FitzClarence, having a high opinion of the value of cavalry as a military arm, took great interest in the regiment, and saw a good deal of it. He encouraged and enjoined instruction in and the practice of outpost.[1] He used to give instructions that small parties should be sent in different directions many miles into the surrounding country, and that rough sketches and reports of the country and ground gone over should be sent in to him afterwards both by officers and men, and the Tenth was constantly employed in this way under his own supervision. These exercises and frequent divisional field days at Poona kept the regiment in pretty constant employment.

The following changes took place in 1852 :—Left— Colonel Bonham, by exchange to half-pay; Cornets Hamilton Beckett and Bridgeman and Major Quentin, by sale of commission ; Lieutenant Severne, by exchange to 16th Lancers ; Lieutenant the Hon. C. J. Keith-Falconer, to 4th Light Dragoons. Appointed — Cornet Arthur Ed. Benson, Cornet Dundas R. Gill, Cornet J. M. Burn-Murdoch, from 3rd Light Dragoons, Cornet J.

---

[1] Lord Frederick FitzClarence was the author of a work on outpost duty which was long accepted as a manual for these duties.

Alston Clarke, Lieutenant H. J. Fairlie, from 4th Light Dragoons, Cornet the Hon. M. Fitzmaurice Deane.

On the 14th March, 1853, Major Wilkie and Lieutenant Fairlie joined head-quarters from England, the former after an absence of two years on private leave, and the latter on exchange from the 4th Light Dragoons with Lieutenant the Hon. Charles Keith-Falconer ; and on the 12th December a draft consisting of Cornets Alston Clarke and Richmond, Assistant-Surgeon A. M. Macbeth, M.D., one sergeant, and thirty-three rank and file, arrived at Kirkee from England.

In the course of this year the regiment suffered from an outbreak of cholera at an unusual period, which was further remarkable in that the attacks were confined to men in hospital who were suffering from ailments considered in no way allied or predisposing to this disease, no case being admitted from the troop rooms. The outbreak occurred between the 10th and 18th September, during an interval of intensely hot and oppressive weather, such as is rarely experienced at that period of the year, which was immediately preceded for some days by a heavy downfall of rain, also unusual. This doubtless tended to produce an unhealthy condition of the atmosphere, for much other sickness prevailed. In these few days six men fell victims to the disease. Amongst those who died was a non-commissioned officer of great merit and a universal favourite, Troop Sergeant-Major Haynes. Besides being an excellent soldier, Haynes was a great authority in and promoter of all manly sports and pastimes, and he was deeply regretted by both officers and men.

Beyond the ordinary routine of duties, drills, field days, and the practice of outpost duties, which were continued each season, there is very little to record for 1853 with the exception that, in addition to the usual

regular divisional field days at Poona, a camp of exercise in which the Tenth took part was established in
the autumn by the Commander-in-Chief in the vicinity
of Poona. His Excellency initiated what was at that
time for the English army a new departure—the prac-
tising of troops in evolutions with a combined force on
a larger scale than the ordinary field days of a weak
division. From the different stations and garrisons of

the Presidency Lord Frederick FitzClarence was enabled
to bring together a considerable force, comprising all
arms. Including the Poona garrison, in the aggregate
it amounted to not far short of 10,000 men. The
troops which came from a distance were encamped
within easy reach of the Poona cantonment, so as to
obviate the necessity of moving the regiments composing the Poona garrison under canvas. The Tenth
marched out of the cantonments at Kirkee to join this

force on the 28th November, and was encamped on the
Sholapore road, some distance to the south of Poona.
The manœuvres were continued for nearly a month,
the troops returning to Poona and Kirkee on Christmas
Eve.

On the 13th December, 1853, the retirement of Lieutenant-Colonel Tritton from the service was accepted
by the Indian Government. On leaving the army
this officer brought to a close a very distinguished
career. He entered the service as a cornet in the 24th
Light Dragoons in 1813, then serving in the Bengal
Presidency, and after being six years in that regiment
was appointed to the 11th Light Dragoons, and in it
rose to the rank of captain. From the 11th he was
transferred to the 3rd Light Dragoons on its coming out
to India, and was promoted to a majority in the 10th
Hussars on its augmentation for service in India in
April 1846, as already mentioned. During his service,
which was wholly in India, he was engaged in the
following active military operations: The siege and
capture of Hattras in 1817, the Mahratta campaign in
1817–18, the siege and capture of Bhurtpore in 1825–
26; in the campaign in Afghanistan in 1842 was present
at the following actions: Forcing the Khyber Pass,
storming the Heights of Jugdulluck, action of Fazeen
and Huft Kotul, and the occupation of Cabul under
Major-General Pollock, C.B.; with the army of the Sutlej
in 1845 as Assistant Adjutant-General of the Cavalry
was present at the following actions: The battle of
Moodkee, the battle of Ferozeshah, the celebrated charge
of the 3rd Light Dragoons on the enemy's batteries and
through their entrenched camp, the battle of Sobraon,
where he had a horse shot under him, and accompanied
the 3rd Dragoons when they forced a passage into the
enemy's entrenched position by single files, under H.E.

Sir Hugh Gough, Commander-in-Chief. He especially distinguished himself by capturing with twelve men one of the enemy's guns when sent in pursuit at the close of the action of the 13th September, 1842, and again by capturing a standard from the enemy at the battle of Moodkee, 18th December, 1845. He obtained a silver medal and clasp for the siege and capture of Bhurtpore in January 1826, a silver medal for the campaign in Afghanistan in 1842, and a silver medal and three clasps for the battles of Moodkee, Ferozeshah, and Sobraon in 1845. Colonel Tritton, after leaving the Tenth, was about to proceed to England after a continuous service of nearly forty years in India, and was on his way for that purpose from Kirkee to Bombay when he met with a serious accident. Whilst passing over a bridge his carriage came against the parapet and was upset. He was thrown out, and falling into the stony bed of the river, now dry, sustained injuries which before many weeks proved fatal. He died at Bombay in February 1854. It was a sad ending to a man seeking repose after so eventful a life, in which he had passed scatheless through so many perils.

The changes which took place in the officers' ranks in 1853 were as follows:—Left—Cornet the Hon. Fitzmaurice Deane, appointed to the 2nd Dragoons; Lieutenant Guy Webster, appointed to 1st Dragoons; Lieutenants Fairlie and Clements, by sale of commission; Captain Little, by exchange to half-pay; Captain C. Freville Surtees, by exchange to 3rd Light Dragoons; Lieutenant Musgrave Bradley Dyne, appointed to 2nd Dragoon Guards; Assistant-Surgeon James Macbeth, M.D., by exchange to 33rd Regiment; Lieutenant Stapylton, deceased. Appointments—Cornet Henry F. Richmond, from 12th Lancers; Cornet James J. Neil Buchanan; Cornet Henry Baring, from 2nd Dragoons;

s

Lieutenant F. J. O. Hopson, from half-pay, 3rd Light Dragoons; Lieutenant W. O. Bird, from 15th Hussars; Captain James Cowell, from 3rd Light Dragoons; Cornet John Hudson; Assistant-Surgeon A. M. Macbeth, from 33rd Foot. In January 1854 Sergeant-Major Charles Hickman was appointed Regimental Sergeant-Major.

On the 29th March, 1854, the 10th Hussars was inspected in review order by Brigadier-General F. Schuler, commanding the Poona Division, and next day on foot parade, bringing to a close the drill season.

In 1853 rumours had reached India of war impending between England and Russia, and of the preparations that were being made to meet such a contingency. As may be imagined, such rumours created no small amount of interest amongst the officers and men of the Tenth. Speculation was rife as to the chances of being called upon to take part in any military operations that the country might be engaged in. The proximity of the regiment to the port of embarkation for Europe, the fact of India being at perfect peace within her borders, and the knowledge of the weakness of the English army in cavalry at home, encouraged all to hope that they would be called upon to take part in the campaign if war really did break out. It turned out that their expectations were by no means groundless, but they had to wait for more than a year after these first reports before even the " order of readiness " reached them.

In November of 1853 the Russian fleet bombarded Sinope, a port in the Black Sea, and destroyed the Turkish fleet, upon which England and France contemplated more decisive measures, and warned Russia that they would actively interfere in the event of any further aggression. The Emperor of Russia now withdrew his representatives from London and Paris; but most strenuous efforts were still made in many quarters to maintain peace, and further negotiations followed. 1854 It was all in vain, however, and on the 27th February, 1854, England's ultimatum was despatched to Russia, demanding that she should withdraw her troops across the Pruth before the 30th April, and stating that her declining or failing to do so would be regarded as a declaration of war. To this no answer was received, and war was at once declared by England, in conjunction with the Emperor of the French, for the defence of the Sultan. This was announced in the " London Gazette " of the 24th March, and the news reached India on the 8th May.

Some two months later, the anticipations of the regiment that it would be called upon to take part in the campaign seemed about to be at once realised. It was warned to be in readiness, as it might be required to join the army then proceeding on active service. Preparations were made at once and with great alacrity; superfluous possessions were got rid of, and campaigning kits devised. With the same view the Tenth was inspected with more than usual care as to details by His Excellency the Commander-in-Chief (Lord Frederick FitzClarence), who complimented Colonel Parlby on its efficiency and fitness for service. He congratulated all on the opportunity, so shortly expected, of distinguishing themselves on service in the field. The hopes of officers and men were thus raised to the highest pitch, but only to be doomed to as deep disappointment when, not long afterwards, it was officially intimated that their services would not be required for the present. Still, the position of the regiment in the country, as already stated, encouraged all to entertain the belief that it was only hope deferred, and that the order for active service must sooner or later come. In this, as will presently be seen, they were not mistaken.

s 2

CHAPTER XXX

THE LANDING OF THE ALLIED ARMY IN THE CRIMEA—ORDERS FOR
THE REGIMENT TO LEAVE INDIA FOR THE SEAT OF WAR—
LAST CHRISTMAS AT KIRKEE—DEPARTURE FROM BOMBAY

1854   THE allied army landed in the Crimea at Kalamita Bay
on the 14th September, 1854, and fought the Russians
at the Alma, driving them before them into Sebastopol;
then making a flank march, it took up position on
the south side of Sebastopol, the English occupying
Balaclava with the view of establishing there a secure
base from which the army could obtain its supplies in
the event of the siege of Sebastopol becoming protracted. On the 25th of October following the Russians
attacked the Allies in hopes of obtaining possession of this
vital position, and then the cavalry engagements took
place which have become matters of history for ever
memorable in the records of deeds of arms. In the
early morning of that day the successful attack of the
English Heavy Cavalry Brigade on the Russian cavalry
was made, followed later on by the splendid charge
of the Light Cavalry Brigade. The result of the brilliant actions of this day was to materially reduce the
strength of the British cavalry, especially that of the
Light Brigade, which, weak to begin with, numbering
only 607 sabres on entering this charge, returned with
less than 200.

  The news of these great casualties duly reached
India, and revived the hopes of the regiment. Definite

orders quickly followed for the 10th Hussars and 12th
Lancers to hold themselves in readiness to join the
army in the Crimea as soon as ships could be chartered
and got ready for their conveyance. These orders were
received by the Tenth on the 11th December, 1854.
They had been long and ardently expected; but the
general rejoicing and excitement were, as may be supposed, none the less when at length they did arrive. The
prospect of being so soon employed on active service
after a monotonous sojourn of eight years at the quiet
and retired station of Kirkee was received with delight
by all. Steps were taken without a day's delay to prepare for an immediate move, one of the first being the
despatch of an officer to Bombay for the purchase of
additional horses. In view of the attenuated condition
in respect of horses to which the cavalry in the Crimea
was reported to be reduced, and the known impossibility
of getting remounts there to meet possible casualties,
the officer in command, Colonel Parlby, obtained permission not only to raise the strength in horses to such
a point as to provide for mounting every man in it, but
to go further and to take a number of troopers in excess
of the actual requirements. The officer selected for this
service was Captain Bowles, an officer of long experience in the country, who proceeded at once to Bombay
and succeeded in procuring the number of horses
deemed requisite in time for embarkation with the regiment. They were afterwards broken in and made fit
for the ranks during the time the Tenth was detained
at Cairo. The Indian Government (then the Honourable East India Company) not only approved of this
proposal of Colonel Parlby in regard to taking additional horses, but, with its usual and well-known
liberality, facilitated its being carried into effect by
making provision for meeting the extra service entailed

thereby. They allowed as many as might be considered necessary of the native horse-keepers or grooms
(in Bombay called *ghorawallahs*, in Bengal *syces*) employed to assist in all cavalry regiments in India to
accompany the Tenth as far as Alexandria without any
additional cost to the Home Government. In about a
week's time from the receipt of the orders all was ready,
and the further delay that took place arose from the
difficulty of getting ships suitable for the purpose and
having them fitted up for the conveyance of men and
horses.

During this year the regiment experienced a serious
loss by the death of its surgeon, Dr. Ross, an able
medical officer, and universally esteemed. He served
previously in the 16th Lancers, and whilst in that corps
saw a considerable amount of active service in India,
including the campaign in Afghanistan under Lord
Keane, the capture of Ghuznee, &c. He died on the
4th May, after a lingering illness of several months'
duration. Dr. Webster, of the 78th Highlanders, succeeded him, but his health likewise failed not long
after his appointment, and he was sent to Bombay on
sick leave, where he died on the 15th December, just
as the Tenth was preparing to proceed to the Crimea.
The Assistant-Surgeon (Dr. Fraser) was then, and had
been for some time, practically in sole charge. On him,
therefore, devolved the duty of making the whole of the
medical arrangements for the voyage and the march
through Egypt, and of seeing to the regiment being provided with the proper hospital equipment for service
in the field afterwards. He was promoted, and appointed Surgeon to the Tenth whilst *en route* through
Egypt to the Crimea.

As has been seen, Lord Frederick FitzClarence took
a keen personal interest in the Tenth, and in its being

prepared and properly equipped when the expected call for its services in the Crimea came, and looked forward to seeing it on its way ; but unhappily this was not to be. The Bombay Army had in the meantime lost its able and popular chief. Lord Frederick FitzClarence died on the 30th October, after a short illness, at Poorundhur, a hill station about twenty miles from Poona, where a sanatorium for European troops was being then established in which he took great interest, and where he had gone himself for change. The sad duty fell to the regiment of escorting his remains from Poona for a part of the way to Bombay, from whence they were sent to England. Lord Frederick was succeeded as Commander-in-Chief of the Bombay Presidency by Lieutenant-General Sir Henry Somerset, K.C.B.,[1] and by him the Tenth was inspected on the 6th December, previous to its departure for the seat of war. He was pleased to express himself in very flattering terms on its appearance and thorough fitness for the service on which it was about to proceed.

The 25th December, 1854, found the Tenth still all together at Kirkee, and, as this was to be the last Christmas there for that tour of service in India, arrangements were made for celebrating the day throughout the regiment in a special manner, and in the evening all the officers and the ladies dined at the mess together. Three days later a wing, under Colonel Wilkie, consisting of two captains, four lieutenants, one cornet, eighteen sergeants, two trumpeters, thirteen corporals, four farriers, and 354 privates, with 420 horses, marched out of Kirkee, *en route* for Oolwa, at the mouth of the Panwell River, whence they were to be conveyed in open boats to Bombay. The detach-

---

[1] Sir Henry Somerset commenced his career in the 10th Hussars having been gazetted a cornet on the 5th December, 1811.

ment was accompanied by the band and the remainder of the regiment as far as Dapoorie Bridge, about a mile and a half out of the Kirkee lines, where it was parted with, receiving the farewell cheers and good wishes of its friends and comrades. A fortnight later, the 12th January, 1855, the head-quarters and left wing, under Colonel Parlby, followed. This second detachment consisted of one lieutenant-colonel, two captains, three lieutenants, one cornet, one adjutant, one quartermaster, one assistant-surgeon, twenty-five sergeants, fourteen corporals, seven trumpeters, four farriers, 254 privates, with 318 horses. The Paymaster (Major Elrington) had already proceeded to Egypt in order to be there in advance of the regiment. A depôt was left at Kirkee, under the charge of Lieutenant Gill, who was appointed to accompany it to England, *viâ* the Cape of Good Hope. It consisted of the invalids of the season, with a few men not considered fit for immediate service in the field, and all the women and children.

The following changes took place in the ranks of the officers in 1854 :—Left—Cornet Hathway, promoted in 14th Light Dragoons; Lieutenant-Colonel Tritton, retired by sale of commission; Captain Methuen Stedman, exchanged to half-pay; Lieutenant John Drummond, retired by sale of commission; Surgeon Malcolm M. Ross, deceased ; Surgeon A. C. Webster, deceased. Appointed—Cornets Charles Hill Uniacke, Augustus A. de Bourbel, W. Mayne, Sydney Vyse, and Surgeon A. C. Webster.

The right wing, under Colonel Wilkie, arrived at Oolwa on its way to Bombay on the 5th January, 1855. There the men and horses were embarked in open native boats, and conveyed to the vessels prepared and now waiting for them in Bombay Harbour. The principal of these was the " Punjab," a vessel belonging to the Indian Navy, and only just off the stocks, a steamer, but not yet fitted up with machinery or engines; in short, a mere hulk. Being well adapted, however, for this service on account of the large accommodation available in her for horses, she was expressly fitted up for the purpose, and became practically a huge floating stable, and, the intention being that she should be chiefly towed by a steamer to Suez, was simply jury-rigged for the occasion. She was able to receive 220 horses between her hold and decks, and that number was put on board of her. The other vessels of the little fleet conveying the right wing were the "Sultana," sailing ship, the "Auckland" and "Victoria," steamers. The latter was told off to tow the "Sultana," and the former the "Punjab." The embarkation being completed, all the vessels sailed together for Suez on the 10th January, 1855. The left wing, under Colonel Parlby, following the same route, in due course reached Bombay, there embarked, and sailed for Suez on the 1st February. This wing was broken up into five detachments and distributed between the "Precursor" and "Feroze," steamers, the "Clare," "Jessica," and "Earl Grey," sailing ships. The "Precursor" had the "Clare," and the "Feroze" the "Jessica" in tow. The "Earl Grey," with only one troop on board, sailed independently, and took a line of her own across the Indian Ocean, whereas the other sailing vessels, with their respective steamers—though they did not keep pace nor were even in sight of each other after the first day or so—followed pretty nearly the same and a more direct course towards their destination. As each detachment left the beautiful harbour of Bombay the whole of the ships lying at anchor "dressed" with ensigns and streamers, and on shore many Europeans and natives assembled to bid adieu to the regiment.   Yards were manned as the vessels passed down the harbour, the men sending cheer after cheer of farewell and goodwill, in which the crowds on shore freely joined.   Sir Henry Leeke, the naval commander at the station, accompanied each of the small squadrons in his yacht until he saw them fairly on their way, then sailing alongside the several ships shouted a good bye and " God speed " to all, which was heartily responded to by the troops.

Of the second fleet, the " Jessica " had the largest number of horses on board, 102.   Besides being undermanned, she was so hampered with a heavy deckload of hay, reaching apparently half way up to the crosstrees, that she could not use her sails under any circumstances, and in a heavy storm, encountered about half way up the Red Sea, ran a narrow risk of being cast adrift helpless.   The captain of the " Feroze " signalled that she must be prepared to go independently, as the strain was too great ; but, on being told of the utter unfitness of the " Jessica " to do so for the reason mentioned above, it was decided not to throw her off so long as the rope held out.   Fortunately the storm soon abated, and in due time the ship reached Suez in safety. The " Sultana " and " Clare " were also towed the whole way ; but the " Punjab " was found to sail so well— though only jury-rigged—that when the wind was strong she became independent of her tug, beating the little steamer " Auckland " so easily that she had to heave to from time to time until the latter got up to her.

On the voyage from Bombay to Suez the horses gave endless trouble on board ship ; but it must be remembered they were all entire, and, there being no other partition between them than a single bale of wood, they managed to get at one another and fight viciously. This appears to have been more especially the case

on board the " Punjab," on the occasion of a severe
storm three days after leaving Aden, in which considerable damage was sustained. Many of the horses got
loose, and it is related by an officer on board at the
time who witnessed it, that they not only fought with
one another, but that "some of them were seized with
uncontrollable excitement and became so ferocious,
foaming at the mouth like mad animals, that they were
destroyed by order of the veterinary surgeon and thrown
overboard." In addition to these losses, there was an
outbreak of glanders after leaving Bombay, when eight
or ten horses had to be shot, and a charger, the property
of Lieutenant Cass, died of congestion of the lungs.

The first detachment (the right wing, under Colonel
Wilkie), landed at Suez on the 10th February, and was
encamped in the desert outside Suez. After halting
there three days it commenced the march across the
desert to Cairo, and arrived there on the 17th February.
The fleet conveying the left wing and head-quarters
arrived at Suez, with the exception of the " Earl Grey,"
in the following order : the " Feroze " and " Jessica " on
the 19th February; the " Precursor " and " Clare " on
the 22nd. The first arrived troops disembarked on
the 20th, and marched to Cairo on the 25th. Those
on board the " Precursor " and " Clare " disembarked
on the 23rd, and marched on the 28th.

The site selected for the encampment of the several
detachments as they arrived at Suez was about two
miles from the town, close to Jacob's Well, in the desert.
This old well furnished a sufficient supply of water for
the horses, but it was of so brackish a quality as to be
quite unfit for human use. Water for the troops was
brought from the Nile on camels, the nearest point to
Suez from which it could be obtained being ninety
miles; but of course with each day's march this distance

lessened. This carriage of water was a serious labour, considering the large quantity required, but the supply provided was fairly ample, and, as a rule, punctually delivered.

At Suez each detachment, after disembarking horses and men, saddlery, stores, &c., rested sufficiently long to get everything ready for the march across the desert to Cairo. This march took four days, being at an average of about twenty-two miles a day, and the whole of the regiment, with the exception of the troop on board the " Earl Grey," was assembled at Cairo by the 3rd March, the last detachment, with Colonel Parlby and head-quarters, coming in on that day. The " Earl Grey" was still reported at sea, and it was afterwards ascertained that this ship had sprung a leak and had to put back to Aden. The troop on board of her— G troop—was landed there and encamped until the vessel was repaired and able to proceed. She at length reached Suez on the 13th March, and the troop arrived at Cairo on the 21st.

CHAPTER XXXI

MARCH FROM SUEZ—ARRIVAL AT CAIRO—THE VICEROY ENTERTAINS
THE REGIMENT—VISIT TO HAMIL PASHA—REVIEW OF THE 10TH
HUSSARS BEFORE THE VICEROY

THUS far the progress of the Tenth towards its desti-   1855
nation was eminently satisfactory. The voyage from
Bombay to Suez was accomplished by all the vessels
employed without any misadventure, with the exception of that just mentioned in the case of the "Earl
Grey." The embarkation on board the native boats
at Oolwa for conveyance to Bombay, an operation new
to all hands and carried out under unfavourable circumstances, was effected without serious difficulty, and
the disembarkation at Suez (likewise by means of
native boats somewhat unsuitable for the purpose) was
equally successful. The only mishap that occurred was
that both in the embarkation at Bombay and debarka-
tion at Suez a horse managed to slip his head collar
and jump out of the boat into the water. On the first
occasion, instead of making for land as might have
been expected, the horse took to the open sea and got
out some distance before he was overtaken by one of
the men (Private Nutt), who plunged in after him, and
succeeded in bringing him back to land. This soldier contracted disease of the chest shortly afterwards,
from which he died, and it was considered not unlikely
to have had its origin in the long immersion which
he had undergone on this occasion. The other case

1855   occurred at Suez. After having been safely transferred from the " Punjab " to the boat for landing, one of the horses, before he was properly secured, jumped out again. This happened close to the ship in deep water, the anchorage being between two and three miles from Suez. One of the Lascar crew (a boatswain), seeing what had happened, immediately seized a piece of rope, attached it to the horse sling, and jumping overboard dived with it under the animal, and brought it up at the other side, and the horse was then speedily lifted out of the water and replaced in the boat.

On the march from Suez to Cairo a very great deal of trouble was experienced from the horses breaking loose from their lines, owing to the picketing pegs not holding in the sandy soil of the desert. This was in a measure overcome by fastening the ropes to corn sacks filled with sand and sunk in the ground. In every other respect the march was accomplished with ease. This was largely, if not entirely, due to the admirable arrangements made to facilitate it by the two officers of the Honourable East India Company's Service who were sent in advance of the regiment by the Indian Government—Major Fraser, of the Commissariat, and Captain Gell,[1] of the Quartermaster-General's department, Bombay Army. Before the arrival of the troops, these officers had water troughs constructed for watering the horses, and established depôts for the supply of provisions for the men and forage for the horses at each of the stations in the desert at which it was decided that the halts should take place. They had also arranged with the Egyptian Government for the necessary carriage of all supplies, regimental baggage and stores, as well as the daily supply of water from the Nile. In this service several hundred camels were

[1] Afterwards Quartermaster-General of the Bombay Army.

employed. The daily marches were long and dreary, more dreary than they otherwise would have been, as they were made in the night in order to avoid exposure to the midday heat. The nights were found to be bitterly cold, and, as it was impossible to proceed otherwise than at a walk for the first three hours, or until daylight appeared, it was more keenly felt. Reveillé sounded between one and two A.M., and the march usually commenced about two, the troops getting into camp at the next station between seven

and eight, or even earlier. As it would have been otherwise quite impossible to find the way through the desert, the Egyptian Government provided a guide, who marched in advance of the column with a lantern suspended from the end of a pole carried over his shoulder. Though there was doubtless a more or less beaten track made by the passenger vans going every fortnight or so between Suez and Cairo, this was of course quite invisible at night. The stars were the only available directors of the way, and they were not sufficient guides for those unaccustomed to go by them. The Egyptian Government also provided an official to accompany and attend upon each detachment, to give whatever assistance he could. He was chiefly required to act as interpreter, and to direct and keep in order the small army of camel drivers and other followers, who were not too amenable to control, and would have been quite unmanageable without this help.

On arrival at Cairo the Tenth was quartered in the Cavalry Barracks at Abbasiyeh, about three and a half miles from the town eastward, on the edge of the desert, and here, instead of a few days as was at first expected, it had to remain nearly six weeks. The regiment was, however, by no means idle. Besides turning the time to good account in breaking in the remounts purchased just before embarkation at Bombay, and also some officers' chargers, likewise newly acquired specially for the campaign, commanding officer's field days and adjutant's drill were held, which served to keep the horses exercised and the men sufficiently employed. For this detention at Cairo various reasons were assigned—the want of suitable vessels for the transport of horses at Alexandria, the scarcity of forage in the Crimea, and the inadequacy of the supply to meet the requirements of two additional regiments of full strength, &c. But whatever the real reason was, seeing that the operations then going on at the seat of war were not of a nature in which cavalry could take an active part, the delay in getting there was not regretted, as under different circumstances it would have been, and the sojourn at Cairo was found a very acceptable and enjoyable break in the long journey from India. Saïd Pasha, who was then the Viceroy, did everything in his power to make their stay in the country under his rule agreeable to the officers. From the moment of their setting foot on Egyptian soil he insisted on their considering themselves his guests, and treated them with an Oriental hospitality truly regal. A regular mess was established in the barracks for the officers quartered there, under the management of a steward, and a staff of servants who provided for all their wants. Plate, linen, glass, china, cooking utensils, and every requisite were supplied; while the married officers, who, with their wives and children, were put up at Shepheard's Hotel in Cairo, lived there likewise as the Viceroy's guests. The Viceroy also honoured the officers with an invitation to dinner at one of his summer residences down the Nile, near the Barrage, and provided a steamer to take them there and back and carriages to drive them from and to the barracks. Colonel Parlby and nearly the whole of the officers availed themselves of this invitation. At Boulac, the port of Cairo, they found on arrival there from the barracks the steamer in readiness, and on board waiting to receive them were Mahomet Pasha and several other native gentlemen of distinction, with Mr. Bruce (afterwards Sir Frederick Bruce), Her Majesty's Consul-General in Egypt. A little over an hour and a quarter with the stream and fast steaming brought the party to the Barrage, a splendid piece of engineering work, intended not only to serve as a bridge across the Nile, but as a *bund* or dam (hence the name) for irrigation purposes. On landing, the party walked to the Viceregal Palace, where His Highness was waiting to receive them. The officers, having been all duly presented, were entertained at an excellent luncheon, and after spending some hours in the gardens and grounds returned to Cairo by steamer in the evening.

Some days after this an entertainment which greatly interested the officers was given to them by

T

1855 Hamil Pasha, son of the late Viceroy, Abbas Pasha.
That, however, was of an entirely private nature,
whereas that of the Viceroy, Saïd Pasha, was more or
less an official *levée*, in full dress. Hamil Pasha paid
the Tenth an informal visit at the barracks, and was
shown round the stables to see the horses, a subject evidently of great interest to him. He then invited
the officers to a luncheon at his residence some little
distance from Cairo, and afterwards to visit his stables,
where he kept a large number of thorough-bred mares.
This was considered an unusual compliment, as amongst
owners of Arab horses some superstition prevails with
respect to brood mares being looked upon by infidel
eyes, or indeed the eyes of any stranger. Later in the
day feats of horsemanship were exhibited by mounted
Arabs; amongst others what is described by an eye-
witness as a sort of tournament with the *jereed*.

Amongst the many objects of interest which must
be seen before leaving Cairo stood, of course first and
foremost, the great pyramids of Ghizeh. But besides
these and other similar objects of curiosity and interest
in the neighbourhood of Cairo, at that time not so well
known to travellers as now, the exploration of the city
itself proved more than enough, presenting as it did
such endless variety. On the other hand, the Tenth
did not fail to do all in its power to show its apprecia-
tion of the friendly and hospitable reception it met with
on all hands. Several reviews and field days were held,
which seemed to prove a great attraction, judging by
the large numbers of people who came out to witness
them. The band of the regiment, too, which frequently
played in public, appeared to afford much gratification
to many people in Cairo. A grand review was held
for the Viceroy, at which the Duke and Duchess of
Brabant and the *élite* of Cairo were present. On one

occasion there was a parade for Mustapha Pasha, and on another an inspection by His Royal Highness the Duke of Brabant, and the barracks were frequently visited by crowds of native gentlemen wishing to see the horses in their stables, objects of special interest to them as connoisseurs of Arab blood.

CHAPTER XXXII

DEPARTURE FROM CAIRO— MARCH TO ALEXANDRIA—A CHALLENGE
FROM AN ARAB SHEIK—REGIMENT EMBARKS — ARRIVAL AT
BALACLAVA — FIRST ENCAMPMENT — REDUCED CONDITION OF
THE BRITISH CAVALRY DIVISION

1855   AT length the time arrived that the interrupted journey
must be resumed. The 12th Lancers, following the
Tenth from India for the same destination, were now
close at hand, and the barracks at Abbasiyeh had
to be vacated to make room for them. As the first
day's march was to be a short one, only a few miles
out of Cairo, it was decided not to start till 2.30 in the
afternoon, in order that the men should have their
dinners once more in comfort, as it was thought likely
that they might not do so again for some time to come.
At that hour, therefore, on the 26th March the regiment moved out of barracks at Cairo to commence its
march to Alexandria, and, proceeding first through
Cairo and then along the right bank of the Nile, crossed
the river by a bridge of boats at Ghizeh, a village
directly opposite the Pyramids of Ghizeh, and encamped
about a mile and a half down the river on the other
side. The country now passed through was very
different from that between Suez and Cairo, for though
the desert route could not boast of made roads any
more than the country between Cairo and Alexandria,
yet there was a track practicable for wheel convey-

ances, in constant use for many years, whereas now
the route lay across an almost wholly trackless country,
with the exception of the last two marches, and over
ground so broken that no carriage of any sort could
accompany the column. Boats had therefore to be
provided for the transport of baggage, stores, supplies,
&c., and for men falling sick by the way, and, as each
day's encampment must of necessity be within easy
reach of the river on account of water being nowhere
else obtainable, this arrangement answered very well.
Captain Gell, of the Bombay Quartermaster-General's
Department, one of the officers already mentioned as
having been sent by the Indian Government in advance
of the troops to conduct them through Egypt and make
all the necessary arrangements for the march, had already been twice over the ground, and selected the best
line to take and the most suitable halting-places, having
regard to the peculiar requirements of the case, and it
was estimated that, by the route chosen, the march
to Alexandria would cover at least 165 miles. The
Tenth, having halted at Ghizeh on the following day,
proceeded on the 28th to its next encampment at
Ecksas, a mile and a half below the Barrage, marching
at about 5.30 A.M. On the journey from Cairo to Alexandria it was not possible to begin the march before daylight, as had been done between Suez and Cairo, owing
to the nature of the country over which the route lay.
On this second day's march the horses had in many
places to go in single file, and even then a very circuitous
route had to be taken to escape from serious obstacles.
It was reckoned that the distance gone over could not
be less than sixteen miles, though if a more direct course
could have been followed it would not have been,
perhaps, more than half as much.

On the 29th, setting out, as on the day before, about

dawn, the regiment marched to Guta. The first part of the way was along the top of one of the numerous embankments made for effecting the irrigation of the country on the rising of the Nile, and was fairly firm ; but the last five miles were over a stretch of desert, where the sand was very deep, heavy, and trying for the horses. The next day, however, was worse, the route from Guta to Benisalameh being over a similar tract of deep sand the whole way. A very pretty site had been selected for the encampment at Benisalameh, and the intention was to halt there for a day, but unfortunately, the ground being very much of the same nature as that traversed on the march, and very unsuitable for picketing, the intention had to be abandoned, and the march was continued next morning for Meschleh, a distance of fourteen miles, over very rough ground. At this place the camping ground held the picketing-pegs well, and the halt intended to be made at Benisalameh was made here, though the site of the camp had the disadvantage of being a mile and a half from the river.

On the 2nd April, at 5.30 A.M., the march was resumed, and as it was over a very fine track, being along the bank of a canal nearly the whole way, the horses were for the first time able to proceed at a trot. Taking advantage of this for a distance of seven miles without a check, the regiment arrived in its next encampment at Kaffir-Bulin by 9.30 A.M., a much earlier hour than usual. Here the horses were picketed in what looked like, and was at first supposed to be, a field of full-grown clover, and hitherto untouched. It was not, however, clover, but a plant very much resembling it, called *burseem*, a course of feeding on which at this season is considered to be particularly wholesome for horses ; and the horses availed

themselves of the opportunity thus offered them very
freely.

The next day's march was to Gubaris, about fifteen miles. Here an incident occurred which proved a source of considerable amusement. Shortly after arrival on the ground, and just as the officers were returning from "midday stables," an Arab sheik, attended by a small bevy of followers, rode into camp, and, on being introduced by an interpreter, announced himself to be the chief personage in these parts, and the possessor of a thorough-bred Arab, which he was prepared and desirous to race against any horse in the regiment over any distance short or long. The challenge was accepted, the terms quickly settled, and the stake (30*l.*) agreed upon. The surprise of all was great on seeing the Arab " racer," a grey horse, good-looking enough and apparently well-bred, but evidently just off a clover field and unfit for a gallop. A charger of Lieutenant Hudson's had been selected for the match, to be ridden by Lieutenant Townley, and as soon as everything was ready a start was made. For the first half mile the sheik got off better than could have been expected, but it need hardly be told what the result was with a fat shoeless horse against another in hard condition ridden by an expert. The sheik paid his money readily enough—that was seemingly a very small matter; but that he could no longer boast of being the possessor of a horse that nothing could approach, and enjoy the corresponding respect such a treasure ensured him, was the sore point, and he went away very crestfallen indeed.

From Gubaris the Tenth marched to Damanhour, a distance of fifteen miles, on the 4th April, and halted there over next day. This was found to be a place of more importance than had yet been met with.

The town was of considerable size, and could boast of a bazaar on a small scale, in which a variety of commodities were exposed for sale. There were also a number of coffee-shops and a good many other shops at which drinks of a less innocuous character could be obtained. The regiment was particularly warned against the latter, the liquor being said to be of the vilest description, and accordingly precautions were at once taken to prevent resort to them.

The next day's march being a long one (twenty-three miles), it was commenced at 4.30 A.M. So early a start was possible, as the road was much better, one that could be followed independently of daylight, and the next halting-place, Kaffir-Dowar, was reached at 10 A.M. It proved a very tedious march; but that of the following day, the 7th April, from Kaffir-Dowar to Alexandria, was a still longer and more fatiguing one, the distance being estimated at over thirty miles. Though an early start was made, Alexandria was not reached till towards midday. On arrival here the s.s. " Etna" was found waiting, and next day (Sunday, the 8th), the first detachment, consisting of D and H troops, under the command of Colonel Wilkie, embarked on board that vessel, and sailed next morning for Balaclava. The second detachment embarked on the 9th on board the "Himalaya," and sailed on the morning of the 10th. It consisted of the head-quarters, under Colonel Parlby, and as many troops and horses [1] as the vessel could accommodate. It arrived at Constantinople on the 13th April about seven P.M., and off Balaclava on the 15th in the course of the forenoon, but was not able to come inside the harbour till towards evening.

Colonel Parlby went on shore at once to report his arrival at head-quarters, and was immediately appointed

---

[1] The " Himalaya " took 350 horses.

to the command of the Cavalry Division during the temporary absence of General the Hon. James Yorke Scarlett on leave.

The first detachment had arrived on the 14th, but
was not yet landed. Its disembarkation was not
commenced till the morning of the 16th, and that of
the head-quarters not till early on the 17th; by the
afternoon of that day the disembarkation of both was
completed, and the regiment found itself encamped in
the Crimea, the journey from India having occupied a
period of 109 days, from the departure of the first
detachment from Kirkee to the arrival of the head-
quarters at Balaclava, including the detention at Cairo.
A considerable portion of the regiment had still to
come. Owing to the want of available transports,
170 men and 168 horses, under the command of Major
Harrison, had to be left behind at Alexandria. A
small detachment had been likewise left at Cairo, to
come on by steamer to Alexandria, its departure to be
timed so as to meet the regiment on its arrival there.
It consisted of Lieutenant Burn-Murdoch in command,
Assistant-Surgeon Macbeth, fifty men left either sick in
hospital or because unfit to march, the Indian Hospital
Staff, and a few native followers. The whole of this
party arrived at Alexandria on the morning of the 9th
April. With the exception of five men, the sick were
now all fit for duty, and were sent to their respective troops. Lieutenant Burn-Murdoch rejoined his
troop on board the "Himalaya." Assistant-Surgeon
Macbeth was sent home to England on sick leave
and did not again rejoin. The five men still too ill
for active service in the field were sent under his
charge to Malta. The Indian Hospital Staff and other
native followers, ghorawallahs, &c., were left at Alexandria, whence they were sent back to Bombay; and a

transport, the screw steamer " Trent," having shortly afterwards arrived, the last detachment came on by her to the Crimea, and disembarked at Balaclava on the 19th April.

The site first selected for the encampment of the Tenth in the Crimea was about two miles from Balaclava and three-quarters of a mile from the little hamlet of Karani, up the valley along which ran the road to Sebastopol. It was close to, but on a higher level than, the position occupied by the rest of the cavalry in the lower and more open part of the same valley. The contour of the ground, however, appeared so unfavourable for camping, that it was objected to on sanitary grounds by the surgeon of the regiment immediately on landing. It sloped gently from all sides towards the centre, so as to form, as it were, a shallow basin, from which there was no outlet, and was, therefore, certain to become flooded in the not unlikely event of a heavy fall of rain. But the position having been already decided on, the lines laid out, the greater portion of the tents pitched, and the troops actually disembarking, no change could then be made. In a few days, however, permission was received to move to any other ground in the neighbourhood which the commanding officer might consider more eligible. A site was, therefore, selected on a ridge of at least 200 feet higher level than the first position and quite out of the valley, a pretty turf-covered slope on which no rain could lodge, overlooking all the other camps in the neighbourhood (French and English), and the Balaclava plain up to the Tchernaya and the heights beyond. Unfortunately, before the change could be made rain fell and the encampment became a swamp. The Indian cotton tents, sodden with wet, were so heavy that they could not be carried up the comparatively steep ascent that led to the new ground. It was not until the weather and the condition of the tents admitted of it that the regiment was moved to what turned out to be its permanent encampment whilst in the Crimea. This position was a little further from Balaclava and nearer Karani. The distance from the rest of the cavalry was considerable, but not sufficiently far to prevent loose horses from the Tenth finding their way to their neighbours (a not unfrequent occurrence), where they were anything but welcome visitors. They gained for themselves a very evil reputation on account of their aggressive propensities, as they did also from mounted officers and others passing along the road to and from the front, whom they often chased, with great impartiality and without regard to person or rank.

The landing of the Tenth in the Crimea excited a good deal of interest, not only in the Cavalry Division, whose ranks it came to reinforce, but in the army generally. Crowds of officers of all ranks and men came down from the front to witness the disembarkation. The beautiful Arab horses were objects of special admiration, and the smart and soldierlike appearance of the men seemed to meet with much approval. It may be mentioned here that the moment the final orders were received for the regiment to proceed to the Crimea, Colonel Parlby abolished razors and pipeclay, so that the men by this time, with their well-grown beards, buff belts, slings, and gloves, looked more like old campaigners than men newly arrived in the field. After the camp was pitched the Indian tents evoked an amount of admiration and envy of which they were in reality anything but worthy. They were not the single pole-tent with double roof and flies issued to European troops in India, but the common " routie " (so called in Bombay), used by native troops and servants. As compared with the bell-tent of the English army, they looked roomy and comfortable, and they were so in fine, dry, sunshiny weather; but in wet weather they were scarcely any protection whatever, and gradually they were all given up in exchange for the English canvas tent.

CHAPTER XXXIII

A RECONNAISSANCE—DAILY DUTIES OF THE CAVALRY—ARRIVAL OF
THE SARDINIAN ARMY—THE QUEEN'S BIRTHDAY—THE LINE
OF THE TCHERNAYA OCCUPIED—THE SECOND BOMBARDMENT OF
SEBASTOPOL—AN ADVANCE UNDER GENERAL DE LA MARMORA

THE regiment arrived in the Crimea to find the army   1855
only recovering from the hardships and severity of an
especially hard winter, with but scanty resources in the
way of shelter, food, or other comforts to resist it. The
cavalry, already cut down and reduced by the actions
of the preceding October, was now almost extinct, the
number of horses left in the light cavalry at the end
of the winter being barely sufficient to mount even a
squadron. The arrival of the Tenth at this time was,
therefore, of great value, as it added at least 500 sabres
to the strength of the Cavalry Division, and it was soon
made to realise that at last it was actually taking part
in the work of the campaign. On the morning of
the 18th April, the very next day after its disembarkation, the regiment was turned out at 3.30 A.M.,
on account, it was said, of an expected advance of
the Russians towards the Tchernaya, but after remaining under arms till daybreak this proved to be a false
alarm. Next day, the 19th, a reconnaissance was made,
with the view of ascertaining the real strength and
position of the enemy on the Tchernaya. This was
deemed necessary by Omar Pasha, who occupied at that

time the right of the allied position with the Turkish army, and in order to enable him to carry it out effectually additional troops were placed at his disposal by the French and English commanders (Generals Canrobert and Lord Raglan), the former sending a body of cavalry and a battery of horse artillery, under General Feroy, and the latter two squadrons of heavy cavalry, the 10th Hussars, and half a battery of horse artillery, under Colonel Parlby. With these detachments and twelve battalions of Turkish infantry the Turkish general proceeded at daybreak over the plain extending from Balaclava towards the Tchernaya. " As the force moved on, evidences of the fatal and glorious 25th October became thick and painful. With the clash of drums and the shrill strains of the fife, with the champing of bits and ringing of steel, man and horse swept over the remnants of their fellows in all the pride of life. The Scots Greys and Inniskillings, the 4th and 5th Dragoon Guards, all had been there, and the survivors might well feel proud when they thought of that day. The 10th Hussars were conspicuous for the soldierly and efficient look of the men and the fine condition of their light, sinewy, and showy horses." [1] As the force descended into the plain it extended its right flank towards Kamara, and its left advanced towards Tchorgoun. On this side of the river the enemy showed only a few Cossacks, who stood on a height overlooking Tchorgoun ; from this they were quickly driven by a few discharges of rockets from the English horse artillery. On the other side, behind the bridge, only a small force of four guns was visible. Omar Pasha did not think it desirable to cross the river, but spent some time with Lord Raglan and the French generals in surveying the surrounding country from

[1] W. H. Russell, *Times'* Correspondent.

Kamara and the neighbouring heights, the summits of which had been attained and were now occupied by his troops. After satisfying himself that the enemy was not in strength, he withdrew, the troops returning to camp, covered by the cavalry and artillery. Before moving off the ground the 10th Hussars filed past Omar Pasha, who seemed very much gratified and pleased at the appearance of men and horses.[1] In the meantime the last detachment of the regiment was being disembarked, and joined head-quarters in camp in the course of the day. It arrived too late to take part in this reconnaissance.

The daily routine of the cavalry at this time consisted of reconnoitring, outpost, convoy, and orderly duty. Owing to the scarcity of horses in the Cavalry Division, these duties fell very heavily on the Tenth until the arrival of the 12th Lancers, and even for some short time after that ; but the voids in the ranks of the skeleton regiments that had passed the winter in the Crimea and had served throughout the war were being gradually filled up by large drafts of men and horses from England, and before long two more regiments, the Carabiniers and 1st Dragoon Guards, were added to the strength of the Cavalry Division.

On the night of the 8th May General De la Marmora, with a portion of the contingent sent by Sardinia to join the army of the Allies before Sebastopol, arrived off Balaclava, to the number of 5,000 men. The General landed next morning, and was received and escorted to head-quarters by a troop of the 10th Hussars.

On the 24th May, being the anniversary of the Queen's birthday, the whole of the British cavalry were reviewed on the open high ground between Karani and St. George's Monastery. The muster was not a large

[1] *Illustrated London News*, 12th May, 1855.

one, being about 1,400 sabres in all, of which the 10th Hussars and 12th Lancers contributed 800. The whole of the Light Cavalry Brigade (excepting the 10th and 12th) only mustered one squadron of not much more than 100 men. It should be mentioned, however, that the 8th Hussars had sent 50 men with the Kertch expedition, which had just started the day before, while a like number of the same regiment were employed at head-quarters as guards and for orderly duty. The cavalry and horse artillery were drawn up in one very extended line until the arrival of Lord Raglan, General Pelissier (who had assumed command of the French army a few days before), and Omar Pasha. These generals were attended by a numerous staff and strong escort, conspicuous amongst the former being the picturesque figure of an Arab sheik. The usual review formula of marching past was then gone through, after which the line was again formed and a general salute given, with three cheers for the Queen. About the same time a royal salute was fired by the fleet lying off Sebastopol and Kamiesch, which was well in view from the ground on which the parade was held. At the close of the review Lord Raglan expressed his satisfaction at the manner in which the 10th Hussars was mounted.

About eight o'clock the same evening the Tenth received orders to turn out during the night and to move down and be drawn up near Canrobert's Hill by three A.M. It paraded a little after two A.M., and, marching down to Kadikoi, halted before dawn near the place appointed. As the day broke troops of every arm and of no less than four nations could be seen advancing into the plain and spreading out like a fan from the village of Kadikoi. The only British troops present on this occasion were the Marines, the 10th Hussars, and the 12th Lancers, with two troops of horse artillery, under Colonel Parlby. The Marines occupied the heights on the extreme right, and between them and the English cavalry was a body of Turks. The main body of the Sardinian contingent moved forward to the left of the English cavalry, while the French, with some Turks, occupied the extreme left, more in the direction of Inkerman. The force numbered altogether about 20,000 men, the larger portion being composed of French troops, with a division of the Sardinian army, 5,000 Turks, and the small force of British troops above mentioned. The general forward movement was made almost simultaneously. The Tenth went over nearly the same ground as on the occasion of the reconnaissance of the 19th April, having the solitary church of Kamara close on the right, and drew up on the banks of the Tchernaya, not far from the bridge across the river on the Woronzow road. Whilst there some heavy firing was heard over the hill to the left, which was afterwards ascertained to have proceeded from a Russian redoubt, placed on a distant range of the heights running towards Inkerman. It had opened fire on the French, whilst attacking a large redoubt to their front, which was taken at the point of the bayonet. It was found, contrary to all expectation, that the guns had been removed, and that the work was defended by an inconsiderable force.

Whilst this was going on on the left, the 10th Hussars and 12th Lancers, with the horse artillery and some Sardinian riflemen, remained halted as mentioned above, but presently General De la Marmora, who commanded that wing of the force, rode up and gave orders to Colonel Parlby to send out a small body of cavalry in advance of the column. Whereupon a troop of the Tenth, commanded by Lieutenant Hopson, was ordered

U

to go forward by the Woronzow road, and to be followed by another commanded by Lieutenant Burn-Murdoch in support. The first advanced until it came upon a village into which some Cossacks were seen galloping back as it approached. Here two men, who said they were Greeks, came out of the village and voluntarily surrendered. Others of the inhabitants, men and women, were seen hurriedly departing and leading some horses away with them. On a report of the circumstances being conveyed to the officer commanding the brigade, the party was ordered to proceed no farther, but to remain halted where they were, attack forming no part of the forward movement. After a time they were withdrawn to the main body, and the Tenth slowly retired and halted on the ground near the church at Kamara with the rest of the brigade. In this advance the only opposition met with was on the left ; but the enemy was nowhere in force and offered little resistance, retreating rapidly into the hills. An active fire, however, was kept up from the batteries on the side of the Inkerman heights, but the shells usually burst short in the air; and the shot, although falling as far as the redoubt near Tchorgoun, failed to do any execution.

Whilst the troops engaged in the more advanced position served to attract the attention of the enemy and cause him to retire, the occupying forces behind them were making all arrangements for, and busily engaged in, taking up a new position on the line of the Tchernaya, fortifying it, and permanently encamping themselves. This being at length accomplished, and the object of the advance attained, the covering troops were withdrawn, and the Tenth, with the rest of the cavalry and artillery, after having stood several hours at Kamara, marched back to Kadikoi. On the way back they found large bodies of French and Sardinians already encamped, and their tents pitched on ground where the day before Cossacks only were to be seen. The Tenth got back to its camp at two P.M., having been out nearly twelve hours. The occupation of the line of the Tchernaya was a great relief to the Cavalry Division, as it was then no longer required for outpost duty and outlying piquet in that direction, duties which fell very heavily on it during the months of its attenuated strength.

During the time the Tenth had been engaged in the preceding movements, the siege of Sebastopol had been progressing slowly. On Easter Monday, the 9th April, the second bombardment had commenced, but it was not until the 7th June that the Allies felt justified in making an assault. On that day the English attacked and took the Quarries, and all through the following night repelled the repeated attacks of the Russians to retake them. The French at the same time captured the more important position of the Mamelon with great gallantry and immense loss. It was now decided to develop the assault as soon as possible. On the 17th a heavy cannonade was opened upon the Redan and Malakoff, and on the following day these two powerful works were gallantly attacked, but without success, the losses being exceedingly heavy.

On the 3rd June a reconnaissance was made on Baidar by a body of French troops under General Morris and General Canrobert and a column of the Sardinian corps under General De la Marmora. The former proceeded by the Woronzow road and pushed their cavalry several miles beyond Baidar,[1] while the latter operated on the left through a mountainous district and advanced into Baidar without seeing more of the enemy than a small number of Cossacks. It was

[1] Lord Raglan's Despatch, 5th June, 1855.

after that deemed expedient to make an advance from the right of the allied position before the assault on Sebastopol, with the view of creating a diversion. Accordingly, on the 17th June the Sardinian troops under General De la Marmora and the Turkish troops under Omar Pasha crossed the Tchernaya and occupied positions, the former in front of Tchorgoun and the latter in the Baidar Valley. On the 18th, between eleven and twelve o'clock at night, the Tenth received orders to send out a wing to join the Sardinian force. By eight o'clock next morning a detachment under the

command of Colonel Wilkie, consisting of four troops, numbering about 240 men, with three captains and four subalterns, moved out of camp for this purpose, and marching by Kadikoi over the Balaclava plain and across the Tchernaya, in due course arrived at Tchorgoun. Here the regiment halted for about half an hour. General De la Marmora had his head-quarters in the village, and to him Colonel Wilkie was directed to report and to await his orders. On receiving these, the Tenth, resuming its march, proceeded further up the Tchioulu Valley at right angles to the Tchernaya and in the direction of the great range of heights which extend from the Inkerman Valley towards Baidar and the sea. After advancing about a mile and a half it came upon a piece of flat table-land, fresh and green and dotted over with walnut and other trees, and there encamped. From this spot the Sardinian advanced post was not more than 500 yards to the front, with about the same distance between it and the enemy's outposts. It had been thought as probable that the whole number of Russians to be found nearer than the scarped summit of the Inkerman range above mentioned would barely exceed a handful or two of Cossacks. When, however, the Sardinians reached this position on the 17th, the enemy retired before them in some numbers, throwing a few shot and shell from light field guns as they retreated. No time was lost in turning the services of the Tenth to account. A squadron was at once ordered for outlying piquet at 5.30 P.M. and to patrol the heights to the left, looking towards the Mackenzie Farm. Several officers (staff and others) came into camp in the course of the afternoon, and in the evening General De la Marmora rode up, accompanied by a small staff.

Next morning, the 20th, the usual precautions in face of an enemy were taken, and the regiment turned out saddled and ready an hour before daylight. The officer in command was not satisfied with his position as suitable for cavalry, having a wooded country immediately in his front, and thought it advisable to withdraw his camp a couple of hundred yards. This was done in the course of the day. The duties here consisted of outlying piquets night and day, and patrolling the ground along the front of the position. The night piquet was relieved at 5.30 A.M. and the day piquet at 5.30 P.M.

On the 21st orders were received to ascend the

Baidar Valley and join the Turkish army, but were
afterwards countermanded, and the detachment was
directed to continue at the disposal of General De la
Marmora, some further movement being in contempla-
tion for the next day.   On the 21st the camp had been
again shifted, and moved this time half a mile farther
back.

On the 22nd reveillé sounded at 12.30 A.M.   The
regiment struck camp, was paraded and ready before
daylight, but no further instructions were received
until an officer returned from head-quarters with directions to wait till General De la Marmora's arrival.   It
then transpired that a reconnaissance was to be made in
considerable strength to the upper end of the Tchioulu
Valley as far as the village of Aitador, and on to the
base of the Mackenzie range, the main body of the
Sardinian army in the meantime to retire down the
Tchioulu Valley and resume its old position on the
Tchernaya, with Kamara immediately in the rear.   The
detachment of the Tenth was to retire after the reconnaissance and encamp on the Woronzow road.   This
programme was carried out.   When the reconnoitring
force arrived in the valley into which the Tchioulu
Valley debouches, lying along the base of the Mackenzie
range, it halted, and skirmishers were thrown out in
front and to the left, while General De la Marmora,
attended by a small party of the Tenth, rode up to the
village of Aitador.   As the skirmishers advanced a
slight fire of musketry was opened on them from the
crest of the Mackenzie range above, facing them, but
the shot passed over their heads without inflicting any
injury, the height being so great as to make good
practice scarcely possible.   Meantime a small field work,
of recent construction, situated a little below the great
range, opened fire on General De la Marmora and his

party, throwing one or two shells and some rockets on them; but, though the practice was good, fortunately no damage resulted. Great alarm, however, was created amongst the villagers lest the fire should be drawn upon them. Shortly after this the reconnoitring party retired, the rear of the column being covered by the Tenth. Leaving a brigade at Tchorgoun to protect that point, the main body of the Sardinian army proceeded to encamp near Kamara, the position assigned for the encampment of the Tenth being between the village and the river on the Woronzow road. The day's work had been severe, and all were fairly knocked up, neither officers nor men having had anything to eat before starting in the morning. General De la Marmora, on coming into camp in the evening, announced that it was not likely there would be any move on the morrow. This was very welcome news; a day's rest would refresh men and horses, as both had gone through much hard work during the last few days.

CHAPTER XXXIV

THE REGIMENT JOINS OMAR PASHA—STORM AT BALACLAVA—OUT-
BREAK OF CHOLERA—RETURN TO KARANI—DEATH OF LORD
RAGLAN—BATTLE OF THE TCHERNAYA—SIEGE OF SEBASTOPOL

1855   ON the 23rd June the head-quarters and remaining
troops received orders to move early next morning to
join the army under Omar Pasha in the valley of Varnootka, on the road to Baidar, leaving only a depôt with
the sick at Karani. The detachment with the Sardinian
army, having had the expected day's rest, received
similar orders in the course of the afternoon, and the
departure of that and the head-quarter detachment
from their respective encampments was so timed that
they should meet at a certain point on the way and
proceed together.

The same evening about eight o'clock a terrific
storm of wind and rain, accompanied by thunder and
lightning, suddenly burst over Balaclava and the valley
of the Tchernaya, from which the head-quarters at
Karani and the detachment at Kamara equally suffered.
The rain poured down in sheets of water. The lower
parts of the valley and neighbourhood of Balaclava
were flooded. Water-courses which had been almost
dry were swollen into foaming torrents, in crossing
which it was reported lives were lost, and much damage
was done both on shore and in the harbour. Officers
who had to march with the troops next morning sat up
all night in their cloaks, on their blankets instead of

lying under them, in a vain effort to keep, at all events, the latter dry, but expecting every moment to find their tents blown away with all they contained. Bad as was the outlook for the marching kit inside, it was even a more serious consideration how the soaked tents were to be moved and carried next morning. The storm, however, had expended its fury some time before dawn, and was succeeded by a bright, still, warm, beautiful morning, and the head-quarter wing left camp after an early breakfast to rejoin its comrades, which it did early in the afternoon. The other wing at Kamara, on break-ing up its camp, paraded before daybreak, and marching first by the Woronzow road, and crossing the Tchernaya by the Tractir bridge, made a *détour* to the left towards Teliou, a small country house with farm buildings. Here, with a battalion of chasseurs and three guns, two of the squadrons halted and took up a position, while the other squadrons went forward to reconnoitre in the direction of the village of Urkusta, by the road which passes by that village up to Ogenbash and the country beyond. On retiring from this reconnaissance the wing continued its march to join the Turkish army, and in the course of the afternoon the whole regiment, with the exception of the small depôt left at Karani, found itself encamped in the valley of Varnootka, in close proximity to the Turkish camp. The site selected here for its encampment seemed all that could be desired—an elevated, dry, gently sloping plateau, sur-rounded by most lovely scenery, wood-clad heights and rich tree-dotted valleys, intersected with small streams. The change from the bare, parched heights of Karani was felt by every one to be a great relief, and the expectation of active employment instead of the monotony of a stationary camp excited much satisfac-tion ; in short, there was a general rejoicing on all being brought together again. Unfortunately, however, this was not to be of long duration. That same night, shortly after sundown, Captain Bowles, one of the most esteemed officers in the Tenth, beloved by all, who marched into camp that afternoon apparently in perfect health, was struck down with cholera and was dead before ten o'clock next morning. Of this officer Lord Raglan writes in one of his last despatches before his own death: " With much sorrow I have to report the very sudden death of Captain Charles Bowles, of the 10th Hussars, an officer of great merit, who had served in India with distinction, and is much regretted in his regiment." This sad event, coming so suddenly and unexpectedly, cast, as may be imagined, a deep gloom over the whole regiment, which was not diminished by this first case being quickly followed by others. Before many days several deaths took place in rapid succession, though these were comparatively few in proportion to the number of attacks. The rapidity with which the fatal cases ran their course was most remarkable, and caused the outbreak to make a deeper impression than perhaps it would otherwise have done.

The veterinary surgeon of the Tenth, Mr. Siddell, a great friend of Captain Bowles, and who had been deeply affected by his death and greatly depressed in spirits, was taken ill on the 30th and died in the short space of about five hours. A few days later Farrier Jones and Private Lawler met with the same fate. Besides the cases of true Asiatic cholera, there was a large prevalence of a complaint presenting much the same character but of a less fatal type, and from this both officers and men alike suffered. The surgeon of the regiment sent a special report of the outbreak to the principal medical officer of the army, Sir John Hall, who came personally from head-quarters before

Sebastopol to pay a visit to the camp, but he could suggest nothing to improve its sanitary condition. The site of the camp had been already once changed, in the hope of bettering it, without any benefit. Notwithstanding the sickness that thus prevailed, the military duties demanded by the situation could not be neglected. The first day after arrival at Varnootka a reconnaissance in force was made to the north of Baidar, in which a squadron of the Tenth advanced very far to the front and came upon the outposts of the enemy, and no day passed in which it did not take part in some expedition or another.

In the meantime other changes became necessary. For some reason Omar Pasha considered it expedient to raise his camp. It may have been because the Russian troops in the neighbourhood of Baidar had lately been strongly reinforced; or possibly, the objects of the advance on that side having been attained, his army was no longer required there; or yet again, a change may have been considered advisable on account of the amount of sickness prevailing amongst the troops. In any case, on the 5th July orders for a move were suddenly and unexpectedly received, and the Turkish army, with the exception of one brigade, at once retired to take post again at Kamara on a high piece of ground to the right of the Sardinian position between Kamara and the sea, and the Tenth returned to its camp at Karani. Up to the last cases of cholera continued to occur from time to time at Varnootka, one of the latest victims being Sergeant-Major Davis, the paymaster's clerk, a much valued and respected non-commissioned officer. The total number of deaths, including two officers, was nine in the twelve days in camp at Varnootka. The regiment did not speedily recover from the state of ill-health into which it had fallen during its short sojourn with the Turkish army in the beautiful valley of Varnootka, and some fatal cases of cholera occurred immediately after the return to camp at Karani; but by the middle of the month (July) epidemic cholera might be said to have quite disappeared.

On the 28th June the English army heard with great regret of the death of its commander, Lord Raglan. On the 3rd July the remains were conveyed on board H.M.S. " Caradoc " with great ceremony. The road from the French head-quarters to Kazatch Bay was lined with the French Imperial Guard and the 1st Corps. Bands were placed at intervals, and field batteries (French) on the high ground fired minute guns. The procession to escort the body consisted of two squadrons 12th Lancers, two squadrons Piedmontese light cavalry, four squadrons of Chasseurs d'Afrique, four squadrons French cuirassiers, two troops of French horse artillery, and Major Brandling's troop of horse artillery. The band of the 10th Hussars was placed on the left of the line. On the death of Lord Raglan, the command of the English army devolved on General Simpson, as being the next senior officer, and he was confirmed in the appointment in the " London Gazette " on the 21st July.

On the 1st August the 10th Hussars paraded in marching order, and was inspected by Major-General the Hon. Sir J. Yorke-Scarlett, who on return from leave of absence resumed the command of the Cavalry Division from General Parlby.

On the 16th of August the Russians made their long-threatened attack upon the line of the Tchernaya. The movement, which ended in the complete defeat of the enemy, was no doubt intended as a vigorous attempt to force the Allies to raise the siege of Sebastopol. The Russian force engaged was estimated at 60,000 men, with 160 pieces of artillery. To these were opposed 12,000 French and 10,000 Sardinian troops, the English troops being principally held in reserve. Some batteries of English artillery were actively employed during the battle and did good service, the cavalry under General Scarlett being held in the plain of Balaclava prepared to take advantage of any circumstance that might present itself.[1] "Our light and heavy cavalry brigades were formed in two heavy masses, supported by artillery, in the plain behind the second Fedukhine hillock, two miles in advance of Kadikoi. The Allies had, in fact, not less than 6,000 very fine cavalry that day in the field, but they were held in check for fear of the artillery, which there is no doubt they could have captured, in addition to many thousands of prisoners, if handled by a Seidlitz or a Murat. But the French General (Pelissier) would not allow a charge to be executed, though French and English cavalry leaders were eager for it, and so this noble force was rendered ineffective."[2] During the battle a squadron of the Tenth, under Captain Walrond Clarke, acted in support of a battery of French horse artillery. The Russian attack proved unsuccessful at all points, and the enemy was in full retreat some time before midday, and thus ended the battle of the Tchernaya. The English cavalry and artillery fell back upon their camps, much discontented that they had had no larger share in the honours of the day.

" On the day following this battle the bombardment was resumed, and the English and French opened a terrific fire upon the enemy. The cannonade continued daily till the beginning of September, when with the usual lull which precedes a storm the fire from the opposing batteries became slower and less frequent."[3]

[1] General Simpson's Despatch.
[2] W. H. Russell in *Times*' correspondence.   [3] Douglas.

" The English cavalry were employed during this time in frequent reconnaissances in the Baidar Valley and also in collecting forage. Every morning they might be seen moving over the ground where their comrades fell, and watching an opportunity to avenge them. The effect was imposing—perfect, one might say, if anything human could be called so. Horses and men were in excellent condition, as fit for work as any cavalry could be."[1]

On the morning of the 5th September the sixth and last bombardment of Sebastopol commenced. More than two hundred pieces of artillery of large calibre played incessantly on the hostile lines, and the total number of guns of the Allies at this time was no less than 830.[2] A perpetual fusillade of musketry was carried on every night on the face of the Russian works, some 150,000 rounds being expended each night. In the early morning of the 8th a strong force of cavalry, under Colonel Hodge, of the 4th Dragoon Guards, received orders to move up to the front and form a chain of sentries in front of Cathcart's Hill and all along our lines. No person was allowed to pass this boundary. Another line of sentries in the rear of the camp was intended to stop stragglers and idlers from Balaclava. After a vigorous cannonade and bombardment the French advanced from their trenches and succeeded in entering the Malakoff, but from twelve till seven in the evening they had to meet and repulse the repeated attempts of the enemy to regain the work. As soon as the tricolour was observed waving over the parapet of the Malakoff, as had been previously arranged, the English attacked the Redan with two divisions. The troops had to pass over 230 yards from the nearest approach to the parapet

---

[1] W. H. Russell.   [2] *Ibid.*

of the Redan, and in this they lost a large proportion of their officers. Reinforcement after reinforcement was brought up, and the desperate fight continued some time; but at last, after terrible carnage, the generals had to admit the failure of the English attack, and the remnant of troops was withdrawn. In the night the Russians began quietly to evacuate Sebastopol. About two A.M. flames were seen to break out in various parts of the town; then followed the strange roar of exploding magazines, and just as dawn broke two large forts crumbled into ruins. The ships in the harbour had all been sunk, and when the southern side of Sebastopol fell it was little better than an empty shell.[1] In the afternoon the allied generals visited the town, and the 10th Hussars provided a squadron as an escort to the Commander-in-Chief.

On the 14th September the Commander-in-Chief received a telegraphic communication from the Queen congratulating the army on the triumphant issue of the siege, and on the following day Her Majesty's gracious permission to bear the word "Sebastopol" on the colours, standards, &c., was notified to all the regiments serving in the Crimea.

[1] W. H. Russell.

CHAPTER XXXV

EXPEDITION TO KERTCH—CAPTAIN PERCY SMITH—THE CAVALRY DIVISION LEAVES THE CRIMEA—THE TENTH AT ISMID—PROPOSALS FOR PEACE—OCCUPATIONS AT ISMID—DEPARTURE FOR ENGLAND

1855 AN expedition of English and French troops had been sent to the Sea of Azoff in May, under General Sir George Brown. Captain J. Lyons, in command of the naval squadron, forced the Straits of Kertch, searched the towns and villages on the coasts of the Sea of Azoff from end to end, burning and destroying the ships and trading vessels of the Russians. The troops landed at Ambalaki and followed the enemy to Kertch, which was occupied as well as Yenikale. The magazines and stores at these two places were captured or destroyed, large quantities of corn were found, and in the dockyard and military establishments much valuable property was taken.

The force under Sir George Brown held these positions for two months; but, that general finding that he required additional cavalry if he was to gain further footing inland, a squadron of the 10th Hussars and a squadron of Chasseurs d'Afrique, the whole under the command of Colonel d'Osman, of the latter corps, embarked on board the "Himalaya" at Balaclava on the 3rd September, and were conveyed to Kertch. The strength of the squadron of the Tenth was Captain the Hon. F. FitzClarence, Captain J. Walrond Clarke,

Lieutenants Cass, Hatfield, and Buchanan, Cornet Hudson, Assistant-Surgeon Lofthouse (attached), and Veterinary Surgeon Partridge (17th Lancers), eight sergeants, one trumpeter, and 111 rank and file. On arrival off Fort St. Paul's, near Kertch, the horses were disembarked on rafts, and as soon as all were landed the detachment marched to the town, some four or five miles distant. Barracks were improvised out of some of the larger buildings, and the troops were comfortably housed. Piquets were sent out and a line of outposts formed some miles inland, the Tenth taking up the ground to the west of the town. The large number of Cossacks in the neighbourhood kept the advanced posts perpetually on the alert by continually showing a front and hovering round our vedettes.[1]

Before a fortnight had passed an opportunity was given to the cavalry to advance and discover the strength of the enemy. "On the 20th September information was received that considerable bodies of Cossacks were within a few miles of Kertch, plundering and carrying off forage. In consequence of this intelligence Colonel d'Osman received orders to take the detachments of the 10th Hussars and the 2nd Chasseurs d'Afrique and make a reconnaisance." The Cossacks were supposed to have assembled their "arabas"[2] at two villages, named Koss Serai Min and Seit Ali, equidistant from Kertch about fifteen miles, and from one another six and a half miles. Captain FitzClarence's troop was ordered to the first village and Captain Walrond Clarke's to the latter. At these villages each was to be joined by a troop of the Chasseurs d'Afrique. On arriving at Koss Serai Min, Captain FitzClarence

---

[1] "A Ride with the Cossacks at Kertch," *Cornhill Magazine.* Written by W. Douglas.

[2] Country carts, used by the Russians in their transport.

X

found both troops of the French dragoons, and immediately sent off an order to Captain Clarke to join him that night. This letter, conveyed by a Tartar villager, was unfortunately not delivered until the following morning,[1] and there appears to be no doubt that he went first to the Cossack camp and gave the Russian general the information of the position of Captain Clarke's troop.

Captain Clarke arrived at Seit Ali late in the evening after dark, and, finding no French chasseurs there, had to make his own dispositions for the safety of his party, posting his vedettes and sending out patrols to the front. A foraging party searched the neighbourhood for provisions, &c., with some success, and the party passed the night *en bivouac* without unsaddling. On the messenger arriving at daybreak from Captain FitzClarence, the outposts were called in and the troops marched to join the rest of the force. On crossing a small stream some little distance on the road a body of the enemy was seen advancing, covered by scouts. Captain Clarke formed up his troop, and after driving in the advanced parties charged the main body, which turned and fled. Following the enemy for two miles, the troop entered a narrow gorge, which was passed through, and on emerging found that there was a body of 300 Cossacks forming up near their camp. It then became obvious that retreat was imperative; but as the Cossacks followed through the pass some men were dismounted to check them with their carbines. This stopped the pursuit for a time, but the Cossacks still hovered round the flanks, and two guns were brought up from the rear, which, however, got into some marshy ground and were unable to come into action. Several prisoners had been taken in the advance,

---

[1] General Simpson's Despatch of 29th September, 1855.

but now they were set free, after disarming the men and shooting the horses. " Still retreating, we kept in the direction where Captain FitzClarence's troop was expected, and had gone about a mile when we heard a shout, and saw a strong body of the enemy forming across our line of retreat. There was no other course open but to penetrate this newly arrived force, so, drawing in his scouts, Captain Clarke wheeled about and charged through their centre. The Cossacks met this charge with a volley (mounted), which was quite harmless. The troop of the Tenth had thus the advantage of encountering the enemy at a halt, and, after cutting its way through, it made good the retreat. This was not done, however, without loss—two privates reported killed, one wounded, one troop sergeant-major, one farrier, thirteen men, and fifteen horses missing." [1]

A junction was now made with Captain FitzClarence and the squadron of chasseurs, who were also engaged with the enemy, having two regiments of Cossacks opposed to them. Colonel d'Osman fell back slowly with his whole force towards Kertch, halting when a good opportunity was afforded to charge the enemy. In one of these charges one private of the Tenth was shot and another received a lance wound ; eight French chasseurs were killed and several more wounded. The losses of the enemy were not known. In his despatch reporting this reconnaissance, General Simpson writes as follows : " From information received, the Cossacks were supported by eight squadrons of hussars and guns. Colonel Ready, commanding the troops, informs me that nothing could exceed the coolness and courage of the troops in presence of such overwhelming numbers of the enemy."

The English and French prisoners taken by the

[1] W. Douglas.

Russians were very well treated. Troop Serjeant-Major Finch, who from his appearance and gold lace on his uniform was taken for an˜officer, was specially cared for. Sergeant Parsons, Privates Bolter and Boys, who had been severely wounded, were left behind; but the remainder were marched on foot the next morning to Kaffa. On arrival there, they were taken before the general, a Pole, who had lost an arm. He received the prisoners very kindly, and spoke to them in English. After remaining at Kaffa a few days they continued the march, and, leaving the Crimea, were sent on by stages to Odessa. On the road the men had to ration themselves, and were given an allowance for this of ten kopecks a day, Sergeant-Major Finch receiving twenty kopecks. On the 5th January, 1856, they arrived at Odessa, in bitterly cold weather, and were put into a private house and comfortably lodged. They were allowed to walk about, but were escorted on all occasions by two Cossacks. An Englishman and his wife, named Hunt, were exceedingly kind to their countrymen, and provided them with blankets, underclothing, and tea.[1] The cavalry continued to perform the duties of outpost in the neighbourhood of Kertch until peace was proclaimed. The Tenth detachment then embarked in steamers and rejoined the head-quarters, then stationed at Ismid, in Turkey.

On the 15th September Colonel Parlby, now brigadier-general in command of the Hussar Brigade, sailed from Balaclava to proceed to England on the recommendation of a medical board. For some weeks the state of health of their old commander had been causing serious concern, and the feeling of regret was deep and universal when it became known that

---

[1] *Soldiering in Sunshine and Storm*, by W. Douglas, late Private 10th Hussars.

his condition had become such as to compel him to leave the Crimea. He was taken ill with the Crimean fever and dysentery and placed on the sick list two or three days before the battle of the Tchernaya, and his medical attendant (Dr. Fraser, of the Tenth), knowing him to be seriously ill and unfit to be out of bed, was greatly shocked to find him up and at the head of his brigade on the morning of that day ; but the general would listen to no advice or remonstrance, and remained on the field till the battle was over and the Cavalry Division withdrawn. The consequence of this was to seriously aggravate his illness and to incapacitate him for any further service in the Crimea ; but, being a man of sound constitution, the voyage and change to England soon restored him to health, and early in the spring, and before his sick leave had expired, he returned to duty, and resumed the command of his brigade at Scutari.

Towards the end of September the adjutant of the regiment, Captain Percy Smith, also left the Crimea on being promoted to a troop in the 2nd Dragoon Guards. This officer had served with the 16th Lancers throughout the campaign in Afghanistan under Lord Keane, and, as already mentioned, exchanged into the Tenth in 1848. After joining the 2nd Dragoon Guards he was appointed Adjutant of the Cavalry Depôt at Canterbury, and after the Crimean war Brigade Major at the Curragh, where he served under his old chief, General Parlby, but rejoined his regiment on its being ordered to India, and took part in the campaign during the Indian Mutiny. Early in 1858, previous to the relief of Lucknow, he commanded two squadrons of the Bays, and two of Lancers detached from the main body of the British force, and coming across some of the enemy's cavalry and infantry he was ordered by Brigadier-

General Hagart to pass round and attack them on their right, and so cut off their retreat on Lucknow. Percy Smith made his attack with great rapidity, and pressed the enemy back. The mutineers then began to open fire from the town, and their troops collected and made a stand. Seeing three of their infantry together, two loaded and one loading, he called on Captain Seymour, of the Bays, and two others, and rode at these men, when he was shot dead. Brigadier-General Hagart writes: " No one has ever fallen more universally beloved by officers and men, and more respected. I do not only speak of his own regiment, the Bays, but of the whole brigade."

There was now a lull in the campaign, and nothing of importance took place during the autumn beyond an expedition which was sent to Kinburn under General the Hon. A. Spencer, in conjunction with a French force under General (afterwards Marshal) Bazaine. In October two drafts arrived from England to recruit the strength of the Tenth. One, under the command of Lieutenant Branfill, consisting of two corporals and forty-four privates, arrived on the 15th, and another of one sergeant, one corporal, and 120 privates, joined head-quarters on the 24th.

As there was no immediate prospect of further military operations, nor any likelihood of the service of the cavalry being required during the winter months, it was decided to remove the Cavalry Division from the Crimea to more suitable winter quarters, leaving only a sufficient number for orderly and escort duties. The bulk of the division was quartered in Scutari, but one brigade was sent up the Sea of Marmora to the town of Ismid, which by road was about eighty miles from Scutari. This brigade consisted of the 8th Hussars, 10th Hussars, and 17th Lancers, under the command of Brigadier-General Shewell, of the 8th Hussars. The Tenth was conveyed from Balaclava to Ismid in the " Himalaya," " Assistance," and " Kangaroo." The first detachment, under Major Harrison, sailed on the 13th November, and the remainder of the regiment, with head-quarters, in the " Himalaya " on the 16th. The latter, stopping a night at Constantinople, arrived at Ismid a little after midday on the 19th. The disembarkation took some time, being interrupted by the state of the weather, but the whole regiment, with the exception of the squadron still at Kertch, was landed and in quarters on the 22nd.

Ismid is a seaport town situated on the acclivity of a hill rising from an inlet of the Sea of Marmora called the Gulf of Ismid. It was the ancient Nicomedia, and many interesting monuments of its former history are still to be met with here and there. By far the greater part of the town is built on the slope of the hill in terraces, which are approached by steep narrow streets ; but there is a quarter of considerable extent occupied by houses of the poorer class, stores, bazaars, &c., lying between the base of the hill and the sea. It was in this part that accommodation was found for the troops and stabling for the horses. The officers of the Tenth had a good large house assigned to them, from which a Turk and his family had to turn out for the occasion. Though the ground floor was available for storage only and such-like purposes, the house was of sufficient size to accommodate the whole of the officers and for the establishment of a mess. Steps were at once taken to procure sufficient furniture, tables, chairs, &c., and cooking appliances. Here for the first time since leaving Cairo the officers all lived together and passed the winter. The officers of the other regiments were similarly quartered in Turks' houses vacated by

1855   the owners, no doubt compulsorily; but the Tenth was
the only one provided with a house of sufficient size
to admit of all the officers messing together. Being
all under one roof added greatly to their comfort.
The troops were distributed through various quarters
of the lower portion of the town. The men of the
8th Hussars occupied the lower, the 17th Lancers the
centre, and the 10th Hussars the upper part of it.
Stabling was provided for the horses in large wooden
store-houses by the seashore. Those which were al-
lotted to the Tenth were handed over in such a condition that it seemed at first sight hopeless to expect that
they ever could be made into wholesome shelters for
horses. They were filled several feet deep with rotting
straw, dung, and rubbish of all sorts, the accumulation
of months, if not of years; but after much labour, out
of this chaos order, sweetness, cleanliness, and comparative comfort were evolved. The men's quarters
were at some distance from the stables in a higher and
better position, and, although the rooms were somewhat
limited in cubic space and destitute of the most ordinary accessories to comfort, the men were considered
to be well housed for troops on active service. They
were also fairly well rationed, and by the end of the
year all were settled down to the ordinary routine of a
regiment in quarters and enjoying a period of comparative rest and repose after their much-varied experience
and knocking about on sea and land during the last
twelve months.

Several changes took place amongst the officers during this year. These were as follows :—Left—Lieutenant T. Burn-Murdoch, appointed to the 6th Dragoons ;
Lieutenant F. T. O. Hopson, by exchange to the 19th
Foot ; Brevet-Captain T. Percy Smith, promoted and
appointed to the 2nd Dragoon Guards ; Lieutenant H. F.

Richmond, appointed to the 3rd Dragoon Guards; Lieu-
tenant T. Alston Clarke, appointed to the 15th Hussars;
Lieutenant Theodore Williams, retired by sale of com-
mission; Captain Charles Bowles, deceased; Veterinary
Surgeon Siddell, deceased. Joined—Lieutenant Ed.
Levett, from the 19th Foot; Assistant-Surgeon L. G.
Hooper.

At the close of 1855 and beginning of 1856 the
prospects of peace were not encouraging. On the contrary, the impression rather gained ground that war
would be resumed on a still wider scale. Proposals of
peace had been submitted, though not by the Allies,
but the Czar declined to entertain them. Russia was
still strong, and had many chances in her favour, and
it was considered that only larger successes on the part
of the Allies in the North as well as the South would
compel her to yield. A spring campaign was therefore
generally anticipated, and it was felt that every effort
must still be made to ensure the utmost efficiency on
taking the field. After a short period of rest, riding and
foot drills had been practised unremittingly at Ismid during the winter; labours brightened, however, with such
amusements as were available. For those who had the
requisite appliances (not usually part of a campaigning
kit), excellent shooting was to be had in the immediate
neighbourhood, and a certain number in each regiment
in the brigade were able to indulge in this sport. Beyond the town, further up the Gulf of Ismid, there was
a large tract of marshy land, some miles in extent,
which abounded with snipe and wild fowl of various
kinds. Woodcock, more inland, were to be found in
large numbers, and other game, but in more limited
quantity.

Although the first overtures for peace made by
Austria and Prussia were rejected, Russia before the

end of January announced that she was prepared to accept the Austrian proposals as " a basis of negotiation." No great faith was placed in this concession by the Allies, who were well aware that a somewhat similar offer had been made nearly twelve months before without any result. On this small beginning, however, hopes of peace, though perhaps but faint at first, began to be entertained. The Allies raised no difficulties in the way of renewed negotiation, which, being undertaken, culminated in an agreement between the Powers concerned, and on the 2nd April of this year a general order announced to the army that a treaty of peace had been signed. The prisoners of war rejoined from Russia, and those non-commissioned officers and men of the Tenth who had been captured near Kertch returned to the regiment at Ismid. Troop Sergeant-Major Finch, the senior non-commissioned officer amongst the prisoners, received the French war medal, which was distributed in certain numbers to the British army for conspicuous conduct in the field.

On the 21st April orders were received for the Hussar Brigade to be broken up, preparatory to embarkation, and Brigadier-General Shewell issued his parting order. Preparations were made at once by the Tenth for its departure, and orders were received that the horses were to be disposed of prior to leaving. Twenty were sold by auction at Ismid, and fair prices obtained. On the 5th May the Tenth marched from Ismid, and encamped two days later in the neighbourhood of Scutari. On the 18th a divisional order was issued that the horses of the 10th Hussars were to be made over to the Turkish Government on the 20th, and on that day officers of the Sultan came to the place appointed to receive them. To be obliged to leave behind their beautiful little Arab horses that had carried the men so well and had proved themselves such good campaigners, caused the deepest regret to all ranks. It will be understood that, even with the prospect of returning to England again after so many years' foreign service, it was a sad day for the men parting with the horses with which they had been associated in India, had ridden across Egypt, and which had carried them through the Crimean campaign.

On the 23rd May Captain Walrond Clarke and a detachment embarked on board the " Trent," and on the 5th June another under Major Harrison on board the " Brenda " for England. The head-quarters, under Colonel Wilkie, embarked on the 7th June on board the s.s. " Hindostan," and, sailing from Scutari the same day, arrived at Portsmouth on the 28th June. This was the last to arrive, and the whole of the regiment was now landed in England, thus bringing to a close a tour of foreign service which, including the Crimean campaign, extended over a period of ten years and two months.

Portsmouth was the port of disembarkation for all the detachments, and as each party arrived it was sent on to Birmingham, Coventry, and Brecon. The head-quarters, with Colonel Wilkie in command, came direct from Portsmouth to Birmingham immediately on landing, the detachment at Coventry being commanded by Major Harrison. At the various stations at which it halted on the way—Portsmouth, Oxford, and other towns—as well as at the final destinations of the several detachments, the regiment was greeted with hearty and enthusiastic cheers of welcome on its return from active service.

The depôt troop, which during the war and the service of the Tenth in India had been stationed at Maidstone, marched on the 4th June, under the command of Captain R. Playne Smith, with Lieutenants Benson and Stacey and Cornets Fife and Panmure-Gordon as his subaltern officers, and proceeded to Birmingham to join the head-quarters on arrival there; but on reaching Coventry, whilst *en route*, Captain Playne Smith and Lieutenant Stacey and part of the depôt troop were ordered to remain, and Lieutenant Benson and Cornets Fife and Gordon to go on with the remainder to Birmingham.

In recognition of the services of the Tenth in the Crimea, all ranks received a medal and clasp for Sebastopol, and also the Turkish medal, the field officers in addition the decoration of the Order of the Medjidieh; and the word "Sebastopol" was added to the honours of the regiment.

CHAPTER XXXVI

THE REGIMENT REDUCED—IN THE MIDLAND COUNTIES—CHANGE IN
THE DRESS OF HUSSARS—COLONEL PARLBY—REDUCTION OF THE
REGIMENT—THE INDIAN MUTINY AND CONSEQUENT INCREASE—
ALDERSHOT—COLONEL WILKIE—FIRST REGIMENTAL STEEPLE-
CHASES—COUNTRY QUARTERS

WITHIN a short time after its arrival in England the   1856
strength of the regiment was reduced from nine troops
(including the depôt troop) to six. This reduction
caused Captains Walrond Clarke and Arthur Loftus to
be placed on half-pay during this year, and the following amongst the officers in excess of the strength were
transferred to the Carabiniers—viz. Major Lord George
Beauclerck, Captain Rosser, and Lieutenants Bird, Buchanan, Davies, Hudson, Uniacke, De Bourbel, and
Vyse. These officers joined their new regiment in
India, and were present at Meerut on the outbreak of
the Mutiny on the 10th May, 1857, and took part in
the various engagements that ensued. The following
amongst them were killed and wounded :—Lieutenants
Hudson and Vyse were killed in the charge of the
Carabiniers at Gungaree ; Captain Rosser was severely
wounded at the taking of Delhi, and died from his
wounds some years afterwards at Sandhurst, where he
held the appointment of ridingmaster ; Lieutenant De
Bourbel was severely wounded and lost a great portion
of one hand at the battle of Hindun.

From Birmingham the following detachments were
found. On the 30th June Captain Alexander marched

with his troop to Brecon, and on the 1st July the two troops commanded by Captains Cowell and Clarke followed him there. In September a move was again made, when Captain Cowell's and Captain Alexander's troops marched from Brecon to Coventry. On the 19th September the Tenth was inspected by Major-General the Earl of Cardigan, Inspector-General of Cavalry.

The dress of hussars had undergone an alteration during the Crimean War, the changes being published in the Dress Regulations of 1855. The Tenth being then on active service, the new uniform was only now introduced. The hussar jacket with pelisse and the gold and crimson sash were abolished, and a tunic with skirt was introduced. The rank of officers was distinguished by more or less braid worn on the collar and sleeves.[1] Strapped overalls were worn for mounted duties.

The 10th Hussars on its return from the seat of war had been mounted on horses transferred from other regiments. In June, 207 horses were received from the Carabiniers. In July, fourteen horses joined from the 3rd Light Dragoons, and again in August another fifty horses came from the same regiment. In September, forty-six horses arrived from the German Legion. On the other hand, as regards the men, the strength of the regiment having to be reduced, fifty non-commissioned officers and men joined the Carabiniers and thirty-two men were discharged. About 100 non-commissioned officers and men were invalided, and twelve sergeants and twelve privates volunteered to the Cape Mounted Rifles and the 7th Hussars.

On the 10th August Lieutenant-Colonel Parlby was placed upon half-pay, and Lieutenant-Colonel Wilkie was gazetted to the command. Colonel William Parlby entered the army as a cornet in the 8th Hussars in

[1] *Vide* Dress Regulations, 1855.

1816. Eight years later he became a lieutenant, and in the following year was transferred to the 12th Lancers. In 1826 he was promoted to be captain in the 4th Light Dragoons, obtained a brevet majority in 1841, and in January 1846 was appointed to the command of that regiment. In August of the same year he exchanged with Lieutenant-Colonel Vandeleur, becoming second in command of the 10th Hussars. He succeeded Colonel Bonham in command five years later, and remained in that position during the rest of the service of the regiment in India. He embarked at Bombay in command of the 10th Hussars on its proceeding on active service from India to the Crimea, and marched with it through Egypt. On arrival at the seat of war, Colonel Parlby was at once appointed to the command of a brigade, and received the rank of brigadier-general on the 30th July, 1855. He also commanded the Cavalry Division from April to July of that year, and the Hussar Brigade from July to September. He served throughout the remainder of the Crimean campaign; was present with the reconnaissance under Omar Pasha, and the battle of the Tchernaya. He was mentioned in despatches, received the medal and clasp, the Sardinian and Turkish medals, and Fourth Class of the Medjidieh. On his return to England Major-General Parlby was appointed to command the Cavalry Brigade at the Curragh Camp, and afterwards in Dublin. He was appointed Colonel of the 21st Hussars in 1865, and transferred to the 4th Hussars in 1880. He became a lieutenant-general in 1869, and general in 1876. He died 26th October, 1881.

The regimental changes in 1856 were:—Officers retired—Lieutenant R. W. Hatfield, by sale of commission. Transfers or exchanges—Cornet J. Fife, from 7th Dragoon Guards; Major Lord George Beauclerck,

Captain C. P. Rosser, Lieutenants W. O. Bird, J. J. N. Buchanan, G. S. Davies, J. Hudson, C. H. Uniacke, A. F. De Bourbel, S. Vyse, to 6th Dragoon Guards. Appointments—H. J. Toulmin and H. A. Bowyer to be cornets.

At the commencement of 1857 a further reduction took place. One sergeant and thirty-one privates volunteered to the 3rd Dragoon Guards, thirty-two rank and file and twenty-five horses were transferred to the Military Train in February, and twenty-two men in March. As a consequence, however, of these reductions, when the Indian Mutiny broke out recruiting had to be again opened in the spring, and in the course of this year and the next 410 recruits joined. These rapid changes in the establishment and the reduction of the regiment to such a weak strength, followed by an equally rapid increase—viz. 626 men, 428 horses—involved upon Colonel Wilkie a most difficult task; but he succeeded in having the whole of these recruits in the ranks ready to take part in the drills at Aldershot on the Tenth proceeding there. This gave constant occupation to all ranks throughout the summer passed at Birmingham.

On the 28th March B troop marched to Kidderminster in aid of the civil power, and remained there until 22nd April. On the 1st May Lieutenant John Fife was appointed Adjutant in succession to Lieutenant T. R. Cuthbert, promoted. In the following October the head-quarters left Birmingham and proceeded to Sheffield, and were joined by the detachment from Coventry. The week after its arrival the 10th Hussars took part in the ceremony of laying the foundation-stone of the Crimean Monument in that town, which was performed by H.R.H. the Duke of Cambridge. The Tenth remained during the winter and following spring at Sheffield. Almost immediately after its arrival at Sheffield, the surgeon (Dr. Fraser) was sent to Egypt to superin- tend the medical arrangements for the troops despatched to India on account of the mutiny in their transit and embarkation at Suez. He also established a hospital at the latter place. He was selected for this duty on account of his experience with his own regiment on its march through Egypt *en route* to the Crimea from India. Dr. Fraser rejoined at Aldershot, after having accomplished his mission, in January 1859.

The regimental changes in 1857 were :—Officers retired—Captain Holmes, Lieutenant Benson, Captain the Hon. F. C. G. FitzClarence, Captain J. W. Clarke. Transfers or exchanges—Captain V. Baker, from 12th Lancers ; Captain and Brevet-Major W. Murray, to 12th Lancers ; Veterinary Surgeon J. G. Philips, from 7th Hussars ; Veterinary Surgeon J. Barker, to 7th Hussars ; Lieutenant B. A. Branfill, to 8th Hussars ; Lieutenant F. H. Suckling, from 65th Foot. Appointments—J. Gore, E. J. Howley, E. L. Lovell, Lord R. D. Kerr to be cornets ; Sergeant E. Simpson to be ridingmaster.

On the 8th June, 1858, the head-quarters, under the command of Colonel John Wilkie, were moved from Sheffield, in the first instance halting at Birmingham for the purpose of assisting in the inauguration of Aston Hall and Park by Her Majesty the Queen. The regiment then proceeded on the 16th to Aldershot, to be quartered on arrival in the North Camp.

The changes in 1858 were :—Retirements—Captain D. R. Gill, Captain T. M. Townley, Lieutenant Panmure Gordon, by sale. Exchanges or transfers—Lieutenant Baring, promoted in 17th Lancers ; Lieutenant E. Stacey, promoted in 18th Hussars ; Lieutenant E. P. Baumgarten, from 4th Dragoon Guards ; Captain J. D. Cowell, promoted in 6th Dragoons ; Captain R. C. Sawbridge, from 8th Hussars ; Captain T. Wirgman, to 8th

Hussars; Captain F. Coates, from 7th Hussars. Ap-
pointments—C. T. Vandeleur, T. S. Ball, O. R. Slacke,
G. Houstoun, A. Barthorp, E. A. Wood, T. J. W.
Bulkeley, and W. M. Maunder to be cornets.

In January 1859 the Tenth moved into the South
Camp, Aldershot, the men occupying half the block of
the West Infantry Barracks nearest the Farnham Road,
the East Kent Militia occupying the other half. The
horses were in the Cavalry Barracks opposite, then in
course of being built. The officers were distributed
among the officers' quarters, West Infantry Barracks, and
the huts in D Lines, South Camp. On the completion
of the West Cavalry Barracks the whole regiment occupied these new quarters during the remainder of its stay
in the camp. The officers' mess-house being unfinished,
the officers messed in the sergeants' mess-room, and occupied the staff-sergeants' quarters over the officers' stables.
In July 1859 Major Broadley Harrison, who had entered the 11th Hussars in 1839, and four years afterwards joined the Tenth, was promoted as lieutenant-
colonel into his old regiment, and Captain V. Baker
obtained the majority. Lieutenant H. Bowyer was
appointed to the vacant troop. On the 6th May Lord
Ralph Kerr was appointed adjutant, *vice* J. Fife, promoted to be captain.

During the summer of 1859 the Government made
arrangements to utilise Woolmer Forest for manœuvres,
and on the 9th July it was used for this purpose for the
first time. A flying column of all arms, under Colonel
Ellis,[1] of the 24th Foot, marched on that day, the cavalry
being represented by a wing of the Tenth, under Major
Valentine Baker. This force encamped at Woolmer in
the evening, and remained there some days. Her
Majesty the Queen visited the camp between five and

[1] Afterwards General Sir Charles Ellis.

six P.M. on the following Sunday, and after driving round the camp and partaking of the soldiers' bread and tea returned to Windsor.[1]

Major-General the Earl of Cardigan and Major-General Lawrenson inspected the regiment on the 23rd August and 8th October respectively.

In August 1859 the head-quarters and three troops marched to Hounslow. On this march, as each squadron passed by Littleton Park, it was most hospitably entertained by Colonel Wood, the owner of that place, Colonel of the East Middlesex Militia and A.D.C. to the Queen. This officer took special interest in the regiment, as he had had a brother in it at Waterloo, and subsequently three sons, a grandson and a great nephew, in addition to his brother-in-law, the Marquis of Londonderry, who commanded the Tenth. C and G troops were detached to Hampton Court, and B troop, under Captain J. Fife and Cornet E. A. Wood, to Kensington.

The badges of rank on officers' uniform introduced in 1857 were in this year embodied in the Dress Regulations. They were as follows :—

Colonel—Crown and star. Collar laced all round with gold lace three-quarters of an inch wide, a figured braiding within the lace. Sleeve ornament, knot of gold chain lace with figured braiding eleven inches deep.

Lieutenant-Colonel—Crown.

Major—Star.

Captain—Crown and star. Collar laced round the top with gold lace and a figured braiding. Sleeve ornaments, knot of gold chain lace and figured braiding eight inches deep.

Lieutenant—Crown. Collar laced round the top with gold lace, with a plain edging of gold braid within

[1] W. Douglas.

Y 2

1859   the lace. Sleeve ornaments, knot of gold chain lace edged with braid seven inches deep.

Cornet—Star. Collar badges in silver embroidery.

The regimental changes in 1859 were :—Retirements—Lieutenant E. J. Howley, Captain W. Mayne. Transfers or exchanges—Major and Brevet Lieutenant-Colonel B. Harrison, promoted in 11th Hussars; Captain J. Gore, to 7th Hussars; Captain R. N. Pedder, from 7th Hussars; Veterinary Surgeon W. Thacker, from 15th Hussars. Appointments—W. Brougham, H. P. Holford, and T. A. St. Quintin to be cornets.

1860   On the 27th February, 1860, two troops, under Captain Cass, proceeded from Hounslow and Hampton Court to Woolwich. On the 31st March Lieutenant-Colonel Valentine Baker succeeded to the command of the regiment, *vice* Colonel John Wilkie, who retired upon half-pay after twenty-two years' service in the 10th Hussars, five of which were in command. Captain Playne Smith succeeded to the majority and second in command, but retired before the close of the year ; he served with the Tenth in India and the Crimea.

Colonel Wilkie entered the service on the 11th May, 1838, as a cornet in the 10th Hussars, and rose through the several grades until he was gazetted lieutenant-colonel on the 10th February, 1854, Colonel Parlby being the senior and in command. He obtained the rank of colonel (brevet) on the 28th November, 1854. Immediately on the arrival of the Tenth in the Crimea Colonel Parlby was appointed to the command of the Cavalry Division in the absence of General Yorke Scarlett, and the command of the regiment at once devolved on Colonel Wilkie. On General Scarlett's return and resuming the command of the division, Colonel Parlby received the command of a brigade, which he retained until the close of the war ; and, as

he did not rejoin after its return to England, Colonel
Wilkie had been continuously in command of the
Tenth from the date of its landing in the Crimea in
April 1855 until he retired on half-pay on the 30th
March, 1860. The reduction on its return from the
Crimea, and the consequent loss to the regiment of
several good officers and about 300 smart, well-trained,
seasoned soldiers and fine men, and not many months
afterwards, owing to the outbreak of the Indian Mutiny,
its sudden increase to eight troops, called forth all the
energy and experience of Colonel Wilkie as a strict
disciplinarian and organiser. It was all at once flooded
with a large number of recruits from the manufacturing towns, of a different stamp from those formed
soldiers discharged so short a time before. They
had, however, to be made as rapidly as possible into
efficient hussars, and to that difficult task Colonel
Wilkie applied himself with characteristic zeal. That
his labours were crowned with success he had the
satisfaction of being well assured by the high praises
repeatedly bestowed upon the Tenth on its first appearance after this at Aldershot by H.R.H. the Duke of
Cambridge, Commanding-in-Chief. Three years later he
handed over to his successor, Colonel Valentine Baker,
a regiment thoroughly disciplined and carefully drilled,
and well fitted to undertake those rapid movements introduced by that brilliant leader. As already mentioned,
Colonel Wilkie retired on half-pay on the 30th March,
1860, and was not again actively employed. He
was promoted major-general on the 6th March, 1868,
and appointed Colonel of the 14th Hussars on the
15th May, 1873. He attained the rank of lieutenant-
general on the 6th October, 1876, and that of general
on the 21st December, 1878. For his service in the
Crimea he received the medal and clasp for the siege

and fall of Sebastopol, the Fifth Class of the Order of the Medjidieh, and the Turkish medal. He died on the 30th April, 1882.

In March 1860 regimental steeplechases took place for the first time, and were held on Shepperton Range. Lieutenant-Colonel Baker presented a bronze challenge cup to be run for, to be won twice by the same officer before becoming his property. The first year it was won by Captain Baumgarten, the horse being ridden by Cornet E. A. Wood, and the next year at Norwich by Mr. Thacker, the veterinary surgeon, a very fine horseman. In 1862 Lieutenant T. J. Williams-Bulkeley won the cup at York, and the following year Mr. Thacker, by winning it a second time, carried it off permanently. Colonel V. Baker then presented another cup, a silver-gilt Danish flagon, to be won three times by the same officer. This cup still (1890) remains in the regiment. It has been won by the following officers :—1864, Mr. St. Quintin's Ballyragget; 1865, Captain Slacke's Planet; 1866, Mr. Gabbett's Standard Bearer; 1867, Mr. Gabbett's Mabel; 1868, no races; 1869, Lord Valentia's Ventpiece; 1870, no races; 1871, Lord Valentia's Wellington; 1886, Mr. Kavanagh's Highlander; 1887, Mr. Baird's Garnet; 1888, Mr. Baird's Victoria; 1889, Lord W. Bentinck's Avalanche.

On the 17th May the 10th Hussars was inspected by Brigadier-General Lord George Paget, C.B., commanding the Cavalry Brigade at Aldershot. On the 22nd June it marched to London to be present at the review of the Volunteer Forces in Hyde Park before Her Majesty the Queen, returning in the evening.[1] On the 11th July, two squadrons, numbering 120 men and horses, were practised in embarking in trains from the

---

[1] The Volunteer Force had been raised in 1859, and at this time was in its infancy. Since then it has steadily increased in strength and popu-

Islington and Holloway Railway Stations, one troop 1860 saddled and the other unsaddled. They were conveyed to Willesden Station on the London and North-Western line, with the object of testing the capabilities of the accommodation for the transport of troops. On the 12th July the two troops at Woolwich, A troop and E, joined head-quarters at Hounslow. On the 13th the Tenth was reviewed at Wormwood Scrubs, in brigade with the 1st and 2nd Life Guards, by Major-General Lawrenson, now Inspector-General of Cavalry. On the 17th, B troop marched from Kensington to Aldershot, and on the following day the head-quarters, with five troops and the two troops from Hampton Court, marched for the same destination.

The Tenth remained at the camp for the summer drills, and on the 18th September left for the following country quarters : B and F troops, under Captain Coates, Captain Fife, Lieutenants Holford, Bulkeley, and Slacke, for Northampton ; C and G, under Captain Pedder and Captain the Hon. E. Stourton, for Ipswich, Major Levett commanding. On the 19th, A troop marched to Ipswich, and H to Norwich ; and on the 20th the head-quarters, with C and E troops, also left for Norwich. A detachment which had remained at Hounslow, consisting of eighteen men and horses, marched on the 21st, and joined the head-quarters at Romford while *en route* to Norwich. On the 4th October the head-quarters were inspected by Major-General Lawrenson.

The head-quarters of the regiment passed the winter, which was a very severe one, at Norwich, and both officers and men found it a very pleasant station. Those on detachment were equally satisfied with their quarters. Ipswich afforded good shooting, and much hos-

larity, so that, after thirty years, it has reached the large number of over 200,000 efficient men.

pitality was received from all around ; while Captains Coates and Fife and the officers of the squadron at Northampton had a good opportunity of testing their powers of riding in the " Shires," of which they availed themselves with great success.

The regimental changes in 1860 were :—Retirements—Colonel J. Wilkie, to half·pay; Major R. P. Smith, Quartermaster J. Fenn. Promotions—Major V. Baker to be lieutenant-colonel ; Cornet T. J. W. Bulkeley to be lieutenant ; Troop Sergeant-Major J. H. James to be quartermaster. Transfers or exchanges— Ensign C. S. Fremantle, from Rifle Brigade ; Captain E. P. Baumgarten, to 7th Hussars ; Captain the Hon. C. C. Molyneux, from 7th Hussars ; Lieutenant R. S. Liddell, from 15th Foot ; Lieutenant T. S. Ball, to 15th Foot ; Captain the Hon. E. Stourton, from 8th Hussars ; Captain E. L. Lovell, to 8th Hussars. Appointments— C. B. Ponsonby, H. Davies-Evans, A. Wyatt-Edgell, and J. C. Russell to be cornets.

On the 1st April the established strength was reduced to 601 men and 400 horses. On the 23rd July the Tenth was inspected by Major-General Lawrenson, Inspector-General of Cavalry, on Mousehill Heath, Norwich. He expressed a wish to see the regiment ride over the jumps that had been placed there for training the horses. Colonel Baker, therefore, took it over in sections, and the general himself, who was a very fine horseman, was unable to resist the temptation, so placed himself with his staff at the head, and led the way over the fences, mounted on Duchess, the property of Captain the Hon. C. C. Molyneux.

On the 9th October Sergeant Benjamin Rickards was appointed Regimental Sergeant-Major, *vice* Hickman, who retired on his pension, and became a riding-master in a well-known establishment in London.

The Tenth remained a little under the year in these quarters, and commenced marching on the 27th August for the North of England. A troop from Ipswich and E troop from Norwich moved to Leeds, under the command of Captain Cass; head-quarters, with D and H troops, under the command of Captain Bowyer and Captain the Hon. C. C. Molyneux, marched from Norwich to York on the 3rd September; on the 16th of the same month B and F troops, under Captain Fife, left Northampton *en route* for York; a squadron from Ipswich, consisting of C and G troops, under Captain the Hon. E. Stourton, marched on the 3rd September for the same destination. In August Lieutenant Lord Ralph Kerr was promoted to be captain, and was succeeded in the adjutancy by Lieutenant Owen Slacke.

CHAPTER XXXVII.

YORK—DEATH OF THE PRINCE CONSORT—A SECOND WINTER AT YORK—THE EARL BEAUCHAMP TRANSFERRED TO THE 2ND LIFE GUARDS—H.R.H. ALBERT EDWARD PRINCE OF WALES APPOINTED COLONEL—THE REGIMENT MOVES TO IRELAND—DUBLIN—THE CURRAGH—NON-PIVOT DRILL INTRODUCED—CAHIR—GENERAL ELECTION

1861   ON the first arrival of the Tenth at York Barracks there was only room for six troops, and the accommodation for officers was so short that five or six subaltern officers had to be lodged in the town; but two months later the stabling which was in course of construction was finished, and the squadron under Captain Cass was marched in from Leeds and joined head-quarters on the 19th November. The regiment was now once more together, and all considered themselves most fortunate in being in so excellent a quarter as York. At this time considerable changes were introduced into the cavalry drill, and Colonel Valentine Baker, who had visited many of the Continental armies, and had observed their cavalry, more especially that of Austria, became a strong advocate for a greater simplicity of drill. He also insisted upon the necessity of all movements of cavalry being carried out with great rapidity, therefore the drill of the Tenth at this time became very fast.

Shortly after the arrival of the Tenth, the Yorkshire Hussars (Yeomanry Cavalry) underwent its annual training in York, and, as Colonel Baker was the inspecting officer, this regiment naturally took much interest in the new movements then being introduced, several of which it set to work, under the command of the Earl of Harewood, to carry into practice. The adjutant of the Yorkshire Hussars at this time was a very distinguished old officer of the Tenth, Captain Slayter Smith, whose services at Waterloo, &c., have been already alluded to in these memoirs.

The winter of 1861 was passed in the ordinary routine of a country quarter, the officers taking advantage of the numerous packs of hounds and excellent sport shown in the various hunting fields in Yorkshire, and it was soon found that there was nothing more calculated to endear them to the people of that county than by turning out in large numbers at all the meets of the foxhounds. These circumstances laid the foundation of the very intimate connection between the Tenth and the inhabitants of York and its neighbourhood, which lasted during the whole of the nineteen months that it remained stationed there, and left many pleasant mutual recollections.

Towards the close of this year (14th December), the severe illness which attacked H.R.H. the Prince Consort had a fatal termination, and the Queen and the whole nation had to mourn the loss of this inestimable Prince. On the 23rd December the 10th Hussars took part in a funeral procession at York Minster, where a service was held at the same time that the burial of His Royal Highness took place at Windsor.

Regimental changes in 1861 :—Retirements—Lieutenant R. Lomax, Captain F. Coates. Transfers or exchanges—Captain G. Hanbury, from 8th Hussars ; Captain R. N. Pedder, to 8th Hussars ; C. E. Frederick and W. C. Fitzherbert to be cornets.

In July 1862 Major-General Lawrenson, Inspector-General of Cavalry, made his inspection, and on the 12th of this month E troop proceeded dismounted to Scarborough, under the command of Captain Cass, for musketry instruction, and each troop went there in its turn for the same purpose. While going through this course the men were quartered in the Castle, and the officers were billeted close by. During the time that E troop was there a fire took place in the town, which was extinguished entirely by the exertions of the men of the Tenth. In doing this a great deal of their clothing was destroyed, principally by the water used. The insurance office, however, gave the men compensation as well as some reward, making at the same time the stipulation that their doing so should be kept secret. It was afterwards said that this was owing to the company being managed by Quakers, who did not wish it known that any reward had been made to the fighting element of the country.

The 10th Hussars, under command of Lieutenant-Colonel V. Baker, was inspected on the Racecourse, Knavesmire, by H.R.H. the Duke of Cambridge on the 8th September, and on the 27th of the same month Lieutenant-General Sir George Wetherall, commanding the Northern District, saw it in the York Barracks.

There were no regimental changes amongst the officers in 1862.

The Tenth remained a second winter at York, very much to the satisfaction of all ranks. As a proof of the friendly relations existing between the town of York and the regiment, at this time the Lord Mayor and Corporation gave permission to the officers to build a boathouse and attach a raft to the path known as the Lord Mayor's Walk. As this was considered a great innovation, it gave rise to considerable discussion in the rival local papers.

On the 27th October the Tenth was again inspected by Major-General Lawrenson.

In January 1863 a great civic function took place in York, on the occasion of the opening of a very handsome iron bridge at Lendal, one of the suburbs of the town. A troop of the Tenth took part in the procession. On the 16th January, on the retirement of Major E. Levett, Captain Arthur Herbert Cass was promoted to the majority and second in command. Major Edward Levett, who had served in the Crimea, exchanged from the 19th Regiment into the Tenth Hussars in 1856.

In April, Earl Beauchamp, Colonel of the 10th Hussars, was transferred to the command of the 2nd Life Guards. Lord Beauchamp entered the army on the 9th July, 1803, as a cornet in the 13th Light Dragoons, and was promoted lieutenant the following year. In 1807 he became a captain, and was transferred to the 16th Light Dragoons, in which regiment he was promoted major in 1812. He served in the 16th in the Peninsular War from March 1809 to September 1810. He was present at the capture of Oporto, the battle of Talavera, and the passage of the Coa, and was severely wounded in the neck on the 28th August, 1810, in Massena's advance previous to the battle of Busaco. He again served in the Peninsula from February 1814 until the end of the campaign. He received the war medal with clasp for Talavera. Lord Beauchamp was transferred as major to the 1st Life Guards on the 18th June, 1815, which regiment he commanded in 1821. He became a major-general in 1837, Colonel of the 10th Royal Hussars in 1843, lieutenant-general in 1846, general in 1854, Colonel of the 2nd Life Guards in April 1863, and died in September 1863.

On the 16th April, 1863, His Royal Highness Albert Edward Prince of Wales was gazetted to the command of the 10th Hussars, in succession to Earl Beauchamp, this being the second time that the regiment had the distinguished honour of having the Prince of Wales at its head.

In the early spring of this year orders of readiness for the march to Ireland arrived, and on the 13th April a squadron consisting of G and E troops, under Major Cass, Captain the Hon. E. Stourton, Captain Vandeleur, Cornets Fremantle and Davies-Evans, left York for Liverpool, to embark there for Dublin. Colonel Baker marched with head-quarters. The other squadrons marched during succeeding days by the same route. This march was principally through the manufacturing districts of Yorkshire and Lancashire, but after leaving the town of Halifax a very wild moorland was passed. With this exception the route was not picturesque. On the day before reaching Liverpool each squadron was met and most hospitably entertained by Sir Robert (afterwards Lord) Gerard at his country place. On the arrival of each squadron at Liverpool it proceeded at once to the docks, the saddlery was packed in the corn sacks, and the horses led on board a small hired transport, which conveyed it across the Irish Channel. The head-quarters and first squadron disembarked at Dublin on the 17th April and marched to the Royal Barracks. The remaining three squadrons, under Major Cass, marched to Newbridge.

On the 7th May the head-quarters were inspected by Major-General Key, Inspector-General of Cavalry in Ireland, and on the 8th the inspection of the three squadrons at Newbridge was made by the same officer.

On the promotion of Cornet J. Fremantle to be lieutenant, Mr. Edward S. Watson was gazetted to the 10th Hussars. This officer, whose father, the Hon. R. Watson, had served for some years in the Tenth, had

been in the naval service, and was A.D.C. to Captain
Peel, R.N., of H.M.S. "Shannon," and took part with
the Naval Brigade at the capture of Lucknow during
the Indian Mutiny.

On the 22nd June the head-quarters, with the squadron in Dublin, marched to Newbridge, to be present
during the Curragh drill season. In addition to the
Tenth, the 4th Light Dragoons and a battery of horse
artillery under Captain Saunders were stationed in the
Newbridge Barracks. The officers of this battery, Cap-
tians Saunders and Strangways, Lieutenants B. Arbuth-
not, the Hon. R. Dillon, and Lieutenant Walton, lived
with the Tenth at this time, and they became to be considered almost as a part of it.

During the latter part of the drill season at the Curragh, in accordance with a new order by which officers
passing out of the Staff College had to spend some
months with those branches of the army in which
they had not served, three officers were attached to the
Tenth—Major Pomeroy Colley, 2nd (Queen's) Regiment,
afterwards Sir George P. Colley, killed at Majuba;
Captain Arthur Griffiths, 63rd Regiment; and Lieutenant Nolan, Royal Artillery, all of whom afterwards
became men of note.

On the 31st July and following day the 10th
Hussars was inspected by Major-General Lawrenson,
Inspector-General of Cavalry. On the 1st October a
squadron, composed of C and E troops, marched to
Portobello Barracks, Dublin. On the 16th Major-
General the Hon. Alexander Gordon, commanding the
troops at the Curragh, inspected the six troops at
Newbridge. On the 2nd November head-quarters and
two troops marched to Portobello Barracks, and on
the 17th the remaining four troops followed. During
the winter months the troops proceeded each in turn

to the Pigeon House Fort for musketry instruction. On the 13th November Major-General Key made his inspection.

Mr. Thacker, who had been veterinary surgeon of the Tenth for some years, was promoted to the Staff. This officer was not only remarkable as a professional man of the greatest ability, but was one of the finest horsemen that ever got into a saddle.

The regimental changes in 1863 were :—Retirements—Major E. Levett and Lieutenant W. Brougham. Promotion—Captain A. H. Cass to be major. Appointments—W. H. Watkins, E. S. Watson, and the Hon. H. G. L. Crichton to be cornets.

This winter was passed in Portobello Barracks, Dublin, where nothing unusual beyond the ordinary routine of a garrison town took place. On the 10th May, 1864, 576 Westley-Richards breech-loading carbines were received. On the 17th June the Tenth marched to the Curragh Camp and was encamped in Donnelly's Hollow. The first few days after arrival were very wet, but on the whole it was more fortunate in this respect during its encampment than it was on some other occasions.

At this time the non-pivot system of drill, adapted from the Austrian service by Colonel Baker, and the formation of the squadron in three divisions of twelve front each, was introduced into the Tenth, and was much discussed in military circles. In the regiment there were never at any time two opinions on the subject, the simplicity of the drill, enabling a great reduction in the number of movements to be made, the greater rapidity of execution, and the ease in leading, presenting great advantages. Colonel Baker had obtained official sanction to carry out this drill in place of that laid down in the Regulations.

The Tenth was inspected by Major-General Lawren- son on the 12th July. At the end of the drill season at the Curragh the regiment was ordered to the South of Ireland, and on the 18th July one squadron, A and F troops, under Captain Sawbridge and Lord R. Kerr, marched for Cork; another, H and G, under Captains Bowyer and the Hon. E. Stourton, for Fermoy; and a third, B and D, for Cahir; and on the 19th, C and E troops, together with the head-quarters, left the Curragh for Cahir. The Tenth remained during the remainder of the summer and throughout the winter at these stations, and with the exception of some moves for election duties was very stationary. These country quarters were very much appreciated, and at head-quarters an excellent pack of hounds was purchased from the neighbouring town of Cashel, known as the Rock Harriers, and, with Captain the Hon. C. C. Molyneux as huntsman, Lord Valentia and Private Thomas Bowkett as whips, capital sport was shown in the Golden Valley of Tipperary.

On the 26th and 28th September the detachments, and on the 29th the head-quarters, were inspected by Major-General Key.

On the promotion of Lieutenant Owen Slacke to a troop, *vice* Bowyer retired, on the 18th October, Lieutenant John Cecil Russell was appointed Adjutant. The regimental changes in 1864 were:—Retirements—Cornet W. C. FitzHerbert, Captain G. Hanbury, Cornet H. P. Holford, Lieutenant A. Wyatt-Edgell, Captain H. A. Bowyer. Transfers and exchanges—Veterinary Surgeon H. Withers, from 3rd Hussars; Captain W. Chaine, from 7th Dragoon Guards; Captain C. T. Vandeleur, to 7th Dragoon Guards; Lieutenant D. F. Gabbett, from 2nd Life Guards; Lieutenant J. C. S. Fremantle, to 2nd Life Guards. Appointments—U. E. P. Okeden, Viscount Valentia, T. A. Smith-Dorrien, and E. Hartopp to be cornets.

z

On the 2nd February a troop, under Lord Ralph Kerr, accompanied by Cornet the Hon. H. L. Crichton, proceeded from Cork to Tralee in aid of the civil power during the election of The O'Donoghue, and on the 12th another troop, under Captain Slacke, was sent from Fermoy to the same place. This troop was detained at Killarney for a few days, when Lieutenant Liddell relieved Lieutenant Bulkeley as its subaltern officer, the latter having been ordered to go through a course of musketry at Fleetwood. Lieutenant Frederick was sent from Cork on the 8th with twenty-nine men and horses to reinforce Lord Ralph Kerr's troop at Tralee. A large number of troops of cavalry, artillery, and infantry, the whole under command of Colonel Norcott, Assistant Adjutant-General, Cork District, were collected for this election, which was a very heated one, as The O'Donoghue was the favourite of the peasantry, while Mr. McKenna was strongly supported by the people of property and the tradesmen of Tralee. The O'Donoghue having been elected, everything went off quietly. The troops left the town on the 21st, and the squadron of the Tenth had a march through the beautiful country of Killarney.

On the 24th February a troop, under Captain the Hon. C. C. Molyneux, with Cornet the Hon. H. L. Wood, proceeded to Clonmel in aid of the civil power, and on the 25th Captain Barthorp and Cornet Smith-Dorrien were ordered with a troop to Nenagh on the same duty. Captain the Hon. Everard Stourton's troop marched from Fermoy to Cashel, and was billeted there during the election; while Captain Slacke's troop was moved from Fermoy to Cahir to strengthen the head-quarters. On the 26th February Lieutenant Ponsonby and Cornet the Hon. H. L. Crichton, with forty men and horses, were sent to Thurles, and Captain Slacke and Lieute-

nant Liddell, with another troop, to the town of Tipperary, also on election duty. The general election
being over, the various troops returned to their former
stations.

When the 10th Hussars was quartered at Cahir, a
subaltern joined the regiment who was a man so remarkable in every way, and especially for the geniality
and kindness of his disposition, that his old comrades
would consider these memoirs incomplete if Edward
Hartopp was not specially mentioned in them. A giant
in height and strength, he had also an unusually great
share of mental quickness and power, as well as many
accomplishments. He was an excellent musician and
was possessed of a splendid voice. He was known as
one of the most daring riders and best heavy weights
that ever crossed a country in Ireland. He constantly
hunted hounds himself, and his stentorian "holloas," full
of music, will never be forgotten by those who heard
them. After leaving the army he became Master of the
Kilkenny Hounds, in which county he showed great
sport and unbounded hospitality, and was beloved by
all, rich and poor. His great power and fine hands
made him so good a whip that few more competent
coachmen ever mounted a box, and he was devoted to
all other forms of sport with hound and gun by flood and
field. He served for some years on the personal staff of
Lord Spencer in Ireland, and afterwards on that of Lord
Northbrook, Governor-General of India. His health,
broken by the Indian climate, prevented him from
remaining in the service, and he died at a comparatively early age, a man who had all the personal qualifications to attain distinction in his profession, but to
whom the fitting opportunity was denied.

CHAPTER XXXVIII

THE PRINCE OF WALES VISITS IRELAND—ESCORTS OF THE TENTH—
IN AID OF THE CIVIL POWER—THE FENIAN MOVEMENT—FLYING
COLUMNS—SECOND VISIT OF THE PRINCE OF WALES

1865 IN the spring of this year it became known that H.R.H. the Prince of Wales would pay a visit to Ireland, and in consequence of this the 10th Hussars received an order of readiness to march to Dublin, so as to be present during his stay in Ireland, and that the escorts for His Royal Highness might be performed by his own regiment. On the 21st April the head-quarters left Cahir, and the other troops followed in succession, the whole arriving by the end of the month in Dublin, and taking up their quarters in Island Bridge Barracks. On the 8th May a squadron, under Captain the Hon. C. C. Molyneux, proceeded to Westland Row Station to escort H.R.H. the Prince of Wales to the Viceregal Lodge on his arrival in Dublin for the purpose of opening the International Exhibition. At the same time a smaller escort of twenty-five men, under Lieutenant Liddell, formed an escort to H.R.H. the Duke of Cambridge. On the following day the regiment found escorts for H.R.H. the Prince of Wales from the Viceregal Lodge to the Dublin Exhibition on the occasion of its opening, and also during the remainder of the day. On the 10th May the whole of the troops in the garrison were reviewed in the Phœnix Park. On the 11th the Prince of Wales again visited the Exhibition and other places of interest in Dublin, and was escorted by a squadron of the Tenth.

On the 12th the visit of His Royal Highness came to an end, when this squadron again formed an escort for him to the railway station.

On the 19th May Major-General Key, Inspector-General of Cavalry in Ireland, made his inspection.

On the 31st May Corporal Frederick Green, with Troop Horse D 35, was selected as an orderly to H.R.H. the Prince of Wales, and proceeded to London, where he was attached to the 2nd Life Guards. This non-commissioned officer afterwards became Troop Sergeant-Major Green, and lost his life during the Afghan campaign, 1878–9, in the disastrous passage by night of the Cabul River at Jellalabad.

During this summer the Tenth was frequently employed in aid of the civil power. On the 11th July Captain Sawbridge's troop marched to Wexford, on the 19th Captain the Hon. E. Stourton's to Garristown, and on the same day Captain the Hon. C. C. Molyneux's troop was despatched to Balbriggan. On the 15th July it was inspected in the Phœnix Park by Lieutenant-General Sir Hugh Rose, G.C.B., commanding the Forces in Ireland. On the 20th July Lord Ralph Kerr's troop proceeded to Dunleer. On the 5th August the regiment marched to the Curragh Camp for the drill season and was encamped in Donnelly's Hollow. Major-General Lord George Paget, Inspector-General of Cavalry, made his annual inspection on the 25th September, and on the 29th it returned to Island Bridge Barracks, Dublin.

At this time the Fenian movement in Ireland began to attract notice, and several of the leaders were arrested and placed upon their trial. This entailed considerable extra duties on the military. One troop of the Tenth was sent daily to the Linen Hall Barracks, the Castle, and Portobello Barracks, taking this duty in conjunction with the 5th Dragoon Guards. Daily escorts were also found for the prison vans to and from the trials. Extraordinary precautions were taken to guard all the barracks and magazines. Rumours of proposed desperate attacks on and destruction of these were in constant circulation.

The regimental changes in 1865 were :—Promotion—Lieutenant-Colonel V. Baker to be colonel. Transfer Assistant-Surgeon G. Hooper, promoted on the Staff. Appointment—Staff Assistant-Surgeon J. T. Milburn to be assistant-surgeon.

On the 27th April, 1866, the Tenth was inspected by Major-General Cunynghame, commanding the Dublin Division. On the 2nd July it was again broken up : Captain Slacke's troop marched to Belfast, Captain the Hon. C. C. Molyneux's troop to Belturbet, and that of Captain the Hon. E. Stourton to Athlone. On the 3rd and 4th of this month the head-quarters and the young horses marched for Dundalk, arriving there on the 5th, 6th, and 7th. On the 10th July Captain Sawbridge's and Captain Barthorp's troops marched for Downpatrick on account of disturbances expected during the Orange meetings on the 12th July. A squadron, under Lord Ralph Kerr and Captain Chaine, proceeded to Dungannon on the same duty. On the 15th August Captain Sawbridge's troop marched to Banbridge in aid of the civil power. On the 29th August Sergeant-Instructor of Musketry W. King was appointed Regimental Sergeant-Major, *vice* Rickards, who retired on his pension and afterwards became Regimental Sergeant-Major of the East Kent Yeomanry Cavalry. The remainder of this year was spent quietly in country quarters, which was very welcome after the constant moves that had taken place during the preceding months.

The head-quarters were inspected by Lord George Paget on the 8th October, and by Brigadier-General

White on the 12th and 13th. After these inspections
all the sporting pursuits of the neighbourhood were
entered into. A pack of hounds was established at
head-quarters, under the management of Lord Valentia,
Mr. Hartopp having a pack of beagles ; while at Belturbet Captain Molyneux undertook to hunt the County
Cavan Harriers, and showed excellent sport in that very
rough country.

Colonel Baker in this year introduced the "Regimental Call" into the 10th Hussars, which is in use
at the present time (1890). It was taken from the
opening movement in "The Song of the Huguenot
Soldiers," from the opera of "The Huguenots." About

the same time a custom which still prevails in the
regiment was initiated by Colonel V. Baker—the playing of two hymns by the band every evening between
the first and second post of watch-setting, followed by
"God save the Queen." This has been carried out since
1866 wherever the Tenth may have been, in quarters,
in camp, on active service, or on board a ship.

The only regimental change in 1866 was :—Promotion—Surgeon T. Fraser, M.D., to be surgeon-major.

On the 22nd February a fire broke out at Haig's
Distillery at Dundalk, which was ultimately extinguished principally by the exertions of the men of the
regiment who were sent down with the fire engine.
The resident magistrate of the town sent a letter of
thanks to the officer commanding.

In the spring of this year Fenianism, which had
been smouldering since 1858 under the name of the
Phœnix Conspiracy, came to a head. It was a secret

revolutionary society, led at this time by a man named
James Stephens, who had been concerned in the
schemes of Smith O'Brien in 1848. He had since
lived in Paris, and there became initiated into the
system of secret societies then forming throughout
Europe. The members of this society were enrolled
in "circles," each "circle" presided over by a "centre."

At the close of the American Civil War in 1865
a large number of Irish Americans only anxious for
further fighting and quite incapable of settling down to
peaceful pursuits were let loose. Thousands of these
now arrived in Ireland, with arms, ammunition, and
money. In September 1865 the English Government
had taken notice of these proceedings by arresting
some of the leaders, suppressing newspapers, and also
taking possession of the telegraph wires. The head-
centre, James Stephens, was also arrested, but contrived
to make his escape from Richmond Prison, and went
to Paris, directing the conspiracy from that capital. For
a time the steps taken had put a check on Fenianism ;
but the centres again became busy at the beginning of
1866, and nightly drills and recruiting were carried on
in the South of Ireland. Men were even enlisted into
the ranks of the British army to act as "centres," and
to try and induce the Irishmen in the different regiments
to join the movement. One of these, a man named
Boyle O'Reilly, entered the Tenth, a remarkably intelligent, well-educated, active young fellow, a man who
soon made himself popular with all ranks, and appeared
likely to rise. O'Reilly was eventually apprehended as
a "centre," and was tried, and sentenced to penal ser-
vitude and transported. Some years later a ship was
sent from America to Australia to assist him and some
other Fenians in making their escape, and this was successfully carried out.

At length the long-threatened rising of the Fenians

took place. On the 5th March, 1867, they " took the
field!" the southern counties, with Dublin and Louth,
giving the principal lead. The whole affair, however,
was a *fiasco*. The Government was provided with
every information, and the Fenian Commander-in-Chief,
General Massey, was arrested at Limerick Junction as
he got out of the train to assume command. The
Fenians were also anticipated in all their moves, and
troops were placed at all the principal points where
risings were expected a few days previous to the date
fixed upon by them to assemble. A flying column, under
the command of Colonel Baker, was formed at Thurles,

in Tipperary; fifty mounted and fifty dismounted men,
under Captain the Hon. C. C. Molyneux, Captain Slacke,
Lieutenant Bulkeley, Lieutenant and Adjutant J. C. Russell, Cornets the Hon. H. L. Crichton and H. Wood,
proceeded by train through Dublin to join it. A troop
under Captain Chaine was ordered to Cullin for the
especial protection of Lord Massereene's place, Oriel
Temple, was there four days, during which the country
was under deep snow, returning to head-quarters when
the snow melted; and the troop from Belturbet, under
Lieutenant Liddell, was stationed at Mullingar until the
collapse of the Fenian movement.

Although it was a complete failure, the Fenian outbreak entailed considerable work on the military. On the 5th March a snowstorm commenced which lasted some days, and the whole country was deep in snow until the 21st; and, although this helped very much to disperse the Fenians, it also made patrolling the country, driving about in cars at night, and clearing away the snowdrifts, less agreeable for the soldiers. With Colonel Baker's column there were, besides the Tenth, five officers and 120 men of the 2nd (The Queen's) Regiment, twelve Engineers, a Commissariat officer, and Captain Talbot, a stipendiary magistrate. This column remained in Tipperary until the end of the month, when it returned to Dundalk, as well as the other detached portions of the Tenth. On the 16th March Captain Lord Ralph Kerr's troop was sent to Dunleer in aid of the civil power, and rejoined on the 18th.

On the 12th April, at Dundalk, Brigadier-General H. D. White, C.B., commanding the Cavalry Brigade, made his inspection. The field day took place in drill order on the sands in the midst of an incessant downpour of rain. On the 15th, D troop, under the command of Captain the Hon. C. C. Molyneux, joined head-quarters at Dundalk, and was succeeded at Belturbet in May by G troop, from Athlone, under the command of Captain the Hon. Everard Stourton.

On the 10th May a letter was received from the Adjutant-General, Dublin, conveying the approval of the Lord-Lieutenant, H.R.H. the Field-Marshal Commanding-in-Chief, and Lord Strathnairn, Commander-in-Chief in Ireland, for the exertions of the army in Ireland during the Fenian outbreak. Lord Strathnairn also thanked officers and men for the good feeling displayed, and, amongst others, specially mentioned the Thurles Flying Column as worthy of commendation.

On the 16th June another fire broke out in Dundalk, which was extinguished by the regiment, and the
Mayor expressed his thanks in a letter to the commanding officer.

A squadron, under Captain Fife, proceeded to Porta-
down, and another to Dungannon, on the 8th July, under
Captain Sawbridge, in anticipation of Orange riots.

On the 13th July Major Arthur Herbert Cass retired upon half-pay, after a service of seventeen years.
He joined the Tenth in India in 1850, accompanied it
through Egypt, and served throughout the Crimean
campaign. He was succeeded by Captain John Fife,
Lieutenant E. A. Wood getting the troop, and Cornet
Edward Watson the lieutenancy.

The Tenth was inspected on the 20th September by
Major-General Lord George Paget, C.B., Inspector-
General of Cavalry. The following month it was moved
from the North of Ireland. The first squadron marched
from Dundalk for Newbridge on the 15th October, one
troop of which was detached to the Curragh Camp.
One squadron marched on the 16th, another squadron
on the 17th, and the troop from Belfast on the 21st,
and by the 29th of the month the whole regiment was
brought together again at Newbridge. On the 21st
December, 520 Snider rifled carbines converted into
breech-loaders were received, and the Westley-Richards
carbines returned into store.

The regimental changes in 1867 were :—Retire-
ments—Major A. H. Cass, to half-pay; Lieutenant H. D,
Evans, Lieutenant D. F. Gabbett. Appointments—R.
Thorold, H. A. Coventry, and the Hon. W. T. W. Fitz-
William to be cornets.

In February, Lieutenant T. J. Williams-Bulkeley
was promoted to a troop, *vice* Captain Owen Slacke,
who retired. Captain Slacke had been adjutant, and soon

1868 after leaving the service was appointed a stipendiary
magistrate in Ireland. On the 9th March a squadron,
under the command of Captain Barthorp, proceeded by
train to Ballincollig, to be at hand during the Fenian
trials taking place in Cork. Colonel Baker was also
ordered there at the same time.

In April of this year H.R.H. the Prince of Wales
again paid a visit to Ireland, for the purpose of being
invested with the Order of St. Patrick. A squadron
of the Tenth, under the command of Captain the Hon.
C. C. Molyneux, with Captain E. A. Wood, Viscount
Valentia, and the Hon. H. L. Crichton, proceeded to
Dublin on the 13th April to form an escort for His
Royal Highness during his stay, and it was quartered
in Portobello Barracks. The Marquis of Abercorn was
at this time Lord-Lieutenant of Ireland, and the cere-
monials carried out during this visit were done with
great magnificence. The Prince of Wales landed on the
15th April, and was escorted by the Tenth squadron.
On the 16th and 17th His Royal Highness was present
at the Punchestown Races, where his regiment had the
honour of entertaining him at luncheon in a private
race stand that was erected for the occasion. On the
18th the Investiture of the Order of St. Patrick took
place in St. Patrick's Cathedral. Captain the Hon.
C. C. Molyneux was Esquire to His Royal Highness,
and unfurled his banner inside the cathedral. Several
other officers of the Tenth took part in the proceedings,
and the same escort again accompanied the Prince
of Wales. On the 22nd a grand ball was given in
the Exhibition Palace to the Prince. The following
day His Royal Highness left for England, and on the
24th the escort squadron marched back to Newbridge.

CHAPTER XXXIX

THE TENTH RETURNS TO ENGLAND—MARCH TO ALDERSHOT—VO-
LUNTEER REVIEW—THE CROWN PRINCE OF PRUSSIA INSPECTS
THE TENTH— SQUADRON ORGANISATION—REGIMENT PROCEEDS TO
SHORNCLIFFE—REGIMENTAL RACES — AUTUMN MANŒUVRES —
PRINCE OF WALES TAKES COMMAND OF A CAVALRY BRIGADE—
ILLNESS OF THE PRINCE OF WALES

AFTER five years' service in Ireland, the 10th Hussars   1868
received orders to return to England. It marched by
squadrons from Newbridge to Dublin, and embarked on
the 8th, 11th, 13th, and 15th May, on board the steamer
"St. Patrick." The dismounted party proceeded on
board the "Lady Eglinton" on the 20th from Dublin,
and disembarked at Portsmouth on the 23rd. The
mounted portion landed at Birkenhead, and marched *via*
Chester, Whitchurch, Wellington, Stourbridge, Alcester,
Moreton-in-the-Marsh, Witney, Reading, to Aldershot,
arriving there on the 21st, 23rd, 26th, and 28th May.

On arrival at Aldershot the Tenth was quartered in
the East Cavalry Barracks, and on the 13th June was
inspected by Brigadier-General Dalrymple White, C.B.
The drill, which had been conducted for some time on
the non-pivot system and by divisions, as before mentioned, was now brought more prominently forward.
Several other commanding officers had obtained permission to adopt it, but opinions throughout the service
were very much divided. Visitors, both official and
others, constantly came to see this drill, but eventually,
after a trial of two or three years, and after securing

the full approval of all who took part in it, it was abolished, and the pivot system adopted again. Yet a few years later the Tenth had the satisfaction of seeing it embodied in the Cavalry Regulations and made the established drill of the service.

In May Captain the Hon. E. Stourton retired from the service by the sale of his commission, and not many months after, to the regret of the whole regiment, died. He had served during the Indian Mutiny in the 8th Hussars. Lieutenant Liddell obtained the troop, Lord Valentia the lieutenancy, and Hugh Sutlej Gough became cornet.

On the 19th June the regiment marched to Ascot and encamped on the Heath. By kind permission of the Stewards, the Grand Stand on the racecourse was used by the officers for their mess, and the stabling of the paddock for their horses. On the following day the 10th Hussars was present and kept the ground in Windsor Park for the Volunteer Review, which took place before Her Majesty the Queen. It encamped again at Ascot that evening, and returned to Aldershot the following day. On the 23rd Lord George Paget made his inspection.

On the 3rd July Her Majesty the Queen held a review of the troops at Aldershot, at which H.R.H. the Prince of Wales took command of the Tenth, and marched past at the head of it.

On the 28th September Lieut.-General Sir James Scarlett, commanding the troops at Aldershot, inspected the regiment, and on the 3rd October the autumn inspection by Brigadier-General White took place.

On the 13th November G troop, under Captain Liddell and Lieutenant R. Thorold, was ordered to Trowbridge on election duty. Having remained there a short time, the civil authorities asked for the troop to be sent to Chippenham for the election in that borough.

After returning to Trowbridge this troop marched to Horfield Barracks, Clifton, to be present during the contested elections in Gloucestershire, returning three weeks later to Aldershot. Lieutenant the Hon. H. Crichton joined it at Horfield.

On the 11th December the Crown Prince of Prussia[1] paid a visit to Aldershot, and inspected the Tenth in its barracks.

The regimental changes in 1868 were :—Retirements—Captain O. R. Slacke, Captain the Hon. E. Stourton. Appointments—H. S. Gough and the Hon. R. G. Molyneux to be cornets.

On the 3rd March, 1869, Cornet H. S. Gough proceeded to Chatham to go through a course of military signalling, which had just been introduced into the service. On the 13th March Cornet the Hon. H. L. Wood was appointed Aide-de-Camp to the Governor-General of India. On the 3rd April Lieutenant the Hon. H. L. Crichton received the appointment of Adjutant, *vice* Russell, who was appointed A.D.C. to Major-General White.

In this month cavalry regiments were formed into four squadrons for administrative as well as tactical purposes, instead of eight troops. This step was taken principally on the strong representation of Colonel Baker. Great opposition was shown throughout the service to it, mainly from the reluctance of the four junior captains to give up the command of their troops. The purchase system, which was still in existence, had something to do with this feeling, as it was thought that their value would be depreciated. It is only fair to add that the four junior captains of the Tenth entered cheerfully into the scheme, and fully testified to the advantage of the system as a matter of organisation.

On the 6th May the regiment was inspected by

[1] Afterwards the Emperor Frederick of Germany.

Major-General White, C.B., in the Long Valley. During this drill season the cavalry at Aldershot was divided into two brigades—the 10th Hussars and Inniskillings, commanded by Colonel Baker ; the 5th Dragoon Guards and the 7th Dragoon Guards, under Colonel the Hon. S. Calthorpe. Major-General Lord George Paget inspected the Tenth on the 3rd June.

On the 1st July Her Majesty the Queen reviewed the troops, when His Royal Highness the Prince of Wales took command of the regiment in the field. In the evening His Royal Highness honoured the officers with his company at dinner. On the 14th July a flying column, under the command of Sir Alfred Horsford, of which the Tenth formed part, marched to Chobham and encamped, *en route* for Wimbledon. On this march the system of signalling with flags was utilised for the first time under Lieutenant Gough. Communication by this means was maintained between the columns as they advanced on the opposite bank of the river Thames. On the 16th the flying column encamped in Bushey Park, when a large number of visitors came down from London to see the camp. It was on this occasion that the Tenth for the first time adopted flags for every tent in its camp of the regimental colours, at that time blue and yellow, with one very large flag on a high flagstaff in front of the officers' mess. On the 16th the column proceeded to Wimbledon and encamped on the Common, where already a large body of Volunteers had been collected. On the 17th the troops were reviewed in the presence of royalty and an immense number of spectators from London and all parts of the country. A sham fight also took place, the cavalry— namely, the 10th Hussars and the 17th Lancers, under Colonel Drury-Lowe—being brigaded under the command of Colonel Valentine Baker. On the 19th the

camp was broken up, and the Tenth returned to Alder- 1869
shot by the same route as it came, and arrived there
on the 22nd.

On the 24th July Lord George Paget, Inspector-
General of Cavalry, made his inspection, and shortly
after this the regiment received orders to move to
Brighton and Shorncliffe.

Lieutenant Liddell was appointed A.D.C. to Lieutenant-General the Hon. Sir Augustus Spencer, the
Commander-in-Chief in Bombay, and embarked for India
on the 5th August. On the 23rd August A and B
squadrons, under command of Captain Sawbridge and
Captain the Hon. C. C. Molyneux, proceeded to Shorncliffe, arriving there on the 28th. On the 24th, D
squadron, under the command of Captain Lord Ralph
Kerr, marched to Brighton. On the same day Quartermaster James and a dismounted party proceeded by
train. On the 25th, C squadron, under Captain Barthorp, marched also to join head-quarters at Brighton.
On the same day a dismounted party went by train
to Shorncliffe. On the 10th September Major-General
Brownrigg, commanding at Shorncliffe, inspected the
head-quarters at Brighton, and on the 6th October
H.R.H. the Duke of Cambridge inspected the regiment.

The regimental changes in 1869 were :—Retire-
ments—Veterinary Surgeon Withers, Lieutenant C. B.
Ponsonby. Transfers and exchanges—Veterinary Sur-
geon W. Appleton, from Military Train ; Sergeant-Major
D. Walsh, from Cavalry Depôt, to be ridingmaster ;
Ridingmaster E. Simpson, to half-pay.

The Tenth remained at Brighton and Shorncliffe 1870
during the winter of 1869–70 without any particular
incidents occurring beyond the ordinary routine of duty.
On the 21st March, much to the regret of all ranks,
Major R. J. Elrington, for many years paymaster of the

regiment, died of scarlatina, and on the 24th the whole of the head-quarters and officers from the detachments paraded to attend his funeral.

On the 29th March the depôt of the 11th Hussars was attached to the Tenth, under the command of Captain Balfe. Lieutenant Cheape and Cornet Verelst were the subaltern officers. This arrangement was in consequence of the Cavalry Depôt at Canterbury being abolished, and in its place the depôt troop of each regiment in India was attached to the head-quarters of a regiment at home. On the 4th April the squadron organisation, which had been on trial for one year, was abolished, and the organisation by troops was reverted to. Cavalry regiments at home on the Indian roster were formed into seven troops; the depôt troop of the regiment attached to them making up eight troops.

On the 24th June the 10th Hussars commenced its march to Aldershot, and was encamped on Cove Common for the purpose of taking part in the summer drills.

On the 9th July Her Majesty the Queen paid a visit to Aldershot, and reviewed the troops. On this occasion His Royal Highness the Prince of Wales took command of the Tenth, and marched past Her Majesty at the head of his regiment. On the 23rd July Major-General White, C.B., commanding the Cavalry Brigade, made his inspection.

On the 4th August a party of thirty-six men and nineteen horses of Captain Wood's troop, under the command of Lieutenant Viscount Valentia, marched from Aldershot to Kensington Barracks for escort and orderly duty. This was the last year that the Queen's travelling escorts were furnished by light cavalry, the Life Guards undertaking these duties in 1871. The following day the head-quarters and five troops marched to Hounslow, and C troop to Hampton Court.

On the 16th August Major John Fife retired, when an excellent soldier and a brilliant horseman was lost to the service. He had been adjutant of the regiment from the 1st May, 1857, to the 5th May, 1859. Captain the Hon. C. C. Molyneux became major; Lieutenant T. A. St. Quintin, captain; and Cornet E. Hartopp, lieutenant. In this month the strength of the regiment was increased to 480 rank and file and 380 horses.

On the 9th November a party consisting of six officers and 150 men, under command of Captain St. Quintin, proceeded to London, and took part in the procession on Lord Mayor's Day.

The regimental changes in 1870 were :—Retirements—Captain R. C. Sawbridge and Major J. Fife. Transfer—Paymaster L. Lyons Montgomery, from 5th Dragoon Guards, *vice* Honorary Major and Paymaster R. J. Elrington, deceased. Appointment—Lord Naas to be cornet.

On the 1st February, 1871, the establishment was altered; eight troops took the place of seven, and the strength was raised to 607 rank and file and 384 horses.

On the 18th March the Queen's Guard at the Horse Guards was furnished by the Tenth. On the 29th, on the occasion of Her Majesty opening the Albert Hall, the 10th Hussars lined Hyde Park from Albert Gate to Prince's Gate.

On the 31st March the regimental races took place at Down Barn, when the Prince of Wales was present, and also ran a horse. His Royal Highness's colours were worn by Captain Bulkeley, who lost his chance of winning by a fall. The Challenge Cup was won for a second time by Viscount Valentia with his

horse Wellington, ridden by Captain Wood. Amongst
other events there was a Hunt Race, all the riders wearing hunting dress, and the race being from point to
point. Although the Tenth had at a former meeting
in Ireland held one of these races, it was at this time a
novelty. The cup for this race was presented by His
Royal Highness the Colonel, and was won by Lieutenant H. S. Gough, Captain Wood being second, and
Captain Bulkeley third, riding Lord Valentia's chestnut
mare Brilliant.

On the 31st May the depôt of the 11th Hussars,
attached to the regiment since March 1870, left, and
marched to Canterbury on the re-formation of the Cavalry Depôt.

On the 30th June the 10th Hussars formed part of
the force reviewed by Her Majesty the Queen in Bushey
Park. His Royal Highness the Prince of Wales took
command of the regiment, and marched past at the
head of it. The Crown Prince of Prussia (afterwards
the Emperor Frederick) reviewed the 10th Hussars at
Wormwood Scrubs on the 12th July. On the 17th July
Major-General H.S.H. Prince Edward of Saxe-Weimar
made his inspection.

On the 30th August the head-quarters and six
troops, under command of Lieutenant-Colonel V. Baker,
marched from Hounslow to Aldershot to take part in the
autumn manœuvres, and encamped on Cove Common, the
strength being 406 men and 340 horses. The cavalry
force consisted of the 1st and 2nd Life Guards, the Royal
Horse Guards, the 2nd Dragoon Guards, the 7th Dragoon Guards, the 10th Hussars, and 12th Lancers. On
the 8th September H.R.H. the Prince of Wales, Lord Valentia acting as his aide-de-camp, took command of the
Cavalry Brigade of the Second Division, which was composed as follows : the 7th Dragoon Guards, 10th Hussars,

and 12th Lancers. The manœuvres took place in the neighbourhood of Aldershot and lasted until the 26th September. The first encampment was at Hazeley Heath, and on the 9th September the division moved to Bramshill and remained there until the 14th. On the 15th, Frensham Common was occupied, and the following day the First Division was met with at Cove Common and driven back. On the 18th, the Second Division encamped at Sandhurst, and after a sham fight on the Fox Hills on the 21st, and a march past before H.R.H. the Duke of Cambridge on the 22nd, the manœuvres were concluded.

The Tenth marched from Aldershot, Hounslow, Hampton Court, and Kensington to Colchester, commencing the movement on the 23rd September. During the month of October it was inspected by Major-General Freeman Murray, commanding the district, and by Sir Thomas MacMahon, Inspector-General of Cavalry. The 10th Hussars remained at Colchester during the winter.

On the 1st November the rank of cornet was abolished, and that of sub-lieutenant substituted.

During this year the purchase system, which, since the reign of Charles II., had been recognised as the means to carry out a flow of promotion and provide retirements for the officers of the army, was abolished. It was not, however, without long and close debates in both Houses of Parliament that this measure was eventually carried, and then only by the exercise of the royal prerogative, by the Prime Minister (Mr. Gladstone). What followed was that the State paid the over-regulation money on retirement to those officers who had already purchased, as long as any purchase officers remained, and an enforced retirement for age was introduced and pensions granted to induce officers to retire.

The regimental changes in 1871 were :—Transfer—

1871   Cornet the Hon. R. G. Molyneux, promoted in the 1st
       Dragoons.   Appointment—Viscount Campden to be
       cornet.

       On the 22nd November the alarming intelligence
       was announced that His Royal Highness the Prince of
       Wales was suffering from an attack of typhoid fever.
       On the 29th, the illness having become more serious,
       Her Majesty the Queen proceeded to Sandringham, and
       the anxiety of the nation became very great. " With
       the exception, perhaps, of certain periods of the Crimean
       War and Indian Mutiny, public feeling had never been
       so deeply touched in the present generation.   Bulletins
       were posted up in all places of public resort.   News-
       papers were eagerly bought . . . and wherever two or
       three friends met, the condition of the Prince was not
       only the first but the single topic of discussion."[1]   The
       climax was reached on the 13th December ; but, hap-
       pily, after this date the fever gradually lost its hold ;
       still it was not until the 13th January that the final
       bulletin was issued announcing that His Royal High-
       ness was making satisfactory progress and daily gain-
       ing strength.

1872   On the 27th February, 1872, the Queen, with the
       Prince and Princess of Wales and other members of the
       royal family, accompanied by all the high officers of
       the Crown, proceeded in state to St. Paul's Cathedral to
       join in a thanksgiving service for the recovery of the
       Prince of Wales.   In order to take part in this cere-
       mony two squadrons of the 10th Hussars, under the
       command of Captain Barthorp, consisting of Captain
       Bulkeley, Lieutenant and Adjutant the Hon. H. L.
       Crichton, Lieutenants Okeden and Thorold, Assistant-
       Surgeon Milburn, Quartermaster James, 202 non-com-
       missioned officers and men, with 212 horses, proceeded

       ---

       [1] *The Annals of Our Time,* by Joseph Irving.

from Colchester to Woolwich on the 21st February. An
additional party of selected men and horses was also
sent from Colchester to form an advanced guard in
the procession, under command of Captain E. A. Wood,
accompanied by Viscount Valentia. Several officers of
the regiment also attended the thanksgiving service in
the Cathedral. On the 27th the detachment of the
Tenth marched from Woolwich to London to take
part in the thanksgiving ceremony. The procession
proceeded from Buckingham Palace to St. Paul's Cathedral by the Green Park, Pall Mall, the Strand, Fleet
Street, and Ludgate Hill, returning by the Holborn
Viaduct, Oxford Street, Hyde Park, and Constitution
Hill. On the 2nd March the squadrons returned to
Colchester. During this month the regiment was inspected by Major-General Sir Edward Greathed.

At the annual regimental dinner in London on the
3rd June His Royal Highness the Prince of Wales
presented the officers with a bronze statuette of himself, mounted on his charger, executed by the sculptor
Boehm. His Royal Highness is represented in his
uniform as Colonel of the 10th Hussars.

CHAPTER XL

SALISBURY MANŒUVRES—ORDERS TO PREPARE FOR INDIA—FARE-
WELL DINNER GIVEN BY THE PRINCE OF WALES—THE 7TH
HUSSARS' DINNER—COLONEL VALENTINE BAKER

1872   On the 2nd August the head-quarters and six troops, under Colonel V. Baker, commenced to march from Colchester to Blandford to take part in the autumn manœuvres in the neighbourhood of Salisbury, arriving on the 13th. The strength of the regiment on this occasion was nineteen officers, 434 non-commissioned officers and men, with 409 horses. The Tenth formed part of the First Division of the First Army Corps, under the command of Lieutenant-General Sir John Michel, G.C.B. The Cavalry Brigade of this corps was composed of the 7th and 10th Hussars and the 12th Lancers, with Colonel Valentine Baker as brigadier, Captain Maillard, 16th Lancers, brigade major, and Lieutenant Smith-Dorrien, A.D.C. Major the Hon. C. C. Molyneux commanded the Tenth. Regiments were exercised in brigade drills until the 24th, when the division marched to Bottle Bush. On the 26th a sham fight took place with the Second Division, and the next day the First Division returned to Blandford.

On the 31st August the regiment marched to Long Crichel Park, the seat of Mr. Sturt (now Lord Alington), to meet His Royal Highness the Prince of Wales on his arrival to take part in the manœuvres. About ten A.M. the 10th Hussars, with Major Strangways' battery of

Royal Horse Artillery, marched into the Park, with Colonel Baker at its head, riding his grey charger, and whilst waiting for the Prince's arrival the troops were entertained with great hospitality by Mr. Sturt. The Duke and Duchess of Teck, the Prince and Princess of Saxe-Weimar, and Lord Lucan were amongst the guests assembled to meet the Prince. The troops marched past the Prince of Wales and Duke of Cambridge, and before leaving the ground Lord Ashley, who was present, asked permission to present to the Prince an old Waterloo veteran, Pensioner Hiscott, who had formerly served in the Tenth, and had come to the Park to see His Royal Highness and his old regiment. The old man was brought tottering up, and the Prince spoke a few kind words to him. The Prince, having made his inspection, expressed to Colonel Baker the pleasure he felt at meeting his regiment and finding both men and horses so fit for service. In the evening the Tenth encamped on Fonthill Down.

The forces which were gathered together in August 1872 were divided into two armies of equal strength, to contend with each other in mimic war under the leadership of Sir Robert Walpole and Sir John Michel respectively. Sir Robert Walpole's force had its point of concentration at Aldershot, while that of Sir John Michel's army was in the neighbourhood of Blandford. The 10th Hussars found themselves serving under the last-named commander. The other Cavalry Brigade in this army consisted of the 2nd, 3rd, and 6th Dragoon Guards, under Sir Thomas MacMahon, who was also in general command of all Sir John Michel's cavalry. It was not until the beginning of September that Sir R. Walpole and Sir J. Michel moved to meet each other in the larger encounters, and these manœuvres continued until the 12th September.

During the whole period of his command, Colonel Baker had given very particular attention to the training of the 10th Hussars in those detached duties which are so especially the *rôle* of cavalry in modern war; and in the constant collisions with Sir R. Walpole's mounted men which preceded the engagements of masses of infantry and artillery the Tenth received the highest commendation for the energetic and intelligent manner in which all ranks worked, and for the effective part which it took in outpost and scouting operations. In one respect the 10th Hussars was especially remarkable. In purchasing remounts Colonel Baker had always made a point of selecting horses with as much breeding as possible, preferring to depend upon blood for hard continuous work rather than upon size and imposing appearance. The correctness of his judgment in this matter was proved by the way in which the Tenth horses, which many people had condemned as too small and slight, sustained very severe exertions for many successive days without at all deteriorating in working power.

The army of Sir John Michel had, in these manœuvres on the Wiltshire Plains, according to the published judgment of the umpires, almost uninterrupted success, and, in gaining that success, it is not too much to say that the General was indebted to his brigade of light cavalry in as great a measure as to any other part of his remarkably efficient army corps. The manœuvres concluded on the 12th September near Amesbury by a grand parade of both the contending armies, and probably so striking a military spectacle has never been seen in England, nor one to which the surrounding circumstances were more favourable. The range of Beacon Hill, the top of which is the highest spot in this part of the country, partly encloses an immense natural amphitheatre, covered with the smoothest turf and measuring nearly two miles in every direction. The slopes of the hill were occupied by spectators, while in the level space were gathered about 30,000 soldiers, all in the highest perfection of military condition and equipment. Nothing was wanting to the completeness of the spectacle, and a bright sun and cloudless sky added to the perfection in appearance of every detail. After the usual inspection and march past the cavalry were formed in two lines, which charged in succession up to the saluting point, and nothing more splendidly striking could be seen than the rapid advance of these divisions, each composed of six regiments.

The autumn manœuvres of 1872 were the last great military exercises in which the 10th Hussars took part previous to its departure for India, and it may well be supposed that many of the lessons which officers and men then learned remained of special value in their subsequent varied service. On the 16th the force commenced to disperse, and the Tenth returned to Colchester, arriving there on the 23rd. On the 30th the inspection took place by Sir Thomas MacMahon.

Lieutenant C. Frederick was promoted to be captain, *vice* J. C. Russell, transferred to the 12th Lancers. Captain Russell entered the army as a cornet on the 18th September, 1860, was adjutant from October 1864 to April 1869, and served in the 10th Hussars until the 3rd August, 1872, when he was transferred as a captain to the 12th Lancers. From June 1869 to November 1874 he served as A.D.C. to the Brigadier-General commanding the Cavalry at Aldershot. From December 1873 to February 1874 he was A.D.C. to Brigadier-General Sir Archibald Alison in the Ashanti expedition. He was mentioned in despatches, and received the medal with clasp and brevet-major. In March 1875 he was appointed Equerry to H.R.H. the Prince of Wales. Major Russell proceeded on special service to South Africa on the 31st May, 1878, and was present at the various actions during that campaign until July 1879 ; mentioned in despatches, medal with clasp, and brevet lieutenant-colonelcy. Lieutenant-Colonel Russell succeeded to the command of the 12th Lancers in July 1881, and in April 1887 was appointed Commandant of the Cavalry Depôt.

On the 18th October Quartermaster John James retired, and Regimental Sergeant-Major William King was appointed in his place. Mr. (afterwards Captain) James served in the Tenth thirty years, and was universally esteemed for his uprightness and charm of character. On leaving he was appointed Assistant-Adjutant of the Corps of Commissionaires, the duties of which he carried out in the same exemplary manner as he had done those of his regiment, and died in London on the 26th August, 1887, aged sixty-six. On the 2nd November Sergeant-Major Thomas Stuart was appointed Regimental Sergeant-Major.

On the 18th November the 10th Hussars received orders to prepare for embarkation for service in India, upon which the regiment was formed into six service troops and one depôt troop. On the 11th December the depôt troop, under the command of Captain Chaine, with sixty-six non-commissioned officers and men, eight women, and twenty-two children, proceeded to Canterbury to join the Cavalry Depôt. On the 20th the 20th Hussars arrived from India, and took over the horses of the Tenth at Colchester.

At this time Dr. Thomas Fraser, after twenty-seven years in the 10th Hussars, was transferred to the Staff. Until 1873 the medical officers of regiments were gazetted actually to individual corps, and formed as much an integral part of it as any other officer. The system had very many advantages, as the doctor, knowing intimately and being a personal friend of each officer and man, found his professional sympathy and experience enhanced and strengthened by long social acquaintance with all ranks under his care. No medical officer ever took a higher position socially and professionally than Dr. Thomas Fraser. He entered the army as assistant-surgeon of the 10th Hussars in 1845, and it was a piece of good fortune, both for himself and the corps, that when he became surgeon he was promoted in his own regiment. He served with it in India, and proceeded with it on its march through Egypt and throughout the campaign in the Crimea. He served continuously on its return to England in 1856 until 1872, when he was appointed to the medical charge of the Canterbury Cavalry Depôt, and afterwards to the Military College at Sandhurst, which last position he occupied till he retired from the service in 1882.

On the 21st His Royal Highness the Prince of Wales honoured the officers of the 10th Hussars by inviting them to dinner at Marlborough House on their departure for India. The 7th Hussars also entertained the officers of the Tenth at a farewell dinner at Willis's Rooms on the 7th January, 1873, prior to their embarkation, and this hospitable treatment helped to perpetuate the good feeling at all times existing between the two corps. The 7th and 10th had been so frequently brigaded together and been so intimate with each other, that the two regiments were often spoken of as the "Seventeenth."

The regimental changes in 1872 were :—Retirements —Lieutenant Viscount Valentia, Quartermaster and Honorary Captain J. H. James. Transfers and exchanges— Surgeon-Major T. Fraser, M.D., to Staff; Surgeon W.

Cattell, from 20th Foot; Lieutenant the Hon. C. C. W. Cavendish, from Coldstream Guards; Assistant-Surgeon J. T. Milburn, to Staff; Captain J. C. Russell, to 12th Lancers; Lieutenant the Earl of Mayo, to Grenadier Guards. Appointments—H. H. R. Heath, W. F. Montresor, and the Hon. J. P. Napier, to be sub-lieutenants; Staff Assistant-Surgeon H. Cornish to be assistant-surgeon, Sergeant-Major King to be quartermaster, Staff Assistant-Surgeon E. A. Rowe to be assistant-surgeon.

On the 7th January A troop proceeded by train dismounted from Colchester to Portsmouth, as baggage guard. On the 8th the Tenth was inspected by Major-General Greathed, and on the following day, under the command of Major the Hon. C. C. Molyneux, left Colchester by train, and embarked on board H.M.S. " Jumna," commanded by Captain Richards, R.N.[1]

Colonel Valentine Baker did not accompany the Tenth to India, but went on half-pay, after commanding it for thirteen years. He was succeeded by Major the Hon. C. C. Molyneux, who was gazetted lieutenant-colonel on the 26th March, 1873. On the same day Captain Lord Ralph Kerr was appointed major and second in command.

Colonel Baker commanded the 10th Hussars from the 30th March, 1860, till the 26th March, 1873. Within three years of his appointment to the command of the 10th Hussars it again had the distinguished honour of seeing a Prince of Wales assume the position of its full colonel, and there can be no doubt that much of the success in command which Colonel V. Baker owed in the first instance to his own ability and energy was secured to him by the encouragement and assistance of His Royal Highness.

---

[1] Eleven years later the same ship conveyed the regiment from India to the Soudan and afterwards to England.

Colonel Baker entered the army in the Ceylon Rifles in August 1848, was transferred to the 10th Hussars in April 1852, and from it to the 12th Lancers in the following May, and joined that regiment in time to take part in the Kaffir campaign of that year. He was present at the action of the Berea and other operations of the war. The 12th Lancers proceeded to India from the Cape, and afterwards was moved to the Crimea in 1855. Captain Baker was present at the siege and fall of Sebastopol, and served on the Commander-in-Chief's escort. He was also present at the battle of the Tchernaya. The 12th returned to India after peace was proclaimed, when Captain Baker, who had been promoted to a troop in 1853, exchanged to the 10th Hussars with Captain Murray in May 1857, and obtained his majority in 1859, and command of the regiment in 1860. In 1863 Colonel Baker brought forward, as the result of a visit which he had paid to the Austrian army, a system of non-pivot drill as applicable to the British cavalry, which has already been alluded to.

During the service of the Tenth in Ireland the Fenian movement took place, and among other important employments Colonel Baker was placed in command of one of the small flying columns which were organised by Sir Hugh Rose, then Commander-in-Chief. For the way in which this service was performed, Colonel Baker received the highest commendation. On the return of the Tenth to England, Colonel Baker was a prominent figure at the series of autumn manœuvres on a large scale which were carried out in 1870, 1871, and 1872. The manner in which he directed the operations of a light cavalry brigade in the latter year will not soon be forgotten by either those who served under him or those who were opposed to him. In March 1873 Colonel Baker went on half-pay. Before being again actively

1873

employed he utilised his period of leisure in travelling through Persia as far as it was at that time possible to go, for the purpose of studying the Central Asian question and learning the exact position of the Russian advance eastward. The result of his observations and information gained in Persia was published by Colonel Baker in a very powerfully written work, "Clouds in the East," which attracted much notice in 1876. In September 1874, after his return from Persia, Colonel Baker was appointed Assistant Quartermaster-General at Aldershot, which position he occupied till August 1875, when he ceased to serve with the British army.

In 1877, war, which had long been threatening, broke out between Russia and Turkey, and Colonel Baker took service under the Sultan and was employed with the rank of major-general in the Ottoman army. The most brilliant service performed by General Baker in the war was during the retreat of Suleiman Pasha from the Balkans. In this retreat on several occasions he exercised independent command in a manner showing the highest genius for war and an extraordinary power of inspiring his troops with confidence under trying circumstances. The action at Takhessen in particular will always remain as a model of a rear-guard engagement scientifically, stubbornly, and successfully fought. A very graphic and spirited account of the war in Bulgaria was published by General Baker in 1879.

After the campaign in Egypt in 1882, the appointment of its Commander-in-Chief was offered to General Baker, now lieutenant-general in the Ottoman army. He at once resigned his position in the Sultan's service in order to accept the offer. The British Government did not, however, confirm this appointment, and General Baker was placed in command of a large semi-military force of Gendarmerie, which was to be organised principally with a view to guaranteeing civil order in Egypt Proper. In 1884 the revolutionary movement in the Soudan had gained considerable ground, and General Baker was sent to encounter the rebels with such force of his Gendarmerie as he was able to collect for the purpose. His high sense of duty made him obey orders, though he felt the impossibility of his task with the material placed in his hands, and at the head of an army of about 5,000 men unwilling to fight, many of whom had to be sent in chains from Cairo, he proceeded to Suakim.

The result of the first and only engagement at El Teb was what General Baker had foretold, and which everybody who knew the conditions under which it was fought must have foreseen. The Egyptian force was panic-struck, broke into helpless confusion when charged by the Arab rebels, and it was only its demoralised remains which succeeded in returning to Suakim. Nothing indeed but the able leading and devoted conduct of General Baker saved it from complete annihilation. The British expedition then sent under Sir Gerald Graham is fully described in a later chapter of these memoirs.

General Baker served during this campaign on the British army staff as Chief of the Intelligence Department, where his experience and advice were found invaluable. The earthworks around Suakim and Trinkitat thrown up by him were the admiration of all, and showed very considerable engineering skill. He was severely wounded at the battle of El Teb, but he refused to leave the field while his services were necessary, and rode during the whole day with an iron slug two ounces in weight lodged in his face, and after the engagement his first thought was to ride to his old regiment and inquire after the part taken by it in the action.   General Baker remained at the head of the Egyptian Gendarmerie until his death.   His end was sudden and most unexpected.   He died in Egypt on the 17th November, 1887, in a small steamer on the Sweet Water Canal.   His last resting-place is in the European Cemetery at Cairo.

Valentine Baker had all the tastes and qualifications which peculiarly fit a man to distinguish himself as a soldier and to impress his influence on others.   He was an enthusiastic sportsman, a bold and determined rider, and he shared the daring adventurous spirit of his brother Sir Samuel, the well-known African traveller and administrator.   As a commanding officer and military instructor he was able to invest the dry details of drill with the highest interest, and in his time it was a common remark among the subalterns of the Tenth that a colonel's field-day was as good fun as a day's hunting.   He had the power of expressing himself most forcibly, simply, and distinctly, either in speaking or writing, and no one could ever be in his company without being impressed with the clearness and vigour of his mind.   Generous, brave, and kind-hearted, he left a reputation in the 10th Hussars which will not soon be forgotten.

CHAPTER XLI

THE REGIMENT EMBARKS FOR INDIA—FROM BOMBAY TO MUTTRA—
DURBAR AT AGRA—LIFE AT MUTTRA—THE PRINCE OF WALES'S
VISIT TO INDIA—THE CAMP AT DELHI—AGRA—LIEUTENANT-
COLONEL THE HON. C. C. MOLYNEUX

HER MAJESTY'S troopship "Jumna," conveying the 1873
Tenth to India, sailed from Portsmouth on the 10th
January, reached Malta on the 20th, Port Said on the
25th, and, passing through the Suez Canal, arrived at
Suez on the 27th, continuing the voyage the same day.
She anchored for a short time at Aden, and arrived at
Bombay on the 11th February. The regiment disembarked on the 13th, and proceeded by train to Deolali.
After a halt of five days there, the Tenth left on the
18th, stopping at the rest camps of Khundwa, Sohaj-
poor, Jubbulpore, Allahabad, and Agra. At the latter
place the camp equipage and native establishment of the
20th Hussars was taken over, and Ahmed Hossain, who
came in charge, was appointed "Kotwal" of the regiment. This worthy native for seven years had served
the 14th Light Dragoons in the same capacity, and
the 20th Hussars for fifteen years. Now for eleven
years he was to remain with the Tenth, during the
whole of its service in India, and with such success did
he carry out his duties that all the work connected
with the regimental bazaar, the native establishment,
consisting of syces, grass cutters, bheesties, &c., who
were under his charge, was carried out smoothly and

B B 2

efficiently, without any trouble of any kind ever arising. On the departure of the Tenth from India in 1882, the officers presented Kotwal Ahmed Hossain with a handsome sword of honour with gold belt, which was given to him on a parade of the whole regiment.

The regiment was inspected on the 25th February by Lord Napier of Magdala, the Commander-in-Chief in India, and on the 26th commenced its march to Muttra, halting and encamping at Secundra, Runkutta, and Fara, and marched into Muttra on the 1st March, taking over the horses of the 20th, which were in charge of a detachment of the 11th Hussars.

The first sight of its Indian mounts was anything but gratifying, after the highly-bred English horses the Tenth had been accustomed to ride. They were principally composed of stud-breds, country-breds, a few Persians, and perhaps one or two Australians—called Walers. Colonel Molyneux set to work to weed out vigorously as many as he could, and by degrees a better class of horse was introduced from the Government breeding establishments and from Australia. At first the remounts from the latter country were like dromedaries; but afterwards an improvement took place and some valuable animals were received from the Colonies, in a large manner owing to the care with which they were selected by Mr. Thacker, the Government agent, formerly veterinary surgeon of the Tenth. The officers' chargers were all Arabs, some of great beauty. All these were brought from Bombay in the first instance, and afterwards many others were picked up from officers leaving the country.

Muttra is an important civil station, but the garrison consists of only one cavalry regiment, and is retained for its use as more suitable than Agra on account of the excellent quality and quantity of dhub grass for forage. It also possesses an extensive drill ground. It was originally selected as a cavalry station to exercise a moral effect on the Maharajah of Bhurtpore, whose ancestors at one time were possessors of the town. It is thirty-six miles distant from Agra. The native city, with its 40,000 inhabitants, is one of the holy places of pilgrimage dedicated to the worship of Krishna or Vishnu, and is surrounded by other sites connected with his legendary history. Many thousands of pilgrims attend annually the shrines around. The cantonments lie below the native city, on the right bank of the river Jumna. The nearest railway station on the arrival of the Tenth was Hattras Road, thirty miles distant; but three years later a light railway was opened between Muttra and the main line. This station was a very popular one with all ranks. The non-commissioned officers and men found excellent sport shooting in the immediate neighbourhood, while the officers, in addition, had good pig-sticking. The health of both officers and men at Muttra was very good, although in the hot weather the heat was great.

On the 7th April Major-General Travers, V.C., C.B., commanding the division, made his inspection. On the 3rd August Ridingmaster D. Walsh died, and Sergeant-Major C. Sandes, 2nd Dragoons (Scots Greys), was appointed in his place.

On the 6th November the regiment, under the command of Lieutenant-Colonel the Hon. C. C. Molyneux, marched to Agra to take part in the Durbar held at that station by His Excellency Lord Northbrook, the Viceroy of India. On the 8th it encamped on the Maidan and escorted the Viceroy on his entry into Agra on the 14th. On the conclusion of this visit the Tenth returned to Muttra, arriving there on the 26th November. On the 27th Lord Northbrook paid a visit to Muttra and dined with the regiment. On the 21st December Lieutenant H. S. Gough was appointed Adjutant, *vice* Crichton, promoted.

Captain Crichton soon after this left by exchanging into the 21st Hussars. He entered the army as cornet in the 10th Hussars in 1863, and held the appointment of Instructor of Musketry in 1864. He was appointed Adjutant in 1869, and during that time introduced an excellent system of pitching and striking camp, which has been since perpetuated, besides many other improvements. After exchanging he was appointed A.D.C. to the Inspector-General of Cavalry in England from 1874 to 1877, and to the Inspector-General in Ireland from 1877 to 1878; and Brigade-Major of Cavalry in Ireland from 1878 to 1883. In 1884 he retired from the service as lieutenant-colonel, and two years later was appointed to the command of the Hampshire Yeomanry Cavalry.

Regimental changes in 1873:—Death—Ridingmaster D. Walsh. Retirements—Colonel V. Baker, to half-pay; Captain A. Barthorp, Lieutenant E. S. Watson, Captain W. H. Watkins, Lieutenant R. Thorold. Promotions— Major the Hon. C. C. Molyneux to be lieutenant-colonel, Captain Lord R. D. Kerr to be major. Transfers and exchanges—Captain B. A. Combe, from 21st Hussars; Captain C. E. Frederick, to 21st Hussars; Sergeant-Major C. Sandes, from Cavalry Depôt, to be ridingmaster; Lieutenant R. F. P. Startin, from 94th Foot. Appointments—Lieutenant R. C. S. Drury-Lowe, from 52nd Foot; R. T. Dalton to be sub-lieutenant.

On the 12th February the Tenth was inspected by Major-General the Hon. A. Hardinge, commanding the Meerut Division. On the 27th a draft consisting of ten men, under the command of Lieutenant Drury-Lowe, arrived from England. On the 27th March, one sergeant, one corporal, thirteen privates, four women, and seven children left Muttra *en route* for England, under charge of Captain E. A. Wood.

In this year there was a serious famine in India, when Lieutenant Heath and other officers were employed on relief duty.

The life at Muttra was that common to most Indian stations in the Plains, and consisted of the ordinary routine of drills and other regimental duties. As regards amusements, in the winter months a pack of English fox-hounds brought out from England in 1873 was hunted by Colonel Molyneux, and afforded fair sport hunting jackal. In the summer months it was necessary to send them to Naini Tal, the nearest hill station. There was excellent shooting in the neighbourhood, consisting of black-buck, coolan and black partridge, duck of all kinds and snipe in the jheels or lakes, The jungles surrounding Muttra were full of boar, and the pig-sticking meets were constant, and gave excellent sport. The favourite jungles were Kawal, Baharban, Maat, Goroiya, and Areeng. It was not long before the game of polo, introduced by the Tenth into England, became the principal source of exercise and amusement. The ground at Muttra was very suitable, and, in addition to the officers' game, there was also a non-commissioned officers' club.

In India, every Thursday is a recognised holiday, and on this day many of the non-commissioned officers and men went out shooting, some distance from the cantonments, and contributed largely to the troop messes by their sport. In the hot weather polo and shooting were still maintained, and after sunset, when the moonlight allowed, open-air concerts were held. A platform was erected among some trees, decked with Chinese lanterns ; the ladies and officers sat on chairs and benches in front, and the men, with the women and children, sat round to listen to the songs and join in the choruses. A regimental theatre was also started, and an excellent troupe worked indefatigably in providing a weekly entertainment for the garrison. A good stock of theatrical properties was brought out from England. The scene-painting was cleverly carried out by Privates Walter Brown, Stevenson, and Fraser, and none who witnessed Corporal Moon will forget the admirable manner in which he put his plays on the boards, nor the spirit he threw into the representations. Corporal Leonard also proved a good actor.

During its stay at Muttra the Tenth did its share in improving the appearance of the station. In 1874 Colonel Molyneux commenced some works which altered the face of the cantonments. Amongst others, he removed the dry mud walls dividing the compounds or enclosures round the bungalows from the main roads, and substituted neat open-work brick walls, and in a similar manner erected brick walls round the young trees which were now planted ; and in 1875 he laid out a new road with avenues of trees leading from the Officers' Mess to the lines. In 1876 these improvements were continued by Lord Ralph Kerr, who planted avenues of flowering trees and mangoes, and also small topes or clumps about the cantonment.

On the 30th October a party of nine men, one woman, and four children, under Troop Sergeant-Major Linden, proceeded to England to join the regimental depôt.

The regimental changes in 1874 were :—Retirement—Lieutenant T. A. Smith-Dorrien. Transfers and exchanges—Captain R. C. D'E. Spottiswoode, from 21st Hussars ; Captain the Hon. H. G. L. Crichton, to 21st Hussars ; Lieutenant M. C. Wood, from 66th Foot ; Lieutenant the Hon. H. J. L. Wood, promoted in the 12th

Lancers; Sub-Lieutenant W. E. Phillips, from 19th Hus- 1874
sars. Appointments—J. P. Brabazon (who had already
served in the Grenadier Guards and seen service in
Ashanti) to be lieutenant, E. T. Rose to be sub-lieutenant.

Major-General the Hon. A. Hardinge made his in- 1875
spection on the 10th February. On the 22nd February
Colonel Marshall and officers of the 9th Lancers, on
journey up country to Sealkote, were entertained at
Toondla Camp by the officers of the 10th Hussars.
On the 5th March one staff-sergeant, one corporal, and
fifteen privates left for England invalided.

A change in the dress was made during this year
by the abolition of strapped overalls, and in their place
pantaloons and jack-boots were taken into wear. This
alteration had been sanctioned in 1872, prior to the
Tenth leaving England, but owing to changes in India
being in arrear a fresh issue of strapped overalls was
made in 1874, and the new equipment not adopted until
1875. Blue serge jackets were also introduced for
the non-commissioned officers and men to replace the
cloth stable jackets for general use, more especially in
the hot and rainy season; they were subsequently used
regularly on the march, and in marching-order drills
during the winter season.

During the course of this hot season (1875) a couple
of brass 6-pounder guns, which were already in the
station, were utilized for teaching gun drill to the men,
under tuition of a sergeant of the Royal Artillery. This
hard exercise was found to be most conducive to the
health of all engaged. Harness was subsequently obtained, and troop horses trained to work with the guns,
with the result that a well-appointed section of artillery
attended all commanding officer's drills, and earned the
special commendation of Major-General the Hon. A.
Hardinge at his inspection in 1877.

Captain Bulkeley proceeded to join the depôt of the regiment at Canterbury, *vice* Chaine, retired upon half-pay. On the 1st April Captain E. A. Wood was appointed Adjutant of the Cavalry Depôt at Canterbury. On the 8th April Lieutenant-Colonel the Hon. C. C. Molyneux went to England on fifteen months' leave, and the command of the regiment was assumed by Major Lord Ralph Kerr.

On the 5th May F troop moved into the sanitarium of Aurungabad Barracks for ten days, and in August D troop also went there. This was owing to a slight outbreak of cholera, from which disease Shoeing-Smith Beck died. On the 11th October Lieutenant R. F. Startin was appointed Adjutant, *vice* Gough, promoted. On the 18th November the regiment, under command of Lord Ralph Kerr, moved into camp at Jeyt, owing to an outbreak of cholera in the city of Muttra. On the 1st December, to the great regret of the whole regiment, Lieutenant and Adjutant R. Startin was accidentally killed by falling on a spear while pig-sticking at Baharban jungle. The following day the regiment marched into Muttra to attend this officer's funeral, returning to Jeyt in the evening. A handsome stained glass east window was put up in the church at Muttra in memory of Lieutenant R. Startin.

At this time sanction was given for a silver Prince of Wales's feather to be worn on the undress sabretache of the officers.

In the cold weather of 1875 the Prince of Wales left England for the purpose of making a tour in India. In November of that year the 10th Hussars received orders to proceed to Delhi, to take part in the assemblage of troops in honour of the visit of His Royal Highness. The regiment marched from Jeyt *en route* for that place on the 4th December, halting at Chatuh

Hodul on the 5th, Bhamanikera on the 6th, Baghola 7th and 8th, Bulubgurh 9th, Buddarpore 10th, Delhi on the 11th. As it marched into Delhi (strength 311 horses), many officers rode out from the camp to meet it, amongst them Major Stanley Clarke, 4th Hussars (afterwards Colonel S. Clarke and Equerry to His Royal Highness the Prince of Wales); Major Richard Clayton, 9th Lancers, and Brigade-Major of the Cavalry Brigade. The Tenth encamped on broken ground in the old cantonments, about a mile from the famous " Ridge," the scene of glorious exploits during the siege of Delhi in 1857.

Colonel Watson, of the Scinde Horse, commanded the Cavalry Division; Colonel Charles Gough, the brigade consisting of the 10th Hussars, the 4th Bengal Cavalry, and the 10th Bengal Lancers. The first brigade drill was held on Monday, the 13th, and as the Tenth had up to this time been out in a cholera camp, it had been prevented having regular regimental drills this season. Men and horses worked, however, most steadily. The four following days divisional days took place, and on the 15th the 2nd Mooltan Horse joined the brigade. On the 20th, manœuvres of the division were held over a very rough country, with boulders of rock and fields intersected by ditches, for irrigation purposes. Lieutenant Cunard on this day broke his collar-bone.

The regimental changes in 1875 were :—Retirement—Lieutenant R. C. S. Drury-Lowe. Promotion—Lieutenant H. S. Gough to be captain. Transfers and exchanges—Captain W. Chaine, to half-pay; Captain W. A. Battine, from half-pay, late 17th Lancers; Lieutenant the Hon. J. P. Napier, to Indian Staff Corps. Appointments—Lieutenant R. B. W. Fisher; Lieutenant P. F. Durham ; Lieutenant E. Cunard; Sergeant-Major

E. M. L. Inman, from 19th Hussars, to be sub-lieutenant ; Captain W. Yeldham, from 18th Hussars ; Captain U. E. P. Okeden, to 18th Hussars.

On the 1st January a polo match took place between the 10th and 13th Hussars, the former winning by three goals to none. On Monday, the 3rd January, an experiment in embarking horses by rail was made by the regiment on a system introduced by Major-General Sir Charles Reid. A squadron of the Tenth marched to the station—seven officers, 120 horses and men, with baggage, tents, ponies, and followers. The train consisted of twenty-one trucks, which were covered, but open at each end. One troop formed up at each end of the train; the horses were led up a ramp into the trucks and filed on till they met in the centre ; six horses were placed in each truck. Thirty-five minutes were occupied in loading the horses and twenty minutes in packing the tents and baggage. The train then steamed out a mile into the country, disembarked in twenty-two minutes, re-embarked in twenty minutes, and finally unloaded in sixteen minutes.

At this time a system of working by dismounted sections was introduced by Lord Ralph Kerr for advanced cavalry work, and was shown to the authorities at Delhi ; the special object being to launch as strong a body of hussars as possible to a given point with all speed, to dismount and hold the ground, three men out of each section being dismounted, with their carbines, their horses being led away at the gallop to nearest cover by the mounted man of the section, and brought back in a similar manner when required. This practice has now been introduced into the service, and is embodied in the Cavalry Regulations.

The Tenth camp at Delhi was on the north side of the Ridge, close behind that of His Royal Highness the

Prince of Wales. The ground was not very favourable
for a military encampment, but by a little management
was made into one that was exceedingly pretty. The
horse lines and troop tents were ranged along a level
front, interspersed with large peepul and neem trees.
Behind rose the first slopes of the Ridge, covered with
babool trees; behind again was the Brigadier's camp.
The officers' and mess tents had to be pitched as best
could be arranged on the Ridge. The mess tent, with
its shameeanas on the left, was approached by a gravel
road with ornamental shrubs and plants on either side.
The commanding officer's tent and shameeana, and the
street of officers' tents, brilliant with flags of the regimental colours, were on the right. All pegs, poles of
mess tent, &c., as well as every tent throughout the
camp, showed the regimental colours, and a large em-
blazoned blue and yellow flag with regimental device
for the bazaar completed the general effect.

On the 11th January the 10th Hussars paraded to
receive His Royal Highness the Prince of Wales on
his arrival at Delhi, and lined the road up to the
Prince's durbar tent. A squadron consisting of 100
men and horses was told off as a personal escort during
the visit of His Royal Highness. On Sunday, the 16th,
the Prince gave a dinner to the non-commissioned
officers and men of the Tenth. He visited them during
the entertainment, and his health was proposed by
Regimental Sergeant-Major Stuart. On the 17th the
regiment paraded for the inspection of the Prince of
Wales, who commanded that expression should be
made to the officers, non-commissioned officers, and
men of the 10th Hussars of the pleasure he felt at
meeting them in India, and his satisfaction at their high
state of discipline, appearance, and soldierly bearing
both in the field and in camp. On the 18th January

1876   a squadron of 114 men and horses, under command of Captain Boyce Combe, with Lieutenant Manners Wood, Lieutenant Inman, and Dr. Roe, left Delhi by train for Agra, and from there by road to Gwalior, on escort duty during the visit of the Prince of Wales to the Maharajah Scindia. On the 19th, a detachment, under command of Captain Hartopp, with native followers, bazaar, &c., marched on return to Muttra. On the 20th, the head-quarters, under Major Lord Ralph Kerr, proceeded by rail to Agra, to be present during the Prince of Wales's visit to that station.

On the 25th January His Royal Highness arrived at Agra at 4 P.M., and was received by an escort of 100 of the 10th Hussars. Sir John Strachey, the Lieutenant-Governor of the North-West Provinces, made the officers his guests during the Prince's stay at Agra. On the 26th a march past of troops of the various rajahs took place before His Royal Highness. The scene was gorgeous, but seemed to be borrowed from the last century. Among others, the Maharajah of Bikhaneer was especially remarkable with his camel guns and camels, sowars in armour, his infantry with match-locks, elephants and horses steeped in henna and covered with armour and silver mail trappings. Some of the horses had steel helmets, with a shield of plate armour hanging from the nose. On the 29th the Prince of Wales visited Futtehpore Sikri, his carriage being drawn by artillery horses. In the evening he returned to Agra. On the 31st His Royal Highness in the same manner visited Gwalior, the capital of the Maharajah Scindia. At Gwalior the squadron of the Tenth, under Captain Boyce Combe, awaited the arrival of the Prince. The Maharajah Scindia held a parade of his troops, and gave an admirable field day. On the 2nd February the Prince returned to Agra, and on the

4th proceeded by rail to Bhurtpore and then to Jeypore. On the 5th His Royal Highness went out into
the jungle with the Maharajah of Jeypore, and there
shot his first tiger.

On the 7th the Prince returned to Agra. In the
evening the squadron of the 10th Hussars turned out
and accompanied him to the Taj. The squadron was
there dismissed, but Lieutenant-Colonel Lord Ralph
Kerr and the whole of the officers accompanied him as
personal escort to the station, and there took leave of
him. The Prince of Wales presented a silver medal
commemorative of his visit to India to all the officers
who had acted as personal escort to him. On the 4th
February the remainder of the squadron at Gwalior left
by route march, and returned to Muttra, arriving there
on the 13th. Head-quarters left Agra on the 9th and
reached Muttra on the 11th.

On the 13th February Lieutenant the Hon. C. C.
Cavendish was appointed Adjutant, *vice* Startin, deceased. On the 12th and 13th March the Tenth was
inspected by Brigadier-General H. Brown, commanding
at Agra. On the 3rd April a prize sword was awarded
by the Commander-in-Chief in India to Private Dowie,
as the best shot in the cavalry in India for 1875.

On the 31st May Lieutenant-Colonel the Hon. C. C.
Molyneux retired from the service, and Lord Ralph Kerr
was appointed to the command. Lieutenant-Colonel the
Hon. C. C. Molyneux entered the army as cornet in the
7th Hussars on the 6th June, 1856. He was promoted a
lieutenant in 1858. He served with the 7th during the
Indian Mutiny from February 1858 to March 1859. He
was present at the repulse of the enemy's attack on the
Alumbagh, the siege and capture of Lucknow, affairs of
Barree and Sirsee, the action of Nawabgunge, the occupation of Fyzabad, throughout the Byswarra campaign,

also the Transgogra campaign, with the pursuit to the Raptee and the advance into Nepaul. For this he received the Indian Mutiny medal and clasp. He was promoted captain in March 1860, and exchanged into the 10th Hussars on the 1st June of the same year. He became major and second in command on the 17th August, 1870. From this time until the Tenth embarked for India, Major Molyneux had frequent opportunities of taking command, owing to Colonel Baker being on the Continent during the Franco-German war, and also on his paying visits to foreign armies. At other times, during the manœuvres in England at Salisbury and near Aldershot, Major Molyneux also was at the head of the regiment while Colonel Baker was acting as brigadier. During the last few months of its stay in England, at Colchester, the preparations for Indian service were left in the hands of Major Molyneux, and on arrival in India at the small station of Muttra, where there were no other troops or even civilians to give assistance, his experience of the country and his ready resource stood the Tenth in good stead and enabled all ranks to settle down and accommodate themselves to conditions of service and the requirements of a climate, both new to them, with such ease as to conduce greatly to their comfort and well-being. Major Molyneux was in command of the regiment on its leaving Colchester for embarkation in January 1873, and was gazetted lieutenant-colonel on the 26th March following. After commanding for three years he retired from the army by the sale of his commission. He was a brilliant rider and a most accomplished horseman in every detail. The many excellent lessons, not only in the drill field but in the hunting field, that he taught those under his command have been remembered and valued ever since.

On the 4th June Lieutenant-Colonel Montgomery, Paymaster of the Tenth, died at Saharunpore of heat apoplexy. On the 12th July Captain R. S. Liddell was appointed Adjutant of the Cavalry Depôt, Canterbury, *vice* Captain E. A. Wood, promoted to the majority of the 10th Hussars.

CHAPTER XLII

THE IMPERIAL ASSEMBLAGE — PROCLAMATION OF HER MAJESTY
EMPRESS OF INDIA — MARCH TO RAWUL PINDI—DIFFICULTIES IN
AFGHANISTAN — THE TENTH ORDERED ON SERVICE—HOSTILITIES
COMMENCE — SQUADRON IN THE KURRAM VALLEY — PEIWAR
KOTAL—KHOST VALLEY—THE SQUADRON MARCHES TO JOIN
HEAD-QUARTERS AT JELLALABAD—MOVEMENTS OF THE HEAD-
QUARTERS—ALI MUSJID—JELLALABAD

1876   THE 10th Hussars marched from Muttra on the 13th
December for Delhi, to take part in the Imperial Assemblage, when Her Majesty the Queen was to be proclaimed Empress of India.   It arrived at Delhi on the
22nd, and with the 4th Bengal Cavalry, the 3rd Bombay Cavalry, and a detachment of the Hyderabad
Contingent, the whole under Colonel Palliser, formed
the First Brigade of the Cavalry Division, commanded
by Major-General Neville Chamberlain.   The other European cavalry regiments present were the 11th and 15th
Hussars.   On the 27th, the officers of the Tenth and the
whole of the men, who attended voluntarily, were present at the funeral of Captain R. Clayton, 9th Lancers,
who was accidentally killed while playing polo.   On
the 29th December the regiment paraded in review
order to escort the Viceroy of India from the railway
station to his camp, the road being lined the whole way
by our own troops and those of the native rajahs.

   The regimental changes in 1876 were :—Death—
Lieutenant R. F. P. Startin.   Retirements—Lieutenant

Viscount Campden, Lieutenant-Colonel the Hon. C. C. 1876 Molyneux, Lieutenant B. S. C. L. Tottenham. Promotions—Major Lord R. D. Kerr to be lieutenant-colonel, Captain E. A. Wood to be major. Transfers and appointments—Sub-Lieutenant Lord Ogilvy, from Scots Guards ; Sub-Lieutenant B. S. C. L. Tottenham, from 106th Foot ; Lieutenant H. H. R. Heath, to Indian Staff Corps ; R. H. F. W. Wilson.

On the 1st January the 10th Hussars paraded in 1877 review order to attend the proclamation of Her Most Gracious Majesty the Queen as Empress of India, which was declared by His Excellency the Viceroy, Lord Lytton. A salute of 101 guns[1] was given, and three *feux de joie* were fired by the 92nd Regiment, the Rifle Brigade, and the Ghoorkas. This was followed by a march past of the troops. The daïs erected in the Maidan for the proclamation of the Queen as Empress of Hindostan was a large polygonal raised platform, surmounted by a chatri or dome tapering to a point, and crowned with an Imperial crown, the whole covered with heavily embroidered silk bands of red and white alternately. The draperies on the sides were embellished with heraldic devices of arms and emblems of the United Kingdom, with banners at the angles, the base covered with beautiful needle-work, lilies, &c. Around the daïs was an open space, and enclosing this raised semicircular ranges of seats, with ornamental roofs, for rajahs and visitors. A commemorative proclamation medal in silver was struck, and one was given to the Tenth. It was awarded to Regimental Sergeant-Major Stuart. The regiment also received a silver trumpet, with banderol and sling, to be

---

[1] During the salute a stampede occurred amongst the elephants belonging to the native princes, when several people were killed and others seriously injured.

retained as a memento of the Imperial Assemblage at Delhi.[1]

On the 3rd January there were general sports for the troops, and on the 4th the Viceroy held a review. On the 8th January the Tenth left Delhi *en route* for Muttra, arriving at that station on the 15th. On the 11th March Major-General the Hon. A. Hardinge, commanding the division, made his inspection.

On the 1st April Ridingmaster C. Sandes was appointed Acting-Adjutant, *vice* the Hon. C. C. Cavendish, who exchanged into the 16th Lancers. Captain Cavendish (afterwards Lord Chesham) shortly after retired from the army, and for many years was Master of the Bicester Hounds, succeeding Lord Valentia in this position. Lord Chesham's father also served for many years in the Tenth. On the 9th, Lieutenant-Colonel Lord Ralph Kerr proceeded on leave to England, and Major E. A. Wood assumed command.

The summer of 1877 was an exceptionally hot one, no rain falling during the monsoon. The health of the regiment happily remained good. During this summer the Tenth lost a very valuable life by the accidental death of Lieutenant Edward Cunard while playing polo at Shorncliffe. This young officer was full of promise, accomplished, a brilliant musician, a good rider, and his loss was felt deeply by all who knew him.

On the 15th November, after having been stationed at Muttra for four years and eight months, the Tenth was ordered to march to Rawul Pindi, in relief of the 4th Hussars. It was under command of Major E. A. Wood, and proceeded by Delhi, Kurnal, Umballa, Jullundur, Umritsur, Lahore, and Jhelum. The river Beas had to be crossed by boats, but no accident of any kind occurred, although the baggage camels were

---

[1] This is now kept in the Officers' Mess.

especially troublesome. At Wazirabad the officers of the 9th Lancers from Sealkote met and entertained the officers of the Tenth. A detachment, under command of Captain Bulkeley, with Lieutenant R. B. Fisher, together with the women and children of the regiment, remained at Muttra until the 1st January, 1878, joining the head-quarters at Jhelum on the 7th.

The regimental changes in 1877 were :—Deaths— Paymaster L. L. Montgomery, Lieutenant E. Cunard. Retirement—Captain E. Hartopp. Transfers and exchanges — Captain W. Chaine, from half-pay; Paymaster and Honorary Captain S. Murphy, from 4th Hussars ; Captain W. Yeldham, to half-pay. Appointments—C. S. Greenwood, H. T. Allsopp, the Hon. G. L. Bellew, F. H. Harford, Lieutenant E. M. L. Inman, Lieutenant R. T. Dalton, Lieutenant W. F. Montresor, to Indian Staff Corps ; Lieutenant the Hon. J. P. Napier, from Indian Staff Corps ; Ridingmaster C. Sandes to be lieutenant.

The Tenth arrived at Rawul Pindi on the 15th January. Rawul Pindi is a large military cantonment, one of the most advanced posts of the Punjaub. The garrison consisted of one European and one native cavalry regiment, two European and two native infantry regiments, with three batteries of artillery. The climate is very cold in winter and hot in summer, but the hot season is of short duration. At that time it was very healthy ; but in later years it has not retained this character, fever being prevalent. The hill station of Murree, over 6,000 feet high, is within a few hours' ride.

Ridingmaster H. McGhee, from the 11th Hussars, was appointed Ridingmaster, *vice* Sandes, appointed Adjutant. On the 15th February Major-General F. Maude, V.C., C.B., commanding the Rawul Pindi Division, inspected the regiment.

A letter was received on the 7th March from the Adjutant-General, Horse Guards, notifying that His Royal Highness the Field-Marshal Commanding-in-Chief approved of the officers of the 10th Hussars continuing to wear the undress sword-belt and slings of crimson morocco leather edged with gold wire, " as it would appear to have been in use by the 10th Hussars for a lengthened period."

In the autumn of 1878 the difficulties which had arisen between the Government of India, at this time under the viceroyalty of Lord Lytton, and the Ameer of Afghanistan (Shere Ali) showed every indication of ending in hostilities. In October an Embassy sent to Cabul, under General Sir Neville Chamberlain, accompanied by a small escort, was stopped by order of the Ameer on arrival at Ali Musjid, in the Khyber Pass, and sent back to India. On account of this occurrence Shere Ali was called upon by the British Government to render an explanation of his conduct before the 20th November, and was informed that if by that time no satisfaction was given, his territory was to be invaded. For this purpose British and native troops were collected at the mouths of the Khyber and Kurram Passes. On the 5th October a squadron of the 10th Hussars was ordered to march *en route* to Kohat to form part of the Kurram Valley Field Force, under command of Major-General F. Roberts, V.C., C.B. The first squadron of the Tenth, consisting of E and B troops (ninety-six officers, non-commissioned officers, and men), under command of Captain and Local Major J. T. Williams-Bulkeley, was selected for this duty. Captain W. Barker, Lieutenants Fisher and Durham, and Surgeon-Major Jeffcoat accompanied the squadron. On the 14th October it arrived at Kohat; on the 20th it was joined by Lieutenant J. P. Brabazon. On the 6th November it marched from Kohat *en route* to Thull, arriving there on the 20th.

The period of grace given to the Ameer Shere Ali having now expired, hostilities commenced, and at one A.M. on the 21st the force under Major-General Roberts advanced towards the Kurram River. The Cavalry Brigade of this force consisted of one squadron of the 10th Hussars, the 12th Bengal Cavalry, and 5th Punjaub Cavalry, the 14th Bengal Lancers joining later. Brigadier-General Hugh Gough, V.C., C.B., commanded the brigade, and Lieutenant Brabazon, 10th Hussars, was his brigade-major. The squadron of the Tenth formed the advanced guard of this force, and had the honour of being the first of the British troops to cross the Kurram River into Afghan territory on the night of 19th November. The river was swollen and a roaring torrent, and the passage a difficult and dangerous one; two or three men were swept away, but escaped from drowning. The forts of Capiange and Ammadi Shama were occupied without opposition on the 21st, our troops encamping at the latter place. On the 22nd the squadron of the Tenth, as advanced guard, marched to Hazir Pir and encamped, and on the 24th, continuing its march, reached the south end of the Durwaza Pass. On the 25th it took part in the operations against the Kurram Fort, which was captured. The advance into the Kurram Valley was now proceeded with, until it was found that the position of the Peiwar Kotal was strongly held by the enemy, and that the further progress of the force under Major-General Roberts would be disputed. On the early morning of the 31st November General Roberts made his dispositions for the attack of this formidable position. About ten o'clock on the night of the 1st December he moved out of camp with the main body, the Moun-

1878 tain Battery, 72nd Highlanders, 5th Ghoorkas, 28th Bengal Infantry, and 3rd Punjaubis, and made a long flank march during the night round the enemy's position.   In the early morning of the 2nd a front attack, as a feint, was made by the 8th Regiment and a battery of artillery, the cavalry in support.   General Roberts then decided on making a bold stroke for victory, and made a still further *détour* in rear of the enemy.   The front attack pressed on, and the Peiwar Kotal was captured.   The Afghans retreated, having abandoned their guns, their dead and wounded, stores, and munitions of war.

The country was not a suitable one for cavalry, and the squadron of the Tenth was held in reserve while the action was carried on.   Lieutenant Brabazon was specially mentioned in despatches.   On the 24th December the squadron marched from Kurram to Hazir Pir, through the Durwazza Pass, arriving there on the 28th.   On the 29th a reinforcement of ten men and nineteen horses joined from the head-quarters of the regiment.

1879 On the 2nd January the squadron, consisting of seventy-eight men and horses, marched to Gaga Maidan, forming the advanced guard of an expedition ordered to be made into the Khost Valley.   General Roberts accompanied it in person, Colonel Barry Drew acting as brigadier.   On the 6th January the force arrived at Matun Fort, and on the following day the enemy came down in large numbers and completely surrounded the camp of the British force, with the intention of liberating prisoners, to the number of about eighty, confined under a strong guard of the Punjaub Native Infantry.   The cavalry, consisting of the Tenth squadron and a squadron of the 5th Punjaub Cavalry, the whole being under the command of Colonel Hugh Gough, V.C., C B., were turned out at 1.30 P.M., and drove back the enemy, estimated at about 1,500 men, into the hills. Colonel Gough in his despatch specially commended the steadiness and precision with which this duty was performed, and General Roberts thanked the squadron in complimentary terms. On the 8th January B troop, under Captain Barker and Lieutenant R. B. Fisher, made an extended reconnaissance into the enemy's country. About eight o'clock the same evening the enemy again advanced and fired into the camp. E troop turned out at once, and was thanked by the Major-General for the rapidity with which it did so. On the 13th the force continued its advance to the head of the Khost Valley, the Tenth again forming the advanced guard, being followed by a battery and 200 of the 72nd Highlanders.

The force encamped at Deghan. On the 27th the squadron marched to Sabri, and on the 29th returned to Matun Fort, which had been surrounded by the enemy in force. Having relieved the fort, the grain was burned and the treasure carried off. The infantry and guns fell back, and the cavalry covered the retirement. The enemy, seeing the cavalry left to themselves, rushed down from the hills and advanced over the plain at a rapid pace, their numbers being estimated at 5,000; one troop was dismounted by sections, and opening a brisk fire killed and wounded a great many of the enemy, and the squadron retired after a skirmish, in which the head Moolah was killed. The dismay of the Afghans at seeing the cavalry dismount and fire was so great that it checked their advance, and presently they fell back. Major-General Roberts expressed in orders his satisfaction at the manner in which this duty had been carried out.

On the 31st January the squadron returned to

1879   Hazir Pir, and there received orders to join the head-
quarters of the Tenth at Jellalabad, forming part of
the force under the command of Sir Samuel Browne,
K.C.S.I.   On this occasion the following order was
published by Major-General Roberts :—

> The squadron of the 10th Hussars has been ordered to join
> its regimental head-quarters at Jellalabad.   In wishing it good-
> bye General Roberts desires to express his deep regret at losing
> so fine a body of men from his command, and to record his high
> appreciation of the assistance they have afforded him.   The
> Major-General congratulates Major Bulkeley, the officers, non-
> commissioned officers, and men on the excellent state of disci-
> pline of the squadron.   No soldiers could have behaved more
> steadily in quarters or done better service in the field.   The
> regret and admiration the Major-General feels are shared in by
> all ranks of the Kurram Column.

On the 9th February the squadron arrived at Kohat,
remaining there until the 12th, when it proceeded on
its march to Peshawur *viâ* the Kohat Pass.   On the
20th February it left Peshawur, and marching through
the Khyber Pass formed the escort of H.E. Sir Frederick
Haines, the Commander-in-Chief, on his way to Jellalabad to visit the force under General Sir Samuel
Browne.   On the 28th February it joined the head-
quarters of the regiment.

Eight days after Captain Bulkeley's squadron had
proceeded from India on active service in the Kurram
Valley the head-quarters and remainder of the 10th
Hussars at Rawul Pindi had been ordered to the front
also, and on the 28th October, 1878, marched *en route*
to Nowshera, arriving at that place on the 2nd November, Major E. A. Wood being in command.   On the
12th November the Tenth marched *en route* to Muthra
Thana, to join the Cavalry Brigade of the First Division,

Peshawur Valley Field Force, under command of Lieutenant-General Sir Samuel Browne. The Cavalry Brigade consisted of the 10th Hussars, the Guides Cavalry,
and 11th Bengal Lancers, under command of Brigadier-
General C. Gough, V.C. On the 14th November the
force advanced to Muthra Thana and encamped.

On the 21st, hostilities having commenced, an advance was made into the Khyber Pass for the purpose
of storming the fort of Ali Musjid. The First and
Second Infantry Brigades, under Brigadier-General
Macpherson, were sent to work their way in rear of the
fort, the one to proceed along the Rhota's heights until
it reached a point commanding it, the other to make a
wide *détour* and take up a position closing the defile
through which it was expected the garrison might attempt to escape. The remainder of the division, under
Sir Samuel Browne himself, was to storm the enemy's
position in front. A detachment of the Tenth, consisting of forty non-commissioned officers and men, under
the command of Lieutenant H. Allsopp, accompanied
the advanced guard of the force under Colonel Apple-
yard, and formed the escort to I-C Royal Horse Artillery in the attack on Ali Musjid.

The Cavalry Brigade marched at seven A.M.,
entered the Khyber Pass and arrived at the Shajai
Ridge, opposite Ali Musjid, about one P.M. The Tenth
was formed up in line in rear of rising ground under
cover. The horses were linked, and remained saddled
and bitted. Each man lay in front of his horse. About
noon the enemy opened fire, when I-C Royal Horse
Artillery, under the command of Major the Hon. Alexander Stewart, was the first to reply. Within the next
hour the whole of the artillery was in action, at ranges
from 2,000 to 2,500 yards, and remained engaged all
day. At 2.25 P.M., in view of the probability of the

First and Second Brigades having reached their destination, a general advance was ordered. I-C battery, with the escort of the 10th Hussars, descended towards the Khyber stream, and took up the most suitable position for silencing the enemy's guns. At 3.30 P.M. the troops were in sharp conflict and remained so until dark. Day was now closing in, and as yet there was no sign of Macpherson's turning movement; the troops were therefore ordered to make no further advance, but hold their positions until the following morning. At daybreak on the 22nd it was noticed that the enemy's fire was not continued, and from other indications it became apparent that the Ameer's troops had abandoned Ali Musjid during the night.[1] The Cavalry Brigade was moved forward, and bivouacked on the right bank of the Khyber River under Ali Musjid.

On the 23rd November the Cavalry Brigade again moved forward, and, meeting with no opposition, bivouacked at Lundi Kotal. C troop, under command of Lieutenant Rose, was left at Lundi Kotal as escort to I-C Royal Horse Artillery, while the Cavalry Brigade moved forward on the 24th and bivouacked at Dhaka. C troop rejoined the head-quarters on that day. Here a halt was made for a week, when the force again advanced on the 1st December, through the Khoord Khyber Pass, and encamped at Bassawul until the 13th, when the Tenth marched back to Dhaka.

Dr. Cornish, who had served with the regiment for some years, was now struck off the strength, and the services of a very valuable officer were lost to it. He afterwards served in South Africa, and was killed at Majuba Hill.

On the 16th the Cavalry Brigade commenced its ad-

[1] Shadbolt's *Afghan Campaign.*

vance on Jellalabad, which place it reached on the 20th, and, finding it evacuated, marched through the city and encamped.

The town of Jellalabad stands on the right bank of the Cabul River, and is surrounded by a wall. The principal street runs from the Peshawur to the Cabul Gate. The bazaar is fairly supplied with cloth, leather, pottery, and grain. The neighbourhood is much subject to earthquakes, and the effects are visible on the walls and houses. The standing camp at Jellalabad was pitched on the east side of the city, about half a mile from the Peshawur Gate. It was on arable land, and, although very soft at first, soon became hardened by traffic. An irrigation canal ran close by, and supplied the greater part of the water for the camp. A sandy plain and low hills were to the south, and at a distance of some seven or eight miles was the lofty range of the Safed Koh. The small pass at Ali Boghan, by which the Jellalabad Plain was entered, was four miles from camp.

The regimental changes in 1878 were:—Retirements—Captain and Brevet-Major W. Chaine, to half-pay. Transfers and exchanges—Captain W. Barker, from 16th Lancers; Captain the Hon. C. C. W. Cavendish, to 16th Lancers; Captain M. M. Slade, from 18th Hussars. Appointment — Sub-Lieutenant C. M. Grenfell.

On the 11th January twenty-five non-commissioned officers and men of the Tenth, under command of Lieutenant E. T. Rose, marched to Ali Boghan to support and co-operate with a force under Brigadier-General Jenkins sent out to capture some Seyeds who were reported to be endeavouring to raise the tribes on the north of the Cabul River. The Seyeds were captured. On the 29th January Captain Manners Wood, Sub-

Lieutenant C. Grenfell, with sixty-eight non-commissioned officers and men, and twenty-four horses, arrived
at head-quarters from Rawul Pindi.

On the 7th February, it having been reported that
a large body of men from the Mohmund tribes to the
north of the Cabul River were advancing and threatening the line of communication and the signal posts,
Brigadier-General Macpherson, V.C., C.B., was sent out
with a mixed force and crossed the Cabul River at
4.30 A.M. D troop, 10th Hussars, under command of
Captain T. A. St. Quintin, accompanied these troops,
and about midday came up with the rear guard of the
enemy, retreating into the hills. Skirmishers were sent
out, who opened fire dismounted; but, as the enemy
scattered over the hills and the range was very great, it
could not be ascertained whether any loss was inflicted
on them. The main body of the enemy, variously estimated at from 5,000 to 15,000, escaped into the mountains the previous evening.

The Cavalry Brigade, under command of Brigadier-
General C. Gough, V.C., C.B., marched at six A.M. to
Ali Boghan to co-operate with the infantry, but as no
enemy could be seen it did not cross the river. On
the 21st February, F troop, 10th Hussars, under command of Captain F. Slade, and accompanied by Lieutenant Lord Ogilvy and Sub-Lieutenant F. H. Harford,
formed part of a force under Brigadier-General Jenkins
sent into the Lughman Valley, where it remained for
four days. On the 28th February, as before related,
B and E troops, under the command of Major Bulkeley,
joined the head-quarters from the Kurram Valley. On
the 12th March a troop, under command of Captain
St. Quintin, accompanied by Lieutenant the Hon. J. P.
Napier and Lieutenant C. S. Greenwood, escorted Major
Tanner on survey duty, remaining away from Jellalabad

five days.   On the 20th March Lieutenant-Colonel Lord
Ralph Kerr, returning from sick leave in England, arrived at head-quarters and resumed command of the
regiment.   Soon after this the weather became very
hot, and preparations were made for moving the troops
to higher ground towards Jugdulluck, on the road to
Cabul.

CHAPTER XLIII

AN EXPEDITION ORDERED AGAINST THE KHUGIANIS—DISASTER IN THE CABUL RIVER—LIST OF THOSE DROWNED—ACTION OF FUTTEHABAD—TELEGRAMS FROM THE QUEEN AND PRINCE OF WALES—DEATH OF SHERE ALI—TREATY OF GUNDAMUCK—WITHDRAWAL OF TROOPS TO INDIA — CHOLERA — HONOURS GRANTED FOR THE CAMPAIGN

1879   ORDERS were now issued for a mixed force. under Brigadier-General Charles Gough to proceed early on the morning of the 1st April with the purpose of engaging the Khugiani tribe, which was reported to have assembled in the neighbourhood of Futtehabad.   At the same time an expedition was determined on to co-operate against the tribes on the left bank of the Cabul River. A small force, composed of one squadron of the 10th Hussars and one of the 11th Bengal Lancers, the whole under the command of Major E. A. Wood, of the 10th Hussars, was directed to cross over the Cabul River the previous evening (the 31st), so as to take up a position in rear of the enemy.   The officers with the Tenth squadron were Captain Spottiswoode, who had just arrived from Rawul Pindi, Lieutenant the Hon. J. P. Napier, Lieutenant Greenwood, Sub-Lieutenants Grenfell and Harford.   These squadrons paraded at 9.30 P.M., and were taken down to the bank of the river at the point selected by the staff for fording.   The native cavalry led, and an Afghan guide was placed in

1879

front of them to show the line of the ford. The squadron of the Tenth received orders to follow closely on the Lancers, and on no account to leave the slightest distance between them, the peculiar and dangerous nature of the ford being apparently well understood by the Staff. Its track was somewhat similar in shape to the letter S, and the current at this part running at the rate of six miles an hour made a crossing in the dark a difficult task. The Bengal Cavalry entered the ford in half-sections, its long column, no doubt slightly and imperceptibly affected by the strong current, having a tendency to give way to the stream till its rear files must have been near the edge of the ford, which consisted merely of boulders and a gravel bed at the head of the rapids. Two baggage mules followed, and immediately touching behind them came the leaders of the Tenth squadron, in accordance with their orders. At a turn in the ford the two mules, giving way to the stream, were taken off their legs and swept down. The Tenth leaders, following in the dim moonlight, left the ford, and, those in rear doing the same, were carried rapidly and silently away in the dark and cloudy night. Not a sound was heard for some moments but the rushing water, and no one seemed to be aware of what was taking place. The whole squadron, officers, men, and horses, were struggling for life in the water, but everything was against them. On account of the night march each man had a tunic on under his khaki; thirty rounds of ammunition were carried, and the havresacks were well filled with the next day's rations, so that although many amongst them were excellent swimmers they found it now of no avail; the water was bitterly cold from the melting snows, and the poor fellows were quickly numbed.

The night being so dark, the nature of the calamity
was not at first apparent to the leaders and the few men
who reached the opposite bank in safety. It was
thought and hoped at first that the remainder were
waiting at the other side, and the guide was sent across.
The regimental call was sounded by the trumpeter, but
it failed to bring in the missing men. Five had in the
meantime succeeded in reaching the shore—Privates
Byatt (afterwards quartermaster-sergeant), Lynch,
McIntosh, Murrell, and Parker—and this they owed to
being able to get rid of their belts and arms. Some
others had been able to reach the bank on the Jellalabad
side.[1] In the meantime the camp was startled by the
return of a large number of riderless horses, their wet
saddles and kits making it apparent that some disaster
had occurred. A search party was at once despatched
to the scene of the accident, with elephants, under
Captain J. R. Slade, R.H.A., but the darkness was so
great that only one body was recovered. At daybreak
the search was continued down stream, and nineteen
bodies were soon discovered. That of Sub-Lieutenant
Harford was found by some villagers about a mile
below the scene of the disaster, and some others were
carried as far as Dakka, a distance by river of sixty
miles. In all, one officer and forty-six non-commissioned
officers and men were lost, and fourteen horses. The
names of the officers, non-commissioned officers, and men

---

[1] A graphic account of this sad disaster was given by the two men of
the rear guard who returned to camp to report the event. The camp was
struck, and officers and men were awaiting the order to mount and march
to Futtehabad, when these two men rode up to Lord R. Kerr, who asked
why they had returned. They answered, " We don't know how it
happened, but we were riding down the bank in the rear of the column
We were talking and watching the squadron filing across the ford in
half sections, when suddenly they all turned their horses to the right,
galloped down stream into the darkness, and disappeared without a
sound."

drowned in the Cabul River on the 31st March, 1879,
were :—

Lieutenant J. H. Harford.	Private G. Haslett.
Sergeant F. Green.	,, W. Hobbs.
,, I. Batten.	,, W. Huett.
Lance-Sergeant H. S. Hayes.	,, H. James.
Farrier R. Gillham.	,, H. Keble.
Corporal C. Skinner.	,, E. Lemon.
Lance-Corporal T. Kemble.	,, P. Loftus.
Private H. Allen.	,, W. McKee.
,, C. Badger.	,, T. Mandeville.
,, G. H. Brown.	,, J. Massey.
,, T. Burke.	,, H. Murrell.
,, H. Cant.	,, W. Nash.
,, P. Cappa.	,, W. Osborne.
,, W. Chamberlain.	,, W. Read.
,, W. Charge.	,, J. Richards.
,, T. Downes.	,, J. Roach.
,, C. Dudley.	,, W. Simms.
,, C. Gaisford.	,, G. Skevington.
,, W. Gould.	,, G. Tidey.
,, T. Gravett.	,, J. Twining.
,, J. Green.	,, W. Wilkins.
,, G. B. Hall.	,, G. Wilson.
,, J. Hall.	,, C. Wooding.
,, J. Hart.	

Several instances of gallantry worth recording took place during this terrible calamity, and none more so than the conduct of Lieutenant Charles Greenwood, who, although almost exhausted by his efforts, had extricated himself from the quicksands and found himself on an island. Hearing cries for help, he again entered the water and found a man thirty yards out, unable to move in the deep gravel, and almost drowning. Lieutenant Greenwood failed in getting the man out alone, when Lieutenant Grenfell, hearing the shouts, came to his assistance, and together they brought the man in safety to the shore.   This was Private Goddard, afterwards a farrier-sergeant.   Lieutenant Greenwood received the Humane Society's medal for his conduct on this occasion.   Private Crowley, who had swum with his horse a considerable distance and remained with it until it succumbed, had great difficulty himself in reaching the shore, and on doing so went to the assistance of Lieutenant the Hon. J. Napier, whom he helped to rescue.   On his return to India, Lieutenant Napier presented him with a gold watch and chain.   The remains of Sub-Lieutenant Harford (who had only recently joined from England) and the forty-six non-commissioned officers and men were interred in one large grave in the Cemetery of Jellalabad.   Major E. A. Wood proceeded with the remainder of his force to its destination and secured the position ordered to be taken up, but the enemy had escaped into the mountains.   Another squadron 11th Bengal Lancers was sent out as a reinforcement.

On the same night (the 31st March), at midnight, the first and third squadrons and head-quarters paraded, under command of Lieutenant-Colonel Lord Ralph Kerr, and accompanied by Major Bulkeley, Captains M. Wood, M. Slade, Lieutenants E. Rose, R. Fisher, P. Durham, Lord Ogilvy, R. Wilson, Lieutenant and Adjutant C. Sandes, Second Lieutenants H. Allsopp and the Hon. G. Bellew, Paymaster Captain Murphy, Riding-master McGhee, Veterinary Surgeon Appleton, and Surgeon-Major Cattell, took part in an expedition under Brigadier-General C. Gough to operate on the south side of the Cabul River.   Captain St. Quintin on this occasion acted temporarily on the staff of General Gough.   The force, consisting of I-C Royal Horse Artillery, under Major the Hon. A. Stewart, two squadrons 10th Royal Hussars, the Guides Cavalry, the 1-17th Regiment, and the 45th Sikhs, arrived at Futtehabad at nine A.M. on the 1st April, and encamped. A party of thirty non-commissioned officers and men of the Tenth, under command of Lieutenant E. T. Rose, sent out on the 2nd April to reconnoitre in the direction of Gundamuck, and if possible to ascertain the strength of the enemy, was fired upon by a considerable body of them. Having exchanged shots and successfully accomplished his task, Lieutenant Rose retired some distance, sending a message to the camp with intelligence of the enemy's movements, and that he was watching them assembling in large numbers on a table-land to the southeast of Futtehabad. At one P.M. E, D, and B troops, under command of Lieutenant-Colonel Lord Ralph Kerr, two squadrons of the Guides, under Major Battye, and I-C Royal Horse Artillery, under Major the Hon. A. Stewart, the whole under command of Brigadier-General C. Gough, proceeded in the direction of Lookhai. F Troop, 10th Hussars, under Captain Slade and Lieutenant Lord Ogilvy, remained behind as a guard to the camp.

The enemy, numbering about 5,000 men of the Kughiani tribe, was found occupying a strong position on the crest of rising ground behind "sungas" (stone parapets), which they were still in the act of building. The reconnoitring party, under Lieutenant Rose, which had come in, was now detailed as an escort to I-C battery of Horse Artillery. The brigade moved over rough stony ground and arrived at the end of a long plateau bounded on both sides by deep nullahs. On the south was the ridge of hills where the Afghans were posted, and from which they fired a few shots. The battery was now brought up and opened fire at about 1,000 yards, the first shell exploding in the midst of a dense mass of men, killing and wounding several, the rest retiring behind the crest. The guns were then advanced, the troop under Lieutenant Rose supporting them on the left. A squadron of the Tenth and two squadrons of the Guides were on the right. The guns continued firing, but the enemy came on, sending two parties along the nullahs on the right and left to turn the flanks. The Afghans crept along the edge of the nullahs, close to the flank of the battery, on which they opened fire, killing a horse or two and wounding a few men. Some of the shots also fell among the squadron of the Tenth and wounded a few men. As the troops were unable to stop this attack, General Gough ordered the guns to retire, covered by the cavalry, who dismounted and opened fire. At the same time he sent for the infantry. The Cavalry Brigade fell back to the north end of the plateau, and shortly afterwards a detachment of the 17th Foot and the 45th Sikhs arrived and drove the enemy out of the left nullah, during which operation Lieutenant Wiseman and a colour-sergeant were killed. At the same time the Tenth and Guides charged the party on the enemy's left, and, sweeping over the nullah, came upon small bodies of the enemy, some of whom stood their ground, and were cut down, while others attempting to escape shared the same fate. It was here that Major Battye was killed, charging at the head of the Guides.

The cavalry continued to advance, and, galloping up to the enemy's position, occupied the "sungas," which were evacuated by the Afghans as the cavalry approached them. The Tenth dismounted beyond the "sungas" and opened fire upon the enemy, and, again mounting, pursued with the Guides for a distance of several miles, the Afghans flying in all directions. It was late in the afternoon before the pursuit ended, and, as the Tenth and Guides fell back towards the camp of Futtehabad, Captain Manners Wood, accompanied by Lieutenant R. B. Fisher and B troop, was sent across

the nullah towards the left, and making a *détour* round
some low hills the advanced guard discovered a party
of the enemy holding a conical hill.   Captain Manners
Wood and Lieutenant Fisher dismounted with most of
the men, leaving as few as possible to hold the horses,
and advanced up the hill in skirmishing order to dislodge the Afghans, who were firing upon them from
their strong position.   On approaching the top, Captain
Wood and Lieutenant Fisher, who were well in front,
noticed a Ghazi lying on the ground pointing his jezail
at them.   Having fired and missed, this powerful
Afghan jumped up and rushed at Captain Wood with
his big knife, and cut at his head, but his helmet and
puggree saved him.   As he lay on the ground at the
mercy of the Ghazi, Lieutenant Fisher rushed at the
Afghan and felled him with the butt end of a carbine
that he was carrying at the time.   The men now fired
two well-directed volleys into the enemy, which completely dispersed them, and the troops returned to the
camp at Futtehabad.   The casualties in the Tenth
during this action were seven men wounded, one horse
killed, eleven wounded, and one missing.

On the 4th April the following telegram was received
from His Royal Highness the Prince of Wales, addressed
to Lord Ralph Kerr : " Express condolence and sympathy with regiment at disaster crossing Cabul River."
On the 8th a telegram from Her Majesty the Queen
to the Viceroy of India was received by the regiment :
" I am deeply grieved at the sad loss of squadron of
10th Hussars.   I am anxious for details.   Please communicate this telegram to regiment."

On the 5th April the force under Sir Samuel Browne
commenced a further advance into Afghanistan.   A and
C troops joined head-quarters from Jellalabad on that
day, and on the 13th the whole regiment marched

towards Gundamuck, arriving on the 14th at Safeyd Sung (White Stone), where it encamped. The weather was becoming very hot in the middle of the day, and the dry winds and dust caused a great deal of suffering from inflamed eyes. To remedy this in some measure the ground under the tents was dug out to the depth of four or five feet. After the force had remained at this place for a fortnight, pneumonia and typhoid fever became so prevalent, it was decided to move the camp, and on the 3rd May the troops crossed the stream, and encamped a mile from the old cantonment of Gundamuck, occupied by the British troops in 1844. This place is considerably higher than Jellalabad, and the ground rises gradually up to the Safeyd Koh. It stands on the road to Cabul, and the entrance to the Jugdulluck Pass is plainly visible.

Early in March the death of Shere Ali, the Ameer of Afghanistan, had been confirmed, and at first it was believed that his son and successor, Yakoob Khan, had less intention of submitting to us than his father, and the hopes of all in camp were raised by the prospect of advancing on Cabul. However, early in May, he sent in his submission, and on the 8th a squadron of the Tenth, under Captain Wood, and a squadron of the Guides, the whole under Major E. A. Wood, accompanied by Major Cavagnari, went out to meet the Ameer on the Cabul road and escorted him into Gundamuck. For about three miles the road was lined with the remainder of the Tenth, the 11th Bengal Lancers, and I-C battery of Horse Artillery, the Guides being employed on the communications to Jellalabad. Having met the Ameer, the procession was formed, the Ameer riding between Majors Wood and Cavagnari; his Prime Minister and Commander-in-Chief following. About two miles from the camp Sir Samuel Browne met the Ameer and rode beside him. Two days later the treaty of Gundamuck was signed, and the usual presents were distributed. Officers were requested to send up to head-quarters any horses that they might wish to dispose of, so that, if approved by a committee, they might be purchased by the Indian Government to be presented to the Ameer. The following horses, the property of officers of the regiment, were selected :— Major E. A. Wood's Arab horse Tarquin, Captain St. Quintin's grey Arab Vivian, Captain St. Quintin's bay Waler The Fop, Captain Bulkeley's grey Waler gelding.

Peace having been proclaimed, the Government decided on the immediate withdrawal of the army to India during the hot weather, leaving a certain number of troops to guard the new frontier. At the same time a mission under Sir L. Cavagnari, with a small escort, was to proceed to Cabul.

On the 1st June the 10th Hussars left Gundamuck for Rawul Pindi. Those who took part in this retirement from Afghanistan will not readily forget what has been well called the "Death March." The regiment marched with I-C battery of Horse Artillery and reached Jellalabad on the 3rd, where the heat in the day-time was very great, although the nights were cool. At Ali Boghan, on the evening of the 4th, the first warning of what was to come was experienced, when two men died of cholera. Before the next two days' march were completed twenty-two non-commissioned officers and men had succumbed, and a gloom came over the regiment as men saw their comrades well in the morning and gone by night. Everything was done that could be done to improve matters, and the example set by the Colonel, Lord Ralph Kerr, will always be cherished in the Tenth. The disease continued until Ali Musjid was reached, when the total of deaths was thirty-eight.

Died from Cholera.

Orderly-room Clerk J. Davis.
Sergeant W. Hitchens.
Farrier J. Grist.
Corporal W. Wren.
Lance-Corporal H. Gee.
Private G. Blood.
    ,,   J. Brown.
    ,,   J. Carter.
    ,,   F. Chapman.
    ,,   G. T. Clarke.
    ,,   C. Clerrington.
    ,,   J. Dix.
    ,,   P. Fagan.
    ,,   E. Farrance.
    ,,   B. Field.
    ,,   J. Finnimore.
    ,,   T. Hacket.
    ,,   G. Harwood.
    ,,   H. Holt.

Private H. Huggins.
    ,,   T. Ing.
    ,,   W. Johnson.
    ,,   N. R. Jones.
    ,,   G. Luck.
    ,,   J. Lyons.
    ,,   J. McAllister.
    ,,   G. Millenick.
    ,,   J. Orford.
    ,,   H. Ramscara.
    ,,   W. Rookwood.
    ,,   G. Sanders.
    ,,   J. A. Sankey.
    ,,   J. Slattery.
    ,,   J. Slaymaker.
    ,,   J. Sorrell.
    ,,   G. Taverner.
    ,,   E. White.
    ,,   F. Woolard.

The following also died during the campaign from other diseases :—

Troop Sergt.-Major Roper, 28th April, 1879.
Sergeant I. Jones, 23rd June, 1879.
Lance-Corporal G. Mooney.
Private G. Boyes.
    ,,   A. Glover.
    ,,   T. Godding.
    ,,   T. Gutheridge.

Private Haslett.
    ,,   W. Johnson.
    ,,   G. Jones.
    ,,   T. King.
    ,,   G. Lifford.
    ,,   A. Myers.
    ,,   T. Oakley.
    ,,   C. Simms.
    ,,   C. Tinney.

Hurri Sing Ki Boorgh, near Peshawur, was reached on the 10th June, and, though the heat was much greater, all were glad to see the plains of India once more, especially as it was felt that the cholera was shaken off. The bridge over the Indus was reported as likely to be swept away owing to the floods, so the 1879 regiment made two double marches, reaching Attock, fifty-four miles distant, in two days, on the 13th June. The river was crossed, the march continued, and on the 18th June the Tenth arrived at Rawul Pindi.

The following extract from the report of the services of the First Division Peshawur Valley Field Force by Lieutenant-General Sir Samuel Browne was received by the regiment in August :—

. . . . But if the above officers are specially mentioned, I by no means wish to detract from the high reputation which the conscientious performance of their duties by every man of that fine regiment, the 10th Prince of Wales's Own Royal Hussars, has earned for it. The regiment is one that any service in the world would be proud of. Tried in the field at Futtehabad against greatly superior numbers, tested in many and long days' reconnaissance and outpost duty, in the accident at the ford of the Cabul River, and in the attack of cholera while passing through the Khyber, the high discipline and soldierlike qualities of this noble regiment have ever shone forth, proving no less the efficiency of the present officers than the careful training it has received in the past.

On the 10th January, 1880, the following extract from the "London Gazette" of the 21st November, 1879, was republished in India :—

The Queen has been graciously pleased to give orders for the appointment of the undermentioned officers to be Ordinary Members of the Military Division of the Third Class or Companions of the Most Honourable Order of the Bath :—Lieutenant-Colonel the Lord Ralph Kerr, 10th Hussars. . . .

The Queen has been graciously pleased to approve of the following promotions being conferred on the undermentioned officers in recognition of their services during the late Afghan campaign, 1878–9, dated 22nd November, 1879 :—

BREVET.

To be Lieutenant-Colonel—Major Edward Alexander Wood, 10th Hussars.

To be Majors—Captain T. Williams-Bulkeley, Captain Thomas A. St. Quintin, Captain Boyce A. Combe, 10th Hussars.

A medal, with clasp for " Ali Musjid," was granted to all those who took part in this campaign, and in commemoration of it the Queen was graciously pleased to permit the 10th (Prince of Wales's Own) Royal Hussars to bear the words " Ali Musjid," " Afghanistan, 1878–1879," upon its appointments.

A memorial window, and underneath it an alabaster slab surrounded by Venetian mosaic, was placed in All Saints' Church, Aldershot, by the past and present officers, non-commissioned officers, and men of the regiment, in memory of their comrades who lost their lives in the Afghan campaign. This beautiful piece of work was designed by Messrs. Clayton & Bell.

On the 11th November Captain W. Barker, 10th Hussars, died at Jhelum. This officer had served for some years in the 16th Lancers, until he exchanged with Captain the Hon. C. Cavendish.

CHAPTER XLIV

THE TREATY OF GUNDAMUCK—OUTBREAK OF SECOND CAMPAIGN—
OFFICERS AND NON-COMMISSIONED OFFICERS OF THE TENTH
EMPLOYED—THE REGIMENT MARCHES TO MIAN MIR—BRIGADED
WITH THE 15TH HUSSARS—LUCKNOW — LORD RALPH KERR—
VISIT OF THE DUKE AND DUCHESS OF CONNAUGHT—ORDERS
FOR ENGLAND RECEIVED

THE Treaty of Gundamuck, arranged in June 1879, previous to the departure of the British troops from Afghanistan, had for its principal object the direct representation of the English Government at Cabul, and in pursuance of this Sir Louis Cavagnari, with an escort of twenty-five sowars and fifty sepoys of the Guides, was received at the Court of Yakoob Khan. Every outward honour was paid to the Embassy, but from the commencement the Ameer had the Residency watched. In August some Herati troops reached Cabul, and these soldiers, not having been opposed to the English, taunted those who had been beaten by them, and disturbances commenced. On the 3rd September an outbreak occurred, and the Afghan troops marched on the Residency and attacked it with fury. A gallant defence was made by Cavagnari and those under him, but, overcome by numbers, they had to give way and all were massacred. Upon this news being received in India, a force was at once organised under Sir Frederick Roberts, and advanced from the Kurram Valley to Cabul.

On the outbreak of the second Afghan campaign it

1879

1879 was naturally the wish of the whole regiment that it should take part in it, but, owing to the reduced numbers and continued sickness, the Commander-in-Chief was unable to sanction this desire, and it remained at Rawul Pindi. Although the 10th Hussars was not permitted to participate in this campaign, four officers and five non-commissioned officers and men were fortunate enough to do so.

Major Boyce Combe was employed as Assistant-Quartermaster-General, Captain J. P. Brabazon as Brigade Major of Cavalry, and Lieutenants R. B. Fisher and R. H. W. Wilson as Transport officers to the Cabul Field Force. These officers accompanied this force on the march to and capture of Cabul, the defence of Sherpur, on the subsequent march to Candahar, and also at the battle of Candahar and defeat of Ayoub Khan's army. They each received the clasp for Cabul and Candahar, and also the Bronze Star given to commemorate the Candahar march, and were all mentioned in despatches. The following non-commissioned officers and men of the 10th Hussars were employed as signallers during the second campaign :—Sergeant John Gibbard, Corporal William Brown, Corporal William Smith, Corporal William Byatt, and Private John George. Their services were found particularly valuable from their knowledge of the country in the former campaign. Corporals Byatt and Smith formed part of a reconnaissance towards Safeyd Sung, where a heliograph station was erected. At this place a mud enclosure was found containing stores, &c., left intact as handed over to Yakoob Khan by the British force at the end of the previous campaign. Heliographic communication was established from Peshawur to Cabul, and, owing to all telegraph wires being cut by the Afghans, its use was found invaluable.

On the 1st April of the following year (1880), the 1879 Queen was graciously pleased to approve of the follow-promotions being made : Captain and Brevet-Major Boyce Combe to be brevet lieutenant-colonel, and Captain J. P. Brabazon to be major. On Brevet Lieutenant-Colonel B. Combe being seconded for service on the Staff, Lieutenant the Hon. J. P. Napier was promoted captain. Dr. Cattell left at the close of the Afghan War. He was appointed to the Tenth in 1873, and served with it continuously in India until 1879. His devotion to duty during the outbreak of cholera in Afghanistan was much appreciated by all ranks.

The regimental changes in 1879 were:—Retirement—Lieutenant R. T. Dalton. Death—Captain W. Barker. Transfers and exchanges—Lieutenant Lord A. F. Compton, from Grenadier Guards; Lieutenant E. M. L. Inman, to Grenadier Guards ; Second Lieutenant C. G. B. Saunders was appointed.

On the return of the Tenth from Afghanistan the 1880 health of the men had suffered considerably, and many were drafted off to the Hills. Fever was very prevalent, and there were some cases of cholera, in consequence of which the married soldiers and their families had to go out into camp. The summer of 1880 was also one of a great deal of sickness, and it was thought that the numbers of troops and followers, and the incessant flow of transport animals, of which large numbers died on the road, passing through the station to and from the second phase of the Afghan campaign, added much to the unhealthiness of it. On the 29th April Lieutenant Saunders, who had only recently joined from England, died of typhoid fever at the hill station of Murree.

In October, at the termination of the second campaign in Afghanistan, the 10th Hussars was ordered to change its quarters, to be relieved by the 8th Hussars on the return of that regiment from the front. On the 8th of this month the head-quarters, under Lieutenant-Colonel Lord Ralph Kerr, with seventeen officers and 363 non-commissioned officers and men, left Rawul Pindi *viâ* Rewat and Jhelum *en route* for Mian Mir. Considerable difficulties were encountered during this march, owing to the feeble condition of the camels. The Afghan campaign had reduced the supply of these animals to a minimum, and those that were left were poor and weak. On the 14th the Tenth crossed the Jhelum in boats by squadrons independently, and continued the march, encamping at Gujerat, Wazirabad, &c., and crossed the Chenab River, and thence to Muridki, to Shaddera, on the Beas River, opposite Lahore, and here made a halt of several days. While encamped at Shaddera the life of an excellent soldier, Private Orris, was lost by the bite of a snake.[1] He was servant to Lieutenant-Colonel Lord Ralph Kerr.

On the 28th October the Tenth marched into Mian Mir, and was encamped beside the 15th Hussars, under Lieutenant-Colonel George Luck. This regiment had arrived previously by rail from Candahar, where it had taken an active part during the second phase of the Afghan War. A brigade of cavalry was now formed to take part in the ceremonies attending the visit of the Viceroy, and Lieutenant-Colonel Lord Ralph Kerr was appointed to the command of it. It consisted of the 10th and 15th Hussars, the Central India Horse, and the 3rd Bengal Cavalry. Major T. W. Bulkeley, being the next senior officer present, assumed command of the Tenth. On the 29th the troops took part in the Durbar held by the Viceroy, Lord Ripon, and a few

---

[1] It was supposed that while asleep his arm was hanging out of bed with his hand on the ground when the snake attacked him.

days later His Excellency did the officers of the regi- ment the honour of taking luncheon with them.

It had been intended that the Tenth should proceed by route march from Mian Mir to Lucknow, but owing to the difficulty of procuring camels and bullock carts it was decided to send it by rail. On the 17th November the first squadron, under Lord Ogilvy, left for its destination, halting the first day at Meerut. At this station the officers and men were entertained by the 1st Dragoon Guards, who had themselves only lately arrived in India. The second halt was at Bareilly, Lucknow being reached on the 20th. The second and third squadrons left Mian Mir on the 18th and 19th, and by the 21st November the whole regiment was assembled in its new cantonments.

The only regimental change in 1880 was :—Appointment—Harvey Alexander to be second lieutenant.

Lucknow, the capital of Oudh, lies on the banks of the river Gumti. The native city is a very large one, three miles from the military cantonment. Viewed from a distance, some of the native buildings, mosques, and minarets have an imposing appearance; but the chief interest of a European centres in the Residency, with its memorial cross, recalling the heroic defence made by the British garrison in 1857, and the glorious deaths of Henry Lawrence and Henry Havelock, and the final relief by Lord Clyde. The cantonment lies to the east of the native town, and is healthily and well situated. It is beautifully laid out with excellent roads shaded by fine trees. In the hot weather many of these trees flower, even the largest, and every variety of colour is to be seen. Public gardens are kept up by the Government—the Horticultural as well as those of the Dilkusha Palace. Flower gardens surround most of the bungalows, and beautiful roses and every variety of English flowers are grown.   The Mohammed Bagh is maintained by the garrison for cricket and other recreations, and in the evenings, when the Europeans, military and civil, usually congregate, a regimental band plays there.   The cavalry lines are situated in the Dilkusha, and the men's barracks touch upon the palace of that name.   The building was occupied by Sir Colin Campbell in the second relief of Lucknow, and again when he permanently recovered it.

During the cold weather, the usual drills were carried out—regimental, brigade, and divisional.   The surrounding country was very suitable for the movements of cavalry on an extended scale, although in many places it was much broken by nullahs and fissures in the ground.   For cavalry drills, the racecourse adjoining the cavalry lines was used, and for the divisional parades and reviews the ground near the infantry lines.   The horses on which the Tenth at this time was mounted were principally Australians (called Walers), the country-bred horses gradually disappearing.   Although they cannot be said to have been exceedingly good-looking horses, they were of a wiry, useful stamp, and thoroughly fit for any work that they might have been called upon to perform.   The officers all continued to ride Arab chargers, and were particularly well mounted.

Many outdoor amusements were organised both by officers and men.   Polo was played three times a week by the former, and the non-commissioned officers and men also had a club.   Many cricket matches were played on the Mohammed Bagh ground between the various regiments of the garrison, and also with clubs from a distance.   The Tenth had an excellent eleven, and kept up the character it has always borne as a good cricketing corps.   The shooting in the neighbourhood was not very good, but officers and men occasionally went out and obtained some sport with black buck, and at certain times of the year there was good quail shooting. Officers got excellent duck shooting by going a night's journey in the train. Very good pig-sticking was also had at Cawnpore, and most of the officers belonged to a club at that place.

In the " cold season " a large number of civilians and their families take up their residence in Lucknow, and there is a great deal of society. The officers of the Tenth gave a ball at the Chutter Munzil Palace (now the United Service Club) on the 31st January, 1881, to which a great number of people from all parts of India came. The rooms in this building are thoroughly Oriental in style of architecture, and lend themselves to this kind of entertainment, and with the electric light, large blocks of ice, plants and shrubs from the Horticultural Gardens, a very beautiful effect was produced. A novelty was also introduced by having a piquet, with its horses and the men dressed as in the Afghan campaign, outside one of the verandahs. A camp fire was kept burning, around which the men sat or slept.

Once a month at full moon the non-commissioned officers and men gave moonlight concerts, which, with the assistance of the band and glees, were a great attraction. A temporary stage was erected out of doors, and seats for ladies, officers, and all the men were provided. Amongst many excellent singers the following were the most prominent:—Sergeant Moon, Private Dowie, Private Jones (who also usually acted as Master of the Ceremonies), Sergeant Taylor, Corporal Howard, Sergeant Parker, Private Lynn, and Private Hayes. Monthly sports for the men were also held in the cold weather, and during the hot season these meetings were made weekly, as they were found to break the *ennui* of this trying time of the year. There was also a very good regimental theatre, at which some excellent plays and extravaganzas were produced. Of these, perhaps " Aladdin " was the most successful, the scenery being painted by Captain McGhee, the Riding-master. Sergeant-Major Bradshaw, Sergeant Hooper, Private Davies, Corporals Carter, Richardson, and Xenos, Privates Fuller, Leonard, and Maltby were the leading actors at this time.

On the 25th March, 1881, Lord Ralph Kerr proceeded to England in anticipation of his period of command ending a few months later, having completed five years' service as regimental lieutenant-colonel, and Lieutenant-Colonel E. A. Wood assumed the command.

Colonel Lord Ralph Kerr entered the army on the 24th November, 1857, as cornet in the 10th Hussars. In June of the following year he was promoted to be lieutenant. On the 6th May, 1859, he was appointed Adjutant and remained in that capacity until he obtained his troop in August 1861. He served with the Tenth throughout its service in England and Ireland, and embarked with it when it proceeded to India in 1873 as major and second in command. On Lieutenant-Colonel the Hon. C. C. Molyneux proceeding to England on leave in April 1875, he took command and was gazetted lieutenant-colonel on the 31st May, 1876. During the first phase of the Afghan campaign, 1878–79, Lord Ralph Kerr commanded from the 20th March, 1879, and was present at the head of the regiment at the action of Futtehabad. He was mentioned in despatches, and created a C.B. On the return from Afghanistan to India, he commanded during the terrible outbreak of cholera that visited the regiment as it passed through the Khyber Pass, and by his example and devotion assisted to alleviate the results. He accompanied the Tenth from Rawul Pindi to Mian Mir in October 1880, and at a Durbar held at that time by the Viceroy of India he commanded a brigade consisting of the 10th and 15th Hussars, the Central India Horse, and the 3rd Bengal Cavalry. An Army Warrant now having come into force limiting the command of regiments to five years, Lord Ralph Kerr was placed on half-pay on the 31st May, 1881. He attended the manœuvres of the Italian army in the autumn of 1881 for the purpose of reporting on the cavalry of that country. He afterwards held the post of Inspector of Auxiliary Cavalry at York from the 3rd April, 1883, until the 2nd April, 1888. He was promoted to the rank of major-general in January 1890. On the 31st May Major and Brevet Lieutenant-Colonel E. A. Wood was gazetted to the command of the regiment, *vice* Lord Ralph Kerr, placed on half-pay. At the same time Brevet Major T. J. W. Bulkeley became the major and second in command.

On the 25th June a Royal Warrant was issued, by which the major of a regiment was given the rank of lieutenant-colonel, and after four years as such, whether as second in command or in command, he obtained the rank of colonel. At the same time he could only remain a regimental lieutenant-colonel for six years, either four years as second and two in command, or *vice versâ*, after which he had to be placed on half-pay. The three senior captains were also given the rank of major. In consequence of this the following regimental promotions took place :—Major T. J. W. Bulkeley to be lieutenant-colonel; Captain R. S. Liddell, Captain and Brevet Major T. A. St. Quintin, Captain and Brevet Lieutenant-Colonel Boyce Combe, to be majors. Lieutenant-Colonel Combe being on the Staff, Captain R. C. Spottiswoode was also promoted.

In July 1881 Sergeant-Major James Marsland was appointed Regimental Sergeant-Major.

In September news was received with great regret by the whole regiment that Lieutenant-Colonel T. J. Williams-Bulkeley had died suddenly in England on the 12th of that month, when travelling in a railway carriage. This officer had been twenty-three years in the 10th Hussars. He was a fine horseman and excellent sportsman, and the name of "Donjie" Bulkeley, by which he was known in and out of the regiment, will long be remembered. Major R. S. Liddell was promoted to be lieutenant-colonel, and Captain H. S. Gough to be major, dated the 13th September.

During the winter of 1881–82 a reconnaissance and a military survey was made of the Nepaul frontier. Sergeant Adams, Corporal Sullivan, and Private Lyons, of the 10th Hussars, accompanied this party and made military sketches. The portion of the sketch executed by the non-commissioned officers of the Tenth was exhibited at the Lucknow Soldiers' Exhibition, and was awarded the first prize for military topography.

The regimental changes in 1881 were :—Deaths—Lieutenant C. G. B. Saunders and Major and Brevet Lieutenant-Colonel T. J. W. Bulkeley. Retirement—Lieutenant and Brevet Colonel Lord R. D. Kerr, C.B., to half-pay. Promotions—Major and Brevet Lieutenant-Colonel E. A. Wood to be lieutenant-colonel, Captain and Brevet Major T. J. W. Bulkeley to be major, Major T. J. W. Bulkeley to be brevet lieutenant-colonel, Captain R. S. Liddell to be major, Major R. S. Liddell to be brevet lieutenant-colonel. Appointment—Gentleman Cadet C. B. Harvey to be second lieutenant.

On the 3rd February, 1882, a draft arrived from England, consisting of Major T. A. St. Quintin, Lieutenant P. Durham, one sergeant, and fifty-one men.

The 10th Hussars was inspected by Lieutenant-General C. B. Cureton, C.B., commanding the Oudh Division, on the 13th and 14th February.

General Sir Donald Stewart, Commander-in-Chief in India, accompanied by the Adjutant-General (Sir G. Greaves), the Quartermaster-General (Sir Charles Macgregor), Colonel Chapman, Military Secretary, &c., arrived at Lucknow on the 25th February. On the 27th the Commander-in-Chief held a review of the whole garrison, and after the march past the Cavalry Brigade, with Royal Horse Artillery, drilled before His Excellency under Colonel E. A. Wood. At twelve noon the Commander-in-Chief held a Levée, at which all officers attended. In the evening Sir Donald Stewart saw the 10th Hussars' polo team, about to take part in the inter-regimental contests, play a match with the second team. On the 28th the Commander-in-Chief left the station.

On the 7th April the meeting of the Cawnpore Pig-sticking Club took place, when Lieutenant the Hon. George Bryan won the Ganges Cup.

On the 18th April Major Spottiswoode was appointed Aide-de-Camp to Lieutenant-General Cureton, and Lieutenant Rose to the Lieutenant-Governor of the North-West Provinces. On the 13th May, 1882, Lieutenant-General Cureton, commanding the Lucknow Division, presented the Afghan medals to the 10th Hussars.

On the 24th the Queen's birthday was celebrated, when the regiment appeared for the last time in white clothing, as khaki colour was ordered to be taken into wear in its place. On the 31st May Sergeant-Major F. Bradshaw was appointed Regimental Sergeant-Major.

From the 1st July, 1881, regimental sergeant-majors and bandmasters were granted the rank of Warrant

officers.   Regimental Sergeant-Major Bradshaw and
Bandmaster Green were the first recipients of this new
grade in the 10th Hussars.

Major St. Quintin was placed on the Seconded List
for service as Remount Agent at Calcutta, the appointment to date from the 18th April.   Captain Manners
Wood was promoted to be major, *vice* Spottiswoode;
Captain Slade to be major, *vice* St. Quintin; Lieutenant
Rose obtained his troop, but, being also seconded for
service on the Staff, Lieutenant Phillips was promoted
to be captain ; Lieutenant Fisher to be captain, *vice*
Slade.

In July the first Egyptian campaign took place,
when the 2nd Bengal Cavalry, stationed at Lucknow,
was despatched to the seat of war.   The Tenth assisted
in entraining the horses and received the thanks of the
Lieutenant-General, the names of Sergeants Bower,
Thaine, and Adams being especially mentioned.   Lieutenant R. H. W. Wilson, 10th Hussars, received orders
to proceed to Egypt, and left Lucknow at once *en route*
to Bombay for embarkation.   On the 8th August Lord
Alwyne Compton was appointed Aide-de-Camp to His
Excellency the Viceroy.

On the 9th October, to the regret of all ranks, the
sudden death of Quartermaster W. King in England
was announced.   This officer joined as a private in
1852, and became a sergeant in 1859.   He held the
appointments of Sergeant-Instructor of Musketry and
Regimental Sergeant-Major, and on the retirement of
Captain James was appointed Quartermaster on the
2nd November, 1872.   This post he held until his
death, and performed most valuable service, both at
the time of the embarkation of the regiment for India
and on the preparations being made for the Afghan
campaign and during the whole of that war.   He died

on the 12th September, 1882. He was succeeded by Quartermaster-Sergeant A. E. Poole.

In December Lieutenant the Hon. A. Lawley and Lieutenant A. Hughes-Onslow joined from England. On the 15th December a surveying party, under command of Major Kemble, 2nd Bengal Cavalry, left Lucknow to make a reconnaissance of the country lying between the river Rapti and the Nepaul frontier. Corporal Carter, Privates Grace, Lyons, and Walton, of the 10th Hussars, were attached, and received great credit for the manner in which they carried out their duties.

The regimental changes in 1882 were :—Death— Quartermaster W. King. Appointments—Gentleman Cadet Hon. A. Lawley to be lieutenant, A. E. Poole to be quartermaster, and A. Hughes-Onslow to be lieutenant.

In January 1883 the regiment marched out into camp for exercise in reconnaissance and outpost duties, and on its return to Lucknow was inspected by Lieutenant-General Cureton. In March Lieutenant the Hon. Julian Byng joined on appointment from England. On the 8th April the band proceeded to Naini Tal for the hot weather.

Lieutenant and Adjutant C. Sandes, who had been promoted captain in the 6th Dragoons on the 24th January, was succeeded by Lieutenant the Earl of Airlie on the 21st April. Captain Sandes commenced his service in the 2nd Dragoons, and after four and a half years' service was attached to the Cavalry Depôt Staff at Canterbury. On the 6th September, 1873, he was appointed Ridingmaster in the 10th Hussars, and on the 24th November, 1877, he became Adjutant. He served in this position in the Afghan campaign, 1878–79, and was present at Ali Musjid and the action of Futtehabad. He performed the duties of Brigade Major of Cavalry at the Durbar assemblage at Lahore in October 1880. After serving a short time as a captain in the 6th Dragoons, he entered the Army Pay Department, and was appointed Paymaster to the Hampshire Regiment, and afterwards to the North Lancashire Regiment.

On the 10th August Lieutenant C. Grenfell was directed to proceed to Egypt to take up an appointment in the Egyptian army, and was placed on the Seconded List.

On the 12th December their Royal Highnesses the Duke and Duchess of Connaught, accompanied by Viscount and Lady Downe, Sir Maurice Fitzgerald, and Dr. F. B. Scott, paid a visit to Lucknow. Their Royal Highnesses were met at the railway station by Lieutenant-General C. Cureton, commanding the division, whose guests they were during their stay at Lucknow. They proceeded at once to the General's house with an escort of the 10th Hussars, under Lieutenant the Hon. A. Lawley. On the 14th, a review of all the troops in garrison was held by the Duke, and in the evening their Royal Highnesses did the officers of the regiment the honour of dining with them. The following day the Duke of Connaught inspected the cavalry lines, and saw a squadron of the Tenth ride over the steeplechase course. His Royal Highness held a Levée, and at the same time the Duchess of Connaught received the ladies. Afterwards the Duke and Duchess witnessed a game of polo, dined with the officers in the evening, and left by train for Meerut.

Orders of readiness for the Tenth to prepare for embarkation to England had been received in June, and in the first instance that it should proceed to Mhow by march route in relief of the 17th Lancers, changing regimental native establishments at Saugor. This, however, a few weeks later, was countermanded, and the Tenth was ordered to proceed by rail to Bombay on being relieved by the 17th Lancers. On the 4th December the welcome order was received to prepare for embarkation on board H.M.S. "Jumna" on the 2nd February, 1884. Active steps were now taken to dispose of the various properties of the regiment accumulated after such a prolonged service in India. On the 15th and 17th December a sale of the officers' horses and polo ponies took place, when representatives from many stations north and south attended, and most satisfactory prices were obtained. On the 16th, the day between the sale of the horses and the ponies, the officers gave a ball at the Chutter Munzil. On the 23rd a farewell ball to the regiment was given by the civilians of Lucknow.

Volunteers were called from the Tenth to other regiments for men desirous of continuing their service in India. Fifty-nine responded.

The regimental changes in 1883 were:—Transfers and exchanges—Lieutenant C. Sandes, promoted into the 6th Dragoons; Captain R. P. Sandeman, from 6th Dragoon Guards; Captain W. E. Phillips, to 6th Dragoon Guards. Appointment—Lieutenant the Hon. Julian Byng.

CHAPTER XLV

THE NATIVE CAVALRY REGIMENTS PRESENT THE TENTH WITH A
CUP—EMBARKATION AT BOMBAY—STOPPED AT ADEN—ORDERED
TO THE EASTERN SOUDAN—PREPARATIONS FOR A CAMPAIGN—
ARRIVAL AT SUAKIM—GENERAL VALENTINE BAKER—THE REGI-
MENT MOUNTED—PROCEEDS TO TRINKITAT—CAUSES OF THE EX-
PEDITION—EL TEB

1884   BEFORE leaving the country the officers of the Tenth
received a silver cup of Indian design and manufacture
from the officers of the Native Cavalry, highly valued
not only for its intrinsic worth but for the feeling that
prompted the gift, and which is kept in the Officers'
Mess as one of the most prized pieces of plate. The
inscription on it is as follows :—

" Presented by the Officers of the Bengal and Punjab
Cavalry and Central India Horse to Lieutenant-Colonel Wood
and the Officers 10th Royal Hussars on the regiment leaving
India in 1884, in commemoration of the Native Cavalry Polo
Tournament of March 1883."

Dr. Berkeley, who had been attached to the Tenth
since 1880, remained in India, and thus, much to the
regret of all, the regiment lost his services. Although
the surgeon had long since ceased to be a regimental
officer, in India it was still possible to continue that
system, and through Dr. Berkeley's arrangements a
separate hospital was kept for the Tenth, and all ranks
felt that he was specially and solely in charge of it,
and a warm feeling existed towards him.

The regiment left Lucknow on the 28th January, 1884 and halted for that night at Allahabad, at Jabalpur on the 29th, at Khandwa on the 30th, and at Deolali on the 31st. After remaining five days at the latter place, the regiment proceeded on the evening of the 5th February by train to Bombay, and embarked on the following morning on board H.M.S. "Jumna,"[1] commanded by Captain Uvedale Singleton, R.N. In the afternoon the Governor of Bombay (Sir James Fergusson) came on board the ship and bade farewell to the Tenth. Having also embarked M-I battery Royal Artillery, under Major Holley, the ship sailed from Bombay Harbour at ten A.M., and proceeded down the coast to Vingorla, and embarked the 2nd battalion Royal Irish Fusiliers the following day. The "Jumna" then proceeded northwards, and steered her course for Aden. On approaching that place on the 14th February, while many were celebrating St. Valentine's Day by exchanging pictures, flattering and otherwise, the work of amateur artists, and congratulating one another on the completion of one stage of the journey homewards, a small steamer belonging to the Government of India was observed approaching, hoisting signals, and on coming nearer it proved to be the despatch vessel "Amberwitch," sent out from Aden to intercept the "Jumna," with instructions for her to call at that port for orders. Conjectures and opinions of all kinds were ventured, and the excitement and curiosity of everyone on board was very great. It was known before leaving India that Egyptian troops had been sent to the Eastern Soudan under Baker Pasha to relieve the garrisons of Sinkat and Tokar, but it was not thought that the English

---

[1] Considerable enthusiasm was displayed by the regiment on finding itself on its return to England embarking on board the same good ship that had brought it to India eleven years previously.

Government would participate in these operations, so that on the arrival of the " Jumna " in Aden Harbour it was perhaps a surprise to the troops to find that they were ordered to take on board camp equipment and disembark at Suakim, a port on the eastern coast of the Soudan.   The orders were read out to the troops by Colonel E. A. Wood, commanding on board, and were received with loud cheering, and great delight was expressed by the regiment on having another opportunity of seeing active service before returning to England.

The whole night was occupied in taking on board camp equipment and in coaling, but going on shore was not allowed on account of quarantine.   As no one either was permitted on board, everything, including the coaling, was carried out by the soldiers.   The coaling was done entirely by the 10th Hussars, the men entering cheerfully into the unaccustomed work.   Probably this was the first time that the *coaling* of one of Her Majesty's ships had been performed by a cavalry regiment.   When all was completed the "Jumna" sailed on the following afternoon (the 15th), and the three days in the Red Sea were occupied in preparing for the landing, arranging for the service kits of the men, and getting the officers' saddlery out of the baggage holds.

The ladies and women were busily employed in providing useful articles for the campaign, and the captain, officers, and men of the ship spared no pains to assist the regiment in its preparations.   Fortunately, the officers and men had retained their Indian helmets, khaki clothing, putties, &c., so in respect of clothing were fully prepared for a campaign in a hot climate.   The men's saddlery had, according to custom, been left with the horses in India, and it seemed very uncertain in what manner the Tenth was to be mounted on landing, even if mounted at all.

The navigation of this portion of the Red Sea is very intricate amongst the coral reefs, and, the weather being rough, a head wind blowing, it was not until the 18th that the "Jumna" arrived at Suakim. The entrance to the harbour is exceedingly narrow, and, as coral reefs run out some way into it, the channel did not appear to afford too much space for the passage of a vessel so large as the "Jumna." On reaching the further end of it, it opens out, and here the vessel swung round with her bows to the open sea and anchored. Lying close by was H.M.S. "Euryalus," the flag-ship of Admiral Sir William Hewett, and on board her was General Valentine Baker Pasha, formerly colonel of the Tenth. A few other English men-of-war lay in the harbour, and one Italian, some transports, and a condensing steamer. The town of Suakim, the principal part on an island, was at the west end of the harbour.

In the afternoon General Valentine Baker came on board the "Jumna" to visit his old regiment, and was received by a guard of honour, the whole of the Tenth turning out and cheering him enthusiastically, the band playing "Auld Lang Syne." He then announced that he proposed to offer the horses of his three regiments of Egyptian Gendarmerie to mount the Tenth. At the conclusion of this visit General Baker, accompanied by Colonel Wood and the field officers of the regiment, landed, the horses were carefully inspected, and a sufficient number of them selected to mount officers, non-commissioned officers, and men, 300 in all. The next morning (the 19th) at daylight the Tenth disembarked, and, marching to the camping ground on the west of the town, pitched the Indian tents, which had been landed at the same time. As soon as the camp was ready and the horse lines prepared, the horses were led down by the Egyptians and picketed. The saddles were of a rough description, mostly an old French cavalry pattern, with no means of attaching the carbines; the bits were of a very severe kind, the Mameluke bit. No heel-ropes and a very few head-ropes came with the horses, no nosebags, and altoge- ther very little kit. Admiral Sir William Hewett and the officers and men of the fleet rendered the great- est assistance in every matter and helped to remedy all the deficiencies. Sailmakers were landed, who set to work to make nosebags, head- and heel-ropes. The *main-tack* of H.M.S. "Euryalus" was cut up into lengths of long rope for picketing in standing camp, and car- bine buckets were improvised by cutting a hole through the shoe cases, through which the carbines were passed, the muzzles fitting into a small leather bucket that the Egyptians had used. In the evening the horses were ridden for the first time, when taken to the wells to water.

Colonel E. A. Wood assumed command of the troops on shore, Lieutenant-Colonel R. S. Liddell command of the 10th Hussars. Major H. S. Gough was appointed Brigade Major, and Lord Alwyne Compton acted as adjutant, *vice* the Earl of Airlie, who was on his way from England to join the regiment.

On the following morning (the 20th) the Tenth paraded at 8.30 A.M. for the first time on its new horses, and went into the country outside the earthworks for a field day. On return it was employed, with the assist- ance of the Royal Navy, in completing the preparations for taking the field, in fitting the saddles, getting horse equipment ready, and in sharpening the swords. On the 22nd the regiment paraded outside the town and went through a field day in the presence of General Baker and a number of Staff officers. In the afternoon General Graham, commanding the expeditionary force sent from Lower Egypt, inspected the regiment in its lines. Major Giles, late of the Scinde Horse and now in the Egyptian Gendarmerie, was attached to the Tenth as interpreter, with seventy-two Egyptians, who were made use of for fatigue duties. M-I battery, under Major Holley, was landed and encamped, but the 89th Regiment remained on board the "Jumna." On the 23rd orders were received for the Tenth to embark with its horses to take part in an expedition for the relief of the garrison of Tokar, a town lying about twenty miles inland from Trinkitat, a harbour four hours' steam south of Suakim. The order was given to be ready to turn out in marching order as soon as the transports coming from Suez were signalled. The transport "Zag-a-zig" having arrived in sight, the first and third squadrons marched down to the harbour, and were conveyed, horses and men, in small boats to the ship and embarked. The second squadron, B and E troops, bivouacked for the night on the wharf, the camp equipment being packed, but the transport not yet ready.

The "Zag-a-zig," with the head-quarters, sailed at 6.30 A.M. on the 24th; the second squadron embarked on board the transport "Hodeida," and sailed at 11.30 A.M. the same day. The former arrived at Trinkitat at midday, the latter in the evening. The disembarkation was commenced at once; A and C troops, with the large portion of the camp equipage, were landed by sunset. The transports were anchored as close to shore as possible; but as there was no landing-place nor for some time even a pier, and as there was a considerable swell rolling in, landing the horses from the ship's boats on to the shelving beach caused some difficulty. A large number of other transports were also unloading at the same time, so that there was full occupation for every boat in the harbour, and it was only owing to

the untiring energy of the Royal Navy that so large a
force, with its camp equipage and stores, was landed
without an accident on an open beach in such a rapid
manner.   Occasion must here be taken to refer to the
services of Captain Singleton, R.N., and the other
officers and men of H.M.S. " Jumna."   The ship itself,
throughout this brief campaign, was looked upon by
the Tenth as its home ; everything that could be provided to reduce the discomforts of a campaign necessarily so hastily organised was willingly given by
officers and men, and nothing was left undone to help
the regiment to prepare itself for active service.   The
ship also became the hospital for the wounded and
sick, and the ladies and women remained on board
and were treated with the greatest thoughtfulness.
Amongst the officers of the fleet who conspicuously
assisted, if not invidious to mention names, it seems
almost necessary to perpetuate in the memoirs of the
Tenth those of Admiral Sir William Hewett, Flag
Captain Hastings, Captain Singleton, First Lieutenant
Morrish, Lieutenant Broadley, and all the officers, petty
officers, and men of the " Jumna ;" Lieutenant Lindsay,
R.N., A.D.C. to General Graham ; and Lieutenant Caul-
field, of H.M.S. " Euryalus."

On the 25th February the remainder of the Tenth
was rapidly disembarked, the rafts from H.M.S. "Jumna"
being used, and some temporary piers were erected on
the shore.   The Tenth camp was pitched between the
19th Hussars and the 42nd Highlanders, and Colonel E. A.
Wood was appointed to command the Cavalry Brigade,
Colonel R. S. Liddell the regiment.   The remainder of
the troops composing the force under General Graham
had been brought from Cairo, and consisted of the 19th
Hussars, the 60th Rifles, the 42nd and 79th Highlanders.
The 89th, which had accompanied the Tenth from India

and remained on board the "Jumna" at Suakim, was now disembarked; Major Holley's battery of artillery, which had also come from India, being left at Suakim as part of the garrison of that place. The 65th Regiment, stationed at Aden, and ordered to England in H.M.S. "Serapis," was also detained for service in the Soudan, and joined the force at Trinkitat on the 27th. No artillery accompanied the troops, but a Naval Brigade, with machine guns, was formed and took a conspicuous part in the campaign.

It will now appear appropriate shortly to refer to the causes that led the English Government to despatch an expedition to the Eastern Soudan. Early in 1884 the revolution against the Egyptian Government in the Soudan had reached very alarming dimensions, and intelligence had been received of the annihilation of the army under Hicks Pasha by the Mahdi's forces. Such garrisons in the Soudan as had not fallen into the hands of the rebels were closely invested by them. Tokar and Sinkat, two towns on the east coast littoral, fifty and thirty miles distant respectively from Suakim, were among these. To relieve these two places Baker Pasha was sent with a force of the Gendarmerie to Suakim. On the 4th February he started from Trinkitat to attempt the relief of Tokar, and on reaching El Teb the Egyptian square was charged by the Arabs, broken into confusion, and defeated with a loss of about 2,500 men killed. General Baker led back the remainder of the force, which was more or. less demoralized, to Suakim. The relief of Tokar by Egyptian troops having failed, and Sinkat having fallen into the hands of the rebels, the British Government now decided to step in, and the force already described, of which the 10th Hussars was the first to arrive, was collected in less than three weeks.

On the 27th a Cavalry Brigade field day took place on the sands outside the earthworks of Trinkitat, under the command of Colonel E. A. Wood. On this day Lieutenant C. Grenfell, 10th Hussars, who had been seconded for service in the Egyptian army, was attached to the regiment. Lieutenant F. H. Probyn, 9th Bengal Lancers, was also attached. In the evening Brigadier-General Herbert Stewart, C.B., arrived from England and took command of the Cavalry Brigade, and Colonel Wood reverted to the command of his regiment. At the same time Brigadier-General Redvers Buller arrived and assumed command of an infantry brigade, Brigadier-General Davies having command of another brigade. On the 28th orders of readiness to advance were issued to the force, the camp was struck, and the tents and baggage collected, to be left at Trinkitat under guards. In the afternoon the horses were taken to the troughs of condensed water the last thing before marching, as no further opportunity of watering the horses would occur until the enemy's wells were captured. At 5 P.M. the cavalry moved off, and crossing a lagoon of deep mud and water the Tenth reached Fort Baker after sunset, and with the remainder of the force bivouacked until the next morning. Heavy rain fell in the night. The following morning (the 29th) the force paraded immediately after the men's breakfasts and advanced at 8.30 A.M. The Infantry Division moved off in a large square, covered about a mile in advance by the first squadron of the 10th Hussars, under Major H. S. Gough and Lieutenant Durham. The remainder of the Cavalry Brigade and mounted infantry were echeloned from their right in rear of the left corner of the infantry square, the 10th Hussars in front line, 19th Hussars in second.

The force passed over the line of Baker Pasha's late

retreat only three weeks previously, and the bodies of the Egyptians lay thick about the plain, being 2,500 in number, and from the dry climate and hot sun they had been preserved in an extraordinary manner. The infantry square was led, under the guidance of General Baker himself, to the right of this line, in order to avoid this demoralizing sight as far as possible, but owing to the cavalry being echeloned on its left the latter passed over the ground where these bodies lay thickest. The advanced parties of the cavalry were engaged in a desultory manner with the enemy during this advance, and discovered the enemy's position on the sandy hillocks surrounding the wells of El Teb. The ships from the harbour opened fire to cover the advance, but as their shot fell far short of the mark it had to be stopped by signal from Fort Baker. The infantry square now made frequent halts and moved along leisurely, inclining towards the left of the enemy's position. The cavalry moved forward and drew the enemy's musketry fire from the right of his position. The exact disposition of the enemy's line now being ascertained, the cavalry moved slowly back to its original position on the left rear of the infantry square and waited for the attack to commence, and while carrying out this movement at a walk was under a very considerable musketry fire, but, owing to the bad practice made, only a very few men were killed and wounded. The Krupp guns of the enemy opened fire upon the infantry square, and one shell exploding in the centre of it, besides causing other casualties, severely wounded Baker Pasha in the face. The guns also directed their fire on the cavalry, but the range was not accurate and the shells passed over their heads. The Arabs now descended in considerable numbers from their entrenched position, and rushed with splendid courage on the left corner of the infantry square, howling, firing, and throwing boomerangs. The fire of the rifles and machine guns was too deadly to allow of success, and although here and there one or two of these gallant savages may have reached the square, all were shot down as soon as they arrived at a certain point, from 150 to 200 yards distant.

The Cavalry Brigade now received orders to advance, and as it passed on the right or outward flank of the square the infantry gave a round of cheers. The brigade, under Sir Herbert Stewart, moved forward at a rapid pace, the 10th Hussars in first line, the 19th Hussars in support, and, having cleared the position to the front, took a few prisoners and was in the act of driving in some cattle when intelligence was brought that the left squadron of the 19th, echeloned in rear, had been attacked in flank by a body of the Arabs, who had suddenly sprung up out of the grass and nullahs. The brigade was at once brought back nearer to the infantry square, which was hotly engaged while wheeling round and outflanking the left of the position of El Teb, and thus enfilading the Arabs in their entrenchments. The Cavalry Brigade now found large numbers of the enemy among the bush, and the two regiments charged again and again and eventually dispersed them. The ground in many places was covered with high mimosa bush, the thorns of which the horses avoided, and, as this caused gaps in the ranks, opportunities were given to the active enemy of rushing out from their hiding-places and of ham-stringing the horses and stabbing their riders. In this manner Major Slade, 10th Hussars, while wheeling his squadron from the flank, was attacked by several Arabs on all sides and killed. Lieutenant Probyn (attached to the Tenth), who, as he entered the action, had asked special permission to exchange his position of serrefile to ride in front of the squadron, was also killed; but from the appearance of his sword afterwards it was seen that some of his opponents had paid dearly for their success. Sergeant J. Cox, too, as fine a soldier as ever served in the regiment, who often had carried off the regimental prize for swordsmanship, thinking he saw a good opportunity, left the flank of his squadron, and charged a group of savages, but being overpowered by numbers he lost his life. Three private soldiers of the Tenth were killed in these charges and several wounded. The enemy being dispersed, the squadrons were then halted; some troops were dismounted and opened fire on the enemy retiring through the bush. The infantry continued to advance through the enemy's position round the wells, keeping up a tremendous fire, and, passing over the rifle pits and entrenchments, completed the victory. The British force upon this was massed round the wells, the horses were taken to water, a bivouac was formed with the cavalry in the centre, and in this manner the night was passed.

Parties went out to search for the killed in the evening, and brought in the bodies of Major M. M. Slade,[1] Lieutenant F. Probyn, of 9th Bengal Cavalry (attached), Sergeant J. Cox, Private J. Brinsley, Private J. Douglas, Private F. Stride. Corporals W. Green, J. Cramp, and J. Lee were very severely wounded; Major Brabazon, Sergeant M. Palmer, Private J. Rumble slightly. The 19th Hussars also suffered severely—one officer and five men killed, the gallant Major Percy Barrow[2] most severely wounded, and many non-

---

[1] Captain Slade, R.A. (then in the Egyptian army), brother of Major Slade, accompanied the searching parties, and his brother's body was found pierced with seven spear wounds, his horse ham-strung to the bone.

[2] This officer died a year later in consequence of this wound, while taking part in some sports at Cairo.

1884 commissioned officers and men. The total loss of the
British force was twenty-eight killed, two missing, and
142 wounded; that of the enemy was calculated at over
2,500, the dead lying in heaps in their entrenchments
and rifle pits. Four Krupp guns, two brass howitzers,
and a Gatling, besides a quantity of arms and ammunition, were captured.[1]

[1] All these had been taken by the Arabs from the force under
General Baker.

CHAPTER XLVI

AFTER THE ACTION—THE TENTH HORSES—TROOPER HAYES—
" A TALE OF THE 10TH HUSSARS "—MARCH TO TOKAR—THE
REGIMENT DESTROYS THE ARMS AND AMMUNITION OF THE
ENEMY—RETURN TO TRINKITAT AND SUAKIM—TAMAII

BEFORE the bivouac was formed, Baker Pasha, severely   1884
wounded as he was, with a bullet still in his face below
the eye, rode into the Tenth lines to inquire after his
old regiment and congratulate it on the day. The
Admiral (Sir William Hewett) also visited the regiment to gather information of its welfare, and, returning
at once to his flag-ship, he signalled to the ladies on
board the " Jumna " the names of those of the Tenth
he had personally seen uninjured after the action.

Thus ended a gallant fight. " Inch by inch the rebels
had fought the ground for three and a half hours, with
a courage that only fanaticism could give, and no higher
praise can be given our men than that they met a worthy
enemy." [1] The small Egyptian horses or ponies upon
which the Tenth was mounted proved their powers of
endurance. They had had no water since the afternoon
previous, but they showed no signs of fatigue. Still,
the want of size, weight, and pace was felt, and the de-
ficiency in these respects was against the thoroughly effective use of the regiment as cavalry. The ground, too,
with its surface covered to a considerable extent with
bush, though not sufficient to interfere with rapid movements, was very favourable to the safety of such a foe.

[1] General Graham's Despatch.

Many individual acts of gallantry might be recorded of this day, but one of which special mention was made was the conduct of Private Hayes, a bandsman in the 10th Hussars. This man, who was skilled as a pugilist, being annoyed during the action with the difficulty of approaching his active and lithesome adversaries, dismounted from his horse, and, attacking a group of Arabs, knocked them down with his fists and then again mounted. This soldier was afterwards thanked by General Graham for his courage, and the following year had the honour of receiving from Her Majesty's own hands at Windsor Castle the Distinguished Service Medal. His name, too, was also brought prominently forward before the public in some lines published in " Punch," which attracted a good deal of notice at the time, as the country felt that the references to General Baker Pasha in the " Tale of the Tenth Hussars " were most opportune.[1]

[1] A TALE OF THE TENTH HUSSARS

When the sand of the lonely desert has covered the plains of strife
Where the English fought for the rescue, and the Arab stood for his life,
When the crash of the battle is over, and healed are our wounds and scars,
There will live in our island story a tale of the 10th Hussars.

They had charged in the grand old fashion with furious shout and swoop,
With a " Follow me, lads ! " from the Colonel and an answering roar
    from the troop ;
On the Staff as the troopers passed it, in glory of pride and pluck,
They heard, and they never forgot it, one following shout, " Good luck ! "

Wounded and worn he sat there, in silence of pride and pain,
The man who'd led them often but was never to lead again !
Think of the secret anguish—think of the dull remorse,
To see the hussars sweep past him, unled by the old white horse.

An alien, not a stranger, with heart of a comrade still,
He had borne his sorrow bravely, as a soldier must and will ;
And when the battle was over, in deepening gloom and shade,
He followed the Staff in silence and rode to the grand parade ;
For the Tenth had another hero all ripe for the General's praise,
Who was called to the front that evening, by the name of Trooper Hayes.

The night of the 29th was very cold, and, having no kits or blankets, those who were able to do so collected materials from the Arab huts, and lit large camp fires, round which the troops collected and slept after the fatigues of the day. On the following morning, the 1st March, at reveillé, having performed the sad office of burying the dead on the outward slopes of the entrenchments of El Teb, as soon as the horses were watered and fed and the men had had their breakfasts, the force fell in and continued its march for the relief of Tokar. Before leaving El Teb the following telegram was received from Her Majesty the Queen : "Pray convey my congratulations and deep sense of his services and of those under him to Sir Gerald Graham, as well as my sorrow for the loss of the distinguished officers and men and my anxiety for the wounded."

The 42nd Highlanders remained at El Teb with the captured guns to hold the position, and rapidly formed

He had slashed his way to fortune, when scattered, unhorsed, alone,
And in saving the life of a comrade he managed to guard his own.
The General spoke out bravely, as ever a soldier can,
"The army's proud of your valour, the regiment's proud of its man."

Then across that lonely desert, at the close of the General's praise,
Came a cheer, then a quick short tremble on the lips of Trooper Hayes.
"Speak out," said the kindly Colonel, "if you've anything, lad, to say,
Your Queen and your dear old country shall hear what you've done to-
    day."

But the trooper gnawed his chin-strap, then sheepishly hung his head.
"Speak out, old chap," said his comrades. With an effort at last he said :
"I came to the front with my pals here, the boys, and the brave old tars ;
I've fought for my Queen and country, and rode with the 10th Hussars ;
I'm proud of the fine old regiment——" Then the Colonel shook his
    hand.
"So I'll ask one single favour from my Queen and my native land.

"There sits by your side on the Staff, sir, a man we are proud to own,
He was struck down first in the battle, but never was heard to groan ;
If I've done aught to deserve it "—then the General smiled, "Of course."
"Give back to the Tenth their Colonel, the man on the old white horse."

fresh entrenchments, and were occupied in burying the
Arab dead. The Europeans who were killed in Baker
Pasha's fight were recognised on the field and buried,
crosses being placed over their graves.

The infantry advanced in a square at 8.30 A.M.,
two squadrons of the Tenth covering the front with
scouts well advanced, the flanks of the square also
being guarded by the 10th and 19th Hussars. The
direction taken—for there was no road or even beaten
track—lay through thick mimosa bush, and, the country

being very flat and some mirage existing, it was not an
easy matter to find the town of Tokar. The scouts of
the Tenth at last came in sight of the mud walls, and
were received by a few scattering shots. At the same
time numbers of Arabs were seen leaving the town, and
an interchange of musketry took place between the advanced parties and the rebels until the main body came
up. On the approach of the infantry square and the
whole of the troops, the civil authorities of the town
came out, with such of the Egyptian garrison as were
left, and announced that none of the enemy remained

in the place. Upon this General Graham and his staff, escorted by the 10th Hussars, marched round the town, to make sure that none of the enemy remained there. A position was then selected in an open plain about 1,000 yards from the town, where the whole force bivouacked in a large square, the mounted branches in the centre.

On the 2nd March the second and third squadrons of the 10th Hussars, and the mounted infantry, were sent out, under Lieutenant-Colonel R. S. Liddell, to reconnoitre and examine a large camp of the enemy reported to be at Dubbah, three miles distant. This was found deserted, and on being examined the whole of the guns, rifles, ammunition, stores, and baggage captured by the Arabs from Baker Pasha's force were discovered. The Tenth destroyed over 1,300 Remington rifles and bayonets, buried the ammunition, and carried away on the ten camels provided as transport the property of the English officers of Baker's force. The men of the 10th Hussars, superintended by Regimental Sergeant-Major Bradshaw, dragged the mountain and Gatling guns back to Tokar, a work of some difficulty in the deep sand. In the evening the regiment received a telegram from H.R.H. the Prince of Wales, congratulating it on its success at El Teb, and inquiring after the wounded.

On the 3rd the 10th Hussars paraded with the Naval Brigade and Gatlings, and, after hearing the general order issued by Sir Gerald Graham read,[1] marched at nine A.M. on its return to Trinkitat. The Naval Brigade halted at El Teb, but the Tenth continued its march,

---

[1] Extract from General Orders, dated Camp, Tokar: " The object of the expedition has been achieved. Tokar has been relieved. The rebels in arms have been defeated. . . . The cavalry showed all the dash and almost reckless gallantry in action that have characterised that arm in our military record. They have also rendered invaluable service in reconnaissance and scouting duties."

and arrived at two P.M. In the evening the Naval
Brigade followed, and the Tenth went out to meet
it, and the good feeling between the two was so great
that the sailors allowed the men to assist them with
their guns, which hitherto they had refused to any
other corps.

The Earl of Airlie, who had preceded the Tenth
from India to England, on arrival at Marseilles, hearing of his regiment being ordered to the Soudan, re-
traced his steps. He bought a horse in Marseilles,
engaged a French servant, embarked on board the first
vessel he could find proceeding eastward, and rejoined
the regiment on its return from Trinkitat and resumed
the duties of adjutant. On the 4th the whole force returned to Trinkitat, escorting the Egyptian garrison and
those of the inhabitants of Tokar who were desirous of
returning to Egypt. Thirty-eight horses of the Tenth
were found unfit for further service and were cast.

On the evening of the 4th the officers of the Tenth
gave a dinner to the General and Staff and the captain
and officers of H.M.S. " Jumna." It is needless to say
that the regiment was not in the position to provide this
entertainment itself, but, owing to the kindness of its
friends of the " Jumna," everything, from the cook to
the tables and chairs, came from that hospitable ship.
In the evening an open-air concert was given, at which
the naval and military commanders and most of the camp
attended. On the 29th March the ladies and women
and children of the Tenth, who up to this time had remained on board the " Jumna," and had witnessed the
action of El Teb in the distance from the deck of the
ship, were transferred to the " Serapis," and the following morning sailed for England.

The return of the expedition to Suakim having been
decided on, the regiment commenced its embarkation

on board the transport " Osiris " on the morning of the 5th April. Besides the horses, baggage, and camp equipage, fifty camels and some mules were placed in the ship, the work being completed by sunset. On the 6th the " Osiris " sailed at eleven A.M., and arriving at Suakim at four P.M. the unloading of the ship was at once commenced, and was carried on all night. The camp was now formed on fresh ground on the south of the harbour. Forty fresh horses were supplied to the Tenth from the Egyptian Gendarmerie, and English saddlery that had been sent from Cairo was given out. On the 10th the second squadron, under Major Brabazon, was employed on outpost duty to prevent natives from entering or leaving the town.

It had been thought that the Arabs would show no further resistance after their crushing defeat at El Teb, but intelligence was now received that Osman Digma had collected a large force at Tamaii, at the foot of the hills, a few miles inland. The 42nd Highlanders were sent out about nine miles to Baker's Zareba to reconstruct and hold it, and the cavalry was employed in protecting the convoys to and from that place. The following day a Cavalry Brigade field day was held, under Brigadier-General Herbert Stewart, and in the evening the whole of the Infantry Division marched to the zareba formed by the 42nd Highlanders.

It was now decided to attack the tribes collected in their stronghold of Tamaii, and on the 12th March the cavalry moved out to Baker's Zareba, and arrived there at ten A.M. After a halt of a few hours the whole force, under General Graham, advanced six miles further to the foot of the hills, the first squadron of the Tenth, under Major Gough, covering the front. About four P.M. the scouts discovered the position of the enemy, and shots were interchanged. The British force on this occasion was accompanied by the battery of artillery under Major Holley, armed with 9-pounders drawn by mules, and these now opened fire on the enemy, who were showing on the ridge and following the cavalry, but a few shells having burst among them they speedily retired. The infantry formed a zareba about a thousand yards from the enemy's position, and the Cavalry Brigade retired to Baker's Zareba for the night, on account of water. At five A.M. on the 13th the Cavalry Brigade advanced again to rejoin the infantry, arriving at the advanced zareba at seven A.M. The whole force was then ordered to advance on the enemy's position. The cavalry went forward to reconnoitre, and the infantry moved in two squares, or, to speak more correctly, as the flanks of the squares were in fours, in a formation that could at once form square. The Second Brigade was in advance, under Brigadier-General Davis, with whom was General Graham himself and his staff. The First Brigade was echeloned on the right rear of the Second Brigade, under Brigadier-General Redvers Buller; the cavalry was echeloned from its own right in three lines on the left rear of the Second Infantry Brigade— the first line under Colonel E. A. Wood, the second under Major Brabazon, the third under Colonel Webster, 19th Hussars. As the force approached the steep side of the valley or broad nullah in which the enemy, to the number of about 10,000, was collected, numerous bodies of the rebels came out, but retreated in front of the fire that was poured into them. On the leading square arriving close to the nullah it received the order to charge, and this not being heard by the flanks caused a gap to occur. This the gallant enemy was not slow to take advantage of, and, rushing in in hundreds, stabbed the men in the rear rank, rushed upon the sailors and their machine guns, and the square in disorder fell back some distance. Seeing this, and in order to create a diversion, the cavalry was brought rapidly up and received the order to charge from Sir Herbert Stewart. The position held by the enemy proving to be behind a sheer precipice of rocks, Colonel Wood halted the first line just in time, and the second squadron, under Lieutenant Allsopp, was dismounted, and opened an enfilading fire upon the enemy, which checked the attack on their right. At the same time Major Holley, with his battery, which held ground between the two squares, opened such a withering fire that the enemy were unable to come up, and General Buller, bringing on the First Brigade, fought his way up to the brink of the nullah, where he poured a murderous fire into the rebels below, who were soon in hot retreat. The Second Brigade had now rallied, and, again advancing, picked up the Gardner guns which had been left behind, and arriving in line with the other brigade assisted in completing the discomfiture of the enemy.

After a short halt the First Brigade entered the nullah slowly, and took the opposite heights at the charge and descended the next hill into Osman Digma's camp and the villages of Tamaii. The three villages, about half a mile from one another, were built of mats and grass, and there were also a number of round tents. Bags of money were found, Korans, talismans, orders, &c., showing that the English success was not expected. Osman Digma's standard was taken and one of Tewfik Bey's was recaptured. Cavalry outposts were posted, and the troops were taken down to the water, which ran fast and clear, but was very brackish in taste. A long halt took place in the enemy's position, when dinners were eaten while the horses fed. Some long-distant desultory shots still fell during this time, causing some casualties; amongst others, the horse of

G G

Lieutenant the Hon. J. Byng, 10th Hussars, was shot. The whole force then fell back for the night, the infantry to the nearest zareba, the cavalry to the further. The loss on this day was seventy killed and over 100 wounded; the 42nd, the 65th, and the Naval Brigade suffering the most. The enemy was reckoned to have lost between two and three thousand men. The only casualties in the Tenth were Sergeant A. Dowson and Private W. Loretto slightly wounded. The following morning (the 14th), at 5.30, the cavalry advanced and marched straight to the watering place of the day before, supported by the infantry. A good deal of desultory fire was kept up by individuals of the enemy among the rocks, and replied to by the cavalry advanced parties. As soon as the horses were watered, the cavalry and mounted infantry advanced over several of the smaller ranges towards the higher hills, and small parties of the enemy fled to the mountains. The infantry entered the villages and searched the huts, while the cavalry crowned all the surrounding heights. This being done, the cavalry was drawn back and ordered to set fire to the village, and this afforded a wonderful spectacle. Boxes of Remington cartridges exploded as if musketry fire was being carried out in volleys, the grass huts burnt rapidly and furiously, and spreading at last to an enclosure where all the shell, powder, rifles, and other stores were placed, the whole went up into the air with tremendous explosions, producing a fine effect, and causing wonderful changes of colour in the mountain scenery. The villages of Tamaii having been burnt, and the horses again watered, the whole force fell back to Baker's Zareba, the cavalry continuing its march and arriving at Suakim at night, Captain Singleton and the officers of H.M.S. " Jumna " coming out to meet the regiment.

CHAPTER XLVII

CONVOY DUTIES—AN ADVANCE INLAND—THE CAMPAIGN BROUGHT
TO A CLOSE—HONOURS AWARDED—ARRIVAL AT PORTSMOUTH—
SHORNCLIFFE—THE DUKE OF CAMBRIDGE INSPECTS THE TENTH
—THE PRINCESS OF WALES PRESENTS THE MEDALS TO THE
REGIMENT—OFFICERS ORDERED ON THE NILE EXPEDITION

ON the 15th March, Major Brabazon, in command of an
escort, accompanied by Major Wood, of the Intelligence
Department, proceeded to the wells of Handoub, on the
route to Berber, to select a camp and interview friendly
tribes, returning to Suakim in the evening. Other
parties of the Tenth were employed daily on convoy
duty, but nothing of importance occurred for some
days. On the 18th the 19th Hussars and the 75th
Regiment marched out to Handoub, and on the 21st
the Tenth marched fifteen miles on the Tokar road to
intercept a convoy expected for Osman Digma. The
regiment remained hidden in a nullah with scouts out
till the evening and then returned, only seeing a few of
the enemy. On the 24th the 89th marched out ten
miles due west, and, being joined by the 75th from
Handoub, formed a fresh zareba, preparatory to another
advance. On the 25th the whole division moved out
from Suakim at 1.30 P.M., after the men's dinners, the
first squadron of the Tenth covering the front. The
remainder of the regiment and the 19th Hussars followed, watering the horses on the way. The heat was

1884

G G 2

extreme, and the infantry suffered very much and made
very slow progress. The zareba was not reached till
after dark, when the whole force bivouacked in rear of
it, the cavalry in the centre. Half the cavalry slept,
with their arms beside them, on the flanks of the position, the remainder lay at their horses' heads. Early
in the morning of the 26th the Cavalry Brigade and
mounted infantry, under General Herbert Stewart, advanced, covered by the first squadron of the Tenth
under Major Gough. After five miles through bush,
the hills were reached, the cavalry scouting carefully
both in front and on the flanks, mounting every height
from which a good view could be obtained, the 10th
Hussars covering the right flank and the 19th the left.
Four miles further on the advanced parties were fired
upon from the position of Tamanieb. The mounted
infantry advanced along rough ground on the left,
while Major Gough, with the first squadron, pushed
on towards the centre. Some desultory firing took
place on both sides, but as the position was unassail-
able for mounted troops General Stewart fell slowly
back.

The cavalry retired to the foot of the hills and met
General Buller's infantry brigade advancing in support,
and the whole falling back a short distance formed a
fresh zareba for the night, in conjunction with General
Davis's brigade, which now came up. On the 27th the
whole force paraded at 5.30 A.M., and advanced towards
the enemy's position; the 10th Hussars' scouts on the
right and front, the 19th Hussars on the left, the
mounted infantry supporting. On the arrival of the
scouts opposite to Tamanieb, the enemy opened fire,
but the cavalry held the ground until the arrival of
the infantry. On Major Holley's guns being brought
up, and two rounds fired, the enemy, who at no time

appeared in great numbers, dispersed. The mounted branches at once descended to the stream and watered, and the horses drank with avidity, as this was the first opportunity afforded to them of tasting water for forty hours. After an hour's rest and feeding the horses, the cavalry and mounted infantry proceeded up a dry river bed on the road to Sinkat, destroyed one of Osman Digma's villages, and captured some cattle. The enemy having entirely evacuated this portion of the country, the whole force retired out of the mountains, and the Cavalry Brigade returned to Suakim that night, a distance of twenty-four miles. The small Arab horses had carried the regiment well, and, with their heads towards home and the sea breeze blowing in their faces, came into Suakim still fresh and willing, after being mounted off and on since 5.30 A.M., having covered forty miles of rough country, and this with very little water.

On the 28th orders were received to prepare for embarkation, the English Government being of opinion that the object of the expedition had been attained. A telegram was received from Her Majesty the Queen congratulating the troops on the success of the campaign. The Tenth was occupied the whole day in handing in the saddlery and equipment, and the horses were given over to the Egyptians. In the evening the officers entertained General Herbert Stewart at a farewell dinner.

On the 29th reveillé sounded at 3.45 A.M., when the tents were packed and given into ordnance store for return to Aden, the baggage was sent on board H.M.S. "Jumna," the camping ground was carefully cleaned up, and the regiment embarked at seven A.M. The 65th and 89th Regiments, together with M-I battery Royal Artillery, embarked at the same time, and soon after

Sir Gerald Graham came on board, made an address, and bade farewell to the troops. Admiral Sir William Hewett, V.C., K.C.B., also visited the ship. Before leaving, Colonel Wood received a letter from the Quartermaster-General of the Force, desiring it to be made known to his regiment the great satisfaction of General Graham at the manner in which it had embarked and the perfect state in which the camping ground had been left. This letter was handed over to Quartermaster A. E. Poole, to whose excellent arrangements and devoted interest to the comforts of everyone throughout this campaign the thanks of the whole regiment were due.

In commemoration of this campaign the 10th Hussars was permitted to bear the words "Egypt, 1884," on its appointments. A silver medal was granted to all who took part in the operations, the two actions "El Teb" and "Tamaii" being inscribed on one bar. Bronze stars were afterwards presented by His Highness the Khedive of Egypt. Colonel E. A. Wood received the Companion of the Bath, Lieutenant-Colonel R. S. Liddell the Third Class of the Order of the Medjidieh, and Lieutenant and Adjutant the Earl of Airlie the Fifth Class of that Order. Colonel Wood, Lieutenant-Colonel Liddell, and Major Gough were mentioned in despatches. Majors Gough and Brabazon became brevet lieutenant-colonels, Private F. Hayes received the Distinguished Service Medal. The thanks of the House of Lords and the House of Commons were given to the troops engaged in the Eastern Soudan on the 13th August, 1885.

A memorial tablet of marble, surrounded by a mosaic border in Venetian glass, was erected in All Saints' Church, Aldershot, in memory of those of the regiment who lost their lives in this campaign. This monument was placed under the window put up by the regiment after the Afghan campaign.

On the afternoon of the 29th March H.M.S. "Jumna" steamed out of Suakim Harbour, and after passing through the Suez Canal met with adverse winds in the Mediterranean and Bay of Biscay, so that it was not until the 21st April that she arrived at Portsmouth. On that day, about ten A.M., H.M.S. "Jumna" arrived off Spithead, and was met by a Government steamer with a large number of the old officers of the regiment and relatives of those on board. Nothing could have been more enthusiastic than the meeting, and the good feeling that prompted so many to come, some of them great distances, and to wait at Portsmouth until the ship, which had been detained four days by contrary winds, arrived, was thoroughly appreciated by every officer and man of the 10th Hussars. This day will be handed down among the brightest recollections of the regiment. A telegram was received from H.R.H. the Prince of Wales congratulating the Tenth on its return, and regretting that he was prevented from greeting it in person on its arrival.

The officers who disembarked from the "Jumna" were Colonel E. A. Wood, Lieutenant-Colonel R. S. Liddell, Major H. S. Gough, Brevet-Major J. P. Brabazon, Captain Durham, Lieutenants Wilson, Greenwood, Lord A. Compton, Allsopp, Harvey, Lawley, Hughes-Onslow, Byng, Major and Paymaster Brett, Quartermaster Poole, and 294 non-commissioned officers and men. Lord Airlie received permission to proceed home overland. In the evening the old officers present at Portsmouth entertained the regiment at dinner.

On the 22nd the troops disembarked, and were inspected by Lieutenant-General H.S.H. Prince Edward of Saxe-Weimar, commanding at Portsmouth, proceeding afterwards by railway to Shorncliffe Camp. On the following Sunday the whole regiment was taken over by train to Canterbury to attend a thanksgiving service in the Cathedral, and was afterwards entertained at a public dinner in St. George's Hall.

On the 28th H.R.H. the Duke of Cambridge, Commanding-in-Chief, visited Shorncliffe and inspected the 10th Hussars.

On the 23rd May it was notified that the Queen had approved of scarlet pantaloons being worn by the officers at Levées and in the evening when in full dress. Her Majesty also approved of the officers wearing in full dress, in review order only, a scarlet shabracque and shell bridle, breastplate, and crupper. This dress and these appointments, which had formerly been worn and were now reintroduced into the regiment, had apparently fallen into disuse on the return of the Tenth from the Crimea in 1856.

On the 27th June the Prince of Wales inspected the regiment. His Royal Highness was accompanied by H.R.H. the Princess of Wales, who did the 10th Hussars the honour of presenting the medals to the officers, non-commissioned officers, and men for the recent operations in the Soudan. The Princess also presented to Mrs. J. Cox, the widow of Sergeant Cox, who was killed at El Teb, the medal of her husband, accompanying it with a few kind words. The Prince of Wales then addressed the regiment : " I was glad," he said, " to have the pleasure of seeing you in India. Since then you have been through the campaign in Afghanistan, and you have only lately returned from an arduous expedition in the East." After further congratulations His Royal Highness added : " It is now twenty-one years since Her Majesty conferred upon me the honour of Colonel of the 10th Hussars, and I feel proud to be connected with it."

At the first regimental dinner after its return to England, the old officers of the Tenth presented an oil painting of the "Charge at El Teb" to the Officers' Mess. The picture was painted by Mr. G. D. Giles, who was present with the regiment at the action. Many of the officers and men represented are very truthful portraits. At the same time Colonel E. A. Wood presented a picture to the 10th Hussars' Mess of H.M.S. "Jumna," the vessel that conveyed the regiment to India in 1873, and again brought it back eleven years afterwards in 1884, as well as doing such excellent service for it during the short campaign in the Eastern Soudan.

Of the next few months at Shorncliffe there is not much to record. As many of the officers and men who had returned from India as could be spared were permitted to proceed on furlough, and as the depôt, 200 strong, from Canterbury, under command of Captain R. B. Fisher, had joined head-quarters, and only about 150 horses taken over from the 7th Dragoon Guards were on the strength, a great portion of the regiment was able to avail themselves of the privilege. The horses of the 7th left in England on their proceeding to India were considered too heavy for an hussar regiment, and many had been disposed of before the arrival of the Tenth. When opportunities occurred a large portion of the remainder were gradually drafted to other corps, and replaced by remounts from Ireland. In 1884–85 no less than 187 remounts were bought by Colonel Wood.

The 10th Hussars was inspected on the 16th July by Colonel the Hon. E. G. Curzon, commanding at Shorncliffe, and on the 30th by Major-General Charles Fraser, V.C., Inspector-General of Cavalry. The summer was passed at Shorncliffe in training the young horses and in drilling the recruits. The Tenth was placed on the peace establishment, and the old soldiers who had served in India gradually retired on their pensions or were passed to the Reserve.

During the following winter the officers kept a pack of drag hounds, and twice a week had excellent gallops over the Vale of Ashford. The officers also set to work to re-establish their reputation in the polo field, and before they had been three months in the country played a match with one of the strongest teams in England.

On the 22nd September orders were received for Brevet Lieutenant-Colonel J. P. Brabazon, Lieutenant the Hon. G. Bryan, Troop Sergeant-Major Turner, two sergeants, three corporals, one trumpeter, and thirty-eight privates, to proceed to Aldershot to form part of a Light Camel Corps being prepared for service with the Nile expedition under Lord Wolseley. On the 25th they embarked at Portsmouth and sailed the same day. Captain and Adjutant the Earl of Airlie proceeded at the same time to Egypt as Brigade-Major to Brigadier-General Sir Herbert Stewart. Captain R. H. W. Wilson, in February 1885, was also selected for special service in the Eastern Soudan, and was afterwards attached to the staff of Brigadier-General Ewart.

Lieutenant-Colonel H. S. Gough received orders to proceed to South Africa, to take part in an expedition into Bechuanaland, under Colonel Sir Charles Warren. He embarked at Dartmouth on the 14th November, 1884.

The regimental changes in 1884 were:—Death—Major M. M. Slade, killed in action. Retirement—Captain R. P. Sandeman. Exchanges—Honorary Captain and Ridingmaster J. Perry, from 17th Lancers, to be ridingmaster; Ridingmaster McGhee, to 17th Lancers. Appointments—Lieutenant F. R. Bowlby, Lieutenant C. T. McM. Kavanagh, and Lieutenant E. Baring.

On the 18th February, 1885, Lord Alwyne Compton was appointed Adjutant, *vice* the Earl of Airlie.

Orders were now received to move to Aldershot, and on the 29th June the head-quarters, with E and H troops, left Shorncliffe and marched *via* Cranbrook, Tunbridge Wells, Horsham, and Godalming, C and G proceeding by Ashford, Maidstone and Sevenoaks, Reigate and Guildford. On the 30th, A and B troops marched by the former route, and D and F by the latter. The whole regiment was assembled at Aldershot by the 3rd July, and was inspected by Major-General Sir Drury Lowe, K.C.B., Inspector-General of Cavalry, on the 7th.

CHAPTER XLVIII

PRINCE ALBERT VICTOR APPOINTED TO THE REGIMENT—RETURN OF
THE OFFICERS AND MEN FROM THE NILE EXPEDITION—THE
REGIMENT INSPECTED BY THE PRINCE OF WALES—COLONEL
E. A. WOOD

1885   THE 10th Hussars, on arrival at Aldershot, occupied the South Cavalry Barracks, and immediately afterwards Lieutenant H.R.H. Prince Albert Victor, who had been gazetted to the regiment on the 7th June, accompanied by Captain the Hon. Alwyne Greville, 60th Rifles, as his equerry, joined and took up his quarters in barracks. The distinguished honour that was now conferred by the Prince of Wales in placing his eldest son as junior subaltern in the 10th Hussars had been notified by His Royal Highness at the regimental dinner in the month previous. Now, for the first time, the regiment was able to point with pride to the "Army List," showing a Prince of Wales and his son as its senior and junior officer.

  On the 12th June Captain R. H. W. Wilson rejoined from active service in the Eastern Soudan, where he had acted on the staff of Brigadier-General H. Ewart. On the 9th July the Earl of Airlie rejoined from the Nile expedition, where he had taken part in the desert march, in the attempted relief of General Gordon at Khartoum, as brigade-major of the combined Camel Corps. Lord Airlie was wounded at the actions of Abu Klea and Gubat, and at the latter his

Albert Victor Capt.

X Royal Hussars.

chief, Sir Herbert Stewart, received his death wound.
Lord Airlie was mentioned twice in despatches, and
received for his services two clasps and a brevet majority. On the 24th Lieutenant-Colonel J. P. Brabazon,
Lieutenant the Hon. George Bryan, and the men composing the Light Camel Corps, rejoined from Egypt.
Of those men of the Tenth who served in this campaign,
the following lost their lives :—Corporal Hawkins, Privates Evans, Milner, and Dengate. Troop Sergeant-
Major Turner, 10th Hussars, who had acted as regimental sergeant-major of the Light Camel Corps, was
commanded to attend at Windsor Castle on the 26th
November, and received from Her Majesty's hands the
medal "for distinguished conduct in the field."

A memorial of alabaster and Venetian mosaic was
erected in All Saints' Church, Aldershot, to the memory
of those of the Tenth who lost their lives in this campaign, and was placed under the Afghan window. The
authorities at this time granted the entire space at the
end of the south aisle of this church for the sole use
of the regiment, on account of the window and monuments already placed there.

On the 26th July Lieutenant-Colonel H. S. Gough
returned from service in Bechuanaland. This officer
had, while under the orders of Sir Charles Warren,
raised a regiment of cavalry, known as the Diamond
Fields Horse, which performed most excellent service.
In recognition of the manner in which he carried out
his duties, the Companionship of St. Michael and St.
George was conferred upon Lieutenant-Colonel Gough
on the 27th January, 1887.

On the 19th August the Tenth was inspected by
Field-Marshal H.R.H. the Prince of Wales. His Royal
Highness was accompanied by the Grand Duke of
Hesse, the Duke of Connaught, Prince George of Wales,

1885 and many other distinguished officers.   After the inspection their Royal Highnesses did the regiment the honour of taking luncheon with the officers, and afterwards a photograph was taken of all those present.   After the inspection His Royal Highness proceeded to unveil the statue of the Duke of Wellington, which had been removed from Hyde Park Corner and erected on a prominent hill near the Queen's Pavilion.   The whole of the Aldershot Division was formed up opposite the statue and presented arms as His Royal Highness performed the ceremony.

On the 30th September the Tenth was inspected by Major-General Sir Drury Lowe, K.C.B.

The regimental changes in 1885 were:—Appointment—Lieutenant H.R.H. Prince Albert Victor of Wales and Lieutenant E. W. D. Baird.

1886   On the 31st March, 1886, Colonel E. A. Wood, C.B., retired on half-pay, and was appointed Inspector of Auxiliary Cavalry and second in command of the Cavalry Brigade at Aldershot.   Colonel Edward Alexander Wood joined the 10th Hussars as cornet on the 16th July, 1858, was promoted lieutenant in 1862, and captain in 1867.   He proceeded with the regiment to India in 1873, and served in that country until 1875, when he returned to England and was appointed Adjutant of the Cavalry Depôt at Canterbury on the 1st of April of that year.   This post he held until promoted to the majority and second in command on the 31st of May, 1876.   On Lord Ralph Kerr proceeding on leave to England in April 1877, he assumed command, marching the 10th Hussars from Muttra to Rawul Pindi during that winter, and on the war breaking out in Afghanistan in 1878 made all the preparations for the regiment proceeding on active service ; was in command of the 10th Hussars during the assault on Ali Musjid, and remained in command at Jellalabad until the return of Lord Ralph Kerr in March, 1879. He was present at the operations in the Lughman Valley, was mentioned in despatches, received a brevet of lieutenant-colonel and medal with clasp. He was employed during the campaign in various independent commands, and on the arrival of Yakoub Khan at Gundamuck with Sir L. Cavagnari, escorted him to his camp. He succeeded to the command of the 10th Hussars on the 31st May, 1881, on the retirement of Lord Ralph Kerr, remained in command during the remainder of the service of the regiment in India, and embarked with it for England in February 1884. He commanded the Tenth during the campaign in the Eastern Soudan, and, until the arrival of Sir Herbert Stewart from England, was appointed to the command of the Cavalry Brigade. He was present at the actions of El Teb and Tamaii, received a medal with clasp, the bronze star and Companion of the Bath, and was mentioned in despatches. Colonel Wood returned to England in command of the regiment, and remained at its head until the 31st March, 1886, when he was appointed Inspector of Auxiliary Cavalry. He served on the Staff as A.D.C. to the Major-General Commanding a Brigade at Malta from 1862 to 1863; A.D.C. to the General Officer Commanding the Forces in Ireland from 1863 to 1864; A.D.C. to the General Officer Commanding, Dublin, from February 1866 to December 1866. He attended the manœuvres of the Austrian army in September 1884, for the purpose of reporting on the cavalry manœuvres. After holding the appointment of Inspector-General of Yeomanry for four years, he was appointed to the command of the Regimental District at Hounslow. As already mentioned, Colonel Wood belongs to a family many members of which have served in the Tenth: two great-uncles, three uncles, a cousin, and himself. Colonel Wood was an excellent horseman, and took a prominent part in the regimental races, in many of which he rode winners, and was a regular player at polo. For many years also he was in the cricket eleven of the regiment.

On the 1st April Colonel R. S. Liddell was appointed to the command of the 10th Hussars, and Major T. A. St. Quintin was promoted to be lieutenant-colonel and second in command.

The regiment was inspected on the 12th and 13th May by Major-General Sir Drury Lowe, K.C.B.

In the spring of 1886 a "point to point" steeple-chase took place between five subalterns of the Royal Horse Guards and five subalterns of the 10th Hussars, a cup being presented by H.R.H. the Prince of Wales. The course, which was close to Stratton Audley, Oxfordshire, was selected by Lord Chesham (late 10th Hussars), Master of the Bicester Hounds, and Viscount Valentia (late 10th Hussars), late Master of the Hounds. The Prince of Wales, Prince Albert Victor, and a large number of people were present. The following officers represented their respective regiments :—

Royal Horse Guards.	10th Royal Hussars.
Lord Binning.	Hon. George Bryan.
Mr. Ferguson.	Mr. Hughes-Onslow.
Mr. Fenwick.	Mr. Baird.
Mr. Vaughan Lee.	Hon. A. Lawley.
Mr. Williams.	Mr. Kavanagh.

The Tenth won the race, having two out of the first three in at the finish—viz. Hon. G. Bryan first, Mr. Hughes-Onslow third.

On the 1st June H.R.H. the Prince of Wales inspected the Cavalry Brigade at Aldershot. On the 2nd July the Prince and Princess of Wales, accompanied by the Princesses Louise, Victoria, and Maud of Wales, paid a visit to Aldershot, and did the officers the honour of taking luncheon with them, on the occasion of Her Majesty the Queen reviewing the Division. Their Royal Highnesses inspected the Tenth in barracks, and the regiment filed past on its way to join the rest of the Division. Prince Albert Victor on this occasion rode at the head of his troop. The inspection by Her Majesty took place in the Long Valley at five P.M.

On the 14th July, with the sanction of H.R.H. the Field-Marshal Commanding-in-Chief, the 10th Hussars marched out for three days for the purpose of carrying out a " cavalry raid ; " the conditions being that the public should be put to no expense and only regimental transport should be used, with the exception of one waggon, carrying twenty-five tents, and an ambulance cart. Private arrangements were made with the owners of property for permission to encamp, which was kindly granted, Mr. R. Combe, of Pierrepoint, and others, permitting their land to be used and giving every assistance. Active service dress was worn, and a change of clothing, a waterproof sheet and cloak were carried on the saddle. Saddles were stripped of their panels, and two blankets, one for the man and one for the horse, placed between the saddle and the numnah. The regiment marched to Frensham, and, after examining the country in front for some miles, pitched its camp, outposts being left out till a late hour at night. On the 15th it marched to Haslemere and Liphook by different roads and made a reconnaissance, after which it fell back to Woolmer and encamped on Keeper's Hill, with outposts thrown out three miles in front on Weaver's Down. On the 16th it moved north-west, proceeding by the two roads past Hind Head and the Devil's Jump, and on Hankley Common was opposed

H H

by the 5th Lancers, sent out from Aldershot to act against the Tenth. The Aldershot force falling back, the Tenth encamped near Tilford. On the 17th it returned to Aldershot.[1]

On the 11th August Lieutenant-Colonel T. A. St. Quintin exchanged into the 2nd Dragoon Guards (the Bays) with Lieutenant-Colonel Viscount Downe, who had recently been appointed to that regiment from the 2nd Life Guards. Lieutenant-Colonel T. A. St. Quintin entered the army as a cornet in the 10th Hussars on the 30th December, 1859. From that time he served continuously with it in England and India until 1882. In April of that year he was appointed Remount Agent at Calcutta, and he held this post until May 1887. In March 1886 he was promoted to be lieutenant-colonel, and in August exchanged. In July 1887 Lieutenant-Colonel St. Quintin was selected for the command of the 8th Hussars. While in the 10th Hussars this officer had always taken a lead in every sport and amusement. An excellent rider, he was one of the keenest supporters of polo and one of the most brilliant players, and a good cricketer. He served with the 10th Hussars throughout the Afghan campaign, 1878–9, and received the medal with clasp.

On the 18th August Troop Sergeant-Major John Crisp was appointed Regimental Sergeant-Major.

On the 8th and 9th September the Tenth was inspected by Major-General Sir Drury Lowe, K.C.B.

Orders of readiness for detachments to be formed by the regiment from Aldershot were received, and on the 21st September the first squadron, under Lieutenant-

---

[1] On the 15th a letter was received from the Horse Guards expressing His Royal Highness's commendation for the manner in which this flying column's march was carried out, " which reflects the greatest credit on the regiment."

Colonel H. S. Gough, C.M.G., and Captain Greenwood, marched to Hampton Court. At the same time Major the Earl of Airlie, Lieutenant the Hon. A. Lawley, and thirty-five non-commissioned officers and men, proceeded to Kensington Barracks to take up the orderly duties in London. Twenty horses belonging to the 7th Hussars, about to proceed to India, were transferred from the detachment of that regiment at Kensington to the Tenth, and attached to the party under the command of Lord Airlie. On the 20th Lieutenant the Hon. Julian Byng was appointed Adjutant, *vice* Lord Alwyne Compton, resigned.

On the 3rd November four officers, 127 non-commissioned officers and men, and 132 horses, under the command of Major Manners Wood, proceeded from Aldershot to London for duty with the Lord Mayor's procession. On the 9th Lieutenant Lord Alwyne Compton and twenty-six men from Hampton Court, and Major the Earl of Airlie and fourteen men from Kensington, took part in this duty.

On the 20th November the officers of the Tenth gave a farewell dinner at the Hôtel Métropole, Charing Cross, to the officers of the 7th Hussars, on their departure for India.

During this year the 10th Hussars received permission to introduce a Nordenfelt machine-gun as part of its equipment, and during the whole of the summer drill season it accompanied the regiment in the manœuvres, under the immediate superintendence of Major Wilson. The gun was mounted on a two-wheeled galloping carriage, introduced into the service by Colonel Liddell. About 2,000 rounds were carried in the boxes, which formed the two seats for the men, and the gun was placed above these. It proved of such great advantage for cavalry service that six of the same pattern,

1886 with some improvements, were issued to other cavalry regiments.

The regimental changes in 1886 were :—Retirements—Captain E. T. Rose ; Lieutenant-Colonel and Colonel E. A. Wood, C.B., to half-pay ; Lieutenant C. M. Grenfell. Promotions—Lieutenant-Colonel and Colonel R. S. Liddell to command the regiment ; Major T. A. St. Quintin to be lieutenant-colonel. Transfers and exchanges—Lieutenant-Colonel Viscount Downe, C.S.I., from 2nd Dragoon Guards ; Lieutenant-Colonel T. A. St. Quintin to 2nd Dragoon Guards.

1887 On the 19th March H.R.H. the Prince of Wales proceeded to Berlin to be present at the celebration of the ninetieth birthday of the Emperor William I. of Germany. His Royal Highness did the 10th Hussars the honour of selecting the commanding officer, Colonel Liddell, to accompany him in his personal suite. Private Tritton, 10th Hussars, proceeded on duty with the party. The visit lasted a week, during which time the Prince of Wales, accompanied by his staff, attended the various festivities that took place, and, in addition, inspected the Hussars of the Guard at Potsdam, at that time commanded by His Imperial Highness Prince William of Prussia.

On the 31st March the head-quarters and B, E, F, and H troops, under command of Colonel R. S. Liddell, marched from Aldershot to Hounslow Barracks. The remaining two troops, C and G, before leaving, completed their course of musketry and rejoined at Hounslow on the 6th April. On the 22nd the regiment was inspected by Major-General R. Gipps, C.B., commanding the Home District, the detachment at Kensington marching down to Hounslow for the inspection. The General afterwards visited Hampton Court.

On the 14th May the head-quarters and the squadron

from Hampton Court marched to London, and, after being joined in Hyde Park by the detachment from Kensington Gate, proceeded to the Marble Arch, and lined the streets from Paddington Station to Holborn on the occasion of Her Majesty opening the People's Palace at the East End. The head-quarters and the band were placed at the Marble Arch. On the completion of this duty the Tenth marched back to quarters in the evening.

On the 3rd May it marched to Wimbledon and took part in a field-day with the 1st and 2nd Life Guards and B-B Royal Horse Artillery. The brigade was commanded by Colonel R. S. Liddell. On the 23rd of the same month the brigade again assembled in the same manner. H.R.H. the Duke of Cambridge was present on this occasion.

CHAPTER XLIX

THE JUBILEE OF HER MAJESTY QUEEN VICTORIA—CELEBRATION OF
THE FIFTIETH ANNIVERSARY OF HER ACCESSION—PRINCE ALBERT
VICTOR PROMOTED TO BE CAPTAIN—HIS IMPERIAL HIGHNESS
PRINCE WILLIAM OF PRUSSIA VISITS THE REGIMENT—JUBILEE
REVIEW AT ALDERSHOT—COLONEL R. S. LIDDELL

1887 THIS year being the Jubilee of Her Gracious Majesty the Queen, the 10th Hussars, having the good fortune of being stationed so near London, had many opportunities of taking part in the general rejoicings and festivities. The regiment marched to London on the 21st June (Jubilee day), and had the honour of taking part in the celebration of the fiftieth anniversary of the accession of Her Majesty the Queen. It paraded at 7.30 A.M., and proceeded in the first instance from Hounslow and Hampton Court to "Olympia." This building was in the most handsome manner placed by the directors at its disposal. The regiment formed up in the arena and dismounted, the horses were watered and fed, and the officers and men had breakfast. After this it moved on to London and lined the streets from Buckingham Palace up Constitution Hill along Piccadilly to its junction with St. James's Street. Twenty-five horses, selected for their appearance and colour (all brown), were provided by the Tenth to mount the Indian native officers who took part in the procession. The weather was magnificent, and the proceedings of the whole day were a splendid success. In the evening the Tenth marched back to Hounslow, halting again for a short time at "Olympia." On this day H.R.H. Prince Albert Victor of Wales, K.G., was promoted to be a captain in the 10th Hussars in excess of the establishment. At the same time he was appointed Aide-de-Camp to the Queen. These honours were granted on the occasion of Her Majesty's Jubilee.

On the 25th His Imperial Highness Prince William of Prussia,[1] who had come to England on the occasion of the Jubilee, did the 10th Hussars the honour of paying it a visit at Hounslow. His Imperial Highness was accompanied by General Löwe, commanding an army corps on the Rhine, a distinguished cavalry officer. Prince William, after inspecting the regiment, rode with it through its manœuvres, and charged with it, riding beside the commanding officer. He afterwards witnessed the whole regiment ride over the jumps erected on the field. It was then formed up, when the Prince made a most flattering and inspiriting address in English. On returning to barracks Prince William honoured the officers by taking luncheon with them. A short time afterwards His Imperial Highness sent a portrait of himself in the uniform of the Hussars of the Guard to Colonel Liddell, with his autograph and the following words written below:—
"In remembrance of the 25th of June, spent with the 10th Prince of Wales's Own Hussars at Hounslow, 1887."

At the end of June orders were received for the Tenth to proceed to Aldershot to take part in the Jubilee review of the troops by Her Majesty the Queen in the Long Valley. On the 3rd July the Kensington detachment, under the Earl of Airlie, arrived at Hounslow in order to proceed with the regiment, and on

---

[1] Afterwards Emperor of Germany.

the 5th the head-quarters, under Colonel Liddell, and the Hampton Court detachment, under Lieutenant-Colonel Gough, marched to Farnborough and encamped on the Swan Plateau on Cove Common. On the 7th the Tenth marched out of camp to Brookwood and formed part of a force under Sir Baker Russell marching in from Guildford, having orders to attack the remainder of the troops encamped at Aldershot, under the command of Sir Drury Lowe. A cavalry sham fight took place on the Fox Hills, but the infantry did not come into contact.

On the 9th July the 10th Hussars took part in the Jubilee review before Her Majesty the Queen in the Long Valley. About 48,000 troops of all arms were present. The cavalry regiments consisted of two squadrons 1st Life Guards, two squadrons 2nd Life Guards, the Royal Horse Guards, the Royal Dragoons, the Royal Scots Greys, the 5th Lancers, the 10th Royal Hussars, the 18th Hussars, the 21st Hussars. Detachments of the 14th and 20th Hussars kept the ground, and two squadrons of the Oxford Yeomanry (Lord Valentia, late 10th Hussars, being present with them), the Hampshire Yeomanry, under command of Colonel the Hon. H. L. Crichton, late 10th Hussars, also took part in the proceedings. Field-Marshal His Royal Highness the Prince of Wales, K.G., marched past the Queen at the head of the 10th Hussars, Prince Albert Victor commanding the right troop of the leading squadron.

On the 12th July the Tenth broke up its camp on Cove Common and marched back to its quarters at Hounslow, Hampton Court, and Kensington. On the 30th July the head-quarters and detachments marched to Wormwood Scrubs to take part in a brigade field day with the 1st and 2nd Life Guards and B-B Royal Horse Artillery, for the inspection of H.R.H. the Duke

of Cambridge. On this occasion the brigade was commanded by Colonel R. S. Liddell.

On the 2nd and 3rd August Major-General Sir
Drury Lowe, Inspector-General of Cavalry, made his
annual inspection of the Tenth.

At this time an invitation was received from the
Emperor of Germany for the commanding officers of
the four regiments which had been inspected by His
Imperial Highness Prince William of Prussia during his
recent visit to England to proceed to Berlin. In conformity with this, Colonel the Hon. R. Talbot, commanding 1st Life Guards, Colonel R. S. Liddell, commanding
10th Royal Hussars, Colonel Stracey, commanding Scots
Fusilier Guards, and Colonel Slade, commanding Rifle
Brigade, left for Germany on the 9th August. On
arrival at Berlin, Colonels Liddell and Talbot received
an intimation from Prince William of Prussia to proceed
at once to Potsdam, and join the regiment under His Imperial Highness's command, the Hussars of the Guard.
These officers were received in the most hospitable and
courteous manner, and for three weeks lived as members of this distinguished regiment and attended all
the regimental, brigade, and divisional drills that took
place. At most of these the Emperor William I. was
present himself.

On the occasion of this visit, by desire of H.R.H.
the Prince of Wales a Nordenfelt machine-gun on a
galloping carriage of the same pattern as the one used
by the 10th Hussars was sent as a present from England
to Prince William of Prussia. Corporal Hustler,[1] 10th
Hussars, was sent in charge of the gun, and had the
honour of explaining its use to the Emperor William I.
and Prince William. The gun afterwards accompanied
the Hussars of the Guard throughout the manœuvres.

---

[1] Afterwards Troop Sergeant-Major Hustler.

Private Tritton, 10th Hussars, accompanied Colonel Liddell on this visit.

Major the Hon. J. Napier was appointed Brigade-Major on the Staff at Shorncliffe, and Lieutenant the Hon. Herbert T. Allsopp was promoted to be captain, dated the 11th July, 1887. Mr. Cameron Barclay was appointed to the regiment, *vice* Lieutenant Lord Alwyne Compton retired, and Lord Southampton in succession to the Hon. H. Allsopp.

At this time a new busby of a lower and lighter pattern, with all the ornaments on it of a smaller size, was tried in the regiment. It met with so much approval that the pattern was adopted for all hussars and horse artillery in Army Orders of February 1888.

On the 13th September, Colonel R. S. Liddell, having completed six years as regimental lieutenant-colonel, was placed on half-pay in conformity with the Royal Warrant of 1881.[1] Colonel Robert Spencer Liddell entered the army as an ensign in the 15th Foot on the 28th March, 1858, and in November 1860 exchanged as a lieutenant into the 10th Hussars. He was promoted to be captain in that regiment on the 2nd May, 1868 ; major on the 1st July, 1881 ; and lieutenant-colonel and second in command on the 13th September following ; colonel in the army in 1885. On the 1st April, 1886, he succeeded to the command of the Tenth. Colonel Liddell was employed on the Staff as A.D.C. and interpreter to the Commander-in-Chief in Bombay from 27th August, 1869, to June 1872, and as Military Secretary from June 1872 to October 1874 ; Adjutant 1st West York Yeomanry, from 1875 to 1876. On the 12th July, 1876, he was appointed Adjutant of the Cavalry Depôt, Canterbury,

---

[1] This Warrant was now altered, the command of a regiment being fixed at four years, with the power of extending it, the senior major to be the second in command.

and held this post until July 1880, when he rejoined
his regiment in India. He accompanied the Tenth on
its return from India in 1884, and took part with it
in the various operations in the Eastern Soudan. On
Colonel E. A. Wood being appointed to command the
Cavalry Brigade, Colonel Liddell assumed command of
the regiment until the arrival of Sir Herbert Stewart
from England. He received the medal and clasp for El
Teb and Tamaii, the bronze star, and Third Class of the
Order of the Medjidieh. He was mentioned in despatches. In the autumn of 1878 he was ordered to
France to attend the manœuvres of the 6th and 7th
Corps d'Armée, and afterwards the review of the 4th
Army Corps under Marshal MacMahon at Vincennes.
In August 1882 he proceeded, with General Sir Frede-
rick Haines, to St. Petersburg, and was present at the
manœuvres at Krasnoe Selo, which took place in the
presence of the Emperor of Russia. On the 19th March,
1886, he had the honour of accompanying H.R.H. the
Prince of Wales to Berlin in order to be present at the
celebration of the ninetieth birthday of the Emperor
William I. In August 1887, on the invitation of the
Emperor of Germany, Colonel Liddell went to Potsdam,
and was attached for three weeks to the Hussars of the
Guard, commanded by His Imperial Highness Prince
William of Prussia, and witnessed the regimental, brigade, and divisional drills of the Cavalry of the Guard.
On the 13th September Colonel Liddell was placed on
half-pay. After remaining on half-pay until the 8th
June, 1889, he was appointed to the command of the
23rd Regimental District. In September 1890 he com-
manded a brigade at the cavalry manœuvres on the
Berkshire Downs.

CHAPTER L

VISCOUNT DOWNE APPOINTED TO COMMAND—INSPECTION BY H.R.H.
THE DUKE OF CAMBRIDGE—THE REGIMENT MARCHES TO YORK—
VISIT OF H.R.H. THE PRINCE OF WALES

1887 ON the 13th September Lieutenant-Colonel Viscount
Downe, C.S.I., was appointed to command the regiment.
Lord Downe entered the army as a cornet in the 2nd
Life Guards in August 1865, and served with that regi-
ment until he was placed on half-pay as a lieutenant-
colonel in 1886. He was appointed second in command
of the 2nd Dragoon Guards, and exchanged into the
10th Hussars in the same year. He served in the
South African campaign in 1879—the Zulu campaign;
was A.D.C. to Major-General Fred Marshall (late 10th
Hussars and 2nd Life Guards), commanding Cavalry
Brigade, Cape of Good Hope; served in Bengal as
A.D.C. to Major-General H.R.H. the Duke of Connaught
from 1883 to 1885. He received the Companion of the
Star of India.

On the 9th November Captain Greenwood, Lieutenant Hughes-Onslow, Lieutenant E. Baird, and 126
men, under command of Major Manners Wood, marched
to London, and took part in the Lord Mayor's procession, returning to Hounslow in the evening.

The regimental changes in 1887 were :—Retirements—Lieutenant Lord A. F. Compton; Lieutenant-
Colonel and Colonel R. S. Liddell to half-pay. Appoint-

ments—Lieutenant-Colonel Viscount Downe, C.S.I., to command the regiment ; Lieutenant the Hon. George Bryan to be captain ; Lord W. A. Cavendish-Bentinck, Gentleman Cadet C. Barclay, and Gentleman Cadet Lord Southampton to be second lieutenants.

On the 19th January, much to the regret of the whole regiment, Lieutenant F. R. Bowlby died in London. He had had a serious attack of rheumatic fever, but was recovering when he caught a chill and died. He was a promising young officer, a good horseman, and fine polo player. On the 14th March Ridingmaster and Honorary Captain J. Perry retired, and was succeeded some months later by Captain Kelly, Ridingmaster of the 5th, and formerly of the 9th Lancers.

On the 6th April the 10th Hussars was inspected on Hounslow Heath by H.R.H. the Duke of Cambridge, Commander-in-Chief of the Army. The detachments from Hampton Court and Kensington attended. His Royal Highness afterwards took luncheon with the officers.

At the Grand Military Meeting held at Sandown Park in April of this year the Tenth was particularly fortunate. The winner of the Gold Cup, Mr. Fenwick's Bertha, was ridden by Mr. Hughes-Onslow (10th Hussars). The Hunters' Flat Race was won by Mr. Kavanagh's (10th Hussars) Silverwood, ridden by owner ; the United Service Hunters' Plate by Captain Fisher's (10th Hussars) Meerschaum, ridden by Mr. Hughes-Onslow ; the Grand Military Hunters' Hurdle Race by Mr. Baird's (10th Hussars) Playfair, ridden by owner. The regiment also had the satisfaction of winning the Grand National Race at Liverpool this year, Lieutenant Baird's horse Playfair coming in first.

Orders were received in the spring of this year for the Tenth to prepare to change its quarters, and on the 9th April the head-quarters, with A and E troops, under command of Lieutenant-Colonel Viscount Downe, proceeded to York. The route taken was by High Wycombe, Aylesbury, Stony-Stratford, Northampton, Market Harborough, Leicester, Nottingham, Mansfield, Worksop, Doncaster, and Pontefract. On the same day the second squadron, under Captain Fisher, and on the 16th the third squadron (F and G troops), under command of Captain C. Greenwood, marched by Edmonton, Ware, Peterborough, Grantham, Retford, Doncaster, and Selby. On the 21st the Kensington detachment marched to Hampton Court, under Lieutenant the Hon. A. Lawley, and on the 23rd marched with B and D troops, under the command of Major Manners Wood, *viâ* Maidenhead, Aylesbury, &c., and the whole regiment was assembled at York on the 4th May. On the march the head-quarters were entertained on the 18th by the Duke of Portland at Welbeck Abbey, and afterwards marched through Sherwood Forest, the park, and the subterranean passages which lead from the Abbey to Worksop.

Twenty-five years had elapsed since the 10th Hussars had been quartered at York, and not one officer, non-commissioned officer, or private soldier was now in the regiment who had been in it at that time.

On the 5th May the Tenth was inspected by Major-General C. Daniell, C.B., commanding the Northern District. On the 17th May the establishment was reduced to twenty-four officers, two Warrant officers, 443 non-commissioned officers and men, and 290 horses.

Major-General Sir Drury Lowe, Inspector-General of Cavalry, made his inspection in the field and in barracks on the 8th and 9th August, and on the 25th September H.R.H. the Duke of Cambridge paid a visit to York and inspected the garrison on Knavesmire. He afterwards did the officers of the Tenth the honour of

taking luncheon with them. In the afternoon he saw a
party of non-commissioned officers and men ride over
the jumps that had lately been put up in a field attached
to the barracks, and also saw the many improvements
carried out by the regiment, such as gardens for the
canteen, kitchen gardens for the non-commissioned officers and men, &c.

Captain the Hon. Alwyne Greville, 60th Rifles, who
had up to this time been Equerry to H.R.H. Prince Albert

Victor, much to the regret of the 10th Hussars, retired
from this position, and was succeeded by Captain George
Holford, 1st Life Guards.

During this summer the Tenth took part in the field
days held at Strensall Camp, near York, where regiments of infantry were encamped for the drill season.
It was also present at the inspection of the Volunteers by Major-General Daniell which was held there.

The cricket season this year was a most successful
one for the regiment. Twelve matches were played,
and it was victorious in all. The Tenth was very for-

tunate, when stationed at York, in having amongst its players Captain the Hon. H. Allsopp, who had been in the Cambridge University Eleven, Mr. Hughes-Onslow in the Eton Eleven, Captain Fisher twelfth man of the Harrow Eleven, besides other excellent players, such as Captain Greenwood and Captain Harvey, the Hon. A. Lawley and Lieutenant Baird. In addition to this a large number of matches were made between the various troops, and the cricket ground in barracks, upon which great care had been bestowed, was in daily occupation by the cricketers. The following year a great addition to the cricketing strength took place on Lord George Scott being gazetted. He had been in the Oxford University Eleven, and had also played for the Gentlemen of England. Later on another addition was made by Mr. Brand being appointed. He had been captain of the Eton Eleven.

The regimental changes in 1888 were :—Death— Lieutenant F. R. Bowlby. Retirement—Hon. Captain and Ridingmaster J. Perry. Transfer—Captain and Ridingmaster P. Kelly, from 5th Lancers, to be riding-master. Appointment—B. C. C. S. Meeking to be second lieutenant.

At the commencement of this year a fund was raised by the British Army to perpetuate the memory of General Valentine Baker by presenting a sum of money to the Gordon Boys' Home and erecting a tablet in the church at Cairo. In response to this the Committee of the Home granted to the 10th Hussars a permanent nomination for a boy in this institution. On the 14th February the following memorandum was received from the chairman of the Committee :—

In consideration of the sum of 350*l*., received from the 10th Royal Hussars, through the hands of General Sir Frederick Stephenson, together with an assurance made by him on behalf of the regiment that a further capital sum of 50*l.* should be added to this fund . . . the Committee hereby grant a perpetual nomination to the Gordon Boys' Home to the 10th Royal Hussars under the conditions set forth in paragraph (*c*) rule 48, page 16, edition 1889, the said condition being modified and extended by special vote of Committee passed on the 14th February, 1889— viz. "the nomination of the officer in command of the 10th Royal Hussars for the time being will be accepted."

(Signed)   G. W. HIGGINSON, Lieutenant-General,
Vice-Chairman of Committee.

On the 16th March Captain Charles Greenwood retired from the service, receiving a gratuity for twelve years' service.

On the 18th March Field-Marshal His Royal Highness the Prince of Wales, accompanied by Lieutenant-General Sir Dighton Probyn and Major-General Arthur Ellis, C.S.I., arrived in York and assumed command of the 10th Hussars. During his visit he took up his quarters in barracks. To meet His Royal Highness the four late commanding officers of the regiment were invited to York—viz. Colonel the Hon. C. C. Molyneux, Colonel Lord Ralph Kerr, C.B., Colonel E. A. Wood, C.B., and Colonel R. S. Liddell. On the 19th the Prince inspected the Tenth, under Lieutenant-Colonel Viscount Downe, on Knavesmire, and afterwards marched at its head on its return to barracks. On the 20th His Royal Highness inspected the troop stables, barrack-rooms, and institutions, afterwards attending the regimental point to point race, which took place near Marston, some six miles from York. Mr. Hughes-Onslow won the race. H.R.H. Prince Albert Victor rode his own horse and came in fourth. On the 21st the Prince of Wales's visit terminated, and he left York, after expressing in orders his satisfaction at the state in which he found the regiment. On the 26th March Lieutenant Harvey

Alexander was promoted to be captain, *vice* Greenwood, retired ; Lieutenant Kavanagh was placed on
the Seconded List for service as Aide-de-Camp to the
Governor of Jamaica. On the 27th March Lord George
Scott was gazetted as a second lieutenant in the regiment. On the 21st May Brevet-Major the Earl of Airlie
was seconded for service as Adjutant of Yeomanry
Cavalry. On the 23rd May H.R.H. Prince Albert Victor
of Wales was promoted to be major in the regiment in
excess of the establishment. On the 8th June Mr. A.
Farquharson of Invercauld was appointed to the regiment, and on 30th July Lieutenant Charles Harvey was
promoted to be captain, *vice* the Earl of Airlie.

On the 10th August Colonel H. S. Gough was
selected to command the 18th Hussars. He joined that
regiment, and proceeded with it in the autumn to India.
Colonel Gough entered the 10th Hussars as cornet on
the 2nd May, 1868, and was promoted lieutenant in
1871. He embarked for India with it in 1873, and
was appointed Adjutant in December of the same year.
He was promoted to be captain in 1875, and in the
following year was appointed Aide-de-Camp to Sir
Frederick Haines, Commander-in-Chief in India. While
holding this appointment he was present during the
Afghan war of 1878–9 at the assault on Ali Musjid,
for which he received the medal and clasp. Captain
Gough rejoined from the Staff in 1881, and was promoted major on the 13th September. In 1884 he embarked at Bombay with the Tenth, and was present
with it throughout the campaign in the Eastern Soudan,
for which he received the medal and clasp for El Teb
and Tamaii, the bronze star, a brevet majority, and
was mentioned in despatches on the 27th March and
6th May. He was employed in the Bechuanaland expedition under Sir Charles Warren in 1884–5, and raised

a regiment called the Diamond Fields Horse. For this he was honourably mentioned and received the C.M.G. On the 21st May, 1884, he was promoted to be a brevet lieutenant-colonel, and in 1888 colonel. In 1876 he accompanied H.R.H. the Prince of Wales as orderly officer on his return journey from India to England. In the autumn of 1889 he proceeded to India in command of the 18th Hussars.

On the 22nd and 23rd August Sir Drury Lowe made his annual inspection of the 10th Hussars.

On the 28th Brevet Lieutenant-Colonel J. P. Brabazon was appointed Aide-de-Camp to Her Majesty the Queen, and to have the rank of brevet colonel. Lieutenant the Hon. A. Lawley was promoted to be captain, *vice* Brabazon, promoted regimental major in succession to Colonel Gough.

During this summer some excellent cricket matches were held, in many of which the Tenth was successful, and the game was again well supported by the troops in barracks. The non-commissioned officers and men were also permitted to go on the river in fatigue dress, the result being that several very good four-oars appeared, and the various troops competed with each other on the Ouse. The White Rose Rowing Club offered a prize, in which four troop boats competed, and an exciting race was won by E troop.

On the 19th September the 6th Dragoon Guards (the Carabiniers) marched into York from Leeds, and was accommodated in the Tenth barracks. On the 21st the two regiments were inspected by H.R.H. the Duke of Cambridge on Knavesmire; Colonel Duncombe, Inspector of Yeomanry Cavalry, being in command of the brigade. After the review the Carabiniers were entertained by the Tenth on the ground, and then marched back to Leeds. His Royal Highness returned to York

1889 Barracks and did the officers the honour of taking luncheon with them.

Major H.R.H. Prince Albert Victor proceeded on leave of absence for a lengthened tour in the East, and after visiting Greece continued his journey to India, in which country he passed the winter. Captain C. B. Harvey, 10th Hussars, and Captain George Holford, 1st Life Guards, had the honour of accompanying His Royal Highness on this tour.

The regimental changes in 1889 were :—Retirement—Captain C. Greenwood. Appointments—A. Farquharson, Lord G. W. M. D. Scott, and T. W. Brand, to be second lieutenants.

1890 The regimental changes in 1890 were :—Retirement—Captain the Hon. H. T. Allsopp. Appointments—A. W. Waite to be ridingmaster; Gentlemen Cadets the Earl of Shaftesbury and· Caryl R. Molyneux to be second lieutenants.

*   *   *   *   *

The period is now reached at which it has been decided to close these memoirs. The regiment is still full of vitality, and each day may add something to its history worthy of record. It must be left to its present members and those who may succeed them to see that no incident of its daily life is allowed to pass unnoted; so that the future chronicler may find it an easy task to carry on what has been here attempted.

APPENDIX I

Regimental Staff

Colonels

	Appointed		Appointed
Humphrey Gore . .	. 1715	H.R.H. George Augustus	
Charles Churchill .	. 1723	Frederick, Prince of Wales	1796
Richard Viscount Cobham	. 1745	The Marquis of Londonderry	1820
Sir Charles Mordaunt .	. 1749	The Earl Beauchamp .	. 1843
Sir William Augustus Pitt	. 1780	H.R.H. Albert Edward, Prince	
		of Wales . . .	. 1863

Lieutenant-Colonels Commanding Regiment

	Appointed		Appointed
Peter Hawker . .	. 1715	Henry Wyndham . .	. 1822
Charles Powlett . .	. 1720	Lord Thomas Cecil .	. 1833
Philip Gery . . .	. 1733	John Vandeleur . .	. 1838
Anthony Lamelonière .	. 1737	H. F. Bonham . .	. 1847
John Jordaine . .	. 1741	W. Parlby . . .	. 1852
Henry Whitley . .	. 1748	John Wilkie . . .	. 1856
William Pitt . . .	. 1759	Valentine Baker . .	. 1859
T. Osbert Mordaunt .	. 1770	The Hon. C. C. Molyneux	. 1873
William Newton . .	. 1786	Lord Ralph Kerr . .	. 1876
William Cartwright .	. 1794	Edward A. Wood . .	. 1881
George Leigh . .	. 1804	Robert S. Liddell . .	. 1886
George Quentin . .	. 1810	Viscount Downe . .	. 1887

Adjutants

	Appointed		Appointed
T. Carver . . .	. 1739	Percy J. Smith . .	. 1850
D. Bell	. 1743	John Rawlinson Cuthbert	. 1855
B. Knigge . . .	. 1755	John Fife . . .	. 1857
R. Brickenden . .	. 1765	Lord Ralph Kerr . .	. 1859
Thomas Lewis . .	. 1768	Owen R. Slacke . .	. 1861
Peter Shadwell . .	. 1784	John Cecil Russell . .	. 1864
J. McDermot . .	. 1794	Hon. Henry L. Crichton	. 1868
T. Souter . . .	. 1800	Hugh S. Gough . .	. 1873
T. Smith . . .	. 1805	R. F. P. Startin . .	. 1875
H. Duperries . .	. 1808	Hon. C. W. Cavendish .	. 1875
S. Bromley . . .	. 1811	C. Sandes . . .	. 1877
S. Hardman . . .	. 1814	The Earl of Airlie . .	. 1882
S. Wells . . .	. 1816	Lord Alwyne Compton .	. 1884
James Preston . .	. 1826	The Hon. Julian Byng .	. 1886
Sir James Baird . .	. 1835	The Hon. A. Lawley .	. 1890
George Webb . .	. 1839		

Quartermasters

J. C. McClellan . .	. 1825	William King . .	. 1872
John Fenn . . .	. 1846	A. E. Poole . . .	. 1882
John Hill James . .	. 1860		

Regimental Sergeant-Majors

Henry Ash . . .	. 1825	Benjamin Rickards .	. 1861
Thomas Cross . .	. 1831	William King . .	. 1866
Robert Clements . .	. 1845	Thomas Stuart . .	. 1872
John Fenn . . .	. 1846	James Marsland . .	. 1881
Richard Peck . .	. 1846	F. Bradshaw . . .	. 1882
William Draycott . .	. 1851	John Crisp . . .	. 1886
Charles Hickman . .	. 1854		

OFFICERS APPOINTED FROM THE FORMATION OF THE REGIMENT IN 1715 TILL THE PUBLICATION OF THE ANNUAL ARMY LISTS IN 1754

NAME	APPOINTED	DATE	REMARKS
Brigadier Humphry Gore	Colonel . .	22nd July, 1715	Appointed Col. of the Royal Regiment of Dragoons 12th Jan., 1722
Col. Peter Hawker .	Lieut.-Colonel .	22nd July, 1715	Resigned 8th March, 1719
Major Paston Knyvet	Major . .	22nd July, 1715	Succeeded 5th Sept., 1717
Balthazar Guidet .	Captain . .	22nd July, 1715	Resigned 25th Dec., 1717
George Treby . .	Captain . .	22nd July, 1715	Transferred to 1st Foot Guards 16th Jan., 1719
John Wittewrong .	Captain . .	22nd July, 1715	Half-pay 12th Dec., 1718
Israel Presley . .	Capt.-Lieut. .	22nd July, 1715	Resigned 1st Jan., 1723
Robert Blount. .	Lieutenant .	22nd July, 1715	Succeeded 2nd July, 1717
John Jordain . .	Lieutenant . Capt.-Lieut. . Captain . . Major . . Lieut.-Colonel .	22nd July, 1715 1st Jan., 1723 21st May, 1733 11th Dec., 1739 4th Feb., 1740	Appointed Colonel of a Regiment of Marines 15th March, 1747
Henry Courtney .	Lieutenant . Captain . .	22nd July, 1715 1st Jan., 1719	Succeeded 12th July, 1723
Henry Gore . .	Lieutenant .	22nd July, 1715	Lieut. Royal Regiment of Dragoons 3rd Oct., 1732; Capt.-Lieut. in Royal Regiment of Dragoons 19th Dec., 1738
Andrew Purcell .	Lieutenant .	22nd July, 1715	Half-pay, late Fielding's Regiment of Foot, 25th December, 1721
Peter Chaban . .	Cornet . . Lieutenant . Capt.-Lieut. . Captain . . Major . .	22nd July, 1715 1st Jan., 1719 3rd Nov., 1735 25th Aug., 1739 31st Aug., 1744	Retired on his pay as Major 28th Jan., 1755
William Prosser .	Cornet . . Lieutenant .	22nd July, 1715 26th Jan., 1721	Died. Succeeded 24th July, 1724
Thomas Crawley .	Cornet . .	22nd July, 1715	Half-pay (late Rook's) 1st Nov., 1718

OFFICERS APPOINTED FROM 1715 TO 1754—*continued*

NAME	APPOINTED	DATE	REMARKS
Thomas Hincks	Cornet	22nd July, 1715	Transferred to Otway's Foot 24th March, 1720
William Stannus	Cornet	22nd July, 1715	Resigned 10th Sept., 1722
Francis Boucher	Cornet	22nd July, 1715	—
Josiah Hort	Chaplain	22nd July, 1715	Resigned 1st May, 1721
Robert Walkinshaw	Surgeon	22nd July, 1715	Succeeded 17th March, 1726
Lieut. Peter Bradshaw, from half-pay, late Lt.-Gen. Stanhope's Dragoons	Lieutenant	2nd July, 1717	Exchanged to half-pay 19th Aug., 1726
Major T. Croasdale, from half-pay of Major-General Rook's late Regiment of Foot	Major	5th Sept., 1717	Succeeded 1st Jan., 1719
Cornet Philip Gery	Captain	25th Dec., 1717	Died. Succeeded 9th July, 1737
	Major	1st Jan., 1719	
	Lieut.-Colonel	21st May, 1733	
Ensign Godfrey Shipway, from half-pay of Major-Gen. Rook's late Regiment of Foot	Cornet	1st Nov., 1718	—
	Lieut.	24th Feb., 1728	
Capt. Samuel Woodward, from half-pay of Col. Maurice Nassau's late Regiment of Foot	Captain	12th Dec., 1718	Succeeded 12th July, 1723
Capt. Walter Molesworth, from half-pay	Captain	16th Jan., 1719	Half-pay 22nd May, 1730
Barrett Bowen	Cornet	7th March, 1719	Resigned 8th Dec., 1722
Major Charles Powlett, from Lord Mark Kerr's Regiment of Foot	Lieut.-Colonel	8th March, 1719	Appointed Lieut. and Lieut.-Col. 1st Troop of Horse Guards 3rd April, 1733
George Buckley	Cornet	24th March, 1720	Half-pay of Churchill's Marines 1st June, 1750
(*vice* Jordan)	Lieutenant	1st Jan., 1723	
(*vice* Chaban)	Capt.-Lieut.	25th Aug., 1739	
(*vice* Jekyll)	Captain	25th April, 1741	
William Cross	Chaplain	1st May, 1721	Resigned 2nd Feb., 1721
Capt. Mathew Fitz-Gerald, from half-pay of Col. Fielding's late Regiment of Foot	Lieutenant	25th Jan., 1721	Resigned 26th Jan., 1721

OFFICERS APPOINTED FROM 1715 TO 1754—*continued*

NAME	APPOINTED	DATE	REMARKS
James Manwaring .	Cornet . .	26th Jan., 1721	—
Daniel Soyer . .	Chaplain . .	2nd Feb., 1721	Succeeded 28th Oct., 1737
Charles Burroughs .	Cornet . .	10th Sept., 1722	Exchanged to Brig.-Gen. Napier's Regt. of Horse 6th May, 1725
John Graham . .	Cornet . .	8th Dec., 1722	Half-pay. Appointed from half-pay to be Lieut. to Maj.-Gen. Hunter's Independent Company of Foot in Jamaica 10th May, 1732
Col. Charles Churchill	Colonel . .	12th Jan., 1722	Died. Succeeded 1st June, 1745
John Whitworth .	Captain . .	12th July, 1723	Died. Succeeded 3rd Nov., 1735
William Elliott .	Captain . .	12th July, 1723	Appointed Major 2nd Troop of Horse Grenadier Guards 13th July, 1737
Robert Walkinshaw	Cornet . .	29th July, 1723	Retired 19th March, 1740
	Lieutenant .	21st May, 1733	
Edward Cater . .	Cornet . .	1st Jan., 1723	Died. Succeeded 29th April, 1725
Lieut. Thos. Jekyll, from Brig. Grove's Regt. of Foot	Lieutenant .	24th July, 1724	Died. Succeeded 31st Aug., 1744
	Capt.-Lieut. .	21st May, 1733	
	Captain . .	3rd Nov., 1735	
	Major . .	24th Feb., 1740	
Ensign Arthur Maynwaring, from Col. Cotton's Regt. of Foot	Cornet . .	29th April, 1725	Half-pay. Captain in Harrison's Regt. 25th June, 1736
Cornet Thos. Bloodworth, from Brig. Napier's Regt. of Horse in Ireland	Cornet . .	6th May, 1725	Capt. Royal Regiment of Fusiliers, commanded by Lord Tyrawley, 26th Dec., 1726
Edward Goddard .	Cornet . .	17th Aug., 1725	Retires on Capt. Pitt's half-pay (late Dejean's) 12th June, 1749
	Lieutenant .	3rd Nov., 1735	
	Capt.-Lieut. .	14th July, 1743	
	Captain . .	31st Aug., 1744	
Lieut. Thomas Bruce, from the half-pay of Col. Foissac's Regiment of Dragoons	Lieutenant .	19th Aug., 1726	Half-pay 25th Sept., 1731
Peregrine Lascelles .	Captain . .	25th Dec., 1726	Half-pay. Capt.-Lieut. 1st Foot Guards 5th June, 1731

OFFICERS APPOINTED FROM 1715 TO 1754—*continued*

NAME	APPOINTED	DATE	REMARKS
Francis Thompson .	Captain . .	25th Dec., 1726	Appointed Lieut.-Col. in Col. Wm. Robinson's Regt. of Marines 24th Nov., 1739
	Do., half-pay		
	Captain . .	22nd May, 1730	
	Major . .	21st May, 1733	
William Gee . .	Captain . .	25th Dec., 1726	Appointed Captain in Ligonier's Regt. of Horse 10th May, 1731
Charles Hamilton .	Lieutenant .	25th Dec., 1726	Retired on the half-pay and "en second" pay of Lieut. Davenport, late 2nd Troop of Horse Guards, 2nd March, 1754
	Do., half-pay		
	Lieutenant .	25th Sept., 1731	
	Capt.-Lieut. .	25th April, 1741	
	Captain . .	14th July, 1743	
Richard Lucas .	Lieutenant .	25th Dec., 1726	Transferred to Wade's Horse 24th Feb., 1728
Edward Meadows .	Lieutenant .	25th Dec., 1726	Died. Succeeded 29th Oct., 1736
Edward Draper .	Cornet . .	25th Dec., 1726	Transferred to His Majesty's Own Regt. of Horse (1st Dragoon Guards) 2nd August, 1734
Philip Meadows .	Cornet . .	25th Dec., 1726	—
Francis Scott (commonly called Viscount Hermitage)	Cornet . .	25th Dec., 1726	Transferred to Queen's Own Royal Regt. of Horse (2nd Dragoon Gds.) 28th Dec. 1727
Ensign David Chapeau, from Col. Harrison's Regt.	Cornet . .	25th Dec., 1726	Half-pay 13th April, 1732
Samuel Aubery .	Surgeon . .	17th Mar., 1726	Resigned 26th Nov. 1751
Gilbert White . .	Cornet . .	29th Dec., 1727	Transferred to Queen's Own Royal Regt. of Horse, dated 1st Jan., 1728–9
Robert Campbell .	Cornet . .	12th Mar., 1728	Half-pay 8th Nov., 1732
Ensign Philip Townshend	Cornet . .	29th Mar., 1729	—
Cornet Chas. Churchill, from Col. Cathcart's Regt. of Dragoons in Ireland	Cornet . .	13th April, 1732	Transferred to Coldstream Guards, 3rd Jan., 1738
	Lieut., *vice* E. Meadows	29th Oct., 1736	
Cornet Chas. Draper, from the half-pay of Major - Gen. Honywood's Regt. of Dragoons	Cornet . .	8th Nov., 1732	Capt. Independent Company at Hull 5th Jan., 1754
	Lieutenant, *vice* Churchill	15th Feb. 1738	
	Capt.-Lieut., *vice* Goddard	31st Aug., 1744	

OFFICERS APPOINTED FROM 1715 TO 1754—*continued*

NAME	APPOINTED	DATE	REMARKS
Quartermaster Richard Philips	Cornet . .	21st May, 1733	Half-pay Tatton's Foot, 1st February, 1743
	Lieutenant .	25th Aug., 1739	
Cornet Samuel Medland, from Col. Nevill's Regt. of Dragoons in Ireland	Cornet . .	2nd Aug., 1734	Succeeded 12th Mar., 1738
Quartermaster John Tempest, from Royal Regt. of Horse Guards	Cornet . .	5th July, 1735	Incapable of service 26th Aug., 1746
	Lieutenant .	19th Mar., 1740	
Quartermaster Sam. Gowland	Cornet . .	3rd Nov., 1735	Refuses to serve 26th Aug., 1746
	Lieutenant .	25th April, 1741	
Thos. Mathews .	Cornet . .	29th Oct., 1736	Appointed Capt. in Col. D. Houghton's Regt. of Foot 26th January, 1740
Major Anth. Lamelonière, from 2nd Troop of Horse Grenadier Guards	Lieut.-Col. .	9th July, 1737	Appointed Lieut.-Col. and Second Lieut. 3rd Troop of Horse Guards 17th March, 1740
Lord Charles Fitzroy, from Ensign 1st Foot Guards	Captain . .	13th July, 1737	Died. Succeeded 25th Aug., 1739
Robert Hitch . .	Chaplain . .	28th Oct., 1737	Died. Succeeded 3rd Feb., 1741
Thos. Carver . .	Cornet . .	15th Feb., 1738	Succeeded as Lieut., being incapable of .service, 26th Aug., 1746
	Adjutant . .	17th Mar., 1739	
	Lieutenant .	14th July, 1743	
Robert Winde . .	Cornet . .	12th Mar., 1738	Capt. in Hawley's Dragoons 31st Oct., 1751
	Lieutenant .	1st Feb., 1743	
Quartermaster Christopher Buckhard Reyhlin	Cornet . .	25th Aug., 1739	—
Cornet the Earl of Hume, from the Queen's Regt. of Horse	Captain . .	10th May, 1740	Appointed Capt.-Lieut. 3rd Regt. of Guards 13th April, 1743
Edward Harvey .	Cornet . .	19th Mar., 1740	Capt. Queen's Regt. of Dragoons (Sir John Cope's) 6th Feb., 1746
	Lieutenant .	31st Aug., 1744	
David Bell . .	Cornet . .	12th Aug., 1741	—
	Adjutant . .	20th Jan., 1743	
	Lieutenant .	26th Aug., 1746	
	Capt.-Lieut. .	28th Jan., 1755	

OFFICERS APPOINTED FROM 1715 TO 1754 —*continued*

NAME	APPOINTED	DATE	REMARKS
Thomas Martin	Cornet, *vice* Mathews	12th Aug., 1741	Died. Succeeded 30th Oct., 1741
William Beckwith	Cornet	30th Oct., 1741	Retired. 3rd March, 1747
	Lieutenant	26th Aug., 1746	
Horace Hamond	Chaplain	3rd Feb., 1741	—
Quartermaster Jas. Lister	Cornet	10th May, 1742	—
Samuel Carter	Cornet	14th July, 1743	—
	Lieutenant	26th Aug., 1746	
William Augustus Pitt	Cornet	1st Feb., 1743	—
	Lieutenant	28th Feb., 1746	
	Capt., Dejean's Regt.	16th April, 1748	
	Capt., hf.-pay, do.	25th Dec., 1748	
	Capt., 10th Dragoons	12th June, 1749	
	Major, do.	28th Jan., 1755	
Quartermaster Robert Atkinson	Cornet	31st Aug., 1744	—
	Lieutenant	5th Mar., 1750	
Field-Marshal Richd. Lord Cobham	Colonel	1st June, 1745	Died. Succeeded 1st Nov., 1749
Michael Greenhow	Cornet	30th July, 1745	Retired on half-pay 25th Feb., 1748
Purbeck Langham	Cornet	5th Sept., 1746	Capt. 2nd Dragoon Guards 25th Jan., 1750
	Lieutenant	3rd Mar., 1747	
Henry Buckston	Cornet	12th Dec., 1746	Retired 21st April, 1753
	Lieutenant	1st Dec., 1748	
John Palmer Boteler	Cornet	9th Jan., 1746	Retired on Cornet Tryon's half-pay 22nd May, 1749
— Ferguson	Cornet	28th Feb., 1746	—
Second Lieut. John Vaughan, from Paulet's	Cornet	9th April, 1748	—
	Lieutenant	10th Dec., 1751	
	Capt.-Lieut.	5th Jan., 1754	
	Captain	28th Jan., 1755	
Major Henry Whitley, from Lieut.-Gen. Bland's Regt. of Dragoons	Lieut.-Col.	15th Mar., 1747	—
Francis Grose	Cornet	1st Dec., 1748	Retired 12th Oct., 1751
Thomas Strong Hall	Cornet	25th Feb., 1748	—
	Lieutenant	21st April, 1753	
Cornet William Tryon, late of the Duke of Cumberland's Dragoons	Cornet	22nd May, 1749	Lieut. 1st Foot Guards 12th Oct., 1751
Major-Gen. Sir John Mordaunt, K.B.	Colonel	1st Nov., 1749	—
Robert Sloper	Captain	1st June, 1750	—

OFFICERS APPOINTED FROM 1715 TO 1754—*continued*

NAME	APPOINTED	DATE	REMARKS
Thos. Reynolds .	Cornet . .	15th Sept., 1750	—
	Lieutenant .	5th Jan., 1754	
Peter Renouard .	Cornet . .	5th Mar., 1750	—
	Lieutenant .	28th Jan., 1755	
Ensign Sam. Evans, from Folliot's	Cornet . .	12th Oct., 1751	—
John Brown . .	Surgeon . .	26th Nov., 1751	—
Ensign Clement Wolseley, from Herbert's	Cornet . .	10th Dec., 1751	—
Ensign Sam. Duckinfield, from Rich's	Cornet . .	16th Jan., 1752	—
Anthony Lovebond .	Cornet . .	21st April, 1753	—
William Morrice .	Cornet . .	5th Jan., 1754	—
Lieut. Richard Davenport, from the Horse Guards	Captain . .	2nd Mar., 1754	—
— Duff . . .	Cornet . .	18th Mar., 1755	—

TENTH REGIMENT OF DRAGOONS, FROM THE PUBLICATION OF THE
FIRST ANNUAL ARMY LIST.

	1754	1755	1756
Colonel . .	Sir John Mordaunt	Sir John Mordaunt	Sir John Mordaunt
Lieut.-Col. .	Henry Whitley	Henry Whitley	Henry Whitley
Majors . .	Peter Chaban Wm. Augustus Pitt	Wm. Augustus Pitt	Robert Sloper
Captains .	Wm. Augustus Pitt Robert Sloper Richard Davenport John Vaughan	Robert Sloper Richard Davenport John Vaughan	Richard Davenport John Vaughan Samuel Carter
Capt.-Lieuts. .	John Vaughan Samuel Carter	Samuel Carter	Thos. O. Mordaunt
Lieutenants .	David Bell Samuel Carter Robert Atkinson Thos. Strong Hall Thomas Reynolds Peter Renouard Clement Wolseley	Robert Atkinson Thos. Strong Hall Thomas Reynolds Peter Renouard Clement Wolseley	Thos. Strong Hall Peter Renouard S. Duckinfield Anthony Lovebond William Morrice
Cornets . .	Peter Renouard Samuel Evans Clement Wolseley Sam. Duckinfield Anthony Lovebond William Morrice George Duff William Tancred	Samuel Evans Sam. Duckinfield Anthony Lovebond William Morrice George Duff William Tancred	George Duff William Tancred John Jones Bodo Knigge Charles Erskine LIGHT TROOP
Captain . .	—	—	Robert Atkinson
Lieutenant .	—	—	Lord Wallingford
Cornet . .	—	—	F. Caldwell
Chaplain .	Horace Hammond	Horace Hammond	Horace Hammond
Adjutant .	David Bell	Bodo Knigge	Bodo Knigge
Surgeon .	John Brown	John Brown	John Brown

TENTH REGIMENT OF DRAGOONS—*continued*

	1757	1758	1759
Colonel . .	Sir John Mordaunt	Sir John Mordaunt	Sir John Mordaunt
Lieut.-Col. .	Henry Whitley	Henry Whitley	William Aug. Pitt
Major . .	Robert Sloper	Robert Sloper	Richard Davenport
Captains .	Richard Davenport	Richard Davenport	John Vaughan
	John Vaughan	John Vaughan	Samuel Carter
	Samuel Carter	Samuel Carter	Robert Atkinson
	Robert Atkinson	Robert Atkinson	Thos. O. Mordaunt
Capt.-Lieut. .	Thos. O. Mordaunt	Thos. O. Mordaunt	Thos. Strong Hall
Lieutenants .	Thos. Strong Hall	Thos. Strong Hall	Peter Renouard
	Peter Renouard	Peter Renouard	Anthony Lovebond
	Sam. Duckinfield	Sam. Duckinfield	William Morrice
	Anthony Lovebond	Anthony Lovebond	William Tancred
	William Morrice	William Morrice	John Jones
	William Tancred	William Tancred	Henry A. Fellowes
Cornets . .	John Jones	John Jones	Bodo Knigge
	Bodo Knigge	Bodo Knigge	Frederick Caldwell
	Henry A. Fellowes	Henry A. Fellowes	Charles Erskine
	Frederick Caldwell	Frederick Caldwell	Richard Briscoe
	Charles Erskine	Charles Erskine	James Foreman
	Richard Briscoe	Richard Briscoe	Robert M. Lewis
	James Foreman	James Foreman	William Forrester (*Second Cornet*)
			Charles Henchman
Chaplain .	Horace Hammond	Horace Hammond	Horace Hammond
Adjutant .	Bodo Knigge	Bodo Knigge	Bodo Knigge
Surgeon .	John Brown	Thomas Eddington	Thomas Eddington

TENTH REGIMENT OF DRAGOONS—*continued*

	1760	1761	1762
Colonel . .	Sir John Mordaunt	Sir John Mordaunt	Sir John Mordaunt
Lieut.-Col. .	William Aug. Pitt	William Aug. Pitt	William Aug. Pitt
Major . .	Richard Davenport	George Marriott	George Marriott
Captains .	Samuel Carter	Thos. O. Mordaunt	Thos. O. Mordaunt
	Robert Atkinson	Thos. Strong Hall	Thos. Strong Hall
	Thos. O. Mordaunt	William Morrice	William Morrice
		William Tancred	William Tancred
Capt.-Lieut. .	Thos. Strong Hall	Peter Renouard	Peter Renouard
Lieutenants .	Peter Renouard	John Jones	Bodo Knigge
	William Morrice	Henry A. Fellowes	Frederick Caldwell
	William Tancred	Bodo Knigge	Charles Erskine
	John Jones	Frederick Caldwell	James Foreman
	Henry A. Fellowes	Charles Erskine	Robert M. Lewis
	Bodo Knigge	Richard Briscoe	Charles Henchman
	Frederick Caldwell	James Foreman	Montagu Wilkinson
Cornets . .	Charles Erskine	Robert M. Lewis	Richard Dayrell
	Richard Briscoe	Charles Henchman	R. Brickenden
	James Foreman	Montagu Wilkinson	Augustus Floyer
	Robert M. Lewis	Richard Dayrell	William Newton
	Charles Henchman	R. Brickenden	John Tyler
	Montagu Wilkinson	Augustus Floyer	George Harrington
	Richard Dayrell	Sir W. Fowler, Bt.	Edward Butler
		William C. Lister	
Chaplain .	Horace Hammond	Horace Hammond	Horace Hammond
Adjutant .	Bodo Knigge	Bodo Knigge	Bodo Knigge
Surgeon. .	Thomas Eddington	Henry Griffiths	Henry Griffiths

K K

TENTH REGIMENT OF DRAGOONS—*continued*

	1763	1764	1765
Colonel . .	Sir John Mordaunt	Sir John Mordaunt	Sir John Mordaunt
Lieut.-Col. .	William Aug. Pitt	William Aug. Pitt	William Aug. Pitt
Major . .	George Marriott	Thos. O. Mordaunt	Thos. O. Mordaunt
Captains .	Thos. O. Mordaunt	Thos. Strong Hall	William Morrice
	Thos. Strong Hall	William Morrice	Robert M. Lewis
	William Morrice	Robert M. Lewis	Samuel Gibbs
	W. Tancred	Samuel Gibbs	
Capt.-Lieut. . .	Frederick Caldwell	Bodo Knigge	Bodo Knigge
Lieutenants .	Bodo Knigge	Charles Erskine	Charles Erskine
	Charles Erskine	Charles Henchman	Charles Henchman
	James Foreman	R. Brickenden	R. Brickenden
	Robert M. Lewis	Richard Dayrell	Richard Dayrell
	Charles Henchman	William Gregory	William Gregory
	Montagu Wilkinson		
	Richard Brickenden		
Cornets . .	Richard Dayrell	Augustus Floyer	Augustus Floyer
	Augustus Floyer	William Newton	William Newton
	William Newton	George Harrington	George Harrington
	John Tyler	George Gould	George Gould
	George Harrington	Thomas Ince	Thomas Ince
	Edward Butler	Chas. Brickenden	Chas. Brickenden
	William Knowles		
	John Yarker		
Chaplain .	Horace Hammond	Horace Hammond	Horace Hammond
Adjutant .	Bodo Knigge	R. Brickenden	R. Brickenden
Surgeon .	Henry Griffiths	Henry Griffiths	Henry Griffiths

TENTH REGIMENT OF DRAGOONS—*continued*

	1766	1767	1768
Colonel .	Sir John Mordaunt	Sir John Mordaunt	Sir John Mordaunt
Lieut.-Col. .	William Aug. Pitt	William Aug. Pitt	William Aug. Pitt
Major .	Thos. O. Mordaunt	Thos. O. Mordaunt	Thos. O. Mordaunt
Captains .	William Morrice Robert M. Lewis Samuel Gibbs	William Morrice Robert M. Lewis Samuel Gibbs	William Morrice Robert M. Lewis Samuel Gibbs
Capt.-Lieut. .	Bodo Knigge	Bodo Knigge	Bodo Knigge
Lieutenants .	Charles Henchman R. Brickenden Richard Dayrell William Gregory William Newton	Charles Henchman R. Brickenden Richard Dayrell William Gregory William Newton	Charles Henchman Richard Dayrell William Gregory William Newton George Harrington
Cornets .	George Harrington George Gould Thomas Ince Chas. Brickenden Sunderland Warmold G. Poyntz Ricketts	George Harrington George Gould Chas. Brickenden Sunderland Warmold G. Poyntz Ricketts Robert Parker	George Gould Chas. Brickenden Sunderland Warmold G. Poyntz Ricketts Robert Parker William J. Arabin
Chaplain .	Horace Hammond	Horace Hammond	Horace Hammond
Adjutant .	R. Brickenden	R. Brickenden	Thomas Lewis
Surgeon .	Henry Griffiths	John Drew	John Drew

TENTH REGIMENT OF DRAGOONS—*continued*

	1769	1770	1771
Colonel . .	Sir John Mordaunt	Sir John Mordaunt	Sir John Mordaunt
Lieut.-Col. .	William Aug. Pitt	William Aug. Pitt	Thos. O. Mordaunt
Major . .	Thos. O. Mordaunt	Thos. O. Mordaunt	William Morrice
Captains .	William Morrice	William Morrice	Rob. Mason Lewis
	Rob. Mason Lewis	Rob. Mason Lewis	Francis Aug. Eliott
	Francis Aug. Eliott	Francis Aug. Eliott	Charles Henchman
Capt.-Lieut. .	Bodo Knigge	Charles Henchman	Richard Dayrell
Lieutenants .	Charles Henchman	Richard Dayrell	William Gregory
	Richard Dayrell	William Gregory	William Newton
	William Gregory	William Newton	George Harrington
	William Newton	George Harrington	G. Poyntz Ricketts
	George Harrington	G. Poyntz Ricketts	Wm. John Arabin
Cornets . .	Sunderland War-mold	Robert Parker	Robert Grenville
	G. Poyntz Ricketts	Wm. John Arabin	Wm. Orby Hunter
	Robert Parker	Robert Grenville	Wm. Cartwright
	Wm. John Arabin	Wm. Orby Hunter	Thos. Ph. Dayrolles
	Robert Greville	Wm. Cartwright	Harry Porter
	Wm. Orby Hunter	Thos. Ph. Dayrolles	Everard Fawkiner
		Henry Porter	
Chaplain .	Horace Hammond	Horace Hammond	Horace Hammond
Adjutant .	Thomas Lewis	Thos. Lewis	Thos. Lewis
Surgeon . .	John Drew	Morgan O'Brien	Morgan O'Brien

TENTH REGIMENT OF DRAGOONS--*continued*

	1772	1773	1774
Colonel .	Sir John Mordaunt	Sir John Mordaunt	Sir John Mordaunt
Lieut.-Col. .	Thos. O. Mordaunt	Thos. O. Mordaunt	Thos. O. Mordaunt
Major .	William Morrice	William Morrice	William Morrice
Captains .	Rob. Mason Lewis	Rob. Mason Lewis	Rob. Mason Lewis
	Francis Aug. Eliott	Francis Aug. Eliott	Francis Aug. Eliott
	Charles Henchman	Charles Henchman	Charles Henchman
Capt.-Lieut. .	Richard Dayrell	Richard Dayrell	Richard Dayrell
Lieutenants .	William Gregory	William Gregory	William Gregory
	William Newton	William Newton	William Newton
	George Harrington	George Harrington	George Harrington
	G. Poyntz Ricketts	Wm. John Arabin	R. F. Greville
	Wm. John Arabin	R. Fulke Greville	John Barlow
		John Barlow	
Cornets .	Robert Grenville	Wm. Orby Hunter	Wm. Orby Hunter
	Wm. Orby Hunter	Wm. Cartwright	Wm. Cartwright
	Wm. Cartwright	Thos. Ph. Dayrolles	Thos. Ph. Dayrolles
	Thos. Ph. Dayrolles	Harry Porter	Harry Porter
	Harry Porter	Everard Fawkiner	Everard Fawkiner
	Everard Fawkiner	William Mordaunt Milner	William Mordaunt Milner
Captain .	Horace Hammond	Horace Hammond	Horace Hammond
Adjutant .	Thomas Lewis	Thomas Lewis	Thomas Lewis
Surgeons .	Morgan O'Brien	Morgan O'Brien	Morgan O'Brien
		Peter Bernard	Peter Bernard

TENTH REGIMENT OF DRAGOONS—*continued*

	1775	1776	1777
Colonel . .	Sir John Mordaunt	Sir John Mordaunt	Sir John Mordaunt
Lieut.-Col. .	Thos. O. Mordaunt	Thos. O. Mordaunt	T. O. Mordaunt, K.B.
Major . .	William Morrice	William Morrice	William Morrice
Captains .	Robt. Mason Lewis	Robt. Mason Lewis	Robt. Mason Lewis
	Francis Aug. Eliott	Francis Aug. Eliott	Charles Henchman
	Charles Henchman	Charles Henchman	William Gregory
		Richard Dayrell	
		William Gregory	
Capt.-Lieuts. .	Richard Dayrell	Richard Dayrell	William Newton
		J. Newton	
		William Gregory	
Lieutenants .	William Gregory	William Gregory	John Barlow
	William Newton	William Newton	Wm. Cartwright
	Hon. R. F. Greville	John Barlow	Thos. Ph. Dayrolles
	John Barlow	Wm. Cartwright	Harry Portal
	W. O. Hunter	Thos. Ph. Dayrolles	W. Sotheby
	Wm. Cartwright	Harry Portal	
	Thos. Ph. Dayrolles	W. Sotheby	
Cornets . .	Wm. Cartwright	Harry Portal	Richard Lumley
	Thos. Ph. Dayrolles	Everard Fawkiner	Chas. Gunter Legge
	Harry Porter	W. M. Milner	Wm. Arme Villettes
	Everard Fawkiner	W. Sotheby	Thos. Moncrieffe
	W. M. Milner	Richard Lumley	R. Tipping
	Wm. Sotheby	Chas. Gunter Legge	F. Gregory
	Richard Lumley	Wm. Arme Villettes	W. Rowley
	Chas. Gunter Legge	Thos. Moncrieffe	
		Robert Tipping	
		Francis Gregory	
Chaplain .	Horace Hammond	Horace Hammond	Horace Hammond
Adjutant	Thomas Lewis	Thomas Lewis	Thomas Lewis
Surgeon .	Peter Bernard	Peter Bernard	Peter Bernard

TENTH REGIMENT OF DRAGOONS—*continued*

	1778	1779	1780
Colonel . .	Sir John Mordaunt, K.B.	Sir John Mordaunt, K.B.	Wm. Augustus Pitt
Lieut.-Col. .	Thos. O. Mordaunt	Thos. O. Mordaunt	Thos. O. Mordaunt
Major . .	William Morrice	Robt. Mason Lewis	Robt. Mason Lewis
Captains .	Robt. Mason Lewis	Charles Henchman	William Gregory
	Charles Henchman	William Gregory	William Newton
	William Gregory	William Newton	Wm. Cartwright
		Wm. Cartwright	
Captain-Lieut. and Capt.	William Newton	Harry Portal	Harry Portal
Lieuts.	John Barlow	Wm. Sotheby	Wm. A. Villettes
	Wm. Cartwright	Hon. R. Lumley	Chas. J. Clavering
	Thos. Ph. Dayrolles	Wm. A. Villettes	Hon. F. Lumley
	Harry Portal	William Rowley	— Dickens
	W. Sotheby	Chas. J. Clavering	R. O'Brien Boyle
	Richard Lumley	Hon. F. Lumley	
	Chas. Gunter Legge		
Cornets	Richard Lumley	William Rowley	Thomas Lewis
	Chas. Gunter Legge	Hon. F. Lumley	William Henry Pitt
	Wm. A. Villettes	— Dickens	Hon. W. M. Maitland
	Robert Tipping	R. O'Brien Boyle	
	Francis Gregory	Thomas Lewis	Thomas Hawkins
	William Rowley	William Henry Pitt	C. H. Bulkeley
	Chas. J. Clavering	Hon. W. M. Maitland	John Slade
	Frederick Lumley	land	Harry Mount
Chaplain .	Horace Hammond	Horace Hammond	Horace Hammond
Adjutant .	Thomas Lewis	Thomas Lewis	Thomas Lewis
Surgeons .	Peter Bernard	R. Bloxham	R. Bloxham
	R. Bloxham		

TENTH REGIMENT OF DRAGOONS—*continued*

	1781	1782	1783
Colonel . .	W. A. Pitt	W. A. Pitt	W. A. Pitt
Lieut.-Col. .	T. O. Mordaunt	T. O. Mordaunt	T. O. Mordaunt
Major . .	George Leathes	George Leathes	G. Newton
Captains .	Wm. G. Williams	Wm. Newton	W. Cartwright
	Wm. Newton	Wm. Cartwright	W. A. Villettes
	Wm. Cartwright	W. A. Villettes	Hon. F. Lumley
Captain-Lieut. and Capt.	Francis Gregory	Francis Gregory	F. Gregory
Lieutenants .	W. A. Villettes	Hon. Fred Lumley	— Dickens
	Hon. Fred Lumley	— Dickens	T. Lewis
	— Dickens	Thomas Lewis	H. Stewart
	Thomas Lewis	Henry Stewart	W. H. Pitt
	Henry Stewart	W. H. Pitt	Hon. W. M. Maitland
Cornets . .	W. H. Pitt	Hon. W. M. Maitland	T. Hawkins
	Hon. W. M. Maitland	Thomas Hawkins	J. Slade
	Thos. Hawkins	John Slade	H. Mount
	John Slade	Harry Mount	J. Kaye
	Harry Mount	John Kaye	William Graham
	John Kaye	William Graham	George Sturt
Chaplain .	Horace Hammond	Horace Hammond	Horace Hammond
Adjutant .	Thos. Lewis	Thomas Lewis	T. Lewis
Surgeon .	R. Bloxham	R. Bloxham	R. Bloxham

TENTH REGIMENT OF LIGHT DRAGOONS—*continued*

	1784	1785	1786
Colonel . .	W. A. Pitt	W. A. Pitt	W. A. Pitt
Lieut.-Col. .	T. O. Mordaunt	T. O. Mordaunt	T. O. Mordaunt
Major . .	G. Newton	G. Newton	W. Newton
Captains .	W. Cartwright	W. Cartwright	W. Cartwright
	W. A. Villettes	W. A. Villettes	W. A. Villettes
	Hon. F. Lumley	Hon. F. Lumley	Hon. F. Lumley
Captain-Lieut. and Capt.	F. Gregory	F. Gregory	F. Gregory
Lieutenants	W. H. Pitt	W. H. Pitt	W. H. Pitt
	J. Slade	J. Slade	J. Slade
	H. Mount	J. Kaye	J. Kaye
	J. Kaye	W. Graham	H. L. Templer
	W. Graham	H. L. Templer	G. Kerr
Cornets . .	G. Sturt	G. Kerr	T. A. Deane
	Henry L. Templer	T. A. Deane	J. Cotton
	George Kerr	C. Coleman	E. Turton
	Thos. An. Deane	Hon. John Hope	Patrick Blake, Bt.
	Charles Coleman	Josiah Cotton	Peter Shadwell
		Edward Turton	
Chaplain .	Horace Hammond	Horace Hammond	Horace Hammond
Adjutant .	Peter Shadwell	P. Shadwell	P. Shadwell
Surgeon .	James Barton	J. Barton	J. Barton

TENTH REGIMENT OF LIGHT DRAGOONS — *continued*

	1787	1788	1789
Colonel . .	W. A. Pitt	W. A. Pitt	W. A. Pitt
Lieut.-Col. .	W. Newton	W. Newton	W. Newton
Major . .	W. Cartwright	W. Cartwright	W. Cartwright
Captains .	W. A. Villettes	W. H. Pitt	W. H. Pitt
	Hon. F. Lumley	J. Slade	J. Slade
	W. H. Pitt	J. Kaye	J. Kaye
Captain-Lieut. and Capt.	F. Gregory	F. Gregory	F. Gregory
Lieutenants	J. Slade	H. L. Templer	H. L. Templer
	J. Kaye	G. Kerr	George Kerr
	H. L. Templer	T. A. Deane	T. A. Deane
	G. Kerr	J. Cotton	J. Cottin
	T. A. Deane	E. Turton	E. Turton
Cornets . .	J. Cotton	P. Blake, Bt.	P. Blake
	E. Turton	P. Shadwell	P. Shadwell
	P. Blake, Bt.	N. Starkie	N. Starkie
	P. Shadwell	C. P. Milloway	C. P. Milloway
	Nicholas Starkie	Hon. W. Lumley	Hon. W. Lumley
	Chas. P. Milloway	William Churchill	W. Churchill
Chaplain .	Horace Hammond	Horace Hammond	Horace Hammond
Adjutant .	P. Shadwell	P. Shadwell	P. Shadwell
Surgeon .	J. Barton	John Scott	J. Scott

Tenth Regiment of Light Dragoons—*continued*

	1790	1791	1792
Colonel . .	W. A. Pitt	W. A. Pitt	W. A. Pitt
Lieut.-Col. .	W. Newton	W. Newton	W. Newton
Major . .	W. Cartwright	W. Cartwright	W. Cartwright
Captains .	W. H. Pitt J. Slade J. Kaye	F. Gregory W. H. Pitt J. Slade	F. Gregory W. H. Pitt J. Slade
Captain-Lieut. and Capt.	F. Gregory	H. L. Templer	H. L. Templer
Lieutenants .	H. L. Templer G. Kerr T. A. Deane J. Cottin E. Turton	T. A. Deane J. Cottin P. Shadwell Hon. W. Lumley W. Churchill	T. A. Deane J. Cottin P. Shadwell Hon. W. Lumley W. Churchill
Cornets . .	P. Shadwell C. P. Milloway Hon. W. Lumley W. Churchill William Powell Robert Hamilton	W. Powell R. Hamilton Richard Moore Hon. A. W. Mac-Donald George Leigh Thomas Gooch	R. Moore Hon. A. W. Mac-Donald G. Leigh T. Gooch William Fuller Emelius Delmé
Chaplain .	H. Hammond	H. Hammond	H. Hammond
Adjutant .	P. Shadwell	P. Shadwell	P. Shadwell
Surgeon .	J. Scott	John Hannay	Thomas Merrick

TENTH REGIMENT OF LIGHT DRAGOONS—*continued*

	1793	1794	1795
Colonel-Com..	—	H.R.H. the Prince of Wales	H.R.H. the Prince of Wales
Colonel . .	W. A. Pitt	W. A. Pitt	W. A. Pitt
Lieut.-Cols. .	W. Newton	W. Newton W. Cartwright	W. Cartwright W. H. Pitt
Majors . .	W. Cartwright	W. Cartwright W. H. Pitt	J. Slade H. L. Templer
Captains .	F. Gregory W. H. Pitt J. Slade	J. Slade H. L. Templer T. H. Deane J. Cottin William Tyndale George Leigh	J. Cottin Hon. W. Lumley George Leigh T. Gooch James Hare Lord R. E. H. Somerset
Captain-Lieut. and Capt.	H. L. Templer	P. Shadwell	William Fuller
Lieutenants	T. A. Deane J. Cottin P. Shadwell Hon. W. Lumley W. Churchill	Hon. W. Lumley W. Churchill George Leigh T. Gooch W. Fuller E. Delmé James Hare James Shadwell Lord R. E. H. Somerset James H. Blake Henry Seymour	J. Shadwell James H. Blake H. Seymour J. Locke Hon. W. Bligh G. Quentin R. Skeen W. Peachey
Cornets . .	Hon. A. W. Mac-Donald G. Leigh T. Gooch W. Fuller E. Delmé Jas. Henry Blake	James H. Blake Lord A. E. H. Somerset Henry Seymour John Locke Stephen E. Poyntz C. Payne Galway Hon. William Bligh George Quentin Frederick Manners Robert Sheen William Peachey	George Brummell Edwd. F. Newman James M'Dermot
Chaplain .	H. Hammond	Horace Hammond	Horace Hammond
Adjutant .	P. Shadwell	James M'Dermot	James M'Dermot
Surgeon .	T. Merrick	E. Fabian Newman	Edwd. F. Newman

TENTH REGIMENT OF LIGHT DRAGOONS—*continued*

	1796	1797	1798
Colonel-Com..	H.R.H. the Prince of Wales	H.R.H. the Prince of Wales	H.R.H. the Prince of Wales
Colonel .	W. A. Pitt	—	—
Lieut.-Cols. .	W. Cartwright J. Slade	W. Cartwright J. Slade	W. Cartwright J. Slade
Majors .	H. L. Templer J. Cottin	J. Cottin G. Leigh	J. Cottin G. Leigh
Captains	George Leigh T. Gooch W. Fuller James Hare Lord R. Somerset J. H. Blake	T. Gooch W. Fuller Lord R. Somerset H. Seymour Hon. W. Bligh G. Brummell	T. Gooch W. Fuller Lord R. Somerset Henry Seymour Hon. W. Bligh George Brummell
Captain-Lieut. and Capt.	Henry Seymour	George Quentin	G. Quentin
Lieutenants	Hon. W. Bligh G. Quentin R. Skeen G. Brummell James M'Dermot Lord Charles Kerr Thomps Bradyll John Chambers	R. Skeen J. M'Dermot Lord C. Kerr T. Braddyll J. Chambers — Garside G. A. Legh F. W. Elliott W. L. G. Thomas Charles Palmer	R. Skeen J. M'Dermot Lord C. Kerr T. Braddyll J. Chambers G. A. Legh C. Palmer W. L. G. Thomas
Cornets .	— Garside George A. Legh Thomas Chadwick Freeman W. Elliott	Charles Palmer Bayles Wardell Jas. A. Heseltine Philip De Vesme Joseph Cook James Bird William Sparling	Bayles Wardell J. A. Heseltine P. De Vesme J. Cook W. Sparling James Bird
Chaplain .	Horace Hammond	Horace Hammond	—
Adjutant .	James M'Dermot	James M'Dermot	J. M'Dermot
Surgeons .	— Marignac	— Marignac and Chambers	— Chambers
Assist.-Surgns.	—	William Taylor — Grant	William Taylor — Grant
Vet. Surgeon .	—	John Denny (first recorded)	John Denny

TENTH REGIMENT OF LIGHT DRAGOONS—*continued*

	1799	1800	1801
Colonel . .	H.R.H. the Prince of Wales, K.G.	H.R.H. the Prince of Wales, K.G.	H.R.H. the Prince of Wales, K.G.
Lieut.-Cols. . .	W. Cartwright J. Cottin	W. Cartwright G. Leigh	W. Cartwright G. Leigh
Majors . .	G Leigh T. Gooch	T. Gooch W. Fuller	T. Gooch W. Fuller
Captains .	W. Fuller Lord R. E. H. Somerset Henry Seymour Hon. W. Bligh J. Chambers J. M'Dermot	H. Seymour G. Quentin J. Chambers J. M'Dermot C. Palmer B. Wardell	H. Seymour G. Quentin J. M'Dermot C. Palmer Charles Viscount Petersham J. L. Cook Hon. A. Macdonald
Captain-Lieut. and Capt.	G. Quentin	Charles Viscount Petersham	Lord C. Manners
Lieutenants	R. Skeen Lord C. Kerr C. Palmer W. L. G. Thomas Bayles Wardell J. Cook W. Sparling J. Bird	R. Skeen J. Cook W. Sparling J. Bird Hon. A. Macdonald Lord C. Manners Lord J. Murray H. C. E. Vernon Robert Oliver	R. Skeen Lord J. Murray H. C. E. Vernon R. Oliver Lord R. Manners J. Carruthers T. Souter Hon. F. Ponsonby John Trant F. G. Carmichael
Cornets . .	R. Rochfort Lord C. Manners Lord Jas. Murray Hon. C. E. Vernon Lord R. Manners	Lord R. Manners Joseph Carruthers Thomas Souter	Ernest Otto Tripp William Sloane Godschall Johnson
Paymaster .	Richard Manby (first on record)	Richard Manby	Richard Manby
Adjutant .	J. M'Dermot	T. Souter	T. Souter
Surgeon .	— Chambers	— Chambers	— Chambers
Assist.-Surgns.	W. Taylor	William Taylor — Grant	William Taylor — Grant
Vet. Surgeon .	J. Denny	J. Denny	John Denny

Tenth Regiment of Light Dragoons—*continued*

	1802	1803	1804
Colonel . .	H.R.H. the Prince of Wales, K.G.	H.R.H. the Prince of Wales, K.G.	H.R.H. the Prince of Wales, K.G.
Lieut.-Cols. .	W. Cartwright G. Leigh	W. Cartwright G. Leigh	W. Cartwright G. Leigh
Majors . .	W. Fuller H. Seymour	W. Fuller H. Seymour	W. Fuller H. Seymour
Captains .	G. Quentin J. M'Dermot C. Palmer Charles Viscount Petersham Hon. Arch. Macdonald Lord Jas. Murray H. C. Edward V. Graham	G. Quentin J. M'Dermot C. Palmer Charles Viscount Petersham Hon. Arch. Macdonald	G. Quentin C. Palmer Lord C. Manners Lord Jas. Murray Fred. Baron Eben Robert Oliver Lord R. Manners Hon. F. Ponsonby
Capt.-Lieut. and Capt.	Lord C. Manners	Lord C. Manners	(*This rank disappears*)
Lieutenants .	R. Skeen R. Oliver Lord R. Manners T. Souter Hon. F. Ponsonby J. Trant F. G. Carmichael Hon. Hen. Murray E. O. Tripp W. Sloane Godschall Johnson C. Edw. Bouverie Edward Warner	R. Skeen R. Oliver Lord R. Manners T. Souter Hon. F. Ponsonby J. Trant F. G. Carmichael E. D. Tripp William Sloane	T. Souter J. Trant E. O. Tripp Godschall Johnson Hon. Fred Howard Thomas N. Hill Augustus Quentin
Cornets . .	E. S. T. Ruthven Temple French Richard Taylor Thomas Noel Hill G. A. Lord Rancliffe Augustus Quentin Lord A. Gordon Ralph B. Johnson George Augustus Bouverie	E. S. T. Ruthven Temple French Richard Taylor Thomas Noel Hill G. A. Lord Rancliffe Augustus Quentin Lord A. Gordon Ralph B. Johnson	R. B. Johnson Geo. Aug. Bouverie Fred. Joseph Darby Chas. Webb Dance Thomas Sheridan George Milbanke Hon. H. Devereux
Paymaster .	R. Manby	R. Manby	R. Manby
Adjutant .	T. Souter	T. Souter	T. Souter
Surgeons .	— Chambers W. G. Taylor	— Chambers W. Taylor	W. Taylor John Denny
Assist.-Surgeon	— Grant	— Grant	Charles Morrison
Vet. Surgeon	John Denny	John Denny	Edward Gaskoin

TENTH REGIMENT OF LIGHT DRAGOONS (HUSSARS) —*continued*

	1805	1806	1807
Colonel . .	H.R.H. the Prince of Wales, K.G.	H.R.H. the Prince of Wales, K.G.	H.R.H. the Prince of Wales, K.G.
Lieut.-Cols. .	G. Leigh	G. Leigh William Payne	G. Leigh W. Payne
Majors . .	W. Fuller H. Seymour	Geo. Quentin Charles Palmer	G. Quentin C. Palmer
Captains .	G. Quentin C. Palmer Lord C. Manners F. Baron Eben R. Oliver Lord Robt. Manners Hon. Fred. Ponsonby John Trant E. O. Tripp Hon. F. Howard	Lord C. Manners Fred. Baron Eben R. Oliver Lord R. Manners Hon. Fred. Ponsonby E. O. Tripp Hon. F. Howard T. N. Hill Lord W. G. H. Somerset Geo. Aug. Bouverie	Lord C. Manners R. Oliver Lord R. Manners Hon. F. Howard Lord W. G. H. Somerset G. A. Bouverie F. J. Darby G. J. Robarts H. F. Mellish A. Goddard
Lieutenants .	T. N. Hill Lord Wm. G. H. Somerset Geo. Aug. Bouverie F. J. Darby G. J. Robarts Henry Milbanke Hen. Fras. Mellish Ambrose Goddard C. Edw. Bouverie T. Smith	F. J. Darby G. J. Robarts H. Milbanke H. F. Mellish H. Goddard C. E. Bouverie T. Smith T. Bowen Geo. West Barnes R. E. Williams Simon G. Newport A. de Grammont	H. Milbanke C. E. Bouverie T. Smith T. Bowen R. E. Williams S. G. Newport G. de Grammont C. J. Gordon N. Brown Hon. F. C. Stanhope
Cornets . .	Francis Carleton Thomas Bowen A. de Grammont Rowland Edward Williams	Charles Haggerty Chas. John Gordon F. W. Elliot Nicholas Brown	C. Haggerty F. W. Elliot Henry Duperier Simon H. Stuart Wm. J. Coventry
Paymaster .	R. Manby	John Roberts	J. Roberts
Adjutant .	T. Smith	T. Smith	T. Smith
Surgeon. .	W. Taylor	W. Taylor	W. Taylor
Assist.-Surgs.	J. Denny C. Morrison	J. Denny C. Morrison	J. Denny C. Morrison
Vet. Surgeon .	Edward Gaskoin	Edward Gaskoin	Edward Gaskoin

TENTH REGIMENT OF LIGHT DRAGOONS (HUSSARS)—*continued*

	1808	1809	1810
Colonel . .	H.R.H. the Prince of Wales, K.G.	H.R.H. the Prince of Wales, K.G.	H.R.H. the Prince of Wales, K.G.
Lieut.-Cols. . .	G. Leigh W. Payne	G. Leigh G. Quentin	G. Leigh G. Quentin
Majors . .	G. Quentin C. Palmer	C. Palmer Lord C. Manners	C. Palmer Lord C. Manners
Captains .	Lord C. Manners R. Oliver Lord Rob. Manners Hon. F. Howard Lord W. G. H. Somerset G. A. Bouverie F. J. Darby G. J. Robarts H. F. Mellish A. Goddard	R. Oliver Lord Rob. Manners Hon. F. Howard F. J. Darby G. J. Robarts H. Goddard T. Bowen S. G. Newport T. Smith R. E. Williams	Lord Rob. Manners Hon. Fred. Howard G. J. Robarts H. Goddard S. G. Newport T. Smith A. de Grammont C. J. Gordon Henry Wyndham J. R. L. Lloyd
Lieutenants .	T. Smith T. Bowen R. E. Williams S. G. Newport A. de Grammont C. J. Gordon N. Brown Hon. F. C. Stanhope W. John Coventry Benjamin Harding	A. de Grammont N. Brown C. J. Gordon W. J. Coventry B. Harding Hon. H. F. Cavendish Richard Jebb Henry Duperier S. H. Stuart	N. Brown Benjamin Harding Hon. H. F. Cavendish Richard Jebb H. Duperier S. H. Stuart Geo. FitzClarence Sir Bellingham Graham, Bart. Andrew Finucane J. W. Webster
Cornets . .	C. Haggerty Henry Duperier S. H. Stuart Geo. FitzClarence	C. Haggerty Geo. FitzClarence Andrew Finucane J. W. Webster Joseph Smyth	J. Smith Edward Turner Charles Synge John G. Lambton Lord A. M. W. Hill Samuel Bromley
Paymaster .	J. Roberts	J. Roberts	J. Roberts
Adjutant .	H. Duperier	H. Duperier	H. Duperier
Surgeon .	W. Taylor	W. Taylor	W. Taylor
Asst.-Surgeons	J. Denny C. Morrison	J. Denny C. Morrison	C. Morrison
Vet. Surgeon .	(*None*)	(*None*)	(*None*)

TENTH REGIMENT OF LIGHT DRAGOONS (HUSSARS)—*continued*

	1811	1812	1813
Colonels .	H.R.H. the Prince of Wales, K.G.	H.R.H. the Prince Regent, K.G.	H.R.H. the Prince Regent, K.G.
Lieut.-Cols. .	G. Quentin C. Palmer	G. Quentin C. Palmer	G. Quentin C. Palmer
Majors . .	Lord C. Manners Lord Rob. Manners	Hon. F. Howard G. J. Robarts	Hon. F. Howard G. J. Robarts
Captains .	Hon. F. Howard G. J. Robarts A. Goddard S. G. Newport A. de Grammont C. J. Gordon H. Wyndham J. R. L. Lloyd B. Harding Hon. F. C. Stanhope	A. Goddard A. de Grammont C. J. Gordon H. Wyndham J. R. L. Lloyd B. Harding Hon. F. C. Stanhope R. Jebb S. H. Stuart Geo. FitzClarence	A. de Grammont C. J. Gordon H. Wyndham J. R. L. Lloyd B. Harding Hon. F. C. Stanhope R. Jebb S. H. Stuart G. FitzClarence J. Smyth
Lieutenants .	Richard Jebb S. H. Stuart G. FitzClarence Andrew Finucane J. W. Webster J. Smyth Edward Turner C. Synge J. G. Lambton Robert Giveen Lord A. M. W. Hill Samuel Bromley	J. Smyth E. Turner C. Synge R. Giveen Lord A. M. W. Hill S. Bromley J. Cottin E. Fox Fitzgerald Henry, Marquis of Worcester Charles Eversfield Fred., Baron Leon	E. Turner C. Synge Lord A. M. W. Hill S. Bromley J. Cottin E. F. Fitzgerald Henry, Marquis of Worcester C. Eversfield Charles Holbern George Wombwell Charles Wyndham
Cornets . .	John Cottin E. Fox Fitzgerald T. Montgomery	George Wombwell Charles Wyndham	Charles Boultbee Horace Seymour H. Somerset F. Page Turner John Chas. Turner Aug. F. Bulkeley
Paymaster .	John B. Wilkinson	J. B. Wilkinson	J. B. Wilkinson
Adjutant .	Samuel Bromley	S. Bromley	Samuel Bromley
Quartermaster	James Rogers	J. Rogers	J. Rogers .
Surgeon .	W. Taylor	C. Morrison	C. Morrison
Asst.-Surgeons	C. Morrison James Ainge	James Ainge W. B. Rogers	W. B. Rogers Geo. Samuel Jenks
Vet. Surgeon	H. C. Sannerman	H. C. Sannerman	H. C. Sannerman

TENTH REGIMENT OF LIGHT DRAGOONS (HUSSARS)—*continued*

	1814	1815	1816
Colonel .	H.R.H. the Prince Regent, K.G.	H.R.H. the Prince Regent, K.G.	H.R.H. the Prince Regent, K.G.
Lieut.-Cols. .	G. Quentin C. Palmer	G. Quentin Lord R. Manners	G. Quentin Lord R. Manners
Majors .	Hon. F. Howard G. J. Robarts	Hon. F. Howard Hon. H. C. Lowther	Hon. H. C. Lowther Thos. W. Taylor
Captains .	A. de Grammont C. J. Gordon J. R. L. Lloyd B. Harding S. H. Stuart G. FitzClarence J. Smyth E. Turner R. Giveen C. Synge Lord A. W. M. Hill Samuel Bromley	S. Bromley Thos. W. Taylor H. R. C. Stapylton John Grey John Gurwood Charles Wood Valentine Jones Henry Floyd Arthur Shakespear Hon. John Jones	S. Bromley H. R. C. Stapylton John Grey John Gurwood Charles Wood Valentine Jones Henry Floyd Arthur Shakespear Hon. John Jones John W. Parsons
Lieutenants .	E. F. Fitzgerald Henry, Marquis of Worcester Charles Eversfield Charles Holbern George Wombwell Charles Wyndham Horace Seymour Henry Somerset Francis P. Turner H. F. Bulkeley Henry FitzClarence John H. Powell Josias Jackson Jas. A. Richardson E. F. Meynell	Charles Holbern E. F. Meynell Robert Curtis John W. Parsons W. Slayter Smith Hon. John Burn Robert Arnold C. J. Allingham Wm. Cartwright Samuel Hardman Geo. O. Gunning J. C. Wallington E. Hodgson Wm. C. Hamilton Anthony Bacon	Charles Holbern E. F. Meynell Robert Curtis W. Slayter Smith Hon. John Burn Robert Arnold Wm. Cartwright Samuel Hardman J. C. Wallington E. Hodgson Wm. C. Hamilton Anthony Bacon W. H. B. Lindsay Wm. Drummond
Cornets .	J. E. M. Douglas	W. P. Jervis Wm. Lindsay	John S. Brown William Gale Charles Harvey D. Toler Curtis Wm. C. Langmead Robert Burdett Thos. Otway
Paymaster .	H. B. Wilkinson	John Tallon	John Tallon
Adjutant .	(None recorded)	Samuel Hardman	Samuel Hardman
Quartermaster	J. Rogers	James Rogers	J. Rogers
Surgeon .	C. Morrison	C. Morrison	Robt. A. Chermside
Asst.-Surgeons	W. R. Rogers G. S. Jenks	W. R. Rogers G. S. Jenks	W. R. Rogers G. S. Jenks
Vet. Surgeon .	H. C. Sannerman	H. C. Sannerman	H. C. Sannerman

TENTH REGIMENT OF LIGHT DRAGOONS (HUSSARS)—*continued*

	1817	1818	1819
Colonel . .	H.R.H. the Prince Regent, K.G.	H.R.H. the Prince Regent, K.G.	H.R.H. the Prince Regent, K.G.
Lieut.-Cols. . .	G. Quentin Lord R. Manners	G. Quentin Lord R. Manners	G. Quentin Lord R. Manners
Majors . .	Hon. H. C. Lowther Thos. W. Taylor	Thos. W. Taylor H. R. C. Stapylton	Thos. W. Taylor H. R. C. Stapylton
Captains .	S. Bromley H. R. C. Stapylton John Grey John Gurwood Charles Wood Valentine Jones Henry Floyd Arthur Shakespear	John Grey John Gurwood Charles Wood Valentine Jones Henry Floyd Arthur Shakespear Hon. J. Jones E. F. Meynell	John Grey John Gurwood Charles Wood Valentine Jones Sir H. Floyd, Bart. Hon. J. Jones E. F. Meynell Robert Arnold
Lieutenants .	Charles Holbern E. F. Meynell W. Slayter Smith Robert Arnold Wm. Cartwright J. C. Wallington E. Hodgson W. C. Hamilton Wm. Drummond	W. Slayter Smith Robert Arnold Wm. Cartwright J. C. Wallington E. Hodgson W. C. Hamilton Wm. Drummond William Gale Thos. Otway	W. Slayter Smith Wm. Cartwright J. C. Wallington E. Hodgson W. C. Hamilton Wm. Drummond William Gale Thos. Otway Charles Harvey
Cornets . .	John S. Brown William Gale Charles Harvey D. Toler Curtis Wm. C. Langmead Robert Burdett Thos. Otway Samuel Wells	Charles Harvey Wm. C. Langmead Samuel Wells Lord Thomas Cecil John, Earl of Wiltshire Hon. R. Watson John Trollope F. G. D'A., Marquis of Carmarthen	Wm. C. Langmead Samuel Wells . Lord Thomas Cecil John, Earl of Wiltshire Hon. R. Watson John Trollope F. G. D'A., Marquis of Carmarthen Lord J. Bentinck
Paymaster .	John Tallon	John Tallon	John Tallon
Adjutant .	Samuel Wells	Samuel Wells	Samuel Wells
Quartermaster	J. Rogers	J. Rogers	J. Rogers
Surgeon .	Rob. A. Chermside	Rob. A. Chermside	Rob. A. Chermside
Asst.-Surgeons	W. R. Rogers G. S. Jenks	W. R. Rogers G. S. Jenks	W. R. Rogers
Vet. Surgeon .	H. C. Sannerman	H. C. Sannerman	H. C. Sannerman

TENTH REGIMENT OF LIGHT DRAGOONS (HUSSARS)—*continued*

	1820	1821	1822
Colonel . .	C. W. Vane, Lord Stewart, G.C.B.	C. W. Vane, Lord Stewart, G.C.B.	C. W. Vane, Lord Stewart, G.C.B.
Lieut.-Col. .	G. Quentin	G. Quentin	Sir G. Quentin, Kt.
Majors . .	Thos. W. Taylor H. R. C. Stapylton	Thos. W. Taylor H. R. C. Stapylton	Thos. W. Taylor H. R. C. Stapylton
Captains .	John Grey John Gurwood Charles Wood Valentine Jones Sir H. Floyd, Bart. Hon. J. Jones E. F. Meynell Robert Arnold	John Grey John Gurwood Charles Wood Valentine Jones Hon. J. Jones E. F. Meynell Robert Arnold Wm. Cartwright	John Gurwood Valentine Jones Hon. J. Jones E. F. Meynell Robert Arnold Wm. Cartwright
Lieutenants .	Wm. Cartwright J. C. Wallington E. Hodgson W. C. Hamilton Wm. Drummond William Gale Thos. Otway Charles Harvey Robert Burdett Samuel Wells	J. C. Wallington W. C. Hamilton Wm. Drummond Thos. Otway Charles Harvey Robert Burdett Samuel Wells Lord Thomas Cecil J., Earl of Wiltshire Hon. R. Watson	J. C. Wallington W. C. Hamilton Charles Harvey Samuel Wells Lord Thomas Cecil John, Earl of Wilt- shire Hon. R. Watson R. S. C., Viscount Beauchamp
Cornets . .	Lord Thomas Cecil John, Earl of Wilt- shire Hon. R. Watson John Trollope F. G. D'A., Marquis of Carmarthen Lord J. Bentinck C. Stuart Wortley	Sir J. Trollope, Bt. Lord J. Bentinck C. Stuart Wortley R. S. C., Viscount Beauchamp Chas. J. Brandling Thomas Wood Thomas Trollope	Sir J. Trollope, Bt. C. Stuart Wortley C. J. Brandling T. Wood R. Dent
Paymaster .	John Tallon	John Tallon	John Tallon
Adjutant .	Samuel Wells	Samuel Wells	Samuel Wells
Quartermaster	J. Rogers	J. Rogers	J. Rogers
Surgeon .	Rob. A. Chermside	Rob. A. Chermside	Rob. A. Chermside
Asst.-Surgeon	W. R. Rogers	W. R. Rogers	W. R. Rogers
Vet. Surgeon.	H. C. Sannerman	H. C. Sannerman	H. C. Sannerman

TENTH REGIMENT OF LIGHT DRAGOONS (HUSSARS)—*continued*

	1823	1824	1825
Colonel . .	Chas. W., Marquis of Londonderry, G.C.B., G.C.H.	Chas. W., Marquis of Londonderry, G.C.B., G.C.H.	Chas. W., Marquis of Londonderry, G.C.B., G.C.H.
Lieut.-Col. .	Sir G. A. Quentin, K.C.H.	Sir G. A. Quentin, K.C.H.	Henry Wyndham
Majors . .	Thos. W. Taylor Val. Jones Græme	T. W. Taylor Val. Jones Græme	Val. Jones Græme Hon. J. Jones
Captains .	Hon. J. Jones R. Arnold W. C. Drummond R. Burdett W. C. Hamilton Lord T. Cecil	Hon. J. Jones R. Arnold W. C. Drummond R. Burdett W. C. Hamilton Lord T. Cecil	R. Arnold W. C. Drummond R. Burdett W. Hamilton Lord T. Cecil J. C. Wallington
Lieutenants .	J. C. Wallington C. Harvey S. Wells John, Earl of Wiltshire Hon. R. Watson R. S. C., Earl of Yarmouth Sir John Trollope C. S. Wortley	J. C. Wallington C. Harvey S. Wells Hon. R. Watson C. Stuart Wortley C. J. Brandling W. H. Wood F. G. D'A., Marquis of Carmarthen	C. Harvey S. Wells Hon. R. Watson C. Stuart Wortley C. J. Brandling W. H. Wood F. G. D'A., Marquis of Carmarthen Robert Dent
Cornets . .	C. J. Brandling T. Wood R. Dent Lord Jas. FitzRoy John Surman L. A. J., Lord Muncaster	R. Dent Lord Jas. FitzRoy John Surman Wm. Battier G. L. L. Kaye E. B. Beaumont	Lord Jas. FitzRoy John Surman G. L. L. Kaye E. B. Beaumont Anth. Macdonell Rob. Giffard
Paymaster .	J. Tallon	J. Tallon	J. Tallon
Adjutant .	S. Wells	S. Wells	S. Wells
Quartermaster	J. Rogers	J. Rogers	Fred. Kenkie
Surgeon .	Rob. A. Chermside	J. M. Roberts, M.D.	J. M. Roberts, M.D.
Asst.-Surgeon	W. R. Rogers	W. R. Rogers	W. R. Rogers
Vet. Surgeon .	H. C. Sannerman	H. C. Sannerman	H. C. Sannerman

TENTH REGIMENT OF LIGHT DRAGOONS (HUSSARS)—*continued*

	1826	1827	1828
Colonel . .	C. W., Marquis of Londonderry, G.C.B., G.C.H.	C. W., Marquis of Londonderry, G.C.B., G.C.H.	C. W., Marquis of Londonderry, G.C.B., G.C.H.
Lieut.-Col. .	H. Wyndham	H. Wyndham	H. Wyndham
Majors . .	Val. Jones Græme R. Arnold	Val. Jones Græme W. C. Drummond	Lord T. Cecil R. Burdett
Captains .	W. C. Drummond R. Burdett Lord T. Cecil J. C. Wallington C. Harvey Hon. R. Watson	Lord T. Cecil J. C. Wallington Hon. R. Watson W. H. Wood Lord J. FitzRoy G. L. L. Kaye	J. C. Wallington Hon. R. Watson W. H. Wood Lord J. FitzRoy G. L. L. Kaye Anth. Macdonell
Lieutenants .	S. Wells W. H. Wood Lord J. FitzRoy J. Surman G. L. L. Kaye Anth. Macdonell George Knox R. Giffard William Osborne	J. Surman Anth. Macdonell Robert Giffard W. Osborne C. H. Nicholson Stephens Lyne Stephens Dudley Heneage L. R., Visct. Frankfort de Montmorency S. C. Oliver	J. Surman Robert Giffard W. Osborne C. H. Nicholson S. L. Stephens Dudley Heneage S. C. Oliver John Musters Sir St. Vincent Cotton, Bart.
Cornets . .	Stephen Lyne Dudley Heneage L. R., Visct. Frankfort de Montmorency S. Charles Oliver Charles J. Whyte	Charles J. Whyte John Musters Sir St. Vincent Cotton, Bart. F. S. Wedderburn James Preston	F. S. Wedderburn James Preston Hon. W. H. Beresford George Vandeleur Duncombe Pyrke
Paymaster .	John Wardell	S. Wells	S. Wells
Adjutant .	S. Wells	James Preston	James Preston
Quartermaster	Jas. C. McClellan	Jas. C. McClellan	J. C. McClellan
Surgeon. .	Henry West	Henry West	Henry West
Asst.-Surgeon	W. R. Rogers	John Riach, M.D.	J. Riach, M.D.
Vet. Surgeon.	H. C. Sannerman	H. C. Sannerman	H. C. Sannerman

TENTH REGIMENT OF LIGHT DRAGOONS (HUSSARS)—*continued*

	1829	1830	1831
Colonel . .	C. W., Marquis of Londonderry, G.C.B., G.C.H.	C. W., Marquis of Londonderry, G.C.B., G.C.H.	C. W., Marquis of Londonderry, G.C.B., G.C.H.
Lieut.-Col. .	H. Wyndham	H. Wyndham	H. Wyndham
Majors . .	Lord T. Cecil R. Burdett	Lord T. Cecil R. Burdett	Lord T. Cecil R. Burdett
Captains .	J. C. Wallington Hon. R. Watson W. H. Wood Lord J. FitzRoy G. L. L. Kaye Anth. Macdonell	J. C. Wallington Hon. R. Watson W. H. Wood G. L. L. Kaye Anth. Macdonell Robert Giffard	J. C. Wallington W. H. Wood G. L. L. Kaye Anth. Macdonell Robert Giffard W. Osborne
Lieutenants .	J. Surman Robert Giffard W. Osborne C. H. Nicholson Dudley Heneage S. C. Oliver John Musters Sir St. Vincent Cotton, Bart. F. S. Wedderburn James Preston	J. Surman W. Osborne C. H. Nicholson Dudley Heneage Sir St. Vincent Cotton, Bart. F. S. Wedderburn James Preston Hon. W. H. Beresford Duncombe Pyrke R. O. Ward	J. Surman C. H. Nicholson Dudley Heneage F. S. Wedderburn James Preston Hon. W. H. Beresford Duncombe Pyrke R. O. Ward C. FitzHerbert Thomas Coltman H. F. Bonham
Cornets . .	Hon.W.H.Beresford G. Vandeleur Duncombe Pyrke Richard Fawkes	Chas. FitzHerbert Hen. F. Bonham Hon. P. Moreton John Rowley	Hon. P. Moreton John Rowley H. Norman
Paymaster .	S. Wells	S. Wells	S. Wells
Adjutant .	James Preston	James Preston	James Preston
Quartermaster	J. C. McClellan	J. C. McClellan	J. C. McClellan
Surgeon . .	W. R. Rogers	W. R. Rogers	W. R. Rogers
Asst.-Surgeon	John Riach, M.D.	John Riach, M.D.	Frederick Goodwin
Vet. Surgeon .	H. C. Sannerman	H. C. Sannerman	H. C. Sannerman

TENTH REGIMENT OF LIGHT DRAGOONS (HUSSARS)—*continued*

	1832	1833	1834
Colonel . .	C. W., Marquis of Londonderry, G.C.B., G.C.H.	C. W., Marquis of Londonderry, G.C.B., G.C.H.	C. W., Marquis of Londonderry, G.C.B., G.C.H.
Lieut.-Col. .	H. Wyndham	H. Wyndham	Lord T. Cecil
Major . .	Lord T. Cecil	Lord T. Cecil	J. C. Wallington
Captains .	J. C. Wallington W. H. Wood G. L. L. Kaye Robert Giffard W. Osborne C. H. Nicholson	J. C. Wallington W. H. Wood G. L. L. Kaye Robert Giffard C. H. Nicholson F. S. Wedderburn	W. H. Wood G. L. L. Kaye Robert Giffard F. S. Wedderburn A., Visct. Fincastle R. O. Ward
Lieutenants .	F. S. Wedderburn James Preston Hon.W.H.Beresford R. O. Ward C. FitzHerbert H. F. Bonham Hon. P. Moreton Hon. H. A. Savile John Rowley Henry Norman	James Preston Hon.W.H.Beresford R. O. Ward H. F. Bonham Hon. P. Moreton Hon. H. A. Savile John Rowley Henry Norman Geo. A. F. Quentin Mat. McDonough	James Preston H. F. Bonham Hon. P. Moreton John Rowley Henry Norman Geo. A. F. Quentin Mat. McDonough E. D. C. Hilliard Sir J. G. Baird, Bt. Bertie B. Mathew
Cornets . .	Geo. A. F. Quentin Mat. McDonough E. D. C. Hilliard Sir James G. Baird, Bart.	E. D. C. Hilliard Sir J. G. Baird, Bt. Bertie B. Mathew Dudley Heneage	Dudley Heneage Charles Wombwell Wm. G. Cavendish
Paymaster .	S. Wells	S. Wells	S. Wells
Adjutant .	James Preston	James Preston	James Preston
Quartermaster	J. C. McClellan	J. McClellan	J. McClellan
Surgeon . .	W. R. Rogers	W. R. Rogers	W. R. Rogers
Asst.-Surgeon	F. Goodwin	F. Goodwin	F. Goodwin
Vet. Surgeon .	H. C. Sannerman	John Gloag	J. Gloag

TENTH REGIMENT OF LIGHT DRAGOONS (HUSSARS)—*continued*

	1835	1836	1837
Colonel . .	C. W., Marquis of Londonderry, G.C.B., G.C.H.	C. W., Marquis of Londonderry, G.C.B., G.C.H.	C. W., Marquis of Londonderry, G.C.B., G.C.H.
Lieut.-Col. .	Lord T. Cecil	Lord T. Cecil	Lord T. Cecil
Major . .	J. C. Wallington	J. C. Wallington	J. C. Wallington
Captains .	G. L. L. Kaye	G. L. L. Kaye	G. L. L. Kaye
	Robert Giffard	Robert Giffard	H. F. Bonham
	F. S. Wedderburn	H. F. Bonham	William Houstoun
	H. F. Bonham	William Houstoun	Hon. P. Moreton
	William Houstoun	Hon. P. Moreton	John Rowley
	Hon. P. Moreton	John Rowley	G. A. F. Quentin
Lieutenants .	James Preston	Geo. A. F. Quentin	Mat. McDonough
	John Rowley	Mat. McDonough	E. D. C. Hilliard
	Geo. A. F. Quentin	E. D. C. Hilliard	Sir J. G. Baird, Bt.
	Mat. McDonough	Sir J. G. Baird, Bt.	Bertie B. Mathew
	E. D. C. Hilliard	Bertie B. Mathew	Charles Wombwell
	Sir J. G. Baird, Bt.	Charles Wombwell	Robert Hume
	Bertie B. Mathew	Robert Hume	Wm. G. Cavendish
	Charles Wombwell	Wm. G. Cavendish	William Tomline
	Robert Hume	William Tomline	N. E. Blackall
	Wm. G. Cavendish	N. E. Blackall	Robert B. Wood
Cornets . .	William Tomline	Robert B. Wood	A. W. Williams
	N. E. Blackall	A. W. Williams	John Long
	Robert B. Wood	John Long	Hon. A. A. Harbord
Paymaster .	S. Wells	S. Wells	S. Wells
Adjutant .	James Preston	Sir J. G. Baird, Bt.	Sir J. G. Baird, Bt.
Quartermaster	J. McClellan	J. McClellan	J. McClellan
Surgeon. .	W. R. Rogers	W. R. Rogers	W. R. Rogers
Asst.-Surgeon	F. Goodwin	F. Goodwin	W. Stewart
Vet. Surgeon.	J. Gloag	J. Gloag	J. Gloag

TENTH REGIMENT OF LIGHT DRAGOONS (HUSSARS)—*continued*

	1838	1839	1840
Colonel . .	C. W., Marquis of Londonderry, G.C.B., G.C.H.	C. W., Marquis of Londonderry, G.C.B., G.C.H.	C. W., Marquis of Londonderry, G.C.B., G.C.H.
Lieut.-Col. .	Lord T. Cecil	John Vandeleur	John Vandeleur
Major . .	J. C. Wallington	J. C. Wallington	J. C. Wallington
Captains .	G. L. L. Kaye H. F. Bonham W. Houstoun J. Rowley G. A. F. Quentin E. D. C. Hilliard	G. L. L. Kaye H. F. Bonham W. Houstoun J. Rowley G. A. F. Quentin E. D. C. Hilliard	G. L. L. Kaye H. F. Bonham J. Rowley G. A. F. Quentin E. D. C. Hilliard Sir J. G. Baird, Bt.
Lieutenants .	M. M'Donough Sir J. G. Baird B. B. Mathew C. Wombwell W. G. Cavendish W. Tomline N. E. Blackall R. B. Wood W. H. Duff A. W. Williams	M. M'Donough Sir J. G. Baird, Bt. W. G. Cavendish W. Tomline N. E. Blackall A. B. Wood W. H. Duff A. W. Williams J. Long R. E. Ward	M. M'Donough W. G. Cavendish W. Tomline N. E. Blackall R. B. Wood A. W. Williams J. Long R. E. Ward Andrew Cathcart H. E. Surtees
Cornets . .	J. Long Hon. A. H. Harbord R. E. Ward	H. E. Surtees John Wilkie Lord G. A. Beauclerck	J. Wilkie Lord G. A. Beauclerck George Webb
Paymaster .	S. Wells	S. Wells	S. Wells
Adjutant .	Sir J. G. Baird, Bt.	Sir J. G. Baird, Bt.	George Webb
Quartermaster	J. McClellan	J. McClellan	J. McClellan
Surgeon .	W. R. Rogers	W. R. Rogers	W. R. Rogers
Asst.-Surgeon	W. Stewart	W. Stewart	W. Stewart
Vet. Surgeon .	J. Gloag	J. Gloag	J. Gloag

TENTH REGIMENT OF LIGHT DRAGOONS (HUSSARS)—*continued*

	1841	1842	1843
Colonel . .	C. W., Marquis of Londonderry, G.C.B., G.C.H.	C. W., Marquis of Londonderry, G.C.B., G.C.H.	C. W., Marquis of Londonderry, G.C.B., G.C.H.
Lieut.-Col. .	J. Vandeleur	J. Vandeleur	J. Vandeleur
Major . .	J. C. Wallington	J. C. Wallington	J. C. Wallington
Captains .	G. L. L. Kaye H. F. Bonham G. A. F. Quentin E. D. C. Hilliard Sir J. G. Baird, Bt. Wm. Armstrong	H. F. Bonham G. A. F. Quentin E. D. C. Hilliard Sir J. G. Baird, Bt. W. Tomline R. B. Wood	H. F. Bonham G. A. F. Quentin W. Tomline R. B. Wood A. W. Williams A. Cathcart
Lieutenants .	M. M'Donough W. Tomline R. B. Wood A. W. Williams J. Long R. E. Ward H. Cathcart H. E. Surtees Lord J. Beresford J. Wilkie	M. M'Donough A. W. Williams R. E. Ward A. Cathcart H. E. Surtees J. Wilkie Lord G. A. Beau- clerck R. H. Smith Barry G. Webb	M. M'Donough H. E. Surtees J. Wilkie Lord G. A. Beau- clerck R. H. Smith-Barry G. Webb William A. Hyder R. Pate Sir T. Munro, Bt.
Cornets . .	Lord G. A. Beau- clerck G. Webb J. Robarts	J. Robarts Robert Pate James C. Ferrier R. G. Townley	J. C. Ferrier R. G. Townley Francis Leigh T. T. S. Carlyon
Paymaster .	S. Wells	S. Wells	E. Bentley Frith
Adjutant .	G. Webb	G. Webb	G. Webb
Quartermaster	J. McClellan	J. McClellan	J. McClellan
Surgeon .	W. R. Rogers	D. Murray, M.D.	D. Murray, M.D.
Asst.-Surgeon	W. Stewart	A. Anderson, M.D.	A. Anderson, M.D.
Vet. Surgeon .	J. Gloag	J. Gloag	J. Gloag

TENTH REGIMENT OF LIGHT DRAGOONS (HUSSARS)—*continued*

	1844	1845	1846
Colonel . .	Hon. H. Beauchamp Lygon	Hon. H. Beauchamp Lygon	Hon. H. Beauchamp Lygon
Lieut.-Col. .	J. Vandeleur	J. Vandeleur	J. Vandeleur
Major . .	J. C. Wallington	J. C. Wallington	J. C. Wallington
Captains .	H. F. Bonham G. A. F. Quentin W. Tomline R. B. Wood A. Cathcart F. O. H. Bridgeman	H. F. Bonham G. A. F. Quentin W. Tomline J. Wilkie Broadley Harrison Lord G. A. Beauclerck	H. F. Bonham G. A. F. Quentin W. Tomline J. Wilkie B. Harrison Lord G. A. Beauclerck
Lieutenants .	M. M'Donough J. Wilkie Lord G. A. Beauclerck R. H. S. Barry G. Webb W. A. Hyder R. Pate Sir T. Munro, Bt. J. C. Ferrier	M. M'Donough R. H. S. Barry G. Webb W. A. Hyder R. Pate Sir G. Munro, Bt. J. C. Ferrier R. G. Townley F. Leigh	M. M'Donough R. H. S. Barry G. Webb W. A. Hyder R. Pate Sir T. Munro, Bt. R. G. Townley T. T. S. Carlyon C. F. Surtees Hon. F. C. G. Fitz-Clarence
Cornets . .	R. G. Townley F. Leigh T. T. S. Carlyon C. F. Surtees	T. T. S. Carlyon C. F. Surtees C. H. S. G., Lord Garvagh Edward Shelley	C. H. S. G., Lord Garvagh E. Shelley W. McFarlane Wardrop
Paymaster .	E. B. Frith	E. B. Frith	E. B. Frith
Adjutant .	G. Webb	G. Webb	G. Webb
Quartermaster	J. McClellan	J. McClellan	J. McClellan
Surgeon .	D. Murray, M.D.	D. Murray, M.D.	D. Murray, M.D.
Asst.-Surgeon	A. Anderson, M.D.	A. Anderson, M.D.	T. Fraser, M.D.
Vet. Surgeon .	J. Gloag	J. Gloag	J. Gloag

TENTH REGIMENT OF LIGHT DRAGOONS (HUSSARS)—*continued*

	1847	1848	1849
Colonel . .	Hon. H. Beauchamp Lygon	Hon. H. Beauchamp Lygon	Hon. H. Beauchamp Lygon
Lieut.-Cols. .	H. F. Bonham	H. F. Bonham	H. F. Bonham
	William Parlby	W. Parlby	W. Parlby
Majors . .	John Tritton	J. Tritton	J. Tritton
	G. A. F. Quentin	G. A. F. Quentin	G. A. F. Quentin
Captains .	J. Wilkie	J. Wilkie	J. Wilkie
	B. Harrison	B. Harrison	B. Harrison
	Lord G. A. Beauclerck	Lord G. A. Beauclerck	Lord G. A. Beauclerck
	W. P. Waugh	W. P. Waugh	W. P. Waugh
	Thomas Lloyd	T. Lloyd	T. Lloyd
	R. H. Smith Barry	Sir T. Munro, Bt.	Sir T. Munro, Bt.
	Sir T. Munro, Bt.	Methuen Stedman	M. Stedman
	R. G. Townley	William Murray	W. Murray
	T. T. S. Carlyon	C. F. Surtees	C. F. Surtees
Lieutenants .	G. Webb	G. Webb	G. Webb
	C. F. Surtees	Hon. F. C. G. Fitz-Clarence	Hon. F. C. G. Fitz-Clarence
	Hon. F. C. G. Fitz-Clarence	C. H. S. G., Lord Garvagh	C. H. S. G., Lord Garvagh
	C. H. S. G., Lord Garvagh	T. S. Little	T. S. Little
	Robert Walsh	M. R. L. Meason	M. R. L. Meason
	Thomas S. Little	R. S. Parker	R. C. Holmes
	M. R. L. Meason	R. C. Holmes	R. Playne Smith
	Robert S. Parker	R. Playne Smith	C. P. Rosser
	Robert C. Holmes	C. P. Rosser	T. Wirgman

TENTH REGIMENT OF LIGHT DRAGOONS (HUSSARS)—*continued*

	1847	1848	1849
Lieutenants .	R. Playne Smith	T. Wirgman	J. W. Thompson
	Charles P. Rosser	J. W. Thompson	W. McF. Wardrop
	Theodore Wirgman	W. McF. Wardrop	R. E. Blake
	Edward Shelley	R. E. Blake	A. J. Loftus
	John W. Thompson	A. J. Loftus	J. W. Clarke
	W. McF. Wardrop	J. W. Clarke	C. MacMahon
	Richard E. Blake	C. MacMahon	J. Percy Smith
	Arthur J. Loftus	John Percy Smith	B. M. Giveen
	Lord James De	B. M. Giveen	B. A. Branfill
	Burgh Browne	B. A. Branfill	J. Drummond
	John W. Clarke		
Cornets . .	Charles MacMahon	R. Clements	R. Clements
	Robert Clements	J. Dummond	E. J. S. Blair
	Butler M. Giveen	E. J. S. Blair	T. Williams
	B. A. Branfill	T. Williams	E. Stacey
	John Drummond	E. Stacey	H. Alexander
	E. J. S. Blair	Theo. H. Dury	J. R. Cuthbert
	Theodore Williams	Henry Alexander	Hon. F. Dimsdale
	Edward Stacey	John R. Cuthbert	F. B. H. Carew
Paymaster .	E. B. Frith	E. B. Frith	R. G. Elrington
Adjutant .	G. Webb	G. Webb	G. Webb
Quartermaster	J. Fenn	J. Fenn	J. Fenn
Surgeon .	M. J. McL. Ross	M. J. McL. Ross	M. J. McL. Ross
Asst.-Surgeons	T. Fraser, M.D.	T. Fraser, M.D.	T. Fraser, M.D.
	J. E. Stephens, M.D.	J. E. Stephens, M.D.	J. E. Stephens, M.D.
Vet. Surgeon .	James Robertson	J. Robertson	Thomas Siddell

TENTH REGIMENT OF LIGHT DRAGOONS (HUSSARS)—*continued*

	1850	1851	1852
Colonel . .	Hon. H. Beauchamp Lygon	Hon. H. Beauchamp Lygon	Hon. H. Beauchamp Lygon
Lieut.-Cols. .	H. F. Bonham W. Parlby	H. F. Bonham W. Parlby	W. Parlby J. Tritton
Majors . .	J. Tritton G. A. F. Quentin	J. Tritton G. A. F. Quentin	G. A. F. Quentin J. Wilkie
Captains .	J. Wilkie B. Harrison Lord G. A. Beauclerck W. P. Waugh Sir T. Munro, Bt. M. Stedman W. Murray C. F. Surtees	J. Wilkie B. Harrison Lord G. A. Beauclerck Sir T. Munro, Bt. M. Stedman W. Murray C. F. Surtees Hon. F. C. G. Fitz-Clarence C. H. S. G., Lord Garvagh	B. Harrison Lord G. A. Beauclerck M. Stedman W. Murray C. F. Surtees Hon. F. C. G. Fitz-Clarence R. C. Holmes Charles Bowles R. Playne Smith
Lieutenants .	G. Webb Hon. F. C. G. Fitz-Clarence C. H. S. G., Lord Garvagh T. S. Little M. R. L. Meason R. C. Holmes R. Playne Smith C. P. Rosser	T. S. Little M. R. L. Meason R. C. Holmes R. Playne Smith C. P. Rosser Theo. Wirgman J. W. Thompson A. J. Loftus	T. S. Little C. P. Rosser Theo. Wirgman J. W. Thompson A. J. Loftus J. W. Clarke J. P. Smith B. M. Giveen

TENTH REGIMENT OF LIGHT DRAGOONS (HUSSARS)—*continued*

	1850	1851	1852
Lieutenants .	Theo. Wirgman	J. W. Clarke	B. A. Branfill
	J. W. Thompson	C. MacMahon	J. Drummond
	A. J. Loftus	J. P. Smith	R. Hatfield
	J. W. Clarke	B. M. Giveen	Theodore Williams
	C. MacMahon	B. A. Branfill	R. Clements
	J. P. Smith	J. Drummond	E. Stacey
	B. M. Giveen	R. W. Hatfield	H. Alexander
	B. A. Branfill	Theodore Williams	J. R. Cuthbert
	J. Drummond	R. Clements	T. M. Townley
	R. W. Hatfield	E. Stacey	Hon. C. J. Keith
	Theodore Williams	H. Alexander	J. E. Severne
Cornets . .	R. Clements	J. R. Cuthbert	H. Beckett
	E. Stacey	T. M. Townley	E. M. R. Stapylton
	H. Alexander	Frederick Marshall	A. H. Cass
	J. R. Cuthbert	Hon. C. J. Keith	G. Webster
	F. B. H. Carew	Hamilton Beckett	W. G. Bridgman
	Thos. M. Townley	J. Edward Severne	H. W. M. Hathway
	Frederick Marshall	E. M. R. Stapylton	M. J. B. Dyne
	Hon. C. J. Keith	Arthur Her. Cass	H. E. Benson
Paymaster .	R. G. Elrington	R. G. Elrington	R. G. Elrington
Adjutant .	George Webb	J. Percy Smith	J. Percy Smith
Quartermaster	J. Fenn	J. Fenn	J. Fenn
Surgeon .	M. J. McL. Ross	M. J. McL. Ross	M. J. McL. Ross
Asst.-Surgeons	Thos. Fraser, M.D.	Thos. Fraser, M.D.	Thos. Fraser, M.D.
	J. E. Stephens, M.D.	J. E. Stephens, M.D.	Jas. Macbeth, M.D.
Vet. Surgeon .	Thomas Siddell	Thomas Siddell	Thomas Siddell

M M

TENTH REGIMENT OF LIGHT DRAGOONS (HUSSARS)—*continued*

		1853	1854	1855
Colonel .	.	Earl Beauchamp	Earl Beauchamp	Earl Beauchamp
Lieut.-Cols.	.	W. Parlby	W. Parlby	W. Parlby
		J. Tritton	J. Wilkie	J. Wilkie
Majors .	.	J. Wilkie	B. Harrison	B. Harrison
		B. Harrison	Lord G. A. Beauclerck	Lord G. A. Beauclerck
Captains	.	Lord G. A. Beauclerck	W. Murray	W. Murray
		M. Stedman	Hon. F. C. G. Fitz-Clarence	Hon. F. C. G. Fitz-Clarence
		W. Murray	R. C. Holmes	R. C. Holmes
		C. F. Surtees	C. Bowles	C. Bowles
		Hon. F. C. G. Fitz-Clarence	R. Playne Smith	R. Playne Smith
		R. C. Holmes	J. W. Thompson	J. W. Thompson
		C. Bowles	James Cowell	J. Cowell
		R. Playne Smith	A. J. Loftus	A. J. Loftus
		J. W. Thompson	J. W. Clarke	J. W. Clarke
		T. S. Little	B. M. Giveen	B. M. Giveen
Lieutenants	.	C. P. Rosser	C. P. Rosser	C. P. Rosser
		Theo. Wirgman	Theo. Wirgman	Theo. Wirgman
		A. J. Loftus	J. Percy Smith	J. Percy Smith
		J. W. Clarke	B. A. Branfill	B. A. Branfill
		J. Percy Smith	J. Drummond	R. Hatfield
		B. M. Giveen	R. Hatfield	Theodore Williams
		B. A. Branfill	Theodore Williams	E. Stacey
		J. Drummond	E. Stacey	H. Alexander
		R. Hatfield	H. Alexander	J. R. Cuthbert

TENTH REGIMENT OF LIGHT DRAGOONS (HUSSARS)—*continued*

	1853	1854	1855
Lieutenants .	Theodore Williams	J. R. Cuthbert	T. M. Townley
	R. Clements	T. M. Townley	A. H. Cass
	E. Stacey	A. H. Cass	A. E. Benson
	H. Alexander	A. E. Benson	D. R. Gill
	J. R. Cuthbert	D. R. Gill	F. T. O. Hopson
	T. M. Townley	F. T. O. Hopson	J. M. B. Murdoch
	A. H. Cass	W. O. Bird	W. O. Bird
	Hugh J. Fairlie	J. M. B. Murdoch	James A. Clark
	George Webster	James A. Clark	H. F. Richmond
	E. M. R. Stapylton	H. F. Richmond	J. J. N. Buchanan
Cornets . .	H. W. H. Hathway	J. J. N. Buchanan	George S. Davies
	M. J. B. Dyne	Henry Baring	John Hudson
	A. E. Benson	George S. Davies	Chas. H. Uniacke
	D. R. Gill	John Hudson	A. A. de Bourbel
	J. M. B. Murdoch	Chas. H. Uniacke	W. Mayne
	James A. Clarke	A. A. de Bourbel	S. Vyse
	Hon. M. F. Deane		
Paymaster .	R. G. Elrington	R. G. Elrington	R. G. Elrington
Adjutant .	J. Percy Smith	J. Percy Smith	J. Percy Smith
Quartermaster	J. Fenn	J. Fenn	J. Fenn
Surgeon .	M. J. McL. Ross	M. J. McL. Ross	Thos. Fraser, M.D.
Asst.-Surgeons	Thos. Fraser, M.D.	Thos. Fraser, M.D.	Alexander M. Macbeth, M.D.
	Jas. Macbeth, M.D.	Alexander M. Macbeth, M.D.	
Vet. Surgeon .	Thomas Siddell	Thomas Siddell	Thomas Siddell

TENTH REGIMENT OF LIGHT DRAGOONS (HUSSARS)—*continued*

	1856	1857	1858
Colonel . .	Earl Beauchamp	Earl Beauchamp	Earl Beauchamp
Lieut.-Cols. . .	W. Parlby J. Wilkie	J. Wilkie	J. Wilkie
Majors . .	B. Harrison Lord G. A. Beau- clerck	B. Harrison	B. Harrison
Captains .	W. Murray Hon. F. C. G. Fitz- Clarence R. C. Holmes R. P. Smith J. W. Thompson J. Cowell C. P. Rosser H. Alexander	W. Murray Hon. F. C. G. Fitz- Clarence R. C. Holmes R. Playne Smith J. W. Thompson J. Cowell	R. P. Smith J. W. Thompson J. Cowell Val. Baker F. M. Townley D. R. Gill Theo. Wirgman Edward Levett
Lieutenants .	Theo. Wirgman B. A. Branfill R. Hatfield E. Stacey J. R. Cuthbert F. M. Townley A. H. Cass A. E. Benson D. R. Gill W. O. Bird J. J. N. Buchanan	Theo. Wirgman B. A. Branfill E. Stacey F. M. Townley A. H. Cass A. E. Benson D. R. Gill Edward Levett	A. H. Cass W. Mayne J. Fife F. H. Suckling H. A. Bowyer R. Lomax J. Gore E. J. Howley
Cornets . .	W. Mayne	W. Mayne J. Fife H. P. Gordon H. A. Bowyer J. Gore	E. L. L. Lovell Lord R. D. Kerr C. T. Vandeleur
Paymaster .	R. G. Elrington	R. G. Elrington	R. G. Elrington
Adjutant .	J. R. Cuthbert	J. Fife	J. Fife
Ridingmaster	—	—	E. Simpson
Quartermaster	J. Fenn	J. Fenn	J. Fenn
Surgeon . .	Thos. Fraser, M.D.	Thos. Fraser, M.D.	Thos. Fraser, M.D.
Asst.-Surgeon	L. G. Hooper	L. G. Hooper	L. G. Hooper
Vet. Surgeon .	John Barker	John Barker	J. G. Philips

TENTH REGIMENT OF LIGHT DRAGOONS (HUSSARS)—*continued*

	1859	1860	1861
Colonel .	Earl Beauchamp	Earl Beauchamp	Earl Beauchamp
Lieut.-Col. .	J. Wilkie	Valentine Baker	Valentine Baker
Major .	B. Harrison	R. P. Smith	Edward Levett
Captains .	R. P. Smith Valentine Baker Edward Levett A. H. Cass W. Mayne J. Fife R. C. Sawbridge F. Coates	Edward Levett A. H. Cass J. Fife R. C. Sawbridge F. Coates H. A. Bowyer R. N. Pedder E. P. Baumgarten	A. H. Cass J. Fife R. C. Sawbridge F. Coates H. A. Bowyer R. N. Pedder Hon. C. C. Molyneux E. L. L. Lovell Hon. E. Stourton
Lieutenants .	H. A. Bowyer R. Lomax J. Gore E. J. Howley E. P. Baumgarten E. L. L. Lovell Lord R. D. Kerr C. T. Vandeleur T. S. Ball	R. Lomax E. L. L. Lovell Lord R. D. Kerr C. T. Vandeleur T. S. Ball O. R. Slacke A. Barthorp E. A. Wood W. M. Maunder	R. Lomax Lord R. D. Kerr C. T. Vandeleur O. R. Slacke A. Barthorp E. A. Wood W. M. Maunder T. J. W. Bulkeley Robert S. Liddell
Cornets .	O. R. Slacke G. Houstoun A. Barthorp E. A. Wood W. M. Maunder T. J. W. Bulkeley W. Brougham	T. J. W. Bulkeley W. Brougham H. P. Holford T. A. St. Quintin C. B. Ponsonby J. C. S. Fremantle H. D. Evans	W. Brougham H. P. Holford T. A. St. Quintin C. B. Ponsonby J. C. S. Fremantle H. Davies-Evans A. Wyatt-Edgell J. C. Russell
Paymaster .	R. J. Elrington	R. J. Elrington	R. J. Elrington
Adjutant .	Lord R. D. Kerr	Lord R. D. Kerr	Lord R. D. Kerr
Ridingmaster	E. Simpson	E. Simpson	E. Simpson
Quartermaster	J. Fenn	J. Hill James	J. H. James
Surgeon .	Thos. Fraser, M.D.	Thos. Fraser, M.D.	Thos. Fraser, M.D.
Asst.-Surgeon	L. G. Hooper	L. G. Hooper	L. G. Hooper
Vet. Surgeon .	J. G. Philips	William Thacker	W. Thacker

TENTH (PRINCE OF WALES'S OWN ROYAL) HUSSARS—*continued*

	1862	1863	1864
Colonel . .	Earl Beauchamp	Earl Beauchamp	H.R.H. the Prince of Wales, K.G.
Lieut.-Col. .	V. Baker	V. Baker	V. Baker
Major . .	Edw. Levett	A. H. Cass	A. H. Cass
Captains .	A. H. Cass J. Fife R. C. Sawbridge H. A. Bowyer Hon. C. C. Molyneux Hon. E. Stourton G. Hanbury Lord R. D. Kerr	J. Fife R. C. Sawbridge H. A. Bowyer Hon. C. C. Molyneux Hon. E. Stourton G. Hanbury Lord R. D. Kerr C. T. Vandeleur	J. Fife R. C. Sawbridge H. A. Bowyer Hon. C. C. Molyneux Hon. E. Stourton G. Hanbury Lord R. D. Kerr C. T. Vandeleur
Lieutenants .	C. T. Vandeleur O. R. Slacke A. Barthorp E. A. Wood W. M. Maunder T. J. W. Bulkeley R. S. Liddell W. Brougham H. P. Holford	O. R. Slacke A. Barthorp E. A. Wood W. M. Maunder T. J. W. Bulkeley R. S. Liddell W. Brougham H. P. Holford T. A. St. Quintin	O. R. Slacke A. Barthorp E. A. Wood T. J. W. Bulkeley R. S. Liddell H. P. Holford T. A. St. Quintin C. B. Ponsonby J. C. S. Fremantle
Cornets ..	T. A. St. Quintin C. B. Ponsonby J. C. S. Fremantle H. Davies-Evans A. Wyatt-Edgell J. C. Russell C. E. Frederick W. C. FitzHerbert	C. B. Ponsonby J. C. S. Fremantle H. Davies-Evans A. Wyatt-Edgell J. C. Russell C. E. Frederick W. C. FitzHerbert W. H. Watkins	H. Davies-Evans A. Wyatt-Edgell J. C. Russell C. E. Frederick W. C. FitzHerbert W. H. Watkins E. S. Watson Hon. H. G. L. Crichton
Paymaster .	R. J. Elrington	R. J. Elrington	R. J. Elrington
Adjutant .	O. R. Slacke	O. R. Slacke	O. R. Slacke
In. Musketry .	A. Barthorp	A. Barthorp	A. Barthorp
Ridingmaster	E. Simpson	E. Simpson	E. Simpson
Quartermaster	J. H. James	J. H. James	J. H. James
Surgeon. .	Thos. Fraser, M.D.	Thos. Fraser, M.D.	Thos. Fraser, M.D.
Asst.-Surgeon	L. G. Hooper	L. G. Hooper	L. G. Hooper
Vet. Surgeon	W. Thacker	W. Thacker	Hicks Withers

TENTH (PRINCE OF WALES'S OWN ROYAL) HUSSARS—*continued*

	1865	1866	1867
Colonel . .	H.R.H. the Prince of Wales, K.G.	H.R.H. the Prince of Wales, K.G.	H.R.H. the Prince of Wales, K.G.
Lieut.-Col. .	V. Baker	V. Baker	V. Baker
Major . .	A. H. Cass	A. H. Cass	A. H. Cass
Captains .	J. Fife	J. Fife	J. Fife
	R. C. Sawbridge	R. C. Sawbridge	R. C. Sawbridge
	Hon. C. C. Molyneux	Hon. C. C. Molyneux	Hon. C. C. Molyneux
	Hon. E. Stourton	Hon. E. Stourton	Hon. E. Stourton
	Lord R. D. Kerr	Lord R. D. Kerr	Lord R. D. Kerr
	A. Barthorp	A. Barthorp	A. Barthorp
	W. Chaine	W. Chaine	W. Chaine
	O. R. Slacke	O. R. Slacke	O. R. Slacke
Lieutenants .	E. A. Wood	E. A. Wood	E. A. Wood
	T. J. W. Bulkeley	T. J. W. Bulkeley	T. J. W. Bulkeley
	R. S. Liddell	R. S. Liddell	R. S. Liddell
	T. A. St. Quintin	T. A. St. Quintin	T. A. St. Quintin
	C. B. Ponsonby	C. B. Ponsonby	C. B. Ponsonby
	H. Davies-Evans	H. Davies-Evans	J. C. Russell
	J. C. Russell	J. C. Russell	C. E. Frederick
	C. R. Frederick	C. E. Frederick	D. F. Gabbett
	D. F. Gabbett	D. F. Gabbett	W. H. Watkins
Cornets . .	W. H. Watkins	W. H. Watkins	E. S. Watson
	E. S. Watson	E. S. Watson	Hon. H. G. L. Crichton
	Hon. H. G. L. Crichton	Hon. H. G. L. Crichton	U. E. P. Okeden
	U. E. P. Okeden	U. E. P. Okeden	Arthur, Viscount Valentia
	Arthur, Viscount Valentia	Arthur, Viscount Valentia	T. A. Smith-Dorrien
	T. A. Smith-Dorrien	T. A. Smith-Dorrien	Hon. H. J. L. Wood
	H. J. L. Wood	H. J. L. Wood	Ed. Hartopp
	Ed. Hartopp	Ed. Hartopp	R. Thorold
Paymaster .	R. J. Elrington	R. J. Elrington	R. J. Elrington
Adjutant .	J. C. Russell	J. C. Russell	J. C. Russell
In. Musketry .	Hon. H. G. L. Crichton	Hon. H. G. L. Crichton	—
Ridingmaster	E. Simpson	E. Simpson	E. Simpson
Quartermaster	J. H. James	J. H. James	J. H. James
Surgeon . .	Thos. Fraser, M.D.	Thos. Fraser, M.D.	Thos. Fraser, M.D.
Asst.-Surgeon.	L. G. Hooper	J. T. Milburn	J. T. Milburn
Vet. Surgeon .	Hicks Withers	Hicks Withers	Hicks Withers

TENTH (PRINCE OF WALES'S OWN ROYAL) HUSSARS—*continued*

	1868	1869	1870
Colonel . .	H.R.H. the Prince of Wales, K.G.	H.R.H. the Prince of Wales, K.G.	H.R.H. the Prince of Wales, K.G.
Lieut.-Col. .	V. Baker	V. Baker	V. Baker
Major . .	J. Fife	J. Fife	Hon. C. C. Molyneux
Captains .	R. C. Sawbridge Hon. C. C. Molyneux Hon. E. Stourton Lord R. D. Kerr A. Barthorp W. Chaine E. A. Wood T. J. W. Bulkeley	R. C. Sawbridge Hon. C. C. Molyneux Lord R. D. Kerr A. Barthorp W. Chaine E. A. Wood T. J. W. Bulkeley R. S. Liddell	Lord R. D. Kerr A. Barthorp W. Chaine E. A. Wood T. J. W. Bulkeley R. S. Liddell J. C. Russell T. A. St. Quintin
Lieutenants .	R. S. Liddell T. A. St. Quintin C. B. Ponsonby J. C. Russell C. E. Frederick W. H. Watkins E. S. Watson Hon. H. G. L. Crichton U. E. P. Okeden	T. A. St. Quintin J. C. Russell C. E. Frederick W. H. Watkins E. S. Watson Hon. H. G. L. Crichton U. E. P. Okeden Arthur, Viscount Valentia T. A. Smith-Dorrien	C. E. Frederick W. H. Watkins E. S. Watson Hon. H. G. L. Crichton U. E. P. Okeden Arthur, Viscount Valentia T. A. Smith-Dorrien Hon. H. J. L. Wood. Ed. Hartopp
Cornets . .	Arthur, Viscount Valentia T. A. Smith-Dorrien Hon. H. J. L. Wood Ed. Hartopp R. Thorold H. A. Coventry Hon. W. T. Fitz-william Hon. R. G. Molyneux	Hon. H. J. L. Wood Ed. Hartopp R. Thorold H. A. Coventry Hon. W. T. Fitz-william Hon. R. G. Moly-neux H. S. Gough	R. Thorold Hon. W. T. Fitz-william Hon. R. G. Moly-neux H. S. Gough D. R. Wyndham, Lord Naas
Paymaster .	R. J. Elrington	R. J. Elrington	L. E. Montgomery
Adjutant .	J. C. Russell	Hon. H. G. L. Crichton	Hon. H. G. L. Crichton
Ridingmaster	E. Simpson	E. Simpson	David Walsh
Quartermaster	J. H. James	J. H. James	J. H. James
Surgeon . .	Thos. Fraser, M.D.	Thos. Fraser, M.D.	Thos. Fraser, M.D.
Asst.-Surgeon.	J. T. Milburn	J. T. Milburn	J. T. Milburn
Vet. Surgeon .	Hicks Withers	Wm. Appleton	W. Appleton

TENTH (PRINCE OF WALES'S OWN ROYAL) HUSSARS—*continued*

	1871	1872	1873
Colonel . .	H.R.H. the Prince of Wales, K.G.	H.R.H. the Prince of Wales, K.G.	H.R.H. the Prince of Wales, K.G.
Lieut.-Colonel	V. Baker	V. Baker	Hon. C. C. Molyneux
Major . .	Hon. C. C. Molyneux	Hon. C. C. Molyneux	Lord R. D. Kerr
Captains .	Lord R. D. Kerr A. Barthorp W. Chaine E. A. Wood T. J. W. Bulkeley R. S. Liddell J. C. Russell T. A. St. Quintin	Lord R. D. Kerr A. Barthorp W. Chaine E. A. Wood T. J. W. Bulkeley R. S. Liddell T. A. St. Quintin C. E. Frederick	W. Chaine E. A. Wood T. J. W. Bulkeley R. S. Liddell T. A. St. Quintin C. E. Frederick W. H. Watkins
Lieutenants .	C. E. Frederick W. H. Watkins E. S. Watson Hon. H. G. L. Crichton U. E. P. Okenden Arthur, Viscount Valentia T. A. Smith-Dorrien Hon. H. J. L. Wood Ed. Hartopp	W. H. Watkins E. S. Watson Hon. H. G. L. Crichton U. E. P. Okeden T. A. Smith-Dorrien Hon. H. J. L. Wood Ed. Hartopp R. Thorold H. S. Gough C. W. F., Viscount Campden (*Sub-Lieutenant*)	Hon. H. G. L. Crichton U. E. P. Okeden T. A. Smith-Dorrien Hon. H. J. L. Wood Ed. Hartopp R. Thorold H. S. Gough Hon. C. C. W. Cavendish C. W. F., Viscount Campden R. F. P. Startin (*Sub-Lieutenants*)
Cornets . .	R. Thorold Hon. W. T. Fitzwilliam H. S. Gough D. R., Lord Naas C. W. F., Viscount Campden	H. H. R. Heath	H. H. R. Heath W. F. Montresor Hon. J. P. Napier R. T. Dalton
Paymaster .	L. E. Montgomery	L. E. Montgomery	L. E. Montgomery
Adjutant .	Hon. H. G. L. Crichton	Hon. H. G. L. Crichton	Hon. H. G. L. Crichton
Ridingmaster	D. Walsh	D. Walsh	D. Walsh
Quartermaster	J. H. James	J. H. James	W. King
Surgeon . .	Thos. Fraser, M.D.	Thos. Fraser, M.D.	W. Cattell (*Surgeon-Major*)
Asst.-Surgeon	J. T. Milburn	H. Cornish	—
Vet. Surgeon .	W. Appleton	W. Appleton	W. Appleton

TENTH (PRINCE OF WALES'S OWN ROYAL) HUSSARS— *continued*

	1874	1875	1876
Colonel . .	H.R.H. the Prince of Wales, K.G.	H.R.H. the Prince of Wales, K.G.	H.R.H. the Prince of Wales, K.G.
Lieut.-Col. .	Hon. C. C. Molyneux	Hon. C. C. Molyneux	Lord R. D. Kerr
Major . .	Lord R. D. Kerr	Lord R. D. Kerr	E. A. Wood
Captains .	W. Chaine E. A. Wood T. J. W. Bulkeley R. S. Liddell T. A. St. Quintin B. A. Combe R. C. D. Spottiswoode	E. A. Wood T. J. W. Bulkeley R. S. Liddell T. A. St. Quintin B. A. Combe R. C. D. Spottiswoode U. E. P. Okeden W. A. Battine Ed. Hartopp H. S. Gough	T. J. W. Bulkeley R. S. Liddell T. A. St. Quintin B. A. Combe R. C. D. Spottiswoode W. A. Battine Ed. Hartopp H. S. Gough W. Yeldham
Lieutenants .	U. E. P. Okeden Ed. Hartopp H. S. Gough Hon. C. C. W. Cavendish C. W. L., Viscount Campden R. F. P. Startin R. C. S. Drury-Lowe M. C. Wood J. P. Brabazon	Hon. C. C. W. Cavendish C. W. L., Viscount Campden M. C. Wood Hon. J. P. Napier R. F. P. Startin H. H. R. Heath W. F. Montresor J. P. Brabazon W. E. Phillips R. T. Dalton	Hon. C. C. W. Cavendish M. C. Wood H. H. R. Heath Hon. J. P. Napier W. F. Montresor J. P. Brabazon R. T. Dalton W. E. Phillips P. Durham B. S. C. L. Tottenham R. H. F. W. Wilson
Sub-Lieuts. .	H. H. R. Heath W. F. Montresor Hon. J. P. Napier R. T. Dalton E. T. Rose	E. T. Rose R. B. W. Fisher Ed. Cunard E. M. L. Inman	E. T. Rose R. B. W. Fisher Ed. Cunard E. M. L. Inman D. S. W., Lord Ogilvy
Paymaster .	L. E. Montgomery	L. E. Montgomery	
Adjutant .	H. S. Gough	—	Hon. C. C. W. Cavendish
Ridingmaster	C. Sandes	C. Sandes	C. Sandes
Quartermaster	W. King	W. King	W. King
Surgeon . .	Wm. Cattell	Wm. Cattell	Wm. Cattell
Vet. Surgeon .	W. Appleton	W. Appleton	W. Appleton

TENTH (PRINCE OF WALES'S OWN ROYAL) HUSSARS —*continued*

	1877	1878	1879
Colonel . .	H.R.H. the Prince of Wales, K.G.	H.R.H. the Prince of Wales, K.G.	H.R.H. the Prince of Wales, K.G.
Lieut.-Col. .	Lord R. D. Kerr	Lord R. D. Kerr	Lord R. D. Kerr
Major . .	E. A. Wood	E. A. Wood	E. A. Wood
Captains .	T. J. W. Bulkeley R. S. Liddell T. A. St. Quintin B. A. Combe R. C. D. Spottis-woode W. A. Battine Ed. Hartopp H. S. Gough	T. J. W. Bulkeley R. S. Liddell T. A. St. Quintin B. A. Combe R. C. D. Spottis-woode H. S. Gough W. Barker M. C. Wood M. M. Slade	T. J. W. Bulkeley R. S. Liddell T. A. St. Quintin B. A. Combe R. C. D. Spottis-woode H. S. Gough W. Barker M. C. Wood M. M. Slade
Lieutenants .	W. Chaine Hon. C. C. W Cavendish M. C. Wood Hon. J. P. Napier W. F. Montresor J. P. Brabazon R. T. Dalton W. E. Phillips R. B. W. Fisher E. M. L. Inman P. Durham D. S. W., Ld.Ogilvy R. H. F. W. Wilson	Hon. J. P. Napier J. P. Brabazon E. T. Rose R. T. Dalton W. E. Phillips R. B. W. Fisher E. M. L. Inman P. Durham D. S. W.,Ld.Ogilvy R. H. F. W. Wilson C. S. Greenwood C. Sandes	Hon. J. P. Napier J. P. Brabazon E. T. Rose W. E. Phillips R. B. W. Fisher P. Durham D. S. W., Ld.Ogilvy R. H. F. W. Wilson C. S. Greenwood C. Sandes Lord A. F. Compton
Sub-Lieuts . .	E. T. Rose C. S. Greenwood	F. H. Harwood C. M. Grenfell	C. M. Grenfell
Second-Lieuts.	—.	H. T. Allsopp Hon. G. L. Bellew	H. T. Allsopp Hon. G. L. Bellew
Paymaster .	Stephen Murphy	S. Murphy	S. Murphy
Adjutant .	Hon. C. C. W. Cavendish	C. Sandes	C. Sandes
Ridingmaster	C. Sandes	H. McGhee	H. McGhee
Quartermaster	W. King	W. King	W. King
Surgeon .	Wm. Cattell	W. Cattell	—
Vet. Surgeon .	W. Appleton	W. Appleton	W. Appleton

TENTH (PRINCE OF WALES'S OWN ROYAL) HUSSARS—*continued*

	1880	1881	1882
Colonel . .	H.R.H. the Prince of Wales, K.G.	H.R.H. the Prince of Wales, K.G.	H.R.H. the Prince of Wales, K.G.
Lieut.-Cols. . .	Lord R. D. Kerr	E. A. Wood R. S. Liddell	E. A. Wood R. S. Liddell
Majors . .	E. A. Wood	T. A. St. Quintin B. A. Combe R. C. D. Spottis-woode	T. A. St. Quintin B. A. Combe R. C. D. Spottis-woode H. S. Gough M. C. Wood
Captains .	T. J. W. Bulkeley R. S. Liddell T. A. St. Quintin B. A. Combe R. C. D. Spottis-woode H. S. Gough M. C. Wood M. M. Slade Hon. J. P. Napier J. P. Brabazon	H. S. Gough M. C. Wood M. M. Slade Hon. J. P. Napier J. P. Brabazon	M. M. Slade Hon. J. P. Napier J. P. Brabazon E. T. Rose W. E. Phillips
Lieutenants .	E. T. Rose W. E. Phillips R. B. W. Fisher P. Durham D. S.W., Ld.Ogilvy R. H. F. W. Wilson C. S. Greenwood C. Sandes C. M. Grenfell Lord A. F. Compton	E. T. Rose W. E. Phillips R. B. W. Fisher P. Durham D. S. W., Ld. Ogilvy R. H. F. W. Wilson C. S. Greenwood C. Sandes C. M. Grenfell Lord A. F. Compton H. T. Allsopp Hon. G. L. Bryan H. Alexander C. B. Harvey	R. B. W. Fisher P. Durham D. S. W., Earl of Airlie R. H. F. W. Wilson C. S. Greenwood C. Sandes C. M. Grenfell Lord A. F. Compton H. T. Allsopp Hon. G. L. Bryan H. Alexander C. B. Harvey Hon. A. Lawley A. Hughes-Onslow
Second-Lieuts.	H. T. Allsopp Hon. G. L. Bellew H. Alexander		
Paymaster .	S. Murphy	S. Murphy	Wm. Montgomery
Adjutant .	C. Sandes	C. Sandes	C. Sandes
Ridingmaster	H. McGhee	H. McGhee	H. McGhee
Quartermaster	W. King	W. King	W. King
Surgeon. .	—	—	—
Vet. Surgeon .	W. Appleton	—	—

TENTH (PRINCE OF WALES'S OWN ROYAL) HUSSARS— *continued*

	1883	1884	1885
Colonel . .	H.R.H. the Prince of Wales, K.G.	H.R.H. the Prince of Wales, K.G.	H.R.H. the Prince of Wales, K.G.
Lieut.-Cols. . .	E. A. Wood R. S. Liddell	E. A. Wood R. S. Liddell	E. A. Wood R. S. Liddell
Majors . .	T. A. St. Quintin B. A. Combe R. C. D. Spottis-woode H. S. Gough M. C. Wood M. M. Slade	T. A. St. Quintin B. A. Combe R. C. D. Spottis-woode H. S. Gough M. C. Wood M. M. Slade Hon. J. P. Napier	T. A. St. Quintin B. A. Combe R. C. D. Spottis-woode H. S. Gough M. C. Wood Hon. J. P. Napier
Captains .	Hon. J. P. Napier J. P. Brabazon E. T. Rose R. B. W. Fisher P. O. Sandeman	J. P. Brabazon E. T. Rose R. B. W. Fisher P. Durham D. S. W., Earl of Airlie R. H. F. W. Wilson	J. P. Brabazon E. T. Rose R. B. W. Fisher P. Durham D. S. W., Earl of Airlie R. H. F. W. Wilson C. S. Greenwood
Lieutenants .	P. Durham D. S. W., Earl of Airlie R. H. F. W. Wilson C. S. Greenwood C. M. Grenfell Lord A. F. Compton H. T. Allsopp Hon. G. L. Bryan H. Alexander C. B. Harvey Hon. A. Lawley A. Hughes-Onslow Hon. J. H. G. Byng	C. S. Greenwood C. M. Grenfell Lord A. F. Compton H. T. Allsopp Hon. G. L. Bryan H. Alexander C. B. Harvey Hon. A. Lawley A. Hughes-Onslow Hon. J. H. G. Byng C.T.McM.Kavanagh F. R. Bowlby	C. M. Grenfell Lord A. F. Compton H. T. Allsopp Hon. G. L. Bryan H. Alexander C. B. Harvey Hon. A. Lawley A. Hughes-Onslow Hon. J. H. G. Byng C.T.McM.Kavanagh F. R. Bowlby E. Baring E. W. D. Baird H.R.H. Prince Albert Victor C. E. of Wales
Paymaster .	W. Montgomery	Art. Brett	Art. Brett
Adjutant .	Earl of Airlie	Earl of Airlie	Lord A. Compton
Ridingmaster	H. McGhee	H. McGhee	John Perry
Quartermaster	A. Ed. Poole	A. Ed. Poole	A. Ed. Poole

TENTH (PRINCE OF WALES'S OWN ROYAL) HUSSARS—*continued*

	1886	1887	1888
Colonel . .	H.R.H. the Prince of Wales, K.G.	H.R.H. the Prince of Wales, K.G.	H.R.H. the Prince of Wales, K.G.
Lieut.-Cols. .	R. S. Liddell H. R., Visct. Downe	H. R., Visct. Downe	H. R., Visct. Downe
Majors . .	R. C. D. Spottiswoode H. S. Gough M. C. Wood Hon. J. P. Napier	H. S. Gough M. C. Wood Hon. J. P. Napier	H. S. Gough M. C. Wood Hon. J. P. Napier
Captains .	J. P. Brabazon R. B. W. Fisher P. Durham D. S. W., Earl of Airlie R. H. F. W. Wilson C. S. Greenwood	J. P. Brabazon R. B. W. Fisher P. Durham D. S. W., Earl of Airlie R. H. F. W. Wilson C. S. Greenwood H.R.H. Prince Albert Victor C. E. of Wales, K.G. Hon. H. T. Allsopp	J. P. Brabazon R. B. W. Fisher P. Durham D.S.W., Earl of Airlie R. H. F. W. Wilson C. S. Greenwood H.R.H. Prince Albert Victor C. E. of Wales, K.G. Hon. H. T. Allsopp Hon. G. L. Bryan
Lieutenants .	C. M. Grenfell Lord A. F. Compton Hon. H. T. Allsopp Hon. G. L. Bryan H. Alexander C. B. Harvey Hon. A. Lawley A. Hughes-Onslow Hon. J. H. G. Byng C.T.McM.Kavanagh F. R. Bowlby Hon. E. Baring E. W. D. Baird H.R.H. Prince Albert Victor C. E. of Wales	Hon. G. L. Bryan H. Alexander C. B. Harvey Hon. A. Lawley A. Hughes-Onslow Hon. J. H. G. Byng C.T.McM.Kavanagh F. R. Bowlby Hon. E. Baring E. W. D. Baird	H. Alexander C. B. Harvey Hon. A. Lawley A. Hughes-Onslow Hon. J. H. G. Byng C.T. McM. Kavanagh Hon. E. Baring E. W. D. Baird
Second Lieuts.	—	C. Barclay C. H., Lord Southampton	C. Barclay C. H., Lord Southampton Lord W. A. Cavendish-Bentinck Bertram C. C. S. Meeking
Paymaster .	Art. A. W. Bright-Smith	Art. A. W. Bright-Smith	Art. A. W. Bright-Smith
Adjutant .	Lord A. Compton	Hon. J. Byng	Hon. J. Byng
Ridingmaster	J. Perry	J. Perry	Philip Kelly
Quartermaster	A. E. Poole	A. E. Poole	A. E. Poole

TENTH (PRINCE OF WALES'S OWN ROYAL) HUSSARS—*continued*

	1889	1890	1891
Colonel . .	H.R.H. the Prince of Wales, K.G.	H.R.H. the Prince of Wales, K.G.	
Lieut.-Col. .	H. R., Visct. Downe	H. R., Visct. Downe	
Majors . .	M. C. Wood Hon. J. P. Napier H.R.H. Prince Albert Victor C. E. of Wales, K.G. J. P. Brabazon	M. C. Wood Hon. J. P. Napier H.R.H. Prince Albert Victor C. E., Duke of Clarence and Avondale, K.G., K.P., A.D.C. J. P. Brabazon, A.D.C.	
Captains .	R. B. W. Fisher P. Durham D. S. W., Earl of Airlie R. H. F. W. Wilson Hon. H. T. Allsopp Hon. G. L. Bryan H. Alexander C. B. Harvey Hon. A. Lawley	R. B. W. Fisher P. Durham D. S. W., Earl of Airlie R. H. F. W. Wilson Hon. G. L. Bryan H. Alexander C. B. Harvey A. Hughes-Onslow Hon. J. H. G. Byng C.T.McM.Kavanagh Hon. E. Baring	
Lieutenants .	A. Hughes-Onslow Hon. J. H. G. Byng C.T.McM.Kavanagh Hon. E. Baring E. W. D. Baird C. Barclay C. H., Lord Southampton Lord W. A. Cavendish-Bentinck B. C. C. S. Meeking	E. W. D. Baird C. Barclay C. H., Lord Southampton Lord W. A. Cavendish-Bentinck B. C. C. S. Meeking Lord G. W. Douglas Scott	
Second Lieuts.	Lord G.W.Douglas-Scott A. Farquharson T. W. Brand	A. Farquharson T. W. Brand A. A. C., Earl of Shaftesbury C. R. Molyneux	
Paymaster .	A. A. W. Bright-Smith	—	
Adjutant .	Hon. J. Byng	Hon. A. Lawley	
Ridingmaster	P. Kelly	A. W. Waite	
Quartermaster	A. E. Poole	A. E. Poole	

APPENDIX II

RECORD OF SPORTS

---◆---

CRICKET

THE game of Cricket has always been well supported both by officers and men of the 10th Hussars, and at no period, perhaps, has it been better represented than at the present time (1890).

It is impossible to obtain records of more than fifty years ago, and difficult to obtain scores and other details until a recent date; but in these memoirs an account has already been given of the matches played in India at Kirkee and Poona between the years 1846 and 1855; and amongst the officers at that time perhaps Captain Tom Townley and Lieutenant de Bourbel, who had been twelfth man for the Harrow Eleven, were the principal players.

After the Crimean War the game was again taken up, and matches took place wherever the Tenth was stationed. At Norwich a very good team was got together in 1860–61, when amongst others who took part in the matches were Captain the Hon. C. C. Molyneux, Lieutenants A. Barthorp, E. A. Wood, Liddell, St. Quintin, Wyatt-Edgell, Corporal Parsons of the band, and Private Ellis, bowlers; with Regimental Sergeant-Major Rickards and Corporal Templeman, useful men in the field. The most important matches at this station were played at Blickling, the Marquis of Lothian's place in Norfolk; at Gunton, belonging to Lord Suffield, and at Norwich itself. In 1861–2, at York, the same regimental team played, with the addition of Corporal Weir, an excellent bowler.

In Ireland many matches took place with the Viceregal

Lodge and all the regiments in the various garrisons, Lieutenants Smith-Dorrien and Edward Watson being great additions to the strength of the eleven.

On the Tenth proceeding to India in 1873 the game was not much played at first, except by individual officers; but at Lucknow a small ground was prepared for the men and was well patronised in the cold weather, amongst the best cricketers being Quartermaster-Sergeant Byatt, Corporal A. Hayter, and Corporal Barth. Conspicuous amongst the officers at this time were Colonel E. A. Wood, as wicket-keeper; Major Slade and Captain R. B. Fisher, twelfth man of the Harrow Eleven, useful bowlers and bats; Herbert T. Allsopp, late of the Cheltenham and Cambridge University Eleven, a fine exponent of the game whether with bat, ball, or in the field; and Charles S. Greenwood, a steady bat. Major Spottiswoode and Captain the Hon. J. Napier also were useful bowlers. In 1882 the team was considerably strengthened by the arrival from England of Lieutenants C. B. Harvey (a useful player), the Hon. Arthur Lawley, and A. Hughes-Onslow, the latter late of the Eton Eleven. During this season Lieutenant Allsopp had several scores of over one hundred accredited to him.

On the return of the Tenth to England in 1884 several new players were added to the Eleven—Lieutenants the Hon. J. Byng (an enthusiastic supporter of cricket), C. T. McM. Kavanagh, the Hon. E. Baring, E. W. Baird, F. R. Bowlby, and Private Seymour.

At Shorncliffe, on first arrival, it was seldom the regimental team could be got together, and only two or three matches were played; but Captain Fisher, Hon. H. T. Allsopp, Hon. A. Lawley, and A. Hughes-Onslow frequently played with success for the Shorncliffe Garrison, the former on one occasion contributing a score of 180.

In the summer of 1885 the Tenth moved to Aldershot, where it held a most successful season, defeating the 2nd Life Guards, the Royal Artillery, the 7th Hussars, a Calcot Park Eleven, and a strong team at Sendholme, losing a match against the Ascot Club, and drawing the remaining two events. The chief scores made during the season were—H. T. Allsopp, 60, 48, and 40; E. W. Baird, 38, and Private Seymour, 49 and 38; whilst the bowling honours were shared chiefly by Allsopp and Hughes-Onslow, assisted by the Hon. E. Baring and C. T. McM. Kavanagh.

In 1886 fourteen matches played resulted in seven wins, five losses, and two draws, the victories being over the 2nd battalion Rifle Brigade (twice), 1st Life Guards, Royal Artillery, Scots Greys, and Calcot Park and Buckhurst Elevens; whilst defeat was suffered at the hands of the 7th Hussars at Hounslow; the 1st battalion Grenadier Guards by four runs, after an exciting match, at Windsor; the Broadwater Club at Broadwater, and the Royal Artillery and Mr. C. R. Dent's Eleven at Aldershot. A. Hughes-Onslow this year was well at the head of the batsmen, with scores of 33, 39 (not out), 97, 55, 39, 61, and 56, and much assistance was rendered at different times by Hon. H. T. Allsopp 46, E. W. Baird 61 (not out) and 37, Private Seymour 57 (not out), Captain Greenwood 34, Hon. A. Lawley 33, and J. Byng 44; whilst the wickets were captured chiefly by the same bowlers as in the previous year.

In 1887, whilst at Hounslow, seventeen matches took place, resulting in six victories, seven defeats, three draws, and a tie. This latter match, against the Royal Horse Artillery, took place at Woolwich on the 27th August; the Royal Horse Artillery, who went in first, making 181, the Hon. E. Baring obtaining wickets with three successive balls. The 10th Hussars then obtained 85 for the first wicket, but with nine wickets down for 132 defeat seemed imminent; the Hon. E. Baring, however, again came to the rescue, but, after rapidly knocking up 41 runs, including a seven, a six, and three fours, he was bowled, when the score was a tie. The chief scores made on behalf of the regiment during the season were—Hon. H. T. Allsopp, 35, 31, 78, and 31; A. Hughes-Onslow, 31, 73, 82, 59, and 50; Captain Fisher, 30, 38, and 55 (not out); E. W. Baird, 30, 54, 51, 32, 55, and 34 (not out); F. R. Bowlby, 37 and 39; the Hon. E. Baring, 41 and 33 (not out); and Corporal Seymour, 34.

In 1888 Lord Southampton and Lieutenant Meeking were added to the cricketing strength, and whilst the regiment was stationed at York it played ten matches, including a two days' match at Welbeck Abbey and a contest with the Gentlemen of Northumberland at Newcastle. Of these it was successful in nine, drawing the remaining match. The same batsmen and bowlers were again to the fore, and B. C. Meeking was of much assistance as wicket-keeper. The chief scores made were— Captain H. T. Allsopp, 36, 58, 35, and 47; A. Hughes-Onslow, 55 and 39; E. W. Baird, 46 and 60; B. C. Meeking, 35 and 50; Captain Greenwood, 50 (not out); Captain Fisher, 41 (not out); and Lord Southampton, 32. The cricket-ground in barracks was greatly improved, and the non-commissioned officers and men played numerous matches with neighbouring clubs, in the majority of which they came out successfully. Amongst the best players at this time were Corporal Seymour, Quartermaster-Sergeant Byatt, Sergeant Williams, Sergeant King, Corporal Dilley, and Private Pearce.

In 1889 the regimental team was greatly strengthened by Lord George Scott, who had been in the Eton and Oxford Elevens and had played once for the Gentlemen against the Players; and this year, whilst serving in the Tenth, he was able to make the highest score on his side in the Inter-University match. Lieutenant-Colonel Lord Downe also took part in the matches. Out of twelve matches played, five resulted in victories and four in defeats, the remainder being drawn. Out-matches were played at Welbeck, Babworth, Hovingham, Escrick, and Everingham, and a strong team from Scarborough was defeated. The only regimental team played against—viz. that of the York and Lancaster—was also beaten. The chief scores made were— Captain the Hon. H. T. Allsopp, 30, 31, 58, and 35 (not out); Lord George Scott, 32, 53 (not out), 31, 139, 105, and 56; A. Hughes-Onslow, 51 and 52 (not out); Sergeant Seymour, 62 and 30; Captain Fisher, 41 and 36; the Hon. J. Byng, 30, 31 (not out), and 43; B. C. Meeking, 31; and Private Dicks, 32. An exciting match against Hovingham ended in a victory by one run, the last two wickets falling to Lord Downe's lobs at the same total.

The non-commissioned officers and men played twenty-two matches during the season, winning no less than twenty and only losing once; Sergeant Seymour, Quartermaster-Sergeant Byatt, Sergeants King and Williams, Corporal Hendry, and Privates Dicks and Shelton being amongst the best players.

At the end of this season a great loss was sustained by the retirement of Captain the Hon. H. T. Allsopp, who had for several years ably carried out the duties of Captain and contributed very largely to the success of the team.

In 1890 a very useful bowler and bat joined in the person of Lieutenant T. W. Brand, who had formerly been Captain of the Eton Eleven, and the captaincy of the regimental team was taken up by Captain the Hon. A. Lawley. Great care had been taken of the ground in barracks during 1888 and 1889, and it was now in excellent condition.

In May a match was played at Wynyard Park, where the Tenth team met with a severe defeat, and it was shortly afterwards beaten at Escrick Park in spite of a score of 55 (not out) by Lord George Scott. It next played Hovingham, when it was easily victorious, Sergeant Seymour making 75 and Meeking 37. An eleven brought by Captain W. Lloyd beat the Tenth, T. W. Brand heading the regimental side with a score of 44.

A return match at Hovingham again counted a victory, chiefly through the batting of Lord George Scott (35), Captain the Hon. A. Lawley (43), and Corporal Hendry (30). On the 10th June, with only four wickets down for a score of 347, to which Sergeant Seymour contributed 125 and Captain A. Hughes-Onslow, 123 (not out), the regiment defeated the officers of Strensall Camp, who scored 112, Captain A. Hughes-Onslow securing eight wickets for 31 runs. Victory again sided with the regimental team against the Durham Light Infantry, Lord George Scott making 55 (not out), and obtaining four wickets for 15 runs.

An eleven brought by Captain the Hon. H. T. Allsopp on the 12th July proved too strong in spite of scores of 37 by Lord George Scott, 59 by Captain Onslow, and 45 by B. C. Meeking; and the regimental team was defeated again by the Artillery of the North-Eastern District, Captain Hon. E. Baring making 36, and B. C. Meeking 36 (not out). A match at Warter Priory again saw the team defeated, Sergeant Seymour and Corporal Hendry, with scores of 46 and 27, being the chief contributors. A return match against the Durham Light Infantry ended in a draw greatly in favour of the 10th Hussars, who declared their innings at an end after making 253 for four wickets, of which Sergeant Seymour made 97 and Lord George Scott 114 (not out). A match against Deighton Grove on the 14th August placed a victory to the credit of the regiment, for whom Captain A. H. Onslow scored 39.

Up to the middle of August in this year the non-commissioned officers and men had played sixteen matches, of which they were successful in twelve and lost two, the remaining ones drawn. On the 4th August they played the officers and defeated them by 183 to 165; Sergeant Seymour making 42, Corporal Hendry 27, and Sergeant Hall 25 for the former; whilst Lord George Scott with 96, and Captain Onslow with 35, received but little assistance from their side.

POLO.

The game of Polo was introduced into England in 1870 by the officers of the 10th Hussars, from a description of the game, as played by the Manipuri tribe in India, which appeared in the " Field " newspaper. Lord Valentia, Mr. E. Hartopp, and Mr. George Cheape of the 11th Hussars, attached to the regiment, were the originators.

The first game that was ever played took place at Aldershot on a piece of ground below Cæsar's Camp. Amongst those who took part in it on this day were Lieutenant Hartopp, the Hon. Thomas Fitzwilliam, Lieutenant Edward Watson, &c. The officers rode their chargers, and golf sticks and billiard balls were used; later on it was found that a cricket ball, whitened, was more suitable for the purpose.

The 9th Lancers adopted the game the following year, and assisted materially by introducing an improved stick. On the 23rd June, 1871, the first match in England was played, between the 9th Lancers and 10th Hussars, at Hounslow; the latter winning by three goals to one. The names of the competitors were:

9TH LANCERS.	10TH HUSSARS.
R. Clayton.	T. A. Smith-Dorrien.
Lord W. Beresford.	E. Hartopp.
R. Moore.	Hon. Thos. Fitzwilliam.
Hon. E. Willoughby.	Lord Valentia.
W. Fife.	W. Chaine.
P. Green.	T. A. St. Quintin.
— Palairet.	H. S. Gough.
— Grissell.	E. Watson.

The polo was preceded by a cricket match between the two regiments, which was left unfinished. A great number of people came down from London to witness the novel sight of a polo match, and Hounslow Heath was crowded with spectators.

On arrival in India, as soon as the Tenth was settled down in its new quarters, the game was again set on foot, and from the facility of purchasing ponies of the proper stamp, the flat and even nature of the ground affording a good choice of sites, and the suitability of the game to a country where short and good exercise is much required for health, all tended to make polo a great success, and it became, as it were, a regimental institution during the whole time the Tenth remained in India. The game was played assiduously three times a week in the evenings until the sun went down, and many brilliant players soon began to show themselves in the regiment.

At the Imperial Proclamation assemblage at Delhi in 1876–7, inter-regimental polo matches were first arranged, and, the 9th Lancers also being in India, the two regiments renewed the friendly contests in the game that they had already inaugurated in England. Captain St. Quintin, 10th Hussars, was appointed secretary for the proposed tournaments, and the first meeting was fixed to take place at Meerut in March, 1877.

During the Imperial Assemblage a fatal accident at polo took place, which cost Captain R. Clayton, 9th Lancers, his life on Christmas Day. This excellent officer and companion had been brigade-major of the cavalry brigade to which the Tenth was attached in the previous year at Delhi, and had endeared himself to all as a good soldier, a first-rate sportsman, and staunch friend. There were few men better known and more popular than poor " Dick Clayton."

At the first polo tournament in 1877, at Meerut, four regiments competed, the 9th Lancers and 10th Hussars being left in to play the final match. The Tenth team was represented by Captain St. Quintin, Lieutenant the Hon. C. Cavendish, Lieutenant Brabazon, and Lieutenant Fisher. The 9th gained a goal in the first few minutes, when a great contest ensued, and time was called without either side again scoring, the 9th Lancers thus winning the first match by one goal to nothing.

In 1878 the second meeting took place, again at Meerut,

when the two regiments were once more left in for the final ties. In this match the 9th Lancers defeated the 10th Hussars by five goals to two. The Tenth was represented by Captain St. Quintin, Lieutenants Fisher, Durham, and Greenwood.

Owing to the Afghan War no meetings were held in 1879 or 1880. After this, Lord Ogilvy, 10th Hussars, became secretary of the tournaments, succeeding Mr. Watson, of the 13th Hussars, and, throwing himself into the work with his characteristic energy, the next meeting in 1881, held at Umballa, was quite the most successful that had hitherto taken place. The following regiments entered:—The Carabiniers, the 8th Hussars, the 9th Lancers, 10th Hussars, 4th battalion Rifle Brigade, the 100th Regiment, and the 12th Bengal Cavalry. The 9th Lancers and 10th Hussars drew each other in the first ties, and after a brilliant game the Tenth defeated its opponents by six goals to two. The final match, on the last day of the week, between the Tenth and the Rifle Brigade, ended in a tie, neither side obtaining a goal, and the game was played over again on the following Monday, the 10th Hussars winning the tournament by two goals to one. The names of the Tenth team were :—Lord Ogilvy and Lieutenant Greenwood (forward), Lieutenant Fisher (half back), Lieutenant Allsopp (back).

Lord Ogilvy having gone to England on leave, Mr. Greenwood became captain of the regimental team and secretary of the tournament, and the meeting for 1882 was arranged to take place at Meerut. Seven regiments entered, viz. : The 8th, 10th, and 13th Hussars, the 9th Lancers, the Rifle Brigade, the 11th and 54th Regiments. The Tenth met the 11th Regiment in the first ties and won easily. In the second, the 10th Hussars played its old opponents, the 9th Lancers, and defeated them by three goals to one, after a brilliant game. In the final ties the Tenth met the Rifle Brigade and won the Cup. The team was composed as follows :—Lieutenant Greenwood, Lieutenant Fisher, Lieutenant Allsopp, and Lord Alwyne Compton.

In 1883 the inter-regimental meeting took place at Umballa, Major the Hon. W. Legge, of the 9th Lancers, performing the duties of secretary. This perhaps was the most brilliant of all the contests that had yet taken place. Twelve regiments entered, and the following eight competed :—The Carabiniers, the 8th, 10th, and 13th Hussars, the 9th Lancers, the King's Own Borderers, the King's Royal Rifles, and the Rifle Brigade. One hundred and seventy-one ponies were brought by the different regiments, and it was generally remarked that a better lot of animals had never been assembled together.

The 9th Lancers and 10th Hussars again met, and a hotly-contested game commenced without either side being able to score a goal. In the middle of the game Lieutenant Durham received a blow on the arm which broke his wrist, and he was unable to play any more. Upon this the Hon. A. Lawley took his place as substitute. The game then continued in the same determined and magnificent manner, without any advantage accruing to either side, until within half a minute of time being called, when the 9th Lancers made a goal and won the game. This regiment easily disposed of the remaining teams and won the Cup. The Tenth team on this occasion was Lieutenant Allsopp, Lieutenant Durham, the Hon. George Bryan, Lord Alwyne Compton, the Hon. A. Lawley (substitute).

A week previous to this meeting, the Native Cavalry held a meeting at Umballa to compete for a challenge cup presented by the officers of the 10th Hussars to the Bengal Cavalry, the Punjab Cavalry, and the Central India Horse. The cup was won the first year by the 12th Bengal Cavalry, after a tie with the 18th; and it was presented to them by Lieutenant-Colonel E. A. Wood, after a dinner given by the 9th Lancers to all the polo teams then assembled at Umballa.

Before leaving India Lord Ogilvy (now the Earl of Airlie) presented a challenge cup to be played for annually by the infantry regiments in Bengal. There was also a Polo Club for the non-commissioned officers and privates of the Tenth, established in the first place at Muttra through the energy of Lieutenant the Hon. C. Cavendish, and afterwards supported by the officers generally and Lord Airlie in particular. The principal players in this club were:—Regimental Sergeant-Major Stuart, Sergeant-Major Assinder, Sergeant-Major Barnard, Sergeant Wright, Corporal Holt, Sergeant Halls, and Privates Fuller, McManus, Baxter, Coles, Cue, Harris, and Smith.

Previous to the departure of the Tenth from Lucknow, David, Earl of Airlie, had a well sunk close to the Divisional Polo

Ground, for the benefit of future players, and it was named after his lordship and had the following inscription on it:—

DAVID'S WELL.

A noble game we played of yore;
    Perchance, my sons, ye play it still,
Perchance, some thirty troops or more
    E'en now the air with thunder fill.

Amen! But if new David's Well
    No longer floods the thirsty ground,
Yet thirsty souls, whilst drinking, tell
    How 'tis that here a well is found.

A.
X. R. H.
June
1883.

As soon as the Tenth arrived in England in May, 1884, the officers were naturally anxious to see if they could be as success-ful in England at polo as they had been in India; but, owing to the difficulties in obtaining good ponies, were unable to enter for the Polo Cup till the year 1885. There was one match, how-ever, arranged by Mr. Philip Green, played in 1884 at Bayham Abbey, Lord Camden's place, and, as the regiment was very soundly beaten by 4 goals to 0, it showed that it was just as necessary to have the best of ponies and to practise hard in England as it had been in India. The teams were: 10th Hussars—the Earl of Airlie, Lieutenant H. P. Allsopp, the Hon. G. Bryan, Lieutenant Hughes-Onslow. Bayham Abbey—Mr. J. Peat, the Earl of Harrington, Mr. Mildmay, and T. S. Kennedy.

In 1885 the Tenth entered for the military tournament at Hurlingham, when its team was composed as follows:—Lieu-tenants Allsopp, Hon. A. Lawley, A. Hughes-Onslow, and Captain Greenwood. The 10th drew the 15th Hussars in the first ties, and, beating them easily, was left in for the final with the 7th Hussars, the winners since 1883. The 7th team con-sisted of Major Hunt, Captain Roper, Lieutenant Hone, and Lieutenant Douglas Haig. A very even and exciting game was the result. In the first twenty minutes no goal was obtained on either side; in the second twenty minutes an unfortunate accident to Mr. Hone, who was struck in the ribs through the head of a stick being broken off, caused a temporary stoppage in the game. On resuming, Mr. Hone, who was quite well again, made a goal for the 7th seven minutes before the call of time, thus making the game one goal all. Two minutes before the call of time, Mr. Haig added another goal for the 7th, who won one of the most even and exciting contests ever played.

In 1886 the Tenth was so unfortunate as to lose, a few days before the matches, the services of its back, Lieutenant Allsopp, through a bad fall. Two teams were, however, entered. First team: the Earl of Airlie, Captain C. T. Greenwood, Lord A. Compton, Lieutenant E. W. Baird; second team: Lieutenants A. Hughes-Onslow, C. Kavanagh, F. R. Bowlby, and the Hon. E. Baring.

The entries this year were not numerous—the 7th Hussars (two teams), the 10th Hussars (two teams), the 11th Hussars, and the 5th Lancers. In the first ties the 10th Hussars' first team beat the 11th Hussars, and the 5th Lancers beat the 10th Hussars' second team. In the second ties the 7th Hussars' first team beat the 10th Hussars' first team easily by 7 goals to 0. In the final the 7th Hussars beat the 5th Lancers and won the Cup.

In the same year the Tenth sent the following team over to Ireland in September to compete for the Irish Military Tournament:—A. Hughes-Onslow, F. R. Bowlby, E. W. Baird, and the Hon. E. Baring. Four teams entered and were drawn as follows:—11th Hussars and 21st Hussars, 10th Hussars and 16th Lancers. The Tenth, after a fine match, beat the 16th Lancers by 4 goals to 2. In the final the 10th Hussars beat the 11th Hussars somewhat easily by 5 goals to 0 and won the Cup.

In the year 1887 the following teams entered for the tournament:—The 5th Lancers, 10th, 13th, 18th, and 21st Hussars, 9th Lancers, and Rifle Brigade. In the first ties the 10th Hussars beat the Rifle Brigade by 7 goals to 0. In the second ties the 10th Hussars was drawn against the 5th Lancers, and the match was one of the closest and fastest ever played for the Military Cup. The sides were: 5th Lancers—Major Cosmo Little, Captains Spicer, H. Jones, and St. John Mundy; 10th Hussars—the Hon. H. Allsopp, A. Hughes-Onslow, the Hon. E. Baring, and E. W. Baird. After a very even match, at the call of time the score stood 3 goals all, and, as it is a rule at Hurlingham that in the event of a tie the game shall be resumed till either side scores a goal, play was resumed, with the result that the 5th Lancers got the goal and won the match. In the final tie the 5th Lancers beat the 9th Lancers and won the cup.

In the year 1888, when the regiment was quartered at York, there was a large entry for the Military Cup, consisting of the Royal Horse Guards, 2nd Life Guards, Royal Artillery, 9th Lancers, 10th, 13th, 15th, and 18th Hussars. In the first ties the 10th drew the 13th Hussars, who scratched. In the second ties the Tenth beat the Blues by 9 goals to 0, thus leaving its team in for the final with the 9th Lancers, whom it beat by 5 goals to 0, and winning the cup for the first time in England. This was a strong team, and excellently mounted. 9th Lancers—Captain Lamont and Jenner, Lieutenants Colvin and Duff; 10th Hussars—Captain C. S. Greenwood, the Hon. H. T. Allsopp, Lieutenants Hughes-Onslow, and E. W. Baird. The regiment was unable this year to enter for the Irish Military Tournament.

In the year 1889, the regiment still being quartered at York, there were seven entries for the Military Tournament at Hurlingham—The Royal Artillery, the Royal Dragoons, the 10th and 13th Hussars, the 9th and 16th Lancers, and the Royal Munster Fusiliers. In the first ties the Tenth beat the Royals by 3 goals to 2. In the second ties the Tenth beat the Royal Artillery very easily by 9 or 10 goals to 0. In the final, the Tenth team was left to play its old antagonists, the 9th Lancers, and, after an exciting match, the 9th Lancers won by 3 goals to 2. The sides were : 9th Lancers—Captains Lamont, Jenner, Little, and Colvin ; 10th Hussars—Captains Fisher and the Hon. H. T. Allsopp, Lieutenants A. Hughes-Onslow and E. W. Baird. Captain Allsopp had had a very bad fall whilst playing a scratch team two days before the tournament. One of his ribs was broken. He, however, played gallantly through the matches, but his crippled condition was much against him. The Tenth did not this year enter for the Irish Military Tournament.

PIG-STICKING.

During both the periods of service in India, the Tenth patronised the sport of pig-sticking most warmly. From Kirkee it was easily attainable, and the officers, with Colonel Parlby at their head, lost no opportunity of enjoying this excellent sport.

On the regiment proceeding a second time to India, it was at once sent to Muttra, where the surrounding jungles, Kawal, Baharban, Maat, Goroiya, and Areeng, teemed with boar, and the sport obtained was magnificent. The Tenth also was fortunate enough to carry off its share of prizes at the annual competitions for the Kadir and Ganges Cups, which took place at Meerut and Cawnpore. In 1877, the Kadir Cup was won by Captain T. A. St. Quintin's grey Arab horse Vivian (Owner up); in 1881, by Lieutenant Fisher's chestnut Arab horse Maiden (ridden by Lieutenant Charles Grenfell); in 1882, by the Hon. George Bryan's grey Arab horse Grey Dawn. In 1877 the Ganges Cup was won by the Hon. C. Cavendish's b. Waler gelding Fop; in 1880, by the Hon. George Bryan's grey Arab horse Uncle G.; in 1882, by the Hon. George Bryan's grey Arab horse Uncle G.

STEEPLECHASES.

Mention has already been made in these Memoirs of the part taken by the Tenth in the early days of steeplechasing, nearly sixty years ago, when the Irish Grand Military Cup was won, in 1832, near Dublin, by Lieutenant the Hon. H. Saville's mare Modesty, ridden by Major Lord Thomas Cecil. Again, in 1840, the first Grand Military Steeplechase in England was won by Captain Sir James Baird, who became the possessor of the Gold Cup. No record has, unfortunately, been kept until recent times of the various sporting events in the regiment; but between 1846 and 1855, in India, many meetings were held and some excellent jockeys were forthcoming, amongst the best being Captain Tom Townley and Lieutenant Wardrop.

After the return of the Tenth from the Crimea, annual regimental steeplechase meetings were instituted, and the first took place in 1860, on Shepperton Range, the regiment being stationed at Hounslow. On this occasion, Lieutenant-Colonel

Baker presented a very handsome bronze flagon as a challenge cup, to be won twice by the same officer before becoming his property. This cup was won in 1860 by Captain Baumgarten's horse Hop the Twig (ridden by Cornet E. A. Wood), Lord Ralph Kerr's grey horse Stumps being second (ridden by Captain John Fife). The 10th Hussars' Cup was won by a horse the property of Captain Coates (ridden by Mr. Thacker.)

In 1861 the Regimental Meeting took place about four miles from Norwich, where the head-quarters were stationed, when Mr. Thacker's mare Ruby won the Challenge Cup.

In 1862, the Tenth being at York, the Steeplechases were held on the 26th April at Poppleton, where Lieutenant T. Williams-Bulkeley's br. m. Mermaid won the Challenge Cup; Lieutenant R. S. Liddell's br. g. Jock o' Hazledean, second; Lieutenant E. A. Wood's (nom.) br. m. Rosamond, third. The 10th Hussars' Cup was won by Lieutenant-Colonel Baker's b. g. The Grubber; Mr. Thacker's ch. m. Choral, second; Captain Bowyer's Piccadilly, third. A Hunt Cup was also presented by the officers for horses the property of members of the Yorkshire Club. This race was won by Sir Charles Slingsby's b. g. Egg Sauce; Mr. Clare Vyner's b. m. Kathleen being second.

In 1863 the Bronze Challenge Cup was won by Mr. Thacker's br. g. Pirate, and, this being the second time he had carried it off, it became his property. The 10th Hussars' Cup was won by Captain the Hon. C. C. Molyneux's gr. g. Blue Ruin, ridden by owner. These races took place at Crockey Hill, near York, the land having been kindly lent by Lord Wenlock.

In 1864 Colonel Valentine Baker presented another cup, a silver gilt Danish flagon, to be won three times by the same officer before becoming his property. This cup has since gone by the name of Baker's Cup. The first year it was won by Lieutenant St. Quintin's Ballyragget (Owner); Lieutenant C. Frederick's Brunette (Owner), second; Captain Sawbridge's Bright Star (Lieutenant Bulkeley), third.

The 10th Royal Hussars' Cup.

Cornet Davies-Evans's Georgia	(Owner)	1
Lieutenant W. Bulkeley's The Fizzer	(Owner)	2
Cornet Davies-Evans's Agnes	(Cornet Frederick)	3

Six starters.

1865.

THE CHALLENGE CUP (BAKER'S CUP).

Captain Slacke's Planet . . . . (Owner) 1
Mr. Davies-Evans's Cornelia . . . . . . (Owner) 2
Mr. Gabbett's Satanella . . . . (Owner) 8

Six starters.

10TH ROYAL HUSSARS' CUP.

Lieutenant St. Quintin's Ballyragget . . . . . (Owner) 1
Captain Chaine's Elvira . . . . . . (Owner) 2
Hon. H. Crichton's The Cornet . . . . . (Owner) 8

Seven starters.

1866.

Island Bridge Barracks.

BAKER'S CUP.

Lieutenant Gabbett's Standard-Bearer . . (Cornet Evans) 1
Lord Valentia's Moccas . . . . (Lieutenant E. Wood) 2
Lieutenant Hartopp's Bernard . . (Cornet the Hon. H. Wood) 8

Four starters.

10TH ROYAL HUSSARS' CUP.

Lieutenant St. Quintin's Ballyragget . . . . . (Owner) 1
Lieutenant Davies-Evans's Cornelia . . . . . (Owner) 2
Lieutenant Davies-Evans's Planet . (Cornet the Hon. H. Wood) 8

1867.

Run over the Mullacurry Course, Ardee.

BAKER'S CUP.

Lieutenant Gabbett's Mabel . . . . (Captain Slacke) 1
Lieutenant Bulkeley's Shooting Star . . . . . (Owner) 2
Lord Valentia's Moccas . . . . (Owner) 8

Six ran.

10TH ROYAL HUSSARS' CUP.

Lieutenant St. Quintin's Ballyragget . . . . . (Owner) 1
Captain Slacke's Vanille . . . . . . (Owner) 2
Lieutenant Gabbett's Mabel . . . . . (Mr. Russell) 8

Four ran.

In 1868 the regiment moved to England, and there were
no races.

1869.

Aldershot.

BAKER'S CUP.

Lord Valentia's Ventpiece	(Owner)	1
Captain Bulkeley's Shooting Star . . .	. (Mr. E. Wood)	2
Lieutenant Smith-Dorrien's Oak Branch . . .	. (Owner)	3

Three ran.

10TH ROYAL HUSSARS' CUP.

Lord Valentia's Ventpiece	. (Owner)	1
Lieutenant Thorold's Ina	. (Owner)	2
Captain Bulkeley's Nigger	. (Mr. E. Wood)	3

Five ran.

1871.

Down Barn, near Hayes.

BAKER'S CUP.

Lord Valentia's Wellington	(Captain Wood)	1
H.R.H. the Prince of Wales's Champion .	. (Captain Bulkeley)	2
The Hon. T. W. FitzWilliam's Punkah . .	. (Owner)	3

Six ran.

PRINCE OF WALES'S CUP. Presented by H.R.H. the Prince of Wales. A point to point race of about six miles. 13st. 7lbs. Hunting kit.

Mr. Gough's The Judge	. (Owner)	1
Captain E. A. Wood's Tortola	. (Owner)	2
Lord Valentia's Brilliant	. (Captain Bulkeley)	3

Ten ran.

10TH ROYAL HUSSARS' CUP.

Captain Bulkeley's Shooting Star	. (Owner)	1
Captain St. Quintin's Crusade	. (Owner)	2
Lord Valentia's Wellington	. (Captain E. Wood)	3

Six ran.

1871.

A Hunt Cup, presented by the officers of the 10th Hussars for horses regularly hunted within twenty miles of Hounslow, had seventeen entries. Mr. Reynolds's War Queen won this race.

1886.

Held at Aldershot with Royal Scots Greys.

BAKER'S CUP.

Lieutenant Kavanagh's Highlander	(Owner)	1
Lord H. Compton's Chance	(Owner)	2
Lieutenant E. Baird's Donovan	(Owner)	3

Five ran.

10TH ROYAL HUSSARS' CUP.

Lieutenant Hughes-Onslow's Ace of Trumps . . .	(Owner)	1
Lieutenant Baird's Violet	(Owner)	2
The Hon. G. Bryan's Nina	(Owner)	3
Colonel Liddell's Vanity	(Lieutenant Baring)	4

SUBALTERNS' CUP.

The Hon. G. Bryan's Fencer	(Owner)	1
H.R.H. Prince Albert Victor's Paddy . .	(Lieutenant Kavanagh)	2
Lieutenant Baird's Lady Jane	(Owner)	3

Seven ran.

1886.

REGIMENTAL POINT TO POINT RACE. Run near Godalming.

Lord H. Compton's Chance	(Hon. H. Lawley)	1
Lieutenant Baird's Donovan	(Owner)	2
Lieutenant Hughes-Onslow's Jack Spraggon . .	(Owner)	3

Ten starters.

In this spring a point to point race took place near Stratton Audley, Oxfordshire, between five subalterns of the 10th Hussars *v.* five subalterns of the Royal Horse Guards. H.R.H. the Prince of Wales was present on this occasion, and there was a very large concourse of spectators.

Hon. G. Bryan's (10th Royal Hussars) Guinea Pig	1
Lieutenant Vaughan Lee (The Blues)	2
Lieutenant Hughes-Onslow's (10th Royal Hussars) Fencer . . .	3
Lieutenant Williams (The Blues)	4
Lieutenant Baird's (10th Royal Hussars) Donovan . . .	5

Unplaced—The Hon. A. Lawley and Lieut. McM. Kavanagh (10th Royal Hussars); Lord Binning, Lieutenant Ferguson, and Lieutenant Fenwick (The Blues).

The cup was presented by H.R.H. the Prince of Wales and won by the subalterns of the 10th Hussars, having two out of the first three in at the finish.

1887.

POINT TO POINT RACE. Near Whitley.

Hon. G. Bryan's Guinea Pig	(Owner)	1
Colonel Gough's G.C.B.	(Owner)	2
Lieutenant McM. Kavanagh's The Slave . . .	(Owner)	3

Ten starters.

The Grand Military Gold Cup of this year was won by Captain Fisher on his own horse, Dalesman, at Sandown.

1887.

Regimental Races held at Aldershot with Royals and Greys.

BAKER'S CUP.

Lieutenant Baird's Garnet	(Owner)	1
Colonel Gough's G.C.B.	(Mr. Hughes-Onslow)	2
Hon. G. Bryan's David	(Owner)	3

Four ran. Won by a length.

SUBALTERNS' CUP.

H.R.H. Prince Albert Victor's Paddy . . .	(Hon. G. Bryan)	1
Lieutenant Baird's Banksia	(Owner)	2
Lieutenant McM. Kavanagh's Highlander . . .	(Owner)	3

Five ran.

10TH ROYAL HUSSARS' CUP.

H.R.H. Prince Albert Victor's Paddy . . .	(Hon. G. Bryan)	1
Lieutenant Baird's Garnet	(Mr. McM. Kavanagh)	2
Lieutenant Baring's General	(Owner)	3

Five ran.

THE CAVALRY BRIGADE CUP.

Lieutenant McM. Kavanagh's (10th Royal Hussars) Abbess	(Owner)	1
Lieutenant Baird's (10th Royal Hussars) Garnet . .	(Owner)	2
Captain Burn Murdoch's (The Royals) Balloon . . .	(Owner)	3

Eight ran.

1888.

Races held at Kempton Park.

BAKER'S CUP.

Lieutenant Baird's Victoria	(Owner)	1
Lord Southampton's Pinafore	(Owner)	2
Lieutenant Alexander's Electra	(Owner)	3

Seven ran.

10TH ROYAL HUSSARS' CUP.

Lieutenant McM. Kavanagh's Sorrow . .	(Mr. Hughes-Onslow)	1
H.R.H. Prince Albert Victor's Paddy . . .	(Captain Bryan)	2
Lord Airlie's Hay Fever	(Lieutenant Baird)	3

Five ran.

SUBALTERNS' CUP (Cup presented by Colonel R. S. Liddell).

Lieutenant Baird's Banksia	(Owner)	1
Lieutenant Baring's General	(Owner)	2
Lord Southampton's Pinafore	(Owner)	3

Five ran.

The Grand National Steeplechase of this year was won by Lieutenant Baird's Playfair, 10st. 7lb., ridden by Mawson.

1889.

Races. Knavesmire, York.

BAKER'S CUP.

Lord W. Bentinck's Avalanche	(Owner)	1
Captain the Hon. H. Allsopp's Bugler . .	(Lieut. Hughes-Onslow)	2
Captain the Hon. G. Bryan's Kirkby	(Owner)	3

Seven ran.

10TH ROYAL HUSSARS' CUP.

Lord W. Bentinck's Ancaster	(Owner)	1
Lieutenant Baird's Victoria	(Owner)	2
Lord Southampton's Marauder	(Owner)	3

Eight ran.

SUBALTERNS' CUP.

Lieutenant Harvey's Lucy	(Owner)	1
Lieutenant Baird's Banksia	(Owner)	2
Lord Southampton's Marauder	(Owner)	3

Five ran.

POINT TO POINT RACE. Skip Bridge to Marston Hill, near York.

Lieutenant Hughes-Onslow's Patch	(Owner)	1
Lieutenant Baird's Pickle	(Owner)	2
Captain the Hon. H. Allsopp's Bugler	(Owner)	3
Captain H.R.H. Prince Albert Victor's Scraptoft		4

Seventeen ran.

Won a good race by half a length. Cup presented by H.R.H. the Prince of Wales, who was present on this occasion.

FOX-HUNTING.

Although the preceding record gives the principal games and sports in which the regiment has partaken during its leisure hours, the Tenth has at all times placed fox-hunting before them all, not only as the King of Sports, but as the one best calculated to give those acquirements most essential to a cavalry officer—a quick eye, knowledge of country, the requisite dash, and *going straight.* It would of course be impossible and, if not, invidious to give the names of all those who have been in the first flight in many a hunting-field in England and Ireland, but it may be fairly said that the 10th Hussars has had its share of them, and will continue to strive to be "*always in front.*"

PRINTED BY
SPOTTISWOODE AND CO., NEW-STREET SQUARE
LONDON